THE EMERGENCE OF GERMAN AS A LITERARY LANGUAGE

Der Genius der Sprache ist also der Genius von der Litteratur einer Nation....Ihr könnt also die Litteratur eines Volkes ohne ihre Sprache nicht übersehen,...denn ihre Vollkommenheit geht mit ziemlich gleichen Schritten fort.   HERDER

THE EMERGENCE OF GERMAN
AS A
LITERARY LANGUAGE
1700–1775

BY

ERIC A. BLACKALL

*Chairman of the
Department of German Literature, Cornell University
Sometime Fellow of Gonville and Caius College,
Cambridge*

CAMBRIDGE
AT THE UNIVERSITY PRESS
1959

PUBLISHED BY
THE SYNDICS OF THE CAMBRIDGE UNIVERSITY PRESS

Bentley House, 200 Euston Road, London N.W. 1
American Branch: 32 East 57th Street, New York 22, N.Y.

©

CAMBRIDGE UNIVERSITY PRESS
1959

*Printed in Great Britain at the University Press, Cambridge
(Brooke Crutchley, University Printer)*

For
WALTER BRUFORD

CONTENTS

Foreword   *page* ix

Textual Note   x

List of Abbreviations   xi

I	THE VINDICATION OF THE LANGUAGE	1
II	THE LANGUAGE OF PHILOSOPHY	19
III	THE LITERARY JOURNALS	49
IV	THE STABILISATION OF THE LANGUAGE	102
V	THE THEORY OF PROSE STYLE	149
VI	THE DEVELOPMENT OF NARRATIVE PROSE	178
VII	THE LANGUAGE OF POETRY	211
VIII	THE DEVELOPMENT OF THE POETICAL MEDIUM	233
IX	THE REVIVAL OF METAPHOR	276
X	THE GRAND MANNER	314
XI	THE PROSE OF MATURITY	351
XII	THE CULTURE OF WIT AND FEELING	387
XIII	THE MYSTICAL APPROACH	426
XIV	THE RETURN TO ORIGINS	451
XV	THE GOLDEN TOUCH	482

General Index   527

Index to Secondary Literature   537

FOREWORD

It is impossible for me to mention all those people who have helped me in the composition of this book over the last ten years. But I should like to thank especially four of my young colleagues at the University of London—Dorothy Knight, Marianne Wynn, Hugh Sacker and Peter Ganz—for their interest and encouragement. The final stages of my manuscript profited greatly from conversations with Elsie Butler, Edna Purdie, Lewis Harmer and Frederick Stopp. It has been my intention to show how the linguistic and literary aspects of our German studies may profitably be brought into closer partnership. I hope I have succeeded, and that this book may have some influence on the teaching of German language and literature at our universities.

This book was written while I was a Lecturer at Cambridge: when it appears I shall be Professor at Cornell. I ask that it may be accepted as a symbol of fruitful co-operation between the scholars of both countries.

E. A. B.

CAMBRIDGE
9 *June 1958*

TEXTUAL NOTE

Owing to the unreliability of the text in some modern reprints, I have found it necessary to quote from actual eighteenth-century editions wherever possible. Where I have had to use a modern reprint, I have done so with caution and mentioned the edition used. In using early editions, I have preferred the earliest edition which was available to me. The large collection of eighteenth-century German books in the British Museum library has been my basis. For some works, however, I have had to visit other libraries. I have usually indicated in a footnote where I found the copy I used. It is hoped that this may be of use to others working on this period. I have been most careful to preserve exactly the original spelling and punctuation, except for a few purely typographical features which I have regularised on the modern pattern. I have used the comma where seventeenth- and eighteenth-century texts used the virgula (/) but also sometimes the comma; this gradually gave way to the comma in all cases. I have used also the normal ¨ to designate *Umlaut* whereas some of my texts use ᵉ. I have used the single hyphen where most early texts use ▪ or ₌. These are purely typographical features, and since my texts do not appear in *fractura* but in roman, it would seem logical to replace the typographical conventions of eighteenth-century *fractura* by those of twentieth-century roman. Except where otherwise stated, italics in my quotations indicate italics in the original texts.

LIST OF ABBREVIATIONS

Dt.Vjs.	Deutsche Vierteljahrsschrift für Literaturwissenschaft und Geistesgeschichte.
EG	Études Germaniques.
Euph.	Euphorion.
GLL	German Life and Letters.
GR	Germanic Review.
GRM	Germanisch-Romanische Monatsschrift.
JEGP	Journal of English and Germanic Philology.
MLR	Modern Language Review.
MPh.	Modern Philology.
NM	Neuphilologische Mittheilungen.
PBB	Paul und Braune's *Beiträge zur Geschichte der deutschen Sprache und Literatur*.
PMLA	Publications of the Modern Language Association of America.
ZfdA	Zeitschrift für deutsches Altertum.
ZfDk.	Zeitschrift für Deutschkunde.
ZfdPh.	Zeitschrift für deutsche Philologie.
ZfdW	Zeitschrift für deutsche Wortforschung.

I

THE VINDICATION OF THE LANGUAGE

IN the preface to a translation of Einhard's Life of Charlemagne published in Germany in 1728, the writer lamented the fact that although the German language had many advantages over Latin, its condition had steadily worsened and it was now almost in its last throes. The statement may seem strange in historical perspective when we think of the great literature that was so soon to follow and the marvellous instrument of literary expression that the German language was to become during that period. But this statement was no isolated cry. It was an utterance characteristic of its time. It voiced a generally felt anxiety and distress which had been prevalent since the last decades of the preceding century. The German language was in a bad way; it needed 'strong medicines' to restore its health. Although the seventeenth century had produced literature of great interest, sometimes of great beauty and depth, there was grave concern in many minds about the state of the German language as a vehicle for literary and intellectual expression. Out of this dissatisfaction emerged one of the great literary languages of modern Europe. One cannot help feeling that without this period of dissatisfaction the German language would never have developed as it did. For the dissatisfaction was no passive despair; it was accompanied by a vigorous determination to improve the situation. The measures applied varied considerably. Some diagnosed the situation and suggested remedies—these were the critics and the grammarians; others preferred to try to make the German language say things in a different way, in a new way, even sometimes to make it say new things—these were the writers. My purpose is to give as clear a picture as possible of this period in the development of the German language—the most important period, I would contend, in its whole history. For it was between 1700 and 1775 that the German language developed into a literary language of infinite richness and subtlety. Some limitation and selectiveness is necessitated by the breadth and complexity of the subject. I cannot deal with every author of this many-sided age; but I have tried to present those facets of the period which seemed to me the most dominating and most significant. The climax and conclusion of my study is represented by the marvellous instrument that the German language showed itself to be in the hands of the young Goethe. That was around 1770. But if one looks at the way German was written in 1700 one can easily understand the general discontent with it as a medium of literary expression at that time. What is not so easy to understand is how the German language of 1700 could ever have developed into that of 1770. How was this miracle possible? But it was not a miracle. It was a process of steady and often quite conscious development in which widely differing forces took part. To disentangle these forces and to describe this development is the aim of this study.

Around the turn of the seventeenth and eighteenth centuries we find dissatisfaction with the German language expressed most strikingly by the greatest intellect in Germany at that time, namely Gottfried Wilhelm Leibniz. The concern which Leibniz felt about the German language sprang from his general concern and affection for the German people, who were then still suffering acutely from the disastrous effects of the Thirty Years War. Even more unfortunate than the disruption of the national economy was the fact that Germany had lost to a considerable degree its national pride and respect. Germans felt themselves to be culturally inferior to their great neighbour France and were too ready to take their tone in all matters from France. This was partly the result of Germany's material prostration; but Leibniz thought it necessary to point out that material conditions would be improved only if the will were there to improve them. Yet the existence of such a will presupposed some sense of national pride. The earlier of his two important essays on the state of the German language, the *Ermahnung an die Teutsche, ihren verstand und sprache beßer zu üben, sammt beygefügten vorschlag einer Teutsch gesinten Gesellschaft* (written probably in 1682–3)[1] begins with a patriotic rhapsody in which Leibniz asserts that love of one's country is a noble and reasonable feeling and there were many reasons why Germans might legitimately be proud of their fatherland—its great natural resources, the inherent honesty of its people, and the fact that, as he asserts, the country was on the whole well governed, with relatively little oppression, and with a kindly dynasty at the head. Germans lacked only the will to be happy, and if this will could but be fostered, then the wounds of war would be healed. One of the first essentials towards the achievement of this end was to increase the number of those people who had higher interests than mere living from day to day, 'those who lead a freer life, who take pleasure in histories and journeys, who sometimes enliven themselves with a pleasant book and, when in society they encounter a learned and eloquent man, listen to him with particular eagerness'. Leibniz laments the lack of a single great cultural centre in his country, although he admits that the multiplicity of courts gave more opportunities for brilliance to show itself. Good books in the German language were rare; all one had, says Leibniz, was, for the most part, books in which reflections in foreign languages were assembled without much coherence, or, if these were in German, then the content was usually absurd and the argument illogical, so that such works offended against reason and thwarted clear understanding. Serious scholarly works were not written in the vernacular. Hence the German language had fallen into disrepute, and with it the intellectual status of the German nation: 'Sind wir also in denen

---

[1] This essay was first published in 1846 by C. L. Grotefend, who thought it was composed about 1680. Onno Klopp placed its composition in 1697, but Paul Pietsch (*Beihefte zur Zeitschrift des Allgemeinen Deutschen Sprachvereins*, Heft 29, 1907) and August Schmarsow, *Leibniz und Schottelius* (*Quellen und Forschungen zur Sprach- und Culturgeschichte der germanischen Völker*, XXIII) (Strassburg, 1877), agree with Grotefend's dating. For the evidence on both sides, see Pietsch and Schmarsow (especially the latter, *op. cit.* pp. 15–16). I follow the text given by Pietsch. On Leibniz and the German language there is an article by A. E. Sokol in the *Stanford University Studies in Language and Literature* (Stanford, 1941) and one by Y. Belaval in *EG*, II (1947).

Dingen, so den Verstand betreffen, bereits in eine Sklaverey gerathen und werden durch unser blindtheit gezwungen, unser art zu leben, zu reden, zu schreiben, ja sogar zu gedencken, nach frembden willen einzurichten.' This state of vassalage and inferiority would continue unless serious-minded Germans turned to their own language with respect and made it an instrument for all including the highest and most serious subjects. The language needed improvement, but this would only come from its employment in serious writing. The general level of writing was low and much of it had features which militated against the spirit of the German language, such as the constant use of foreign expressions and constructions. The justification usually given for this was the assertion that the German language was unfitted to express higher thoughts. But, says Leibniz, in no modern vernacular do the Holy Scriptures sound better. The German language, he asserts, was as much in a state of vassalage to foreign powers as were other aspects of the national life. Language is a mirror of minds, and perfection of a national language seems to be attained in periods of great national prosperity, as the examples of Greece, Rome and France show. But Leibniz is not advocating the ruthless expulsion of all foreign words from the German language, for he admits that some useful and neat expressions had been advantageously absorbed from other tongues. Nevertheless the unnecessary use of foreign words when good German words for the same concepts exist should be avoided. 'Beßer ist ein original von einem teutschen als eine Copey von einem Franzosen seyn.' Leibniz then goes on to propose the establishment of what he calls a 'teutschgesinte Gesellschaft' whose function shall be to encourage the production of serious works (*Kernschriften*) in the German language. This would not only raise the standard of the language but also improve taste, purify the tone of social intercourse and advance the general intellectual prosperity of the nation. For Leibniz language is the foundation of all culture; it is the necessary prerequisite for cultured intercourse and national well-being. The great philosopher is gravely and deeply concerned.

THE VINDICATION OF THE LANGUAGE

In the second essay on language, the *Unvorgreiffliche Gedanken betreffend die Ausübung und Verbesserung der Teutschen Sprache* (written almost certainly in 1697 and first published by his secretary J. G. Eccard in 1717, one year after the death of Leibniz),[1] Leibniz begins by describing language as 'ein Spiegel des Verstandes',[2] and then proceeds to elaborate in more detail his dissatisfaction with the state of the German language at that time. German was rich in words denoting real objects, especially in words connected with occupations like mining,[3] hunting and seafaring; but Leibniz finds it lacking in vocabulary to express those things not experienced by the senses, so that the scholar has been driven to Latin to describe such matters.[4] Again Leibniz expresses his objection to what he now calls the 'puritanical' extirpation of all foreign words from the German vocabulary, asserting that the French by their efforts at purification of the vocabulary had diminished the force and riches of their lan-

---

[1] I follow the text given by Pietsch in Heft 30 of the *Wissenschaftliche Beihefte zur Zeitschrift des Allgemeinen Deutschen Sprachvereins* (Berlin, 1908). Gottsched reprinted the text in full in vol. I of the *Beyträge* (published 1732) with the comment: 'Dieses ist eine unserm Gutachten nach so wichtige Schrift, daß wir uns nicht enthalten können, dieselbe unsern Lesern von Wort zu Wort mitzutheilen' (*op. cit.* p. 368). See below, pp. 111 ff.

[2] Paul Böckmann (*Formgeschichte der deutschen Dichtung*, vol. I (Hamburg, 1949), pp. 482–3) sees in this remark a logical-mathematical conception of language, and uses it to symbolise a 'mathematisch-begriffliche Sprachform' as against the rhetorical style of the baroque age. This is hardly justified. Leibniz is not using *Verstand* in any rationalistic sense. He is merely echoing the famous maxim of Publilius Syrus, 'Sermo animi est imago'. He may have known the English rendering: 'Speech is the picture of the mind', to be found in the *Collection of English Proverbs* by John Ray (Cambridge, 1670, p. 24), for he was familiar with other works by Ray (see below, p. 7, n. 2). I feel sure that in this context '*Verstand*' means 'mind' in its widest sense, and is not to be understood in any narrowly rational sense.

[3] Leibniz asserts that even the Turks in the mines of Greece and Asia Minor use German mining terms '... ut ipsi Turcae in fodinis Graeciae et Asiae minoris vocabulis metallicis Germanorum utantur' (*Die Philosophischen Schriften von G. W. Leibniz*, ed. Gerhardt, vol. IV (Berlin, 1880), p. 144).

[4] 'Am allermeisten aber ist unser Mangel, wie gedacht, bey denen Worten zu spühren, die sich auff das Sitten-wesen, Leidenschafften des Gemüths, gemeinlichen Wandel, Regierungs-Sachen, und allerhand bürgerliche Lebens- und Staats-Geschäffte ziehen: Wie man wohl befindet, wenn man etwas aus andern Sprachen in die unsrige übersetzen will' (*Unvorgreiffliche Gedanken, ed. cit.* § 15).

guage.¹ Some of the learned societies in Germany had also gone too far in this respect, although the situation which they set out to improve had been far more lamentable than their own excess of zeal. Leibniz then reviews the development of German as a literary medium in the preceding two centuries. At the time of the Reformation, he asserts, a fairly pure German had been spoken; but later, and for various obvious historical reasons, Italian, Spanish and French had made great incursions into the language. The peak of this unfortunate development had been reached with the Thirty Years War, when Germany was flooded with foreign peoples who destroyed not only the country but also the language. Since the peace, French had become the language of culture and elegance, and German youths affecting French fashions had brought their own language, and with it their nation, into disrepute abroad. Some gain had been effected by this enslavement to foreign tongues (*Franz- und Fremd-entzen*) but the German language, when feeling the need for enrichment, should return to its own pristine clarity as well as import foreign wares from France '...so wohl unsern innern Kern des alten ehrlichen Teutschen wieder herfür suchen, als solchen mit dem neuen äusserlichen, von den Frantzosen und andern gleichsam erbeuteten Schmuck ausstaffieren'. This was to be one of the main activities of the society which Leibniz wished to see founded, part of its general purpose of raising the standard of intellectual life in Germany: 'Das Haupt-Absehen wäre zwar der Flor des geliebten Vaterlandes Teutscher Nation, sein besonderer Zweck aber und das Vornehmen (oder object) dieser Anstalt wäre auf die Teutsche Sprache zu richten, wie nehmlichen solche zu verbessern, auszuzieren und zu untersuchen.' These three infinitives —*verbessern, auszieren, untersuchen*—are important; they summarise the three types of linguistic activity which Leibniz considered essential for the betterment of the language. It would

---

¹ He also attacks the *Accademia della Crusca* in this context. This famous Florentine academy, founded in 1583, soon attained a reputation for excessive purism, and current Italian phrases like *parlare in crusca, scrivere colla crusca alla mano* testify to its proverbial pedantry.

seem that, by *verbessern*, Leibniz means 'to improve' rather than 'to correct', although both meanings had developed side by side since medieval times. By *auszieren*, he means 'to embellish'. The word *untersuchen*, used elsewhere by Leibniz in the sense of 'erforschen', would seem to imply that sort of analytical investigation which must precede any grammatical codification.[1] He then proceeds to consider vocabulary, and enumerates three methods by which it could be enriched: the rescue of words which are falling or have fallen into disuse, the 'naturalisation' of foreign words of particular value, and lastly, and only where no other method is possible, the considered invention (*wohlbedächtliche Erfindung*) or composition of new words. One of the first works of the new academy would have to be the collection and collation of lexical material. Leibniz advocates the compilation of a *Sprachbrauch* (*lexicon*) for current words, a *Sprach-Schatz* (*cornu copiae*) for technical terms, and a *Sprachquell* (*glossarium*) for archaic and dialect words. This last proposal is interesting, for it shows that Leibniz was fully aware of the rich lexical material preserved in the German local dialects. He urged the study of all dialects, not only those of his native area but also the Upper German dialects.[2] He also advocated the collation of the vocabularies of other Germanic languages, and pointed to the value of a study of Gothic, Old Saxon and 'Old Frankish' (by which, presumably, he meant the Franconian dialects of Old High German).[3] In the last section

---

[1] Cf. 'Wir haben schon zuvor oben unter dem Titl der *Etymologie* oder Untersuchung der Grund-Wurtzelen Teutscher Sprach von denen Stamm-Wörteren gehandlet' (*Parnassus Boicus*, vol. XI (Munich, 1725), p. 406).

[2] On Leibniz's interest in dialects, see Sigrid von der Schulenburg, *Leibnizens Gedanken und Vorschläge zur Erforschung der deutschen Mundarten* (Abhandlungen der Preußischen Akademie der Wissenschaften, Philosophisch-historische Klasse No. 2 (Berlin, 1937)). On his second journey to England in 1676, Leibniz had come across John Ray's *Collection of English Words* (1674) and wrote approvingly of it to Gerhard Meier of Bremen in 1694.

[3] Leibniz mentions the work of Martin Opitz in this connection. Opitz had published the *Annolied* with notes in 1639, and Leibniz, in a letter to Wotton (*Werke*, ed. Duten, vol. VI, 2, p. 218) wrote: 'Martinus Opitius, vir doctrina ingenioque summus, qui primus Poesin Germanicam vel aliarum gentium laudem extulit, in Annonis, Archiepiscopi Coloniensis, qui undecimo saeculo floruit, vitam, a Poëta antiquo carmine Germanico scriptam, notas dedit utiles.' In this

of the essay, Leibniz considers which authors of the past might well serve as models in their use of the German language. He gives honourable mention to Opitz and Zesen, and then, going back in time, to Luther, the older Reichstag documents and town records, *Reinecke Voß*, Rollenhagen's *Froschmäuseler*, Fischart's version of Rabelais, the *Amadis* and the *Teuerdanck*, Aventin and Stumpf as historians, Paracelsus and Hans Sachs.

The three essential qualities which Leibniz would see embodied in any cultured language are characterised in the *Unvorgreiffliche Gedanken* as *Reichthum*, *Reinigkeit* and *Glantz*.[1] This takes up the theme which he had already expounded in an interesting earlier work, the introductory essay to his edition of the *Anti-Barbarus* of Marius Nizolius, an Italian humanist, who in this work attacked scholastic philosophy and in particular its language. Nizolius had demanded more clarity and plasticity in philosophical language. Leibniz, in his introductory essay entitled *De optima philosophi dictione* (1670),[2] claimed that to the qualities of a good speech there belong *claritas* and *elegantia*. These he defines as follows: 'Clarum est quod bene percipitur, itaque clara est oratio cujus omnium vocabulorum significationes notae sunt, tantum attendenti.... Elegans est oratio, quae auditu lectuve jucunda est.' Clarity depends on the words themselves or on the construction in which they are used. Philosophers should be particularly careful about the connotation of the words they use, and should consider both the normal usage and the origin of these words. If origin deviates from usage, usage should be followed. If usage is doubtful or various, the origin of the word should be

---

section of the *Unvorgreiffliche Gedanken*, Leibniz also pays homage to the work of the French Academy, to Ménage's *Origines de la langue française* (1650) because it had collected archaic and popular words, and to Furetière's *Dictionnaire universel pour la langue française* (1690) because it had not excluded technical words.

[1] By *Glantz* Leibniz means 'elegance', as emerges clearly from a passage later in the same work (§ 110) where he says that this *Glantz* depends on 'den Geist und Verstand des Verfassers..., um die Worte wohl zu wählen und füglich zu setzen'.

[2] I have used the text of this work as found in Gerhardt's edition of Leibniz's philosophical works, vol. IV (Berlin, 1880), pp. 138–46.

taken into consideration. Technical words (*privata*) should be avoided by philosophers as much as possible, for there is no concept which cannot be expressed in terms of the vocabulary of normal speech, even though several words may be necessary to replace one special term. No language amongst the current vernaculars, said Leibniz, was better suited to philosophy than German; and this because of its richness in words to denote real things (*realia*), although German was lacking in words to denote non-corporeal things, the fictions of the imagination (*commentitia*). This may seem a strange argument to prove that German is the best language for philosophy, but Leibniz made it quite clear that he wanted philosophy to be more concrete in its vocabulary and, like Nizolius, he censured the scholastics for excessive abstractness. This, he says, is why philosophy in the German tongue appeared so late. Not because philosophy as such was disliked by the Germans, but foreign philosophy of the scholastic type. His ideal for the language of philosophy was that it should be popular, by which he meant accessible to all, and concise: it should possess 'compendiosissimam popularitatem vel popularissimum compendium'.

Leibniz is clearly of great importance in the early stages of the evolution of the German literary language of the eighteenth century. His realisation of the imperfections of the medium was combined with an earnest advocation that it should be employed for serious intellectual purposes, for he believed in its peculiar richness in words denoting *realia* and its potentialities as a medium of expression towards the realisation of which he had made concrete proposals—'verbessern, auszieren, untersuchen'.

In his advocation that German should be used for serious works of scholarship, Leibniz was taking up an admonition that had been expressed before him and stating it more urgently. In the preface to his translation of Terence, published at Tübingen in 1539, Valentin Boltz had said 'Das ist das alt gifft und pestilentzisch Uebel, das wir Teutschen nicht vil acht auff unser Muttersprach gehabt haben, wie sie gepflegt und auffgebracht werd.... Darob werden auch vil stoltz gelerten murren und sagen, es sey nit löblich, daß man alle Ding also in Teutsche sprach bring, das Latein werde dadurch verachtet' and Fischart, in the preface to his *Ehzuchtbüchlin* (1578), stated that he wished to prove by his translation 'das wir Teutschen, wa wir uns der Müh nicht verdrüsen liesen und unsere Sprach excolirten,[1] gleich so wol, ja besser, als andere unvollkommene, gebettelte und gespättelte Sprachen, könten die herrliche Philosophische *Materias* inn unserer unvermengten, reynen und für sich selbs beständigen Mutersprach auspringen'. Similar ideas had also been voiced by the greatest German seventeenth-century grammarian J. G. Schottelius in his *Aüsfuhrliche Arbeit von der Teutschen Haubt-Sprache*, and various passages in the *Unvorgreiffliche Gedanken* suggest that Leibniz knew the work of Schottelius and was indebted to it in various ways.[2] But the extent of Leibniz's dependence on Schottelius has been greatly exaggerated, for Schottelius believed in a standard language regulated by grammarians and schooled by the example of distinguished writers of the past; he seems to have placed little importance on the usage of speech. His 'teutsche Haubt-Sprache' is not based on any one speech-dialect, but accepts as its canon of authority the usage of good writers,[3] and he showed no sign of being interested, as Leibniz was, in the collecting of dialect words. Yet Schottelius had paid like homage to the German language and expressed like regret that it should have fallen into such neglect amongst scholars and serious men of letters. Schottelius had demonstrated the

[1] To cultivate, refine, ennoble; cf. Lat. *excolo*.
[2] Leibniz, in a letter written to William Wotton in 1705, speaks of 'Schottelius, qui non parvo opere linguae Germanicae Grammaticam complexus est, multa habet profutura ad antiquitates Teutonismi noscendas, idemque Scriptores citat' (Duten, vol. VI, 2, p. 218). On the general question of the indebtedness of Leibniz to Schottelius, see Schmarsow, *op. cit.*
[3] 'Die hochteutsche Sprache aber, davon wir handelen und worauff dieses Buch zielet, ist nicht ein *Dialectus* eigentlich, sondern *Lingua ipsa Germanica, sicut viri docti, sapientes & periti eam tandem receperunt & usurpant....* Omnibus dialectis aliquid vitiosi inest, quod locum regulae in Lingua ipsa habere nequit. Lingua haec nostra Germanica per secula gradum fecit & hoc loquendi & scribendi decore induta est, cujus Linguę vera fundamenta ob oculos ponere, eidem artis formam, certitudinis amabilis sedem & aedem struere annitimur, variationum in Dialectis incuriosi' (*Ausführliche Arbeit*, p. 174).

THE VINDICATION OF THE LANGUAGE

richness of the German vocabulary,[1] its wide range of roots and its infinite capacity for forming new derivatives and compounds, in which respect he had likened German to Greek.[2] If once the exact meanings of words were established, then Germans would find that there was no branch of intellectual speculation which could not be given noble expression in their own language.[3] Schottelius was at one with Leibniz in his recognition that the German language needed careful study and improvement. Both he and Leibniz in their admonitions to their countrymen to care for the vernacular and use it for all, even the most serious purposes, were stimulated by a great love of the German language and a sincere belief that it was in danger of running to seed unless it received careful, studied attention and constant use. Schottelius too had realised that if the youth of his country were trained to respect and love their native language, Germany would regain her self-respect; for his book also is permeated by the aftermath of the great catastrophe of the Thirty Years War. In his introductory preface, Schottelius had said that no true knowledge could be attained through the medium of a foreign language. If one neglected one's own language, this implied that one's own nation was inferior in intellectual ability, since one's own language was incapable of expressing intellectual concepts. In all these opinions, Schottelius found a greater and more influential successor in Leibniz. And yet Leibniz continued to publish his works in languages other than the vernacular.

Meanwhile another great figure in the intellectual life of Ger-

---

[1] Schottelius (*op. cit.* p. 1256), like Leibniz, had pointed to the especial richness of the German language in words connected with mining and hunting.

[2] 'Es ist unsere Teutsche Sprache der Grichischen, was die Kunst und Glükk zudoppelen betrifft, vollbürtige Schwester, ja redet noch wol reichlicher in vielen von sich, wie sie denn auch an Menge der Vor- und Stammwörter jener wol zuvorgehet' (*op. cit.* p. 99).

[3] 'Worum solte denn nicht vergönnet, oder vielmehr rühmlich seyn einem Teutschen, deñ leitenden Kräften und grundrichtigem Vermögen seiner Mutter Sprache klüglich und vernünftlich nachzuforschen, nachzufolgen, wol darin zuschürfen, wol zusauberen, und die verborgene Schätze helffen bekant zumachen, damit auch jede Kunst, und jedes Stükke der Wissenschaften gemählig auf Teutsch bekant werden müchte' (*ibid.*).

many at the dawn of the eighteenth century had taken a bold step towards the restitution of true respect towards his native language, but this time in the realm of the spoken word. In the autumn of 1687 Christian Thomasius, celebrated jurist and lecturer at the University of Leipzig, announced in the German language on the screens of the university that he proposed to deliver a course of lectures on the maxims of Balthasar Gracian '...ein Collegium über des Gratians Grund-Reguln, Vernünfftig, klug und artig zu leben'. Both the subject of these lectures and the mode of their announcement were revolutionary, but the important fact for our context is that the announcement was made in the German language and the lectures were delivered in German. This was a blow at the established tyranny of Latin as the language of university instruction, a tyranny which not even Luther had been able to shake. In the seventeenth century there had been isolated voices raised in protest, with the admonition that all instruction should be in the vernacular.[1] There had also been occasional lectures given in the German language by German scholars of distinction, amongst them the humanist Tilemann Heverlingh in Rostock, who had lectured on Juvenal there in German in the year 1501, and Paracelsus himself who had lectured in Basle on medical subjects in the German language round about 1526.[2] But Thomasius seems to have been the first person to *announce* a course of lectures in German. His fixing of the notice in the vernacular to the university screens was a symbolic gesture reminiscent of Luther's nailing his theses to the door of the church

---

[1] Thus, for instance, Wolfgang Radtke (Ratichius) who embodied his proposals in a memorandum presented to the Reichstag in 1612, and Johann Bathasar Schupp who had pointed out, in his *Dissertatio de opinione ex Avellino Marpurgensi* (1655), that a patient could be cured in German just as successfully as in any other language, and that the nature and attributes of God could be studied as well in German as in Latin.

[2] For further details on this topic, the reader is referred to Richard Hodermann, *Universitätsvorlesungen in deutscher Sprache um die Wende des 17. Jahrhunderts* (Diss. Jena; Friedrichroda, 1891) and the article, by the same author, on 'Universitätsvorlesungen in deutscher Sprache: Christian Thomasius, seine Vorgänger und Nachfolger', in the *Wissenschaftliche Beihefte zur Zeitschrift des Allgemeinen Deutschen Sprachvereins*, Heft 8 (Berlin, 1895).

at Wittenberg. It was a gesture to flout authority, a typical gesture from Thomasius whose whole activity was concerned with the overthrow of prejudice and rigid superstition. In Thomasius's mind Latin stood for the weight of past habits of thought, for aristotelianism and scholasticism. Some thirty years later, on looking back at this action, Thomasius declared that nothing had so horrified the University of Leipzig since its foundation, and that the screens might well have been reconsecrated with Holy Water as a result. He himself was eventually persuaded to leave Leipzig. He went to Halle and continued to lecture in the German language. In 1717 Thomasius was able to state that lectures were being given in the German language 'not only at Halle, but at other Protestant universities'.[1] Scholars had now become resigned to the use of German as a language for spoken communication of their learning.

As a preparation to his lectures on Gracian in 1687, Thomasius put out a hastily composed pamphlet addressed to his students and bearing the title *Welcher Gestalt man denen Frantzosen in gemeinem Leben und Wandel nachahmen solle?*[2] The style is lively, direct and attractive. 'Gentlemen,' Thomasius begins, 'if our German forefathers were to rise from the dead and come amongst us, they might think they were in a foreign land.' Everything French seems to be in the fashion—French food, French clothes, French speech, and even French diseases. But, says Thomasius, imitation is not in itself evil, so long as we imitate the *excellence* of our model. The French had evolved an ideal of cultured conduct, denoted by such terms as *honnête homme, homme savant, bel esprit, homme de bon goût, homme galant*. Thomasius considers each of these in turn. The scope of his considerations transcends

---

[1] In a review of Agricola's famous collection of proverbs, in Thomasius's periodical *Summarische Nachrichten von auserlesenen, mehrentheils alten, in der Thomasischen Bibliotheque vorhandenen Büchern*, 23. Stück (1717), p. 917. Copy in the British Museum.

[2] I quote here from the text in *Christian Thomasens Allerhand bißher publicirte Kleine Teutsche Schrifften* (Halle, 1701, p. 21), copy in Central Library, Zürich. There is a modern reprint by Sauer in the *Deutsche Literaturdenkmale des 18. und 19. Jhts*, 'following the original editions of 1687 and 1701', but nevertheless slightly modernised.

the bounds of our subject, but we should notice that Thomasius emphasises the ability to express oneself clearly and with a certain felicity of phrase as a quality of the *bel esprit*. Thomasius also asserts that the great reputation of French scholars was largely due to the fact that they wrote in the vernacular. But as for Germany...

So ist auch offenbahr, daß wir in Teutschland unsere Sprache bey weiten so hoch nicht halten als die Frantzosen die ihrige. Denn an statt, daß wir uns befleißigen solten, die guten Wissenschafften in Teutscher Sprache geschickt zu schreiben, so fallen wir entweder auff die eine Seite aus, und bemühen uns die Lateinischen oder Griechischen *terminos technicos* mit dunckeln und lächerlichen Worten zu verhuntzen, oder aber wir kommen in die andere Ecke, und bilden uns ein, unsere Sprache sey nur zu denen Handlungen in gemeinen Leben nützlich, oder schicke sich, wenn es auffs höchste kömmt, zu nichts mehr, als Histörgen, und neue Zeitungen darinnen zu schreiben, nicht aber die *Philosophi*schen oder derer höhern *Facult*äten Lehren und Grund-Regeln in selbiger vorzustellen.

It is perplexing, however, to find this passage, so close in general tenor to the observations of Leibniz, succeeded by the assertion that it would be difficult to elevate the German language to such a state of perfection for it to be suitable for learned works because this had been tried by the Fruchtbringende Gesellschaft, amongst others, but without success. Thomasius argues from the observation that French was the common language of intercourse in cultured circles in Germany to an admonition that it should be used for the propagation of learning. His position is therefore ambiguous: he deduces the superiority of French scholarship as being largely due to the use of the vernacular, but he would not recommend vernacular writing for the Germans because he finds the German language imperfect. This is characteristic of the uncertainty which prevailed on this topic at this time—as significant in its way as the ambiguity of Leibniz's advocating that Germans should use their own language for scholarly works and yet not doing so himself. But Thomasius's statement of the problem is more significant than the remedy suggested; for this is an early work of Thomasius, and not a major one, nor the fruit of careful thought, it would seem. He may at this time have considered that the German language could better be enriched by the use and study of an already accepted foreign vernacular than by tinkering with the existing vernacular on purist lines such as the Fruchtbringende Gesellschaft had practised. But he must have changed his mind; for in later life Thomasius devoted great attention, both as a teacher and as a writer, to the cultivation and use of the German language for purposes of serious communication.

In the preface, addressed to students, of his *Einleitung zu der Vernunfft-Lehre* (1691),[1] Thomasius justified his use of the vernacular in this work by stating that he wished to appeal to a wide public. The Greeks had not written their philosophy in Hebrew, nor the Romans in Greek—each of these great nations had used its vernacular because they rightly envisaged philosophy as a subject for all men. The French philosophers of recent times had followed the ancients in using the vernacular for their writings. Why should the Germans, by not doing so, suggest to other nations that philosophy and learning could not be written in their language? Latin, Thomasius said elsewhere, was not a necessary prerequisite for learning, although it was, naturally enough, essential to one who would know and understand Latin philosophy.[2] But the knowledge of Latin was not in itself a sign of superior intelligence or learning. In his *Gemischter Discours bey Intimirung fünf neuer Collegiorum* (1691)[3] Thomasius said that after years of lecturing experience he had found that most of his audience were unable to write good German, even though some of them had been able to write good Latin. He implied that excessive and exclusive study of Latin had diminished interest in and respect for the vernacular. He therefore instituted in Halle a course of regular

[1] I have not been able to see the first edition of this work, but quote from the copy of the second edition (Halle, 1699) in the University Library, Cambridge. The British Museum has the fourth edition of 1711.

[2] *Ausübung der Vernunfft-Lehre*, 2nd edn., Halle, 1699, §§ 78, 79. Copy in Cambridge University Library. British Museum has 1710 edition.

[3] Contained in the *Kleine Teutsche Schriften* of 1701 (see p. 13, n. 2 above) and reprinted (ed. Opel) in 1894.

lectures on style, the celebrated *Collegium Styli* of Thomasius, in which he tried to give his students regular and practical training in the writing and speaking of their own language. This he considered to be an essential part of the training of a lawyer. In a handbook which he published for the use of law students,[1] Thomasius recommended to them the study of grammar, poetry and rhetoric. The study of the German language, he said, was neglected in his day and this neglect was fostered by schools and universities. The study of German grammar would teach jurists how to speak correctly, the study of poetry would give the young lawyer many a 'scharfsinnige Fiction' to prove his point when pleading in court, and the study of rhetoric would help him evolve a good oratorical style. For oratory three qualities are essential: *perspicuitas, decentia* and *gravitas*—the language of the lawyer should be *deutlich, anständig, und nachdrücklich*. Natural skill is required, but this could be assisted by the study of rhetoric which distinguishes three styles: *hoch, mittelmäßig* and *niedrig*.[2] The 'high' style was usually recommended for legal oratory, but Thomasius prefers the 'middle' style. He would not, however, discountenance the 'scharfsinnige, schertzhaffte und aufgeweckte Schreibart', which has its uses on appropriate occasions, nor would he reject all 'Zierligkeit der Rede'. But ornamentation should be used moderately and style should consist more 'in einer sittsamen und ungezwungenen Deutlichkeit... als in gekünstelten Worten und Figuren'. We each have our natural style and we should not try to assume another. Thomasius advocates a style which is the mean between the too concise (which tends to be obscure) and the too wordy (which tends to be tiresome); the young lawyer must always make sure that his style is richer in thoughts than in words. Clarity should always come before ornamentation; the lawyer should not aim at oratorical figures but concentrate solely on the clear presentation of the cause of

[1] *Höchstnöthige Cautelen welche ein studiosus juris der sich zu Erlernung der Rechts-Gelahrheit auff eine kluge und geschickte Weise vorbereiten will, zu beobachten hat* (Halle, 1713). I quote from the British Museum copy.

[2] This distinction derives from the rhetorical treatises of antiquity, especially from Cicero.

THE VINDICATION OF THE LANGUAGE

his client. Thomasius recommends his lawyer to study Latin, French and German authors, but laments the lack of good German authors. This, he says,[1] is primarily due to the neglect of the German language, for although the desire to improve it had been present for some years, very little had been achieved in this direction. This strange little work forms an interesting pendant to the *Collegium Styli* of Thomasius which he instituted in Halle as an inherent part of the Law course. He has left us a description of these lectures,[2] and from this we see that they embodied the same principles as he advocated in the *Cautelen*. He used to begin with theoretical lectures on usage, illustrating his precepts by reference to good German authors. Then he would set his students to compose a letter on some given subject, or a speech on some formal occasion, a letter of proposal to a young lady, or just some short anecdote. He would then proceed from these simple exercises to the writing of essays without giving his students any plan to follow, eventually allowing them to choose their own subjects. Clarity and ease of expression were the qualities which he considered essential to good style and which he tried to imbue in his pupils by these exercises.

In the second section of his *Ausübung der Vernunfft-Lehre* (1691),[3] Thomasius drew attention to the fact that learned writers and teachers had quite consciously cultivated a style which had neither clarity nor ease of expression. They had striven after a highly figurative and esoteric style, so that learning had unfortunately become associated with a certain type of bombastic obscurity in the eyes of the general public, who thought that nothing could be profound or learned if it were said simply and clearly. Thomasius's ideal of *Deutlichkeit* involves the avoidance of ambiguity, of excessively figurative language and of bombastic overstatement. One should proceed from the simple to the more difficult in an easily evolving, natural order. The orator must

---
[1] *Op. cit.* ch. 9, §26.
[2] In the *Gemischter Discours* quoted above, 1701 edition, p. 379.
[3] I have used the second edition of 1699; the section is entitled 'Von der Geschickligkeit andern die Erkäntniß des wahren beyzubringen'. Copy in Cambridge University Library.

appeal to the emotions by the turn of phrase which he uses; but the philosopher should only employ the simplest examples and similes (as Socrates did), for truth is most beauteous when she is naked. Thomasius's other desideratum was *Artigkeit*, by which he meant the quality of not being clumsy, disagreeable, disorderly or irritating. The style should be appropriate to the subject, the occasion and the audience. Let me conclude by quoting Thomasius in his own colourful language:

Befleißige dich einer solchen Schreibart, die vernünfftig gelehrten Leuten nicht unangenehm ist, und ihnen mehr Warheit als leere Worte beybringet.

Das ist: Hüte dich, daß du in Schrifften für gelehrte Leute nicht mit gantzen Wägen voll Syllogismis auffgezogen kömmst, und daß nicht auff allen Blättern *Quicquid, Atqui — Ergo, Distinguo, Applico, Limito, Probo Majorem, Conclusio est absurda* u.s.w. zu lesen sey. Denn gewiß die gelehrte Welt ist heut zu tage zu *galant* dazu, daß sie an diesen Disteln...einen Geschmack finden solte....

Der Verstand eines weisen Mannes ist begierig Warheit in deiner Schrifft zu finden, und kanst seine Begierde nicht besser stillen, als wenn du ihm dieselbe mit Hauffen giebst, und mit vergeblichen Worten nicht auffhältest, oder mit verführischen Worten ihn an statt der Warheit Irrthümer beybringen wilst.[1]

Thomasius was no mere theorist. We have seen that his *Programm* of 1687 represented a vindication of German as a language for scholars to use in lecturing, and that he responded to his own challenge by his lectures on Gracian. The course of our considerations has taken us, however, far beyond the lecture-room; for Thomasius was equally anxious, as we have seen, that scholars should use German for the *written* communication of their thoughts. Here, too, Thomasius did not content himself with admonition. He wrote a series of philosophical works in German and he gave to Germany her first literary periodical in the vernacular. It was in these two spheres, the philosophic treatise and the literary journal, that the German language showed itself earliest as an instrument worthy to rank with contemporary French in the period under survey.

[1] *Ausübung der Vernunfft-Lehre*, ed. cit. pp. 143–7.

II

THE LANGUAGE OF PHILOSOPHY

WHEN Christian Thomasius offered his treatise on logic to the Leipzig censor in 1689, the *imprimatur* was refused on the grounds that 'no work could be considered by the censorship in which philosophical matters were treated in the German language'. This event is significant, for although personal antipathy to Thomasius may have been involved in this refusal, the terms of the refusal proved Leibniz's contention that there was a contemporary objection amongst German scholars to the use of the German language for scholarly purposes. This objection was primarily academic; but it did not hold good in Halle, where a newly founded university was priding itself on being up-to-date. This treatise on logic was one of the first things which Thomasius published after his arrival in Halle, where it appeared in 1691 under the title *Einleitung ʒu der Vernunfft-Lehre*. It was not by any means the first philosophical treatise to be published in the German language, although most philosophical works by Germans were still being published in Latin or French at this time, including such important works as Tschirnhausen's *Medicina Mentis* (1689) and Leibniz's *Théodicéé* (1710). But the personality of Thomasius, the public interest which surrounded him at this time of his life, the place of publication and the audience which he envisaged and consciously wrote for, all these considerations make his *Einleitung ʒu der Vernunfft-Lehre* a work of especial significance for our investigation.

Thomasius wrote this treatise for the same type of courtly young men as those to whom he had advocated French ideals of cultured conduct in his *Programm* of 1687. It was intended for a similar audience, although in a different place, to that which he had addressed on the maxims of Gracian. The *Einleitung ʒu der Vernunfft-Lehre* had grown out of his lecturing experience; it was to provide his students with a satisfactory manual and thus relieve them of the necessity of note-taking, a practice which, as Thomasius explained in his *Vorrede an die studirende Jugend*,[1] had its disadvantages both for lecturer and student. Thomasius did not envisage an audience consisting solely of the sons of the rich, for in this same preface he discussed measures by which poor students should be enabled to attend his lectures. But his ideal of courtly conduct was one for all men, for rich and poor alike; and he constantly emphasised the practical uses of the study of philosophy. 'Mein Zweck ist, die zu einem tugendhafften und beglückten Leben in dieser Welt führende Welt-Weißheit fürzustellen',[2] or again: 'Dieses ist keine Gelahrheit zu nennen, die weder in dem menschlichen Leben einigen Nutzen schaffet, noch zur Seeligkeit anführet.'[3] He chose therefore to write in the German language because he wanted philosophy to be accessible and useful to all: 'Die Weltweißheit ist so leichte, daß dieselbige von allen Leuten, sie mögen seyn, von was für Stande oder Geschlecht sie wollen, begriffen werden kan.' Philosophers of all nations had written in their own tongue, including the French of his own day. 'Warum sollen denn wir Teutschen stets während von andern uns wegen dieses Vortheils auslachen lassen, als ob die Philosophie und Gelahrheit nicht in unserer Sprache vorgetragen werden könte.' Thomasius used the language which he

[1] I have used the second revised edition of 1699 (see footnote 1 on p. 15 above).
[2] *Ed. cit. Erstes Hauptstück*, p. 7. The word *Weltweisheit* is common in the eighteenth century as a German term for *Philosophie*. The latter word was already borrowed in M.H.G., hence early N.H.G. *Philosophei*. The eighteenth-century form *Philosophie* represents re-borrowing, this time through French. Adelung (1786) concedes that the word *Weltweisheit* is old (Williram uses *werltwiso* for 'philosopher') but states that it was less commonly used than *Philosophie* because it was vaguer, and because *philosophisch* was a better adjective than *weltweise*. This passage is unchanged in the second edition (1801).
[3] *Ibid*. p. 11. *Gelahrheit* is a by-form of *Gelahrtheit*, meaning 'learning' (Mod.Ger. *Gelehrsamkeit*). Adelung says that *gelahrt* is an 'Upper German' form of *gelehrt*, and that *Gelahrtheit* was then (1775) archaic and had been replaced by *Gelehrsamkeit*. *Gelahrtheit* had, in fact, developed a pejorative sense during the eighteenth century. Gottsched (*Beobachtungen*, 1758—see below, p. 145) says that *Gelahrtheit* means the same as *Gelehrsamkeit*.

expected his audience to understand. His style exactly matched his approach. The construction of this treatise may seem puzzling to the modern reader who comes to it from an acquaintance with the usual manuals of logic. It lacks any strictly mathematical method of exposition, because it antedates the establishment of such a method in German philosophy and also because such a method would have been unsuited to Thomasius's immediate purpose. He was concerned to attract his audience to the subject, and to show them that the study of logic had more connections with the art of living than the highly abstract treatises of others might suggest. He rejected the syllogism as a means to the attainment of higher truth[1] and because his presentation lacks this essential foundation, it appears disjointed and unsystematic. But this was part of his war against the tyranny of scholasticism. He was anxious to remove the stigma of Leibniz's contention that the German universities were monkish establishments, full of dead learning and pedantry, and without any real contact with life and its problems. In these aspirations Thomasius was assisted by the place of his work; for the University of Halle had been founded in this new spirit and Paul von Fuchs in his inaugurating address had stressed the connections of learning with life, and the usefulness of the universities to the nation. Thomasius wanted the discussion of current problems in university classes. He was not prepared to equate the teaching of law with the discussion of Justinian. Philosophy should not consist merely in academic discussions of the philosophies of the past. German learning was cumbersome and remote whereas he admired the graceful and useful learning of the French, their *beauté d'esprit*. His first important philosophical work, written in Latin, had appeared in Leipzig in 1688 under the urbane title, *Introductio ad Philosophiam Aulicam* (later translated into German by another hand as *Einleitung zur Hoff-Philosophie*); and in a German *Programm* of 1689

[1] The title-page promises that 'durch eine leichte, und allen vernünfftigen Menschen, waserley Standes oder Geschlechts sie seyn, verständliche Manier der Weg gezeiget wird, *ohne die Syllogisticâ* das wahre, wahrscheinliche und falsche voneinander zu entscheiden, und neue Warheiten zu erfinden' (my italics). See also the passage from the *Ausübung der Vernunfft-Lehre* quoted above (p. 18).

he had defined logic as the science of clearing the mind of prejudices, and ethics as the art of living pleasantly and agreeably. In the preface to the *Einleitung zu der Vernunfft-Lehre* Thomasius contrasted the scope of this work with that of his *Introductio ad Philosophiam Aulicam*. Its purpose should be 'nicht so wohl die Erforschung der Wahrheit, als die Erkäntniß derer gemeinen Irrthümer'; hence his work would consist rather of short summaries than of detailed discussion...

und fast aus nichts anders, als aus *hypothesibus, definitionibus, axiomatibus, propositionibus* und *observationibus* bestehen, wiewohl ich, um meinen Zuhörern die Lust nicht zu vermindern, nicht jedes von diesen *classen à part tractir*en, sondern mit Fleiß die *axiomata, definitiones, observationes* u.s.w., mit einander vermischen will, doch also, daß die *methode* dadurch nicht *confus* gemacht werde, sondern leicht und *naturell* bleibe.[1]

This style seems to us the very opposite of 'leicht und naturell'; yet it was well suited to Thomasius's purpose and audience. It is studded with foreign words, sometimes Latin and sometimes French. The technical terms are usually the Latin ones then in existence, the French words are usually taken from general cultured vocabulary at the time, such as *à part, confus* and *naturell* in the above passage. Sometimes Thomasius preserves the Latin case-ending, as we see in the terms he uses above, but at other times he does not (e.g. 'aus eben dem *Fundament*'). He often gives foreign words a termination more current in German than the Latin or French ending, but this 'naturalisation' of foreign words is usually confined to those words which we might justly expect to have formed part of the general cultured vocabulary of those days. Thus we find verbs like *attaquiren, continuiren, acceptiren, defendiren*, nouns like *definition, connexion, meditation, protestation* which might be conceived as loans from French but there is also *defension, publicirung, concept* and *scribenten*. Sometimes Thomasius alternates between a naturalised and a non-naturalised form; thus he uses both *odios* and *odiös* in close

---

[1] *Ed. cit.* Vorrede, p. 67.

proximity, *sectae* and *Secten*, *caput* and *Capitel*. It is also a feature of his style to give both the German and the foreign term for the same concept—*Schmähungen oder Calumnien; die hochnöthige doctrin de Praejudiciis oder von denen Vorurtheilen; Zweiffel* on one line and then *dubia* a few lines later. These examples could be multiplied indefinitely, and in this respect the language of Thomasius would not seem to differ very much from that of most other learned men writing in German at that time, except that one does feel that there is a greater dependence than was normal in such circles upon the vocabulary of cultured *speech*. This opinion is strongly reinforced by the many turns of phrase which Thomasius has adopted from quite colloquial speech—images which suggest popular, homely speech rather than the language of courtly youth. In the preface to the *Einleitung zu der Vernunfft-Lehre*, Thomasius deals at length with some criticism he had received, referring to it as 'dieses *Gekeiffe*'. Of the words of his critic, he says: 'Auf mich aber reimen sie sich, *wie eine Faust auf ein Auge.*' 'Der Autor...mir hätte *auff die Haube greiffen* wollen', he had 'Meynungen aus dem Cartesio *erschnapt*'. Other examples of this forceful popular idiom are: 'so hätte vielleicht der Titel dem Leser nicht *das Maul so wässerig gemacht*'; 'Gleichwohl ist die Jugend nachläßig, und will es sich nicht allemahl *ein wenig sauer werden lassen*, absonderlich aber diejenigen, denen Gott für andern Mittel bescheret. Ich will dannenhero auch diesen nach meinem Vermögen *unter die Arme greiffen*'; 'Nachdem er uns das gantze caput...*als ein glaubwürdiges Evangelium hergebetet*'. All these examples have been taken from the early part of this work, which is polemical in nature. Despite this, it must surely be agreed that the general tone is unexpected as an introduction to a philosophical treatise. These two features of the style of Thomasius, namely the use of foreign technical words and of native colloquial speech-phrases, may seem at first glance to be incompatible. Yet on occasions they blend into a strange unity, as we can see from the following sentence which combines foreign philosophical terms with the colloquial metaphors of soldiery: 'Ich wolte aber wünschen, daß er einen angetroffen hätte, der ihm was *suppeditiret*, mit welchem er die bekante *distinction inter primum cognitum & primum principium*, als welche alle seine *objectiones bombardiret*, hätte unterminiren können.'[1] This language, strange as it may seem to us today, would have appealed to the gay young sparks and bloods in Thomasius's audience, for it was applying the language of their own speech to the subject-matter and the concepts of contemporary philosophy.

All German philosophy of this time suffered under the disadvantage that no philosophical terminology had as yet been established in the German language.[2] Some writers had retained the Latin terms intact; others had attempted to find German equivalents, but the equivalents varied from author to author, there was no generally accepted terminology, and we even find the same author using various words for one Latin term without any attempt at differentiation. This linguistic uncertainty was but the external sign of the vagueness of philosophical concepts in Germany at this time. If philosophers worked with ill-defined concepts, one could hardly expect them to evolve a stable German terminology for these wavering concepts. Thomasius approached this question of terminology in the fifth section of the preface to the *Einleitung zu der Vernunfft-Lehre*, and expressed his objection to the fabrication of German equivalents for the Latin technical terms of philosophy. His standpoint is briefly this: if a philosophical concept is naturally and normally referred to by a foreign name, then we should continue to use this name. In this we have the distinguished precedent of Cicero who did not hesitate to use Greek philosophical terms. But if an accepted German equivalent exists and is used in current speech, then let us use that. The philosopher should call things by the names they customarily bear, whether these be foreign or native. Thomasius had in mind

---

[1] *Vorrede*, pp. 61–2. *Suppeditiren* means 'to provide, furnish with'.

[2] For a sketch of the development of philosophical terminology in German since the days of Notker, see Rudolf Eucken, *Geschichte der philosophischen Terminologie* (Leipzig, 1879). Unfortunately the early eighteenth century is dealt with very sketchily.

a particular work, the *Cöthener Logik* of 1621,[1] which had translated all the philosophical terms. To illustrate the absurdity of these translations, Thomasius composes a letter in which he uses some of them. We can see from some of these examples what he disliked in this 'German' terminology: phrases like 'ob der Mensch *eine unterste Art* sey', '*einzele*' (for *individua*), '*ein theilender oder artmachender Unterscheid*' did violence to the spirit of the German language; words such as 'Aufflösungen, Grundsätzen, Eintheilungen, Anfügungen und Begräntzungen' were obscure; the characterisation of hot and cold as 'widerwärtige oder benehmliche entgegengesetzte' was cumbersome and absurd. Thomasius does not explain his objections, he just holds this 'terminology' up to ridicule.[2] He himself advocates the middle way, 'und weder allzusehr affectire, ausländische Wörter in eine Sprache zu mischen, noch auch alle Kunst-Wörter in die Sprache, darinnen man schreibet'. Therefore he will sometimes speak of 'selbständiges Wesen', sometimes of 'Substanz'; he will use both 'Gegenstand' and 'Object', both 'Stoff' and 'Materie'; but on no account will he ever use 'Unterlage' for 'subjectum' or 'Die Zeugemutter aller Dinge' for 'Natur'.[3] His criterion would seem to be, therefore, the avoidance of the unnatural and the absurd; and he seems to be fully aware of the uncontrollable associations which must needs cling to a word transferred from ordinary speech to the special domain of philosophical vocabulary. Christian Weise's attitude was similar. 'Etliche thun hier zu viel, etliche wollen gar zu wenig zulassen' he said in *Der Grünenden Jugend Nothwendige Gedancken*.[4] It would be a good thing if the Germans could denote their virtues without having recourse to

---

[1] Thomasius says that its full title was *Kurtzer Begriff der Verstand Lehre zu der Lehr-Art*. I have been unable to see a copy.

[2] See also the passage from the *Programm* of 1687, quoted above (p. 14).

[3] This is aimed at Philipp von Zesen who had advocated the word *Zeugemutter* for *Natur* (*Adriatische Rosemund*, 1645, ed. Jellinek, p. 269). Schottelius (*Haubt-Sprache*, p. 1368) writes: 'Schendlich ist es, der alten Haubt Sprache dieses Wort Natur entziehen wollen, und eine grosse Zeugemutter mit Zitzen daraus machen....'

[4] I quote from the copy of the 1690 edition in the British Museum. This passage is on p. 307. The one quoted below is on p. 308.

foreign expressions. In philosophy, mathematics and politics, however, there were many technical terms which were difficult to render in German: 'Da soll bey etlichen *Objectum* ein Gegenwurff, *Subjectum* eine Unterlage, *Elementum* ein Urwesen, *Pistole* ein Reitpuffer, *Contrescarpe* ein verdeckter Weg, *Lieutenant* ein Platz-Halter, *Corps de Garde* eine Wach-Versamlung heissen. Doch was richten wir damit aus, als daß wir von wenigen verstanden, und von den meisten ausgelachet werden.' Christian Weise has strayed from the realm of philosophy in his enthusiasm. But he has made his point and made it well.

It was Christian Wolff (1679–1754) who introduced into Germany both the reasoned presentation of philosophy and a stable philosophical terminology. He was, as Kant said later,[1] 'der Urheber des bisher noch nicht erloschenen Geistes der Gründlichkeit in Deutschland'. He taught the Germans how to think in logical progression, and his exposition depended on a foundation of clearly defined concepts which brought with it a set of recognised terms. Wolff evolved this terminology gradually. The coherence of his presentation and style is explained largely by the fact that he came to philosophy by way of mathematics. His exposition reminds one of Descartes, from whom it indeed derived by way of Tschirnhausen with whom Wolff, in contrast to Thomasius, shared his faith in the syllogism as the only foundation of valid argument. Wolff's *Habilitationsschrift* in Leipzig had been a Latin treatise on mathematical method as applied to philosophy, in which he substantially adopted the standpoint of Descartes. His first published work in the German language was a treatise on mathematics, the *Anfangs-Gründe aller mathematischer Wissenschaften* (1710). German treatises on individual branches of mathematics had been quite common in the sixteenth and seventeenth centuries,[2] but Wolff embraced the whole breadth of

[1] *Kritik der reinen Vernunft*, Preface to 2nd edition, 1787.
[2] Notker's arithmetical treatise (probably a version of that by Boethius) is lost. The oldest preserved mathematical treatises in German would seem to be the version of Sacrobosco's *Sphaera Mundi* by Konrad von Megenberg (*c.* 1350) and the *Geometria Culmensis* of about 1400, with Latin text and German translation. The fifteenth century saw several works on separate branches of mathe-

mathematical investigation up to his time, and established a mathematical vocabulary which has remained essentially intact to our own day. The work begins with a defence of mathematical method as 'das sicherste Mittel zu hurtigem Gebrauche der Vernunfft, so wohl in Erfindung der noch verborgenen, als in Beurtheilung der bereits erfundenen Wahrheit zu gelangen, und sich von der schädlichen Herrschafft der Sinnen und Imagination zu befreyen, das ist, alle Irrthümer und Vorurtheile glücklich zu vermeiden'.[1] Let us note in passing the rejection of imagination which can have no place in Wolff's strictly rational argument. Wolff then explains why he wrote the work in German, and his explanation is very simple: 'Ich habe diese Anfangs-Gründe Deutsch geschrieben, weil sie unsern Deutschen zu Dienste stehen sollen.' He then says that he has preserved the technical terms and merely given them terminations suited to the German 'Mund-Art'.[2] This is true in the main for the actual terms of mathematics. Wolff does use 'naturalised' foreign terms like *addiren, substrahiren, multipliciren, dividiren, dupliren, Product, Quotient, Quadrat, Proportion, Linie, Punct*; but he also uses

matics, some using German terms, some retaining the foreign terms. The big increase came at the beginning of the sixteenth century with the printing of various aids to ready reckoning. During this century we find various treatises on arithmetic and several translations of Euclid. Albrecht Dürer's geometrical treatise of 1525 assiduously avoided foreign terms. An important stage was represented by Kepler's translation of his own *Nova Stereometria* (1616) which is preceded by a German–Latin glossary. During the seventeenth century the use of German equivalents for foreign terms in mathematical treatises was more frequent and more thorough. But no agreement on accepted equivalents was achieved.

On this whole subject see Felix Müller, 'Zur Terminologie der ältesten mathematischen Schriften in deutscher Sprache' in the supplement to the 44th Jahrgang of the *Zeitschrift für Mathematik und Physik* (Leipzig, 1899), pp. 301–33. Also Alfred Schirmer, *Der Wortschatz der Mathematik nach Alter und Herkunft untersucht*. Beiheft zum XIV. Bd. der *Zeitschrift für deutsche Wortforschung* (Strassburg, 1912). On Kepler, see A. Götze, *Anfänge einer mathematischen Fachsprache in Keplers Deutsch*, 1919 (=Eberings Germanische Studien, Heft 1).

[1] I quote from the third edition of 1725 (copy in Central Library, Zürich). The British Museum has the fourth edition of 1750.

[2] This word must, of course, be understood in its early eighteenth-century meaning of 'speech'.

native terms like *Wurtzel*, *Zahl*, *Bruch*, *Nenner*. One might deduce from these examples that Wolff, like Thomasius, was employing the term in most general use. This, as we shall see later, is not precisely the case.

The lexical situation is difficult to assess. There had been no lack of suggested German equivalents for the technical terms of mathematics. But no set of terms had established themselves as paramount or absolute. It was this *establishment* of an accepted mathematical vocabulary which Wolff achieved. It is difficult to assess with any degree of accuracy how far he can be said to have *created* this vocabulary. Some of his German terms are found in earlier treatises. This may mean that he was reviving them; it may, however, mean nothing of the sort, for he may well have arrived independently at the same result as someone else centuries before. Thus when Wolff explains 'ein Divisor oder Theiler', this may look like his invention, yet the word is found in a treatise of 1460.[1] On the other hand, 'perpendicular oder senckrecht' embodies a *Verdeutschung* first found in J. C. Sturm's *Teutscher Archimedes* of 1670. But neither of these facts proves that either of these words was a current mathematical expression when Wolff was writing, let alone that it was the *accepted* German equivalent at that time.

Some of the foreign terms are still retained by Wolff. Thus, in the section on the circle, he uses the word *Circul*, despite the fact that the word *Kreis* had been used in the strictly geometrical connotation by Kepler, Harsdörffer and more recently by L. C. Sturm in his mathematical encyclopaedia of 1707.[2] He also uses *Peripherie* for 'circumference', although both *Umkreis* and *Umfang* were in use at the end of the seventeenth century for this same concept. (Pirckenstein, in his translation of Euclid published in 1694, gives 'Umbkreiß, Circumferenz oder Peripheria'; the rather puristic Samuel Reyher, in his Euclid of five years later, gives 'Umbkreyß oder Umbfang'.) But along with these foreign

---

[1] See Schirmer, *Wortschatz der Mathematik*, p. 71.
[2] L. C. Sturm, *Kurtzer Begriff der gesambten Mathesis* (Frankfurt an der Oder, 1707).

terms we find Wolff in this same section using *Mittel-Punct* (a well-established hybrid, used by Dürer amongst others in the sixteenth century but usually given alongside *centrum* in Wolff's day), *Halbmesser* and *Durchmesser* (seventeenth-century renderings of 'radius' and 'diameter'),[1] and *Sehne* for 'chord', first found with this connotation in the sixteenth century.[2] The last example represents the addition of a specifically mathematical connotation to the range of meanings enjoyed by a word already in general use. Wolff frequently employs words from the general vocabulary with a specific mathematical connotation—such as *Schwere, Kraft, Last, Ort, Bewegung, Größe* and *Ähnlichkeit*. This, too, is an important part of his establishment of a native vocabulary for a scientific discipline.

Important for our consideration is the vocabulary of method, for these terms Wolff was to apply to philosophy in general, and from this sphere they passed into the vocabulary of general cultured speech. The terms which Wolff uses for method are almost entirely German, and the *Anfangs-Gründe aller mathematischer Wissenschaften* is prefixed by an essay entitled 'Kurtzer Unterricht von der mathematischen Methode oder Lehrart' in which he defines these terms, and gives their Latin equivalents. Precise definition of concepts leads to precisely delineated terms. He divides *Erklärungen*[3] (*definitiones*) into *Erklärungen der Wörter* (*definitiones nominales*) and *Erklärungen der Sachen* (*definitiones reales*). Here we find the famous word *Begriff*,[4] established in its

---

[1] Both found first in J. C. Sturm's translation of Archimedes (1667). Older terms were: for 'radius', *halber Diameter* or *Semidiameter*, for 'diameter', *Diameter, Mittelriß, Durchzug, Durchschneider* and *Durchschlag*.

[2] See Schirmer, *op. cit.* p. 65, and Müller, *op. cit.* p. 328.

[3] This use of *Erklärung* is an example of stabilisation. In earlier mathematical treatises we find various renderings of *definitio*, amongst them also *Beschreibung* and *Auslegung*.

[4] *Begriff* has quite a range of meanings in M.H.G., most of which show closer connection with the verb *be-grifen*. Thus the meanings 'Umfang', 'Bezirk'. Lexer finds that the noun is used to mean 'Umfang und Inhalt einer Vorstellung' with the mystics. (The *DWb.* gives no example of the meaning 'notio' before Winckelmann and Lessing!) Eduard Brodführer, in Trübner's *Deutsches Wörterbuch*, cites its use by Luther to mean 'Vorstellung', and adds that Wolff used it first as a synonym for *Vorstellung*, later distinguishing carefully between these

precise philosophical connotation by Wolff. The distinction is made between *klare* and *dunckle Begriffe*, with *klar* sub-divided into *deutlich* and *undeutlich*, and *deutlich* into *vollständig* and *unvollständig*. *Lehrsatz* is the term which Wolff uses for 'theorem', *Aufgabe* for 'problem', *Zusatz* for 'corollary'.[1] The statement (*Satz*) is divided into the *Bedingung* (hypothesis) and the *Aussage* (thesis).

In all his philosophical works, Wolff proceeds from a set of concepts which he clearly defines, giving to each its German name. Already in the first of these works, the treatise on logic published in 1712 under the title *Vernünfftige Gedancken von den Kräfften des menschlichen Verstandes und ihrem richtigen Gebrauche in Erkäntniß der Wahrheit*, the Latin terms have almost entirely disappeared. Here is a sample of the language taken from the chapter in which Wolff treats of the various types of statement:[2]

Der Grund, warumb einem Dinge etwas zukommen kan oder nicht, ist entweder in ihm, und zwar in etwas zu suchen, was es beständig an sich hat, oder in etwas, so es nur zu gewisser Zeit unter gewissen Bedingungen hat, oder endlich ausser ihm in etwas anderem. Z.E. Der Grund, warumb der Stein schweer ist, muß in seiner Materie, daraus er bestehet, und also in etwas, daß der Stein immer an sich hat, gesuchet

---

two words ('Hierdurch gelangen wir zu Vorstellungen der Geschlechter und Arten der Dinge, welches man eigentlich Begriffe zu nennen pfleget', *Met.* I (1743), §152). The word first became frequent through its use by Wolff, and it spread into ordinary literary language during the course of the eighteenth century.

[1] *Lehrsatz* would seem to be a creation of the Fruchtbringende Gesellschaft (Weigand[5] gives examples dated 1648 and 1657). J. C. Sturm used it in 1670, but Wolff establishes it in his *Mathematisches Lexikon* of 1716. Other terms included *Betrachtung* and *Beweisstück* (Samuel Reyher, 1697), and *Theorem*. *Aufgabe* is found already in sixteenth-century mathematical treatises. This term was well established by the time of Wolff. *Handgriff* and *Werkstück* were other seventeenth-century terms for this concept. *Zusatz* replaces older *Folge*, *Nachsatz* or *corollarium*. Adelung gives it as synonymous with *Zugabe*. Wolff's own *Mathematisches Lexikon* had given both: 'Zugabe oder Zusatz heißet ein Satz, welcher aus einem andern hergeleitet wird' (quoted in *DWb.*). Three essential aspects of Wolff's achievement are therefore illustrated by these three words: he established *Lehrsatz*, confirmed *Aufgabe* and introduced *Zusatz*.

[2] Text taken from the fourth edition of 1725, pp. 70–2. Copy in British Museum. I have abbreviated most of Wolff's cumbersome titles in the references of this and succeeding chapters, and shall refer to this work as Wolff's *Logic*.

werden. Fraget man aber, warumb der Stein das Bette warm gemacht; so muß der Grund in seiner Wärme, und also in etwas, welches er nur unter gewissen Umständen haben kan, nemlich wenn er lange im warmen, als im heissen Wasser oder auf dem heissen Ofen gelegen, gesuchet werden. Endlich wenn ich frage, warumb der Stein warm ist, so wird der Grund ausser ihm, als etwan im heissen Wasser, darinnen er gehangen, oder in dem heissen Ofen, darauf er gelegen, gesuchet. In dem ersten Falle nun muß allen Dingen von einer Art zukommen, was einem zukommet; in dem andern aber nur etlichen, nemlich die sich unter einerley oder gleichgültigen Umständen befinden. Z.E. Alle Steine sind schweer; aber nur etliche machen warm, die nemlich warm sind: und nur etliche werden warm, die nemlich im Warmen lange liegen. In dem ersten Falle werden die Sätze *allgemein*; in den anderen beyden aber *besondere Sätze* genennet.

...Man siehet aber hieraus, daß ein jeder Satz gar leichte in zwey Theile sich zergliedern lässet. Der erste ist die *Bedingung* unter welcher einem Dinge etwas zukommet, oder nicht zukommen kan, nemlich weil es entweder dieses oder jenes an sich hat, oder auch sich unter diesen oder jenen Umständen befindet. Der andere Theil ist die *Aussage*, welche dasjenige in sich enthält, was einer Sache zukommet, oder nicht zukommen kan. Z.E. In dem Satze, der warme Stein machet warm, ist die Bedingung, daß der Stein warm sey: die Aussage aber, daß er warm mache. Derowegen kan man ihn auch solchergestalt ausdrucken: Wenn der Stein warm ist; so machet er warm. Da zeigen sich die gedachten Theile gar deutlich.

This is a very typical example of Wolff's prose. The exposition is very systematic and very clear, for all implications of every statement are fully explored and each is aptly illustrated. We shall consider later the more general features of this style; let us concentrate for the moment on the vocabulary. For his philosophical concepts Wolff uses German words whose meaning seems to us self-evident. Yet he is careful to define each clearly, and at the end of the volume he gives the Latin equivalents of the more important of these terms. This glossary is interesting because it shows which words he thought it necessary to gloss. Here we find *Begriff* (*notio, idea*), *Satz* (*propositio*), *Aufgabe* (*problema*), *Schluß* (*syllogismus*), *Anmerckung* (*scholion*), *Beschreibung* (*descriptio*), *Erklärung* (*definitio*), *Zergliederung* (*analysis*), *Zusatz* (*corollarium*). From these elementary concepts emerge compounds like *Förder-Sätze* (*praemissae*), *Grund-Satz* (*axioma*), *Heische-Satz* (*postulatum*), *Hinter-Satz* (*conclusio*), *Lehr-Satz* (*theorema*) —all of which are included in the list at the back of this treatise. It is perhaps difficult for us, now that most of these terms belong essentially to German philosophical vocabulary, to appreciate the full magnitude of this revolution. But if we compare the passage I have just quoted from Wolff's *Logic* with the following excerpts from the contemporary German translation of Thomasius's *Introductio ad Philosophiam Aulicam*,[1] the difference is so striking that it hardly needs any further comment. The difference in method between the two philosophers does not permit an exact parallel, but the content of the following passage has several points of contact with the Wolff passage:

Gleich wie aber die *Propositiones* nach den insgemein üblichen Fragen, *quae? qualis? quanta?* pflegen eingetheilet zu werden, also verändern sich auch die *Demonstrationes* solcher *Propositio*nen. Erstlich aber ist von der *Division* derselben in *hypotheticas* und *categoricas* zu *noti*ren, daß ob gleich die *Hypotheticae* können *demonstri*ret werden, und auch das bekanteste Exempel, welches insgemein so pfleget vorgebracht zu werden: Wann ein Esel flieget, so hat er Federn, eine nothwendige *Connexion* mit dem ersten *Principio cognoscendi* hat, dem ohngeachtet aber die *Demonstratio hypothetica*, als die nicht so edel ist, deswegen nicht hieher gehöre, weilen wir bereits oben aus eben der *Raison* die *veritatem hypotheticam* als eine unedlere Wahrheit verworffen haben.

Hernacher ist die *Proposition* entweder *universal* oder *particular*. Die *Universale* wird gezeiget durch eine *Demonstration à priori*, welche durch Beyhülffe der *Induction* zuwege gebracht wird. Die *Particulare* aber wird insgemein durch eine *Demonstration à posteriori* dargethan, nun und denn aber auch vermittelst einer *Demonstration à priori* etc. etc.

This, one might justly say, is not German at all, for the whole sentence-structure is heavily Latinate, and all the essential words are taken almost unchanged from the Latin original. The words 'edel' and 'unedel' (*eine unedlere Wahrheit*)—however German

[1] *Einleitung zur Hoff-Philosophie* (Berlin, 1712), ch. VIII, §§9–10. British Museum copy.

they may appear—are, in fact, almost devoid of meaning in this context. Indeed, so much Latin is needed to understand the passage, that one wonders what was the purpose of such a 'translation'. It could hardly convey any meaning to anyone ignorant of the Latin language, whereas the passage from Wolff's *Logic* just quoted is perfectly clear to anyone. This results largely from the vocabulary used: Wolff has consciously chosen to express himself in words which are part of the ordinary reader's speech-vocabulary. He fixes the meaning a shade more precisely, perhaps, by definition; and if he uses a somewhat less common word or phrase, its meaning is either etymologically perspicuous (*Aussage*) or made clear by the argument (*besonderer Satz*). Both these works were, however, published in the same year.

Wolff's German terminology[1] translates into the natural speech material of his day the meaning of the Latin concepts, or of the new distinctions which he is introducing. Hence his German terminology does not suffer from that obscurity and unnaturalness which Thomasius had deplored in the vocabulary of the *Cöthener Logik*, and thus was far more readily understood and accepted. He rejected such pedantic loan-translations as *Unterlage* for 'subject' and *Gegenwurf* for 'object'. Where he does retain a loan-translation, the word must be well established in ordinary speech, or at least be readily comprehensible to the general reader. Words like *Einfluß* and *Eindruck* had been part of the vocabulary of the medieval mystics. They were loan-translations with powerful pictorial associations and image-character. They survived in speech, and Wolff used them in his philosophical vocabulary; but he stripped them of any sensual or image quality. He treats them as abstracts, using them in constructions which disregard their original metaphorical force. Thus he will use *Einfluß auf* rather than the older and metaphorically more justified *Einfluß in*, and the periphrasis *Eindruck machen* rather than attempt to retain the dynamic verb *eindrücken* which Thomasius is still using.

[1] Paul Piur, *Studien zur sprachlichen Würdigung Christian Wolffs* (Halle, 1903), contains some interesting material, but overstates Wolff's inventiveness. The balance is restored by A. Schirmer, basing himself largely on F. Müller's article of 1899 which Piur should have known.

There was a direct line of stylistic tradition from the medieval German mystics through Nicholas of Cues, Luther, Spee and Böhme to the religious writers of the early eighteenth century. Many expressions from the old mystical vocabulary were still alive in current speech in the early eighteenth century. Leibniz had advocated the study of the mystics as a source of enrichment for the German philosophical vocabulary, and the few essays on philosophical subjects which he wrote in German show this type of expression. Here is a passage from an essay entitled *Von dem höchsten Gute* found amongst Leibniz's posthumous papers:[1]

…so kann man wohl sagen, das Wahre sey das, so mit dem Verstande, und das Gute das, so mit dem Willen Gottes, als des Urwesens, übereintrifft.

Und dieses kann uns auch dienen, das Wahre vom Falschen, und das Gute vom Bösen zu unterscheiden. Denn es befinden sich in uns gewisse *Strahlen* der göttlichen Weisheit und des ewigen Wortes, nemlich die ersten ewigen Wahrheiten, welche ein *Maaß* sind der andern, so daraus *entspringen*. Gleichwie er nemlich ein *Urquell* aller Ding ist, so ist auch alle gründliche Erkänntniß aus dem Erkänntniß Gottes zu leiten, und in seinem *Liecht* sehen wir das Liecht. Es befinden sich in uns auch ebenmäßig *Flammen* des göttlichen Willens, so uns einen Trieb zum Guten geben, und Würkungen seyn des Geistes Gottes. Und gleichwie viel Menschen in *Dunkelheit* bleiben, weilen sie die *reinen Strahlen* des göttlichen *Liechts* von dem falschen *Schein* der sinnlichen Blendungen nicht unterscheiden, also bleiben auch viele im Argen, weilen sie den Trieb des Geistes und des Fleisches nicht wohl zu sondern wissen. Zu beyden wird eine gewisse Ruhe des Gemüths, und *Eingang* in sich selbst erfordert, und das ist eben die rechte Kunst zu denken, von der so viel schreiben, aber darin so wenige einen sonderbaren *Fortgang* haben und tüchtige Proben geben können weilen sie weder die Wahrheit noch das Gute mit Ernst suchen, also sich nicht recht zu Gott wenden, und auch daher dessen Seegen nicht genießen.

Weilen nun Gott ist das vollkommenste Wesen, und der Will nichts anders, als ein verständiger Trieb, so bringt der Wille Gottes mit sich einen vollkommnen Trieb zu einen vollkommenen Erkänntniß, oder

---

[1] My italics. Text from G. E. Guhrauer, *Leibnitz's Deutsche Schriften*, vol. II (Berlin, 1840), pp. 35–6.

THE LANGUAGE OF PHILOSOPHY

zu Nießung und Empfindung der Vollkommenheiten, welche aus dem göttlichen Hauptquell auch in andre Dinge *geflossen*. Solches alles ist bei Gott auf einmal im höchsten Grad beisammen, aber der Creaturen und also auch Unsre Vollkommenheit bestehet in einem ungehinderten starken *Fort-Trieb* zu neuen und neuen Vollkommenheiten.

This language is highly metaphorical. Its images (which I have italicised) belong to those of mystical language, and they are still largely possessed of their pictorial associations. 'Gewisse Strahlen der göttlichen Weisheit und des ewigen Wortes' is still an image, although the incompatible nature of the second dependent genitive might suggest the contrary; but it is clear that Leibniz in this passage, whether instinctively or consciously we know not, preserves his metaphors intact: '...die reinen *Strahlen* des göttlichen *Liechts* von dem falschen *Schein* der sinnlichen *Blendungen* nicht unterscheiden', 'Vollkommenheiten, welche aus dem göttlichen *Hauptquell* auch in andre Dinge *geflossen*'. This style has its dangers. No writer can fully control the external associations aroused by images; no poet is ever sure that the images he uses will have the same associations for the reader as they have for him. This is the magic of poetry and the source of its eternal freshness through centuries of relatively persistent imagery. But it is death to philosophy where the reader must understand a given word in exactly the same sense as the writer. Hence the paramount importance of a clearly defined terminology which must be, in the main, abstract. For images are bound to lead to indistinct comprehension; and if they are defined, they cease to be images. It is the imagic language which makes the works of Jakob Böhme so difficult of comprehension; it was images like 'blond beasts', 'superman', 'midnight' and 'God's death' which led to the misinterpretation of Nietzsche. Christian Wolff must have realised this danger. We find that he uses 'Erkäntnis' for the old mystical expression 'das Licht der Vernunft' which Thomasius was still using. He also rejects the word *Stoff* (which has since been reinstated in philosophical vocabulary) in favour of the more neutral *Materie* which has no general associations. He is suspicious of the word *Gegenstand* because it still has the suggestion of 'opposition', 'standing against' for him (i.e. equivalent to Modern German *Widerstand*).[1] These older metaphorical words become clearly defined abstracts in Wolff's language. He uses the word *Stetigkeit* without any ethical associations (such as M.H.G. *stæte* had) and to mean 'continuity';[2] and he stripped the word *Begriff* of any verbal sense (*be-greifen, angreifen*) which was still associated with it.

Wolff's sharp sense of clear definition caused him to distinguish between some pairs of words which were used almost synonymously in the common usage of his time. He fixes the moral connotation to *Gewissen*[3] which was used almost indiscriminately with *Bewußtsein* by other contemporary writers. He uses *Empfindung* for mental perception (distinguishing it carefully from *Empfindlichkeit* with which it was often used synonymously at that time[4]) and *Gefühl* for sensory perception. He assigns *Begriff* to rational perception, *Vorstellung* to the imagination. He

[1] *Gegenstand* only assumed its modern meaning in this philosophical language of the eighteenth century. Its original meaning was either 'opposition' or 'opposite'. This meaning was still much alive in South German speech at the time of Wolff, and Haller uses this word, where we should use *Gegensatz*, in the earliest editions of his poems, correcting it to *Gegensatz* later. There was considerable opposition to this use of *Gegenstand* from South German circles (see below, p. 147) and Adelung (1796) still recognises a divergence in usage between North and South Germany. But Gottsched had used it regularly to mean 'object'. In the *Beobachtungen* of 1758 he recognised its use with this connotation as a happy enrichment of the language by the philosophers. *Gegenwurf* and *Vorwurf* were loan-translations used by some writers, and these two words are still to be met with in the works of Lessing and Schiller in this sense.

[2] Leibniz had used *Continuität* for 'continuity'. No doubt he considered the various German equivalents too imprecise in connotation for his purpose, and therefore preferred this patently foreign word.

[3] 'Das Urtheil von unseren Handlungen, ob sie gut oder böse sind, wird das Gewissen genennet' (*Thun und Lassen*, 1728 ed., §73) and 'Wir eignen dem Menschen ein Gewissen zu, in so weit er vermögend ist von den freyen Handlungen zu urtheilen, ob sie gut, oder böse sind, und ob man sie vollbringen, oder unterlassen sol' (*Ausführliche Nachricht*, 1726 ed., §138). There is a full discussion of this word in the *DWb*.

[4] E.g. 'Es stehet nun bei ew. maj., was die gesamten anverwandten vor eine empfindlichkeit aus diesem todesfalle tragen sollen' (Christian Weise, quoted in *DWb*.), meaning 'what feelings they should reveal'. Thomasius had used *Empfindlichkeit* in the sense of *Empfindung*. Wolff defines *Empfindlichkeit* as 'Neigung zu schnellem Zorne' (*Von Gott* etc., 1725 ed., §487).

attempts a distinction between *Verstand* and *Vernunft*.[1] *Grund* is sharply distinguished from *Ursache*,[2] and *Kraft* from *Vermögen*.[3] Occasionally we find Wolff using two different German terms for the same Latin term, but close scrutiny of the context usually reveals a true distinction. Thus the fact that Wolff renders *principium mutationis* as '*Quelle* der Veränderung', but *principium contradictionis* as '*Grund* (or *Satz*) des Widerspruches' is no testimony to imprecision but rather to the opposite.

Wolff himself was fully aware of the magnitude of his achievement, for he was not given to self-depreciation. In an interesting work entitled *Ausführliche Nachricht von seinen eigenen Schrifften, die er in deutscher Sprache von den verschiedenen Theilen der Welt-Weißheit heraus gegeben*, and first published in 1726,[4] Wolff describes the evolution of his philosophical language. The initial impetus for him to write in German had been, as with Thomasius, to provide his students with suitable manuals. His works should, however, be intelligible to a wider public than that which attended his lectures. He had therefore determined to write 'pure' German, avoiding Latin words because these were 'just as out of place in the German language as German words would be in the Latin language'. Wolff adopted an extreme standpoint on this subject, and in this he presents a strong contrast to Thomasius. The fact that a foreign word might be part of current usage was, for him, no justification in itself for its use: 'Der gemeine Gebrauch entschuldiget nicht: eine Gewohnheit muß vernünfftig seyn und

---

[1] *Vernunft* is defined as 'die Einsicht, so wir in den Zusammenhang der Wahrheiten haben, oder das Vermögen den Zusammenhang der Wahrheiten einzusehen' (*Von Gott*, ed. cit., §368) and *Verstand* as 'das obere Vermögen zu erkennen...welches den Menschen, aber nicht den Thieren zukommet' (*Ausf. Nachr.*, ed. cit., §93) and 'das Vermögen, das Mögliche deutlich vorzustellen' (*Von Gott* etc., §277).

[2] 'Der Grund ist dasjenige, wodurch man verstehen kann, warumb etwas ist, und die Ursache ist ein Ding, welches den Grund von einem andern in sich enthält' (*Von Gott* etc., §29).

[3] 'Das Vermögen ist nur eine Möglichkeit etwas zu thun; hingegen da die Krafft eine Quelle der Veränderungen ist, muß bey ihr eine Bemühung etwas zu thun anzutreffen seyn' (*Von Gott* etc., §117).

[4] I quote from the copy of this edition in the Central Library at Zürich. British Museum has the revised edition of 1733.

einen guten Grund vor sich haben wenn man sich darnach achten sol.' He believed that German was a better language for scholarship than Latin.¹ Where a German equivalent for a Latin term existed, he would use it only if it were exact. He would accept *gedencken* for *concipere*, but not the rendering of *ontologia* as *Dinger-Lehre*, because although it was etymologically a fairly exact correspondence it was inexact in the meaning it would suggest to the ordinary, cultured, German reader; instead Wolff suggested the term *Grund-Wissenschafft*.² Two general principles had governed the establishment of this terminology: first, as regards the choice of words: 'daß ich die deutschen Wörter in ihrer ordentlichen Bedeutung nähme und darinnen den Grund der Benennung zu dem Kunst-Worte³ suchte'—that is to say, Wolff had followed the connotation of speech-usage, creating, as he says earlier in the same work, the word as if no Latin equivalent existed and without reference to any such existing equivalent. Secondly, as regards the use of these terms: 'Ich schreibe mit Gedancken und gebe einem jeden Worte seine abgemessene Bedeutung bey der ich beständig verbleibe. Wer mich nun verstehen wil, der muß ihm diese Bedeutungen bekandt, und geläuffig machen, damit er in meinen Schrifften keinen Satz anders ausleget, als es die Krafft meiner Worte leidet.'⁴ This second principle is a qualification of the first; for Wolff implies that the connotation which he gives to some words is a special one. Hence

[1] The assertion is expressed somewhat quaintly and without reasoned proof, thus: 'Ich habe gefunden, daß unsere Sprache zu den Wissenschafften sich viel besser schickt, als die lateinische, und daß man in der reinen deutschen Sprache vortragen kan, was im Lateinischen sehr barbarisch klinget' (*ed. cit.* § 16).
[2] 'Ich brauche das Wort Grund-Wissenschafft', he writes, 'weil man in diesem Theile der Welt-Weisheit die ersten Gründe der Erkäntnis erkläret' (§ 17). Similarly, Wolff did not take up the word *Beilage* which Leibniz had used for *attributum*, but revived the old word *Eigenschaft* as being a clearer denotation of the meaning involved. Thomasius had used *attributum* (e.g. *Einleitung zu der Vernunfft-Lehre*, p. 46). Wolff used *Dasein* for *existentia*, whereas Thomasius had used *Seyn* (or *Existenz*).
[3] *Kunstwort* means 'technical term' in the eighteenth century. It was glossed with this meaning by Schottelius and Stieler, but the earliest example quoted in the *DWb.* is from Leibniz's *Unvorgreiffliche Gedanken*.
[4] *Op. cit.* § 18.

just as in the realm of mathematics Wolff had given words which had a general meaning in speech an additional limited meaning in the mathematical context, so too did he give a specific philosophical connotation to words from ordinary speech. In his philosophical vocabulary Wolff uses *Art* to mean 'species', *Ding* to mean *ens*, *Begebenheit* to mean *eventus*, *Zergliederung* to mean 'analysis', and it is only because he has bestowed the special connotation of *propositio* to *Satz* that he can form the compounds *Grundsatz*, *Lehrsatz* and *Heischesatz*. This consideration must always be borne in mind when we read Wolff.

The following short passage, chosen at random from the *Logic*, uses a vocabulary which (apart from the one term *Förder-Sätze* meaning *praemissae*) is in no way different from the vocabulary of ordinary speech usage; yet its meaning is obscure without reference to Wolff's definitions, and liable to be misconstrued, simply because it moves within the sphere of our common speech-vocabulary:

> Nach dieser Erklärung folget der Beweiß. Dieser aber muß so lange fortgeführet werden, biß man in den Schlüssen auf solche Förder-Sätze kommet, die dem andern nicht allein bekandt sind, sondern an deren Richtigkeit er auch keinen Zweiffel hat. Verstehet er aber gar nichts von der Sache, so muß der Beweiß geführet werden biß auf Erklärungen und klare Erfahrungen, oder andere leere Sätze [*misprint for* Lehr-Sätze, *corrected in later editions*]. Denn in uns ist die Überführung entstanden, da wir von den Erklärungen und Erfahrungen an biß auf unseren Satz alles in richtiger Ordnung überdacht.[1]

But the meaning emerges quite clearly when we refer to Wolff's own definitions of his terms. He is using the word *Erklärung* in his special sense of *definitio*, and he defines his conception of *Erfahrung* earlier in the work: 'Wir erfahren alles dasjenige, was wir erkennen, wenn wir auf unsere Empfindungen acht haben' (e.g., that light makes things visible, etc.). By this means Wolff overcame the danger of miscomprehension aroused by the employment of common terms in a specialised context. Whenever

---

[1] *Op. cit.* ch. 13, §3. *Überführung* in this passage means 'persuasion', the usual eighteenth-century connotation of this word.

he uses words of common speech, he is always careful to define exactly in what sense he is using them, to use them only and always in this sense, and not to use any other words for these same concepts. Thomasius had used either foreign terms (with or without German terminations), or words from normal speech without clear definition of their meaning. Thus, for instance, in the fourth chapter of his *Einleitung zu der Vernunfft-Lehre*,[1] Thomasius explains *ens*, *aliquid* as 'ein Ding, Wesen oder Etwas, durch welches ich alles, was ausser dem Menschen oder in demselbigen, und in seinen Gedancken gewesen ist, noch ist, und künfftig seyn wird, verstehe'. He then mentions the distinction to be made between *ens potentiale*, *ens rationis* and *ens reale*, but gives no German equivalents. He continues: 'Von einem jedweden *ente reali* sagt man, daß es ein Wesen (*essentiam*) habe, und daß es sey (*quod existat*).' But *Wesen* had been given as one of the translations of *ens* above! This is typical of Thomasius's lack of clear concepts. He continues in this chapter with an attempt to draw a distinction between *Existenz* and *Wesen* in which he uses the word *Seyn* without ever having defined it. It was Wolff's great achievement that he gave Germany a philosophical vocabulary in which every word had a precisely defined connotation. And this vocabulary was not only precise, it was predominantly German.

It is interesting to turn from Wolff's public writings to his private writings—from his published treatises to his letters and his sketch of an autobiography.[2] For here we find an entirely different language. This is how Wolff pays tribute to one of his

---

[1] 2nd ed. pp. 42–3.

[2] This 'Autobiography' consists of notes made by Wolff in 1743 for the use of a certain Rektor Baumeister in Görlitz. The manuscript remained in the possession of the Bürgermeister of Görlitz, an old student of Wolff's, and was then presented by him to the Milich library in Görlitz in 1760. It has been published from this manuscript by H. Wuttke (Leipzig, 1841), and is prefixed by a long essay from the pen of Wuttke which is full of interesting biographical material and contains liberal quotations from Wolff's letters to Manteuffel. To these letters I shall refer below.

The letters to Leibniz are to be found in the 'Supplementband' of Pertz's great edition of Leibniz's works. They are edited by Gerhardt.

school teachers at the Magdalenäum in Breslau, Christian Gryphius, the son of the famous dramatist:

> Gryphio habe ich auch etwas besonderes zu dancken. Einige wenige worunter er auch mich ausersehen hatte, musten die gantze Lection wehrendes Docirens ex tempore aufschreiben und in einen zusammenhangenden discours bringen, zu Ende der Lection aber, wenn er aufgefordert war, vorlesen. Er war ein sehr hitziger Mann, der gleich zornig ward, wenn das geringste momentum ausgelassen oder etwas nicht nach seinem Sinne niedergeschrieben war. Hingegen lobte er ungemein einen öffentlich, wenn man es recht gemacht hatte. Und dieses war ein stimulus, da man einander aemulirte und zu besonderer attention aufgemuntert worden.[1]

This is Wolff off his guard; writing, no doubt, hastily and without much care for literary expression. The language, we notice, is full of foreign words. The same adulterated vocabulary is found in his letters to Manteuffel; here are a few sentences culled at random[2] from these letters:

> 28 May 1738. ...so vermeinet er hier um so viel gewißer zu reussiren.
>
> 11 Oct. 1739. Die Vocation nach Marburg hatte [ich] schon vorher erhalten, ehe die verdrüßliche Sache in Halle passirte.
>
> ...da ich mich am Caßelischen Hoffe nicht engagiren möchte, indem man mir eine Station in Leipzig geben wollte mit einem Gehalt von 600 Rthl.
>
> 27 Oct. 1739. Wenn ich dem Caßelischen Hoffe so obligiret bin, daß ich an keinem Ort eine Bedienung annehmen darf, wenn die Conditiones noch so vortheilhaft wären....
>
> 15 June 1740. Bey der Societät der Wissenschafften sehe nicht, was sonderliches zu effectuiren....Die beyden letztern Stücke dependiren viel mit von dem Glücke....

This, apparently, was the language in which cultured men of that time were accustomed to write to each other. Wolff's achievement emerges as all the greater when we compare this 'private' style with the carefully nurtured language in which he chose to address his wider audience.

[1] Wuttke, p. 113.
[2] From the extracts given in Wuttke.

Our analysis has so far been concerned with Wolff's vocabulary. But there is more to style than just vocabulary, and Wolff is far more than a coiner of terms. He had a distinctive style of his own in which all his works were written, no matter what field of intellectual investigation they covered. This style is pure, clear and uniform, but it betrays its mathematical origin, for Wolff, as we have seen, moved from mathematics through logic to the other sciences. Everywhere in his writings we observe the same progression from carefully defined terms and the insistence on using these terms and no others. Hence strict adherence to the defined meaning of a word, and to this one word only to denote this defined meaning, is a salient feature of Wolff's method. This naturally involves repetition and leads to a certain monotony of style. Wolff realised this but defended himself in the *Ausführliche Nachricht*. It was a virtue, he said, of normal language that the same word should be used in slightly varying connotations, but this was impossible in a closely knit syllogistic argument, where each statement is proved with reference to preceding statements. The meaning attached to a given word must remain constant throughout the argument if that argument is to be valid. 'Derowegen brauche ich ein Wort, so offt ich an eine Sache gedencke, und frage nichts darnach, ob es offte, oder wenig vorkommet.'[1] Three principles, he said, had always governed his style: to use no word before it had been clearly defined, to use no statement as the foundation of an argument which had not itself been proved, and to deduce each new statement from the preceding statements by the process of logical argument. This style seems apt when Wolff is dealing with mathematics or logic, but when he turns to more human problems, the limitations of his style are apparent, and its restricted vocabulary, which had given strength and coherence to his more abstract speculations, is now a defect. The strictly mathematical argument with its rigid adherence to the syllogism and constant reference back, Euclid fashion, to already proved conclusions, produces a cumbrous and pedantic effect when applied to flesh and blood. Here is a *reductio ad*

[1] *Ausführliche Nachricht*, §21, p. 50.

absurdum of the mathematical method from Wolff's treatise on politics:[1]

> Wiederum, da der Mann das Weib mit zu Rathe ziehen soll in denen Dingen, die beyder Wohlfahrt betreffen (§ 58.); so muß er auch dem Weibe nichts mit Ungestüme anbefehlen, sondern alles mit glimpflichen Worten und einer guten Manier vorbringen, damit sie nicht die Liebe gegen ihn fahren lässet (§ 449. Met.), oder auch wohl gar einen Haß gegen ihn bekommet (§ 454. Met.) und dadurch alle Scheue für ihm verlieret (§ 787. Mor.)....

It is important that we should appreciate not only the range but also the limitations of Wolff's linguistic achievement. For the wide popularity of his works and the general appeal of his subject-matter meant that his style was bound to be influential on prose-writing in general. This philosophic age took a style specially evolved for philosophical writing and applied it to writing in general. This seems to me to be the origin of that wooden, academic stiffness of so much early eighteenth-century German prose. This stiffness is quite different from the heaviness of the highly incapsulated serious prose of the baroque age. Wolff's prose is relatively free from incapsulation, and depends more on a sequence of clauses. This follows from his philosophical method—one statement leads to the next, and each is treated as a whole in itself. Everything is explained in terms already defined, a term once accepted is always used for the thing it expresses, there are no alternative expressions, nothing is left vague, nothing is left to chance, nothing is left to the imagination—an admirable style for rationalistic philosophy but not for more general purposes. For general purposes this style is immensely cold, monotonous both in vocabulary and rhythm.

In the rhythmical pattern of his sentences, Thomasius still belongs more to the seventeenth century:

> Die Bescheidenheit ist eine Tugend, die den Menschen antreibet, daß er allen Menschen, sie mögen seyn von was Stande sie wollen,

---

[1] *Vernünftige Gedanken von dem gesellschafftlichen Leben der Menschen* (1721). I have used the fourth edition of 1736, copy at Central Library, Zürich. British Museum has 1756 edition. This passage is found in ch. 2, § 61.

freundlich und als Menschen, die in diesem Stück seines gleichen sind, begegnet, sie gleiches Recht mit sich geniessen läst, und sich nicht mehr hinaus nimmt, als ihme von Rechtswegen gebühret.[1]

The structure is involved, the flow constantly interrupted. Now let us listen to Wolff defining the same quality:

Wer sich nicht über andere erhebet, sondern einem jeden so viel Ehre giebet, als ihm gebühret; der ist bescheiden. Und also ist die Bescheidenheit eine Tugend jedermann seine gebührende Ehre zu geben.[2]

The rhythm is steady and consistent, moving uninterruptedly towards the final cadence, with each clause complete in itself and following in a train of logical thought from the last. The individual feature of the style of Thomasius is that tendency, which we noticed above, to introduce into the highly artificial sentence-structure a word or phrase of natural vigour—speech-material transfused into a sentence-structure which is as far removed as possible from that of speech. An example of this is the phrase: 'und sich nicht mehr hinaus nimmt' in the above passage. Unless we know Thomasius, it is unexpected in this essentially learned style. These differences are best illustrated by a somewhat lengthier comparison. Here is Thomasius on passion:

Ein Wollüstiger denckt aber immer auff zukünfftige Dinge. Seine ungedultige Begierde treibt ihn an, daß er die gegenwärtigen gleichsam verschluckt, und allezeit nach mehrern trachtet. Ein Wollüstiger ist am *capable*sten, so zu sagen, Schlösser in die Lufft zu bauen, und mit eiteln Gedancken von zukünfftigen Dingen sich was zu gute zu thun. Die feste Eindrückung der gegenwärtig genossenen Dinge, macht ihn bey natürlicher Erinnerung derselben begierig, wiederumb solche zu geniessen; Und weil es unmüglich ist, daß er sie allemahl würcklich geniessen könne, so stellet er sich indessen die Umstände der zukünfftigen *conversation* für, wie er sie gerne sähe, und setzet in solcher Betrachtung tausend angenehme Dinge zusammen. Weil nun dieses offte, auch öffters in der *Conversation* selbsten, wenn sie lange dauert,

---

[1] *Einleitung zur Sittenlehre* (1692), quoting from the fifth edition of 1710, pp. 225–6. British Museum copy.

[2] *Vernünftige Gedanken von der Menschen Thun und Lassen* (1720), quoting from the third edition of 1728, §810. Copy in Central Library, Zürich. British Museum has 1752 edition.

geschiehet, so schärfft so ein Mensch dadurch am allermeisten sein *Ingenium*, und macht sich zu allerhand artigen Erfindungen, Mährgen, Gedichten u.s.w. umb so vielmehr geschickt, umb so vielmehr ein solch offters Nachdencken bey einem Wollüstigen zu wege bringet, daß er würcklich mehr Lust bey seiner zwar sinnreichen aber eitelen Vorstellung geniesset, als bey dem Genuß selbsten.[1]

The general tone is galant and the passage begins in a brisk and sprightly manner, but it soon succumbs to the stereotyped balance and shape of periodic sentence-structure. Wolff on the same subject has neither the gaiety of Thomasius's opening nor the quicksands of his close. He maintains the same even tenor throughout:

> Die Wollust treibet wohl die meisten zur Unmäßigkeit an. Es wird aber hier die Wollust genennet diejenige Lust, welche man durch die Sinnen empfindet. Wer demnach gewohnet ist das Gute und Böse durch die Lust und Unlust, welche die Sinnen gewehren, zu unterscheiden; den nennet man wollüstig. Da wir nun dasjenige wollen, was wir für gut halten: hingegen das nicht wollen, was wir für böse halten (§ 496. Met.); so strebet ein Wollüstiger nach denen Dingen, die ihm durch die Sinnen Lust gewehren, und hat hingegen einen Abscheu für denen, die ihm durch die Sinnen Unlust machen, oder auch die Lust der Sinnen stöhren. Derowegen da die Lust, so durch guten Geschmack und Geruch, ingleichen durch vergnügten Anblick erreget wird, unter die Lust der Sinnen gehöret; so wird ein Wollüstiger zur Unmäßigkeit in Essen und Trincken angetrieben, weil Speise und Tranck wohl riechen und schmecken, oder auch appetitlich aussehen.[2]

We have quoted sufficiently from Wolff's prose to show how monotonous his style can become. Its monotony is due to the extreme regularity of its sentence-rhythm (for almost every sentence consists of a statement preceded by a subordinate clause giving the reason for this conclusion), and the sameness of its vocabulary. This style leaves very little to the imagination, but Wolff, as we have seen, would have nothing to do with imagina-

---
[1] Thomasius, *Ausübung der Sittenlehre* (1696), quoting from fourth edition of 1708, pp. 206–7. British Museum copy.
[2] Wolff, *Vernünftige Gedanken von der Menschen Thun und Lassen*, 1728 ed., § 469.

tion. Nevertheless the clarity and smoothness of this style, excessive as they may appear to us of the twentieth century, were positive qualities which German prose had lacked for many decades. This style is the prelude to the eighteenth century, for it has neither the dusty convolutes of baroque cultured prose nor the rough-and-tumble syntax of popular prose (with a line leading from the chapbooks to Christian Weise). It is the expression of a clear, orderly mind using language with seriousness and respect. It is lacking in colour, but Wolff was concerned solely with making his meaning clear. He wrote 'in thoughts', as we saw above, and disdained all artifice of diction:

> Deswegen...brauche ich keine Künste den Leser durch Worte einzunehmen. Meine Worte fallen, wie ich dencke. Und ich setze keines vergebens. Ich rede nicht so, weil es Mode ist in dergleichen Fällen so zu reden; sondern weil meine Gedancken, welche mir die Sachen vorstellen, diese und keine andere Worte erfordern.[1]

Language and thought stand in a peculiar relationship of interdependence which has always defied conclusive definition. Wolff's highly logical style is the expression of his mathematical thought-processes; similarly the definiteness of his terminology is the expression of the exactness of his thought-concepts. Wolff established not only the language of German philosophy but also its discipline. He countered what Gottsched called 'das ungebundene und unsichere Raissoniren'.[2] Kant, as we have seen, declared that it was Wolff who had introduced 'thoroughness' into German thought; Hegel[3] paid tribute to Wolff's contribution to the 'Verstandesbildung' of the Germans:

> Er ist es erst, welcher nicht gerade die Philosophie, aber den Gedanken in der Form des Gedankens zum allgemeinen Eigenthum

---

[1] *Ausführliche Nachricht*, ed. cit. §21. Cf.: 'Endlich muß ich von meiner Schreib-Art noch dieses erinnern, daß ich niemahls mehr Worte gebraucht, als die Sache erfordert, und mich aller verblühmten und hochtrabenden Redens-Arten enthalten' (*ibid.* p. 51).

[2] *Historische Lobschrift weiland Herrn geheimen Raths und Kanzlers Freyherrn von Wolf* (Halle, 1755), p. 34.

[3] Hegel, *Vorlesungen über die Geschichte der Philosophie*, ed. Michelet (Berlin, 1836), p. 473 ff.

gemacht und ihn an die Stelle des Sprechens aus dem Gefühl, aus dem sinnlichen Wahrnehmen und in der Vorstellung in Deutschland gesetzt hat.

It is possible for men to think clearly and yet write obscurely, especially when they adopt an existing fashionable mode of expression. This Wolff did not do; in the passage from the *Ausführliche Nachricht* last quoted, he had definitely eschewed fashion: 'Ich rede nicht so, weil es Mode ist in dergleichen Fällen so zu reden.' He made his language the exact and perfect expression of his thoughts, working from the mind and not from the feelings, as Hegel truly recognised.

Wolff's influence spread to all classes of society and to foreign lands. His fame became so great that when he was recalled to Halle by Frederick the Great in 1740, his entry into the city was almost a triumphal procession. His works were the first scholarly works in German to be translated into several languages. This fact alone proved that German was now accepted as a suitable language for serious subjects—and this but a few decades after Leibniz's gloomy analysis of the situation. The notorious freethinker Johann Christoph Edelmann, writing in 1740, spoke of the vogue of Wolffian philosophy as widespread; women seemed to be overcome by a veritable 'Lykanthropie (Wolffs-Menschheit)': 'Denn wo an manchen Orten zwei oder drei versammelt sind, da ist der liebe Gott Wolff gewiß auch mitten unter ihnen.'[1] Gottsched tells of a simple peasant who, to the astonishment of all scholars, obtained a complete knowledge of mathematics from Wolff's *Anfangs-Gründe*.[2] Wolff's aspirations to be understood by all had clearly been fulfilled. His vocabulary was to affect indelibly the cultured vocabulary of all Germans of his time. Some of the words which he had culled from speech-usage and to which he had given a specific philosophical meaning, returned to the literary language with this new *nuance* (e.g. *Begriff*, *Eindruck*, *Gewissen*). The plays and novels of the 1740's are full of this terminology. 'Seine Kunstwörter', said Gottsched in

[1] L. Noack, *Philosophiegeschichtliches Lexikon* (Leipzig, 1879), p. 931.
[2] Gottsched, *Historische Lobschrift*, pp. 32–3, footnote.

1755,[1] 'sind nicht nur unter Gelehrten aller Arten, sondern auch unter Rednern und Dichtern, die sich doch billig derselben enthalten sollten, gemein geworden, ja selbst in die artige Welt gedrungen.' Wolff's style with its highly logical sentence-structure and its monotonous smoothness was to remain the model for serious German prose for some time to come. Gottsched admitted that he consciously modelled the style of his learned works on this prose,[2] and it was Gottsched's *Erste Gründe der gesammten Weltweisheit* (1734) which became the popular textbook of philosophy in Germany in the eighteenth century.

[1] Gottsched, *Historische Lobschrift*, pp. 44 ff.
[2] 'Auch mir, der ich in die schönen Wissenschaften ein reines Deutsch einzuführen gesuchet, hat seine Metaphysik zum Muster gedienet, ja mich dazu geschickt gemacht' (*ibid.* p. 44).

III

THE LITERARY JOURNALS

THE first forty years of the eighteenth century were marked in Germany, as elsewhere, by the development of a large and predominantly middle-class literary public. This was certainly the most striking aspect of the cultural life of that period, and there were many contributory causes of the most varied nature. For the majority of Germans, this was a period of peace, and the country was beginning to recover from the devastation of the Thirty Years War. It was an age of austerity which set its face consciously against luxury. In Frederick William I of Prussia, its most distinguished ruler, was embodied rejection of the old prodigality in which the petty princes still lingered. The middle classes were becoming increasingly prosperous and developing a pride and a new social consciousness. The thought of the period opposed the authority of tradition, it was essentially anti-aristocratic. Both philosophic rationalism and pietistic theology addressed their admonitions to man in general. Respect for privilege was diminishing, whether this were the privilege of the lord, the scholar or the priest. All men, said the spirit of the age, could attain to truth, learning and salvation. The gap between the great men and the mass narrowed so that average competence became higher but outstanding distinction rare. It was predominantly an age of popularisation, permeated by a strong pedagogic spirit—the beginnings of the 'Age of Enlightenment' as it was later called. Intellectual curiosity was eager, there was a thirst for knowledge in all fields. But this knowledge had to be communicated in an easily digestible form, for the demand extended far beyond the range of the learned societies and the universities. Some degree of popularisation was therefore necessary, and the age produced a spate of popular manuals. Wolff's philosophical works were, in essence, themselves manuals of this type, although vastly superior in style and presentation to most of their fellows. A new arrival was the literary journal, a regular publication in the vernacular containing essays which either imparted knowledge or discussed moral and social problems. These journals were 'literary' in a double sense; not only had they definite literary pretensions, but they also discussed, directly or indirectly, both literature and language. By the time of Gottsched, the literary journal has emerged fully-grown as a popular production addressed primarily to a middle-class audience. It is never frivolous, for the subjects it treats are serious, but the treatment is light and easy, the style more popular than that of the manuals. The moral content of these journals is often very close to that of contemporary treatises on morals like Wolff's *Vernünftige Gedanken von der Menschen Thun und Lassen*, but the style is quite different. It addresses the reader directly in a much lighter vein, in language which does not seem to be far removed from that of well-mannered conversation. An urbane style was evolved by a process of trial and error. In this fact lies the importance of the journals in the development of the German literary language.

In the journals of this period, however, we can distinguish two main types, both of which might be included under the heading of 'literary journals'. The older type is one that confines itself mainly or entirely to the consideration of books which have recently appeared; the newer type consists predominantly of moral essays on various themes of interest to the middle-class audience. The former is of a more scholarly nature and developed as a conscious imitation of the French *Journal des Sçavans*, the latter was inspired by the English moral weeklies of Addison and Steele. There would seem to be no direct connection between these two types of journal, and the latter type is the more important for our considerations; but there was a certain amount of convergence later in the century, and Thomasius's *Monatsgespräche*, although belonging fundamentally to the former, more scholarly type, did contain elements which anticipate the 'moral weeklies'. His journal contrasts sharply in style with those of

Gottsched. This contrast is in itself instructive for any consideration of the development of style in this period. For all these reasons, Thomasius must figure at the commencement of this chapter; but the fact that the *Monatsgespräche* was the first literary journal to be published in the German language outweighs all other justification.

The literary journal[1] had arrived in Germany with the publication of the first number of the *Acta Eruditorum* at Leipzig in January 1682. It arrived as a fully developed *genre*, consciously modelled on the *Journal des Sçavans* which had been appearing in Paris since January 1665.[2] The editor, Otto Mencke, in his preface to the first number, acknowledged the high example set by both the *Journal des Sçavans* and the *Philosophical Transactions of the Royal Society* of London. Mencke hoped, apparently, to transcend both these models for he welcomed contributions from scholars of all countries. It was no doubt for this reason, and also because Mencke envisaged a public independent of all national frontiers, that the journal was published in Latin. The *Acta Eruditorum* offered little criticism, but confined itself to the excerpting of new books for the benefit of scholars who had not yet seen these, or were too poor to buy them. The works summarised were works of scholarship, often on scientific subjects; *belles-lettres* were not considered. The contributors included such famous persons as Leibniz, Tschirnhausen and Thomasius, but Thomasius made himself unpopular with Mencke by his treatise on bigamy and his championing of the German language. The breach between Thomasius and Mencke was widened with the publication of the first number of the *Monatsgespräche* in January 1688, for this first number ended by snubbing the *Acta Eruditorum*.

[1] For general information on this subject, see Robert Prutz, *Geschichte des deutschen Journalismus* (Hanover, 1845), which is excellent although only one volume was published which does not reach beyond Thomasius. A later work, Ludwig Salomon, *Geschichte des deutschen Journalismus* (2nd ed. 1906), extends further but is very sketchy on our period, and the author is mainly concerned with political journalism.

[2] A Latin translation of the first five volumes appeared in Leipzig between 1665 and 1670. The translator was a lecturer at the University of Leipzig named Friedrich Nitzsche.

Travellers in a post-chaise are discussing the journals, someone asks about the *Acta Eruditorum*, his companion begins: 'Als für etlichen Jahren der Herr Mencke...', but at that point the coach overturns and deposits its inmates in the snow. And so, says Thomasius, 'ihr *Discours* nahme ein beschneietes ENDE'.

This was very insolent. Here was a university lecturer dismissing in this off-hand way the most learned product of his own university town. It was, however, the sort of insolence which appeals to youth, it showed an engaging disrespect for the bigwigs. It was part of Thomasius's campaign against the tyranny of pedantic authority, against the dead letter of unpractical learning. We have seen how this tone characterised his philosophical writings. The periodical is written in the same spirit, except that the attack is sharper and the novelty of the form more sensational. The first number bore the title *Schertz- und Ernsthaffter, Vernünfftiger und Einfältiger Gedancken, über allerhand Lustige und nützliche Bücher und Fragen, Erster Monat oder JANUARIUS*. The periodical appeared at fairly regular intervals until April 1690,[1] the title being varied as time went on. It was bound up into volumes in 1690 under the title *Freymüthige Lustige und Ernsthaffte iedoch Vernunfft- und Gesetz-Mässige Gedancken Oder Monats-Gespräche über allerhand, fürnehmlich aber Neue Bücher Durch alle zwölff Monate des 1688 und 1689 Jahrs*.[2] Hence this periodical is usually referred to as the *Monatsgespräche* of Thomasius. The modification of the original title in the book edition of 1690 was the result of the severe attacks which Thomasius had to suffer owing to the 'frivolity' and the 'bitter, personal satire' of his writing. These titles demonstrate in miniature how different is the tone of this periodical from that of the *Acta Eruditorum*. The *Monatsgespräche* are galant, and stress usefulness and amusement. But the titles also reveal that the *Monatsgespräche* had the same general purpose as the *Acta Eruditorum*, namely the discussion of new books. Its method and approach

---

[1] Except the last few numbers whose publication was delayed.
[2] I shall quote from this edition (in three volumes) correcting a few obvious misprints. Copy in the British Museum.

would be different: the periodical would be addressed to men of the world and not to professional scholars. It was, in fact, a counterblast to the *Acta Eruditorum*. And it was in the German language.

Thomasius begins by an apostrophe to the spirits of pedantry and hypocrisy, consciously spoonerised:

> *A Messieurs Monsieur Tarbon et Monsieur Bartuffe*
> Ich rede euch an *Monsieur Barbon*[1] und *Mons. Tartuffe*, und ihr werdet es mir demnach für eine grosse Nachlässigkeit auslegen, daß ich eure Nahmen in *rubro* nicht recht drücken lassen. Aber *Messieurs*, Ihr werdet mir verzeihen, wenn ich sage, daß ihr euch geirret, und daß *Mons. Tartuffe*, der sonst andere Leute mit einer falschen Scheinheiligkeit zu hintergehen gewohnet ist, sich dieses mahl durch einen falschen Schein selbst betrogen, *Mons. Barbon* aber ein greuliches versehen, daß er eine *ingenieuse Invention* für einen *Solœcismum* gehalten. Ich bin ein wenig *delicat* in *Ceremo*nien, und habe bald Anfangs einen wichtigen Zweiffel bey mir wegen der Herren ihre *Praecedenz* empfunden. Denn so viel euch *Mons. Tartuffe* betrifft, schiene es wohl das Ansehen zu haben, als wenn ihr den Rang über *Mons. Barbon* von rechtswegen verdienetet, weil ihr vielfältig mit beten und singen umbgehet, dieser arme Tropff aber mehrentheils mit *inform*irung kleiner Knaben zu thun hat. Nichts desto weniger habe ich für *Mons. Barbon* auch das andere Ohr offen behalten, der mir durch einen *Syllogismum in Camestres*[2] gleichsam zu sagen schiene, daß er ja so wohl als *Mons. Tartuffe* ein vornehmer Mann wäre, und sich gar zu weilen bey Hoffe auffhielte, und daß weil ihr zum öfftern in einem *subjecto* anzutreffen wäret, er so dann allemahl in ruhiger *possess* sey, daß er seine Residentz in den vornehmsten Theil desselben hätte; denn es wäre nicht zu leugnen, daß die *Pedanterie* im Gehirne sässe, die Heucheley aber im Hertzen....

This style shows that same mingling of popular and learned elements which we noted in the last chapter as being the salient feature of Thomasius's language. Here they are united in a style which is fresh and lively at the first impact, but soon becomes tedious because the humour is so laboured. Its jocularity is that of the scholar, and nothing can disguise that fact. The last

---

[1] This was a popular name for a pedant since Guez de Balzac's satire *Le Barbon* (Paris, 1648). [2] One of the nineteen valid moods of the syllogism.

sentence in the passage quoted has that profusion of dependent clauses and the incapsulated structure so characteristic of serious prose of the later seventeenth century. It is on this highly ornate rack that the slender wit of this passage is distended. This is an outstanding example of a writer constricted by a prevailing mode of writing. Thomasius is trying to use the baroque sentence for purposes for which it was never designed. This is why, despite his obvious intention of striking a light, gay tone, he can begin a sentence with *Nichts desto weniger* and use so many preterite subjunctives. It will not do; it is an utter failure. But we should never forget two things: that this is the first attempt at cultured journalism in the German language, and the first attempt to write a light *feuilleton* style similar to that cultivated by the French. The fact that the attempt was made is more important than the measure of its success. For progress is gained by experimentation. Hence just as the attempt to write philosophy in German had revealed a deficiency in the language, so did Thomasius's *Monatsgespräche* reveal the need for a graceful, light style and the impossibility of adapting the baroque sentence to this purpose. Thomasius seems to have felt this, for he did his best to lighten the texture with colloquial phrases; but this only serves to demonstrate even more potently the unsuitability of the sentence-mould. It is important, however, that we should realise the originality of this style being used in a journal which is to cover the same ground as the *Acta Eruditorum*. It has a personal quality which contrasts with the strict impersonality of the *Acta Eruditorum*.

The journal is cast in the form of a conversation between four travelling companions, a cultured gentleman on his travels, a scholar on holiday, a business-man and a schoolmaster. The schoolmaster is the butt of most of these discussions, for he embodies the spirit of pedantry. Thomasius gives us real discussion, not merely excerptation or summary of the contents, and he conveys his own personal judgments to the reader through these conversations. In the books which he chooses to discuss, Thomasius has the taste of his worldly audience in mind. It is significant that the first number begins with a discussion of two works by Abraham a Santa Clara¹ whose style is praised for its 'seltzamer inventionen' and the unexpected application made of these. By this means Abraham a Santa Clara had held the attention of his audience—in other words, Thomasius recognises that Abraham's style was admirably suited to his purpose as a preacher. Most of the first number is occupied with a discussion on fiction, a sphere into which the *Acta Eruditorum* never ventured. The characters of the four friends are quite well described but there is little difference in the type of language they use. They are characterised more by the content than by the language of their conversation. Indeed these are not very conversational conversations. There is an occasional brisk interchange, and it is true that the speech of all four characters is spiced with lively colloquial phrases and images, for example: 'Herr Benedict lässet ihn mit einer kleinen Haarwusche davon lauffen', 'Predigten, so aus dem Ermel geschüttet werden', 'Allfantzereyen', 'Ich will ihn mit seinen eigenen Waffen schmeissen', 'Nun könte ich wegen dieses Puncts viel zu Markt bringen' (say in my defence), 'gar nicht für eine Magd oder Schuchhadder (shoe-rag) geachtet', 'etwas auf die Nase zu brieffen' (not given by Adelung, but probably equivalent to 'auf die Nase binden, heften'²) 'ein Hümpler (bungler) bleiben', 'Schnitzer begehen', 'mit einem blauen Augen davonkommen'. But apart from this colloquial freshness, the work consists mainly of a series of lengthy speeches.

Here for example is Christoph, the business-man, explaining his taste for novels:

> Es ist dieses Jahr eine solche Historie unter den Titul l'*heureux Page* heraus kommen, in welchen³ der *Autor* vielleicht auff eine warhafftige

---

¹ *Reim dich oder ich liß dich* and *Gack, gack, gack*, both published in the year 1687.
² M.H.G. *brieven* means 'schreiben', 'aufschreiben'.
³ Presumably dative case is meant here. This use of forms in -*en* where normal modern usage would demand the corresponding form in -*em* is very frequent in printed texts of this period. There are two other examples in this passage, one of which *für einen Jahre* shows that there is no question of the accusative being intended. Confusion between these two forms seems to be prevalent in the early decades of this century. See below, p. 130, for Gottsched's regulation of this matter.

Geschichte gezielet, massen bekannt ist, daß für einen Jahre in denen Zeitungen gemeldet wurde, daß eine vornehme Dame hohen Standes einen Cammerdiener geheyrathet habe. In dieser Geschichte nun, die nach Art der Romans eingerichtet ist, und in welcher der glückseelige *Page*, so als ein *Marqvis* und *Heros* der Historie eingeführet wird, nicht gar zu saubere Seide spinnet, ist unter andern *ingenieusen inventionen*, auch diese daß als der Mann der vornehmen Dame, welche von den *Marqvis* bedienet worden, durch seine *jalousie* angetrieben seine Gemahlin ertappen wollen, und nach einer zum Schein angestelten Reise sich in ein Zimmer hinter die Tapeten verstecket, er durch eine bey sich habende schlagende Sack-Uhr verrathen worden, dergestalt, daß man ihn für einen Dieb gehalten, biß er sich mit der grösten *Confusion* seiner selbst, seiner Gemahlin und des *Marqvis* so nebst unterschiedenen andern gegenwärtig gewesen, zuerkennen gegeben, welches alles wegen der darbey eingemischten andern Umstände und sinnreichen Beschreibung recht anmuthig zu lesen ist.[1]

Nothing could be further removed from the normal style of conversation than this language. It is the constricted breathing of the scholar that animates these excessively latinate periods with their strong dependence on participial constructions: 'eine bey sich habende schlagende Sack-Uhr', 'wegen der darbey eingemischten andern Umstände'. The whole structure of the sentences is too involved, the style moves too rigidly in the accepted channels of cultured oratory to convey any sense of the true accents of conversation. Nevertheless the vocabulary is not that of the scholar, it belongs to the man of the world, the cultured gentleman. There is even one colloquial image, when Thomasius speaks of the page who 'nicht gar zu saubere Seide spinnet'. This uneasy contrast between a learned sentence-mould into which is poured the language of a cultured man of the world dominates the prose of the *Monatsgespräche*. There is a constant sense of strain.

But let us not demand too much. The importance of the *Monatsgespräche* in the development of the German language as a medium of literary expression lies not in their literary quality so much as in the fact of their very existence. Here was a literary

[1] *Ed. cit.* p. 25.

periodical in German addressed to an audience far wider than the professional world of scholars, and written in a language which was not that of the specialist. The ordinary cultured man was being encouraged to take an interest in matters of literary taste and in new books generally. For Thomasius did not limit himself to fiction. His commencement with Abraham a Santa Clara had been a defiant gesture—a Catholic, popular writer praised in the teeth of Protestant, learned Leipzig. But in later numbers of this journal he discussed serious works of scholarship like Tschirnhausen's *Medicina Mentis*, offered a spirited defence of the philosophy of Epicurus and had some favourable things to say about Confucius. To us the style of his 'conversations' may seem distressingly inappropriate; to his contemporaries it must have been delightfully inappropriate. For the success of the first numbers is corroborated by the virulence and number of the attacks which Thomasius suffered from his Leipzig colleagues and from scholars further afield. It was claimed that his four characters were recognisable caricatures of actual Leipzig scholars, and so Thomasius modified the form in which his periodical was cast, eventually abandoning the conversation form altogether and confining himself entirely to book reviews of an essay character. This was during the second year of publication when the general tone became far more serious and far less violent—and the whole journal less interesting.

In the second number, which had appeared in February 1688, Thomasius returned to the *Acta Eruditorum* in the course of a general discussion of journals. He lamented the fact that it did not appear in the German language and then went on to praise the author of the *Nouvelles de la République des Lettres* (Bayle) for his 'sonderliche Schreibart, welche mit einen subtilen und durchdringenden Schertz vermischet ist'.[1] This may well be intended as an indirect criticism of the ponderous style of the *Acta Eruditorum*. It is significant that Thomasius should have considered it a good thing for the style of a journal to be transfused with gaiety (*Schertz*). But after publication of the first two

[1] *Ed. cit.* p. 227.

numbers, Thomasius found himself in a stylistic quandary. In the preface to the March number, he tells us that some had found his journal insufficiently serious, while others would have preferred him to be consistently jocular. We find that he often indulges in an affected levity which is reminiscent somewhat of French *préciosité*, as in the protracted 'wit' of the following passage:

[Thomasius had] ...doch dabey dann und wann versucht, der Heucheley und Pedanterey gleichsam unversehens, und wann es mehr aus Einfalt als mit Vorsatz geschähe, auff den Leib zu treten, ümb zu vernehmen, ob diese zwey *Matronen* auch unleidlich wären, und wie weit ich mit ihnen außkommen könte. Ich habe sie in Wahrheit sehr weich und unleidlich gefunden, und haben sie nach ihrer ersten Grundregel mich bald anfangs durch entgegen gesetzte Gewalt ihrem Joch unterwerfen wollen. Gleichwie ich aber dafür gehalten, daß an dem ersten Streit viel gelegen wäre, und dannenhero mich nach Möglichkeit wiedersetzet, als haben sie nach der andern Grundseule ihrer *Politic* eine *Amnestie* mit mir gemacht, und durch falsche *caressen* mich entweder auff ihre Seite zu bringen, oder doch zum wenigsten bey der Nase herümb zu führen, und bey Gelegenheit rechtschaffen zu drücken sich angelegen seyn lassen.... Aber ich habe mir eingebildet, daß ich zum wenigsten auff etliche Jahre genugsam versehen wäre, auch eine Belägerung von ihnen außzuhalten, ihre *Stratagemata* zu verlachen, und ihre *Bombardi*rung mit ein klein wenig Dinte außzulöschen....[1]

This is a very revealing passage. The subject-matter is very serious, for the passage refers to the struggle which had darkened Thomasius's whole life. It had been a bitter fight for which he was paying dearly at the time this passage was written. Yet Thomasius is determined to be bright. The tone and purpose of his journal, the nature of his audience demanded this. But, since he is fundamentally a scholar, however much he may wish to appear a man of the world, his urbanity remains an academic urbanity. He adopts the learned artificiality of the ironic metaphor, a jocular personification, a comic travesty of the heroic. But these are borrowed plumes which sit uncomfortably on the full-bottomed wig of the learned jurist. His attempted urbanity is

[1] *Ed. cit.* vol. III, Vorrede, pp. 7–9 (January 1689).

weighed down by the cumbersome structure of his heavy periods. Thus when Thomasius parodies the absurdities of the heroic novel, he is no less tiresome than his subject:

> Madame Thetis ließ allbereit den Tisch decken, und die Tritones trugen die Teller zu, daß dieselben beyzeiten gewärmet würden; die Wasser-Nymphen aber *praepari*rten ein mit Kümmel und Hermelgen zugerichtetes Fußbad, damit, wann Mons. Phoebus, welcher kaum noch hundert Schuh vom Gestade des Meers war, ankäme, er nicht lange auff seinen Abend-Imbis warten dürffte, als zwischen Franckfurth und Leipzig auff der Land-Strasse 4. Personen im Schnee herumb krochen. ...Mit einem Wort, es war Abend, und unsere 4. Reisegeferten, die wir in vorigem Gespräche im Schnee ligen lassen, stunden wieder auff.[1]

In the long preface to the second year of the periodical, Thomasius stated his intention of writing with more seriousness in future, because the levity and satire of the first numbers had aroused offence. He now asserted that his original intention was to be satirical only in the first number, but that he had found it necessary to continue somewhat longer in this style. He admitted that he had 'einen ziemlich verdrießlichen stylum' in writing about serious matters, and he appealed to the example of Erasmus for justification of the satirical style. To modern readers the style of the *Monatsgespräche* will not seem satirical enough; too little distinction is made between the language of pedantry and the language of those who attack it. Thomasius had not sufficient control of language to use it as a vehicle of characterisation. His talents were hardly those likely to make him a successful satirical journalist. But his work is of immense importance, not only because he wrote in German, but because he used the literary journal to attack certain evils. He showed that this could be done; he started a fashion which others followed.

Satire figured largely in the German 'moral weeklies', although its scope was widened. Whereas Thomasius had set his face against pedantry and hypocrisy, the moral weeklies attacked all forms of affectation. These journals had a middle-class tone from the outset. They were written for a middle-class audience which

[1] *Ed. cit.* vol. I, pp. 115–16 (February 1688).

disapproved of many things which Thomasius's more aristocratic audience might well have condoned. They opposed gambling, duelling, swearing and anything that smacked of aristocratic debauchery and dissoluteness. We are moving towards the world of *Clarissa Harlowe* and *Miss Sara Sampson*.

The first of these moral weeklies, *Der Vernünfftler*,[1] published at Hamburg from 31 May 1713 until 30 May 1714, declared in its first number that it aspired to be the German equivalent of the journals of Addison and Steele, with the same general purpose, namely, 'modestly and gently to reprove the present corrupt manners in the world, and, wherever possible, to reform them somewhat'.[2] No such moral intentions had ever been proclaimed by Thomasius. His fight had been against tyranny, not corruption; he had been striving not to reform the human mind, but to liberate it. The editor of *Der Vernünfftler* was Johann Mattheson, more famous as a musician than as a writer, but the articles were by various contributors. Most of the material was taken directly from *The Spectator* or *The Tatler*. Indeed, many of the numbers are nothing more than translations. Stylistically they are, on the whole, very close translations; and this is a fact of very great importance. Through *Der Vernünfftler* the graceful urbanity of Addison's style exerted a lasting effect on German narrative prose. Addison's prose had two qualities which the language of Thomasius's *Monatsgespräche* had lacked: a lightness of touch and a shapeliness that could be termed 'classical'. In contrast Thomasius's prose was pedantic and cumbrous. *Der Vernünfftler* attains that lightness and urbanity he was seeking after, because

---

[1] The book edition was published in 1721. Its full title is: *Der Vernünfftler. Das ist: Ein teutscher Auszug, Aus den Engeländischen Moral-Schrifften des Tatler und Spectator, Vormahls verfertiget; Mit etlichen Zugaben versehen, Und auf Ort und Zeit gerichtet von Joanne Mattheson* (etc.—his titles follow) (Hamburg, 1721). Each number has four pages. There are 100 numbers. I have used the copy in the Staats- und Universitätsbibliothek, Hamburg. This would seem to be a rare book and there is no copy in the British Museum. There is no pagination; I cite therefore the number of the issue. The Hamburg copy has a 101st number in MS. bound up with the rest.

[2] '...die heutigen *corrumpirten* Welt-Sitten bescheidentlich und gelinde durchzuziehen, auch, wo müglich, einiger massen zu *reformi*ren.'

it is a translation from a language which had already attained these qualities in its prose. It would seem that Addison had been inspired by the fluidity of French prose. *Der Vernünfftler* may therefore represent the influence of French on German through the medium of English. It certainly shows German maturing under the influence of a foreign prose style. This is both interesting and important.

At first the style is somewhat uncertain of itself. In the second number there occurs the following passage:

> Allein *Cupido* ist nicht nur blind heutiges Tages, wie er vor Alters gewesen, sondern stern-blitz-voll, und hat alle seine gute Eigenschafften verlohren. Wie könnte es sonst müglich seyn, daß *Celia* mit aller ihrer Annehmlichkeit so lange Jungfer bliebe? Daß *Corinna* mit allen ihrem Verstand; *Lesbia* mit ihrer himmlischen Stimme, und *Saccharissa* mit allen und jeden diesen, in ihrer eintzigen Persohn versammleten, Vortreffligkeiten, *Opern* und *Assembléen* beywohnen, und die armen Haur-Krakken fast zu Tode jagen möchten, ohne daß ein *Chapeau* bey ihrer Ankunfft die Farbe verändert?

which seems to present an unsuccessful mixture of sophistication and vulgarity in its diction. The words *stern-blitz-voll* and *Haur-Krakken*[1] stand out so grossly from their pallid environment that the passage is robbed of its effect. An attempt at gentle irony has degenerated into crudeness, as we can see if we compare this passage with its English original which runs as follows:

> But *Cupid* is not only Blind at present, but Dead-drunk, he has lost all his Faculties: else how should *Celia* be so long a Maid with that agreeable Behaviour? *Corinna*, with that sprightly Wit? *Lesbia*, with that Heavenly Voice? And *Sacharissa*, with all those Excellencies in one Person, frequent the Park, the Play and murder the poor Tits that drag her to publick Places, and not a Man turn pale at her Appearance?[2]

---

[1] Michael Richey, *Idioticon Hamburgense* (2nd ed. 1754), glosses *Krakke, ohle Krakke* as 'alte Schind-Mähre, die bald umfallen will' and *Hore* as 'Hure'. Otto Mensing, *Schleswig-Holsteinisches Wörterbuch*, gives *Haur* as a by-form, and *Krack* (pl. *-en*) as 'Schinder', 'altes, mageres Pferd' also used of human beings. *Hoorbock* means 'Hurenkerl'.

[2] *The Tatler*, no. 5. It is interesting to note that the word 'tit' also refers originally to horses (but to small horses). Did the translator know this? His knowledge of English seems to be excellent.

The translator has gone just a shade too far; both words are too strong (each in its own way) for the context. But before long *Der Vernünfftler* is reproducing with considerable skill the full tone of the English original. Here is a passage starting with a general reflection and then illustrating this by a piece of imaginative fiction such as might figure in a novel:

But there are none to whom this Paper will be more useful, than to the Female World. I have often thought there has not been sufficient Pains taken in finding out proper Employments and Diversions for the Fair ones. Their Amusements seem contrived for them rather as they are Women, than as they are reasonable Creatures; and are more adapted to the Sex than to the Species. The Toilet is their great Scene of Business, and the right adjusting of their Hair the principal Employment of their Lives. The sorting of a Suit of Ribbons, is reckon'd a very good Morning's Work; and if they make an Excursion to a Mercer's or a Toy-shop, so great a Fatigue makes them unfit for anything else all the Day after. Their more serious Occupations are Sowing and Embroidery, and their greatest Drudgery the Preparation of Jellies and Sweet-meats. This, I say, is the State of ordinary Women;
The Spectator, no. 10.

Allein niemand wird mit dem Vernünfftler mehr gedient seyn, als der weiblichen Welt. Ich habe offtmahls erwogen, daß man sich noch nicht gnugsahme Mühe gegeben, recht anständige Verrichtungen und Ergetzlichkeiten vor das schöne Geschlecht zu ersinnen. Ihn gemeiner Zeitvertreib scheinet ihnen nur zuzukommen, in sofern sie Frauensleute sind, nicht aber als vernünfftigen Geschöpffen: Und ihr gantzer Betrieb schickt sich mehr vor das Geschlecht denn vor die *Species*. Die *Toilette* ist ihre große *Scene*, und das Haar-Auffstecken die vornehmste *Affaire* ihres gantzen Lebens. Wenn ein Kleid mit zugehörigem Band ausgesucht wird, so ist der Morgen wohl angewandt; Und fährt man etwan in eines Seiden-Händlers oder *Galanterie*-Krämers Bude, o! so macht eine solche *Fatigue* die lieben Dinger den gantzen Tag müde und zu allen andern Sachen unlustig. Ihre allerernsthaffteste Verrichtungen sind, wenns hoch komt, das Nähen und Sticken, und die allersaureste Mühe, *Gallart* oder *Confect*, auch wohl, wenn sie es so weit gebracht, Gurcken einzumachen. Dieses, sage ich, ist der Zustand der lieben Kinder insgemein;
Der Vernünfftler, no. 26.

This comparison is instructive. In the German, the little description of the lady's toilet comes out as a lively piece of light satirical writing. If we think back to Thomasius's attempts at such writing, we can see how marked is the achievement. A glance at the English will show how this has come about. The German translator, having well understood the tone of the original (additions like *die lieben Dinger* and *Gurcken einzumachen* show that), has reproduced the sentence-rhythm. The sentences are not of the baroque incapsulated type still favoured by Thomasius. The clauses are kept apart, just as they are in the English. The sentence-structure of English is here helping to transform the sentence-structure of German, and that is a very significant fact. The structural ideal of the chancery style, that of keeping the various parts of the sentence in place by enveloping them with the main verbal complex, is here no longer respected. His first sentence is not: *Allein niemand wird mit dem Vernünfftler mehr als der weiblichen Welt gedient seyn*, but follows the English structure. Similarly he does not write: *Ihr gemeiner Zeitvertreib scheinet ihnen nur in sofern sie Frauensleute sind, nicht aber als vernünfftigen Geschöpffen zuzukommen.* The baroque principle of the one enveloping verb is here replaced by a delicate equipoise of strains and stresses. In the first sentence *niemand* is balanced by *der weiblichen Welt*, the third sentence swings from *Frauensleute* to *vernünfftigen Geschöpffen*, from *Geschlecht* to *Species*. The passage is constantly in movement: *Wenn ein Kleid...so ist der Morgen. ...Und fährt man etwan...o! so macht eine solche Fatigue....* The principle of balance accounts for the fact that an idea may appear as a *pair* of words or phrases: *Verrichtungen und Ergetzlichkeiten; Die Toilette...und das Haar-Auffstecken; Ihre allerernsthaffteste Verrichtungen...und die allersaureste Mühe.* It is lively prose constantly flitting hither and thither, and producing just that effect of lightness that was needed. Lightness, then, came into German narrative prose at this time under the close influence of English prose rhythms.

The same principles of rhythm and structure are demonstrated by the following parallel:

SEMPRONIA is at present the most profest Admirer of the *French* Nation, but is so modest as to admit her Visitants no further than her Toilet. It is a very odd Sight that beautiful Creature makes, when she is talking	Sempronia ist itziger Zeit die geschworne Bewunderin der Frantzösischen *Nation*; allein sie ist dabey so züchtig, daß sie ihre Auffwärter weiter nicht als biß an die *Toillette* kommen läst. Es läst abgeschmackt, wenn diese

Politicks with her Tresses flowing about her Shoulders, [and examining that Face in the Glass, which does such Execution upon all the Male Standers-by.] How prettily does she divide her Discourse between her Woman and her Visitants? What sprightly Transitions does she make from an Opera or a Sermon, to an Ivory Comb or a Pin-Cushion? How have I been pleased to see her interrupted in an Account of her Travels, by a Message to her Footman; and holding her Tongue in the midst of a Moral Reflection, by applying the tip of it to a Patch?
The Spectator, no. 45.

schöne Creatur von Welt-Händeln *raisonnirt*, da ihr alle Haar übers Gesicht hangen. Wie artig kan sie die Unterredungen eintheilen zwischen ihre Cammer-Mädgen und denen die sie besuchen? welche sinnreiche *Transitiones* weiß sie nicht zu machen von einer *Opera* zu einer Predigt, zu einem elffenbeinern Kamm oder wohl*taillir*ten Nadel-Küssen? Wie hat es mich mannichmahl vergnüget, wenn sie die Erzehlung ihrer Parisischen Reise durch einen Befehl an ihren Diener so annehmlich unterbrochen? und wenn sie mitten in einer *moral*ischen Anmerckung stillgeschwiegen, weil sie eben eine *Mouche* auff die Spitze ihrer Zungen angefeuchtet?
Der Vernünfftler, no. 66.

Note how in several cases quite long phrases follow the infinitive which would normally stand in final position—because these phrases are in relief. The rigid sentence-mould is broken for the sake of stylistic effect. Wolff had broken away from the seventeenth-century sentence for the sake of clarity and precision. Here is another breakaway from the same stylistic norm, but this time in the name of gaiety and urbanity. Yet this breaking-away is not achieved by a breaking-down of the old sentence. It represents a new start. There is no direct connection between the language of the *Monatsgespräche* and that of *Der Vernünfftler*. But, as it so happened, both journals cultivated urbanity of style, although they set about it differently. It was *Der Vernünfftler*, the prose of which so closely followed the sentence-rhythm of its English counterpart, which was the more successful and which influenced the whole development of the German literary language.

As part of their campaign against affectation, the 'moral weeklies' attacked Francophile affectations like grandiloquent complimentation and the adulteration of the German vocabulary with French words and phrases. Thomasius had paid no attention to this; his own vocabulary is full of French words, as we have

THE LITERARY JOURNALS

seen. There is a passing reference to this topic in *Der Vernünfftler*[1] but it does not seem to have interested Mattheson very much, for the language of this journal is also full of French words. We read sentences like: 'Man...lasse der Natur ihren Lauff, *die ein jedes Subjectum daʒu destiniret, woʒu es capable*'[2] or: 'Kurtz es gehöret hieher ein jeder, der die Welt als eine Schau-Bühne betrachtet und gerne *einen rechten Gout von den agirenden Persohnen* haben wolte.'[3] It is true that *Der Vernünfftler* does on occasions use French words with stylistic effect, as when 'a very curious piece' is rendered by 'eine rechte rare *Piece*', or 'with which I presented my reader' by 'womit ich meine Leser *regali*ret', or 'a fashionable kind of gaiety and laziness' by 'eine gewisse *Mode* und *galante* Faulheit'.[4] But this is not always the case. This adulteration of vocabulary is strange in a periodical which avowedly owed its whole inception and tone to the example of Addison and Steele who had recognised in the language of their own country a like deterioration and infection with French words. 'The present war', says no. 156 of *The Spectator*,

has so adulterated our tongue with strange words, that it would be impossible for one of our great grand-fathers to know what his posterity have been doing, were he to read their exploits in a modern newspaper.... Our warriors are very industrious in propagating the French language, at the same time that they are so gloriously successful in beating down their power.

Here is another sample from *Der Vernünfftler*, which is this

---

[1] No. 66: 'Es ist sonst zu beklagen, daß wenn solche Herrlein ihr Gütgen in Franckreich zerschmoltzen, sie ausser etlich wenigen Frantzösischen Worten nichts mit zu Hause bringen, als daß sie das hiesige Geld, die ehrliche Hamburgische Sprache, und die Strassen nicht mehr kennen, obgleich ihre Reise mannichmahl nicht anderthalb Jahr austrägt.' This number is modelled on *Spectator*, no. 45 ('On French fashions and fopperies'), but there is no passage corresponding to this.
[2] No. 12. My italics. The original prints *Subjectum*, *destini*[ret], and *capable* so that they stand out from the rest of the text. This is a free rendering of a passage in *Spectator*, no. 157.
[3] No. 26. The corresponding English sentence reads: 'In short, every one that considers the world as a theatre, and desires to form a right judgment of those who are the actors on it' (*Spectator*, no. 10).
[4] The italics indicate italics in the original.

time not in a light vein but nevertheless suggests the influence of Addison's more serious prose style:

> Gewiß, wir sind deßwegen nicht hier, zu essen und zu trincken, zu schlaffen und zu träumen, zu putzen und zu stutzen, sondern GOTT rechtschaffen, uns selbst und unserm Nechsten mit allem Fleiß zu dienen. Wer dieses zu thun sich vorsetzet, und nach Vermögen ins Werck richtet, hat Gelegenheit genug seiner Schuldigkeit wahrzunehmen, und wird die Zeit eher zu kurtz als zu lang finden.[1]

This is rhetorical prose, carefully constructed in order to attain a certain, calculated effect. It is a highly conscious and essentially artificial style, with a strong rhythmical pattern produced by careful balancing of words and of phrases. The first half of the first sentence in the passage just quoted consists of a succession of rhythmical pairs, intensified by the rhyming pair *putzen-stutzen*, which is then followed, in the second half of the sentence, by a triple object extension (*Gott...uns selbst...unserm Nechsten*) which corresponds rhythmically to the three pairs of the first half of the sentence. The rhythmical pattern of the sentence captures the attention and impells it on to the climax *dienen*, which is made all the more effective by being temporarily withheld by the phrase *mit allem Fleiß*. We have the sense of a well-controlled rhetorical sentence, impelling us by its own rhythm towards its natural destination, the climax of the thought-progression which it is expressing. For in this type of sentence, the rhythmical climax falls on the word or words most essential to the meaning of the sentence. One might say that the rhythmical climax coincides with the thought-climax. Hence the structure of this type of sentence, although artificial, is never cumbrous. One does not have the sense of a tyrannical shape imposing itself on refractory material. The effect, although very consciously produced, does not strike one as unnatural. Words are not forced into unnatural places by an overriding pattern, nor non-subordinate ideas into subordinate clauses. Everything remains quite clear, however

---

[1] No. 88. This number is a version of *Spectator*, no. 323 ('Journal of a Fine Lady'), and is satirical. But these sentences from the conclusion replace an anonymous epitaph on Sir Philip Sidney's sister in the original.

studied the effect may be. It is this type of writing which characterises Addison's serious prose style at its best. And no doubt the classical shapeliness of his sentences appealed to the German writer. Addison's prose is more perspicuous than so much of the prose of German manuals and learned works of the time, and much more elegant. It was certainly both more perspicuous and more elegant than the prose of Thomasius. It was so clear that anyone could understand and enjoy it. It was also a national prose, free from foreign adulteration. All these considerations must have appealed to our German editor.

Der Vernünfftler was but the first of countless imitations of the English journals, but not all of them were so well written.[1] Thus, for instance, the short-lived *Der Leipziger Spectateur* (1723), addressed its readers in the following clumsy sentences:

> An dieser Zweyten Speculation des Leipziger Spectateurs wird der vernünfftige Leser hoffentlich sein Vergnügen finden, auch die Intention, so man bey dieser Arbeit führet, gar deutlich daraus ersehen. Warum man diese Arbeit den Spectateure genennet, das werden diejenigen leichtlich begreiffen, denen die Englische Arbeit des Herrn Steelen bekannt ist. Daß man aber solche den Leipziger Spectateur betittult, darzu hat man seine Ursachen, die künfftig sollen gemeldet werden; protestiret aber übrigens wider den irrigen Concept einiger Leser, als wenn man nur die Fehler, Schwachheiten und Laster der Leipziger durch zu ziehen bemühet wäre. Diese Arbeit ist auf gantz Teutschland, ja auf die gantze Welt gerichtet, derselben ihre Vorurtheile, Laster, Fehler und Schwachheiten auf eine ohnpassionirte und modeste Art zu zeigen.[2]

This prose is cumbersome and disagreeable to read. It lacks the shapeliness of the prose of *The Spectator*. If we compare the rhythmical pattern of these sentences with the passages just quoted from *Der Vernünfftler*, the difference is striking. In these sentences the rhythmical climax does *not* coincide with the climax of the content. The most important part of the thought is com-

---

[1] There is a list in M. Kawczyński, *Studien zur Literaturgeschichte des XVIIIten Jahrhunderts*. Moralische Wochenschriften (Leipzig, 1880).
[2] *Avertissement derer Verleger* at the end of the second *Speculation* or number.

municated in the first half of the sentence, whereas the rhythmical pattern produces a climax in the second half of the sentence. The result is that all these sentences peter out, and the twentieth-century writer would probably reverse the order of the two component halves in every case. The whole linguistic expression is corsetted by a rigid shape which accentuates the thought-connections by a cumbersome series of conjunctions which are constantly halting the attention in a forced and unnatural way: '*Warum* man diese Arbeit den Spectateur genennet, *das* werden diejenigen begreiffen...'; '*Daß* man aber solche den Leipziger Spectateur betittult, *darzu* hat man seine Ursachen...'. This pulling back and then thrusting on of the reader is one way of producing emphatic statement; but here it is used so regularly that it has become a mere formal mode and no longer serves to bring into relief some particular part of the sentence.

This journal was severely attacked for its clumsy style, notably by Breitinger in an article entitled 'Der gestäupte Leipziger Diogenes, oder Crittische Urtheile über die erste Speculation des Leipziger Spectateurs' which appeared in the Zürich *Historischer und politischer Mercurius* for February 1723.[1] Breitinger remarks: '*Purschickos*[2] *leben* ist nicht deutsch, weis nicht, ob es Leipzigisch ist?' He objects to a sentence like 'Einige Funken *wollten* ihr Andenken auf meines Freundes Mantel stiften' on the grounds of logic (sparks cannot have an intention). He points to a malapropism like 'einen Treffs auf sein *Capitolium* kriegen', or 'eine Schaubühne mit einem *Excrement* seines Ingenii eröffnen'; he objects to vulgarisms like 'einen mit dem Obergewehr zur Fricassee machen', 'es regnete Brennholz', and (interestingly

---

[1] Diogenes was the pen-name of the author of *Der Leipziger Spectateur*. This essay was reprinted in Gottsched's *Beyträge zur critischen Historie der deutschen Sprache, Poesie und Beredtsamkeit*, 14. Stück (1736), pp. 222–44. I quote from this text. British Museum copy.

[2] This word represents a jocular formation with Greek adverbial suffix -ικῶς. Such formations are characteristic of German student language. Stammler, in *Trübners Deutsches Wörterbuch*, says that this word is first found in Celander's *Der verliebte Student*, 1713. Schiller uses it, but in a clear student context (*Wallensteins Lager*, line 460). Adelung, in the first edition of his dictionary, does not give the word. It is obviously a cant word, which is what Breitinger means here.

enough), 'das Loch suchen, das der Zimmermann gelassen hat' which is still current in colloquial speech.

The *Discourse der Mahlern*,[1] a periodical published at Zürich from 1721 to 1723 by a group of friends in which Bodmer was the leading spirit, was dedicated to the 'illustrious Spectator of the English nation'. It hoped to fulfil the same function in Switzerland as *The Spectator* in England. The very first number expressed admiration not only for the contents of *The Spectator* but for the agreeable way in which it was written.[2] The little society responsible for the production of this periodical devoted considerable time to the study of their English model—through the medium of the French, abridged translation—as we can see from the account of their proceedings which is known as the *Chronick der Gesellschaft der Mahler*.[3] From this work we learn that on 18 October 1721 the society despatched a letter to Steele in the course of which they stated: 'Nous avons pesé vos discours scrupuleusement, fouillé dans le sens de toutes vos pensées, développé periode par periode, confronté discours à discours enfin examiné jusqu'aux mots.'[4] They then proceeded to enumerate some points on which they differed from their model, notably on the relative value of imagination and understanding (they believed

---

[1] There are four series of these 'discourses'. The first three (dated 1721, 1722 and 1722) bear the title *Die Discourse der Mahlern*, the fourth is entitled *Die Mahler, Oder Discourse von den Sitten der Menschen, Der vierdte und letzte Theil*, 1723. The British Museum has no copy, but there are copies at the University Library of Basle and the Central Library, Zürich. Photostats of the whole work are also available at Zürich. There is a reliable reprint of the first series only, by Theodor Vetter, in the *Bibliothek älterer Schriftsteller der deutschen Schweiz* (2. Serie, 2. Heft, Frauenfeld, 1891). I quote from the original edition.

[2] '...die ergetzende Manir mit welcher er seine Gedanken ausgedrücket hat.'

[3] Published from a manuscript in the Zürich library by Theodor Vetter in *Bibliothek älterer Schriftsteller der deutschen Schweiz* (Frauenfeld, 1887). I shall refer to this work as *Chronick*. Cf. p. 10: 'Den 28ten Augusti [1721] ward in der Gesellschaft beliebt unser *original*, ich meine die *Disc.* der Engelländer beßer zu *stud*iren; zu dem Ende wurden von Zeit zu Zeit in der Gesellschaft hin und wieder einige *Disc.* vorgelesen, und darüber so *reflect*irt, daß man die Folge seiner Gedanken, die Richtigkeit seiner Schlüßen, die abänderungen seiner *tours* etc. genau bemerckte.'

[4] *Chronick*, p. 14. No trace of a reply. I have retained the orthography of the original.

the pleasures of the understanding to be higher). This was a reference to Addison's *Essay on the Pleasures of the Imagination* in *The Spectator* (nos. 411–21); but Addison had not asserted that the pleasures of the imagination were in themselves higher than those of the understanding, he had maintained that each was in some ways superior to the other. But for these Swiss, it appeared that Addison's vindication of the imagination had often weakened the reasoning in *The Spectator*:[1] 'Er machet nicht selten absprünge, wenn er anfängt *raisonn*iren.'[2] One of their friends, Zellweger, agreed with this judgment '...car on void bien, quand on y prend garde, que le feu de son Imagination le met quelquesfois hors de gonds de la Raison, et le pousse dans des raisonnements vagues, qui n'ont aucune liaison avec le sujet, qu'il traite'.[3] Another point of difference was what the *Mahler*, in this letter to Steele, called his 'penchant pour le style burlesque' which they considered only worthy to amuse the common people (in whom they, at this time, were apparently not interested!).[4] We shall therefore expect the style of the *Discourse der Mahlern* to eschew vague reasoning and scorn the burlesque.

The first series is predominantly the work of Bodmer and Breitinger. They remained the main contributors in the second, third and fourth series, but a few articles were also contributed by others. All these men belonged to learned professions,[5] and

---

[1] Nevertheless Bodmer reproduced the ideas of Addison's essay fairly closely in the essay on Imagination which forms the 19th Discourse of the first series of the *Discourse der Mahlern*. This essay is important in that it contains the seeds of the later theories of Bodmer and Breitinger which brought them into conflict with Gottsched.

Many of the discourses show close affinity in thought (and sometimes phrase) with *The Spectator*, but there is no question of direct translation, not even from the French translation. For general information on this subject, see Theodor Vetter, *Der Spectator als Quelle der Discurse der Maler* (*sic*) (Frauenfeld, 1887). See also his essay, 'J. J. Bodmer und die englische Litteratur' in the *Bodmer Denkschrift* (Zürich, 1900). [2] *Chronick*, p. 17. [3] *Chronick*, p. 27.

[4] See also the letter to Lauffer on 25 October 1721 (*Chronick*, p. 18): 'wir die *burlesque* Schreibart für kindisch und unvernünftig erklähren, und zu nichts brauchen, als den Pöbel zu *amus*iren.'

[5] The articles were each signed by the name of a celebrated painter, but each contributor used several pseudonyms. Identification of authorship is afforded by a list in the *Chronick* (pp. 78–80).

indeed every page of this journal demonstrates that it is essentially the product of learned men. There is, at first, no attempt at an easy, light style. The general tone is serious, even weighty. We can appreciate the objection of these men to the 'raisonnements vagues' of Addison and the 'style burlesque' of Steele. For this style is heavily reasoned, and certainly never ventures into the burlesque.

Bodmer composed the first number, which begins as follows:

Der ein Buch will in die Welt ausgehen lassen, findet für seine Person gleich viele Ursachen sich einen glücklichen Successe zuversprechen, und das Gegentheil zubefahren.

Wenn er auf der *einen seiten* gläubet, da er seine Materie wol außerlesen, daß er sie mit guten Vernunffts-Gründen unterstützet, daß er seine Gedancken in ihrer wahren Proportion, und in ihrer natürlichen Schönheit ausgebildet habe, so hat er Fondament die Hoffnung zufassen, das Publicum werde solche Sachen die nützlich, vernünfftig sind und wol geschrieben, mit der besten Approbation aufnehmen. Wenn er sonst diese gute Meinung von seiner Schrifft nicht hätte, daß sie wegen ihrer Güte meritirte publiq gemachet zu werden, so hätte er Tort sie den Leuten zudebitieren, weil es zu ihrem und dabey zu seinem eigenen Schaden ausschlagen würde. Das Publicum würde die kostbare Zeit und das Geld verliehren, welches es auf eine Scarteque wenden möchte, es würde die Lügen, die Salbaaderey und die Thorheit kauffen, und sich damit den Kopff zerbrechen: Und er legte seiner seits seine Unwissenheit an den Tag; er gäbe sich einer gerechten Satiren bloß, und sähe sein Buch noch vor seinem eigenen Ende, in den Staube werffen und von den Würmern gefressen werden. Ob demnach zuerste ein Autor selbst einen guten Concept von seiner Schrifft hat (ohne welches er nicht befugt ist, sie der Welt mitzutheilen) so findet er Ursache, die gute Aufnahme derselben in der Hoffnung zuvorzusehen, und diese Rechnung zumachen, daß jedermann ein Werck werde lesen und applaudieren, welches mit seiner Nützbarkeit, mit seiner Vernunfftmässigket und mit seiner Artigkeit jedermann in die Augen leuchtet. Er kan gedencken, daß ein jeder suchen werde sich daraus zuerbauen, daß seine Schlüsse einem jeden precis und starck vorkommen werden, daß seine schöne Beschreibungen jedermann ergetzen werden; Endlich daß die Reüssite seines Buches unfehlbar erfolgen werde.

So bald er aber auf der *andern seiten* die Caprices des Pöbels, und die Uneinigkeit und Leichtsinnigkeit betrachtet, welche sich in den

Urtheilen der Menschen ereignet, so siehet er mehr als eine Ursache
zufürchten, daß seine Schrifft von dem Publico, von welchem die
Ignoranten und die Pedanten die grössere Zahl machen, werde verachtet
werden....

This pompous beginning makes a bad start. The author is presenting simple platitudes through the medium of a highly involved style. There is a jarring disagreement between form and content. A rhetorical note is immediately struck by the contrast of *Successe* and *das Gegentheil* in the first sentence, and this oratorical tone is continued by the broad contrast of the two following paragraphs (*auf der einen seiten...auf der andern seiten*). The stance of the orator is struck, but the eloquence is lacking. The external features of rhetoric are there—imperfect subjunctives in conditional clauses, emphatic repetition of conjunctions or prepositions, emphatic variation (*lesen und applaudieren; precis und starck; Uneinigkeit und Leichtsinnigkeit*)—but the real spirit of rhetoric is lacking. The diction is undistinguished; some simple things are expressed very clumsily (*hat er Fondament die Hoffnung zufassen; meritirte publiq gemachet zu werden*); the elaborate mould is never filled with anything of consequence. Bodmer seems quite unaware of the unsuitability of this language to his subject-matter. He has no sense of style. He writes like a pedant, and sometimes downright badly. The vocabulary contains foreign words which were not even normally current at this period (*Successe, Reüssite, Fondament, Tort, debitieren*). In the rest of this first discourse we find *Descriptionen, disintriciren, Favor, Consideration, das publique Theatrum, auspolirt, Present, Resolution, Membra dieser Societet, obligirt, recitiren, Coteri, Estime, accordiren* and unusual formations like *affrontirlich* and *uncapabel*. Such grossly adulterated language was exceptional even for this period, and contemporary critics recognised this fact. Thus Johann Jacob Lauffer, Professor of History and Eloquence at Berne, whose opinion on the first number of the journal was solicited, replied:

> Wan die *materi* nit nur wol ausgelesen, sonder auch wol ausgeführet wird, wan die Abschilderungen und Vorstellungen lebhafft, die Schreibart fließend und ungezwungen, die Sätze nit allzu weitläuffig,

die Sprüche nit allzu sehr hinter einander gesetzet, sonder die Kürtze und Klarheit beständig mit einander verknüpfet stehen, wan sonderlich die Reinigkeit der teütschen Sprache beybehalten wird, wan nit allzuviel frömde Worte mit untermischet werden, so wird man Ihre Blätter mit großer Vergnügung und Nutzen lesen.[1]

Let us note carefully the objections voiced by this contemporary critic. He is concerned solely with the language. He asserts that the style was not vivid enough, not fluid and unconstricted, that the sentences were too long and too sententious, and there were too many foreign words. It is important to observe that Bodmer's style struck this contemporary observer in almost exactly the same way as it does us. On adulteration of vocabulary, Lauffer continued with detailed criticism:

> Ich bin zwar nit der Meinung, daß man unsre teütsche Sprache mit frömden Wörtern, gleich andern, nit auch solle bereichern. Allein wan ich ein gut teütsches Wort finde meine Gedanken auszudrüken, so wolte ich nit bald ein frömbdes gebrauchen. Ich wolte lieber für *reüssite* guten Ausschlag, für *tort* Unbill, für *coterie* Gesellschaft setzen. Und ist gewüß, daß unsere Sprache, wan man sie wol verstehet, so reich und nachdrüklich als immer eine andre ist, und wan sie mit frömbden Worten nit vermenget, viel besser fließet....

This critic felt that these foreign expressions were objectionable, not because they were foreign, but because they obstructed the easy flow of the style. And he realised, more than Bodmer at this stage, that the journal needed an easy flowing style.

If Bodmer had the style of a pedant, then Breitinger had the style of a preacher. Here is a passage from the fourth discourse of the first series, which Breitinger contributed:

> Wenn ich nun den Menschen auf seinem Sterb-Bette betrachte, in der Zeit, da er in beständigen Sorgen lebt, das Band, welches Leib und Geist zusammen hält, werde zerspringen; so deucht es mich, ich sehe ihn, in einer gleichen Situation stehen, in der er ausser der Societet gestanden hätte: Dannzumal wird der Vorhang allgemach weggeschoben, der Mensch kommet wie zu sich selber, der zuvor eine fremde Person gespielet: Auf der einen Seite siehet er die Welt, die er jetz verlassen soll; und die andere weiset ihm die unermeßliche Ewigkeit,

[1] *Chronick*, p. 83.

die ihm alles Commerce mit den Sterblichen abschneidet: Die Furcht, welche ihn in so viele tausent Formen verstellet hat, verschwindet, weil die Knechtschafft, in der er die Zeit seines Lebens gestanden hat, aufhöret, und ihm die Menschen in zukunfft so wenig Nutzen als Schaden bringen können: Er redet wie es ihm um das Hertze ist, seine Worte sind von besonderm Nachdrück, und aufrichtige Copisten seiner Gedancken; die Vernunfft beginnet sich der alten Freyheit und des Rechtens, welches die Natur ihr mitgetheilet hat, zubedienen, indem die Seele sich von dem groben Kloß des Cörpers loßwindet: das Gewissen, der Verräther unsers Thuns und Lassens führet uns vermittelst des Gedächtnisses zurück, bis auf die frühen Jahre unserer Existentz, es durchgehet alle unsere Verrichtungen nach den strengen Gesetzen der Gerechtigkeit, und fället von uns einen unbestochenen Urtheil-Spruch.

This writing has definite quality. It flows naturally in a rhetorical vein which seems in no wise forced. It is vivid, fundamentally simple, both in its manner of saying things and the way in which the various statements are joined together, and effective because its rhetorical contrasts correspond to a real vivid picture of contrast in the writer's mind. But it is intensely serious. The interesting thing for our speculations here is to notice that Bodmer and Breitinger themselves came to the realisation that this, no doubt their natural style, was unsuited to the objects of the journal. They consciously set about evolving a more easy-flowing, more light-hearted style; they consciously endeavoured to write in a way which should attract an audience beyond the confines of the schoolroom or the church. This periodical shows, in its development, the whole stylistic trend of the times. A learned style had been established, but this was not suitable for all purposes. A lighter style, a more elegant style was needed.

The first step was taken by Bodmer in the sixth discourse of the first series. Here Bodmer discusses the elements of the sentence and suggests that clarity of expression depends predominantly on a skilful use of what he calls *particulae*, i.e., words used to connect statements. If these be carelessly or arbitrarily used, language becomes 'dunckel, ungestalt, unordenlich und schwach'. Clarity also depends, he says, on the order of the words; above all, the verb should not be placed too far from its subject and object. Then, as an example of a bad sentence, he cites the following:

> Der Printz von Conde, unter welchem diese kriegerische Fechter, diese erfahrne Officier, diese grosse Helden, welche durch ihre ruhmwürdige Thaten sich in den letzten Kriegen so bekannt gemachet haben, und welche den Ruhm des Frantzösischen Nahmens allein so hoch getrieben, weil sie diesen Printzen zum Haupt und General gehabt hatten, underwiesen und erzogen worden, hat Franckreich mehr Dienste gethan weder gantze Armeen.[1]

Bodmer remarks that the obscurity of this sentence is due to the excessive use of relative pronouns. He reconstructs the sentence as follows:

> Der Printz von Conde hat Franckreich mehr Dienste gethan, weder gantze Armeen; Unter ihm sind diese kriegerische Fechter, diese erfahrne Officier, diese grosse Helden underwiesen und erzogen worden, die durch ihre Thaten in den letzten Kriegen sich so bekannt gemachet haben, und welche den Ruhm des Frantzösischen Nahmens allein so hoch getrieben, weil sie ihn zum Haupt und General gehabt hatten.

This rearrangement, says Bodmer, is according to the spirit (*Genie*) of the German language. The implication is that good writing should respect the 'spirit' of the language in which it is written. The test of this 'spirit' is current usage, says Bodmer; but there is good and bad usage, and the usage of cultured men should be followed because they have freedom of choice in vocabulary and can reject expressions which they consider unworthy. Their speech is, therefore, the result of critical selection.

This discourse by Bodmer marks a very important moment in the development of the German literary language in the eighteenth century. Others had broken *away* from the seventeenth-century sentence-mould, but here a sentence of the old type is being

[1] This is a version of a passage in Bourdaloue's *Oraison Funèbre de Louis de Bourbon, Prince of Condé*. The original reads: 'De la vient que le prince de Condé valait seul à la France des armées entières... que sous lui se formaient et s'élevaient ces soldats aguerris, ces officiers expérimentés, ces braves dans tous les ordres de la milice, qui se sont depuis signalés dans nos dernières guerres, et qui n'ont acquis tant d'honneur au nom français, que parce qu'ils avaient eu ce prince pour maître et pour chef.'

broken *up* before our eyes and reassembled according to the new fashion. The sentence quoted is typical of the earlier age. It has the characteristic feature of a main clause in which the predicate is separated from the subject by a series of subordinate clauses, so that the main clause acts as a sort of outer envelope surrounding the various subordinate parts and subordinating them to itself. Bodmer feels that this is a 'bad' sentence. It is 'obscure'. In his analysis he decides that this is due to the division of the main clause and to the excessive use of what he calls *particulae*. His reconstruction involves three changes. First he keeps the main clause intact, placing it at the head of the sentence. Secondly he takes a subordinate clause from the old sentence and makes it into the main clause of his second sentence. This is significant, because one of the results of the rigid mould of the incapsulated seventeenth-century sentence was that ideas were expressed in subordinate clauses which really belonged in main clauses. Thirdly Bodmer removes that incapsulation which delayed the verbal predicate *underwiesen und erzogen worden*.

These critical speculations of Bodmer reached a climax in the twenty-third discourse of the first series, in which he went through the earlier discourses and suggested various stylistic corrections. Bodmer was no doubt influenced in this matter by the desire to make his journal more widely popular, for Laurenz Zellweger, an archivist in Trogen, had stated that his peasants liked the journal, once that the style had been explained to them.[1] Bodmer seems to have determined that in future his journal should be accessible to simple folk with little education.[2] In the emendations offered in this twenty-third discourse, the words *disintricieren, Reussite, Entibus, Membra, reciprocierlich, Benevolentz, Attaques, Sexe, Espece* and *Ceremonien* were replaced by German equivalents, but a large number of foreign words were still left unchanged. Thus, if we take as a sample his revised version of

[1] 'Il n'y avoit que le stile, qu'ils n'entendoient pas par tout, parcequ'il n'étoit pas assez coulant et naturel pour eux, et quelques mots François etc. que je fus obligé de leur expliquer' (*Chronick*, p. 30).

[2] 'Die Bauren verdienen, daß man auch ihrer eine Rechnung trage, da sie fast die eintzigen sind, denen die Natur ihre Reden vertraut hat' (*Chronick*, pp. 31–2).

the second main paragraph of the first discourse, we find *Caprices, Scribenten, subtil, penetriren, Imagination, Descriptionen, Requisitis, Disposition, Habit, Statur, Autoritet, Favor, Consideration, Relation, Evidentz, capabel* or *raisonnabel.* This seems puzzling at first sight. We must, however, remember that German-Swiss speech has always been characterised by a stronger admixture of French words than German cultured usage. This is the impression we obtain from the debates between Bodmer and Breitinger on the one hand and Gottsched on the other. It would seem then that Bodmer eradicated only those foreign words which he, as a Swiss, felt to be affected. He was probably animated, not by any nationalistic purism, but merely by the desire to use a vocabulary which should be comprehensible not only to his cultured compatriots but also to the simpler countryfolk.[1]

Bodmer's stylistic revision of the earlier discourses involved, however, not merely the substitution of German equivalents for foreign words, but also the remodelling of whole sentences now felt to be cumbrous or obscure. For instance the entire first section of the passage quoted above on page 71 is replaced by this condensation:

Ein Autor, der wol beredt ist, der die Kunst zu meditieren in einem hohen Grade besitzt, der eine grosse Kenntniß der Sachen zuwegen gebracht hat, wenn er ein Buch in die Welt ausgehen läßt von dem die Materie wol außerlesen, mit guten Vernunffts-Gründen unterstützet, und alle Gedancken in ihrer wahren Proportion und natürlichen Schönheit ausgebildet sind, hätte zwar Recht zu gedencken, daß seine Schrifft sollte gekaufft und gelesen, und die Mühe die er darauf gewandt, von dem erfolgenden Nutzen reichlich bezahlt werden; so lang er die Aufnahm derselben allein nach ihrer Güte abmißt. So bald er aber...

[1] It is interesting in this connection to note that Breitinger in 'Der geställupte Leipziger Diogenes' (see above, p. 68) censured the vocabulary of *Der Leipziger Spectateur* in the following terms: 'Dieser Leipziger könnte noch bey manchem Schweizer in die Schule gehen, der ihn lehren würde, wie *depossedi*ren, *ingenium, speculationibus, corruption, douceurs, bravoure, inviti*ren, *praeservi*ren, *incommodi*ren, *Courage, taliter qualiter, justement, tendresse,* in der deutschen Sprache gesaget wird' (Gottsched, *Beyträge* etc., 14. Stück, p. 236). This was written after the twenty-third number of the first series of the *Discourse der Mahlern*, but nevertheless seems to me significant.

This certainly represents an improvement. Some of the clumsiest phrases have been remodelled and the vocabulary is free from adulteration (although *meditieren* might have been replaced by a native word). The rhetorical cast of the sentence-structure has also been, in the main, abandoned, although certain rhetorical elements (like the emphatic succession of clauses introduced by *der*, dependent on *der Autor*) remain and always will remain in Bodmer's style. There are still far too many *particulae*. The main clause is split into two, even though the predicate comes not at the end of the whole period but half way through it. Some of the subordinate clauses might well be turned into main clauses of new sentences. The period is still involved, the style is verbose. Bodmer has not mastered the easy sentence, even though he has become more sensitive to language. This heightened sense of style is shown by the fact that, in another place, Bodmer transforms a clumsy image like 'daß nichts als die Schneide des Todes capabel ist, diesen harten Knopff der Freundschafft aufzulösen' into 'daß nichts als der Tod, der alles zerreisset, starck gnug seye, dieses feste Band der Freundschafft aufzulösen'. Incapsulated structure as in the sentence: 'Dieß alles ist nun capabel einem neuen Autor Furcht einzujagen, und seine Hoffnung wol zureussiren, genau zubeschneiden' is removed by complete remodelling. All this shows good taste and increasing stylistic sensitivity. Lauffer expressed his satisfaction with these and like improvements; the language of the journal, he said, was now no longer so 'rauh' nor so 'gekünstlet' (strange bedfellows!). He does not doubt that if the authors continue in this way and speak 'mit lachendem Munde, und nit mit allzu ernsthafften Gebehrden' they will win the approbation of both men and women. 'Sie haben', he continues, summarising the whole situation clearly, 'in ihren meisten *discurs*en biß *dato* mit Gelehrten geredt, welche doch den geringsten Theil der menschlichen Gesellschaft ausmachen, wan sie sich aber angewehnen werden, mit jedermann, sonderlich mit dem Frauenzimmer, auf eine angenehme Weise zu reden, so wird die Anzahl ihrer Leser sich um ein merckliches vermehren'.[1] *The*

[1] *Chronick*, p. 97.

Spectator, as Lauffer recognised, owed much of its widespread fame to its women readers. And so the authors of the *Discourse der Mahlern* determined that their second series should be lighter in tone, 'fließender und Schertz-reicher werden, als der erste der zu *systemat*isch ist'; and it should have a greater appeal for women.[1]

In this way, women entered indirectly but nevertheless quite influentially into this complex of disparate influences moulding the German language as an instrument of literary expression during the first half of this century. It was something new for an author to be writing for women. The conscious envisagement of women readers encouraged the definite attempt to be simpler, brighter, wittier and even more elegant. Women read not for instruction, but for entertainment—that was the implication. Reading for them is not a serious occupation but a leisure pursuit. If they can be educated in the process, so much the better; but the prime purpose of the author must be to attract and to amuse. It was considerations such as these which were to fashion the whole tone and style of Gottsched's journals. This we shall examine in due course. For the moment it is important that we should notice these Swiss writers, some four years earlier and under the definite stimulus of *The Spectator*, already visualising the possibility and indeed the advantages of attracting a female reading public. They quite consciously set themselves to adapt both the content and the tone of their journal to this new potential public. It cannot be said that they were very successful. But the measure of their success is less important than their realisation of this new potentiality and their conscious attempt to evolve a suitable style.

Imaginative fiction, satire and humour figure prominently in the later series of this journal. There are satirical attacks on the heroic novel and on false compliments. There is a mock encomium on tobacco and a mock diatribe against beards. Stylistic matters come in for some discussion; there is an attack on rimed verse and on the metaphorical, allusive style of baroque poetry. The

[1] *Chronick*, p. 32.

Addisonian dream-fiction is imitated in the first number of the second series where Bodmer receives a visitation from the spirit of Martin Opitz. We are immediately conscious, in this very first number of the second series, that something quite different is being attempted. The tone is different, the subject-matter is different. Perhaps it is the women that Bodmer has in mind. The new series begins as follows:

> Wenn ich auf meinem Vorwerck[1] bin, so folge ich offtmahlen dem sanfften Strohm einer klaren Bache, die ihr Wasser gemächlich um die Wiesen und Felder desselben herumzingelt, und steige so lange hinauf, biß daß ich endlich zu einem ausgespannten Eichbaume komme, der seine Wurzeln mit den Wellen dieser Bache netzet, die in seinem Schatten hervorstrudeln. Ich sasse an einem schönen Tag unter diesem Baume, und weidete eine Weile meine Augen, die ich von der Höhe auf welcher derselbe stehet, in die Ründe des Thales und der darüber liegenden kleinen Hügeln herum schweiffen ließ; hernach nahme ich meinen Opitz der mein steter Gefehrte ist, aus der Tasche, und lase mit dem größten Ergetzen, was er zum Lobe des Feld-Lebens, von Zlatna, und von Vielgut geschrieben, indem ich von Zeit zu Zeit unter meinen Füssen solche Objecte antraffe, von denen mein Poete Beschreibungen machet, und zuweilen eine so genaue Aehnlichkeit zwischen diesen und denen Gegenständen fande, die ich vor den Augen hatte, daß ich offt im Zweifel stuhnde, ob mich Opitz auf sein Vielgut versetzet habe, oder ob er sein Gedichte von dem Platze gemachet, von welchem mir die Objecte seiner Beschreibungen so natürlich in die Augen fielen.

This represents a definite attempt at descriptive prose of an easy-flowing nature, direct and pleasing in its appeal, straightforward but expressive in its vocabulary. The first sentence seems to fulfil these aspirations, and is quite successful. But only a few lines later this prose returns to Bodmer's normal pedantic type of sentence, not incapsulated but flowing on and on from one clause to the next. After the reference to Opitz and his *Zlatna* there follows a succession of clauses which are not really subordinate ideas and distend the sentence to inordinate length and make it

---

[1] 'Ein Vorwerk bestehet gemeiniglich aus einigen von einem Hauptgute abgesonderten und mit den dazu nöthigen wirthschaftlichen Gebäuden versehenen Ländereyen' (Adelung, 1780).

cumbersome and tedious in its effect. There are still far too many *particulae*. The sentence-mould is far too heavy for the content. In the Essay on Beards the effect obtained is almost ludicrously heavy and the humour is stifled by the language. A very simple idea needs many words to find expression:

> Daneben ist auch ein langer Bart ein grosses Verhinderniß in einem Hand-Gemenge, und kan seinen Mann leichtlich in die Spiesse verwicklen, gleichwie ein grosser Feldherr wol bemercket hat, und dahero seinen Soldaten befohlen, die Bärte vor der Schlacht abzuschneiden, damit solche nicht in die Hände der Feinden fielen, und Beute gemacht würden.

But as time passes, Bodmer and Breitinger see the value of dialogue as a stylistic medium, and in the sixteenth number of the second series something much lighter in texture is achieved, for example:

> Es ist undisputierlich, daß das weibliche Geschlecht für die Kleider-Pracht mehr paßionirt ist, weder die Männer. *Tellesille* ist eine Person, welche ich auf diesem Fusse kenne: Wenn sie daheim mit der Nadel beschäfftiget ist, so sind ihre Unterredungen und Gespräche anders nichts, weder eine Erzehlung von den Moden, die sie an der und dieser Jungfer gesehen hat: Gehe hin, sagt sie zu der Magd, heisse mir den Schneider kommen; daß er mir das seidene Schöpel verändere; ich will daß er mir die Ermel in Falten lege, so wie es *Emilie* trägt: Und so dir etwan die Kappen-macherin begegnet, so kanst du ihr sagen, daß sie diesen Nachmittage meiner nicht vergesse; sie muß den Pusch von meiner Kappen eine andere Stellung geben, denn ich habe wahrgenommen, daß es die neueste Mode ist, daß sich dieselbigen gegen dem Gesicht niederbücken.

or in Number 25 of the same series:

> Als ich den verstrichenen Montag die Jungfer Schildin wiederum heimsuchte, trate Hr. Honigseim von ungefehrd in das Zimmer, in welchem sie mich mit seiner Lebens-Beschreibung unterhielte. Sie ware anfänglich über seiner unvermutheten Ankonfft bestürtzt, weil sie sich nicht versehen hatte, denselben in seiner vorigen Gestalt wieder zu sehen; aber diese Bestürtzung veränderte sich so gleich in ein Gelächter, als sie ihm eine kleine Weile steiff in die Augen gesehen

hatte, sie sprange von dem Sessel auf, lieffe ihm entgegen, und redte ihn unter einem angenehmen Lächeln also an: Wo habt ihr den Bart gelassen Herr Honigseim, daß ihr mit nackendem Kinn hier erscheinet?

We have only to compare these two short extracts with the very first numbers of the *Discourse der Mahlern* (e.g. the passage quoted on page 71 above) to see how there has been a definite progression towards a more jovial, more entertaining style, lighter in the structure of its periods, less affected and more German in its vocabulary, less rhetorical, less involved—and calculated to appeal to a wide audience and not merely to a forum of scholars.

Readers in Germany were, however, displeased by the dialectal features in the language of the *Discourse der Mahlern*, and objections were voiced by various persons. Apart from the large number of foreign words (discountenanced, as we have seen, even by Swiss critics) there were characteristic Upper German features of phonology, morphology and vocabulary which were archaic or incorrect by the standards of important cultural centres like Hamburg, Halle or Leipzig. Gottsched strongly criticised the language of the *Discourse der Mahlern*, and compared it unfavourably with the language of another journal, *Der Patriot*. *Der Patriot*, published in Hamburg from 5 January 1724 until 28 December 1726, was conducted by a group of distinguished Hamburg citizens, some of them writers of repute like Michael Richey and Barthold Heinrich Brockes.[1] The prose of this journal was outstanding for its time; it is spacious, clear prose with a considerable sense of form and at times definite distinction. The general tone is calm, the rhythm and shape of the sentences is leisurely and rounded:

Ich lebe demnach seit einigen Jahren in einer angenehmen Stille, mitten unter dem Lärmen einer unruhigen volkreichen Stadt, wo die kleinen Thorheiten des Pöbels und die grossen Ausschweiffungen der reichen, mich bald zum Gelächter bald zum Mitleid bewegen.

[1] Bound up as *Der Patriot vom Jahre MDCCXXIV, MDCCXXV und MDCCXXVI*, Hamburg, no date but presumably early in 1727. I quote from the copy of this edition in the British Museum.

Such a sentence is obviously conceived with care. It is the expression of a mind which loves balance and shapeliness. It aims at inculcating a sense of the author's 'angenehme Stille' by using calm, measured language. Form harmonises with content. The sentence is from the first number of this periodical which maintains this measured flow; although it can avoid monotony by moving into a short, sharp, rhythmical sequence, as in the latter part of the following passage, also from the first number:

> Durch diese und andere sorgfältige Auffmercksamkeit und Bemühungen ist meine Begierde, zu lernen, so weit vergnüget, und bin ich nunmehro mit mir selber in Gelassenheit zu frieden. So sehr ich mich bestrebe, gegen die täglichen Wunderwercke und Wohlthaten meines GOttes nicht unempfindlich zu seyn; so wenig kan auch etwas widriges mich empfindlich, oder mein Wohlstand mich trotzig, machen. Ich fürchte nichts, ich betrübe mich nicht unmässig, ich schweiffe nicht aus in meiner Freude, ich zürne nicht, ich beneide niemand, und kurtz, mein eintziges Bemühen, ja meine gantze Leidenschafft ist, mit Vergnügen zu sehen, daß es jedermann wohl gehe.

There is a heritage from the seventeenth century (and, I think, ultimately from Latin) in this style. I refer to the tendency to use a pair of words, similar in meaning, instead of one word—usually where the thought in question is an important one for the total meaning, and the sentence needs to be given particular stress at this point. We are familiar with this stylistic device from the language of our own Book of Common Prayer;[1] in the passage just quoted we find 'Auffmercksamkeit und Bemühungen', 'Wunderwercke und Wohlthaten', 'mein eintziges Bemühen, ja meine gantze Leidenschafft'. This rhetorical device which we had seen used to produce balanced movement in the prose of *Der Vernünfftler* is here used for emphasis. Equally emphatic is the

---

[1] E.g. 'erred and strayed', 'devices and desires', 'declare and pronounce', 'pardoneth and absolveth', 'assemble and meet together', 'acknowledge and confess', 'sins and wickedness', 'dissemble nor cloke', etc. Saintsbury (*History of English Prose Rhythm*) traces this back as far as Berners and Fisher in the fifteenth century, and implies influence of classical rhetoric. This influence was reinforced by the writers of the so-called 'Cambridge School'—Cheke, Ascham and Wilson—in the sixteenth century.

enumeration of short clauses in the last sentence of the passage quoted. What gives this passage definite stylistic quality is the combination of these two rhythmical patterns to build up to the final phrase of the passage, and give it full emphasis. The author is not merely concerned in saying something, he is concerned in saying that something with emphasis and persuasiveness.

Now let us take a sample of narrative prose from the same journal. This is from the twenty-first number dated 25 May 1724:

> Sie setzten demnach ihren Stab weiter, bis abermahls die anbrechende Nacht sie nöhtigte, eine Schlaff-Stelle zu suchen. Das Haus, darin sie traffen, hatte einen sehr unfreundlichen Herrn, der ihnen unter offenem Himmel in seinem Hoffe ein Lager machen ließ, und sie die gantze Nacht hindurch dem unangenehmsten regnichten Wetter Preiß gab. Gleichwohl belohnte der Reise-Gefehrte unsers Einsiedlers diese üble und harte Begegnung, wider alles Vermuhten, mit eben demselben Becher, den er seinem vorigen so höflichen Wirthe genommen hatte, und ließ selbigen deßwegen mit Fleiß, jedoch als unversehens, zurück. Philaret verwunderte sich von neuen hierüber, und noch mehr als vorhin, da er zugleich sahe, daß sein Freund den Becher mehr durch einen besondern Einfall, als aus Geitz und Eigennutz, zu sich gesteckt hatte.

This prose is clear and quite pleasant to read, but not very expressive. For a narrative style, it is somewhat lacking in highlights. But, as with all the prose of this journal, it is completely devoid of clumsiness and affectation. Here is the *basis* for a good narrative style. All it needs is a writer with more bite, more wit and more subtlety to make of this style a delicate and graceful medium in which to tell a tale. What *Der Patriot* achieves is writing which definitely aims at being correct, clear and pleasing, and although it is the work of several writers, this same stylistic endeavour seems to dominate the whole.

Another important feature of *Der Patriot* was the extreme purity of its vocabulary. Its authors were firmly opposed to the adulteration of their language with foreign words. They showed by their own style that this was not necessary, and they constantly satirised those who continued in this fashion, which they viewed as a form of affectation.[1] The seventeenth number of *Der Patriot* contains a letter, fictitious no doubt, from a correspondent who complains that the paper contains 'so wenig *curieus*es' and proceeds to offer some samples of local news, one of which reads:

> Viele Eigenthümer der hiesigen *maisons de campagne* haben bereits ihre *bagage* aus Hamburg voraus gesandt, und lassen alle *praeparatori*en vorkehren, bald folgen, um ihr *sejour*, bey dieser schönen *Saison*, hieselbst nehmen zu können.

The journal comments on those adulterators of language who think that nothing is worth saying unless their German is constantly interlaced with Latin, French and Italian words, 'adorned, as it were, with foreign jewels', and goes on to lament that this, alas, was the prevailing mode of writing which had brought the Germans and their language into such disrepute with other nations. *Der Patriot* suggests that this affectation was particularly current amongst the aristocracy. This is a very interesting point, for it shows the middle-class tone of the journal and its reading public. The use of adulterated German now has something rakish and decadent about it. This is a new attitude to the question. It is reinforced by a later number of *Der Patriot*[2] which contains an absurd letter in very adulterated German from an aristocrat named 'Charles de Sotenville'. The postscript runs:

> *A propos.* Ich bitte mich zu *excusi*ren, daß ich so *hardi* bin, gegen Dero *coutûme* vieles aus der *langue francoise* in meiner *lettre* anzubringen.... Um die Wahrheit zu sagen, ich bin so wenig des Teutschen als des Frantzösischen gantz mächtig, und werden sie die *Melange* der beyden *pardonni*ren....

In the fifty-fifth number, the opinion of the poet Besser is cited who lamented the fact that Germans seemed to use their own language only for speaking to servants or with such a strong

---

[1] This represents a certain simplification of the problem, for it cannot be said that Thomasius was indulging in 'affectation', and yet his prose, as we have seen, was full of foreign words. I also cannot believe that Bodmer and Breitinger were 'affected'. They were following too closely their own colloquial speech and paying too little attention to that conscious selection of vocabulary which must needs be a feature of all good writing.

[2] No. 111, dated 14 February 1726.

admixture of foreign words that it became 'like a patched beggar's cloak'. In the conclusion to the last number of this periodical the author laments that a German of those days had to understand French, Latin and Italian in order to be able to read a book in his mother-tongue: but *Der Patriot* had always striven 'durch eine sorgfältige Reinlichkeit und edle Simplicität in der Beredsamkeit diesen verwehnten Geschmack zu bessern, dem bisherigen gelehrten Mischmasch entgegen, der eine Pest unserer Sprache ist, und durch viele bunte Flecken in unsern Büchern sich schon längst geäussert hat'. The fact that the foreign word *Simplicität* can appear in such a context merely shows how deep-set was the affection!

The fifty-fifth number of *Der Patriot* reflects on what constitutes good writing and decides that the most important thing is the avoidance of all that is unnatural and affected. Clear, orderly thinking is essential, but one must also know how to give form to one's expression. Everything should 'come out' as naturally as possible, 'ohne den geringsten falschen Schmuck'. Two lines on the Thames from a poem by Sir John Denham are then offered as a description of the epitome of all good style:

> Zwahr tieff, doch aber klahr: sanfft, aber doch nicht matt:
> Starck, ohne Raserey: voll, ohn sich zu ergiessen.[1]

The anonymous author of this number of *Der Patriot* then proceeds to enumerate the qualities essential to good writing. First there is progressive clarification:

> Nehmt einen eintzelnen Satz vor euch, und richtet beständig euer Augenmerck darauff, damit der Leser allezeit einen so viel deutlichern Begriff davon habe, je weiter er euch folget. Was er zuerst von ferne siehet, scheinet ihm eine Wolcke zu seyn: hernach findet er, daß es ein Berg ist, und endlich ein Wein-Garte. Er gehet hinein, und die Trauben sind reiff.

---

[1] These lines are taken from *Coopers Hill*, published in 1643. In the original they run as follows:
> Though deep, yet clear, though gentle, yet not dull,
> Strong without rage, without o'er-flowing full.

Then plasticity:

> Schreibet, als ob ihr jedes Ding vor euch sähet, davon ihr handeln wollt. Die Gleichniß Reden, so uns eine Sache ins Gesicht bringen, sind die allerlebhafftesten und nachdrücklichsten.

The good author should show cultured taste in his choice of words and expressions:

> Zeiget in euren Schrifften, daß ihr höfflich, edelmüthig und wohl auffgebracht[1] seyd. Bedienet euch keiner niederträchtigen Figuren, noch anderer Pedantischen Zierahten. Denn beydes sind untrügliche Kennzeichen eines schlechten Verstandes.

He should write in a state of enthusiasm and check his work in cool reflection:

> Schreibet nicht anders, als wenn ihr auffgeräumt, und von eurer Sache gantz eingenommen, oder darauff erhitzt seyd. Sehet es aber nach, wenn ihr euch etwas kaltsinnig, oder verdrießlich, und zum schreiben selbst nicht geschickt, befindet.

This author, whoever he may have been, was consciously advocating simple principles in order to combat the affectations and superficialities of the manuals of style put out by the rhetoricians for whom good writing was synonymous with ornamentation. The seventieth number of *Der Patriot* mocks at those who incite their pupils to write 'zierlich, schön und verblümt' rather than 'verständlich und deutlich' so that young heads are so stuffed with recipes of this kind that they are quite unable to express their thoughts in a natural, easy and agreeable way. The main thing is always to write so clearly that the reader can see everything before his eyes; but this can only happen if the writer is moved by what he expresses. If he is moved, then metaphors and figures of speech will come spontaneously to his pen.
Der Patriot admitted that it had consciously cultivated a stylistic mean which should be neither too much below the

---

[1] *auffgebracht:* apparently in the sense of English 'brought up'. Adelung (1774) gives the example 'Sie wird dieses kind schwerlich aufbringen' meaning 'groß ziehen'. But this is not quite the same meaning.

learned reader nor too much above the simple reader, 'comprehensible to everyone and simply demanding the ordinary use of human reason'.[1] The English journals had done much to improve the English language. *Der Patriot*, in its last number, hopes that it has done something to raise the linguistic consciousness and taste of the German nation. There is no doubt that the prose of this journal was generally recognised to be very good. It was much admired by Gottsched, whose first journal, *Die Vernünfftigen Tadlerinnen*[2] (1725-6) had been praised in no. 69 of *Der Patriot* (dated 26 April 1725). Gottsched in his turn praised *Der Patriot* in *Die Vernünfftigen Tadlerinnen* as 'a national glory', suggesting that it should be called 'Der teutsche Patriot'. He praises it for its 'reine Sprache und schöne Schreibart', contrasting it favourably with the *Discourse der Mahlern*. He mentions the lack of foreign adulteration in the vocabulary of *Der Patriot*, and describes its style as 'deutlich, ordentlich, nachdrücklich, fliessend und zierlich'.[3] He ventures to think that *Die Vernünfftigen Tadlerinnen* had much the same objects in view and that was why they had earned the approval of *Der Patriot*. Gottsched's journal was expressly addressed to women readers and purported to be written by a group of women. Each number bears the signature of one of three women. The journal began as a co-operation between Gottsched and two of his Leipzig friends, but the others soon dropped out and therefore it is legitimate to speak of this journal as Gottsched's work. The first number explains that the tone of the journal is conditioned by the fact that it is composed by women, and that the style will not be learned, but flow from 'einem natürlichen Verstande, und einer angebohrnen Lebhafftigkeit'. The second edition of the first volume

---

[1] No. 36, dated 7 September 1724.

[2] *Die Vernünfftigen Tadlerinnen, Erster Jahr-Theil*, 1725 (published in book form, Leipzig bei Joh. Fr. Brauns seligen Erben, no date) and *Andrer Jahr-Theil* (book form, same publisher, Leipzig, 1727). There is also a later reprint. I have used the copy of the first edition in the Central Library of Zürich. The text in the edition of the Gottsched Gesellschaft (ed. Reichel (Berlin, 1903-6), only six volumes published) is incomplete and much doctored.

[3] *Op. cit.* vol. I, p. 163.

is ushered in by a new preface in which Gottsched explains that the nature of his audience had precluded the extreme orderliness and thoroughness which would be expected of a work written for a scholarly audience. He had contented himself with writing in a style that was clear, instructive and pleasant[1]—a style, he adds ironically, which not all scholars were capable of cultivating. Here is a sample of the style, the beginning of the very first number:

> Was ist das nun wiederum vor eine neue Hirn-Geburt? Es wird itzo Mode, daß man gern einen Sitten-Lehrer abgeben will. Haben wir aber nicht von Manns-Personen moralische Schrifften genung; und muß sich das Weibliche Geschlecht auch ins Spiel mischen? Es wird gewiß ein ehrbares Caffeecräntzgen seyn, welches bey dem Uberflusse müßiger Stunden gewohnet ist, alles zu beurtheilen und durchzuhecheln. Die guten Kinder müssen wohl dem Sirach zeitig aus der Schule gelauffen seyn, sonst würden sie seine Lehre besser gefasset haben: Laß dich nicht zu klug düncken, jedermann zu tadeln. Wenn doch die lieben Momus-Schwestern sich wieder in die Aufsicht dieses klugen Hauß-Lehrers begeben wolten, so würde ihnen ihr unzeitiger Kützel, vielleicht zu ihrem eigenen Vortheile, vergehen.
> So haben ohne Zweifel viele geurtheilet, als sie die Uberschrifft von diesem Blatte in den öffentlichen Zeitungen wahrgenommen. Und dies würden gewiß verdienen, ihres unbedachtsamen Ausspruches halber, am ersten von uns getadelt zu werden. Wir vergeben ihnen aber dißmahl ihre Ubereilung. Es ist allerdings was ungewöhnliches, daß sich schwache Werckzeuge zu öffentlichen Richtern aufwerffen.

The passage continues for a short time in this tone and then breaks into something more concrete:

> Phyllis, ein wohlerzogenes Frauenzimmer, fand mich bey einem unvermutheten Besuche, in Lesung einer gewissen Moralischen Betrachtung beschäfftiget. Wie so fleißig, liebe Schwester? war ihre erste

---

[1] In the very last number of this periodical, Gottsched made the following claim: 'Ich habe mich bemühet, deutlich und natürlich zu schreiben, damit mich auch die Unstudirten lesen und verstehen möchten: und mich dünkt, daß ich zum allerwenigsten in diesem Stücke meinen Zweck erhalten habe' (*ed. cit.* vol. II, p. 414). For this use of *zum wenigsten*, cf. an example given by Adelung (1786), 'Wollen sie mir nicht alles geben, so werden sie mir doch zum wenigsten die Hälfte geben'.

Anrede, als sie kaum ins Zimmer getreten war; die ich mit einer freundlichen Bewillkommung und Darlegung meines Zeit-Vertreibs beantwortete. Das letzte that ich um desto williger, je gewisser ich wuste, daß meine Phyllis auch eine Freundin solcher Schrifften war, die auf die Verbesserung unserer Sitten abzielen. Wir hatten uns kaum gesetzt, als wir fast beyde zugleich auf die Gedancken kamen, ob es denn nicht möglich sey, nach dem Exempel der Manns-Personen, eine besondere Schrifft zu verfertigen, darinnen von mancherley Fehlern der Menschen überhaupt, insonderheit aber von den Schwachheiten des weiblichen Geschlechtes, gehandelt würde. Es fielen uns verschiedene Materien ein, die nicht von geringem Nutzen zu seyn schienen, und so viel uns wissend war, noch von keinem gebührend abgehandelt worden. Wir sahen beyde in diesem Vorhaben keine Unmöglichkeit, und der Beystand, den sich eine von der andern versprach, machte uns einen Muth, unsere Absicht ins Werck zu richten.

This style has all the purity and clarity of *Der Patriot* and yet it is far more colourful and lively and gay. It has in fact that very urbanity which we felt was lacking in *Die Discourse der Mahlern*, that lightness of touch which Thomasius had tried but failed to achieve in the *Monatsgespräche*. Thomasius knew that a light style was needed, Bodmer had come to see that a female audience must be envisaged. Gottsched combines these two desiderata and strikes exactly the right tone from the start. Thomasius had tried to lighten the texture of the baroque sentence with colloquial words and phrases, *Der Vernünfftler* and Bodmer had rejected the whole structure in favour of shorter, simpler sentences, *Der Patriot* had seen that simplicity was not enough. Gottsched brings grace and plasticity, ease and fluidity to the style which had been evolving in the journals under direct, or more remote, English influence. That is why he stands at the climax of this chapter, because he built on to his predecessors in this genre and he built for his successors the foundations for a narrative prose style. There is a certain refinement about the vocabulary. But phrases like 'Darlegung meines Zeit-Vertreibs' or 'Schrifft zu verfertigen' or 'gebührend abgehandelt worden' embody not *pedantic* but *careful* diction. Gottsched avoids sloppiness even at the risk of being thought a little stiff. For he never steps outside the bounds of the polite. On the other hand the first passage quoted contains conversational (but not coarse) images (*Hirn-Geburt*; *Lehrer abgeben*; *ins Spiel mischen*; *Caffeecräntzgen*; *durchzuhecheln*; *Kützel*). It represents the thoughts coursing through an imaginary reader's head. This reader is somewhat sceptical, a little pompous perhaps. He (for it is almost certainly a he) is made to think in colloquial images despite his patronising tone. This combination of the conversational and the cautious gives to the style just the right shade of irony. The second paragraph of this same passage marks a change of tone with a change of style. Evenly flowing sentences, unbroken by rhetorical questions or emotional emphasis, are used to communicate general reflections. When Gottsched is writing in this mood his prose is very like the leisurely, well-balanced prose of *Der Patriot*. But his style is very malleable and when his imagination is stirred he can describe with great liveliness and vigour. Here is a portrait of a lady from the seventh number of the first volume of *Die Vernünfftigen Tadlerinnen*:

So gerne sie sonst in ihrem Bette der angenehmen Ruhe geniesset, so munter springet sie Sonntags vor 5. Uhren mit gleichen Füssen heraus. Dann bringet sie drey volle Stunden mit ihrem Ankleiden zu. Im Hembde läufft sie schon vor den Spiegel, um zu sehen, ob die kleine Blatter, die ihr gestern an der Stirne ausgefahren war, verschwunden sey? Alsdenn besiehet sie eine halbe Stunde den Vorrath ihrer Kleidungen. Und was vor Mühe kostet es nicht, ehe sie sich entschliesset, ob sie heute grün, gelbe, roth oder blau erscheinen will. Denn gehet es über den Haupt-Putz her. Sie schläget die Haare bald so, bald anders auff. Jetzt krauset sie einen Pusch derselben, sie schmieret sie mit Jeßmin, sie streuet den Puder darüber. Doch es steht nicht recht: Sie kämmet alles wieder aus, und fängt von neuen an. Auch dieses geräth ihr nicht: Allein sie wird nicht überdrüßig, drey bis viermal einerley Arbeit zu thun. In anderthalb Stunden sind die Haare fertig. Darauf sieht sie nicht anders aus, als eines Müllers Magd, die einen halben Tag in dem dicksten Staube gestanden. Sie schabet den Puder mit Messern vom Gesichte, und wenn sie die Kleider ausschüttelt, wird der Boden ihres Zimmers weisser, als die Strasse ist, wenn es eine Nacht durch geschneyet hat. Gefällt es ihr, ein schwartzes Fleckgen auf das Gesicht zu legen, so kostet es auch eine halbe Stunde, ehe sie mit sich selbst eins wird, wo es liegen soll. Kommt es an die Kleidung, so hat die Aufwärterin ihre Angst. Sich dreyßigmal vor zweyen gegen einander hangenden Spiegeln umzudrehen, das ist was weniges: und da wird bald dem Schneider, bald der Näterin,[1] bald sonst jemanden alles Unheil angewünscht. Zuletzt kommt das Geschmeide. Und wenn man nun dencket, daß endlich alles recht sey, so hat sie doch noch so viel zu verbessern, und zu ändern, daß sie endlich mit dem grösten Verdrusse davon gehen muß, aus Furcht mitten in der Predigt in die Kirche zu kommen.

This passage is fiction, and might well figure in a novel. By the time of Gottsched, the moral weekly has come to include character sketches and little narratives which are so close to the novel in subject-matter that it is no surprise to find the novel taking over this style. In the passage just quoted we have a good sample of how Gottsched writes in this vein. We notice here as elsewhere that Gottsched has the power to use sentence-rhythms expressively. We saw a moment ago how he will use lengthy, slow-moving, well-balanced sentences if his subject is expansive and reflective. Here he is using short, sharp, rhythmic sequences to express restlessness and busy activity. We have moved a long way from the narrative prose of Thomasius where the same cast of sentence was made to express every kind of subject-matter. Whereas Thomasius tells us about something, Gottsched by the expressive use of language is evoking his subject before our eyes by making the very sound and movement of his language reproduce to a certain degree the sound and movement of what he is describing. Yet it is not only rhythm that produces this effect, but also the vocabulary used. This is simple, unaffected German and yet expressive. It is not flat or inexpressive. Concrete rather than abstract, conversational rather than literary, it gives life and colour to the description.

Die Vernünfftigen Tadlerinnen attacks much the same abuses as those which had figured in the earlier moral weeklies. It is attractive to compare the language in which the various journals

---

[1] I.e. *Nähterin*; Adelung (1777) says this form was more frequent than *Näherin*.

discussed one of these topics, for the great superiority of Gottsched's style then becomes strikingly apparent. Here are some extracts from the earlier journals on the subject of false compliments:

(*a*) Mit den *Complimenten* oder sogenandten Ehren-Worten ist es heutiges Tages so beschaffen, daß fast keiner denckt, was er sagt.... Man bedencke nur, was nicht vor ein *Abusus* mit den Unterschrifften in Briefen vorgehet, (wenn es noch gleich mit den Reden hiesse, ein Wort ein Wind) und welche demühtige *Expressiones* es sind, da geschrieben wird: *Votre treshumble et tresobeissant Serviteur?* Es kan schwerlich was submissers erdacht werden, und dennoch ist nichts gebräuchlicher, ja nichts unwahrers in der Welt.

Der Vernünfftler, no. 44.

(*b*) Der Pfarrer bate den Amman nach gemachter Frage, wie es um ihn und die Seine stehe, er möchte doch der erste hineingehen, der Amman zoge den Fuß, bückte den Leib, und schüttelte den Kopff mit den wenigen doch kräfftigen Worten: Es geschieht nicht. Der Pfarrer replicierte: der Herr seye so gütig, ich bitte darum; Der Amman: Es geschieht nicht. Ey der Herr mache doch keine Façons; Es geschieht nicht; Der Herr macht mich gantz beschämt; Ich thu es nicht. Ich bitte inständig: Es geschieht bey meiner Seel nicht. Worauf der Pfarrer sich ergabe, und in einem Sprung und drey Schritten die Treppen auf und in die Stuben fuhr, damit er mit seiner Höfflichkeit dem andern keinen weitern Anlaß zu fluchen geben möchte.

Discourse der Mahlern, III, no. 17.

(*c*) Unter denen Städten, die ich hierum gesehen habe, als Dresden, Leipzig, Berlin.... Görlitz usw usw., ist keine so reich an Complimenten als Leipzig, man trifft überall unterthänige Diener und Dienerinnen an, und die Leute haben ihre Complimentir-Säcke so reichlich gespickt, daß sie aller Orten damit recht verschwenderisch haußhalten. Zumahl distinguiren sich darinn vor andern das Frauenzimmer und die Gelehrten. *Der Leipziger Spectateur.*

Gottsched clinches the matter quite forcibly by introducing the subject in these words:

Die unnützen und gezwungenen Höflichkeiten, die man einander im gemeinen Leben zu bezeigen gewohnt ist, scheinen dem Naturelle unseres Teutschlandes so wenig gemäß zu seyn, daß man auch kein rechtes teutsches Wort hat, womit man das Frantzösische *Compliment* gebührend ausdrücken könte.

Die Vernünfftigen Tadlerinnen, I, p. 11.

Complimentation is for Gottsched merely one aspect of that affectation which he attacks in all its forms. For him complimentation represents a linguistic affectation which, of course, is the expression of mental and emotional affectation. This linguistic affectation appears in two main forms in the German of his day: in bombast, and in the use of foreign words. Gottsched realises that both these abuses proceed from the desire to avoid the ordinary, normal word. Both then are aspects of the same mental affectation. Hence whereas other critics had treated these subjects separately, Gottsched treats them together, probes to the roots of the disease and suggests implicitly the remedy. He gives two examples of letters in this false complimentary style, one is full of foreign words, the other of bombast. The first of these proceeds from the desire to show that one is not plebeian; 'Man muß sich von der *Canaille* auch *en parlant distinguiren*', says Gottsched, expressing himself in the language of his butt. On this topic his attitude is rationalistic; foreign words are foolish because they are unnatural and unnecessary, for every language is rich enough to express all thoughts. He even suggests that German is superior to French, Italian and English because it does not proceed from a mingling of the languages of several peoples—a somewhat strange argument. The bombastic style of the second letter, Gottsched says, proceeds from a type of imagination which is too fiery and tries to outdo itself in expressiveness—in other words, from an imagination not controlled by clear thinking. To counter these two excesses it is proposed that a Society of German Muses be founded to cultivate purity of language and a reasonable mode of expression. In a later number Gottsched brings this stylistic affectation into relationship with bad taste. People without good taste, he says, 'halten es vor eine grosse Zierlichkeit, wenn man was ausländisches in unsre grobe Bauer-Sprache einmischet'.[1]

[1] *Op. cit.* vol. I, p. 39.

A 'Société des galants hommes' is imagined as a counterblast to the Society of German Muses for both the affectation of foreign words and the use of rhetorical bombast are classed by Gottsched as features of *galanterie*.[1] It is interesting to notice that for Gottsched the word *galant* characterises bad taste. We seemed to have turned full circle since the days when Thomasius, in his *Programm* of 1687, had advocated the ideal of the *homme galant* to his students. Now Gottsched can say of this same *galant homme*: 'Es eckelt ihm vor allen Büchern, die in seiner Mutter-Sprache geschrieben werden, wie er denn auch unsre Blätter nicht lesen will, weil es seiner Meynung nach nicht möglich ist, daß diese teutsche Zettel einiger Galanterie fähig seyn solten.'[2] The word *galant*, originally applied only to clothes (ital./sp. *gala*), was extended to courtly behaviour in general by the Hôtel de Rambouillet and its adherents. It comes into German at the end of the seventeenth century, and 'er ist ein galanter Kerl' is glossed by Stieler as 'scitus, venustus, elegans homo est'. Its meaning becomes confined to the external forms of courtly behaviour. These were often little more than empty show. Hence we find a shift of meaning. This is facilitated by the fact that the usage of the word was extended from persons to things. Thomasius in 1687 said it was being used of cats and dogs, tables and chairs, and pen and ink. Gottsched takes up Thomasius's point and says that (in 1725) it was also used for ragoûts, fricassées and joints of meat. Since the word has almost lost all meaning as a characterising epithet, Gottsched would like the concept to disappear completely. What meaning it still had, implied the persistence of artificial, empty civilities. Gottsched

---

[1] The first rule of the constitution of this 'Société' reads: 'Wer in die *Société des galants hommes*, die zur *enrichi*rung unserer *crassen* Mutter-Sprache *institui*ret ist, *recipi*ret zu werden *plaisir* findet, ist *obligi*ret, durch einen wohl *tourni*rten Brief um eine so *honorable* Stelle zu *solliciti*ren, worinnen zum wenigsten *la troisieme partie* der Wörter aus einer *etranger*en Sprache *mutui*ret seyn muß' (vol. I, p. 40). This feature of *galanterie* is censured again in vol. II, no. 23, where Gottsched refers to 'die unnützen Sprachen-Mischer..., die ohne Noth dergleichen ausländische Lumpen auf ihren Teutschen Rock hängen, und sich einbilden recht galant zu reden und zu schreiben'.

[2] *Op. cit.* vol. I, no. 10.

is therefore opposed to all 'galant' behaviour: to excessive flattery, affectations of dress, affectation of a higher station than that to which one belongs. His distaste for the heroic novel includes a strong opposition to the linguistic expression of *galanterie* as being forced, affected and unnatural.

For naturalness is Gottsched's primary criterion in style. 'Hohe Gedanken sind gut, wenn sie bey hohen Sachen gebraucht werden; aber unnötig, ja läppisch, wenn man von niedrigen und gemeinen Dingen prächtig und wunderwürdig reden will. Man zwinge sich derowegen nicht zu einer hohen Schreibart.'[1] He pleads for more simplicity and sincerity in the writing of letters, he opposes in the same manner as Addison and Bodmer affectations of versification like acrostics. Sometimes this desire for reasonableness and naturalness comes near to the rejection of all metaphor as when he criticises the couplet:

> Schallt ihr Paucken und Trompeten
> Daß davon die Stern erröthen

by an argument which asks *inter alia* whether the sound can reach the stars, whether they have ears to hear, whether they can change colour, and so on.[2] As we should expect, Gottsched finds nothing to praise in the highly metaphorical language of Hofmannswaldau and Lohenstein, for their elevated style is forced. It is 'gezwungen' and 'gekünstelt'. In this Gottsched finds himself agreeing with Bodmer. But he thought that Bodmer sometimes was guilty of *trop de zèle*: 'Rubeen ist insonderheit ein solcher Grübler, der, wie man zu sagen pfleget, Flöhe husten höret, und Gras wachsen siehet.'[3] He also thought that Bodmer fell into the same error

---

[1] *Op. cit.* vol. I, no. 12.
[2] *Ibid.* no. 10; although he is right in pointing out that the image is inappropriate because one blushes for *shame*.
[3] *Ibid.* no. 34, withdrawn after the second edition. Rubeen was Bodmer's pen-name in the *Discourse*. *Grübler* used here in the sense of one who 'grubs about' after something. The normal English translation of 'brooder' is often inadequate to render this word which has the subsidiary meanings of 'over-meticulous', 'hair-splitting', 'pedantic', 'sophistical'. Cf. *op. cit.* vol. I, no. 49, where Gottsched uses the word to connote writers of acrostic verses. Adelung (1775) defines the word as 'eine Person, welche zu mühsamen und unnützen

himself and indulged in rhetorical bombast. He instances a very flowery passage from Opitz's address to Rubeen-Bodmer in the first discourse of the second series of the *Discourse der Mahlern*, and criticises Bodmer for using phrases like 'über das Land *spatzierende* Augen', the flowers that 'ihre *Hälse hervorrecken, und die hinterste Strahlen der Morgenröthe nachmahlen*, ja *Gerücht von Balsam, Weyhrauch und Myrrhen* in seine Nase bliesen'. Such phrases, he says, are every whit as unnatural as those which Bodmer had objected to in Neukirch's verses. He calls on Bodmer to defend himself, which Bodmer did in a work entitled *Anklagung des verderbten Geschmackes, oder Critische Anmerkungen über den Hamburgischen Patrioten und die Hallischen Tadlerinnen*, usually known as Bodmer's *Antipatriot*. Publication of this work was delayed until 1728, although it was composed in 1725 or 1726. Meanwhile Breitinger had composed a work entitled *Von dem Einfluß und Gebrauche der Einbildungs-Krafft; zur Ausbesserung des Geschmackes* which appeared in 1727.[1] Both this work and

---

Untersuchungen und Betrachtungen geneigt ist' and quotes the following example:
Ein Grübler trinkt, beseufzt sein Leid,
Und sammelt Flüche, Furcht und Dünste.   (Hagedorn)

The *DWb.* notes that Stieler glossed the word as *scrutator, curiosus, inventor, investigator*, and distinguishes between two classes of meaning in Modern German. One is without derogatory connotation, e.g. 'dem feinen Grübler unter den Philosophen, dem Platon' (Stolberg) and this meaning approximates to that of 'thinker', 'philosopher' in the eighteenth century. Thus Herder speaks of 'die Lehrsäle aller scholastischen und mystischen Grübler' (Suphan xix, 302).

But the normal meaning has a derogatory flavour, and we find it often used with epithets like 'finster', 'phantastisch' 'leer'. This derogatory connotation is very frequent in the eighteenth century, and is intended by Gottsched in this passage. Dornblüth (*Observationes*, 1755, p. 88—see below, pp. 140 ff.), objecting to Gottsched's use of the word *Kunstrichter* for *criticus*, suggests '*Gelehrte* vel in sensu ironico: *Grübler*'.

[1] I have used a copy in the Central Library at Zürich with marginal notes and comments. The press-mark is Gal. III. 302b. The volume also contains the *Antipatriot*, with similar marginal corrections. It looks like a proof copy. The marginal comments are usually concerned with stylistic matters, are in Latin as well as German, and often refer to a 'matron', possibly the periodical *Die Matrone* published at Hamburg from 1728 to 1730 by J. G. Hamann (the uncle of the *Magus im Norden*, and a supporter of Gottsched), or to Gottsched. Thus on p. 7 *Rednerey* has the marginal comment *matrona improbat*; and *Gemein-*

the *Antipatriot* proceeded from a discussion of Gottsched's definition of 'die sinnreiche Schreibart' in no. 37 of the first volume of *Die Vernünfftigen Tadlerinnen*. Breitinger's *Einbildungs-Krafft* (as we shall call it for short) is but the first part of a general treatise on oratory and good writing, of which the other parts were never composed although later works of Bodmer and Breitinger were to cover these topics. It deals with imaginative descriptions and it is here that the famous comparison between painting and poetry—the starting-point for Lessing's *Laokoon*—occurs.[1] Breitinger says that a good description should be complete, should be moving and emphatic (*bewegend und nachdrücklich*), should endeavour to find the apt word and avoid all superfluity, and should be clear in every detail. He is against the mechanical employment of figures of speech. A writer who is really moved by his subject will find his expressions and images quite spontaneously, he will not need to search in a well-stocked memory. Breitinger is mostly concerned with poetry, and the work concludes with a paean on poetic enthusiasm (*Enthusiasmus*). But the fact that this work was concerned also with descriptive prose led Gottsched to assert that Breitinger's description of the superiority of the poet over the painter was as verbose and bombastic as the descriptions which Breitinger was attacking. Gottsched refers the Swiss to a certain descriptive passage in *Der Patriot* which was more plastic and more sober. This is in the fifty-sixth number of Gottsched's second periodical *Der Biedermann* (1727–9), consciously more serious in tone and intended as a successor to the recently terminated *Der Patriot*. Breitinger was really countering the idea that good writing was a question of external trappings. His preface, dedicated to Christian Wolff, says:

Diejenigen, welche über die Beredsamkeit überhaupt geschrieben haben, halten sich eintzig bei der äußerlichen Form der Rede auf....

Büchern: non placet matronae, *Auffschlage*—. To *Critick-Verfasser* there is the comment *Gottsched spottet über dies wort*. To *Begangenschafft*: *über dies wort spottet die Matrone. Lockerinnen*: *ist der Matrone nicht recht.*

[1] The *idea* is, of course, much older and originated in antiquity.

Die Figuren der Rede sind ihre Rhetorick und die Lexica der Bey-Wörter versehen ihnen die Kunst Beschreibungen zu machen....

which, as is clear from the context, was a reference to Gottsched and his Leipzig friends, who, as is also said, are concerned 'aus dem Gedächtnisse *machinalische* [i.e. 'mechanische'] Schlüße zusammen zu fügen, und aus gesammelten Gemein-Büchern ein mannigfaltiges verworrenes Gewebe durch einander zu knüpfen'. Gottsched in his reply accuses Breitinger in this descriptive passage of '*machinalische Gedächtniskünste*, unnötige und aus einem poetischen Lexikon erborgte Beywörter und seltsame Metaphoren oder verblümte Ausdrückungen'.

Gottsched, in admonishing authors to write *naturally*, did not advocate the written reproduction of speech. No man is born master of his native tongue, he says,[1] for speech has faults to which the writer must be sensitive and not write like a bird who sings 'wie ihm der Schnabel gewachsen ist'. It is one thing to tell your friends amusing stories, and quite another to write in such a way as to earn the approbation of 'der klugen Welt'. It is significant that whereas Gottsched at one point in the first edition of *Die Vernünfftigen Tadlerinnen* had praised the example of Christian Weise, he replaced this model by Günther in the later editions;[2] and he definitely disapproved of a colloquial writer like Abraham a Santa Clara.[3] It is clear that Gottsched's ideal was *cultured* prose which should be reasonable in its choice of expression and avoid all falseness. It should be natural, but not uncouth. Gottsched's assertion that good writing should be not only natural (*natürlich*) but also reasonable (*vernünfftig*) set Bodmer arguing in the *Antipatriot*.[4] He objects to these categories, saying that the one infringes on the other, but he also objects to Gottsched's whole conception of *die sinnreiche Schreibart*, to which numbers 34 and 37 of the first edition of *Die Vernünfftigen*

[1] *Die Vernünfftigen Tadlerinnen*, vol. II, no. 2.
[2] *Ibid.* vol. I, no. 12.
[3] *Ibid.* vol. II, no. 2, after expressing the hope that the journals would only praise authors who write well. This may be a dig at the first number of Thomasius's *Monatsgespräche*, see above, p. 55.
[4] I quote from the first edition of 1728, copy in the Central Library at Zürich.

Tadlerinnen were devoted. Bodmer asserts that Gottsched never defines the term *sinnreich*; all he did was to equate it with *witzig* or *artig* without defining either. Bodmer quotes Wolff as having defined it as follows in his *Metaphysics*:

> Der Witz (Esprit) ist eine Leichtigkeit die Aehnlichkeiten der Dingen wahr zu nehmen: Wer hierzu aufgeleget ist, den nennet man sinnreich.[1]

Wolff had also explained that wit proceeds from 'Scharfsinnigkeit und guten Einbildungs-Krafft und Gedächtnis'... 'Wo man scharfsinnig ist, da entdecket man Aehnlichkeiten, die nicht ein jeder gleich wahr nimmet'... 'Je mehr also einer Aehnlichkeiten zu entdecken weißt,[2] je mehr hat er Witz, und je sinnreicher ist er'. Bodmer therefore decides that *das Sinnreiche* depends on 'Vergleichung der Aehnlichkeiten'[3] and proceeds to consider the two main forms of this type of writing, namely metaphorical writing (*die verblümte Schreib-Art*) and burlesque writing (*die possierliche Schreib-Art*). Metaphor clarifies concepts by comparisons and gives more strength, weight and intensity (*Krafft... Gewicht... Nachdruck*); it also gives pleasure by revealing hidden similarities. Bodmer defends his descriptive passage in the first number of the second series of the *Discourse der Mahlern* (which Gottsched had attacked, see above, p. 97) by justifying the metaphors which he had used.

Here we have two critics, both of them intelligent and alert minds, both lovers of literature, both endowed with a respect for language, who seem to have arrived at an entirely different ideal of literary language by experimenting in the writing of a literary journal. Gottsched's ideal is a clear, natural but 'reasonable'

---

[1] This is a paraphrase of §366 of that work.

[2] *Sic* in Bodmer: Wolff has *weiß*. These quotations are from §§858–60 of the *Metaphysics*.

[3] *Sinnreich* is not in common usage nowadays, but this does seem to be the eighteenth-century meaning. Adelung (1780) defines it as: 'Fertigkeit besitzend, mehrere Begriffe mit einander zu verbinden, und ihre Aehnlichkeit zu entdecken.' This *Vergleichung der Ähnlichkeiten* produces aesthetic pleasure (*Ergötzen*) in Bodmer's view. Hence aesthetic judgments are dependent on reason. This view is defended by Bodmer in his correspondence with Calepio.

language—reasonable in that it eschews outlandish extravagances and allows the reason to control everything. Bodmer's ideal is a metaphorical language which is intense, rather elevated, and subject primarily to the imagination. Both these ideals were to bear fruit later. Both are important gains in the progress of German towards becoming a great literary language. Bodmer's ideal, reinforced by his later works and by Breitinger's *Critische Dichtkunst*, was to inspire Klopstock and the *Sturm und Drang*. Gottsched's ideal was to find polish and grace in the prose of Gellert; and to form the basis of narrative prose.

IV

THE STABILISATION OF THE LANGUAGE

GOTTSCHED had the misfortune to be attacked by the greatest of his literary contemporaries. It was a frontal attack from a powerful opponent and he never recovered from it. Time has not redressed the balance in his favour. He undoubtedly had little or no understanding of the true nature of poetry. He had a pedantic attitude to literature. He was, in fact, a pedant. But pedants have their uses. Gottsched made a positive contribution to the development of the German language, and modern criticism has tended to consider this as far the most important part of his activity. This contribution was twofold. By a series of endeavours culminating in the publication of the *Deutsche Sprachkunst* in 1748, he was successful in gaining acceptance for a standardisation of the written language based on the usage of Meissen; and by theory and practice he exerted a valuable influence—valuable, at least, for the time being—on German prose. The first is grammatical, the second stylistic. We shall deal with the first in this chapter, and with the second in the next.

In his stabilisation of the *Schriftsprache* Gottsched produced no ideas which can be termed original; but the achievement was nevertheless considerable. We tend to think that the language had already been stabilised by Luther or that it settled itself in the natural maturing of time. Neither is true, as any study of the language of Germany between Leibniz and Gottsched will reveal. An extreme vagueness is everywhere apparent at this time concerning what is really 'correct' in language. What is 'good German'? Who writes it? Who speaks it? Even the poets are all at sea: for what is to constitute an acceptable rhyme? 'Am besten ists, man richtet die Reime nach dem Orte, da sie hinge-

THE STABILISATION OF THE LANGUAGE

schickt werden', says Christian Weise in 1675;[1] whereas a pseudonymous writer in 1717 states his opinion as: 'Es bleibet eine allgemeine Regul, daß ein ieder reimen soll, wie er das Wort in seinem Laut ausspricht.'[2] Nearly fifty years lie between these two utterances: but both testify to the same linguistic bewilderment. The problem is still there; the solution not found. Between these two poles of time and these two poles of opinion we find Christian Weise in 1693[3] having second thoughts: 'Wer sich aber die Gedancken macht, daß er sein Licht in gantz Deutschland will leuchten lassen, der muß auff dergleichen Reime dencken, die sich an allen Orten annehmlich und bewehrt befinden.' This was the Middle High German opinion; and this was the same problem as had occupied Middle High German poets—still, apparently, unsolved. But how was it to be solved? There were few enough words pronounced in the same way all over Germany. And for the rest, who or what was to decide the correct pronunciation? This was not merely a question of phonetics, not merely one of orthography: morphological features were often involved. Since the first German grammarians, and particularly since the great work of Schottelius, opinion had been divided between accepting one particular dialect as the norm or some form of the language which was above and apart from the dialects. The situation was still further complicated by the fact that there was no general agreement on *which* dialect should be taken as the norm—there were arguments in favour of Silesian, others in favour of Upper Saxon and some (as we shall see) were to be advanced in favour of other dialects; and there was only the very vaguest conception of what the 'language above the dialects' should be, and even here there was a division corresponding roughly to the East Middle German and Upper German *Gemein-*

---

[1] *Der Grünenden Jugend Nothwendige Gedancken*, quoting from the copy of the 1690 Leipzig edition in the British Museum, pp. 326.

[2] 'Musophilus': *Vergnügter Poetischer Zeitvertreib* (Dresden and Leipzig, 1717), p. 286. Quoted in Kåre Kaiser, *Mundart und Schriftsprache* (Leipzig, 1930), p. 56. I have been unable to see a copy of the original work.

[3] *Curiöse Gedancken von Deutschen Versen*, quoting from the copy of the second edition of 1693 (no place; probably Leipzig) in the Central Library at Zürich, p. 9.

sprachen of the sixteenth century (with religious differences still helping to perpetuate this linguistic division). There were some who still looked to Luther's East Middle German *Gemeinsprache* as their decisive canon; others venerated the Upper German *Gemeinsprache* of the Imperial Chancery and its documents. Recent literary tradition was, for the most part, in favour of a Silesian form of the East Middle German norm. But this tradition was neither long-standing nor long-lasting, for it did not extend back beyond the early seventeenth century nor last beyond the early eighteenth century. The German cultural centre had shifted to Saxony, and the spirit of the times was definitely against the galant and baroque culture of seventeenth-century Silesia. It is true that Günther was a Silesian and a genius. But he was dead before Gottsched arrived in Leipzig. And although unquestionably the greatest German writer of the first two decades of the century, his talent was too individual, too isolated, too great to form a school or to continue the cultural hegemony of Silesia. Silesia was sinking into literary sterility. It was Saxony that was in the ascendant.

Gottsched's achievement has sometimes been represented as the final decisive climax to a long struggle between Silesia and Meissen for linguistic supremacy.[1] This formulation is too narrow but it recognises an important element in the total, wider achievement. Both provinces had claimed to be authoritative, and each had her adherents. But sometimes the struggle took the form of divided loyalty, as when Zesen (in the *Deutscher Helikon*) although admitting that Meissen German was, on the whole, the best, expressed his opinion that Silesian was more correct in its distinction between the stem vowels of *ehren* (M.H.G. *êren*) and *nehren* (M.H.G. *nëren*),[2] these two words constituting a pure

---

[1] So, for instance, by Konrad Burdach in an article entitled 'Universelle, nationale und landschaftliche Triebe der deutschen Schriftsprache im Zeitalter Gottscheds' in *Fests. August Sauer* (Stuttgart, 1925), pp. 12–71. My examples in this paragraph are mostly drawn from this essay and from Karl Weinhold's essay on the Silesian dialect (Vienna, 1853), but the marshalling and interpretation of the facts is my own.

[2] In Silesian pronunciation the vowel of *ehren* was an open [ɛ] and that of *nehren* a closed sound.

rhyme in Meissen. Opitz had insisted on this phonetic distinction in his *Buch von der deutschen Poeterey*.[1] Zesen here defends Opitz, whereas Enoch Hanmann of Leipzig (writing some four years earlier) had not considered this a valid argument because Silesian had many rhymes which were equally impure.[2] Many Silesian writers of the seventeenth century went farther than Opitz in their use of Silesian peculiarities. Logau seems to have had no misgivings whatsoever on this score. Others, however, like Peter Titus at the beginning and Hofmannswaldau at the end of the century, felt it necessary to apologise for their provincialisms. It is clear that they certainly did not consider Silesian a model for all Germans. Hofmannswaldau even speaks of the difficulty of 'breaking himself' of these provincialisms.[3] Silesia had nevertheless gained the reputation of being the German Parnassus, and this meant that Silesian poets were looked to as models and mentors. Poets from other areas, such as Fleming, were considered 'rough' by Silesian standards. It was claimed that the Silesian poets had a 'purer language', but without any clear envisagement of what this 'purity' consisted of.[4] And yet Hofmannswaldau, one of the best Silesian poets, finds it necessary to apologise for what were, in his view, impurities. The situation is therefore complex. On the other side, voices in favour of Meissen were heard. The claim that Meissen written German was the best German is, of course, even older than Luther. It was an opinion generally held by the time of Luther, as he himself tells us. Zesen suggests that, despite the cultural ascendancy of Silesia, this opinion was still held by many in 1650. Among the most disputed features were the Silesian lengthening of original short vowels in monosyllabic words (giving rhymes like *sihst*: *ist*, *erkiest*: *ist*, both found in Opitz), retention of old long vowel in a rhyme like *Rath*: *hat* (M.H.G. *hât*), shortening of long vowel

---

[1] Braune's *Neudruck*, p. 36.
[2] Burdach quotes from his *Anmerkungen zu Martin Opitzens Buch von der deutschen Poeterey*, 1645.
[3] 'sich der Mund-Art entbrechen', *Heldenbriefe*, 1696, Vorrede.
[4] For example by the Silesian J. C. Kunckel in his *De Silesiorum in poesi Germanica praestantia*, 1698—especially § 13.

from M.H.G. diphthong as when *Fuß* is allowed to rhyme with *Kuß* (or *Füßen* with *wissen*; both these rhymes are used by Opitz), hardening of final media as when *Berg*: *Werk* is an acceptable rhyme, and certain morphological features, some of which represent archaisms (old unlevelled preterites, weak preterites with juncture -*e*-, certain past participles without *ge*-) whereas others are more modern developments like the final -*e* in *Hertze*, *Glücke*, *zurücke* (which is also found in other dialects at this period).[1] Observation and phonetic sense are often rather hazy; and both sides charge each other with faults found also in their own ranks. The objections expressed here and there to the rhyming of -*ei*- with -*eu*-, -*ü*- with -*i*-, and -*ö*- with -*e*- are characteristic of the current vagueness and confusion; for such rhymes are found in all writers of the period, are not confined to any one district and were still being used by the best poets of the end of the century. In 1707 Erdmann Neumeister, a friend of C. F. Hunold and like Christian Wernicke engaged in attacking the bombast of Silesian poetic diction, suggested that the Silesians were already adapting their language to Meissen usage. This was followed up by Hunold himself, who, in reply to an outraged Silesian, says that most people would agree that the language of Meissen was 'the best and the most pleasant'. This is in 1718, in Hunold's own periodical, the *Vermischte Bibliothek* of Halle. Two years later, in the same periodical, he published an adverse review of a Silesian poem, criticising severely its language. This called forth a reply from an anonymous Silesian in the next year (1721) in which only two authorities are recognised: Silesian poets and Silesian pronunciation. The attitude seems to be stiffening; Silesian writers no longer feel the need to apologise. Other dialect areas were later to voice their claims, notably Low Saxon and Upper German. But for the moment neither of these had any body of serious literature to cite as authority. Up to 1724, the year of Gottsched's arrival in Leipzig, the decisive struggle was still between Silesia and Meissen, and although it is a gross oversimplification to reduce the whole of Gottsched's linguistic

[1] See below, p. 129, footnote.

activity to this one conflict, it was Gottsched who, as *part* of his linguistic activity, fought the final round—and won.

Gottsched's rise to fame in Leipzig was extremely rapid.[1] In three years he dominated Leipzig; in three more years, by 1730, he was the linguistic mentor of all Germany. How is one to account for this? By the success of his periodicals and his treatises, by his reform of the Leipzig stage, and above all by his reorganisation of the *Deutschübende Poetische Gesellschaft*.[2] It is in the framework of this Society that his interest in improving the German language first develops. It had originated in 1697 in meetings of members of the circle of Burkhard Mencke to criticise each other's verses, but its aims and membership had been considerably broadened by the time that Gottsched became a member in 1724. By 1727 Gottsched had been elected *Senior* of the Society, reorganised it and issued a statement of its aims. The very change of name to *Deutsche Gesellschaft* was significant. Still more significant was the programmatic statement, in the statutes of 1727:

Man soll sich allezeit der Reinigkeit und Richtigkeit der Sprache befleißigen; d.i., nicht nur alle ausländische Wörter, sondern auch alle Deutsche unrichtige Ausdrückungen und Provinzial-Redensarten vermeiden; so daß man weder Schlesisch noch Meißnisch, weder Fränkisch

---

[1] There are four general studies of Gottsched: Eugen Wolff, *Gottscheds Stellung im deutschen Bildungsleben*, 2 vols. (Kiel und Leipzig, 1895, 1897); Gustav Waniek, *Gottsched und die deutsche Litteratur seiner Zeit* (Leipzig, 1897); Eugen Reichel, *Gottsched*, 2 vols. (Berlin, 1908, 1912); and Gerhard Schimansky, *Gottscheds deutsche Bildungsziele* (Königsberg, 1939). Of these, Schimansky's treatment is somewhat overstated but nevertheless a useful antidote to the conception of Gottsched as a cultural Quisling; Reichel gives the most information, but his book is marred by excessive length and enthusiasm. (It is difficult to agree with Reichel when he asserts (I, vii) that Gottsched had the biggest vocabulary of any writer in the world, or (I, 69) that he had a 'faustischer Geist'.) Wolff gives valuable quotations from letters to and from Gottsched, and prints the correspondence with Bodmer of 1732–9 in full. Waniek is the best arranged of these works. All draw on T. W. Danzel, *Gottsched und seine Zeit* (Leipzig, 1848), which contains much of Gottsched's correspondence. All are immensely prolix and extremely tedious. There is room for a succinct, balanced, readable account of Gottsched's work and importance.

[2] See Fr. Neumann, 'Gottsched und die Leipziger Deutsche Gesellschaft', *Archiv f. Kulturgeschichte*, XVIII (1928), pp. 194–212.

noch Niedersächsisch, sondern rein Hochdeutsch schreibe; so wie man es in ganz Deutschland verstehen kann.[1]

This was Gottsched's first statement of his ideal Standard. He supports the ideal of the 'language above the dialects',[2] but the possibility of this ideal arising from *purification* of an existing dialect is not excluded by the wording, although we are not told which is to be the dialect or what is to decide what is 'unrichtig'. The formulation is therefore somewhat vague, but it rejects *uncritical* acceptance of either Silesian or Upper Saxon. It comes down on neither side. This looked like a possible basis for future agreement, and it was. It had a certain air of generosity about it. But in the preface to this same *Nachricht*, Gottsched makes it clear that his ideal is to be found in Leipzig. For the fame of this city as a university town, a commercial centre and a book-market brought together there Germans from all areas who, in their concourse with each other, would naturally put away their dialectal predilections of speech. Here then were the most favourable conditions for the evolution of the Standard, *even if the Meissen language itself were not superior to the others*. There is a sting in the tail. For, despite all his protestations, Gottsched from the outset envisaged his Standard German on a Meissen basis. Later when others (like Bodmer) saw no reason why any other dialect should not equally well serve as this basis, he was driven to a more rigid and unflinching defence of Meissen usage. For the moment he took care that the *Nachricht* reached all parts of Germany, for with the statutes it included a collection of essays by the members to demonstrate the excellence of the Upper Saxon Standard, the language used by scholars and men of letters in the cultural metropolis of Leipzig. At home, new members were gained for the Society from university and aristocratic circles. Poems were published, public orations held on suitable occasions;

---

[1] Included in *Nachricht von der erneuerten Deutschen Gesellschaft in Leipzig und ihrer ietzigen Verfassung*, 1731. See Eugen Wolff, vol. II, p. 46.

[2] A statement in the same statutes to the effect that each member should rhyme according to his own native speech may seem to conflict with this. Such inconsistency might equally well be considered significant in its way; and Gottsched's biographers have thought so. But the statement only refers to rhymes.

THE STABILISATION OF THE LANGUAGE

in 1728 appeared the first version of Gottsched's *Redekunst*, in 1730 the *Critische Dichtkunst* and the first volume of the Society's publications of prose and verse. All Germany had plenty of opportunity to get to know this new Saxon Standard German and to see examples of its use. Gottsched was supplementing theory with practice. Sister societies began to spring up all over Germany and most of them kept in touch, either through middlemen or correspondence, with Gottsched and the Leipzig Society. A vast correspondence on linguistic matters developed. Interest in the German language was everywhere apparent; and of all this activity, Gottsched was the fountain-head. However alienated men may have later become by Gottsched's opinions on literary matters, they all, with a few eccentric exceptions, continued to look to Leipzig as the linguistic authority for correct usage.

In 1730 Gottsched was elected a member of the Prussian Academy, the *Societät der Wissenschaften*, which had been founded in 1700 by Frederick I of Prussia at the instigation of Leibniz. It was then at a rather low ebb, its president being the notorious Gundling who, although possessed of some talent for history, had become little more than a drunken court buffoon who, on his death in 1731, was buried by order of the king in a barrel inscribed with filthy verses. The *Societät der Wissenschaften* had achieved very little so far. Its Deed of Foundation, drafted by Leibniz himself, had included amongst its aims, the 'erhaltung der Teütschen Sprache in ihrer anständigen reinigkeit', and the *General-Instruction* of 11 July 1700 had urged that the foundation should ensure that 'die uhralte teutsche Haubtsprache in ihrer natürlichen, anständigen Reinigkeit und Selbststand erhalten werde, und nicht endlich ein ungereimbtes Mischmasch und Unkäntlichkeit daraus entstehe'.[1] It also envisaged the replacement of foreign words and the increase of the vocabulary by the collecting of old and local words. The personality of Leibniz himself shines through the phraseology of the *General-Instruction*; for these are the ideals he had voiced in the *Ermahnung* and the

[1] See Adolf Harnack, *Geschichte der Königlichen Preußischen Akademie der Wissenschaften zu Berlin*, 1900, for these documents.

Unvorgreiffliche Gedanken. But in fact it was King Frederick who had insisted on the linguistic activity of the Academy, for this had not been envisaged in the draft by Leibniz. A section for the cultivation of the German language had been established in 1710, and it had been agreed at a meeting on 19 February 1711, on a proposal from the king, that a German dictionary should be produced. Jablonski, secretary of the Academy at the time of Gottsched's election, had produced a treatise on how such a dictionary might be arranged; and in 1721 the Section had formulated some proposals towards the regulation of orthography. These proposals were sent to Gottsched soon after his election, for consideration and criticism by himself and the Deutsche Gesellschaft of Leipzig. The covering letter of 24 April 1730 testifies to the fame already enjoyed by this society. Jablonski wanted 'einige allgemeine regeln und grundsäze' that should command general agreement—a yard-stick with which to proceed. But general principles are, of course, the most difficult thing on which to get agreement, especially in a fundamental human attribute like language where every man feels himself knowledgeable. Gottsched may well have realised this. Be that as it may, nothing much seems to have come of these negotiations except a report with appended orthographical proposals in the *Nachricht von der Deutschen Gesellschaft zu Leipzig* for 1731, and Gottsched's assertion, in a formal oration delivered late in 1731 or early in 1732, that the Deutsche Gesellschaft of Leipzig should itself set about producing a German dictionary and a German grammar.[1] Indeed after the death of Burkhard Mencke (1732), Gottsched tried to get state recognition and support for the Leipzig Society. The petition sent to the relevant ministry in Dresden defines the Society's objects as the investigation, both analytical and historical, of the German language. Nothing much, either, seems to have come out of his membership of the *Societät der Wissenschaften* except a growing estrangement due to the appointment in 1746 of Maupertuis as president and to the whole policy under Frederick the Great. Gottsched objected to the way in which

---

[1] 'Begrüßungsrede an Lotter' in *Gesammelte Reden*, 1731-2.

THE STABILISATION OF THE LANGUAGE

Leibniz's whole conception was being put aside, especially to the fact that the publications were appearing in the French language. Leibniz had certainly envisaged that German should be the language of the transactions,[1] but they appeared in Latin until the reorganisation under Frederick the Great when they were published in French. Gottsched conceived of the *Societät* as a strongly national institution with fundamentally national tasks. It was certainly in this spirit that it had been founded; and it was in this spirit that Jablonski had solicited Gottsched's help.

The prelude to the *Deutsche Sprachkunst* was the periodical entitled *Beyträge zur Critischen Historie der deutschen Sprache, Poesie und Beredsamkeit* which Gottsched edited from 1732 to 1744. In it we can observe him feeling his way towards the systematic formulation he gave to his standardised German in the *Sprachkunst*. It would be impossible, within the scope of the present study, to attempt an analysis of the eight stout volumes of the book edition of this periodical. It would also be difficult to establish with any degree of certainty the authorship of the various articles. But the driving force behind it was Gottsched and it was his guiding purpose that gave unity to the manifold elements of the periodical. This purpose he stated in the very first number as being to show 'das allmählige Wachsthum der deutschen Sprache, den Fleiß unsrer Landesleute dieselbe zu bessern, die Vollkommenheit so sie schon erlanget, die Fehler so einige von ihnen begangen, und die Mittel selbige zu vermeiden'.[2] This is written in the same year as the petition to the Dresden

---

[1] This is clear from Leibniz's earliest plan, the *Consultatio* of 1676. He appealed to the authority of the French Académie and the Royal Society of London, both of which had, by their achievements, justified their use of the vernacular. Leibniz used this as an argument to solicit the co-operation of the German private linguistic societies (e.g. the Fruchtbringende Gesellschaft). In February 1734 it was agreed that part of the publications should appear in German, but this decision was never implemented. Gottsched in the first volume of his periodical *Das Neueste aus der Anmuthigen Gelehrsamkeit* (1751) reviews the fifth volume of the Academy publications, pointing out that their production in French was running contrary to the intentions of Leibniz and Frederick I. (British Museum copy, pp. 324–5.)

[2] Quoting from the British Museum copy of the original edition. This passage is on p. 4 of the Preface.

ministry, and both lay emphasis on both analytical and historical investigation of the German language. The earlier numbers show considerable interest in etymologies, but this gives way later to a more synchronic, analytical approach. There are attempts to formulate some of the more difficult sections of German grammar, such as the system of strong verbs or the rules of word-order. In the lexical field we note the persistent opposition to all that is not generally comprehensible, either because it is too local or too old or too new or too insufficiently defined. 'Die besonderen Mundarten sind also den Schönheiten der deutschen Sprache nothwendig zuwider', says J. H. Winkler in an article on the beauty of the German language.[1] We observe that the attitude is becoming increasingly intolerant, correctness is becoming more and more closely identified with Meissen usage. The Steinbach dictionary is accused of partiality for Silesian,[2] the championship of Low Saxon by Äpinus is covered with ridicule,[3] the Upper German area is charged with neglect of the vernacular due to its Jesuit schools.[4] All this is leading straight up to the *Deutsche Sprachkunst*. And the need for grammatical formulation is recognised in an article which begins with the words:

Der verschiedene und widrige Gebrauch der Wörter und Redensarten in einer Sprache ist ein Beweis, daß man die Regeln noch nicht gefunden und festgesetzet habe, nach welchen man die Richtigkeit des Ausdrucks zu beurtheilen pfleget.[5]

Bodmer at first sought the authority of Gottsched as his correspondence with Johann Christoph Clauder at Leipzig shows. We find him writing in 1730 both to Mascou and Professor Kapp at Leipzig, asking for someone to correct the language of his writings.[6] Clauder took over this task and prosecuted it until he

---

[1] Vol. I, pp. 55 ff., 70 ff.
[2] Vol. IV, pp. 190 ff., especially p. 211.
[3] Franz Äpinus, *De linguae Saxoniae inferioris neglectu atque contemtu iniusto* (Rostock, 1704), discussed in vol. I, pp. 304 ff.
[4] Vol. IV, pp. 74 ff.
[5] Vol. I, p. 130. *widrig* here means 'entgegengesetzt', a normal eighteenth-century meaning.
[6] Letter from Mascou to Bodmer of 14 January 1731, and from Kapp of 1 February 1731—see Eugen Wolff, *op. cit.*

THE STABILISATION OF THE LANGUAGE

left Leipzig in 1735. In a letter of 19 October 1732 he mentions with particular emphasis two Helveticisms: the use of the termination -*n* in the plural of nouns where it does not belong, and the use of -*e* in the dative singular of nouns whose genitive is monosyllabic. Clauder discussed some of Bodmer's points with Gottsched, for he mentions this fact in his letters. It is interesting to find Clauder praising the Swiss for the care they took in correcting their language.[1] Certainly, the later editions of their works show considerable approximation to the Leipzig Standard. Haller writes in 1735 to Gottsched, thanking him for the criticism of his poems and sending him the new edition in which he had embodied Gottsched's corrections; and Bodmer writes to Gottsched in July 1738 that he would like to submit his translation of *Paradise Lost* to Gottsched's correction but recoils at the thought of the labour this would entail. This is shortly before the outbreak of the literary feud, but there is no contradiction involved. The fact that Bodmer sought correction of the external form of his written German did not mean that he had in any way modified his basic disagreement with Gottsched on stylistic matters. This had emerged in the *Antipatriot* of 1728; and it recurred in the fifth volume of the *Beyträge*[2] (dated 1738), where there is an exchange of views concerning Winkler's article on the beauty of the German language (see above, p. 112). For Winkler the beauty of a language consisted in clarity and comprehensibility; for Bodmer the criterion was expressiveness. Gottsched's reply is rather ineffective, but shows that the gulf has not been bridged. The Swiss wanted to inculcate *markige* and *herzbewegliche Wörter* into the Saxon Standard. Bodmer, like any conscious dialect-speaker, felt the lack of certain expressions and wished to supply them from his own dialect. Gottsched would have none of this. This tension, between an ideal of clarity and an ideal of expressiveness, forms the linguistic aspect of the battle on poetics which we shall consider in a later chapter.

In 1746 there appeared at Zürich a revised and extended edition

---

[1] See Kürschner, *Deutsche National-Litteratur*, vol. 42, p. lviii; letter of 27 February 1733.   [2] *Ibid.* pp. 428 ff.

of the *Discourse der Mahlern* entitled *Der Mahler der Sitten*. The whole periodical is marked by opposition to Gottsched's linguistic strictures,[1] and one number contains an attack on the tyranny of Meissen, asserting that Swiss Alemannic is richer in sound and vocabulary, more concise, avoids cacophonic successions of final *-en* syllables by reducing them to 'ein leises *-n*', distinguishes the mutated vowels more clearly, avoids ugly diphthongisations 'mit gähnendem Mund' as in *Kraut* or *mein*, but preserves the good old diphthongal pronunciation of *Dieb, Liebe*. This is going back to a pre-Luther situation and is so ludicrously eccentric that it has been thought not to be the work of Bodmer.[2] The crux of the article runs as follows:

> Lasset uns derowegen alle Furcht für den Sachsen beyseite setzen, und unsers Rechtes und Eigenthums uns mit der Freyheit und Geschicklichkeit bedienen, daß unser Dialekt durch die Ausputzung und Erweiterung seines glücklichen und von Alter hergebrachten Schwunges zu einer für sich selbst bestehnden, und für sich zulänglichen Sprache werde.

Here we have the assertion that Alemannic would form as good a basis for Standard German as Upper Saxon. To this there is no logical objection. But there were empirical objections, and this is why Upper German was pilloried by Gottsched just as much if not more than Silesian. It is this antagonism which Burdach has overlooked.

The first edition of Gottsched's grammar was published at Leipzig in 1748. It bore the title: *Grundlegung einer deutschen Sprachkunst, nach den Mustern der besten Schriftsteller des vorigen und jetzigen Jahrhunderts*.[3] In his dedicatory epistle Gottsched

---

[1] Bodmer attacks the '*nervenlose* Sprache der sächsischen Magister' and their avoidance of participial, elliptical and metaphorical constructions.

[2] The article in question is vol. II, no. 102. Waniek suggests that the author was Samuel König, the mathematician. Nevertheless Bodmer published it. Bodmer's authorship is accepted by Max Wehrli in his anthology *Das geistige Zürich im 18. Jahrhundert* (Zürich, 1943), from which I take my text. Waniek quotes more of the same passage.

[3] Reichel says the first edition is a very rare book and that he has never seen a copy. There is one in the British Museum, and it is from this copy that I quote.

THE STABILISATION OF THE LANGUAGE

refers to the difficulty of writing a grammar and pays tribute to his predecessors in this field during the past two centuries.[1] His purpose he defines as 'Erhaltung und Ausbreitung' of the German language. The word *Erhaltung* connotes the essence of all Gottsched's linguistic activity. For he was no great innovator:

> Meine Absichten sind nicht gewesen, Neuerungen in unsrer Sprache zu machen. Ich gehöre nicht unter die Zahl derer, die sich einbilden, sie hätten Fähigkeit genug, ihre Muttersprache zu verbessern, anders einzurichten, und zu verschönern... Alles, was also, meines Erachtens, ein Sprachlehrer thun kann, ist dieses, daß er die verborgenen Schönheiten seiner Muttersprache aufsuche, entdecke, anpreise und bey seinen Landsleuten in Schwang bringen helfe: nicht aber, daß er sich zu einem neuen Gesetzgeber aufwerfe, der ein ganzes Volk nach seinem eigenen Kopfe will reden lehren; und sich Regeln erdichte, die von seiner Nation noch niemals angenommen, oder beobachtet worden.

Despite this assertion, Gottsched did nevertheless become a legislator for the language of the whole nation. To a certain extent he desired this, however modest the tone may be in this first edition of the *Sprachkunst*. The long footnotes[2] added to the later editions are more intransigent. Gottsched seems more inclined to dismiss criticism by reference to such concepts as 'bad' or 'incorrect'. People from all over Germany were seeking his advice on linguistic matters: thus in the fifth edition of 1762 a footnote tells us that certain 'great men in Vienna' had written to him enquiring about the correct use of *derer* and *denen* (as against *der* and *den*).[3] This was only one of many such instances. Gottsched was no doubt flattered by such inquiries, and he grew more conscious of his position. As a result he became more magisterial and adamant in his strictures. But in this passage, from the dedication to the first edition, Gottsched is attacking outlandish innovators. He may

---

[1] Mentioning by name Clajus, Schottelius, Stieler and Bödiker.
[2] I use the term 'footnotes' in a somewhat loose sense. In spirit they are footnotes although they appear after the various paragraphs, not at the foot of the page.
[3] *Ed. cit.* p. 165. Copies of this edition are not rare, and the British Museum has one. There is an article on this question, and an answer by Gottsched in vol. 1 of the *Beyträge* (pp. 342–54). But this was in 1732; and there is no indication that the article originated from Vienna.

later have dictated; but he certainly never dictated 'Regeln... die von seiner Nation noch niemals angenommen oder beobachtet worden'. In this he followed his own ideal of a grammarian. This fact accounts for the widespread interest in and immediate response to the *Sprachkunst*. The norm it advocated must have had sufficient in it to earn the approbation of large numbers of German readers. The book must have been eagerly bought, for the first edition was sold out in a few months. The Preface to the second edition is dated August 1749, and in it Gottsched expressed his delight that so many Germans were showing active interest in their own language. The third edition of 1752 paid tribute to the many suggestions and criticisms which various persons had sent the author. The fourth edition of 1756 referred to the spate of grammatical works, some of them hostile, which the book had called forth. The fifth edition of 1762 was one of the most celebrated and the last to be published during his lifetime. The sixth and last edition was published in 1776, ten years after Gottsched's death.[1]

One assumption underlying Gottsched's *Deutsche Sprachkunst* is that every German will write in his native language. In this respect Gottsched was continuing and completing the work of Leibniz, Thomasius and Wolff. In his memorial lecture on Martin Opitz in 1739, he had deplored those 'lovers of darkness', those 'enemies of their fatherland' who refuse to countenance scholarly works in the vernacular.[2] Like the ancient Egyptians they would make a mystery out of learning, and so keep those who have not studied classical languages—that is to say, the large mass of the nation—in almost bestial ignorance. Gottsched was here appealing for the 'Unstudierten', 'den größten und edelsten Theil eines Volkes' as he now called them, those same 'Unstudierten' to whom, as we have seen,[3] he had addressed himself

---

[1] The British Museum has copies of the first, fifth and sixth editions, all of which I have used.

[2] *Lob- und Gedächtnißrede auf den Vater der deutschen Dichtkunst Martin Opitzen von Boberfeld* etc. (Leipzig, 1739). I quote from the original edition, of which there is a copy in the British Museum. This passage is on pp. 21 ff.

[3] See above, pp. 89 n.

THE STABILISATION OF THE LANGUAGE

in *Die Vernünfftigen Tadlerinnen*, and indeed in all his works. He also continued the fight against French which we have seen him waging in his early periodicals; for the battle was far from won. French was still the language of the courts and the privileged aristocracy, it still had the *cachet* of refinement and was, for this reason, already being widely employed by those sections of the middle classes which had pretensions to culture. It is interesting to find the future Frau Gottsched writing to Gottsched in October 1730 as follows:

> Aber warum wollen Sie mir nicht erlauben, daß ich französisch schreibe? Zu welchem Ende erlernen wir diese Sprache, wenn wir uns nicht üben und unsere Fertigkeit darinnen zeigen sollen? Sie sagen, es sey unverantwortlich, in einer fremden Sprache besser als in seiner eigenen zu schreiben, und meine Lehrmeister haben mich versichert, es sey nichts gemeiner als deutsche Briefe, alle wohlgesittete Leute schrieben französisch....[1]

Gottsched himself complained, in a letter of 28 December 1737 to Manteuffel, that the courts were still enamoured of everything foreign and that the princes themselves hardly understood their own language.[2] It was for this reason that Gottsched was unable to recommend the language of the courts as a model. Equally vigorous was Gottsched's fight against those who wrote in the vernacular but thought it necessary or becoming to interlard their phrases with foreign words. We have already noted above that Gottsched's approach to this matter was entirely rationalistic. He realised that this affectation proceeded from a desire to prove that one was better than one's fellow men and from bad taste. It was unnecessary and unnatural, therefore irrational.[3] This same attitude characterised his whole attitude to the *Fremdwort* question. But his standpoint was reasonable and in no wise extremist. Thus in the *Sprachkunst*, we find him inveighing against the purism of

---

[1] *Briefe der Frau Gottsched*, vol. I (Dresden, 1771), pp. 6 ff. The manuscripts have disappeared, and it is probable that the editor, Frau von Runckel, has modernised the text. See Adolf Lange, *Die Sprache der Gottschedin in ihren Briefen*, vol. I (Uppsala, 1896), Vorwort.
[2] Quoted in Eugen Wolff, vol. I, p. 6.   [3] See above, pp. 94 ff.

the seventeenth-century *Sprachgesellschaften*, recognising that one cannot do without foreign words entirely;[1] but he considered that much recent borrowing, especially from French, was unnecessary. He instances the French terms for army ranks current in Germany at that time, whereas the Imperial army used German terms which he cites. He recommends the naturalisation of foreign words by giving them native German endings. He points to old-established examples of this, such as *Schalmey* from *chalumeau*,[2] *Pastorell* from *pastorella*, *Recitativ* from *recitativo*, *Oper* from *opera*, and *Pilgrim* from *pellegrino*.[3] But this process should only be carried out when no German equivalents existed, and Gottsched proceeds to show how some *Fremdwörter* could easily be replaced by native terms. He selects as his example the vocabulary of music, suggesting German equivalents for the Italian loans. Sometimes Gottsched seems not so opposed to Latin technical terms. Indeed in the *Redekunst* of 1728 he had described those people who germanise technical terms as 'Phantastische, die im Gehirn nicht wohl versehen sind'. But his attitude sharpens throughout the *Beyträge* and in the Preface to his 1744 edition of the *Théodicée*, he expresses the hope that it will soon be possible to 'chase this whole barbarism from German soil'. Gottsched was equally sensitive to Francophile adulteration of German syntax and style. He deplored the use of *mehr* and *minder* with adjectives on the model of French *plus* and *moins*,[4] the modishness of phrases like *der Mensch hat viel Welt* (*du monde*) or *er ist vom Handwerke* (*du métier*),[5] and the imitation of French *faire dire*, *faire savoir* etc., as *sagen machen*, *wissen machen* which, he said, was 'rothwälsch oder hottentottisch' but not German.[6] The use of the salutation

[1] 1st edn. p. 150.
[2] This derivation would seem to be slightly incorrect, in that M.H.G. *schal(e)mî(e)* is obviously derived from O.Fr. *chalemie*.
[3] 1st edn. p. 157. *Pilgrim* seems to have been a normal form current in Gottsched's day, but Adelung in 1777, although appreciating its historical justification, says: 'In der anständigern Sprechart braucht man statt dessen lieber *Pilger*.'
[4] *Sprachkunst*, 1st edn. p. 215.   [5] 5th edn. p. 5.
[6] *Sprachkunst*, 5th edn. p. 473. Cf. the following from *Das Neueste aus der anmuthigen Gelehrsamkeit*, vol. v (1755), p. 124: 'Dieses *machen* ist...ein offen-

THE STABILISATION OF THE LANGUAGE

Heil dir! he considered as a pernicious anglicism, also the use of *die Schöpfung* for *die Welt*, and the adjective *gesegnet* for English 'blessed' which he would render by *teuerster*.¹ Gottsched was prepared to assert, on occasions, that German was superior as a language to both Latin and French. We noted above the curious argument, advanced at one point in *Die Vernünfftigen Tadlerinnen*, that German is superior to French, Italian or English because it does not proceed from the mingling of the languages of several peoples.² In a letter of 1742 we find him asserting that German is more *precise* than either Latin or French.³ In a footnote in the fifth edition of the *Sprachkunst*, he considers the claim of the French that their language was more perfect than any other. He refers to an article by the 'learned and unbiased Father Buffier' in the *Beyträge* which showed what strong prejudices this opinion assumed. The French claim that their language follows the natural order of thoughts, but Gottsched objects that the many short sentences are more suited to conversation than to elegant, oratorical or poetical expression, that German had possessed just this quality some two hundred years earlier but had consciously rejected it on the grounds of euphony. He cites an example like Luther's 'Denn er kömmt zu richten, das Erdreich; er wird den Erdboden richten, mit Gerechtigkeit' (Psalm 96, v. 13).⁴ Already in earlier versions of the *Sprachkunst*, he had stated his opinion that the excellence (*Vollkommenheit*) of a language depended first on the range of its vocabulary, and that German was therefore better now than two or three hundred years ago. A footnote in the fifth edition specifies the spheres in which Gottsched considered the German vocabulary to be particularly rich: handicrafts, hunting, forestry, mining, viticulture

---

barer *Gallicismus*, der sich auf deutsch ohne Fehler nicht nachsagen läßt. Denn wer spricht bey uns: ich will dich gehen, sehen, schlafen, essen *machen*? wie man doch im Französischen gar wohl saget: *Je te ferai marcher, voir, dormir, manger*. Vor solchen *barbarismis* muß man sich sehr in acht nehmen, wenn man eine Sprache nicht verderben will.'

¹ *Sprachkunst*, 5th edn. pp. 5, 507, 539.
² See above, p. 94. ³ Eugen Wolff, vol. I, pp. 10–11.
⁴ *Sprachkunst*, 5th edn. p. 13.

and especially seafaring. This had for the most part already been said by earlier writers in the century, especially by Leibniz. But Gottsched went on to say that German had a rich range of expressions in philosophy and mathematics, 'seit dem die gelehrtesten Männer aufgehöret haben, das vormalige Gemeng zu lieben'.[1] The main argument continued, in the earlier editions, with the suggestion that the excellence of a language depended secondly on clarity, that is to say: 'wenn die Wörter wohl zusammen gefüget, und nach gewissen leichten Regeln verbunden werden'—etymological perspicuity of word-formation (both composition and derivation). The third essential quality was concision, or emphasis (*die Kürʒe, oder der Nachdruck*). Gottsched dismissed the idea that some languages sound nicer than others, as too vague and too much of a generalisation to be a suitable fourth criterion of perfection. Gottsched's three criteria of *Reichthum*, *Deutlichkeit* and *Nachdruck* recall the criteria of Leibniz which were defined in the *Unvorgreiffliche Gedanken* as *Reichthum*, *Reinigkeit* and *Glantʒ*. In this, as in so much else, his dependence on his great predecessor is apparent; and it is perhaps not without significance that he reprinted the *Unvorgreiffliche Gedanken* in the first volume of the *Beyträge*.[2]

There were critics of the seventeenth and early eighteenth centuries who had been stimulated by the force of the opposition to express their admiration for something vaguely known as the 'uralte deutsche Haupt- und Heldensprache'. A moralistic attitude is embodied in such a phrase. German, we notice, is a *Heldensprache*, the language of heroes. Even Leibniz had praised what he termed the 'innern Kern des alten *ehrlichen* Teutschen' (see above, p. 6). Gottsched himself, in the dedicatory epistle to the first edition of the *Sprachkunst*, had spoken of 'die Schönheiten unsrer uralten, *männlichen* und lieblichen Mundart' (using the word 'Mundart' here in its widest possible sense) and later in the

---

[1] 5th edn. p. 14.
[2] He says (*ibid.* p. 368) that he considers the work of great importance, and that it contains proposals and remarks which the Deutsche Gesellschaft of Leipzig had already accepted.

THE STABILISATION OF THE LANGUAGE

same paragraph referred to the German language as having been spoken and written by 'unzählbaren *tapfern Helden*, großen Geistern und gelehrten Leuten'.[1] Yet Gottsched seems to have realised the danger inherent in such Romantic phrases. For in the second chapter of the *Sprachkunst* he deals with those 'Grübler'[2] who thought that the German language had been a more vigorous medium at the time of Maximilian and Charles V. To this assertion Gottsched replies that the 'old roughness' (*alte Rauhigkeit*) of writers before Opitz certainly does sound somewhat more emphatic, but on the other hand the language was now more melodious and less ambiguous owing to a richer vocabulary and more regulated word-order, and yet still capable of forceful expression. Gottsched is convinced that, on all the three criteria he recognised as valid, the development of the German language since the time of Opitz had been in the direction of improvement:

> Aus dieser Ursache nun wäre es zu wünschen, daß unsre Sprache bey der itzigen Art sie zu reden und zu schreiben erhalten werden könnte: weil sie allem Ansehen nach denjenigen Grad der Vollkommenheit erreichet zu haben scheint, darinn sie zu allen Vorfällen und Absichten einer ausgearbeiteten und artigen Sprache geschickt und bequem ist.[3]

The word *artig* is significant. This is Gottsched's counterblast to the *nachdrücklich* and *kräftig* which others had used to describe the older language. Gottsched is here giving expression to the stylistic ideal of his time, an ideal already voiced by Thomasius in the same word *Artigkeit* (see above, p. 18). He agreed that Opitz was the father of all good writing in the German language; but German had continued to improve since his day. It was equally false to cling to the ideal of the old Imperial Chancery language, for the cultural centre of Germany had moved, since the Reformation, to areas more to the north and the east. What, therefore, is more natural than that men from all districts should

---

[1] My italics in these quotations.
[2] On the meaning of this word, see above, footnote to p. 96. This is the reading of the fifth edition, the first edition had *Gelehrte*.
[3] 1st edn. p. 12. The fifth edition improves the punctuation.

be concerned to improve their own language and so contribute to this steady advancement of their mother-tongue?

The Deutsche *Sprachkunst* begins with the famous statement:

Eine Sprachkunst ist eine gegründete Anweisung, wie man die Sprache eines Volkes, nach der besten Mundart desselben, und nach der Einstimmung der besten Schriftsteller, richtig und zierlich, sowohl reden als schreiben solle.[1]

Within one sentence Gottsched is here placing side by side two quite different authorities: 'beste Mundart...beste Schriftsteller.' He is using the word *Mundart* precisely in its modern sense. He does not mean 'way of speaking', but specifically 'regional dialect'. This emerges from his definition in the next paragraph:

Eine Mundart ist diejenige Art zu reden, die in einer gewissen Provinz eines Landes herrscht; in so weit sie von der Art zu reden der andern Provinzen, die einerley Sprache haben, abgeht.

He therefore recognises a regional standard, based on the speech (*cultured* speech, he is quick to explain) of a given area. But alongside this, he recognises the criterion afforded by the usage of the best writers, which represents a standard language independent of and superior to all regional dialects, based not on speech at all but on writing. He amplifies this second point, extending it also to speech, in a footnote to this section in the later editions, where, after recognising the variety of regional dialects in Germany, he goes on to observe:

Es ist aber gar keine Landschaft in Deutschland, die recht rein hochdeutsch redet: die Uebereinstimmung der Gelehrten aus den besten Landschaften, und die Beobachtungen der Sprachforscher müssen auch in Betrachtung gezogen werden.[2]

But the phrase *aus den besten Landschaften* brings us back to the other criterion of *die beste Mundart*, for it represents a sort of

---

[1] Quoting from the first edition of 1748 (British Museum copy). The later editions have slightly amended wording and punctuation. Thus, in the fifth edition of 1762 this first paragraph runs as follows: 'Eine Sprachkunst überhaupt ist eine gegründete Anweisung, wie man die Sprache eines gewissen Volkes, nach der besten Mundart desselben, und nach der Einstimmung seiner besten Schriftsteller, richtig und zierlich, sowohl reden, als schreiben solle.'

[2] 5th edn. p. 403.

THE STABILISATION OF THE LANGUAGE

bridge between these two entirely different criteria. But what are *die besten Landschaften* and what is *die beste Mundart*? The best dialect, says Gottsched, is usually that spoken at the court or in the capital of a country. But if a country has more than one court, then it is the language of the largest court in the middle of the country. He is obviously thinking of ancient Athens, and of the East Middle German area as its modern German successor. He never really explains what qualities make a dialect the 'best'; and is constantly in danger of the vicious circle that the dialect of Meissen is best because it is closest to *Hochdeutsch* which is based on the language of Meissen because it is the best! The geographical argument is the most he can offer, and it is not very persuasive. He repeats this argument later in the book, adding the assertion that it was in the Meissen area that men had most occupied themselves with the perfecting of their language; it was the centre of the book-trade and of German university life, and from this area came the best writers.

By advancing these two criteria for a standard language—the best dialect and the best writers—Gottsched is therefore attempting to reconcile the two opposing attitudes which had prevailed on this question for some time. The psychological basis of his syncretistic standpoint is the fact that he grew up in East Prussia where the High German language of intercourse still had very strong Low German features, and that when he settled in Leipzig at the age of twenty-four he found in Upper Saxon a dialect free from the extensive Low German colouring of his native East Prussian and much closer to the language of literature, and yet with dialectal peculiarities of its own which he felt as not consonant with High German and therefore did not fail to castigate in the *Deutsche Sprachkunst*.[1] But his attitude to the whole problem of the establishment of a standard language had no *logical* basis, for he showed no understanding of the real relation-

---

[1] 'Die Provinzialredensarten aber, nebst denen Wortfügungen, die nur diesem oder jenem Scribenten eigen sind, wollen wir eben so sorgfältig zu verbiethen, und auszumärzen suchen; als die Lateiner die Solöcismen verbothen, und aus der guten Mundart verbannet haben.' Text from first edition, p. 334.

ship between dialect and *Schriftsprache* and offered no estimate of how far the best authors approximate to the best dialect, except the statement that they were then to be found in Leipzig.

But we are here not concerned with the merits of Gottsched's book as a descriptive grammar, nor with its relations to the grammars of the preceding century,[1] but solely with the *effect* of his work on his generation and its contribution to the development of the literary language. As for his criterion of the 'best' authors, Gottsched merely says that a nation usually has no difficulty in recognising its best authors. These will come from many different regions, but by the care which writing naturally engenders, they will have cast off the 'errors of their native dialect'. Gottsched goes on to say that if these good writers differ on points of usage, the final decision must be made by what he calls 'die Analogie der Sprache'. This he defines as 'die Aehnlichkeit in den Ableitungen, und Verwandelungen der Wörter; imgleichen in der Verkürzung, Verlängerung und Zusammensetzung sowohl der Wörter als der Redensarten'.[2] This is nothing more or less than the old principle of *analogia* found in the grammatical discussions of classical antiquity and revived by Schottelius in the seventeenth century. Analogy, says Gottsched, is never absolute in any language; but the greatest number of agreeing examples should constitute the rule. One can therefore establish rules in language; yet these rules are not imposed from outside but emerge from the usage of language itself. He illustrates this from his own dialect in a footnote to the fifth edition; thus many people in Meissen say *ich bin Willens*, which is analogical to *ich bin der Meynung, des Sinnes, des Vorhabens* etc., but others say *ich habe in Willens* to which there is no analogy and which is therefore incorrect. Gottsched recognises that there are phrases and constructions well established in the language which will not stand this test. He would only apply it if there are two competing phrases, as in the example given. He also recognises the im-

---

[1] Both these matters are investigated in great detail by Jellinek, *Geschichte der neuhochdeutschen Grammatik*, vol. I (Heidelberg, 1913).
[2] 1st edn. p. 3.

portance of historical development. He would therefore take into consideration the writers of past times, and the other Germanic languages, for these often throw light on the true origin and significance of a construction. All these sources of information will be used, not in order to deplenish the language, but to establish what is the usage of the best dialect and the best writers, and to consolidate and defend this usage for the benefit of his contemporaries, particularly those in outlying dialect areas, to show them how they may approach to the usage of the *beste Mundart*. Gottsched continued to proclaim that his ideal was a language above the dialects: but it is clear that his norm was cultured Meissen usage.

The first part of the *Deutsche Sprachkunst* deals with orthography. Gottsched presents general principles and then proceeds to details. Throughout he applies the same criteria as he had proclaimed in the preliminary chapters: Upper Saxon cultured pronunciation is taken as the norm, and spelling is considered as a means to represent this pronunciation. His first general rule is: 'Man schreibe jede Sylbe mit solchen Buchstaben, die man in der guten Aussprache deutlich höret.' This use of the word *Buchstabe* shows Gottsched's imprecision in terminology, and the whole sentence postulates a phonetic approach to orthography which is not consistently maintained. Nevertheless, the appeal to Upper Saxon usage is evident as Gottsched's starting-point. But only to cultured Upper Saxon usage, for he rejects pronunciations like *Jott, Jabe* and *jut* (for *Gott, Gabe* and *gut*), or *Bodden* and *Fadden* (for *Boden* and *Faden*) current there in colloquial usage. Gottsched says of the *j*, that it is much softer than *g* and *k*: 'sie steigen stufenweise, *Jahr, Gabe, Kahn*; nicht *Gahr, Jabe*; viel weniger wie einige sprechen: *Kabe, Gahn*.'[1] He repeatedly supports Upper Saxon as against Silesian pronunciation. He notes that Silesians pronounce the words *bin, hin, von,* with a long vowel, and *Blut,*

[1] 1st edn. p. 20. This dialectal approximation of stop and spirant is seen in the letters of King Frederick William I of Prussia who produced forms like *geger* (Jäger) or *guhng* (jung). See H. Hummerich, *Beiträge zur Sprache König Friedrich Wilhelm des Ersten von Preußen* (Diss. Greifswald, 1910). Leopold von Ranke called Frederick William's spelling 'wildgewachsen' and 'kennzeichnend'.

Gut, Mut, with a short vowel—but this, he says, is not so in other dialects and cannot therefore be accepted as a rule. The Silesian long vowel in *Fluß, Schluß* is objected to, because it is short in the Meissen dialect. Two different arguments are therefore used against these Silesian features, which are rejected either as being extreme or simply because they are not Upper Saxon. These features had been embodied in literary Silesian spellings like *Gutt, Mutt, Blutt,* also *verterben, Prister,* but the eminence of Silesian poets of the previous century should not, says Gottsched, persuade us to adopt these spellings which do not represent good, i.e. Upper Saxon, pronunciation. The second criterion, the 'good writers', is invoked to combat illiterate spellings like *jib, kib* or *kip* (for *gib*); these are phonetic spellings, but Gottsched states quite firmly that they come from 'bad' dialects which should endeavour to adapt their 'bad pronunciation' to written usage. On the pronunciation of the diphthong *ei,* he also invokes the authority of the *Schriftbild* and is most explicit about the various dialectal pronunciations: '*Ei* muß weder wie *ai* gesprochen werden, wie es von einigen Oberdeutschen geschieht, die *mein, Bein,* wie *main, Bain,* hören lassen; noch wie *ee* klingen, wie man in Meißen thut, da viele *Stein,* wie *Steen, Bein,* wie *Been, Kleider,* wie *Kleeder* sprechen. Noch ärger ist es mit den Schwaben und Bayern, *Bein* wie *Boan,* und *Stein* wie *Stoan* auszusprechen. Man muß beyde einfache Vocalen zugleich ausdrücken.'[1] This passage is a good illustration of Gottsched's sense, nourished from many sources, of what is the norm and what is the divagation. The third criterion, analogy, is frequently invoked, as in Gottsched's second general rule of orthography which runs: 'Alle Stammbuchstaben, die den Wurzelwörtern eigen sind, müssen in allen abstammenden beybehalten werden.'[2] He also rejects the spelling *Gedult* because its 'similarity' with other words 'of this kind' like *Huld, Schuld* shows that it should be written *Geduld.* Again, we notice, the terminology is hopelessly vague

---

[1] Text from the fifth edition (p. 47) which here expands on the first edition.
[2] The fifth edition adds the modification 'soviel möglich ist' before the *beybehalten werden.*

but the point is clear. The presentation, however, shows confusion between phonetic spelling and spelling-pronunciation. For instance, we are told that *å* (to use the contemporary typographical form) should be pronounced 'wie ein halbes a und halbes e'—which is spelling-pronunciation, pronunciation influenced by the *Schriftbild*; but Gottsched goes on to say that this sound should not be written *ae*, as by some innovators, because this denotes two separate sounds, as in *Danae, Pasiphae, Phaeton*—which is appealing to the ideal of phonetic spelling. All this comes about because of the vagueness of the term *Analogie*. He invokes the authority of tradition in his third general rule: 'Man schreibe so, wie es der allgemeine Gebrauch eines Volkes seit undenklichen Zeiten eingeführet hat',[1]—again a formulation so vague as to be almost meaningless, but Gottsched is really concerned with combating certain outlandish neologisms in orthography, and particularly those of Zesen and his followers. Zesen's spelling had been largely phonetic, but he was also concerned with etymological perspicuity. Gottsched invokes the 'good writers' and the traditions of centuries against Zesen spellings like *hi* (for *hie*), *frei* (for *frey*), *Filosofie, Kwahl, schäẓẓen, hakken, Saẓ, Glük*; he considers that such orthography destroys the beauty of a language and abandons its etymological structure by obscuring its roots. It was, however, the principle of analogy which had led Zesen to such spellings as *wärden, mänsch, ärde*, for he wrote *ä* for [e] where related stems have *a*. This, in Gottsched's eyes, is nothing but 'wunderliche Grillenfängerey', 'nichts als die Begierde nach Neuerungen'. On the question of double consonants Gottsched is guided by the length of the preceding vowel, taking cultured Meissen pronunciation as his norm. Thus he advocates the following types of spelling: *Schlaf* (not *Schlaff*), *in* (not *inn*), *werfen* (not *werffen*), *Schutz* (not *Schuẓ*). He also regulates the use of *h* as a sign of lengthened vowel, and rationalises punctuation.[2]

---

[1] Text from the first edition. In the fifth edition, this is the fourth general rule.

[2] These three criteria of pronunciation, usage of good writers and analogy are well illustrated in Gottsched's argumentation for the spelling *Deutsch* in the

Regulation of orthography may not seem to be of importance in the development of a literary language, but when we consider the chaotic state of German spelling at the end of the seventeenth century, it is clear that a generally agreed orthography was an important part of that stability and security which was coming to the German language. In an excellent study [1] of the period immediately preceding Gottsched's work, Kåre Kaiser has demonstrated the general desire for a stabilised orthography at this time and also the lack of any guiding principles. Some writers had asserted the phonetic principle; but which pronunciation was to be decisive? Schottelius had begged the question by appealing to 'der gut angenommene Gebrauch, und die Grundrichtigkeit der Sprache'; another writer, Omeis,[2] had referred quite vaguely to 'die vernünftige Aussprache', whatever that might be. Kaiser investigates some of the features on which there was dialectal deviation at this time. There was general negligence in the designation of *Umlaut*, and here the printers were often to blame, as Gottsched pointed out;[3] but to this must be added the general absence of *Umlaut* in Upper German written documents, which was a feature of long standing, partly corresponding to pronunciation and partly due to scribal tradition, with a gradual adaptation to the Middle German written usage, but still leaving uncertainty in the minds of some eighteenth-century writers from the Upper German area. In this, as in so much else at this period, morphology and orthography are so inextricably mingled that it is almost impossible to treat them separately.

There were, however, marked Upper German morphological characteristics. The tendency towards apocope of final -*e* and the weakening of the final nasal were strong features of the south. The

essay: *Ob man Deutsch oder Teutsch schreiben solle?* (first written in 1728, and published in the *Nachricht* of 1731, but revised later and included in the third and later editions of the *Sprachkunst*) where they reappear as *Aussprache, Gewohnheit* und *Abstammung* (*Sprachkunst*, 5th edn. p. 676).

[1] Kåre Kaiser, *Mundart und Schriftsprache—Versuch einer Wesensbestimmung in der Zeit zwischen Leibniz und Gottsched* (Leipzig, 1930).

[2] M. D. Omeis, *Gründliche Anleitung zur Teutschen accuraten Reim- und Dicht-Kunst*, 2nd ed. (Nuremberg, 1712).

[3] *Sprachkunst*, 5th edn. p. 50.

apocope of -e led to overcompensation in written German which we find in all dialect areas as an indirect result of dialect usage.[1] Southern German opposition to 'the Lutheran *e*', as it came to be called, had wider effects. There grew up, especially amongst Upper German writers, a distaste for the juncture -e- in compounds. Here again a morphological feature becomes an orthographical prejudice. This was voiced, for instance, by the editor[2] of the 1745 edition of the poems of K. F. Drollinger who was born in Baden and lived most of his life in Switzerland, in a footnote giving Drollinger's expressed opinion: 'Es wird oft in die Mitte der zusammengesetzten deutschen Wörter das (e) ohne Noht und wider den Wollaut eingeschoben. Diesen Fehler haben wir vornemlich den schlesischen und sächsischen Poeten zu danken.'[3] Hence his own usage, as represented by *Folgstern, Reisgesellschaft, Sterbbett*. The weakening or even loss of the final nasal is a dialectal feature associated not only with Upper German but also with certain dialects of Middle German,[4] especially West Middle German.[5] This led to confusion in the distinction in usage between the strong and weak declension of the adjective. Gottsched censures such combinations as *die gelehrte Leute*, and assigns them to what he rather vaguely calls 'gewisse Landschaften'.[6] Another result of this weakening of the

[1] Kaiser quotes examples from Christian Reuter, *der Mensche* (masc.sg.), *Unglücke* (sg.), *ins Gesichte*, and Christian Weise, *der Kerle* (sg.), *in ein Gespräche geriethen*, etc., both of whom were Saxon writers. This feature is also very frequent in the Swiss writers (e.g. in the *Discourse der Mahlern* and in Breitinger's *Critische Dichtkunst*). [2] J. J. Sprengen.

[3] Frankfurt am Main, 1745. British Museum copy, p. 22.

[4] See H. Reis, *Die deutschen Mundarten* (Berlin, 1920), p. 53. Hermann Paul, *Deutsche Grammatik*, vol. III, p. 99. Virgil Moser, *Einführung in die frühneuhochdeutschen Schriftdialekte* (Halle, 1909), p. 168, pointing out that this is no new feature. Gottsched assigns it to 'die Herren Thüringer, Franken und Schwaben' in a footnote to the fifth edition of the *Sprachkunst*, p. 287.

[5] The letters of Liselotte von der Pfalz are full of such forms, e.g. *ich kan nicht glaube, Nun komme wir* (examples from Kaiser, *op. cit.*, quoting Adolf Urbach, *Über die Sprache in den deutschen Briefen der Herzogin Elisabeth Charlotte von Orléans* (Diss. Greifswald, 1899).

[6] 1st edn. p. 206, 5th edn. p. 252. This is not entirely due to loss of final nasal, for it is found at this period in all dialect areas, and testifies to the general vagueness regarding the distinction between strong and weak declension.

final nasal was the confusion between final *-m* and *-n* which was rampant at this period and led to a situation parallel to the confusion of dative and accusative pronouns.[1] On all these points Gottsched perceives clearly which is the original form and which is the weakened form; and he always sides with the original form. He is therefore opposed both to apocope and to overcompensation.

The second part is entitled *Die Wortforschung* and embraces what is usually called Accidence. Gottsched lists the various parts of speech and then proceeds to deal with each in detail. Again we notice constant references to the 'incorrect' forms associated with dialects other than Upper Saxon; again we observe the appeal to the usage of 'good writers' and to the principle of 'analogy'.

The criterion of the cultured Upper Saxon norm is used by Gottsched to admit the diminutive endings *-lein* and *-chen*, but to reject the South German *-l* suffix.[2] He recognises great divergence on the question of gender amongst the different provinces, but decides to adopt Meissen usage without further ado,[3] although he does try to establish some 'rules' according to meaning or termination. In his chapter on noun declensions he expressly mentions with disapproval the *-s* plurals of Low Saxon (although making exceptions for foreign words), Silesian forms like *das Herze*, an analogical form like *des Menschens* and the genitive singular *meiner Frauen*.[4] This last example might be aimed at the Swiss who seem to have clung longer in their

---

[1] See above, p. 55, n. 3.

[2] 1st edn. p. 143 and, with expansions, 5th edn. p. 187. According to Paul (*Deutsche Grammatik*, vol. v, p. 90), *-chen* was predominating over *-lein* by 1700. Gottsched seems to consider *-lein* as more refined and elevated. He compares *Fräulein* and *Herrchen* (5th edn., footnote). Despite the fact that *-chen* originated in Middle German and *-l* in the south, we find by this period that each has spread far beyond its original confines. The Swiss writers make frequent use of the *-chen* suffix, despite the fact that it is quite foreign to their speech-dialects.

[3] '...allen übrigen Landsleuten aber die Wahl lassen, ob sie sich derselben bequemen, oder bey ihrer alten Art bleiben wollen.' 1st edn. p. 160.

[4] 5th edn. pp. 224, 234, 235, 237, some of this material in footnotes and therefore not in the 1748 edition.

THE STABILISATION OF THE LANGUAGE

scribal tradition to the old weak genitive singular in -*en*. The genitive case is, of course, obsolete in spoken dialect, and so this feature is undoubtedly the result of striving after some elevated written norm. Altogether there was a tendency amongst the Swiss to consider -*n* as a genitive plural sign (*Discourse der Mahlern*; *Versuch schweizerischer Gedichten*) which attaches itself to all masculine and neuter nouns. These forms are frequent in the earliest editions of Albrecht von Haller's poems, but he 'corrected' them in later editions. Similar forms are found in Austro-Bavarian texts like the *Parnassus Boicus* (Munich, 1722–37). Other forms which Gottsched rejects as 'Upper German' are *der anderte*, *derley*, and *ich gehete*.[1] He also rejects a Low German solecism like *ich bin sehr hart begegnet worden*.[2]

The practice of the 'good writers' is advocated as a guide on many questions. We are told that the good writers avoid monotony by using both *der* and *welcher* as relative pronouns.[3] Their practice shows agreement that the correct constructions are *mich dünket*, but *mir däucht*.[4] Their usage is invoked against participial constructions like *ein zu lesendes Buch*, representing an attempt at a future participle in German.[5] Gottsched appeals to the authority of the past in his demand that compound nouns should not be hyphenated. Many people, he says, draw a distinction between old established compounds and more recent ones, spelling the latter with a hyphen between the two elements. Gottsched sees no reason for this distinction and therefore advocates the spelling *Hofrath* and not *Hof-Rath*.[6] He justifies his distinction between *zween*, *zwo* and *zwey* by reference to the authority of 'unsere Alten und selbst die deutsche Bibel'.[7] He also refers to Luther's Bible in order to justify *genannt*, *gekannt* as against Meissen *genennt*, *gekennt*;[8] to the German Bible and the best authors to justify *ich rief* as against *ich rufete*.[9] And yet Gottsched is not uncritical of the great authors of the past. In a footnote to the fifth edition of the *Sprachkunst*, he admitted: 'Man sieht unsern Vorfahren bis-

---

[1] 5th edn. pp. 273, 274, 320. [2] *Ibid.* p. 353. [3] 1st edn. p. 238.
[4] 5th edn. p. 372. [5] 1st edn. p. 311. [6] *Ibid.* pp. 138–9.
[7] *Ibid.* p. 221. [8] 5th edn. p. 312. [9] 1st edn. p. 279.

weilen nach, worinn man ihnen nicht nachahmen würde.'[1] He was, for instance, not prepared to accept Luther wholeheartedly as a grammatical model for the eighteenth century. In this he encountered opposition from his Leipzig colleagues J. F. Christ and J. G. Wachter;[2] and he was setting himself up against the authority of an earlier grammarian Johann Bödiker whose *Grundsätze der Deutschen Sprach* had appeared at Berlin in an enlarged edition, edited by J. G. Wippel, just two years before Gottsched published the first edition of his *Sprachkunst*.[3] The original edition had given Luther's Bible translation first place amongst linguistic authorities, but this new edition makes considerable concessions to the spirit of the 1740's, and recognised that the German language had changed considerably since the time of Luther.

Although he admired Luther's style, Gottsched considered Luther too remote from the eighteenth century to serve as a fit model, and found in him features of vocabulary, accidence and syntax which, from the point of view of Gottsched's contemporaries, were definitely obsolete. In this he was following up some remarks made by Leibniz in the *Unvorgreiffliche Gedanken*. Many of Luther's words were discarded as archaic in the *Beyträge*, and it was at Gottsched's instigation that Johann Leonhard Frisch in 1746 published his fifty quarto pages of archaic words, mostly still in use around 1700. Gottsched thought that verbal forms such as *du sollt, du willt* or *ich sahe*, found frequently in Luther's Bible, should not for that reason be considered correct. He called

---

[1] 5th edn. p. 512.

[2] J. F. Christ in *Villaticum* (Leipzig, 1746), and J. G. Wachter in the preface to the 1737 edition of *Glossarium Germanicum*. For the details see Jellinek, *Geschichte der nhd. Grammatik*, vol. I, pp. 223–7.

[3] Bödiker's work was first published in 1690 (at Cölln an der Spree) under the title *Grund-Sätze der Deutschen Sprachen*. In 1701 his son edited the work and published the revised edition under the title *Neu-vermehrte Grund-Sätze der Deutschen Sprachen*. This had a reprint in 1709. Then in 1723 a new edition, radically revised by Johann Leonhard Frisch, was published under the title *Grund-Sätze der Teutschen Sprache*. And finally the edition referred to above with the full title *Johann Bödikers Grundsäze Der Teutschen Sprache Mit Dessen eigenen und Johann Leonhard Frischens vollständigen Anmerkungen Durch neue Zusäze vermehret von Johann Jacob Wippel*.

THE STABILISATION OF THE LANGUAGE

them 'Überreste des Alterthums, die man zwar an Luthern, und unsern andern Vorfahren entschuldigen, aber nicht nachahmen muß'.[1] He also considered the position of the participle in a phrase from the Bible like 'Er ist wie ein Baum, *gepflanzet* an den Wasserbächen'[2] was no longer possible in German. Opitz too is not always held up as unimpeachable, for Gottsched shows how he confused *sich* and *ihm*,[3] and he considers that the use of the verb *tun* to form periphrastic tenses is old-fashioned, absurd and vulgar—despite the fact that Opitz still favoured it.[4] He also objects to Schottelius employing such a construction as *der großer Cicero*, and he comments: 'Dieses hat aber weder vor ihm jemand geschrieben, noch nach seiner Zeit nirgends Beyfall gefunden'[5] (itself a bad sentence which, in both its parts, is a definite overstatement). Gottsched disliked the use of *so* as a relative pronoun, because of its frequent occurrence also in its adverbial sense;[6] and yet this usage was hallowed by many if not all of the great writers of the past two centuries, and later in the *Sprachkunst* Gottsched himself advocated it as a legitimate variant to *der, die, das* and *welcher*.[7]

The principle of analogy is invoked to deal with the confusion between Dative Singular *dem* and *den* prevalent at this time,[8] and to prove that *gewesen* is correct but not *gewest*.[9] To this same 'analogy' (coupled with a natural conservatism) must be attributed Gottsched's insistence on *süßes*, and not *süßen, Weines*.[10] Gottsched is here supporting the logical and the older construction; but the new alternative had been establishing itself in

---

[1] 5th edn. p. 308. Early in the second volume of *Die Vernünfftigen Tadlerinnen*, Gottsched had referred to Luther as 'der erste gute Poet und Redner in Deutschland, der in seiner Muttersprache alle seine Vorgänger weit hinter sich gelassen hat'. He praises the *Sendbrief vom Dolmetschen*. But he goes on to say that the word-order and vocabulary of the Bible translation were now archaic.
[2] 5th edn. p. 483.   [3] *Ibid.* pp. 282–3.   [4] *Ibid.* p. 373.   [5] *Ibid.* p. 252.
[6] 1st edn. pp. 238–9; expanded in 5th edn. p. 290.
[7] 1st edn. p. 342; still there in the 5th edn.
[8] 'In Obersachsen, auch wohl im Reiche.' These words added in 5th edn. p. 166. See above, footnote to p. 55.   [9] 5th edn. p. 302.
[10] 1st edn. p. 208; 5th edn. p. 254. Gottsched returns to the point again on p. 341 of the first edition, when talking of something quite different: 'Voll guter Wissenschaft und unsträfliches Wandels; *nicht unsträflichen*.'

the early eighteenth century, although great uncertainty still prevailed. Hemmer in his *Abhandlung* of 1769 (see below, p. 144) considered the *süßen Weines* type as provincial.[1] It is interesting to find Goethe in 1825 writing almost apologetically: 'Ich kann mich der Flexion "kostlichen Sinnes" nicht entschlagen', but justifying himself by reference to Lessing's *Briefe antiquarischen Inhalts* (1768).[2] It was not until the nineteenth century that the weak declension prevailed in this construction which now presents a peculiar irregularity in the language. Gottsched's principle of analogy often led him to preserve words and phrases which, already at this time, were definitely archaic. Thus he recommends *kreuchst, kreucht, kreuch* as 'correct' forms of the present tense of the verb *kriechen*, although Meissen usage was against them. He justifies his preference by analogy with the vowel-alternation in the present tense of other strong verbs.[3] He writes *dreyʒig* on the analogy of the other decads.[4] He prefers *ich ward* on the grounds of analogy with other strong preterites, but admits *wurde* on the analogy of *würde*. This seems to have been a development in Gottsched's opinion; the fifth edition reads: '*Ich ward, oder wurde*' and then gives a footnote explaining his preference for *ward*; but the first edition had read '*ich wurde, oder ward*'.[5] The principle of analogy is here in conflict with itself. The most extraordinary example, however, was the attempt to establish that the

[1] *Abhandlung über die deutsche Sprache* (Mannheim, 1769), p. 157.
[2] Weimar ed., *Briefe*, XXXIX, p. 203. To C. W. Göttling on 28 May. The passage continues: 'sie [i.e. *die Flexion*] ist so in mein Wesen verwebt, daß ich sie, wo nicht für recht, doch mir gemäß achten muß. Ich habe mich besonnen wie dieser Eindruck in der frühsten Zeit bey mir entstanden seyn möchte und mir sind Lessings Briefe antiquarischen Inhalts eingefallen, auch noch verschiedene andere Beyspiele.' He hopes for enlightenment from Göttling on this point. Göttling's answer is said to be preserved in Goethe-Schiller Archiv, but is not included in the edition of this correspondence by Kuno Fischer (Munich, 1880).
[3] 1st edn. p. 271, 5th edn. p. 332. Dornblüth (see below) rejected these forms categorically, Adelung rejected them as Upper German. It is strange to come across the form *er geneußt* given as the third singular present indicative of *genießen* in the section on syntax (1st edn. p. 378) but *er genießt* in the section on prosody (1st edn. p. 478).
[4] 5th edn. p. 267. But the first edition had the spelling *dreyßig* (p. 219).
[5] 1st edn. p. 248; 5th edn. p. 306.

THE STABILISATION OF THE LANGUAGE

final -*e* should only occur in feminine nouns. This was Gottsched's answer to the fact of apocope, and he attempted to regulate the extremely complex situation by a rationalisation involving the principle of analogy. Faced with the fact that the language had innumerable masculine and neuter nouns in -*e*, he resorted to various devices in order to save his principle. For the masculines he gives some apocopated forms as 'correct' (*Both, Heyd, Schott, Schwed*) and wonders whether it would not be 'better' to write *Bub, Knab, Rab* and *Namen, Samen*.[1] With the neuters he will not countenance any other than apocopated forms (although he had defended the neuter -*e* earlier, in vol. II of the *Beyträge*).[2] Consequentially he cites amongst the feminines *die Bahne*, and he will not accept apocopated feminines like *Kron, Lieb, Gnad*. It must be *der Heyd* (heathen) but *die Heide* (heath). Gottsched's extreme rationalism in linguistic matters is demonstrated by his objection to the word *Achselträger* which, he says, is not a proper compound, because it does not mean a man who carries his shoulders (as the form indicates), but has a meaning which is not expressed by the addition of the two elements.[3] Similarly he will not allow that *Frauenzimmer* can denote an individual, because of its second element—although this meaning had been establishing itself since the early seventeenth century.[4] The word *nachher*, he says, is meaningless by its form; one should therefore use *hernach* or *nachmals*.[5] Sometimes Gottsched invents a rationalisation: faced by the fact that words in -*niß* (Upper German -*nuß*) were of feminine or neuter gender, Gottsched posited the rule that the feminine denotes the abstract and the neuter the concrete meaning. This still holds true with *Erkenntnis* which has double gender; but normally the modern standard language has established one gender for each word, mostly neuter.[6]

---

[1] 1st edn. p. 169.   [2] *Op. cit.* pp. 225 ff., against J. F. Christ.
[3] 5th edn. p. 181.
[4] 'Ein jegliches ehrbares frawenzimmer', Opitz, *Poeterei*, 1624 (Neudruck, ed. Braune, p. 15). And Gottsched uses it himself with this meaning later in the *Sprachkunst*! (1st edn. p. 360).   [5] 5th edn. p. 381 (not in 1st edn.).
[6] They were, according to Kåre Kaiser, predominantly feminine in Upper German, but neuter in Middle German. Gottsched's rule is stated in the *Beo*-

The third part of Gottsched's *Sprachkunst* embraces both word-formation and syntax. It begins by deprecating the cultivation of 'altfränkisch' and emphasising the advances made by the language since the time of Opitz. Indeed, the general attitude seems to be that the syntax of Gottsched's day was the best so far; but that it was not yet accepted by all provinces. This section of the *Sprachkunst* shows the same features as the earlier sections. More interesting than what Gottsched asserts, is what he attacks. Perhaps the most interesting parts are the footnotes to later editions, showing the objections voiced by others or solecisms which Gottsched himself had noticed. Thus he criticises a Meissen colloquialism: 'bey einer Haare'.[1] He objects to the use of the article with proper names, and considers a biblical example like: 'Aber Michal, Sauls Tochter, hatte *den* David lieb', as an archaism and its use by certain Low Saxon authors of his day as unjustified.[2] He objects to unnecessary substantivisation of adjectives[3] and, in the fifth edition, suggests that this new fashion is due to the influence of French. He thinks the 'new' phrases: *ein Mann von Stande, von Vermögen* may be of similar provenance, for to be justified in German they need a qualifying adjective.[4] He criticises those districts where one says: 'Er geht in *der* Kirche.'[5] He admires compound adjectives of measure like *fingerlang, federleicht, feuerheiß*[6] and similar compounds with *-reich, -voll* or *-arm* etc., but he warns against going too far in this, and producing words which are too outlandish. He mentions in this connection 'certain poets of the last century' and the way that Canitz had satirised them; but a footnote to the fifth edition[7] refers to the 'brood of these monstrous and clumsy words' invented by the

bachtungen (see below, p. 146): '*Erkenntniß*...heißt entweder (*subjective*) das Vermögen, etwas zu erkennen oder (*objective*) die Sache die man erkennet. Bedeutet es das erste: so hat es das dritte Geschlechtswort, *das Erkenntniß*. Hat es die letzte Bedeutung: so bekömmt es das zweyte Geschlechtswort, *die Erkenntniß*.' (Original edition, p. 96.)

[1] 1st edn. p. 361.   [2] 5th edn. p. 409.
[3] 1st edn. p. 346: 'Das Schöne, ist also unnütz, denn wir haben schon die Schönheit.'
[4] 5th edn. pp. 421, 434, 518.   [5] 1st edn. p. 352.
[6] 1st edn. p. 353.   [7] 5th edn. p. 428.

Zürich writers. He mentions the confusion between reflexive and personal pronoun in some districts, and repeats the assertion that Opitz sometimes erred in this matter; he censures the form *selbselbst* used by Opitz, although admitting the rather archaic pronominal forms *selbander*, *selbdritte* etc.[1] *Waser* he considers 'altväterisch': *Aus waser Macht thust du das?* should now be *Aus was für einer Macht thust du das?* It is incorrect to use *vor* in this construction, says Gottsched, and it is archaic to 'leave both out' —thus a phrase like: 'Was Schein, was Änderung doch würde diese Zeit ihm zeigen...' calls forth his comment: 'So redet und schreibt man nicht mehr zierlich.'[2] On the use of *so* as a relative, Gottsched admits it in this part of the work, but adds the comment, in the first edition: 'Doch thut man besser, wenn man dieses Wort nicht gar zu häufig brauchet,'—to which he adds, in the fifth edition, 'und entweder nur beym ungewissen Geschlechte [i.e. neuter] oder nach etlichen Wörtern von verschiedenen Geschlechtern'. He then, in both editions, adds the point he had made earlier that *so* occurs so frequently in its other use that its use as a relative might cause confusion or cacophony.[3] 'Altfränkisch' also are *jedermänniglich, männiglich*.[4] In the section on the syntax of the verb, he says that a genitive extension as in *er ist des Erbiethens* or *er ist treffliches Adels* would now be expressed quite differently, or with *von*.[5] The phrase *sich der Sache Meister machen* is incorrect (he makes no suggestion that this is archaic) and should be *sich zum Meister einer Sache machen*.[6] As regards the various constructions with *erinnern*: he approves *ich erinnere mich dessen*, he recognises that many people say *ich erinnere mich das* but does not like it, and he dislikes even more

---

[1] 1st edn. pp. 362–4.

[2] *Ibid.* p. 365. This peculiar form originated in the chancery language of the fifteenth century and was very widely used in the Middle German area during the sixteenth century. It was considered uncommon by Gueintz (1666) and Schottelius; but the phrase *aus waser Macht* (from Luther's Bible) had survived into the eighteenth century.

[3] 1st edn. p. 366; 5th edn. p. 441.

[4] 1st edn. p. 366; 5th edn. adds the observation that the 'Kanzellisten noch damit herumtummeln' (p. 442).

[5] 1st edn. p. 373.

[6] 5th edn. p. 449.

*ich erinnere mich daran.*¹ He chides various Northern dialects for saying: '*An wen* hast du das gesaget, gegeben' instead of using the dative.² The general confusion between dative and accusative in the north was satirised in the play *Der Witzling*, by Frau Gottsched in the sixth volume of *Die deutsche Schaubühne*.³ Upper Saxons were not free from such solecisms, says Gottsched. Later on he says, in a footnote to the fifth edition, that this point was the 'Shibboleth' on which Low Saxons give themselves away. They are also apt to say 'er geht *am Hofe, in der Kirche*' etc., and 'er ist *ins Haus*' and 'er fragt *nach mich*'.⁴ He defends the use of the double accusative with *lehren* against the incursion of the dative personal object.⁵ He conceives a clear distinction of meaning between the perfect and the preterite tense and censures 'certain districts' for not observing this; in the fifth edition he expressly states that the Upper Germans use the perfect tense for both.⁶ Another solecism of the Upper Germans was the declined predicative adjective, says Gottsched.⁷ In the section on auxiliary verbs he refers to certain 'Misbräuche des vorigen Jahrhunderts'. Auxiliary verbs were omitted, sometimes wrongly used.⁸ Gottsched considers that auxiliary verbs should not be omitted without 'dringende Noth, und erhebliche Ursache', otherwise this may lead to obscurity and cacophony. He demands the subject pronoun, and is against its omission in epistolary style. The seventeenth century had also confused the prefixes *ver-* and *vor-*;⁹ Gottsched wants a clear distinction, as he does also between *vor* and *für*, both as verbal prefixes and as prepositions.¹⁰ He objects to the phrase *von Alters her* on the grounds of analogy (*von* takes

---

¹ 1st edn. p. 375; expanded in 5th edn. p. 451.   ² 5th edn. p. 455.
³ This volume appeared in 1745, 2nd edn. 1750.
⁴ 5th edn. pp. 462–4, 469.   ⁵ 1st edn. p. 391.
⁶ 1st edn. p. 403; 5th edn. p. 479.   ⁷ 5th edn. p. 484.
⁸ 1st edn. pp. 412–13. *Hätte sagen würden* is described on p. 416 of the first edition as characteristic of the Mark; similarly, on p. 491 of the fifth edition as a 'märkischer Provinzialfehler' for *würde gesaget haben*.
⁹ 1st edn. p. 422.
¹⁰ *Ibid.* pp. 423–4; see also p. 432 of the same edition, where he rejects *fürnehm* and *fürtrefflich*. There is an article on this matter in the first volume of the *Beyträge* (pp. 130–6).

the dative).[1] He distinguishes between *gegen* and *wider*: 'Gegen heißt *erga*, wider *contra*'—*gegen* has a friendly meaning, *wider* expresses opposition, adding that Low Saxon writers made mistakes on this point.[2]

Dictatorial, pedantic, conservative—these are the epithets that might be used of Gottsched's *Sprachkunst*. They have been used to condemn his attitude to literature, and rightly so. For they connote qualities unconducive to the sensitive comprehension and interpretation of works of creative, individual imagination. But such qualities, in their positive manifestations, are valuable qualities in a grammarian. There is no doubt that the *Deutsche Sprachkunst* succeeded, for what it presents is in almost all respects the fundamental basis of the language of modern German literature. Where it differs, we find that Gottsched is usually clinging to some older usage and is disinclined to accept a linguistic feature of more recent appearance. His success was undoubtedly due in large measure to this cautiousness. But also to his intolerance. It was this magisterial tone which called forth attacks;[3] but it was this grandiose, dictatorial sureness which, in the long run, led to the acceptance of his standard German. He had worked himself into the position of an oracle; and the Germans were no longer eager to argue the case, they simply wanted to follow someone who spoke with conviction.

The immediate effect of this magisterial tone was, however, to provoke counterblasts. These were many and sometimes violent, but none succeeded in shaking the power of the Leipzig dictator in this sphere of his activity. They have been catalogued and, in part, examined by Gottsched's biographers. None of them is of any lasting importance in the history of the German language. One of them is, however, of considerable interest. It is also the fiercest. This is the *Observationes oder gründliche Anmerckungen über die Art und Weise eine gute Ubersetzung besonders in die teutsche*

---

[1] 1st edn. p. 430.   [2] 5th edn. p. 511.
[3] Bodmer, in an article in the second volume of *Der Mahler der Sitten* (Zürich, 1746), pp. 612 ff., tried to oppose the Saxon grammarians 'die mit ihrem Ansehen widerlegen, da sie es mit gründlichen Reden nicht können'.

Sprach zu machen with the subtitle: 'Nebst einer zu disem Vorhaben unentpärlichen *Critic* über Herrn Gottschedens sogenannte Redekunst, und teutsche *Grammatic* oder (wie er sie nennt) Grundlegung zur teutschen Sprache.' It was published at Augsburg in 1755, and its author was the Benedictine Father Augustin Dornblüth from Gengenbach on the Upper Rhine.[1]

The interest of this work is that it represents a flat denial of all that Gottsched stood for. It denies that his attitude to language was governed by the two complementary ideals of *Natur* and *Vernunft*. It claims that Gottsched, in his espousal of all that was new, neglected what was natural in the German language, for the natural was the long-established and Dornblüth's ideal is the chancery language of the seventeenth century. Gottsched claimed to be guided by *Vernunft* when he was merely being arbitrary: he had said that the monks with their barbaric Latin spoilt the German language, yet it was the monks who preserved medieval literature and Luther was a monk whose good German was 'vermutlich nicht erst nach seinem Abfall durch ein übernatürliches Liecht erlangt, sondern zuvor schon als Mönch erlernt'.[2] Gottsched's purported *Allgemeingültigkeit* was a ludicrous assertion; he did not appeal to all and he did not represent general linguistic usage. It was absurd to claim that the *Redekunst* would interest ordinary people, for they will lack the classical knowledge to follow the examples; therefore the work should have been written in Latin. The same argument is used against Gottsched's use of German expressions for Latin technical terms and for *Fremdwörter* in general. Children understand the technical terms of grammar, foreigners understand them; but Gottsched's glossary of his own terms shows that he expected people not to understand them. Gottsched's claim to represent general usage was both preposterous and presumptuous; his 'High German' forms were

[1] I quote from the copy of the original edition in the British Museum. For a fuller account of Dornblüth, see my article, 'The Observations of Father Dornblüth', *MLR*, L (1955), pp. 450–63.

[2] *Op. cit.* p. 60. He mocks at Luther's 'hocherbauliche Tischreden' (p. 102) and commends Gottsched's disapproving remarks on Luther's language in the *Sprachkunst*.

often merely Saxonisms and there was no justification for asserting that Middle German forms like *er läuft* were 'better' than the corresponding Upper German forms without mutation.[1] Many of the meanings given to words by the Saxon writers do not, according to Dornblüth, represent general usage: for example *Handlungen*, he thinks, should mean 'transactions' and not 'actions'; *niederträchtig* is not a term of abuse but merely the opposite to *hochmütig*, and *Leydenschafft* means 'die Hölle, das Feegfeuer, oder ein mit lauter schmertzhafften Krancken angefülltes Spital'![2] He even questions whether Gottsched's usage always represents *cultured* usage, and his tenth chapter contains a list of 'barbarismi vitandi' culled from Gottsched on which figure *verhunzet, verworren,* and *bekommen* in the sense of 'to get'. The severest charge of all was that Gottsched had been misled by his admiration of the French language into the use of gallicisms of vocabulary, syntax and style. Thus *schmäcken* for *goûter* was a Saxon gallicism: the proper German expression is *versuchen, kosten* or (in another meaning) *gutheißen, gut befinden*.[3] The constructions represented by *welch ein Anblick*,[4] or *um* with the infinitive[5] are French but not German. Gottsched's German Grammar was not even German.

Dornblüth obviously realised that Gottsched's *Sprachkunst* had no firm theoretical foundations. His strongest point was the statement that there was no logical justification for saying that a Middle German form was *better* than an Upper German form. He ignored Gottsched's criterion of analogy, probably as unworthy of mention. He saw no logical reason for rejecting any word or construction which was current in his own literary traditions. One could of course turn his own argument against himself and say there was no logical reason to suggest that an Upper German form was better than a Middle German form. Dornblüth would probably agree; but it was not solely the claims of Meissen to legislate for all Germany which annoyed him. He did believe in

---

[1] *Op. cit.* p. 324. Dornblüth, of course, has the spelling *läufft*.
[2] *Ibid.* pp. 80, 12, 23.   [3] *Ibid.* p. 128.
[4] *Ibid.* p. 84.   [5] *Ibid.* pp. 211–12.

the superiority of Upper German. For one thing there was its literary tradition and the prestige given to it by the Habsburg Chancery; then there was the belief that Upper German was more German whereas Saxon was grossly Frenchified; and finally there is the suggestion that Dornblüth, like Bodmer, thought Upper German was more expressive, powerful and manly, for he defends the old incapsulated periodic sentence because it is a means 'denen Worten eine mehrere und eindringende Krafft zu geben';[1] and he says of Gottsched's style that it has not only nothing graceful or stately about it, 'sondern sogar nicht einmahl etwas natürliches, *mannliches oder ernsthafftes* [my italics]....Wegen seinem Franzößlen, komt alles heraus, als wan er immer schertzete.'[2] The first of these arguments could be countered by both an older and a more recent literary tradition, the second involved a sentimentality and really convinced nobody, the third had to prove itself by example. And this is where Dornblüth, like Bodmer, failed. The language they wrote in was too much out of step with recent literary practice, too lacking in standardisation, too unformulated to command approval. And there was no personality like Gottsched to win favour for its cause.

The language of Dornblüth's *Observationes* now appears so archaic that it is difficult to imagine its being published in the very middle of the eighteenth century and only twenty years before Goethe went to Weimar. But this merely reveals the completeness and magnitude of Gottsched's success, for Ewald Boucke has shown that, apart from certain oddities, it corresponds in almost all features to the language of Upper German works emanating from southern German presses in the first half of the century.[3] The very title-page, with its long, involved title has an archaic appearance and the Preface begins with a period of twenty-two lines' length. Both spelling and morphology appear

---

[1] See p. 217. [2] See pp. 350–1.
[3] Ewald Boucke, *P. Augustin Dornblüths Observationes* (Munich, 1895), pp. 20–7. These works are mostly translations. There were no Upper German authors of any quality during this period—except for the Swiss. This is perhaps a significant fact. On this matter, see my article on 'The *Parnassus Boicus* and the German Language', *GLL*, N.S., VII, no. 2 (January 1954).

fantastically archaic to us, and it is interesting to conjecture what Modern German would have been like if Luther and Gottsched had not won the day for East Middle German. An entirely different *Schriftsprache* would have resulted. For Dornblüth represents a very late and very obstinate assertion of the ideal of the southern *Gemeinsprache*. In many respects his language is closer to the chancery of Maximilian than to his own day. It is full of features expressly rejected by Gottsched, features characteristic of the southern *Kanzleisprache*, some of which are medieval survivals, some not. Thus he insists on the adverbial *-en* termination, stating categorically that *schließlich* is adjective and *schließlichen* is adverb.[1] He uses the forms *sie seind, ich siehe, ich hilff, er seye*, and plural *die Wort*. Nomina agentis in *-er* take a plural *-e* (*die Übersetzere, die Zeitungsschreibere*) which perpetuates an older dialectal feature, although Schottelius had accepted such forms as standard. Very odd is the assertion that the Saxons fail to distinguish between the indicative and the subjunctive mood of the 'imperfect', for to *scheinen* there is *er schien(e)* (indicative) and *er scheinete* (subjunctive), and with a weak verb there is a distinction between *forderte* (indicative) and *forderete* (subjunctive).[2] This theory seems to be Dornblüth's own invention, for no such distinction is regularly observed in Upper German of this period; but it represents an interesting attempt at superimposed rationalisation to justify competing forms. It also shows how necessary it was for Gottsched to combat a form like *scheinete*. For what seems to us nowadays an illiterate or ludicrous solecism, was a current form accepted in parts of Germany in Gottsched's day. This example demonstrates the value to us of the *Observationes* as a commentary on the *Sprachkunst*.

No one seems to have supported Dornblüth against Gottsched, and the periodicals either ignored his work or laughed at it. Meanwhile there were many outside of Saxony who sympathised with Gottsched's purpose. Prominent amongst these were Ignaz Weitenauer from Baden, J. J. Hemmer in the Palatinate and H. B. Braun in Bavaria. Weitenauer was Professor of Hebrew

[1] See p. 62.   [2] See pp. 225–6 and elsewhere.

and Greek at the University of Innsbruck. He published in 1764 an essay entitled *Zweifel von der deutschen Sprache*.¹ In his preface he, like so many of his contemporaries, points to the similarity of the Greek to the German language, saying that both have a variety of dialects, that German combines 'den feinen Witz der Athenienser, und die mannhafte Großmuth der Lacedämonier', but whereas the Greeks accepted all dialects as justified variants, he thinks that there should be agreement between the German dialects on essential elements of the language. The pamphlet is directed against those who, like Bodmer or Dornblüth, supported particularism. However varied pronunciation may be, there must be one agreed orthography, says Weitenauer. He characterises the contemporary conflict as follows:

> Eine Seite Deutschlands hat sich eine geraume Zeit her beflissen die Muttersprache zu mildern, und durch Beysetzung einer großen Anzahl leichter Sylben dieselbe gelinder zu machen. Die andere Seite ist bey der alten Strengheit geblieben, und hat sich nicht entschließen wollen, die kurzen Wörter ihrer Vorfahren zu verlängern.²

He calls these two factions 'die Strengen' and 'die Gelinden', mocks at the opinion expressed by 'die Strengen' that 'das vielfältige E thut den Ohren weh, und entkräftet das alte Heldendeutsch mit seinem unangenehmen Singen'³ (in which his ironic use of the epithet 'heroic' is entirely in the spirit of Gottsched) and points out that this argument, if driven to its logical conclusion, would make the language too monosyllabic and very harsh—and foreigners complained already of its harshness. He uses Gottsched's examples and sometimes quotes his words. He is entirely on the side of *die Gelinden*.⁴ Johann Jakob Hemmer was a meteorologist of European repute, a convinced supporter of the lightning-conductor. He also published several works on the German language, notably an *Abhandlung über die deutsche Sprache* (Mannheim, 1769) and a *Deutsche Sprachlehre für die Pfalz* (Mannheim, 1775).⁵ The *Abhandlung* says that the Germans have

---
¹ Copy in the British Museum. It was published at Augsburg and Freiburg.
² See pp. 13–14.   ³ See p. 25.
⁴ But he defends *meine geehrte Leser* (p. 54).
⁵ There is a copy of the *Abhandlung* in the British Museum.

laboured for nine hundred years to improve their language, but have not brought it to a state of perfection comparable to that of other languages. The work proceeds immediately to praise of Gottsched and the Saxons, saying that other provinces (notably Austria and Bavaria) were removing 'die Rauhigkeit und alte Barbarey ihrer Sprache', but not the Palatinate.[1] Yet a language possessed of 'Deutlichkeit und Nachdruck' is essential to the spread of arts and sciences; and Hemmer laments the neglect of the German language both in the pulpit and in the classroom. Palatinate books and documents, and the speech of her court, army, clergy and even of the ordinary people were riddled with unnecessary French words. This 'verdunkelt den majestätischen Glanz unserer Heldensprache' ('heroic' used this time as a term of approval!).[2] Hemmer draws attention to Palatinate provincialisms in orthography, morphology and syntax. Many of them are solecisms mentioned by Gottsched in the *Sprachkunst*. Hemmer's principles and his canons are, in every case, those of Gottsched.[3] Heinrich Braun, whose work is referred to by Hemmer, was the well-known champion of elementary school education in Bavaria. He published a number of works on linguistic matters, all of which are closely modelled on Gottsched's strictures. Amongst them were *Anleitung zur deutschen Sprachkunst* (Munich, 1765), a *Redekunst* (Munich, 1765) and a *Deutschorthographisches Wörterbuch* (Munich, 1767).

Gottsched replied to Dornblüth first with various references in his periodical *Das Neueste aus der anmuthigen Gelehrsamkeit*,[4] and then with his *Beobachtungen über den Gebrauch und Misbrauch vieler deutscher Wörter und Redensarten* (Strassburg and Leipzig, 1758),[5] where he expressly refers to Dornblüth in the Preface:

[1] *Op. cit.* pp. 7–8.   [2] *Op. cit.* p. 76.
[3] But he differs on some details, e.g. he defends the spelling *bässer* on analogy with *baß*. Unfortunately he thinks *unbäßlich* (*unpäßlich*) is related! (p. 105).
[4] For example, vol. v, pp. 527 ff. (ironical in tone) and pp. 612 ff. (more serious, suggesting that Catholics must no doubt distinguish themselves from heretics by language), and vol. vi, pp. 126 ff. (Copy in the British Museum.)
[5] There is no copy of this work in the British Museum, but I have used the copies in the University Library of Basle and the Central Library of Zürich. Since I composed this chapter and the next, the *Beobachtungen* have become easily

'Was sollte man', says Gottsched, 'auch einem Manne antworten, der mir Wörter und Redensarten zur Last leget, die seit hundert und mehr Jahren, ehe ich gebohren worden, in den besten Büchern gestanden; ja nicht nur in Sachsen, sondern auch in Bayern und Schwaben längst geschrieben worden.' Gottsched is defending himself against Dornblüth's charge that he only accepted what was new and what was Saxon. He suggests that Dornblüth was badly read both in the older authors and in the new Saxon authors. He charges him with Catholic prejudice, and now defends Luther: 'Vieles ist durch die Folge der Zeit, bey ihm und andern zeitverwandten Schriftstellern, veraltet: vieles aber ist auch bis auf diese Stunde gut, brauchbar, und nachahmungswürdig geblieben.' It was merely a question of discrimination. The *Beobachtungen* deals with individual points of Upper German usage (with occasional references to the errors of Middle and Low German) and is arranged like a small dictionary. It is inspired, as Gottsched admits, by works like the Abbé Girard's *Synonymes françois*.[1] Gottsched upholds the same overriding principles as in the *Sprachkunst*:

Wem meine Vorschläge nicht gefallen...der behält seine alte Freyheit, auch ohne Regel und Ordnung zu reden, und zu schreiben. Denn wer kann solche Leute zwingen, die nicht aus eigenem Triebe der *Vernunft*, der *Sprachähnlichkeit*, und dem *guten Gebrauche der besten Schriftsteller*, folgen wollen.[2]

The somewhat protesting tone is the result of criticism; and the omission of any reference to Meissen may well indicate that this was no longer necessary.

This eighteenth-century German Fowler—for that is what it is—is a veritable mine of information on the language of the day. It is interesting to learn that, for Gottsched, *niederschreiben* was a new-fangled variant for *aufschreiben*, *pflegen* was strong in the

---

available in a reprint with extensive commentary by J. H. Slangen (Utrecht Litt.D. thesis, in German) (Heerlen, 1955). See my review in *MLR*, LI (1956), pp. 611–12.

[1] 1st ed. published 1718 under the title *Justesse de la langue françoise*. It introduced the distinction between 'principal' meaning and 'accessory' meanings. The third edition of 1740 had the title *Synonymes françois*.

[2] Vorrede; my italics.

meaning of 'to be accustomed' but weak when it meant 'to nurse', that there was confusion current between *Vorsicht* and *Vorsehung* and that Günther may have set the fashion, that the use of *Vorwurf* in the meaning 'subject' (*Vorwurf einer Dichtung*, still used today) was vulgar, that *Auswahl* was 'ein neugebackenes Wort, um eine Elite zu sagen' and the best expression was *Ausbund*, that *eingestehen*, *Eingeständniß* are bad words because the *ein-* is tautological, or that *zuverläßig* is incorrect because one does not say 'darauf ist sich zuverlassen'.[1] Such erroneous expressions might well be found in writers from all areas. But there were also characteristic Upper German solecisms. Amongst these Gottsched mentions *in Betrachtung einer Stadt* (for *bey dem Anblicke*); the plural *Beiner*; the confusion of *beysammen* (*seyn*) with *zusammen* (*kommen*), between *sammeln* (inanimate things) and *versammeln* (animate beings), between *erwachsen* and *gewachsen*; the use of *preisen* to mean 'zieren', and of *tapfer* in a sense close to that of the word *brav* in twentieth-century German; and the form *auferbaulich*. But he also mentions the Low Saxon confusion between *zu Hause* and *nach Hause*, and its false preterite *ich jug* (from *jagen*). *Gelächter aufschlagen* is censured as a Meissen provincialism; so too is a peculiar use of *beginnen* meaning 'to behave, show oneself' as in *er beginnet seiner sehr närrisch* or *er beginnet seiner auf eine närrische Art*.

Throughout the work there are scattered replies to many of the objections raised by Dornblüth. It defends the use of *Gegenstand* for *objectum* against Dornblüth's assertion that it means *oppositum*, the words *Zueignungsschrift* (as against *Übergabsschrift*),

---

[1] I do not give page-references because the book is alphabetically arranged and has a good index. In some of these judgments (*Vorwurf*, *Auswahl*, *eingestehen*, *zuverläßig*) Gottsched has not carried the day. In the example of *niederschreiben* we find Adelung in 1778 and Heynatz (*Versuch eines Deutschen Antibarbarus*) in 1790 already disagreeing with him (see Slangen, *op. cit.* p. 321). His distinction between strong and weak use of *pflegen* seems individual and has no historical justification (see Slangen, p. 331). On the whole Gottsched appears conservative in his strictures on vocabulary ('Eine *Auswahl* treffen ist vollends nicht gut. Warum nicht wählen, eine Wahl treffen, oder vornehmen? Man muß nicht unnütze Neuerungen machen') with a rationalistic attitude to word-formation (*eingestehen*; *zuverläßig*) which eschews metaphor (see below, p. 173).

Dichtkunst (for *Poesie*; or, in a different meaning, *Verskunst*), *Erlaucht, Gelehrigkeit* and *Gelehrsamkeit* (which are not the same), *Geschmack* in a metaphorical sense and *Weibsstück* with depreciatory force. It criticises Dornblüth's adverbs in *-en*, reminds him (*à propos* of *verwirren*) that some verbs can be declined weak and strong with a distinction of meaning, and expresses in round terms his extreme disapproval of the seventeenth-century chancery language. This last point is repeatedly emphasised.

It is in this stylistic opposition—for and against the *Kanzleisprache* and its complex periods—that this significant polemic culminates. And we must now turn our attentions back to the development of prose style. For having, in *Die Vernünfftigen Tadlerinnen* and *Der Biedermann*, given a practical demonstration of how the German language could be used in a light, graceful manner Gottsched had turned his attentions to the theoretical task of establishing principles to benefit the general development of German prose style.

V

THE THEORY OF PROSE STYLE

WHEN invited to contribute to the *Discourse der Mahlern*, Daniel Rodolph, priest at Gränichen in the Swiss canton of the Aargau, declined on the following grounds:

La langue allemande n'est pas un plat propre à servir des mets delicieux. Tout y est dabord froid, et l'on est continuellement occupé à crier au rechaut. Cette langue ne souffre pas le masque, elle ne se laisse pas plier, elle est roide. Elle ne sauroit monter pour le sublime, ni descendre pour le naturel, ni s'insinuer pour le plaisant, sans une affectation continuelle et *obtorto collo*. Point de proportion, semblable à un garçon, der auff Stelzen geht. Der muß sich auff seine Stelzen richten; nit auff d'leüt, denen Er das Stelzen-spectacul gibt.[1]

The implication was that German, in 1720, was vastly inferior to French as a medium of expression. Let us note the detailed charges: it was inflexible, invariable and incapable of being either sublime or natural without becoming artificial and affected.

In the introduction to his celebrated history of eighteenth-century literature, Hermann Hettner described the artistic achievement of the German eighteenth century as 'die Eroberung eines idealen und doch volkstümlichen Stils'. The sixteenth century had produced a style that was *volkstümlich* enough but nothing more. One side of the seventeenth century had developed a consciously artistic style, striving towards the greatest intensity of expression and as far away as possible from the *volkstümlich*. The same century had also seen the emergence of a counter-current demanding naturalness, which had reached farthest in Christian Weise's injunction: 'die Sachen also vorbringen, wie sie naturell und ungezwungen sind, sonst verlören sie alle grâce, so künstlich, als sie abgefaßt werden'. It was the achievement of

---

[1] *Chronick der Gesellschaft der Mahler*, Beilage XVII.

the first half of the eighteenth century to produce a prose style which avoided the excesses of both these tendencies. It lay between the too rhetorical and the too ordinary. It was a plain, lucid style avoiding both flatness and extravagance.

The revival of interest in Latin prose at the time of the Renaissance had led in some countries—notably in England and in France—to the development of two distinct types of prose style. The one was Ciceronian and formed the basis of the chancery language of Europe. It was an involved, periodic style representing the climax of antique rhetoric. The other came in as a reaction against Ciceronian style and was based on the style of Seneca. It shows two types both of which represent a disavowal of Ciceronian features. There was a 'loose' manner which disdained elaborate structure, and a 'curt' manner which eschewed long sentences and favoured *sententiae*. The Ciceronian style has careful symmetry with elaborate connections. The Senecan style has either short clauses built into large sentences with slight, informal connections (in the 'loose' manner), or no connection at all and short crisp sentences (in the 'curt' manner). Bacon in *The Advancement of Learning*, looking back to the predominantly Ciceronian age of Ascham, talks of men hunting after 'the choiceness of the phrase, and the round and clean composition of the sentence, and the sweet falling of the clauses, and the varying and illustration of their works with tropes and figures'; and Fuller admires Seneca for his 'pure, plain and full style'. But Shaftesbury, although admiring the fine sentiments in Seneca, found that he had expressed them 'with little or no coherence, without a shape or body to his work, without a real beginning, a middle or an end'. In short the Ciceronians objected that Seneca neglected form for content, whereas the Senecans objected that Cicero neglected content for form. 'Short-lung'd Seneca' (Cowley) and 'wordy Tully' (Cornwallis) are characteristic descriptions by each side of the other. In general the Ciceronian style seems to predominate in the sixteenth century and the Senecan (in both manners) in the seventeenth. But in Germany it would seem that Ciceronianism lasted longer. This was noticed outside of Germany and this is what Fontenelle meant when he wrote in a letter to Gottsched, dated 24 July 1728: 'Une chose plus considerable et que i'entens reprocher a votre Langue, quoique ce soit plustost la faute des Ecrivains, c'est que uos frases sont souuent extrémement longues, que le tour en est fort embarrassé, le sens longtemps suspendu et confus.'[1] Some of the movements which elsewhere helped to create the taste for a plainer style (Cartesianism, puritanism, the production of scientific works in the vernacular) hardly touch the German seventeenth century. Their force is, however, to be felt quite strongly in the first half of the eighteenth century.[2]

Cicero's ghost haunts most discussions of prose style in Germany at the beginning of the eighteenth century. Sometimes it actually materialises in his own particular formulation of the three characters of style. This doctrine is found in both Cicero and Quintilian. The basic distinction is between a grand style, a middle style and a plain style. It is not known who first advanced this formulation, but a distinction between philosophical and rhetorical style is attributed to Theophrastus. 'The plain style', suggests G. L. Hendrickson,[3] 'is due to the demand, originating with the philosophers, for a more exact and logical system of argument, while the so-called grand style is rhetoric itself in the original conception of it as ψυχαγωγία' (that is, the winning of men's souls). The middle style seems to have come into being as a

---

[1] As quoted in T. W. Danzel, *Gottsched und seine Zeit* (Leipzig, 1848), p. 88.

[2] A great deal has been written of late years on the distinction between Ciceronian and Senecan (sometimes also called Attic) prose in modern literature. I would refer the reader particularly to: G. Highet, *The Classical Tradition* (Oxford, 1949); F. P. Wilson, *Elizabethan and Jacobean* (Oxford, 1945); M. W. Croll, 'The Baroque Style in Prose' in *Studies in English Philology in Honor of Frederick Klaeber* (Minneapolis, 1929), pp. 427–56 and, by the same author, 'Attic Prose in the Seventeenth Century', *Studies in Philology*, XVIII (1921), pp. 79–128; G. Williamson, 'Senecan Style in the Seventeenth Century', *Philological Quarterly*, XV (1936), pp. 321–51 and the same author's *The Senecan Amble* (London, 1951).

[3] 'The Origin and Meaning of the Ancient Characters of Style', *American Journal of Philology*, XXVI (1905), p. 267. See also the same author's article; 'The Peripatetic Mean of Style and the Three Stylistic Characters', *ibid.* XXV (1904), pp. 125–47.

tertium quid between these two essentially rival styles. It is in Cicero's *Orator* that the three styles are most clearly delineated. The plain style is for instruction and suits the philosopher, it does not aim at charm or ornament, it is more concerned with the thought than the word. The grand style is the style of true eloquence, it is the emotional style, the style to move men. The middle style is to delight; it will keep an even tenor, be easy and smoothly flowing, with only a moderate use of figures of speech. *Subtile in probando, modicum in delectando, vehemens in flectendo*, is Cicero's summary. The Middle Ages adopted these Ciceronian categories. St Augustine uses a similar triad of verbs in an important passage on style ('... ut doceat, ut delectat, ut flectat ...'), pointing out that the plain style need not necessarily be simple.[1] It is the style of argumentative, dialectic prose. Thus St Paul's Epistles are, for him, in plain style. Behind the classical doctrine of the three characters there had lain the basic principle that subject-matter should condition style. St Augustine preserved this principle paradoxically, maintaining that in Christianity the highest mysteries express themselves in plain style and the simplest everyday experiences take on a grand style. Erich Auerbach considers this tantamount to removing the foundations of the whole doctrine.[2] But this is surely wrong; Augustine is still preserving the basic principle that subject-matter conditions style. E. R. Curtius has pointed out that the rigid doctrine of the three characters was essentially Cicero's, for even Quintilian, who is his close follower in stylistics, admitted overlapping and continuation of styles, whereas Demetrius distinguished four styles and Hermogenes seven. It was in the form of the Ciceronian triad that the doctrine survived into modern times.[3] It would seem from the material collated by Curtius that the doctrine of the three characters was not rigidly maintained during the Middle

---

[1] *De Doctrina Christiana*, Book IV, ed. Migne, pp. 27 ff.
[2] E. Auerbach, 'Sermo humilis', *Romanische Forschungen*, LXIV (1952), p. 313.
[3] E. R. Curtius, 'Die Lehre von den drei Stilen in Altertum und Mittelalter', *Romanische Forschungen*, LXIV (1952), pp. 57–70 (a criticism of certain assumptions in Erich Auerbach, *Mimesis*, Berne, 1946).

Ages. But it was received in Renaissance times as part of the revival of interest in Cicero. It is from Renaissance poetics that it found its way into Germany.

We find it quite clearly stated as soon as Germans begin to think about literary style at all. Thus Martin Opitz has a division between what he calls a 'hohe', 'mittele oder gleiche' and 'niedrige art zue reden'. He seems to have taken his terminology from Scaliger who distinguished between: (1) *altiloqua*, (2) *media, quam aequabilem vocare liceat nobis* and (3) *infima forma*. The ancient triad often lies behind an apparently different scheme of arrangement. Thus Christian Weise in his *Curiöse Gedancken von Deutschen Briefen* (1691) distinguishes four styles: political, sententious, high and poetic. But the last means either composed in verses or excessively figurative. The basic division is therefore still threefold and coincides roughly with the Ciceronian characters, the high style being distinguished by floridity, the sententious by abruptness, the political by fluidity. Weise tends to think of the sententious style as Senecan and the political style as Ciceronian in build; and hence the model for his 'political' style—the style of polite intercourse—is the court chancery. This is hardly 'plain style' in the old sense. But it is thinking conducted with the old Ciceronian categories.

The same Ciceronian triad is still to be found in Gottsched's treatise on rhetoric. Rhetoric (*Redekunst*) and Poetics (*Dichtkunst*) are clearly distinguished at this time; Rhetoric deals with the composition of prose and Poetics with poetry.[1] Gottsched's treatise was first published in 1729 under the title *Grundriß zu einer Vernunfftmäßigen Redekunst*. It then appeared in a revised and enlarged form of 1736 as the *Ausführliche Redekunst*. It is mostly with this larger version of the work that we shall concern ourselves, since it usually presents the same material in better form, but the *Grundriß* will be quoted when there are significant

---

[1] E.g.: 'Die Poesie ist eine Kunst, etwas in gebundnen, wie die *Rhetoric* in ungebundnen Worten vorzustellen' (Gottlieb Stolle, *Kurtze Anleitung zur Historie der Gelahrheit* (Halle, 1718), p. 208). The distinction between rhetoric and grammar is also quite clear: 'Die *Grammatic* lehret reine, die *Rhetoric* aber zierlich reden und schreiben' (*ibid.* p. 169. British Museum copy).

differences between the two.[1] At the climax of the work a distinction is made between three kinds of style: *natürlich, sinnreich* and *bewegend* (or *beweglich*); Gottsched says that he prefers these terms to the distinction of *niedrige—mittlere—erhabene* (*Schreibart*), because, he says, it is difficult to draw the line between *niedrig* and *niederträchtig*, and between *erhaben* and *hochtrabend*. Nevertheless Gottsched's three terms represent essentially the Ciceronian triad. *Natürlich* style is simple straightforward style unadorned by figures of speech, eschewing all artifice and running easily and clearly. The *sinnreich* style is more artificial, proceeding from wit and expressing itself succinctly, the clauses connected more by ideas than by words. The *beweglich* style is the language of emotions working on the emotions: 'Sie redet nicht so wohl, sondern sie donnert und blitzet vielmehr und setzt also die Leute in Verwunderung' says the *Grundriß* and admits that figures of speech are proper in this style. The *Redekunst* tones down the description of this style: for Gottsched, as we shall see, became more and more opposed to grand style. The *Redekunst* is prefaced by a history of rhetoric, showing how this art has always decayed when it has lost sight of its true function and become too conscious of itself as an art-form. Of the ancients it is Cicero whom Gottsched most admired. Of the moderns it is Opitz. Since his time rhetoric had decayed. Lohenstein and Ziegler were too bombastic, Pufendorf and Ziegler too fond of foreign words.

---

[1] The title-page of the *Grundriß* bears the date 1729, but the dedication is dated 6 October 1728. Perhaps this is why Goedeke (and others following him) give the date as 1728. It was published at Hanover. There is no copy in the British Museum, but I was able to consult one in the library of the Deutsches Seminar at the University of Göttingen, thanks to the kindness of Professor Wolfgang Kayser. Of the *Ausführliche Redekunst* I used the copy of the 1736 edition in the Technische Hochschule at Zürich, but subsequently discovered other copies, one in the Germanic Institute of the University of London. The British Museum has only the fifth edition of 1759. An abridgement for use in university classes appeared in 1759 under the title *Akademische Redekunst*.

The position of Gottsched's *Redekunst* in the history of rhetoric has been considered by Gerhard Wechsler, *Johann Christoph Gottscheds Rhetorik* (Diss. Heidelberg, 1933); its position with relation to German stylistic manuals of the preceding sixty years by Ulrich Wendland, *Die Theoretiker und Theorien der sogenannten galanten Stilepoche* (Leipzig, 1930). See below, p. 159.

Approbation is given to Canitz, Besser and Thomasius; but Christian Weise is completely discredited. We are told that he lacked knowledge of the Ancients and wrote in a hotch-potch of German and foreign phrases, doing more harm than good—for he invented his own style which was not even suited to schoolboys, let alone to men of serious disposition. Yet most rhetoricians seem to have followed in the wake of Lohenstein or of Weise, and both were lamentable as stylistic models. To use the terms (quoted above) used by Gottsched later in the *Redekunst*, it could be said that he considered Lohenstein as having overstepped the line between *erhaben* and *hochtrabend*, and Weise that between *niedrig* and *niederträchtig*. We should note this specification of the Scylla and the Charybdis. For it is the key to the development of prose style, and narrative style in particular, during the first half of the century.

Let us pause for a moment in our consideration of Gottsched's treatise in order to illustrate his point by a demonstration of these two extremes. Here is Lohenstein at his most *hochtrabend*, introducing his hero to the reader:

Hochgeneigter Leser,

HIer stellet sich, unser vor etlichen Jahren gethanen Vertröstung nach, nunmehr der Großmüthige A r m i n i u s auf den Schau-Platz der Welt. Er suchet bey denen Sieg-prangenden Helden dieser Zeit günstige Erlaubnüs, Ihm einen Eintritt in dero Rüst-Kammern zu verstatten; Und lebet der guten Hoffnung: ob Er gleich in der heutigen Kriegs-Kunst, so wol wegen Aenderung der Zeiten, als anderer Zufälle und Gelegenheiten sich nur unter derselben Schüler oder, Lehrlinge zehlen möchte, daß sie ihm dennoch nichts minder seinen theuererworbenen Lorber-Krantz, als auch eine Stelle in denen Ehren-Sälen unter anderer Helden-Bildern gönnen, und ihm den Nahmen eines hertzhafften Feldherrn deßwegen in keinen Zweifel ziehen werden; weil Er die Kriegs-Kunst und Staats-Klugheit zu seiner Zeit an dem Welt-gepriesenen Hofe des mächtigsten Kaysers A u g u s t u s, da die Krieg- und Friedens-Künste gleichsam mit einander umb den Vorzug kämpften, vollkommentlich erlernet, hernach aber bey Antretung seiner Regierung und obristen Feldhauptmannschafft in Deutschland, vor die Beschirmung der gleichsam in letzten Zügen liegenden Freyheit, gegen die stoltzen Römer höchst-rühmlich angewendet; ja nicht allein seinen bedrängten Lands-Leuten das schwere Joch der Römischen Dienstbarkeit, daran einige Römische Kayser so gar selbst einen Greuel gehabt, gäntzlich vom Halse gestreifft, andere deutsche Fürsten zu gleichmäßiger Heldenmüthiger Tapferkeit aufgemuntert, und wider die hochmüthigen Römer in Harnisch gebracht, sondern auch derogestalt siegen gelernet: daß das durch ihn geschwächte grosse Rom unterschiedliche mahl erzittert, Augusten sein Glücke zweifelhafft gemacht, und von derselben Zeit an das streitbare Deutschland vor unüberwindlich gehalten worden.[1]

And here is Christian Weise introducing one of his novels:

Hochwehrter Leser

DIeß Buch hat einen närrischen Titul, und ich halte wohl, daß mancher meinen wird, er wolle seine Narrheit daraus studiren. Doch es geht hier wie mit dem Apothecker Büchsen, die haben außwendig *Satyros* oder sonst Affengesichte angemahlt, inwendig aber haben sie Balsam oder andre köstliche Artzneyen verborgen. Es siehet närrisch aus, und wer es obenhin betrachtet, der meint, es sey ein neuer *Simplicissimus* oder sonst ein lederner Saalbader wieder auffgestanden. Allein was darhinter versteckt ist, möchte ich denenselben ins Hertz wünschen, die es bedürffen. Uber Fürsten und Herren haben andere gnug geklaget und geschrieben: hier finden die Leute ihren Text, die entweder nicht viel vornehmer sind, als ich, oder die zum wenigsten leiden müssen, da ich mich vor ihnen nicht entsetze. Den Leuten bin ich von Hertzen gut: daß aber etliche Laster so beschaffen sind, daß ich sie weder loben noch lieben kan, solches geht die Leute so eigentlich nicht an. Es ist auch keiner gemeint, als wer sichs annehmen will. Und diesem wünsch ich gut Glück zur Besserung, vielleicht wirckt diese Possierliche Apothecker-Büchse bey etlichen mehr, als wenn ich den *Catonem* mit grossen *Commentariis* hätte auflegen lassen.[2]

The mere juxtaposition of these two pieces should suffice to show what Gottsched was driving at. He has seen the situation truly and clearly, and he is to steer a middle course between the down-to-earth of Weise and the up-in-the-clouds of Lohenstein. It is a

[1] I have taken this passage from Kurt May's anthology *Deutsche Prosa im 18. Jahrhundert* (Berlin, 1937). It represents *Arminius* (Leipzig, 1689), b. 4. I have checked with the copy of the original edition in the British Museum.

[2] Christian Weise, *Die drey ärgsten Ertz-Narren* [no place], 1673. Quoted from Braune's reprint in the *Neudrucke* (Halle, 1878).

flat middle course taking few risks and courting no dangers. But it takes him, and others, to the destination for which they embarked. But now to return to the treatise. Gottsched says that all good style must be *deutlich, ordentlich, angenehm* and *nachdrücklich*, meaning by the last of these criteria (as we shall see later) probably little more than *elegantia*. This statement still shows the tradition of classical rhetoric. For Aristotle the only essential quality had been clarity; but his pupil Theophrastus added linguistic correctness (ἑλληνισμός), suitability (πρέπον) and ornament (κατασκευή or κόσμος). Gottsched deals first with the smallest units of style —words. These should be *verständlich*, that is 'generally comprehensible'; the good writer should avoid provincialisms, archaisms, foreign words, neologisms, technical terms and ambiguities. Words should be *ehrbar*, but also suited to the audience. They should be neither too old nor too new. On this point Gottsched shows an attitude of reasonable moderation. He would not reject all somewhat archaic words; if they are good words, he would prefer to increase their currency.[1] He makes fun of the neologising activity of the Fruchtbringende Gesellschaft and the Pegnitzschäfer; but is equally opposed to the excessive use of foreign words. Words should be more *ernsthaft* than *poßirlich*, more *wohlklingend* than *übelklingend*. Tropes are then listed and exemplified, there is an exhortation that they should be used sparingly, and there is an attack on bombast and those writers 'on stilts': '...die niemals natürlich denken oder schreiben; sondern lauter seltsame und ausschweifende Redensarten brauchen.... Kurz, sie reden ganz phantastisch, wenn sie am schönsten zu reden meynen; und wenn sie sich recht zierlich ausdrücken wollen, so sind alle ihre Sätze lauter Räthsel.'[2] Figures, says

[1] Cf. 'Denn ich schließe von unsern Reichthümern auch die alten Wörter nicht aus; ob sie gleich zuweilen von ausländischen, auch wohl ohne Noth neugeprägten einheimischen, verdrungen worden. Ich gestehe es gern, daß sie nicht alle brauchbar sind; weil man viele nicht mehr verstehen würde. Aber viele, ja die meisten, sind ohne ihre Schuld aus der Uebung gekommen, und verdieneten es gar wohl, wider in Schwang gebracht zu werden.' *Sprachkunst*, 5th edn. p. 64.
[2] *Redekunst*, pp. 254–5; cf. 'Alles auf Stelzen gehen; Alles hoch, verblümt, sinnreich und prächtig; oder vielmehr übersteigend, dunkel, schwülstig und hochtrabend klingen.' *Gesammelte Reden*, pp. 604–5. Written in 1728.

Gottsched later in the *Redekunst*, are the expression of passion, and are only justified if they have real emotional value. They therefore belong only to the grand style, and Gottsched is dealing essentially with what is middle style (although he never says so). For of the three this is the only style he really accepts for prose. The criterion of *reasonableness* should enable writers to avoid excesses and aberrations of the fancy and the imagination.

'Man fordere alle ihre Eingebungen vor den Richterstuhl der Vernunft...frage man auch, ob alle tropische Redensarten der Wahrheit, oder der Natur und Gewohnheit zu reden, gemäß sind; oder ob sie über die Schnur hauen.'[1] Amongst writers addicted to bombast he expressly mentions Lohenstein and Ziegler. He defines bombast as 'die falsche erhabene Schreibart' and distinguishes three kinds: lofty expression for lowly matter, bombastic (and not really lofty) expression for high matter, and lastly bombastic expression for lowly matter. 'Hauptsächlich entsteht die falsche Hoheit aus ungeheuren Vergrößerungen, aus unerhörten Gleichnißreden, oder Metaphoren, und Allegorien, aus wunderbaren auf ungewöhnliche Art zusammengesetzten Wörtern, und endlich aus überflüßigen Beywörtern.'[2] In the *Grundriß* the attack is more pointed. There is no value, says Gottsched, in memorising or collecting fine words in order 'auf bedürfenden Fall das magere Gerippe seiner Rede mit Lohensteinischen Purpur-Streifen zu behängen'. The absurdities of the bombastic style, he says, are produced in part by *excess* of metaphor or by conflicting metaphors, and he charges the *Discourse der Mahlern* with this fault.[3] He mentions with express disapproval compound epithets, 'sonderlich wenn sie neu oder gar zu künstlich sind, als z.E. ein flammen-schwangrer Dampf, ein Strahl-beschwänzter Blitz etc.' And as if it were not obvious whom he was attacking, he mentions names, including that of Lohenstein.[4]

The setting of Gottsched's *Redekunst* has been adequately explored by Ulrich Wendland in his investigation of stylistic

[1] *Redekunst*, pp. 329–30.   [2] *Ibid.* pp. 315–16.
[3] *Grundriß*, pp. 50, 57.
[4] *Ibid.* p. 60. The phrases are borrowed from a satire by Canitz, see below, p. 220.

manuals of the early eighteenth century.[1] Since then, some more information has been provided by Bruno Markwardt and others.[2] From these researches a somewhat complex picture emerges. There seems to have been a general feeling that the style of Lohenstein was hardly suited to express the intellectual climate of the new age. We find him acclaimed along with Hofmannswaldau; but neither of the two is advocated as a stylistic model. Thus Benjamin Neukirch, in the preface to his famous anthology of 1695, spoke of the 'liebliche, galante und verliebte schreib-art' of Hofmannswaldau and praised Lohenstein because of 'seines scharfsinnigen und spruchreichen, gelehrten styli'. But in another work, the *Anweisung zu Teutschen Briefen*, the same author warned against any attempt to copy Lohenstein's style: what was 'leicht, scharfsinnig und gelehrt' in Lohenstein would be 'abgeschmackt und pedantisch' in anyone lacking his skill. It was only later, when the full absurdity of imitating these styles had been seen, that there was any reference to *Schwulst* (e.g. in Johann Georg Hamann, *Poetisches Lexikon* (Leipzig, 1726)—and four later editions, the last in 1765). As Lohenstein became more and more associated with bombast, there was a revival of respect for Opitz, now heralded as the master of fine expression and good taste. Apart from this rather venerable authority, we find lip-service to Hans Sachs and less whole-hearted approval of Luther (considered archaic in many respects), while Thomasius and Morhof were respected as scholars rather than as writers. The attitude to Christian Weise is significant. He obviously embarrassed his age by his freshness, which was rather more than they wanted. Hence we find Erdmann Neumeister in his *Die Allerneueste Art, zur Reinen und Galanten Poesie zu gelangen* (written around 1700, first published and provided with this preface by Hunold, Hamburg, 1707) saying that Weise was successful in natural writing

---

[1] Ulrich Wendland, *Die Theoretiker und Theorien der sogenannten galanten Stilepoche und die deutsche Sprache* (Leipzig, 1930) (Form und Geist, vol. 17).

[2] Bruno Markwardt, *Geschichte der deutschen Poetik*, vol. I (Berlin and Leipzig, 1937). See also H. K. Kettler, *Baroque Tradition in the Literature of the German Enlightenment 1700–1750* (Cambridge, n.d. [1943]).

'und wenn allezeit der Geist des Hofmannswaldau oder Lohensteins hervor leuchtete, wolte man ihn unvergleichlich nennen'.[1] This would seem to imply that he had not enough 'style'. Indeed, complaints that he was too conversational and ordinary were frequent enough. This was still the basis of Gottsched's disapproval. Weise, he said on one occasion, had 'vielmahls gar zu natürlich geschrieben'.[2] Gradually a sharp distinction emerged between the followers of the Silesians and the followers of Christian Weise. Andreas Köhler (in 1734) spoke in terms of 'Weisianer' and 'Hoffmannswaldauer'; both had their good qualities, but they cultivated basically different styles.[3] A similar distinction was expressed negatively by C. F. Weichmann (in 1721): 'Jenen fehlet es an Feuer, ihre Gedanken gleichsam in rechten Fluß zu bringen; Diese aber sind wie ein wildes Pferd ohne tüchtigen Reuter, der es in seiner Hitze zu mässigen und auf dem rechten Wege zu halten wisse.'[4] The opposition applied primarily to verse and was based on Weise's demand for prose syntax in verse (see my seventh chapter). But it involved an opposition between grand style and plain style, or between *hochtrabend* and *niederträchtig*, according to the attitude of the observer.

The real 'natürliche und reine Art' was that cultivated by the French. Hence the widespread advocation of French as a stylistic model in these treatises of the early eighteenth century. It was recognised that Hofmannswaldau had successfully cultivated the 'liebliche Art' of the Italians and Lohenstein the 'scharff-sinnige, spruchreiche und gelehrte Art' of the Spaniards. But these were now past fashions. France held the cultural hegemony. Legion at this time were the translations into German of French manuals of letter-writing and of etiquette. But francomania began to fade

[1] The British Museum has the 1722 edition, in which this is on p. 57.
[2] *Critische Dichtkunst* (1730), p. 213.
[3] *Deutliche und gründliche Einleitung zu der reinen deutschen Poesie* (Halle, 1734), pp. 5 ff. and 68. He makes no distinction between the style of Lohenstein and that of Hofmannswaldau.
[4] Prefatory essay to the first part of Brockes's *Irdisches Vergnügen in Gott* (Hamburg, 1721), b. 2.

as the Germans became more sure of themselves. Hunold in 1716 is not so uncritical as before. Bouhours' contempt for Germany seems to have something to do with this, for it had awakened sharp opposition.[1] The admiration for France was often vague or even confused. We find Hunold (*Einleitung zur Teutschen Oratoria*, Hamburg, 1703) praising Boileau *and* Benserade, Neumeister in his Poetics recommending Scudéry *and* Boileau. In the *Querelle des Anciens et des Modernes*, although some ancient authors were still cited as good stylistic models (mostly Silver Latin, prominent amongst them Ovid, Longinus, Claudian, Martial and Ausonius), these German theorists usually took the side of the Moderns. Characteristic is an utterance like: 'Wir schätzen von den Lateinern nur diese Bücher hoch, die bey gelehrten Sachen keinen duncklen und verwirrenden Stylum führen.'[2] Another sign of the influence of France is the cult of letter-writing which set in. Voiture had said: 'Le sonnet m'a semblé fort beau et la lettre fort galante.' No wonder then that it should appeal to a Germany that prided itself on being, or trying to be, galant. Countless manuals of letter-writing appeared in the first decades of the century, most of them translated or imitated from the French and many of them enjoying rapid and repeated reprints. The letter became a serious literary form, and epistolography a serious scientific discipline.

All stylistic manuals of the time suffered under excessive classification. There was no understanding of the true nature and origin of style. There was no attempt whatsoever at formulating a philosophy of style. Style was something mechanical which could be divided up into points, each considered under its separate heading, with alternative solutions offered. Certain vaguely con-

---

[1] On Bouhours and his influence in Germany see (in *Deutschkundliches*, Fests. Panzer, Heidelberg, 1930) the article by Max von Waldberg entitled 'Eine deutsch-französische Literaturfehde', which is unfortunately marred by teutonic touchiness. See also Paul Böckmann's article 'Das Formprinzip des Witzes i.d. Frühzeit d. dt. Aufklärung', *Jb. d. Freien Dt. Hochstiftes*, Halle 1932–3, pp. 62–6 and his *Formgeschichte der dt. Dichtung*, Hamburg, 1949, vol. I, pp. 485 ff. On the general contempt for German amongst Frenchmen of Bouhours' day, see Paul Lévy, *La langue allemande en France*, vol. I, pp. 117 f. (Paris, n.d. [1951]).

[2] Hunold, *Oratoria*, 1703, Vorrede Bl. A 3b.

ceived ideals or general principles have been extracted by Wendland and Markwardt from their examination of these treatises.

Foremost amongst these would seem to be *Höflichkeit*. The Germans still had a widespread reputation for vulgarity and barbarism, and the manuals were anxious to counter this by advocating avoidance of the ordinary, common expressions. This, says Wendland, is the origin of the circumlocutions and polite periphrases so much advocated at this time, such as *meine Wenigkeit* for *ich*, or *Dero Diener* for *mich*. But some of the features he lists (such as omission of subject pronoun *ich*) had been features of chancery style for over a century. It would be truer to say that desire to avoid vulgarity strengthened the prestige of chancery style as well as leading to imitation of some of the more superficial aspects of French politeness. For it was not all new. Sesquipedalian politeness and lickspittle obsequiousness had characterised German official style for over a century. The falseness of this was realised; but many people preferred it to the outspoken roughness of Christian Weise, for they were anxious to cast off their reputation for barbarism.

There was a vague feeling that the style should suit the subject-matter. Decorum is one of the stylistic imponderables of the period, often mentioned but never defined. In some quarters we find an attempt to replace the three characters of style by more casuistical divisions according to the person addressed (rank, character, education, age) and to the situation and occasion of the address. Contemporary voices were raised against the pedantic scholasticism of this atomising classification, such as that of J. D. Longolius: 'Die Sachen, davon ein Stiliste redet, sind ja so unzehlig, und kan also in Ansehung derselben unmöglich eine genugsame Eintheilung des Styli erfunden werden' (*Einleitung zur gründlichen Erkäntniss einer ieden, insonderheit aber der teutschen Sprache*, Leipzig and Chemnitz, 1715).[1] But such outbursts were relatively rare. There was, however, general agreement that the style should remain constant (*aequal*) throughout the work. *Natürlichkeit = Vernünfftigkeit* was a much bandied slogan of the

[1] *Op. cit.* p. 156.

time and would seem to derive ultimately from diffused Boileau. Constant was the exhortation to appear *ungezwungen*, with constant reference to precept and example of the French.

And yet *elegantia* still remained the most vaunted ideal. Still—because it had been the supreme stylistic ideal of the Humanists. But *elegantia* for the early eighteenth century meant something purely external; it was often equated with *Nachdrücklichkeit*, by which was meant at this period not the connotation that Breitinger was later to give it (the forceful use of expressive language) but the use of stylistic figures to charm and delight the reader. This surface elegance was also known as *Zierlichkeit*. It involved such things as unexpected turns of phrase, *pointes*, word-play and bold connections of ideas. It was the German attempt to achieve something akin to French sophistication. This desire for surface brilliance influenced both theory and practice in Germany at this period. *Zierlichkeit*, conciseness and clarity were advocated as the prime rules of style by J. Hübner: 'Die Grundregeln sind diese: 1. Erwecke bey dem Leser eine Verwunderung. 2. Befleissige dich in allen Zeilen der Kürtze. 3. Und vermeide mit aller Sorgfalt Obscurität' (*Kurtze Fragen aus der Oratoria*, 2nd ed. Leipzig, 1706).[1]

Conciseness was an ideal more respected in theory than in practice. As an ideal it was in direct conflict with the conscious elaborateness of chancery style. But although the chancery style was still much in use in the early eighteenth century and still considered a justified model, theoretical objections to it were mounting (e.g. by A. N. Hübner in his *Gründliche Anweisung zum Deutschen Stilo*, Hanover, 1720). Benjamin Neukirch objected to certain aspects of the *Kanzleistilus*, notably (1) too many epithets; (2) excessive and false use of adjectives and participles; (3) unnecessary definitions, descriptions and encomia; (4) too many synonyms; (5) irrelevancies; (6) accumulation of subordinate clauses towards a monstrous conclusion; (7) unnecessary conjunctions and other links.[2] But he also objected to the 'gezwungene

---

[1] *Op. cit.* p. 327.
[2] *Anweisung zu Teutschen Briefen*, 6th edn. (Leipzig, 1745), pp. 510, 532–45.

Kürtze der construction' affected by business-men. Two extremes were to be avoided, the long-winded and the short-winded. Or, in other terms, the Ciceronian and the 'curt' form of Senecan. What eventually remains is the 'loose' manner of Senecan style and it is this that German develops.

Linkage was another subject much referred to, usually under the name of *connexio*, its designation in classical manuals of rhetoric. 'Wenn einer noch so schöne Redens-Arten hätte, der kömmt nicht fort, wenn etwas an der Connexion mangelt. Hingegen mag die Rede noch so schlecht seyn, wenn es nur wohl zusammenhängt, so findet er seine Liebhaber' was the opinion of one of these theorists.[1] This is Ciceronianism rampant. A distinction was usually made between *connexio verbalis* (external linkage) and *connexio realis* (linkage of ideas). The various forms of *connexio verbalis* were often discussed at length and the appropriate conjunctions listed. This again is the essence of Ciceronianism. But the *connexio realis* was usually passed over rather hastily. Here Gottsched was to break new ground in his insistence that what mattered was the *connexio realis*, and not the *connexio verbalis* which was often nothing more than a cloak for the absence of the other. And it was the *connexio realis* which formed the ordering principle of the 'loose' manner of Senecan prose.

In these stylistic manuals of the early eighteenth century we find a general demand for a rich vocabulary. The attitude to neologisms was characterised by caution: society must first have sanctioned them. We encounter opposition to Zesen, particularly amongst those who found themselves in sympathy with Christian Weise. Their ideal of *copia verborum* did not disdain the enrichment of expression by such rhetorical devices as *amplificatio* and *variatio*. *Amplificatio* implies the division of a whole into its constituent parts, and the enumeration of these (or some of them) instead of repeating the whole; *variatio* implies repetition of the idea without repetition of the word. All writers had a horror of repetition of the word. 'Die Anmuth und Lieblichkeit der Rede

---

[1] V. von Wertheim, *Ein allzeit fertiger Briefsteller*, ed. D. von Scharffenberg (Chemnitz, 1724) (first publ. 1711), pp. 47 f. and 77 ff.

wird durch nichts eher verderbet', said one of them, 'als durch öfftere Wiederholung einerley Wörter' (Chr. Schröter, *Gründliche Anweisung zur deutschen Oratorie* etc., Leipzig, 1704).[1] This leads to *circumlocutio, circumscriptio* and *periphrasis*. Lists of circumlocutions were given in some of the handbooks. All this is in direct opposition to the ideals of naturalness and concision, but it is part of the determination to avoid the *niederträchtig* and the *barbare*. The ancient tradition of classical rhetoric and the recent example of French preciosity met here, and they found fertile soil in a society nourished on the rhetoric of German *Kanzleistilus* and the preciousness of German *Hofzeremoniell*. All the handbooks urged avoidance of *niederträchtig* expressions. Choice of words should be governed not only by euphony, decorum and usage, but also by *dignitas*. This is especially true with epithets. Some theorists advocated those based on some trope, others advocated something akin to the *epithète significatif* and *epithète rare* of Ronsard which had been advocated by Opitz. The search for the elevated or the striking epithet should, however, not result in the revival of archaisms. All writers seem united in their opposition to archaisms, and it was at this time that the word *altfränkisch* began to be used with derogatory connotation.[2] Enlargement of vocabulary by composition was also envisaged. 'Zusammengesetzte Wörter nach Art der Griechen aus etlichen Wörtern sind doch die schönsten', said Andreas Köhler in his Poetics (Halle, 1734).[3] (The comparison with Greek is nothing new; it is found already in Schottelius, if not earlier.) Heaping of synonyms as in official, especially legal, language—an instance given was *vollstrecken, vollbringen und vollziehen*—was deemed both pedantic and inelegant—almost as bad as repeating the same word.

Markwardt speaks of 'die allmähliche Verdrängung des barocken Stilideals durch das Ideal der vernunftgemäßen, wohlgeordneten Verständlichkeit' but recognises that in this traditional

---

[1] *Op. cit.* p. 99.
[2] See the article by Lüdtke and Götze in the *ZfdW*, VII (1906), pp. 15 ff.
[3] *Op. cit.* p. 72. For full title, see above, p. 160 n. 3.

galant period we find a combination of late baroque and early rationalistic outlook. Morhof and Weise seem to have been the immediate sources of these two streams of ideas which were sometimes in conflict but sometimes modifying each other. Opposition was mounting against the old cumbrous, rigid style of prose writing based on the *Kanzleistilus*, but also against the immoderate naturalness of Christian Weise. A middle course was to be advocated, a new 'middle style' which is related to but not identical with the old 'middle character of style' in rhetoric. The contradictions contained within the attitude to style we have just depicted, arose from the fact that it derived from two sources—classical rhetoric and French preciosity—which, as the example of seventeenth-century France itself had shown, could sometimes be in direct conflict but more often merely complement each other. Our ideas on preciosity have been considerably modified by recent research.[1] 'On ne confondra plus préciosité et mauvais goût', says M. Bray. It was a striving towards distinction which developed naturally from an earlier esoteric euphuism into the more intellectual and rationalistic ideal of the *bel esprit*. Common to both was the cultivation of elegance—of 'style', in the widest sense of the term. The generation of 1660 turned, however, not only against the excessively figurative language of earlier preciosity but also against the Ciceronianism of what is usually called *le style Louis XIII*. Lanson describes this style as follows:

> Le philosophe, le ministre d'État, la femme du monde construisent la même phrase lentement déroulée, solidement étayée, la phrase d'une pensée qui travaille à se mettre en ordre et prétend, avant tout, manifester son enchaînement. Les mots sont serrés dans le cadre logique que construisent les relatifs, conjonctions et participes présents....On sent un esprit robuste qui se contraint à une discipline nouvelle, à une marche posée et régulière: il se crée une forme un peu lourde, claire et sérieuse.[2]

---

[1] See D. Mornet, *Histoire de la littérature française classique (1600–1700)* (Paris, 1942) and R. Bray, *La Préciosité et les Précieux* (Paris, 1948). See also Odette de Mourgues, *Metaphysical, Baroque and Précieux Poetry* (Oxford, 1953), for a striking attempt to delimit the connotation of these terms.

Gustave Lanson, *L'Art de la prose* (1909), pp. 58 ff.

Its greatest master was Louis Guez de Balzac, and his reputation as a stylistic authority continued for some time after his death in 1654. It was a Ciceronian style marked by nobility, fine cadence but a certain ponderousness. The new generation moved fairly rapidly towards a different type of sentence. Brunot says: 'La génération suivante préférera à cette prose solide, mais massive, qui semble faite surtout pour l'exposition et l'argumentation, la phrase alerte, vive, courte, qui fixe une idée ou porte un trait.'[1] This tendency towards Senecanism eventually developed into the French form of 'curt' style, the *style coupé*, which dominated the first half of the eighteenth century but is developing earlier. The old ideals of classical rhetoric—clarity, orderliness, concision —remained despite the growing opposition to Ciceronianism. Indeed, they were even more zealously pursued after 1660 than before, because of the growing sureness of taste and greater devotion to principles like *bienséance*, *vraisemblance* or *la raison* itself. Most of the ideas we have encountered in German stylistic manuals of the first decades of the eighteenth century are to be found in the France of Louis XIV. We find the same advocation of concision[2] alongside (less frequently) the demand for elaboration,[3] the same dislike of the use of synonyms[4] or superfluous epithets[5] to give *rondeur* to the sentence, the same mistrust of repetition[6] leading to the cultivation of variation and even peri-

---

[1] *Histoire de la langue française*, vol. III, p. 710 (Paris, 1909). The same volume contains the best analysis of *précieux* language of the period before 1660.

[2] For example: 'C'est une grande faute que de dire plusieurs paroles lorsqu'une suffit. Un discours, pour être vif et agréable, ne doit rien avoir de superflus' (Lamy, *Rhétorique* (1688), p. 10).

[3] Jouvency taught his pupils to cultivate *amplificatio*.

[4] 'Les esprits médiocres ne trouvent point l'unique expression, et usent de synonymes' (La Bruyère, *Des Ouvrages de l'Esprit*).

[5] Bary (*Les Secrets de nostre Langue*, 1665) examining the phrase: *d'vne gloire immortelle qui ne souffre point d'éclipse*, says: 'Il ne falloit pas dire ainsi: une gloire immortelle est toûjours éclatante' (1776 ed. p. 165). Similar remarks are to be found *passim* in many authors of the period.

[6] All sorts of arguments were advanced in favour of the avoidance of verbal repetition. But Pascal maintained its value as a means of avoiding confusion, and Bouhours would rather have repetition than risk obscurity. Several of the great writers (La Fontaine, Bossuet and Racine in particular) used repetition as a conscious effect, but the theorists were hesitant.

phrasis. The principle of variation conflicts with that of concision; and it is difficult to maintain it alongside the principle of the *mot juste*[1] and the practice of restricting the lexicon. The eighteenth century still accepted the ideals of regularity and clarity as the highest desiderata. It was now consciously recognised that concision might detract from clarity; but the excision of all unnecessary words was still considered the sure road to beauty. Opposition to enumerated synonyms and meaningless epithets persisted.[2] Opposition to 'irregular' constructions (zeugma, anacoluthia, prolepsis) still obtained. Repetition was to be avoided except for conscious effect.[3] More attention was given to the symmetry of the sentence. An early eighteenth-century theorist writes as follows: 'Qu'entre les parties d'une phrase il s'en trouve qui soient propres à figurer entr'elles, on aime à leur trouver une ressemblance grammaticale. On est agréablement frappé, quand les termes qui les forment et qui les unissent sont pris dans la même classe et rangés dans le même ordre.'[4]

The Ciceronian ideal of sentence construction was the carefully proportioned period, with the various parts clearly connected by integrating *particulae*. But we can see the tide turning against Ciceronianism in Bouhours' warning against *unnaturally* long periods due to 'déplacement de termes' and Bary's objection to grammatical linkage not corresponding to real linkage of ideas. The Ciceronian sentence was apt to dragoon statements into a superimposed, simulated interdependence. Those who still favoured it in the seventeenth century, claimed that it should not have more than four members between which there should be some measure of *correspondance* as regards length and arrangement. In the eighteenth century, the shape of the sentence still

---

[1] The most extreme expression of this idea is to be found in La Bruyère: 'Entre toutes les différentes expressions qui peuvent rendre une seule de nos pensées, il n'y en a qu'une qui soit la bonne' (*Ouvrages de l'Esprit*, no. 17).

[2] For example, Voltaire: 'Ne vous servez jamais d'épithètes que quand elles ajouteront beaucoup à la chose' (on a line in *Sertorius*).

[3] Cf. Voltaire on a line in *Héraclius* (v, 2, 9): 'Il faut éviter les répétitions à moins qu'elles ne donnent une grande force au discours.'

[4] Le chanoine de Gamaches, *Les agrémens du langage réduits à leurs principes* (Paris, 1718), p. 89.

formed the hard core of stylistics. 'Un mot déplacé', said the Abbé Girard in 1740, 'est une aussi grande faute dans le langage qu'un mot corrompu ou non usité.'[1] Anti-Ciceronianism was gaining ground and the new age worked out a logical justification of it. There was talk of a natural order of words, an *ordre direct*. This is to be used for the communication of ideas and is the especial glory of the French language. It is based on linkage of ideas, not on grammatical linkage. Grimarest, thinking of German, urged writers not to make one wait until the last word of the sentence 'pour conoître le noeud de plusieurs propositions jointes ensemble'. Buffier admonished men to 'arranger les mots, les uns après les autres, de la manière la plus propre à se présenter naturellement à l'imagination'.[2] Rapid expression, quick comprehension of the *liaison des idées* had now become the prime consideration in all prose style. Inversions and ellipses were permitted, but only for the sake of concision and vigour. Verbs were not to be removed too far from their subjects since this made for obscurity. In general we find a desire to keep together the words that belong together in meaning. The placing of subordinate clauses in relation to the main clause was most carefully considered. But a subordinate clause must represent a subordinate idea. Gamaches recognised that a better effect was often attained by avoiding subordination. For example instead of saying: 'Dieu, qui est toûjours juste dans les jugemens, ne souffrira pas que l'impie jouisse d'une longue prospérité', it would be better to make two main clauses; and Fénelon writing of Amphitrite: 'Son char sembloit voler sur les eaux, une troupe de nymphes nageoit à l'entour', thereby gained a better effect than if he had written: 'Son char, autour duquel nageoit une troupe de nymphes, sembloit voler sur les eaux.'[3] The Abbé Féraud maintained that 'les pronoms relatifs ne sont bons qu'autant qu'ils sont nécessaires. Il faut les épargner tant qu'on le peut sans nuire à la

---

[1] *Les vrais principes de la langue française*, vol. I, p. 82.

[2] Grimarest, *Eclaircissement sur la langue françoise* (1712), p. 185; Buffier *Grammaire françoise sur un plan nouveau* (1714), no. 767.

[3] Le Chanoine de Gamaches, *Les agréments du langage* etc. (Paris, 1718), p. 41.

clarté'. The tide was firmly set against prolixity and incapsulation. Vividness demands concision. Buffier counselled his readers: 'd'employer les expressions les plus courtes pour exprimer ce qu'on veut dire'.[1] All this amounts to a defence of the 'curt' manner of Senecan style, the *style coupé* as it was called in France. Most French grammarians of the first half of the eighteenth century urge 'cutting' the sentence and eliminating grammatical linkage. The general attitude is perhaps most concisely stated by Gamaches: 'On ne doit point mettre de liaison entre les propositions qui sont unies par le sens.' This, as we shall see, was exactly Gottsched's attitude. Buffier, whose work was certainly known to Gottsched, asserted that there was a principle of order at work in the *style coupé* and defined it as follows:[2]

> Les périodes du stile coupé consistent en plusieurs phrases ou expressions qui souvent prises chacune en particulier semblent faire un sens complet; et pourtant ce ne sont que des phrases ou des propositions particulières subordonnées à une proposition principale, dont elles marquent les diverses circonstances ou les divers regars.

There were still some spirits who lamented this new fashion in prose style, this 'tissu de petites phrases isolées, décousues, hâchées, déchiquetées' as the Abbé d'Olivet called it in 1736. As late as 1770 we find Crevier, the Professor of Rhetoric at the University of Paris, exclaiming:[3]

> Aux fatiguantes périodes de nos devanciers, nous avons substitué de petites phrases, courtes, qui rendent le style brusque, sautillant, haché, qui en font, en un mot, si j'ose dire ce que je pense, un ciment sans chaux. Ce style ne pèche pas contre la clarté, mais il n'a point de dignité.

But *Aufklärung* Germany was less concerned about dignity than clarity. It owed far more to French theories and discussions of style than has been recognised by German scholars.

---

[1] *Grammaire françoise* etc. (1714), no. 775.
[2] *Ibid.* no. 995. For proof of Gottsched's acquaintance with Buffier, see above, p. 119.
[3] *Rhétorique française*, vol. II, p. 48.

THE THEORY OF PROSE STYLE

Gottsched recognises two detrimental developments in German prose style of his day—that is to say, during the first half of the eighteenth century. The one was a tendency towards philosophical abstractness; the other was a craze for metaphor, for *malerische Bildlichkeit*. Both were to be roundly castigated in the *Beobachtungen* of 1758. As for the first—the tendency towards abstractness—we have already noted in the *Sprachkunst* his objection to new abstracts formed by substantivation of adjectives.[1] It is the other objection that must concern us more closely, for it became an important issue and affected the general development of the literary language.

In this matter Gottsched found some support in French writers. Opposition to an excessively figurative style is encountered as early as Malherbe, but this was really an attack on bad taste of a particular type. Metaphorical style persisted in earlier preciosity and was itself attacked, in its exaggerated form, by the generation of 1660, notably by Molière. The reaction was very severe and came near to the rejection not merely of exaggerated imagery but of all imagery. We find Sorel objecting to the phrase *envisager les périls* because dangers have no faces, Bouhours to *la charité agrandit l'âme*. There are signs of a reversal in La Bruyère; but the most explicit realisation of the situation is shown by Rapin:[2]

On est tombé dans une autre extremité par un soin trop scrupuleux de la pureté du langage: car on commença d'oster à la Poësie sa force et son élevation, par une retenuë trop timide, et par une fausse pudeur, dont on s'avisa de faire le caractere de nostre langue, pour luy oster toutes ces hardiesses sages et judicieuses que demande la Poësie: on en retrancha sans raison l'usage des metaphores, et de toutes ces figures qui donnent de la force et de l'éclat aux paroles....[3]

[1] E.g. Das Große, Schöne, Edle... 'gewiß eine neue Metaphysik der Witzlinge'—see above, p. 136.
[2] *Reflexions sur la poetique d'Aristote* etc. (1674), p. 82.
[3] Compare Lessing in 1751, reviewing a French translation of English prose and verse by various authors, who says of the French nation: 'Sie hat den Gebrauch der Metaphern und aller der Figuren allzu sehr eingeschrenkt, welche den Worten Nachdruck und Pracht geben, und hat sich bemüht alle Vollkommenheit dieser wunderbaren Kunst in die Grenzen einer reinen und ausgebesserten Rede einzuschliessen' (Lachmann-Muncker, vol. IV, p. 262).

This, we shall see, was exactly the situation which arose in Germany. For out of Gottsched's attack on Silesian bombast there developed a general attack on figurative style. In the first volume of Gottsched's *Critische Beyträge*, the article by J. H. Winkler on the beauties of the German language (see above, p. 112) contained an attack on what was called 'der widersinnische Ausdruck' which included this passage: 'Also kömmt es sehr abgeschmackt heraus, wenn man dem Witze und der Alberkeit eine Lebensfeder zuschreibt, wenn man den Begierden Segel zueignet, wenn man der göttlichen Vorsehung Speichen andichtet, wenn man die Menschen durch das Rad des Verhängnisses empor heben läßt.'[1] These sentiments must have had the approval of Gottsched since they were printed in his periodical. They are aimed at the baroque metaphor, but the argument involves a principle opposed to metaphor in general. We shall see Gottsched repeating similar arguments in the *Critische Dichtkunst* when we come later to consider Breitinger's refutation. Gottsched objected that this style involved obscurity and often contradiction. 'Man denke nicht: Es klingt doch hübsch, oder neu, oder hoch!', he said in the *Redekunst*, 'Was nicht vernünftig ist, das taugt gar nichts.'[2] It was for the same reason that Gottsched rejected the baroque oxymoron as represented by such phrases as *entsetzlich schön, abscheulich gelehrt, grausam beliebt* or Brockes' phrase *erbärmlich schön* in the *Passionsoratorium* of 1712 (to which he devoted a whole footnote in the fifth edition of the *Sprachkunst*).[3] This is verse; but the same applied to figurative prose. 'Die Sucht, metaphorisch zu reden, wo man deutlich und verständlich reden soll', said Gottsched in the *Beobachtungen*, 'hat alle Sprachen allmählich verderbet, und wird auch die unsrige ihrem Verfalle nähern.'[4] Let us note the contrast of *metaphorisch* with *deutlich und verständlich*: the two things seem to be incompatible for Gottsched. Similar argumentation was used to combat

---

[1] *Op. cit.* p. 63. *Alberkeit* is described by Adelung as a less frequent High German variant of *Albernheit*.
[2] *Redekunst*, p. 330.   [3] *Sprachkunst, ed. cit.* p. 265.
[4] *Op. cit.* p. 37.

the widespread figurative use of verbs like *zeichnen, malen* and *schildern*:

> In metaphorischen Verstande, werden heute zu Tage alle diese Wörter des Zeichnens, Malens und Schilderns bis zum Ekel gemisbrauchet... man malet zuweilen auch Töne, Gedanken, und Geister, die keine sichtbare Gestalten haben. Beschreiben und erzählen kann man solche Dinge wohl, aber das Schildern, Malen und Zeichnen wird dabei nur widersprechend, unmöglich und lächerlich.[1]

He returned to the subject again in connection with the word *entschatten* which he considered a lamentable neologism beloved of those who cultivate a 'varnished style':

> Sie beschreiben nichts mehr, sie schildern, malen, und *entschatten* nur, Sie geben auch keinen Abriß, oder Entwurf mehr von einer Sache; sondern bilden lauter Entschattungen und Kohlenrisse davon. Kurz, es ist eine ganz malerische Schreibart aufgekommen, von der man aber oft denken möchte: Geschmieret ist nicht gemalet.[2]

These passages from the *Beobachtungen* are, of course, later than Breitinger's *Critische Dichtkunst*; and they show that Breitinger's defence of metaphorical expression, so important in the development of German as a literary language, has not caused Gottsched in any way to modify his attitude.

On this matter Dornblüth agreed with Gottsched. In the twelfth section of the *Observationes* he asserted that metaphorical figures are foreign to German which is 'vil zu ernsthaft, als daß dergleichen Schulblümlein zuliesse'. He welcomed Gottsched's support on this matter, but regretted that Gottsched had himself fallen into the error he deplored, writing phrases like 'eine *Armut* in Worten', 'in keinem besondern *Flore*', 'wo keine Gelehrsamkeit *blühet*', '*Stärcke* im Reden' (instead of *Kraft*), '*Quellen* der Vorurteile' (instead of *Ursachen*). He then gave examples of this metaphorical style run to seed from an official document of

---

[1] *Ibid.* p. 183. *Schildern* in its primal usage is, according to Gottsched, confined to portraits. Slangen (*op. cit.* p. 314) quotes Stosch, *Versuch in richtiger Bestimmung einiger gleichbedeutender Wörter der deutschen Sprache* (Frankfurt an der Oder/Berlin, 1773–80), who confirms this but adds that the word is also used for details of a painting. Adelung recognises this second meaning.

[2] *Ibid.* pp. 87–8.

the time and from a sermon by Sebastian Sailer, a praemonstratensian priest best known for his writing in Swabian dialect.[1] Dornblüth claimed amongst other things that this style was obscure. But metaphorical expression was dear to Sailer's heart and he rallied to its defence, appealing to the authority of celebrated orators in order to show the advantages of such a style in pulpit oratory, since the periodic style was unsuited to the pulpit and to the common people. Dornblüth combined his opposition to metaphorical style with an attack on hyperbole, which appeared 'childish' in a serious language like German. Thus a phrase like *in Thränen zerschmeltzen* might sound all right as *fondre en larmes* but it was absurd in German. He noted how commonly the French use *infini, infiniment* and observed that the real equivalents in German were *vil, sehr vil, sehr, Menge, etc.*[2] This reflection suggests an interesting parallel with the Abbé Bouhours who had objected to Spanish as the language of exaggeration ('le faste, des termes vastes et résonnants, la pompe et l'ostentation partout') claiming that French was 'sérieuse' and was therefore naturally opposed to hyperbole and bold metaphor:

> Notre langue n'use que fort sobrement des hyperboles, parce que ce sont des figures ennemies de la vérité; en quoi elle tient de notre humeur franche et sincère, qui ne peut souffrir la fausseté et le mensonge. Pour la métaphore, elle ne s'en sert que quand elle ne peut s'en passer ou que les mots métaphoriques sont devenus propres par l'usage. Surtout elle ne peut supporter les métaphores trop hardies; et nous ne sommes plus au temps du *zénith* de la vertu, du *solstice* de l'honneur et de l'*apogée* de la gloire.[3]

Bouhours' attitude to language was conditioned by his Cartesianism. Gottsched and, as we can here see, Dornblüth were activated by similar rationalistic principles. It was this that lay behind the whole opposition to baroque prose. Clarity was being extolled in place of ornateness.

---

[1] His dates are 1714–77, and his *Sämmtliche Schriften im schwäbischen Dialecte* were edited by K. D. Hassler in 1843. For further details see Hassler's introduction and Goedeke, vol. III, p. 211.
[2] *Observationes*, pp. 185–6.
[3] *Entretiens d'Ariste et d'Eugène*, ed. Radouant, Paris, 1920, p. 49.

This applied not only to baroque figurative language but also to the shape of its sentences. For having in the *Redekunst* dealt with words, Gottsched had proceeded to consider periods. He defined a period as: 'Eine solche Rede nun, die einen völligen Verstand in sich begreift.'[1] Our thoughts sometimes have a 'Zusammenhang' which demands that several statements be combined into one sentence. But this should not be overdone: 'Es ist besser drey oder vier kleine Sätze so vortragen, daß mich ein jeder versteht; als alles zusammen zu schmeltzen, und meinen Leser dadurch zu verwirren, daß er nicht weiß wo er ist.'[2] He is particularly opposed to the artificial linking together of sentences with formal heavy conjunctions. This was a salient feature of the chancery language. But Gottsched raised the question whether this *Hof- und Canzley-Stilus* was a suitable model for 'vernünftige Scribenten'. German courtiers were proud of it, he says, and no wonder; for they had never devoted any attention to language but merely contented themselves with copying the stock manner of the chanceries. They should turn to France and observe how the experienced men of the French court, like Bussy Rabutin, St Evremond and others, cultivated quite a different style from the miserable language of German official documents. Sentences should vary in length and structure. But if one was consciously concerned with sentence-structure, one's style would be affected and unnatural. He formulates the following eminently sensible rule of style: 'Denn überhaupt ist dieses die Regel im guten Schreiben, daß man seine Sache recht verstehen, hernach aber die Gedanken davon so aufsetzen muß, wie sie einem beyfallen; ohne daran zu denken, ob man es mit einfachen oder zusammengesetzten Perioden verrichtet.'[3] There was nothing more absurd than the stiff conjunctions of chancery usage. One should write and speak as in ordinary intercourse with well-mannered people, where such formulas are never used. 'Man wird auch dergestalt viel deutlicher reden und schreiben, als wenn man immer eine Menge von Gedanken in einen weitläüftigen Satz zusammen bindet.' This is Gottsched's proclamation on the subject of

[1] *Grundriß*, p. 62.   [2] *Ibid.* p. 65.   [3] *Redekunst*, p. 267.

connexio (see above, p. 164). What he is here demanding, is that *connexio realis* shall never be sacrificed to *connexio verbalis*.

All this amounts to a complete rejection of Ciceronianism by arguments which are essentially Senecan. And this despite Gottsched's own admiration for Cicero and his expressed disapproval of the 'gebrochene, kraftlose Rede' of Seneca. His rejection of metaphorical style, if taken to its logical conclusion, implies the rejection of the *genus grande*. His opposition to Christian Weise implies a rejection of the extreme form of the *genus humile*. We are left with a *genus mediocre* which embodies the French ideal of cultured naturalness (of which, more later). It is a cross between an uncolloquial 'plain' style and an unmetaphorical 'middle' style. And its basic structural pattern is the loose manner of Senecan prose.

An important part of Gottsched's contribution to the development of prose style was his attack on participial constructions. These would seem to be of Humanist provenance and kept alive particularly in the chancery style but frequently found in all sorts of writers. Gottsched objected to the use of passive participles with active meaning and *vice versa*, in fact to the confusion between active and passive meaning in the German participles. He therefore rejected a construction like *die zu ihm tragende Freundschaft* or *die von ihm habende gute Meynung*, current at the time.[1] We have seen that in the accidence section of his *Sprachkunst* he had rejected attempts to form a German future participle (see above, p. 131). Unfortunately—as Eugen Wolff has pointed out—he formulated some of his objections in too general terms and this led to misunderstanding such as is shown in Haller's review of the *Sprachkunst* in the *Göttinger Gelehrte Zeitungen* for 1749. Gottsched had expressed his objections to participles at the head of a sentence, saying that the use of the present participle in such a construction was an old-fashioned imitation of Latin and Greek which ran counter to the natural spirit (*Schwung*) of the language, and that the similar use of the past participle was an uncouth apeing of French.[2] The constructions he was attacking

[1] *Sprachkunst*, 1st edn. p. 408. [2] 1st edn. p. 409.

are exemplified by: *Dieses sehend, sprach er*... and *Erschrecket durch deine Worte, kann ich dir nichts antworten*, or, with omission of the participle: *Zu schwach, eine Schlacht zu liefern, zog er sich zurück*.[1] Yet he had to admit, in the fifth edition, that a construction like: *Sterbend ging er hin, lebend kam er wieder* was unobjectionable. But he remained generally ill-disposed towards these constructions. Examples from the Bible and the poets he was apt to discount as due to the influence of Hebrew or classical languages, or to the exigencies of metre. On this point Gottsched was frequently attacked, and had to admit that he had nothing against participles as such. For the younger poets had rallied to their defence, and Haller, in his review of the *Sprachkunst*, had referred to the authority of Opitz and many poets of his own age.[2] Dornblüth would allow the past participle, but not the present participle in verbal use—as represented by constructions like *an ihn allzeit gedenckende, ihn anmütig betrachtende, und mit Eyfer liebende*. Gottsched had made this point too. Dornblüth also was opposed to the confusion between active and passive meaning of the participles.[3] This opposition to participial constructions, despite its too extreme formulation, did help to lighten the texture of prose. If we think back to the style of Thomasius in the *Monatsgespräche* and to participial phrases like *eine bey sich habende schlagende Sack-Uhr* or *wegen der darbey eingemischten andern Umstände* (see the passage quoted above on pp. 55–6) we can appreciate the force of his objection. These constructions are unnatural and obscure. Like the periodic sentence they were part of the ornate baroque legacy for which the plainer taste of the new age had no use.

[1] Gottsched's examples.
[2] *Göttinger Gelehrte Zeitungen* (1749), p. 30. Quoted by Eugen Wolff.
[3] *Observationes*, ch. XXI. I have quoted Dornblüth's own examples of these constructions.

VI

THE DEVELOPMENT OF NARRATIVE PROSE

LET us now turn to consider in somewhat more detail Gottsched's attack on the periodic sentence of chancery style, and on chancery style in general. The full development of chancery style began at the time of the Humanists and its basis was Ciceronian. Before then, it had already been characterised by long sentences and by tautological doublets. Now, and to a certain extent as a result of the revival of interest in Latin, we find other stylistic features developing.[1] These were the features still pervading chancery style at the time of Gottsched. They were:

1. Extreme use of *connexio verbalis*. Excessive coupling of clauses by stock conjunctions (*dieweil, als, maßen, wiewohl*, etc.). A particularly noxious form of this was the use of a cumbrous protasis beginning with *wiewohl* or *demnach*, followed by an apodosis introduced by *als*; whereas this *connexio* did not correspond to any such relationship of meaning.

2. Elaborate use of periphrasis and variation. Among the most frequent forms of periphrasis was the use of a virtual double negative for a positive, e.g.: *nicht nur...sondern auch=und*; or a phrase like: *Mir zweifelt nicht, daß... = ich weiß*. Among the more frequent forms of *variatio* was the tautological enumeration of synonymous expressions, including titles.

3. Interlarding with foreign words and phrases. These were at first confined to Latin (under the influence of legal language), but in the seventeenth century we also find adulteration with modern vernaculars, especially French (showing the influence of courtly language).

4. A general tone of obsequious politeness.

---

[1] For this analysis I have drawn on G. Steinhausen, *Geschichte des deutschen Briefes* (see below, p. 197), which contains the best description known to me of chancery style and a great wealth of illustrative material.

All these tendencies had been intensified during the seventeenth century. The conjunctions became still heavier (*allermaßen, alldieweilen*), tautological concatenations reached even greater lengths (*mein ganz hochfleißiges, gebürlich und bittliches ersuchen, berufen und laden;* ...*allhier bei mir erscheinen, an- und einkommen*), adulteration was now mainly with French words but Latinate participial constructions were still frequent. The virtual double negatives still abounded (*Ich kan die Herren semptlich freundtlicher Meinung nicht bergen, sondern vielmehr dieselben avisiren*...). The tone of polite obsequiousness became ever more oppressive. The following is a typical stuffy beginning to an official letter of the time:

Dieweil nun wir dem Herren Jederzeit freindtlichen vnnd in Ehrgebühr mit Schreiben zu Ersuchen vnndt auf zu warten Schultig seindt, Ihm auch vor alle seine Erzeigte vnd Erwießene vnndt an vnnß gethane *Impetiment* zu dancken Jederzeit Bereith sein, derowegen auch also nicht vmbgehen, dem großgünstigen Herren Etwaß von unserer glücklichen vndt wohl *absolvirten* Reiß Bericht zu thun nicht verschweigen können.[1]

A characteristic sample of seventeenth-century chancery style in full fig is afforded by the following passage from a letter, dated 22 October 1631, from the government of Hesse Darmstadt to that of Saxony:

Weil nun das elend hin und wider reichs unaussprechlich gros, auch leider die kriegsnoth dem durchleuchtigen, hochgebornen, unserem gnedigen fürsten und herren, landgraf Georgen zu Hessen theils in, theils nechst an dero fürstenthumb und landen ist, auch dessen continuirung seine fürstl. gn. auch dero herzliebste frau gemahlin, fürstliche kinder und ganzer stat unschuldiger weis ganz unverwinnlichen, nimmer verschmerzlichen schaden und wohl gar den eußersten undergang (welches doch die gütigkeit des allgewaltigen gottes väterlich abwenden und verhüten wolle) herzbekümmerlich empfangen und erleiden möchten, so haben dieselbe umb solcher ihrer eigenen hohen angelegenheit, meistentheils aber umb des *publici* willen nicht umbgehen sollen, mit dem hochwürdigsten unserm genedigsten churfürsten und herren zu Maintz aus denen dingen weiter zu communiciren und

[1] J. C. Behaim, dated 11 February 1622.

mit dessen churfurstl. gn. sich zu bereden, ob den ganz und gar kein einig weiter mittel zu widerstiftung friedens und ruh zu excogitiren, oder ob man eben alles miteinander vollends in die allereußerste stürzung gleichsamb zusehend und stillschweigend ohn anlegung einiger fernern hand gerathen lassen müßte.

The accepted authority of chancery language remained, despite all assertions to its discredit, at the end of the seventeenth century. This showed itself in the most unexpected places. Even Christian Weise, that proud protagonist of naturalness, chose to begin his treatise on letter-writing with a discussion of the various *connexiones*: a sequence of *Demnach...So...Wann dann... Als...Derohalben...Daran* should do for any letter.[1] Works like J. C. Lünig's *Angenehmer Vorrath Wohlstylisirter Schreiben* (Leipzig, 1728) or A. F. Glafey's *Anleitung in einer weltüblichen Deutschen Schreib-Art* (Frankfurt and Leipzig, 1730) contained only productions in chancery style—which is significant in view of the portentous generality of their titles. For Glafey the essence of all good style consisted in a 'wohlgefasten Periodus', and he delighted in the most complex hypotactic sentences.

Gottsched's attack on the *Kanzleistilus* had begun in *Der Biedermann*, where he said that it was disorderly, 'weil er alle Gedanken durcheinander wirft, die doch billig ganz besondre Sätze hätten ausmachen sollen', archaic (in that it uses old-fashioned conjunctions and other formulas and phrases) and consequently also obscure.[2] Three separate objections were here being voiced and the attack was continued in the same terms in his later works: the chancery style was disorderly, archaic and obscure. The first of these charges was aimed at the construction of the periodic sentence. In the *Sprachkunst* of 1748, Gottsched objected to the piling-up of verbs at the end of a sentence and recommended that, in all writing, the verb be placed as near its subject as possible, for the sake of clarity—and the rest of the

[1] *Curiöse Gedanken von Deutschen Briefen*, 1691. I use the British Museum copy of the 1698 edition (Leipzig and Dresden).

[2] No. XXVII, quoted from Gottsched Gesellschaft edition, ed. Reichel (Berlin, n.d.), vol. III, pp. 137–8. Spelling modernised. I have not been able to see a copy of the original edition of this periodical.

sentence should follow, rather than be interpolated between subject and verb. He cites this sentence (by Goldast): 'Es ist billig, dass man den deutschen Landen und Provinzen *ein Haupt*, welches dieselben in sämmtlicher Liebe erhalten, zieren, beschützen, und die Unfurchtsamen, mit dem Zaume weltlicher Gewalt aufhalten möchte, *ordnen sollte*', and comments: 'Hier sieht man wohl, daß die beyden letzten Worte, billig, und viel besser gleich nach den Worten, *ein Haupt*, hätten stehen können.'[1] The confusion and obscurity of this style, thought Gottsched, were primarily due to the verbs being so far separated from their subjects. The second and third charges—archaism and obscurity —were to a certain extent interdependent, except that obscurity could also result from unfamiliar neologisms. Gottsched instanced both the archaisms and the neologisms of the *Kanzleistilus*. It was still using pronominal forms like *männiglich* (*kund und zu wissen sey männiglich*; *wie männiglich bekannt*), apparently representing Old High German *mannogilîh*.[2] It perpetuated the archaic use of *ohn-* as a prefix both with adjectives (*ohnbedächtig*) and participles (*ohnerhört*). It even invented new 'analogical' formations of monstrous build like *ohnvonnöthen* or *ohnermangeln*.[3] Amongst the neologisms Gottsched reckoned unnecessary tautological formations like *alldieweil, ansonsten, anheute, eingestehen* (*gestehen* is enough).[4] He mentioned that a certain abuse of the prefix *an-* was characteristic of Upper German chanceries.[5] He

[1] *Op. cit.* p. 400.
[2] *Sprachkunst*, 5th edn. p. 442. Adelung (1777) says it is archaic, but still current 'im Oberdeutschen': 'Einige hochdeutschen Kanzelleyen haben es noch beybehalten.' The *DWb.* says: 'der gewöhnlichen rede gehört *männiglich* nur im 16. und 17. jahrh. noch an, später steht es bei dichtern und im Kanzleistil, heute ist es völlig veraltet.' Nevertheless it quotes examples from Wieland, Claudius and Musäus amongst eighteenth-century prose writers. *Trübners Deutsches Wörterbuch* even quotes isolated twentieth-century usages (Max Eyth, Schwerin).
[3] *Beobachtungen*, pp. 222-3. Adelung (1777) recognises these still as current 'Upper German' forms, not accepted in 'High German' (except *ohngefähr* and *Ohnmacht*; but even here he agrees that some say *ungefähr* and he prophesies that soon one will say *Unmacht*).
[4] *Sprachkunst*, 5th edn. pp. 381, 528; *Beobachtungen*, pp. 370 and 79.
[5] *Sprachkunst*, 1st edn. pp. 422-3. Weitenauer (see above, p. 144) makes the same point (*Zweifel*, pp. 73-4).

disliked the use of unnecessarily lengthy forms like *sintemal* and *wannenhero*,[1] the use of *entgegen* for *wider* (which he described as one of the 'Barbareyen dieser Schreibart'),[2] the use of *Dero* and *Ihro*.[3] He ridiculed words like *Abmaaß, Obsorge, Vereigenschaftung*—even *Abschluß, Berichtigung* and *Vorkommenheiten* (which seem quite familiar words today)—as formations *unnatural* to the German language.[4] (It was on the same grounds that he had objected to many of the words invented by the Fruchtbringende Gesellschaft.) Gottsched also pilloried the habit of indiscriminately forming adjectives from adverbs and prepositions, saying that this too was characteristic of the chancery style. He cited as examples *soig, nunig, mehrig, kaumig, schonig* and also *sonstig* (which has since established itself).[5] He objected to the confusion of participles in phrases like *die gegen E.H. Gn. tragende* (for *getragene*) *Hochachtung*,[6] and the use of indefinite for definite article (*eine hohe Landesregierung*; *ein hochlöbliches Appellationsgericht*).[7]

In the *Beobachtungen* he objected to unnecessary neologisms like *erinnersam* (for already current *erinnerlich*),[8] or *Zeugenschaft* (used by 'some Austrian preachers' for *Zeugnis*),[9] or *Anbetracht*

---

[1] *Sprachkunst*, 5th edn. p. 528. On *sintemal*, Adelung (1780) comments: 'In der edlern Schreibart der Hochdeutschen ist es veraltet, als welche es gern den Kanzelleyen überlässet, wo man die Wörter und Partikeln nicht vielsylbig genung bekommen kann, und daher wohl gar ein *sintemahl und alldieweil* zusammen setzet, obgleich alle sieben Sylben nichts mehr sagen als *weil, indem*, oder in einigen Fällen auch *nachdem*.'
[2] *Ibid*. p. 512.
[3] *Ibid*. p. 280. *Beobachtungen* (p. 147) call this *-o* 'ein blosser Sprachfehler... ein Schnitzer der Staatsgrammatik'.
[4] *Ibid*. p. 182. Adelung (already in 1774) accepts *Abschluß* and *Berichtigung* without comment, but says that *Vorkommenheit* is only usual in 'Upper German' (1780; unchanged in 1801).
[5] *Ibid*. p. 249. Adelung in 1801 still considers it 'oberdeutsch'. Campe called it 'niedrig', but recognised it. The *DWb.* gives examples from Goethe and Lichtenberg.
[6] *Ibid*. p. 375.   [7] *Ibid*. p. 407.
[8] See p. 94. Adelung (1774 and 1793) considers this 'Upper German' for *erinnerlich*.
[9] See p. 436. Not given in Adelung (1780), nor in second edition (1801). *DWb.* gives some examples from Austrian writers.

for *Absicht* (e.g. *in diesem allerseitigen Anbetracht*).[1] By inventing such words the perpetrators merely reveal either ignorance of the riches of their own language of a ludicrous pride according to which ordinary, comprehensible words are not good enough for them.[2] He also objected to the chancery employment of ordinary words with unusual connotations. 'Warum', he exclaimed at one point in the *Beobachtungen*, 'sollen doch die bekanntesten Wörter in ihrem Munde und in ihren Federn ihre ganze Natur ändern, und etwas sagen, das sie gar nicht bedeuten können?'[3] Thus he objected to the use of *unerfindlich* in the sense of *ungegründet* or *unerweislich*,[4] or *erschießen* in the sense of *eintragen*,[5] *zukömmlich* in the sense of *schuldig*,[6] *Anstand* in the sense of *Zweifel* (*nicht den mindesten Anstand*).[7] There was nothing about the nature, history or tradition of the *Kanzleistilus* to justify accepting it as an authority. 'Was an sich selbst ein Schnitzer ist, wird durch keine Staatsgrammatik recht', says Gottsched, recalling the incident when the Emperor Claudius used a strange Latin expression and was rebuked by a senator with the words: 'Et tu quidem, Caesar, hominibus jus civitatis dare potes; verbis non potes.'[8]

Dornblüth replied to Gottsched's attacks on the *Kanzleistilus*, with an outburst of professional snobbery:

Hierüber aber könte man ihme mit bestem Recht antworten: sutor ne ultra Crepidam! zu Teutsch: der Schulmeister soll dem Cantzler

---

[1] See p. 8. This word is not recognised by Adelung in 1774; but in the second edition, of 1793, he has it with the comment: 'ein völlig Oberdeutsches (*sic*) Wort, welches daselbst gemeiniglich ohne Artikel gebraucht wird. *In Anbetracht seiner Umstände*, in Betrachtung, Erwägung. Eben so unnothig ist *anbetrachten*, fur betrachten.'

[2] See p. 62.   [3] *Op. cit.* p. 372.

[4] *Ibid.* For example: 'unerfindliche Beschuldigungen, Beschwerden', Adelung (both editions) considers this usage an Upper German archaism.

[5] *Ibid.* p. 99. Adelung (1774 and 1793) says this is not a High German usage. The word had meant 'to be useful' in M.H.G.

[6] *Ibid.* p. 440. Not given in Adelung, first or second editions. (*DWb.* gives an isolated example from Arnim.)

[7] *Ibid.* p. 282. Also recognised as an Upper German usage by Adelung in 1774; but not so restricted in 1793.

[8] *Ibid.* p. 409.

nicht einreden... wan er in einer Cantzley gearbeitet oder *practici*rt hätte; würde er wenigist eine periodische Ordnung, *Genuinitatem* et *Copiam Verborum*, und eine Erkantnus des Guten und Schlechten ergriffen, und sich solcher erlernten guten Art... bedient, hingegen unnatürliche französßlende teutsche Schrifften verabscheut... haben.[1]

The *Observationes* are one continuous defence of the *Kanzleistilus* in all its features, and the main line of argument is seen in the passage just quoted: that it was a style natural to the German language which favoured periodic sentence-structure. Gottsched's style was French; not only had it nothing elegant or stately about it, it was not even natural, manly or serious. 'Wegen seinem Französßlen, komt alles heraus, als wan er immer schertzete.'[2] The recent decay in chancery language was also due to Frenchification, to the abandonment of the period-sentence. For German tended towards expansiveness and its natural sentence-form was the incapsulated period with its elaborate system of clauses interlinked by particles. Dornblüth suggested a comparison with French: 'Erfordert... der Teutsche durch vorgemelte *Transition*en, einen *periodi*schen, Zusamenhang; und was der Franzos etwa *per modum Gerundii* erst darnach bringt, will der gute Teutsche *per modum Incisi* vor dem Haubt-*Verbo* gesetzt haben, damit seine Rede bindiger werde, und deutlicher erhelle was zusamen gehört.'[3] This was a defence of *connexio verbalis*, claiming (in direct opposition to Gottsched) that it was the outward expression of *connexio realis*. *Transitiones* are means to the attainment of *connexio verbalis*. Dornblüth devoted a whole chapter to these (XV: *De transitionibus et earum particulis*) in which he gave a list of conjunctions (including some rejected by Gottsched as cumbrous), distinguishing various patterns of relation indicated by groups of conjunctions and the attendant order of words. By these means, good 'transitions' were to be effected: 'Die Erfahrnus beweißt, daß eine Schrifft *cum hac observatione* vil läuffiger und zierlicher ins Gesicht kome.'[4] His ideal is essentially Ciceronian: the period where grammatical links clearly indicate the

---

[1] *Observationes*, pp. 354 ff. [2] *Ibid.* pp. 350–1.
[3] *Ibid.* p. 5. [4] *Ibid.* p. 194.

thought-connections. Gottsched had claimed that these were not essential; for in a well-composed sentence the thought-connections should be self-evident. And the chancery sentence sometimes gave a false external linking to inherently unconnected thoughts. The result was disorder.

Dornblüth was here countering Gottsched's first charge against the chancery style: that it was *disorderly*. But the full defence of incapsulation came in his next chapter, on final position of the verb. He begins thus:

> Im Teutschen müsse das *Verbum* welches die *Construction* binden mus, (wan es *sine Verbo auxiliari* stehet) oder aber die *Verba auxiliaria* die das Haubt-*Verbum conjungi*ren (ausgenomen *in sensu Interrogationis vel Positionis*) gemeiniglich zu letzt gesetzt und die *Construction* darmit geschlossen werden; welches sehr gut und bindig lautet.

We should note this conception of the main verb 'tying up' the whole sentence, making it *gut und bindig*. Dornblüth had used the word *bindig* earlier (in the passage quoted above) when he was defending the periodic sentence. It is his key-word. It denotes, in essence, his stylistic ideal. Prose is to be well ordered, even at the risk of the most pedantic regimentation. Dornblüth went on to complain that translators frequently disregarded this, following either the word-order of the foreign original or, if they were theologians (and most of them were) the style of Luther. (The construction represented by *der du bist im Himmel* was, for Dornblüth, not archaic but un-German; it was *contra naturalem verborum ordinem*.) Gottsched had been a frequent offender and Dornblüth proceeded to take various sentences from Gottsched's works and remodel them in accordance with his ideal of the orderly sentence. For example, here is a sentence from the dedication to the *Redekunst* as Dornblüth quotes it: 'Mehr als einmahl habe ich mirs vorgesetzet, auch meinem vormahligen Landesherren, diejenige Ehrfurcht an den Tag zu legen, die auch in der Fremde niemals in mir erloschen ist.' This he recasts as follows: 'Ich hab mir wohl öffters meinem vormahligen Landesherren, die tiefe Ehrerbietigkeit, die auch in der Fremde niemahl in mir erloschen ist, an Tag zu legen (*sed melius*) zu bezeugen vorgenomen.' The main verb *ich hab mir vorgenomen* envelops the sentence like some outer casing holding all the other parts within itself. Two diametrically opposed attitudes to sentence-structure are here presented. Gottsched contended that the orderliness of the periodic sentence was in fact disorderliness because it forcibly assembled elements which were themselves individual wholes, into a false superimposed whole. Dornblüth's contention was that Gottsched broke into unordered fragments a whole in which various elements coexisted in ordered shape.

For instance we find Dornblüth criticising Gottsched's use of what he called the 'gerund', saying that this was French and not German. He was thinking of *um* with the infinitive (or just the infinitive), *following* the main verbal complex. This construction should never come last, he said, but should be used either as an incapsulation before the main verb, or as a *transitio* at the beginning of the period. Thus one should write, not: 'Dem König aber gefiehle den Argwohn zu verstellen, und eine bessere Gelegenheit zu erwarten, hinter den Handel zu komen und demselben vorzubauen', but rather 'Um aber hinter den Handel zu komen und demselben vorbauen zu könen, gefiel dem König den Argwohn zu verstellen, und eine bessere Gelegenheit abzuwarten.' The 'gerundial' phrase now stands in head-position as *transitio*, and the period rolls towards its main verbs in final position. One can understand Dornblüth's point: in this particular example his sentence turns on the pivot of its main verb *gefiel*. A somewhat more striking example is afforded by this sentence: 'Aber wie viele Mühe würde es denen kosten, Fabeln von Eßlen und Tigerthieren zu machen, die Feinde der Religion abzumahlen' (Mosheim). Here there are no *transitiones*, no *particulae*. To us nowadays the sentence sounds somewhat gawky. For Dornblüth it was a collection of unordered fragments. He recast it with clear links: 'Würde es wohl aber etwas so schwehres seyn, wan man, um die Religions-Feinde abzumahlen, Fabeln von Eßlen und Tigerthieren erfinden wollte?' Here we have the second alternative: 'gerundial' phrase incapsulated before the main verbal complex. The difference between what one might call Saxon and chancery structure is well exemplified by the following comparison:

(*a*) Sind wir dan so sinnreich nicht, daß wir etliche Stunden dazu anwenden könten, Gedichte mit Gedichte (*sic*) abzuweisen?
(Mosheim)

(*b*) Sollten wir dan nicht so geschickt seyn, daß wir Gedichten mit Gedichten abzufertigen (*vel* zu Schanden zu machen) einige Stunden anwenden könten? (Dornblüth)

the second of which has an 'envelope' *daß*-clause.

Behind the antagonism of Dornblüth and Gottsched lies the antagonism between a Ciceronian and a non-Ciceronian prose style. To Dornblüth it appeared as an opposition between German and French. To us it appears nowadays as a conflict between an ornate ceremonious style and a plain everyday style. Both styles are to be found side by side in the prose of the first half of the century. It would be foolish for us here to attempt any overall or exhaustive examination, but a few individual illustrations may be offered and must suffice to point the difference. Let us take our examples from the sphere of narrative prose. For two reasons: first because we have already noted some contrasts in narrative prose in earlier chapters of this book, and secondly because the birth of the modern European novel is one of the most important events in the development of all literary languages during this period.

We have already noticed attacks in the moral weeklies on metaphorical expression and the periodic sentence used for narrative purposes. We have seen Thomasius using the periodic sentence and participial phrases; and even though he himself satirised the metaphorical flowers of the style of 'heroic' narrative, his own prose still had the general shape and character of the Ciceronian style. In contrast we have seen that Gottsched's narrative style in his early periodicals had the general shape and character of the new, more loosely-knit style which corresponds to the loose manner of Senecan prose. Both styles persist for a while in German narrative prose. Let us consider some examples. Here is a passage from *Die Insel Felsenburg*,[1] published in 1731:

> Biß hierher war der *Capitain Wolffgang* damals in seiner Erzehlung kommen, als er, wegen einbrechender Nacht, vor dieses mal abbrach, und versprach, uns bey erster guten Gelegenheit, den übrigen *Rest* seiner *Avantur*en wissend zu machen. Es suchte derowegen ein jeder von uns seine gewöhnliche Ruhe-Stelle, hatten aber dieselbe kaum 3. Stunden gedrückt, als, wegen eines sich erhebenden Sturmes, alle ermuntert wurden, damit wir uns gegen einen solchen ungestümen Stöhrer unserer Ruhe in behörige *positur* setzen könten. Wir verliessen uns zwar auf die besondere Stärcke und Festigkeit des getreuen *Paridis*, als welchen Nahmen unser Schiff führete; da aber das grausame wüten des Windes, und die einmal in Raserey gebrachten Wellen, nachdem sie nunmehro 2. Nacht und 2. Tage ohne einzuhalten getobet, auch noch keinen Stillstand machen wolten, im Gegentheil, mit hereinbrechender 3ten Nacht, ihre Wuth vervielfältigten, liessen wir die Hoffnung zu unserer Lebensrettung gäntzlich sincken, bekümmerten uns fast gar nicht mehr, um welche Gegend wir wären, und erwarteten, theils mit zitterenden, theils mit gelassenen Hertzen, die erschreckliche Zerscheiterung des Schiffs, und das mehrentheils damit sehr genau verknüpffte jämmerliche Ende unseres Lebens.[2]

As narrative prose this is not very successful, so blatant is the incompatibility between violent content and cumbersome form. It has the same deficiency, therefore, as the narrative prose of Thomasius. The general structural pattern of this prose is very similar to that of the *Monatsgespräche*. The sentences are fundamentally periodic with plenty of *connexio verbalis*: thus *damals* in the first clause links on to *als* which introduces the second clause, *derowegen* links the second sentence with the first, then *kaum* is taken up by another *als* which in turn is extended into a *damit* clause. Other features of chancery style are apparent: frequent participial phrases, frequent circumlocutions (*in Raserey gebracht*;

---

[1] *Wunderliche Fata einiger See-Fahrer*, etc. by 'Gisander' (J. G. Schnabel). There is a reliable reprint of the first volume by H. Ullrich in the *Neudrucke* (1902). The British Museum has a contemporary edition made up from various reprints, in four volumes (Nordhausen, 1732–51). I quote from Ullrich's edition, but have checked the text from the British Museum edition.

[2] *Ed. cit.* p. 47.

Stillstand machen), unnecessary doublets (*Stärcke und Festigkeit*), unnecessary parallelism of clauses—all of which slackens and emasculates the narration. But, as with Thomasius, this fundamentally uncolloquial prose is enlivened every now and then by a flash of liveliness which shows that the narrator is galant: here the colloquial phrase 'seine Ruhe-Stelle...*gedrückt*' and the military metaphor 'in *positur* setzen'. When Ludwig Tieck republished this novel in 1828 and first gave it the title *Die Insel Felsenburg*, he found it necessary to rewrite it. Here is his version of the passage we have just analysed:

> Bis hierher war der Kapitain Wolfgang in seiner Erzählung gekommen, als er wegen einbrechender Nacht für diesmal abbrach, mit dem Versprechen, daß er uns bei der ersten Gelegenheit den noch übrigen Theil seiner Begebnisse mittheilen wolle. Jeder von uns suchte nun seine gewohnte Ruhestelle; kaum aber hatten wir drei Stunden auf derselben gelegen, als wir alle wegen eines sich erhebenden Sturmes wieder ermuntert wurden. Wir verließen uns nun zwar auf die Stärke und Festigkeit unseres 'getreuen Paris', welchen Namen nämlich unser Schiff führte; da indeß die Wuth des Sturms und das Toben der Wellen, nachdem es zwei Nächte und zwei Tage ohne Unterlaß fortgedauert, nicht aufhören wollte, im Gegentheil bei Anbruch der dritten Nacht sich noch vervielfältigte, gaben wir alle Hoffnung auf unsere Lebensrettung auf, bekümmerten uns fast gar nicht mehr darum, in welcher Gegend wir uns befänden, und erwarteten theils mit zitterndem, theils mit gelassenem Herzen die schreckliche Zerscheiterung unseres Schiffs und das damit verknüpfte jämmerliche Ende unseres Lebens.[1]

The prose is much smoother and much more easy-flowing. The more artificial *connexiones* have been removed (*damals* from the first sentence, *derowegen* from the second) and so have the (for Tieck) incongruous colloquialisms. Circumlocutions (*wissend machen, in Raserey gebracht, Stillstand machen*) and general wordiness have been resolved into tauter phrases. Tieck's revision shows most clearly the gulf between what he, in his preface,

---

[1] This edition, in six volumes, was published at Breslau in 1828. There is a copy in the British Museum, from which I quote. This passage is on pp. 69–70 of the first volume.

called 'the chancery style of those [former] days' and the literary taste of 1828.

But the style of the book is not even. Käthe Werner agrees that 'In der Insel Felsenburg dominiert noch der mittellange bis lange Periodenbau, den die Barockprosa aus der humanistischen Gelehrtenprosa übernommen hatte', although this is combined with paratactic sequences and even sporadic occurrence of the inversion-type 'und muß ich ihn zum Ruhme nachsagen'.[1] Despite the overall influence of chancery style, the book shows stylistic uncertainty; but this variety of style, Dr Werner thinks, is characterising. In the less turbulent parts of the book, especially in the scenes on the island, the style is less periodic and shows a marked influence of the vocabulary of pietism. Here is a sample from the latter part of the book:

> Die arme kleine *Concordia* fieng nunmehro auch, wie ich glaube, vor Hunger und Durst, erbärmlich an zu schreyen, verdoppelte also unser Hertzeleyd auf jämmerliche Art, indem sie von ihrer Mutter nicht einen Tropffen Nahrungs-Safft erhalten konte. Es war mir allbereit in die Gedancken kommen, ein paar melckende Ziegen einzufangen, allein auch diese Thiere waren durch das öfftere schiessen dermassen wild worden, daß sie sich allezeit auf 20. biß 50. Schritt von mir entfernt hielten, also meine 3. stündige Mühe vergeblich machten, also traf ich meine beyden *Concordien,* bey meiner Zurückkunfft, in noch weit elendern Zustande an, indem sie vor Mattigkeit kaum noch lechzen konten. Solchergestallt wuste ich kein ander Mittel, als allen beyden etwas von dem mit reinen Wasser vermischten Palm-Saffte einzuflössen, indem sie sich nun damit ein wenig erquickten, gab mir der Himmel einen noch glücklichern Einfall. Denn ich lieff alsobald....[2]

The sentences here are straggling rather than rounded, but the links are still heavy. Unimportant words seem to have unnecessarily long forms (*nunmehro* for *nun, allbereit* for *bereit, alsobald*

---

[1] Käthe Werner, *Der Stil von J. G. Schnabels 'Insel Felsenburg'*, typescript diss. (Berlin, 1950). I am indebted to the Humboldt University for the loan of a copy. Asyndetic alignment occurs in the second sentence ('...hatten') and parataxis in the last sentence ('und erwarteten...') of the passage quoted above.

[2] *Ed. cit.* p. 175.

for *sobald*) or a shade too much emphasis (*allen beyden*; *allein auch*; *noch weit elendern*). The result is a general distribution of stress which leads to flatness. In this—as in the circumlocutions and pleonastic doublets—we have a tendency, perhaps even a striving, towards breadth. Even when the style is predominantly paratactic, the effect is still heavy:

> Da aber nicht vor rathsam hielt, gegen die Nacht zu, die gefährlichen Wege hinunter zu klettern, entschloß ich mich, in diesem irrdischen Paradiese die Nacht über zu verbleiben, und suchte mir zu dem Ende auf einen mit dicken Sträuchern bewachsenen Hügel eine bequeme Lager-Statt aus, langete aus meinen Taschen etliche kleine Stücklein Zwieback, pflückte von einem Baume etliche ziemlich reiffe Früchte, welche röthlich aussahen, und im Geschmacke denen Morellen gleich kamen, hielt damit meine Abend-Mahlzeit, tranck aus dem vorbey rauschenden klaren Bächlein einen süssen Trunck Wasser darzu, befahl mich hierauf GOtt, und schlieff in dessen Nahmen gar hurtig ein, weil mich durch das hohe Klettern und viele Herumschweiffen selbigen Tag ungemein müde gemacht hatte.[1]

for the long asyndetic sequence is heavy in its own way and slight overstresses ('kleine Stücklein', 'ziemlich reiffe Früchte', 'gar hurtig', 'ungemein müde') produce flatness. It would seem that whether the style be periodic or paratactic, the cumbersome spirit of chancery style pervades it all. And although the vocabulary differs according to whether the speaker is galant or sentimental, educated or simple, the style lacks vigour and is therefore ill-suited to narrative prose.

Here is a passage from another tale of shipwreck, published at Hamburg in 1720:

> Nachdem ich mich durch den gehabten Schlaff ein wenig erquicket, und der *Paroxismus* vom Fieber gantz vorbey, stund ich auff: Und ob gleich die Furcht und Angst wegen meines Traumes sehr groß, bedachte ich doch, daß das Fieber den andern Tag wieder kommen würde, mithin sey meine Zeit, jetzund etwas zur Hand zu kriegen, um mich, wann ich wieder schwach würde, damit zu stärcken und zu erquicken. Also füllte ich zuförderst eine grosse viereckte Flasche mit Wasser, und setzte sie auf meinen Tisch, daß ichs im Bette langen

[1] *Ed. cit.* p. 121.

konte: um ihm auch die Kälte und die Fieberhaffte Eigenschafft zu benehmen, goß ich den vierten Theil eines Nössels oder Schoppen *Rum* darzu und schüttelte es durch einander. Hernach langte ich mir ein Stück Ziegen-Wildprät, und bratete es auf Kohlen, konte aber gar wenig davon essen. Ich spatzierte umher, war aber sehr matt und dabey über Betrachtung meines elenden Zustandes und der Furcht, daß die Kranckheit den andern Tag wieder kommen würde, von Hertzen traurig und niedergeschlagen. Des Nachts machte ich mir ein Essen von 3 Schildkröten-Eyern, so ich in der Aschen bratete, und, wie man bey uns sonst die gesottene pfleget, aus der Schalen aß. Und dies war, so viel ich mich von meinem gantzen Leben erinnern kan, der erste Bissen, den ich mit Gebeht zu GOtt in den Mund gesteckt!

The beginning of this passage recalls the prose of *Die Insel Felsenburg*. But as it progresses the effect becomes quite different. It shows considerable affinities with the tradition of chapbook prose continued by Christian Weise: the lack of a true link at *mithin*, the colloquial phrase *zur Hand zu kriegen*, the use of *so* as a relative. Certain reminiscences of chancery style are still present: notably the clumsy participial phrase *durch den gehabten Schlaf*, and the use of pleonastic doublets (*Furcht und Angst*; *stärcken und erquicken*; *traurig und niedergeschlagen*) for the sake of emphasis. But there is real emphasis here. And the basic sentence-structure is not that of the chancery style; it is loose and relies on *connexio realis*. The sentence: 'Hernach langte ich mir ein Stück Ziegen-Wildprät, und bratete es auf Kohlen, konte aber gar wenig davon essen' is characteristically un-Ciceronian.

The passage we have just analysed is from the first German translation of *Robinson Crusoe*, published only a few months after the appearance of the book in England. Here is the corresponding passage in the English original:

...Having been somewhat refresh'd with the Sleep I had had, and the Fit being entirely off, I got up; and tho' the Fright and Terror of my Dream was very great, yet I consider'd, that the Fit of the Ague wou'd return again the next Day, and now was my Time to get something to refresh and support myself when I should be ill; and the first Thing I did, I fill'd a large square Case Bottle with Water, and set it upon my Table, in Reach of my Bed; and to take off the chill or aguish

THE DEVELOPMENT OF NARRATIVE PROSE

Disposition of the Water, I put about a Quarter of a Pint of Rum into it, and mix'd them together; then I got me a Piece of the Goat's Flesh, and broil'd it on the Coals, but could eat very little; I walk'd about, but was very weak, and withal very sad and heavy-hearted in the Sense of my miserable Condition; dreading the Return of my Distemper the next Day; at Night I made my Supper of three of the Turtle's Eggs, which I roasted in the Ashes, and eat, as we call it, in the Shell; and this was the first Bit of Meat I had ever ask'd God's Blessing to, even as I cou'd remember in my whole Life.[1]

From this comparison we can see immediately that the translation is very good and very close. The shape of the English sentences is usually well preserved, and this fact accounts for several features in the German: notably the protases of the first two sentences and perhaps the omission of the verb 'to be' and the semantic doublets. Not that these are anglicisms; but their presence in the English original has undoubtedly stimulated the translator to use these particular stylistic possibilities of his own language.

At this point in the narrative there follows a more reflective passage which begins thus:

After I had eaten, I try'd to walk, but found myself so weak that I cou'd hardly carry the Gun, (for I never went out without that) so I went but a little Way, and sat down upon the Ground, looking out upon the Sea, which was just before me, and very calm and smooth: As I sat here, some such Thoughts as these occur'd to me.

What is this Earth and Sea of which I have seen so much, whence is it produc'd, and what am I, and all the other Creatures, wild and tame, humane and brutal, whence are we?

Sure we are all made by some secret Power, who form'd the Earth and Sea, the Air and Sky; and who is that?

Then it follow'd most naturally, It is God that has made it all: Well, but then it came on strangely, if God has made all these Things, He

---

[1] My German text is on pp. 130–1 of the second impression of the original edition, *Das Leben und die gantz ungemeine Begebenheiten des Weltberuffenen Engelländers, Mr Robinson Crusoe*, etc. . . . Die Zweyte Hamburgische Aufflage . . . Hamburg 1721 (copy in the Priebsch Collection of the Institute of Germanic Languages and Literatures, University of London). I have corrected one obvious misprint (*Schaleß aß* for *Schalen aß*). The English text is quoted from a contemporary copy (2nd edn. 1719) in the University Library, Cambridge, in order to show the original punctuation. This passage is on p. 107.

guides and governs them all, and all Things that concern them; for the Power that could make all Things, must certainly have Power to guide and direct them.

If so, nothing can happen in the great Circuit of his Works, either without his Knowledge or Appointment.

And if nothing happens without his Knowledge, he knows that I am here, and am in this dreadful Condition; and if nothing happens without his Appointment, he has appointed all this to befal me.

Such reflections are an important element in *Robinson Crusoe*. Their religious flavour would naturally appeal to a Germany in which pietism was prevalent. The passage appears in the German version as follows:[1]

Nachdem meine Mahlzeit verzehret, probirte ich das Ausgehen, spührte aber eine solche Müdigkeit, daß ich kaum die Flinte tragen konte, (dann ich nahm sie allezeit mit mir:) Also wanderte ich gar nicht weit, setzte mich auff den Boden nieder, sah auffs Meer hinaus, welches mir recht im Gesichte, und gantz still und eben war, und bekam, unterm Sitzen, folgende Gedancken:

'Was ist die Erde und das Meer, wovon ich so ein groß Stück gesehen? Woher sind sie entstanden? und was bin Ich und alle andre Creaturen, Wilde und Zahme, Menschliche und Viehische? Woher sind Wir?'[2]

'So folget dann gantz natürliche Weise, dies alles habe GOTT geschaffen. Gut, fiel mir dann seltzsam ein, hat GOTT alle diese Dinge erschaffen, so führet und regieret Er sie auch alle und was darzu gehöret. Dann diejenige Macht, welche alles machen können, muß gewiß auch die Gewalt haben, sie zu führen und zu regieren!'

'Ist dem also, so mag in dem grossen Umfang seiner Wercke nichts geschehen ohne sein Wissen oder Befehl.'

'Geschicht nichts ohne sein Wissen, so weiß Er ja auch daß Ich hier bin, und zwar in so erbärmlichen Zustand: Und geschieht nichts ohne seinen Befehl, so hat er auch geordnet alles was über mich gekommen ist.'

It is simple, terse prose. This may even account for the absolute participial phrase at the beginning. The vocabulary is straightforward and undistinguished; but it avoids the commonplaceness and colloquialism of Christian Weise.

[1] *Ibid.* pp. 131–2.
[2] The next sentence in the English does not figure in this translation.

THE DEVELOPMENT OF NARRATIVE PROSE

This section of the book builds up to the anguished question: 'Why has God done this to me? What have I done to be thus used?'...

My Conscience presently check'd me in that Enquiry, as if I had blasphem'd, and methought it spoke to me like a voice: 'WRETCH! *dost thou ask what thou hast done?* look back upon a dreadful mis-spent Life, and ask thy self *what thou hast not done?* ask, Why is it *that thou wert not long ago destroy'd?* Why *wert thou not drown'd in* Yarmouth Roads? *Kill'd in the Fight when the Ship was taken by* the Salle Man of War? *Devour'd by the wild Beasts on the* Coast of Africa? Or *Drown'd HERE, when all the Crew perish'd but thy self?* Dost thou ask, *What have I done?*

I was struck dumb with these Reflections, as one astonish'd, and had not a Word to say....

This remarkable passage is rendered in the German as follows:

Bey dieser Frage gab mir mein Gewissen sofort einen Verweiß, als begienge ich eine Gottslästerung, und däuchte mich, es bestraffe mich gleichsam mit diesen Worten: 'O du Ertz-Bösewicht! darffst du noch fragen, womit du es verschuldet? Ey siehe nur zurücke auff dein mit schwartzen Sünden beflecktes und so liederlich zugebrachtes Leben, und frage dich dann selber, womit du es verschuldet? Frage vielmehr, warum du nicht schon längstens aufgerieben worden? Warum du auff der Rheede vor Yarmouth nicht ertruncken? In dem Gefecht mit den Saleeschen See-Räubern nicht getödtet? Auff der Africanischen Cüste von wilden Thieren nicht zerrissen? Oder hier, nicht so, wie alle deine Gefährten, vom Meer verschlungen worden? Und du fragest noch: Womit du es verschuldet?'

Diese Betrachtungen machten mich Mauß-stille, wie ein bestürtzter Mensch da stehet, und ich hatte kein Wörtlein dagegen einzuwenden....[1]

All the expressive power of this very graphic writing has come through in the German translation. The meaning is sometimes strengthened: 'it *spoke* to me'—'es *bestraffe* mich', '*dost* thou ask...'—'*darffst du* noch fragen', 'drown'd...perish'd'—'verschlungen', 'not a word to *say*'—'*einzuwenden*'. This is particularly so at the crucial points in the progression towards the

[1] *Ibid.* pp. 132–3. The whole of the apostrophe in this passage is printed in heavier type in the original.

climax: *Ertz-Bösewicht*; *Ey*; *aufgerieben*. The climax itself is well realised in the German, as is the wonderful silence which immediately follows. The mind of Defoe, we notice, is 'struck dumb' by these immense reflections: the anonymous German is '*Mauß-stille*'. We have not yet reached the ecstatic expression of Klopstock. There is nothing passionate about this language; but there is restrained sincerity behind this clear, simple and rather moving prose.

This would seem to be another instance of English affecting German prose style through the intermediary of a close translation. We have already seen how translations from *The Spectator* had affected the style of the German moral weeklies. The popularity of *Robinson Crusoe* in Germany is attested by the large number of translations and imitations. Our example is therefore neither fortuitous nor irrelevant. This must have been a very widely read book. It was also a very remarkable book. It must have burst on the German novel-reading public as a staggering novelty. For this public still had to content itself in the main with reprints of seventeenth-century heroic novels. Thus the *Asiatische Banise* of Ziegler, first published in 1689, was reprinted in 1690, 1700, 1707, 1716, 1721, 1728, 1733, 1738 and 1753; and in 1753 a revised edition was published and this was reprinted in 1764. A continuation of Ziegler's work, composed by J. G. Hamann and published in 1724, was also popular, for it had run to five editions by 1766. There were also no less than five imitations published at various dates between 1715 and 1754. The novels of Bucholtz were republished during this period (*Herkuliskus und Herkuladisla* in 1713, *Herkules und Valiska* in 1728 and 1744) and also Anton Ulrich's *Octavia* (1711, 1712). Lohenstein's *Arminius* must still have been widely read, even though the only reprint was the revised edition of 1731 prepared by G. C. Gebauer, for references to it are frequent. Translation of English novels into German on a large scale did not begin until the middle of the century, but there is a certain amount before 1750. In this period the translation from Defoe's works far outnumber those from other novelists. *Gulliver's Travels* first appeared in German at

Hamburg in 1728. In the forties we find the first translations of Richardson (*Pamela*, by Mattheson (Hamburg, 1742); *Clarissa*, 1748–53) and Fielding (*Joseph Andrews* in 1745; *Tom Jones* in 1749–51). In narrative fiction, therefore, the first half of the eighteenth century was still dominated by the heroic novel. There were other lesser types, such as the salacious novels of Bohse and the realistic works of Christian Weise and Reuter, but, on the whole, it is true to say that for this period the novel still meant the old heroic-galant novel of the seventeenth century. It is against this background that we must understand the popularity of *Robinson Crusoe* in Germany. It was something entirely new both in content and style. And yet the ceremonious narrative style of the old courtly novel still persisted as a tradition, making itself felt even in Schnabel's notable attempt at a German *Robinson*.

It is now time to return to the manuals of epistolography. Heroic novels often contained letters. This was a tradition going back at least as far as Honoré d'Urfé's *L'Astrée*. The manuals of letter-writing published in Germany during the first decades of the eighteenth century had a close connection with the heroic novels. Letters from novels were used as examples. Sometimes the author of the treatise was himself a novelist. It is interesting to reflect on the fact that *Pamela* was to arise from a collection of model letters. And it is from *Pamela* that the modern psychological novel may be said to spring. The connection between the letter and the novel is therefore attested in more than one way. We must now examine the situation in Germany.

The development of German epistolary style has been traced by Georg Steinhausen.[1] He points to the fact that in the fifteenth century, official letters usually employed the elaborate sentences and tautological formulas of chancery style, whereas private letters show extremely simple sentence-construction and homely vocabulary. The gulf widened with the ever-increasing tortuous-

---

[1] *Geschichte des deutschen Briefes*, 2 vols. (Berlin, 1889 and 1891)—a masterly work to which I am much indebted in this section of my considerations, although it does not, in my opinion, give sufficient weight to the influence of French preciosity. My examples are selected from the vast store embodied in Steinhausen's work.

ness and artificiality of the chancery language until this official style began to infect that of private letters. Already in the late fifteenth century manuals of letter-writing were advocating the use of *synonyma* and *colores rhetoricales*. This artificial rhetoric became fashionable because it was considered to be the sign of culture, and the sixteenth century saw its complete victory in epistolary style. There grew up a conscious striving for complexity, a sickening straining after politeness. The result was pomp and servility. Epistolary style became the extreme antithesis of the natural expression of thoughts.

Seventeenth-century letters show the chancery style with all these features intensified. But the influence of French preciosity with its conscious cultivation of wit also makes itself felt and contributes a counter-current. We now notice a difference between the more Latinate style of official communications as compared with the more Frenchified style of private letters. Both have a highly artificial structure, but private letters are characterised more by *précieux* indirectness than by Ciceronian grandiloquence. A man can write to his brother of the impending birth of a child as follows: 'Bey meiner Frauen ist die mine zum Springen fertig, vnd hastu mit nechsten zu vernehmen, waß bey einnehmung ihres Kindbetts es für Beuten geben werde.' One theologian writes to another: 'Seine Hochwürden v. Magnificenz werden Sich vielleicht anfänglich verwundern, wie Ich rauchendes Döchtlein mich erkühne mit so geringer v. schlechter Feder vor dero hocherleüchte augen zukommen.' Half a century lies between these letters (the first is dated 1645, the second 1700) but the same type of artificial, strained metaphorical style pervades them both. This ornamental diction is a form of *Zierlichkeit*: and seems to have become considered an essential part of cultured letter-writing. We find Cramer apologising to J. F. Mayer in 1707 for not using it: 'Ihr Magnificentz Brieff will ich von Punct zu Punct beantworten ohne alle Zierligkeit der worte, weil die Post wegen des üblen wetters nur umb 10 Uhr kommen.' Sometimes we find in private letters a combination of chancery and *précieux* style. Ciceronian periodicity

THE DEVELOPMENT OF NARRATIVE PROSE

and *précieux* metaphoricalness both proceed from the desire to avoid the commonplace and the vulgar. Both are consciously artificial and consciously avoid the natural. Both are badges of culture.

Heavy complimentation was another feature of this highly artificial style. 'Ogni cosa si celebri con apparato e con solennità', said an Italian concerning seventeenth-century German epistolary style, contrasting it with the grace and freedom of the French.[1] This was a medieval heritage, intensified by Spanish ceremoniousness. It found expression both in the elaborate salutations at the beginning of chancery documents and in the manuals of etiquette so popular at the time. Here again Ciceronianism and preciosity joined hands. The middle classes took over this obsequious politeness as the patina of 'culture'. In this, as in many other things, they took their tone from the court chanceries and court style. This bombastic servility had reached its climax around 1700. In 1715, for instance, we find one Captain Mordeisen(!) beseeching favour of Elizabeth Charlotte of Orleans in these terms:

mithin die hohe Würckung Dero Hochfürstl. Gnade noch anderweitig, obschon unverdient, zugönnen, umb so eher, da Ew. Königl. Hoheit die höchstberührte Gnaden-Strahlen nicht nur auff Lilien und Tuberosen, sondern auch auff geringen Klee und Dero alte Diener zuwerffen, ohne dem Sich jederzeit rühmlichst angelegen seyn lassen.

One could hardly wish for a better example of this strange union between Ciceronianism and *préciosité ridicule*.

Little attention had been paid to private letters in the manuals of letter-writing—the so-called *Briefsteller*—until the seventeenth century, when epistolary style in general became the subject of treatises. Thus a celebrated work like Harsdörffer's *Teutscher Secretarius* (Nuremberg, 1656) deals with every conceivable kind of letter. Towards the end of the century we find a new type of *Briefsteller*: less encyclopaedic, and consisting mainly of a collection of model letters often translated from the French. This type, showing strong French influence, is characteristic of the *galant* period of the early eighteenth century. Amongst those

[1] Panfilo Persico, *Del Segretario* (Venice, 1629), p. 118.

who composed *Briefsteller* at this time were well-known authors like Christian Weise, Benjamin Neukirch, 'Menantes' (Chr. Fr. Hunold) and 'Talander' (August Bohse). But the stress is still laid more on *Zierlichkeit* than on anything else. With Gellert this shifts to the ideal of 'cultured naturalness'. And this change reflects the change in French linguistic taste itself, which we have considered above. Gellert's standpoint brings him often close to Boileau.

The letter had become a literary *genre* in seventeenth-century France. Well composed letters were a mark of culture and afforded opportunities for the display of wit. Hence the vogue of the manuals of letter-writing, the so-called *Secrétaires*. Most popular of all was the *Secrétaire à la mode* of Puget de la Serre, addressed to the *honnêtes gens*. This was first published in 1641 and was reprinted in various editions up to 1700. Amongst the models that La Serre advocated, we find both the ceremonious style of Guez de Balzac and the urbane style of Voiture. La Serre advocated Balzac's style for letters of condolence, but Voiture's for love-letters. The second half of the century saw fewer manuals of epistolography but several important collections of letters. Some of these became well known in Germany, especially Pierre Richelet's *Recueil des plus belles lettres des meilleurs auteurs français* (1689, and several later editions) and, slightly later, the various collections by J. L. Le G. de Grimarest (*Commerce de lettres curieuses et savantes*, 1700; *Traité sur la manière d'écrire des lettres*, 1709).[1] In the theory of epistolography, these French writers of the later seventeenth century made a distinction between *lettres galantes* and *lettres tendres et passionnées*. A different style was required for each. In the galant letter, 'on s'explique d'un air tendre et brillant. L'esprit y a autant de part que le cœur'; in the tender letter, all must be 'simple et naturel' (Richelet). Both styles were accepted. There was, for the moment, no decision in

---

[1] A selection from Richelet's collection was published by 'Menantes' at Hamburg in 1704. A bilingual edition (French and German) of Grimarest's letters was published at Nuremberg and Vienna in two parts (1749, 1751; see British Museum catalogue).

favour of the *simple et naturel*. But this should never descend to the trivial. Richelet demanded for tender letters a style that should be 'vif, & coupé, simple & naturel, *mais sans bassesse*' (my italics). The terms recall Gottsched's strictures in the *Redekunst*. This is the ideal of 'cultured naturalness', advocated in Germany by Gellert. Both styles had been approved in France. But in Germany the one was used to beat the other. It is the ideal of cultured naturalness that won the day.

It would seem that the idea for Gellert's treatise on letter-writing, the *Praktische Abhandlung von dem Guten Geschmacke in Briefen* (1751), came from his friend Rabener.[1] In Cramer's life of Gellert, we read that Rabener urged Gellert to write the work 'zur Verbannung des ihm [Rabener] so verhaßten weitschweifigen Canzeleystyls'.[2] Gellert's Preface states his intention of encouraging young people, especially women, to cultivate a *natural* style and of removing the widespread misapprehension that the German language was not supple and flexible enough to treat of civilised matters and express the tender emotions. These are often the subject of letters. Letters are a substitute for conversation, and should therefore remain closer to conversation than to a more conscious and flowery style. The 'prächtige...kanzleyförmige Schreibart' should be shunned because it is *unnatural*. As an example of what to avoid he imagines a request to a great lord beginning as follows:

Gnädiger Herr,

Nachdem ich in Erfahrung gebracht habe, daß Ew. Hochwohlgebohrnen eines Sekretärs bedürftig sind, und ich mich zu sothaner Bedienung seit vielen verflossenen Jahren auf Schulen und Akademien bestmöglichst geschickt gemacht habe, etc.[3]

We observe that this cumbrous protasis exemplifies several of the features of chancery style noted above. Gellert's analysis is

---

[1] According to Steinhausen (vol. II, p. 250) Gellert had written some *Gedanken von einem guten deutschen Briefe* in 1742; but I have been unable to trace this treatise in any edition of Gellert's works or elsewhere.
[2] Gellert, *Sämmtliche Schriften* (1774), vol. X, p. 68.
[3] Quoting from the *Sämmtliche Schriften* of 1774, Vierter Theil, p. 5.

governed by his ideal of naturalness: the conjunction *nachdem*, he says, is a meaningless link, the phrase in *Erfahrung bringen* is a pompous periphrasis, the use of *bedürftig* and *sothan* is bookish, *verflossen* is superfluous, and *bestmöglichst* is 'durchaus fremd'. It is unnatural in every way. But, says Gellert, we should not fall into the other mistake of writing our letters in clumsy colloquial style. These are the same two extremes, represented most completely by Lohenstein and Weise, which Gottsched had specified in the *Redekunst*. Here they are restated under the influence of the French ideal of 'cultured naturalness'.

The words we use should be the words of polite conversation; but the way we use them should be something more. We should choose our words more carefully, for we have time to do so. We should combine them more carefully, for this makes for elegance. We should choose and combine our words in a manner suited to the subject. 'Wenn wir in einer geschmückten oder prächtigen Sprache von einer geringen und gemeinen Sache reden: so hat der Ausdruck kein Verhältniß, er wird unnatürlich oder abentheurlich'—this had been, in Gottsched's analysis, one of the origins of bombast (see above, p. 158). In terms of antique rhetoric, it was using the grand style for lowly matter. A too consciously *sinnreich* style is also a poor thing; it displeases because of its artificiality. On the other hand there is style which displeases because it is 'too natural', 'die Schreibart, die zwar aus sehr leichten, aber auch sehr leeren, Worten und Gedanken besteht'. As an example of unnatural style he quotes a euphuistic letter of thanks to a patron proclaimed as a model in Benjamin Neukirch's *Galante Briefe*. To illustrate the dangers of too natural a style, he gives a letter reproaching a friend for not having written, in which a bald, flat style debilitates the effect. He then gives in translation a letter with the same content written by Pliny to his friend Paulinus, where the words are chosen and arranged to obtain the greatest effect. Gellert has rejected the grand style, the sententious middle style and the vulgar low style. There remains that same blend between plain middle style and civilised low style which Gottsched had advocated. If we consider this in terms of the Ciceronian–Senecan antithesis, Gellert has rejected the Ciceronian and the curt Senecan styles, leaving only the loose Senecan style. But we must remember that he is only talking of epistolary style.

As for the structure of a letter, it should not be composed too consciously: 'Man bediene sich also keiner künstlichen Ordnung, keiner mühsamen Einrichtungen, sondern man überlasse sich der freywilligen Folge seiner Gedanken, und setze sie nach einander hin, wie sie in uns entstehen.'[1] This is an attack on the treatment of the letter as an oratorical discourse. Grimarest had objected to this, on the grounds that it hampered naturalness. Gellert says that the elaborate recipes with all their formalistic rhetoric, are not worth a fig—for they merely prevent men from writing naturally. This is a complete rejection of the artificial sentence-mould of the chancery style. Gellert is almost ironical: 'Sie [*the manuals*] geben uns gewisse Anfangs- und Schluß-Formeln, gewisse Verbindungswörter, die im Umgange nicht gebräuchlich sind, gleichsam als Hüter, damit unsre Gedanken nicht aus ihren Fesseln entrinnen können.' But he pulls himself up sharp to remind us that this is a serious matter: 'Der Gebrauch dieser Methoden ist unstreitig an dem schlimmen Geschmacke in Briefen hauptsächlich Ursache, der lange Zeit in Deutschland geherrscht hat.'[2] It was all due to the mistaken but widely accepted opinion that the chancery language was the best language and therefore the best language for letter-writing. Gellert realised the crucial point when he says that this had led to a sickly monotony in style, 'weil alles in einer einförmigen Stellung vorgetragen worden'. The rest of the treatise is an elaboration of these points. Persistent is the attack on the chancery language. Objection is made to its abstractness, its obsequiousness and its periodic structure.[3] On the periodic sentence Gellert is quite explicit: it is bad

---

[1] *Op. cit.* p. 37.
[2] *Ibid.* pp. 39 ff.
[3] On abstractness: 'Wir haben Abstracta gemacht und den gnädigen Herrn in die Gnade, den Hochedlen in das Hochedle und so weiter verwandelt', p. 71. On obsequiousness, cf. his objections to the excessive addiction to titles and to artificial pronominal forms like *Dero, Dieselben, Hochstdenselben*, p. 72.

because it forces into one period clauses which naturally would be separate, and because it forces words out of their natural order, so that instead of saying: 'Nachdem ich so glücklich gewesen, Ew. Excellenz Befehle zu vollziehen', as would be natural, one says: 'Nachdem Ew. Excellenz Befehle zu vollziehen, ich so glücklich gewesen bin', which is artificial and ungainly.[1]

Equally firm is Gellert's opposition to forced wit and forced pathos—to the use of the *pathetisch* or *sinnreich* style when the *natürlich* style is demanded. Gellert maintains that letters should by their subject demand the *natürlich* style. He has made it clear that he means a graceful naturalness and not the unconsidered language of real conversation. This is a development of the *genus humile* of antiquity; but it is taking up the moral learnt from the bad example of Christian Weise. His ideal is the epistolary style of Mme de Sévigné; and he expressly rejects the style of Voiture and Balzac who 'squander their hyperboles in encomia and their antitheses in wit'.

Sometimes letters involve narrative. Narrative style, says Gellert, rests on one simple premise: 'Wir wollen eine Sache in den Umständen wissen, durch die sie eine Begebenheit geworden ist; allein wir wollen sie auch bald wissen, und nichts hören, was nicht zur Sache etwas beyträgt.'[2] Therefore clarity and concision are essential, and the secret of a good narrative style is to strike a balance between the two. It should delude the reader into the belief that he is an eye-witness of the action.

No one could ever claim that Lohenstein did this. It would indeed seem doubtful whether he ever had any such intention. His battle-scenes in *Arminius* are so stifled by learned parentheses, *sententiae* and rhetorical circumlocutions that they move at a snail's pace. Christian Weise—to go to the other extreme—was vivid enough. But he lacked that other quality which Gellert praises alongside vividness, namely *Anmuth*, for it is *Anmuth* that remains Gellert's guiding principle and which always has the last word:

Dieses [*vividness*] geschieht durch die kleinen Gemälde, die man im Erzählen von den Umständen, oder Personen, entwirft, insonderheit

[1] *Op. cit.* p. 72.   [2] *Ibid.* p. 77.

wenn man die Personen zuweilen selbst reden läßt, und uns dadurch mit ihrem Charakter bekannt macht. Man redet oft selbst im Erzählen den Andern an, und fragt ihn, wie wir bey einer Sache zu thun pflegen, die wir mündlich erzählen, oder die wir wirklich vorgehen sehen. Man antwortet sich; man streut kleine Betrachtungen ein, die uns unser Witz, oder unsre Belesenheit hergeben. Alles dieses am rechten Orte, mit Anständigkeit, nicht zu häufig, kurz, so thun, daß alles, so sehr es entbehrt werden kann, doch zur *Anmuth* der Geschichte unentbehrlich gewesen zu seyn scheint, dieses ist das Verdienst der Erzählung.[1]

Both in what it rejects and in what it proclaims, this treatise is a theoretical description of the style of which *Das Leben der Schwedischen Gräfinn von G*** (1747–8) is the practical demonstration. Let us examine some examples. Here, first of all, is a passage of narrative from the climax of the novel:

Nunmehr komme ich auf einen Perioden aus meinem Leben, der alles übertrift, was ich bisher gesagt habe. Ich muß mir Gewalt anthun, indem ich ihn beschreibe; so sehr weigert sich mein Herz, die Vorstellung einer Begebenheit in sich zu erneuern, die ihm so viel gekostet hat. Ich weis, daß es eine von den Haupttugenden einer guten Art zu erzählen ist, wenn man so erzählt, daß die Leser nicht die Sache zu lesen, sondern selbst zu sehen glauben, und durch eine abgenöthigte Empfindung sich unvermerkt an die Stelle der Person setzen, welcher die Sache begegnet ist. Allein ich zweifle, daß ich diese Absicht erhalten werde. Wir fuhren, wie ich gesagt habe, dem ankommenden Schiffe eine halbe Stunde entgegen. Es waren zehn bis zwölf Deutsche Reisende auf demselben, und auch etliche Russen. Diese stiegen in unserm Angesichte ans Land, und gratulirten dem Herrn Andreas zur glücklichen Ankunft unsers Schiffes, weil sie hörten, daß er der Herr davon war. Andreas, der die See stets in Gedanken hatte, hörte ihnen begierig zu. Nur mir ward die Zeit zu lang. Ich trat daher mit meinem Manne auf die Seite, und bat ihn, daß er wieder zurückfahren möchte. Da ich noch mit ihm rede, so kömmt einer von den Passagierern auf mich zugesprungen, umarmt mich, und ruft; Ja, ja sie sind es, ich habe meinen Augen nicht trauen wollen; aber sie sind meine liebe Gemahlinn. Er drückte mich einige Minuten so fest an sich, daß ich nicht sehen konnte, wer mir diese Zärtlichkeit erwies. Das Schrecken kam dazu, und ich glaubte nicht anders, als daß ein unsinnig Verliebter mich angefallen hätte. Aber, ach Himmel, wen sah ich endlich in

[1] *Ibid.* p. 78. My italics.

meinen Armen! Meinen Grafen in Rußischer Kleidung, meinen ersten Mann, den ich zehen Jahr für todt gehalten hatte. Ich kann nicht sagen, wie mir ward. So viel weiß ich, daß ich kein Wort aufbringen konnte. Mein Graf stund und weinte. Er erblickte endlich seinen ehemaligen Freund, als meinen itzigen Mann. Er umarmte ihn; doch von beiden habe ich kein Wort gehört, oder vor Bestürzung nichts verstehen können.[1]

We are faced here with a situation of abnormal intensity. The author knows it is so unusual as to be almost incredible. Nevertheless he maintains his demand, expressed also in the treatise on letters, that it shall be described so vividly as to make the reader believe he is present as an eye-witness. The situation is built up swiftly and tersely, with none of the glosses and side-remarks which slow down Lohenstein's battles. No time is wasted on psychological analysis of motives or reactions. On the contrary: 'Ich kann nicht sagen, wie mir ward.' We are living through events as they happen. Nothing is allowed to distract us from the rapid chronology of the experience. Compare this with a brief episode from Lohenstein. Hermann and Eggius, in fierce combat, have dragged each other down:

> Ob nun zwar Herrmann oben zu liegen kam, war doch die Menge der Römer, so diesem Römischen Heerführer zu hülffe kamen, so groß daß Herrmann den unter sich gebrachten Eggius verlaßen, und zu Fuße wider tausend Lantzen und Degen sich vertheidigen muste. Fürst Adgandester, welcher der Oberste unter denen Grafen oder Gefärthen des Feldherrn war, die, wie bey den Galliern die so genannten Soldurier aus dem Kerne des Adels von denen Deutschen Fürsten nichts minder im Friede zur Pracht und allen fürnehmen Hoffämtern, als im Kriege zu ihrer Leibwache pflegen erkieset zu werden, ward dieser dem Feldherrn zustoßenden Gefahr inne. Weil nun dieser Gefärthen Pflicht ist, daß, wie ihr Hertzog ohne Schimpff keinen es ihm darff an Tapfferkeit zuvor thun laßen, also ihnen eine nicht geringere Schande sey, des Fürstens Tugend nicht gleiche kommen, ja ein unausleschliches Brandmahl ihres gantzen Lebens, ohne den Hertzog lebendig aus der Schlacht kommen; Weßwegen sie auch auff dem Helme einen kohlschwartzen Federpusch führen; so drang er nicht alleine durch das Gedränge der

---

[1] Gellert, *Sämmtliche Schriften*, ed. cit., vol. IV, pp. 321–3.

Römer verzweiffelt durch, sondern ermunterte auch durch seyn Beyspiel noch dreißig andere Ritter, welche wie der Fürst für den Sieg, also sie für ihren Fürsten zu streiten, und ihm alle ihre Heldenthaten zuzueignen verbunden, und wenn nur einer für dem andern Ehre einlegen kan, dem Tode selbst das blaue in Augen zu sehen gewohnt sind.[1]

Obviously there is no attempt here to make us feel we are eye-witnesses. The flow of the action is constantly retarded by periphrasis, parenthesis and cumbrous conjunctions. Contrast this with the steady crescendo of short, clipped sentences by which Gellert reaches his climax. Lohenstein has plenty of time and he is often more interested in the side-issues than in reaching any climax. Gellert is concerned solely with the basic movement of the sequence. He does not allow the parts to obscure the whole. Lohenstein is often more interested in the parts than the whole. Hence Lohenstein is expansive, Gellert is concentrated. Each therefore tends toward a different type of sentence. Lohenstein in this mood instinctively casts his thoughts in periodic sentences of Ciceronian build;[2] Gellert uses short simple sentences. The one seems anxious not to hurry the reader; the other wants to get there as quickly as possible. In this we can perhaps feel the difference between a ceremonious and a more practical age.

Here is a more static, descriptive passage from earlier in Gellert's novel:

Wir lebten auf unserm Landgute so ruhig und zärtlich, als jemals. Und damit wir den Verlust unsers klugen Vaters desto weniger fühlten: so nahm mein Gemahl seinen ehemaligen Reisegefährten, den Herrn R.... zu sich. Er war noch ein junger Mann, der aber in einer großen Gesellschaft zu nichts taugte, als einen leeren Platz einzunehmen. Er war stumm und unbelebt, wenn er viel Leute sah. Doch in dem Umgange von drey oder vier Personen, die er kannte, war er ganz unentbehrlich. Seine Belesenheit war außerordentlich, und seine Bescheidenheit eben so groß. Er war in der Tugend und Freundschaft strenge bis zum Eigensinne. So traurig seine Miene aussah, so gelassen

---

[1] Lohenstein, *Arminius* (Leipzig, 1689), vol. 1, p. 35. British Museum copy.
[2] He did not always write in this way; for at times he affected Senecan *sententiae* and even something approaching the curt manner.

und zufrieden war er doch. Er schlug kein Vergnügen aus; allein es schien, als ob er sich nicht so wohl an den Ergötzlichkeiten selbst, als vielmehr an dem Vergnügen belustigte, das die Ergötzlichkeiten Andern machten. Sein Verlangen war, alle Menschen vernünftig, und alle Vernünftige glücklich zu sehen. Daher konnte er die großen Gesellschaften nicht leiden, weil er so viel Zwang, so viel unnatürliche Höflichkeiten und so viel Verhinderungen, frey und vernünftig zu handeln, darinnen antraf. Er blieb in allen seinen Handlungen uneigennützig, und gegen die Glücksgüter, und gegen alle Ehrenstellen fast gar zu gleichgültig. Die Schmeichler waren seine ärgsten Feinde.[1]

This prose is reminiscent of the simply balanced prose of Addison which we have seen, in German dress, in *Der Patriot*. It embodies Gellert's ideals of clarity and concision, just as the narrative passage conformed to his ideal of vividness. The points are made simply and effectively: often by pairs of statements connected by a simple rhythmical swing of poise and counterpoise:

> *Und damit* wir den Verlust unsers klugen Vaters desto weniger fühlten: *so* nahm mein Gemahl....
> Er war *noch* ein junger Mann, *der aber*....
> *Seine Belesenheit* war...außerordentlich, und *seine Bescheidenheit* eben so groß....
> *So traurig* seine Miene aussah, *so gelassen und zufrieden* war er *doch*.

These connections seem to fit quite easily into the natural flow of the prose; they do not conflict with the rhythm, as they do so often in chancery style. One is never held back for the sake of grammar or oratory. And yet these *connexiones* derive ultimately from rhetoric. So does the use in this passage of doublets like *ruhig und zärtlich, stumm und unbelebt, Tugend und Freundschaft, gelassen und zufrieden*. The *connexiones* are there for shapeliness, the doublets for emphasis. But both have been transformed from cumbrous artificiality into a thing of elegance. The *connexiones* are never heavy and assist the rhythm, the doublets are not tautological but enrich the meaning. We can see from this how Gellert's ideal of *Anmuth* transfuses his whole style. Let us note the last few sentences beginning at 'Sein Verlangen...', for they embody Gellert's attitude to all things, including language. Like this

[1] *Ed. cit.* p. 270.

character in his novel, Gellert was opposed to all 'Zwang' and 'unnatürliche Höflichkeiten', all 'Verhinderungen, frey und vernünftig zu handeln'. He was indifferent to *Glücksgüter und Ehrenstellen* (Lohenstein was obviously not). And his greatest enemies were the flatterers. His ideal remained naturalness; but a civilised naturalness, controlled by *Anmuth*.

The stylistic connection between the letter and the novel should by now be apparent from our analysis. The first epistolary novels in German are J. K. A. Musäus's *Grandison der Zweite* (1760–2) and J. T. Hermes's *Sophiens Reise von Memel nach Sachsen* (1769–73). Both use the Gellert type of letter. In his review of Musäus's novel, Thomas Abbt had already expressed the opinion that Gellert's epistolary style should no longer be considered as perfection (*Litteraturbriefe*, no. 314). The new generation, more unabashed in their cult of feeling, were more passionate letter-writers. *La Nouvelle Héloïse* transformed the genre. It is the essential link between *Pamela* and *Werther*. And *Werther* is the crowning demonstration of the very close connection between epistolary and narrative style in the German eighteenth century. It had to be so, in an age which cultivated its own world of feelings in its letter-writing and created fictitious worlds of feeling in its novels.

It is interesting to find Voß in 1773 writing to Brückner:

> Gellert ist ein guter, ein unterhaltender und belehrender Schriftsteller. Aber den Ruhm, den er bei seinen Zeitgenossen verdiente, verdient er jezt in dem Grade nicht mehr. Ich glaube noch immer, daß es gefährlich sei, seine Prosa für ein Muster der Schreibart auszugeben. Denn französisch Deutsch kann unmöglich gut deutsch sein.

This must be understood in the framework of Voß's antipathy to the Saxon norm ('Die Obersächsische ist wirklich die schlechteste Sprache') and his Bodmer-like contention that German had become spineless ('ich studire deswegen die Minnesänger und Luthers Schriften, um die alte Nerve wieder zu bekommen, die die deutsche Sprache ehedem hatte, und durch das verwünschte Latein und Französisch ganz wieder verloren hat'). In 1774, also to Brückner, he expressly fits Gellert into this framework:

Gellert schreibt leicht, aber nicht schön. Er nimt von unsrer starken Sprache nur den kleinen Theil von Worten, die man gebraucht, ein französisches Buch (nicht zu übersezen) zu parafrasiren; nähert sich dem Ton der Gesellschaft, der durchaus nichts taugt, wo der Schriftsteller nicht eben das im Sinn hat, diesen, wie jede andre Sache aus der Natur um uns, nachzuahmen; nimt leicht zu fassende Gegenstände, und gießt dann sein ewiges unausstehliches Wassergeschwäz in solchem Überflusse darüber, daß die dumme Eitelkeit, die doch auch gern *viel* und *schnell* verstehn oder lesen will, volkommen befriedigt wird. Glaub' nicht, daß ich hizig schreibe. Ich versichere dir, daß ich für Gellerts wahre Verdienste eben die Hochachtung habe, die du nur immer haben kannst. Aber mein Urtheil ist das Urtheil des Bundes und Klopstocks.[1]

These remarks indicate the very real limitations of Gellert's prose style. But they belong to a later age—an age which had a deeper and more poetical conception of language.

[1] This passage is from the letter dated 17. xi. 1774 to Brückner in *Briefe von J. H. Voß*, ed. Abraham Voß, 2nd edn. (Leipzig, 1840), vol. I, p. 185. The earlier remark about Gellert is to be found *ibid.* p. 138, the remark about '*Nerve*' is on p. 130.

VII

THE LANGUAGE OF POETRY

It might well be questioned whether this study should concern itself with poetry. Is not the language of poetry too individual to fit into our general scheme of investigation? Does it not spring from personal imagination and mirror the man rather than the age? Does not the language of poetry by definition transcend the language of its time? How then can it be considered in any scheme which is chronological? Shall we not unavoidably be drawn into a pattern of progress which is false and irrelevant? It is good that we should consider these objections at the outset; not because they are valid, but because they indicate the limitations of what we can hope to achieve. No amount of investigation into the language of the time will account for the genius of a great poet. But this is not our intention. We are not concerned with explaining poetic genius. We salute the fact of its existence and we believe that poetry represents language at its highest peak of expressiveness. We cannot therefore ignore poetry. Our subject is the development of an uncouth language into one of the most subtle literary media of modern Europe. We believe that the critical phase in this development was the period from 1700 to 1775. Since poetry represents a higher power of language than prose, it is in the poetry of the period that we shall expect to find the greatest potentialities of the language. We shall also encounter there some of its greatest failures. Achievement did not always match endeavour. Poetic intentions were frustrated by a traditional poetical diction which had to be overthrown before personal feeling could express itself once more in poetry of beauty and power. This liberation, it might be objected, is the primary activity of any great poet. He must find his own language. True enough; but this emerges from a tension with normal speech and accepted 'poetical' diction. The individual language of the poet is therefore related to the language of his time. And the language in general profits and inherits from his achievement. In considering the development of any literary language it is therefore important to note these great periods of refashioning. But if this were all, our path would be an easy progress from one such milestone to the next. Yet it is not only the great poets who develop the poetic expressiveness of a language. The failures often contribute something by their very strugglings. So do the critics and theorists. There was a general feeling in the first half of the eighteenth century that German could be *improved* as a poetical medium. Whether this belief was right or wrong is not my concern; the belief existed and contributed greatly to the development of the language. Theorists and practicians of the art of poetry legislated and experimented in the forging of a richer, subtler language. New spheres of subject-matter were assailed. The language was bludgeoned or cajoled into appropriate moods, often by men of fertile linguistic imagination even though few of them had any clear idea of what poetry really was and still fewer were themselves poets. Thereby the language grew in expressiveness: and this redounded to the advantage, not merely of poetry but of the language as a whole. For this reason both the poets and the theorists of poetic diction must have their place in a study of the language as a medium of literary expression.

Rossetti said of the Englishmen of the reign of Queen Anne that they 'created a style in prose, and wrenched its characteristics to form their poetry'. Much the same can legitimately be said of the Germans between 1700 and 1740. There is no clear distinction between poetry and prose in the minds of most writers. At best, poetry is envisaged as a more elegant, more rhetorical, more unusual, sophisticated and elevated form of expression than prose. The difference was one of degree, not of kind. This is clear from the definitions of poetry in the manuals of poetics. 'Die teutsche Poësie', said Erdmann Uhse in 1719, 'ist eine Geschicklichkeit, seine Gedanken über eine gewisse Sache zierlich, doch dabey klug und deutlich, in abgemessenen Worten und Reimen vorzubringen.'[1]

[1] *Wohl-informirter Poet*, etc., p. 7.

Almost the same words are used by Andreas Köhler in 1734: poetry is defined as 'eine Kunst und Geschicklichkeit, seine Gedancken von einer ieden Sache ordentlich und zierlich in Reimen und richtiger Abzehlung der Sylben also vorzutragen, daß der Leser sich daran delectire'.[1] Poetry is a skill, it gives pleasure. But also instruction: 'Eine schöne und lustige Wissenschafft, dadurch des Menschen Geist auffgemuntert, und angefrischet wird, die auch sehr nützlich, weil unser Gemüth, Sinn und Verstand dadurch zu höhern Geschäfften gleichsam geschärffet und tüchtig gemacht wird.'[2] Poetry, says Christian Weise, is the handmaid of rhetoric, in that it teaches a young man to express his ideas not only clearly but gracefully.[3] It is not uncommon to find mentioned amongst the uses of poetry that it preserves the purity and beauty of the language. Thus Johann Christoph Memmlingen in 1685: 'Vornehmlich aber ist ihr [der Poesie] Nutzen daran zu erkennen, daß die deutsche Sprache desto reinlicher und zierlicher erhalten werde, und ist gewiß, wer einen guten Vers schreibet, der wird auch in der gemeinen Schreib- und Redens Art nicht verstossen...';[4] and Johann Ernst Weise in 1708, rather more urgently: 'Die Poesie soll ja der gefallenen teutschen Sprache wieder auff die Beine helffen.'[5] This skill, like all skills, can be acquired by persistent study. Hence there is some scepticism displayed towards Horace's proud dictum. 'Wann wir unsre Zeiten ansehen, dürffte man fast sagen: *Poeta et fit et nascitur*. Denn wir haben die schönste Gelegenheit, den vollkommensten *Apparatum* und die deutlichsten Anleitungen dazu', says J. G. Neukirch.[6] Männling is even more definite: '*Poetæ non fiunt sed nascuntur*. Ich getraue mir aber gantz richtig den Gegen-Satz zu behaupten, daß Poeten nicht

---

[1] *Deutliche und gründliche Einleitung zu der reinen und deutschen Poesie* (Halle, 1734), p. 1.
[2] *Des Taurenden Poetik* (Nuremberg, 1702), Vorrede.
[3] *Curiöse Gedancken von Deutschen Versen* (Leipzig), vol. II, p. 16. This work was first published at Leipzig in 1691. I have used the copy of the 1693 edition in the Central Library at Zürich.
[4] *Europäischer Parnassus* (Wittenberg, 1685), p. 8.
[5] *Unvorgreiffliche Gedancken von Teutschen Versen* (Ulm, 1708), p. 4.
[6] *Anfangs-Gründe zur Reinen Teutschen Poesie* (Halle, 1725), p. 11.

gebohren, sondern durch gute Unterweisung gemacht würden.'[1] Poetry was therefore within everyone's reach. It was a craft. Hence the vogue of manuals. These often contained lists of poetic expressions from standard authors (mostly seventeenth-century) which could be used to adorn the phrase and avoid the dull flatness of prose. Writers had no qualms about such borrowing. It was part of the trade. Männling said that all good poets of the seventeenth century had borrowed phrases from the ancients. Christian Weise was attacked because his style was said to lack these adornments. The general feeling was that poetry should use the same language as prose, but elevate itself above ordinariness by the use of *ingenieuse Fictiones* or *Inventionen*, by figures of speech involving ingenuity, wit, learning and all other forms of sophistication. 'Vor allen', said J. S. Wahll in 1723,[2] 'soll der *Stylus Poëticus* seyn, welcher so wol nicht wider die teutsche Reinlichkeit und gehörige *Construction* sündiget, als auch die teutsche Sprache durch annehmlichere Zierlichkeiten und lieblichere und nachsinnlichere Redens-Arten erhebet, als im gemeinen Leben, ja auch wohl im *Stylo Oratorio* zu geschehen pfleget.' But the basic structure of this language remains that of prose. This was most stoutly stated in Christian Weise's famous injunction: 'Welche *Construction in prosâ* nicht gelitten wird, die soll man auch in Versen davon lassen.'[3] There is no sharp distinction made at this time between poetry and prose. No distinction of nature is postulated at all; the only difference lies in the figuration. The situation has been pungently described by a critic: 'Poesie als die gewähltere, Prosa als die gewöhnlichere Ausdrucksweise.'[4] The basic structure of the language of poetry, as in the England of Queen Anne, was and remained the structure of prose.

Christian Weise's programmatic statement was aimed at various archaisms sanctioned under poetic licence. He would have none

[1] J. C. Männling, *Deutsch-Poetisches Lexicon* (Frankfurt and Leipzig, 1715), Vorrede.
[2] *Gründliche Einleitung zu der rechten, reinen und galanten Teutschen Poesie* (Chemnitz, 1723), p. 134.
[3] *Curiöse Gedancken von Deutschen Versen*, ed. cit. vol. I, p. 141.
[4] Kåre Kaiser, *Mundart und Schriftsprache* (Leipzig, 1930), p. 70.

of this. Constructions like *die Stube dein, ich bin gewesen da, ich zu dem Freunde gekommen bin* cannot be justified by the necessities of rhyme or scansion. This thought was taken up by others; for example, by Andreas Köhler: 'Man muß des Reimes wegen die *Constructionem prosaicam* der Wörter nicht verderben', or J. G. Neukirch: 'Die Construction, so man in ungebundener Rede gebrauchet, muß auch hauptsächlich in Versen beobachtet werden.' Neukirch disapproves expressly of postposition of epithet, separation of prefix from infinitive, pleonastic repetition of the article (*die Weisheit, die machet*) and free positioning of the verb in main clauses. These constructions had been quite common in seventeenth-century verse. An archaic flavour attached to them. They were now old-fashioned, musty, ramshackle. But not everyone accepted this attitude or Christian Weise's strictures. Morhof thought them exaggerated; a certain freedom of word-order was, he maintained, justified for the sake of emphasis or euphony. Burkhard Mencke (*Unterredung von der Deutschen Poesie*, 1710) admitted exceptions for the sake of 'eine vortreffliche Pensée oder den angenehmen Klang'. In the Breslau *Anleitung zur Poesie* of 1725 (anonymously published) we find an ambiguous situation: Weise is charged with destroying the true spirit of poetry, but his demand for prose-construction is restated emphatically elsewhere in the book: 'Die Construction muß in Versen vollkommen so bleiben, wie sie in Prosa ist.' Other restatements were offered by Wahll (*Gründliche Einleitung*, 1723): 'Was nicht in prosa stehen kann und nicht in denen Ohren klinget, kann auch in versen nicht passiret werden' and Köhler (*Deutliche und gründliche Einleitung*, 1734): 'Von der Construction, die in prosa gebräuchlich, hat man, so viel möglich, nicht leichtlich und ohne Noth abzuweichen.' On the whole, therefore, it can be said that Weise's injunction was accepted by the age; but there were individual protests.[1]

The demand for prose-construction in verse was, as we have

---

[1] See Markwardt, *Geschichte der deutschen Poetik*, vol. I, pp. 273–5 and p. 348. Weise had already adumbrated his demand for prose-construction in the *Nothwendige Gedancken* of 1675.

seen, to some extent a conscious reaction against the artificiality of the seventeenth century. So too was the opposition to metaphor. At first opinion was divided between those who still followed Lohenstein or Hofmannswaldau and those who mistrusted all forms of figurative expression. The opposition party rapidly came to dominate the scene. Indeed, poetry swung away from seventeenth-century fashions more rapidly than prose. The reaction sometimes took the form of resolving all metaphor into simile. Others scrutinised all comparisons with strictly rationalistic criteria. Some avoided all forms of figurative expression and cultivated a self-conscious straightforwardness. This latter resulted in flatness of style: either ceremonious flatness as with Canitz, Besser and König, or commonplace flatness as with Christian Weise. Few were prepared to go as far as Weise's: 'Ich will meine *simplicit*ät im Reden behalten.'[1] But many writers were affected by this change in taste. In our discussion of prose style we saw a similar reaction against grandiloquence. We also mentioned parallel currents in late seventeenth-century France. During the first half of the eighteenth century, France seems to have considered metaphorical style as more proper to poetry than to philosophy. But even in poetry, metaphor was judged by logical and rationalistic precepts. We find Voltaire objecting to the metaphors of Corneille, and La Harpe to those of Voltaire. In the *Journal Etranger* for September 1762, an observer[2] noted: 'Les Français...sont timides en poésie, rejettent les métaphores et les images de l'imagination, remplissent de termes abstraits, arides et muets un langage qui n'admet que des expressions pittoresques et sonores.' This was a cry of regret; for by the 1760's the tide had turned again in favour of metaphor both in France and in Germany. But the description was true of Germany as well as of France. In the first half of the century metaphor fell out of favour and poetical diction moved towards directness. The age, especially in France, was more inclined to philosophy than

---

[1] *Curiöse Gedancken von Deutschen Versen*, ed. cit. vol. I, p. 133.

[2] Suard. Quoted by Alexis François in vol. VI of the *Histoire de la langue française* (ed. Brunot) (Paris, 1932), p. 1263.

poetry. In England, one Samuel Parker had advocated (*A Discourse of Ecclesiastical Politie*, 1670) an Act of Parliament against 'fulsome and lushious Metaphors' as an 'effectual Cure of all our present Distempers'. Absence of metaphor became one of the salient features of the diction of Augustan poetry. 'The poetry of Dryden and Pope differs therefore from earlier and later English poetry in that it is not a poetry of suggestion but of statement', says F. W. Bateson,[1] 'The bareness of diction, the absence of metaphor, and the metrical monotony of Augustan poetry were therefore deliberate and necessary. They ensure the precision and the economy of its strokes.' There is little approaching the merits of English Augustan poetry to be found in the German verse of the time. But there are constant glimpses of pale reflections. And the theory often operated with similar principles.

Metaphorical figuration of language had been accepted by Opitz as part of the *zuebereitung vnd zierh der worte* proper to poetry. This included metaphorical circumlocutions (like *Wolckentreiber* or *Meerauffreitzer* for the North Wind). Collections of these poetic periphrases—the so-called *Schatzkammern*—were published throughout the seventeenth century and lists were often included in manuals of style or grammar. These handbooks of figurative ornamentation became the textbooks of poetic composition. As one author put it: 'Damit ein ieder nach Nothdurfft und Belieben, insonderheit aber die angehende die Poeterey liebende Jugend, sich desselben bescheidentlich gebrauchen, und erfahrnen Meistern glücklicher folgen könne.'[2] In the theoretical comparison of poetry with painting, metaphor was interpreted as one of the primary expressive qualities of poetry. Buchner (*Weg-Weiser*, 1663) demanded: 'daß ein Poet zu förderst sich befleißen solle, schöne Metaphoren zu gebrauchen, dann fast nichts anders die Rede herrlicher, ansehnlicher und auch lieblicher und

---

[1] *English Poetry and the English Language* (Oxford, 1934), pp. 58–9.

[2] Joh. Peter Titz, in his edition of Peschwitz's *Jüngst-Erbauter Hoch-Teutscher Parnaß*, published as *Anmuthige Formeln, Sinnreiche Poetische Beschreibungen und Kunst-zierliche, verblühmte Arten zu reden etc.* in 1663. See Bruno Markwardt, *op. cit.* vol. I, p. 47.

angenehmer macht'.[1] Harsdörffer (*Trichter*, 1647–53) said one recognised a poet by his metaphors as one did a lion by his claws. 'Ohne solche poetische Ausrede ist das Gedicht saft- und kraftloß.' Birken and Neumark were agreed on this primacy of metaphor in poetic language. Ziegler (*Von den Madrigalen*, 1653, 1685) brought an interesting twist into the theory by justifying poetical circumlocutions on the grounds that the single word sometimes did not exist in German. Morhof (1685) was just as definite as Harsdörffer: poetic diction must contain metaphor, 'sonsten kreichet sie bey der Erden und hat nichts, wo durch sie sich erheben kann'. But Morhof opposed excessive use of metaphor. Moscherosch (*Sittewald*, 1642) had already satirised the absurdities of continuous figuration, and Sacer (*Reime dich oder ich fresse dich*, 1673) had mocked at the devotees of the *Schatzkammern* who 'anderer Leute Sachen zusammen lausen und zausen'. Reaction was mounting, provoked by German imitations of the excessively figurative style of the Italian Marino. The real attack on *marinismo* does not come until the eighteenth century; but a certain rationalistic caution regarding metaphor is already visible in the closing years of the seventeenth century. Morhof objected to an English poet talking of sleeping hills and flowers. These were *außspürige Einfälle*, the fruit of uncontrolled fancy;[2] there must be some moderation. It is not only with Morhof that we find at this time an appeal for restraint and moderation. A swing away from figurative style in the direction of plainness, a reaction strongly stimulated by the influence of Boileau, is apparent in the court poets flourishing around 1700 whose duties, like those of our poet laureate, were to compose suitable verses for ceremonial occasions. The most famous of them were Johann von Besser and Johann Ulrich König. They helped to maintain the conception of poetry as a cultured craft, aristocratic and festive both in occasion and language. Their language was not flowery but formal. As their royal masters

---

[1] Cf. Markwardt, *op. cit.* vol. I, p. 61.
[2] Quoted by Markwardt (p. 231). The word means 'outlandish, eccentric', 'aus der Spur gehen'.

imitated Louis XIV, so they themselves followed Boileau's famous apostrophe of that monarch. In his *Untersuchung von dem guten Geschmack*,[1] König pitted Boileau against Marino. Imitation of Marino had undone in Germany the good work done by Opitz, and the school of Lohenstein had vitiated good taste. Boileau had broken the tyranny of bad taste in France; the fashion for Marino was also past in Italy. Something of the kind had also been achieved in Germany, he claims, by judicious study of the Ancients. In a note he mentions Canitz, Besser, and the preface to Wernicke's epigrams. Canitz is pre-eminently a poet of good taste which König defines as 'ein richtiger Begriff des vollkommenen in allen Dingen'.[2] It can be trained by 'Prüfung, Fleiß, Kunst und Übung'.[3] His ideal for language is realised when 'die Redens-Arten rein, gleich, deutlich, zierlich, wohlgewehlt, edel, regelmäßig, und alle diese Stücke nicht zu kurtz, nicht zu lang, sondern wohl zusammen verbunden sind'.[4] This movement towards plainness under the influence of Boileau can be best seen in three minor poets of the beginning of the eighteenth century.

Friedrich von Canitz (1654–1699) never claimed to be a poet. Although he liked making verses, he never published any of them and there is no indication that he ever wished to do so.[5] He was a polished diplomat, versed in many languages, widely travelled, well read, a lover of the Ancients as well as of contemporary France, for whom versifying was an agreeable recreation. He translated from Horace, Juvenal and Boileau; and it was his admiration for Boileau and the principles of his *Art Poétique* that made him oppose, very gently and diplomatically, the galimatias of Silesian metaphorical bombast. In his satire *Von der Poesie*, he wrote:

Kein Wort kömmt für den Tag, das nicht auf Steltzen geht.
Fällt das geringste vor in diesen Krieges-Zeiten,

---

[1] In his ed. of Canitz's poems, 1727; see below.
[2] *Op. cit.* p. 260.   [3] *Ibid.* p. 263.
[4] *Ibid.* p. 316.
[5] His poems were first published anonymously after his death as *Nebenstunden unterschiedener Gedichte* (1700, and eight reprints); but the standard edition is that published by König in 1727. I quote from the British Museum copy of this handsome book.

So, dünckt mich, hör ich schon die Wetter-Glocke läuten:
Ein Flammen-schwangrer Dampf beschwärtzt das Lufft-Revier,
Der Straal-beschwäntzte Blitz bricht überall herfür,
Der grause Donner brüllt, und spielt mit Schwefel-Keilen.

Against this newfangled exaggeration he upheld the pure example of the Ancients. In the second half of the eighteenth century one meets the statement in various places that it was Canitz who brought good taste back to Germany. The famous edition of his poems made by König in 1727 contained König's treatise on good taste to which we have referred above. His verse was characterised by poise, balance and good judgment. He was no poet; but he was sober. And German verse needed an antidote to the euphuistic phantasmagoria it had recently been passing through. König in his preface praised the 'gleiche, männliche, und ungeflickte Schreib-Art' of this verse.[1] Here is the beginning of a poem on the flagellation:

> Unser Heyland steht gebunden,
> Voller Striemen, voller Blut,
> Und fühlt so viel neue Wunden,
> Als der Büttel Streiche thut.
> Seht, was seine Liebe kan!
> Und wir dencken kaum daran,
> Daß Er, wegen unsrer Schulden
> Dieses alles muß erdulden.[2]

What flat, prosaic language! But to understand it historically we must compare it with a treatment of the same subject by a disciple of Lohenstein:

> Dem Himmel gleicht sein bunt-gestriemter Rücken,
> Den Regen-Bögen ohne Zahl
> Als lauter Gnaden-Zeichen, schmücken;
> Die (da die Sünd-Fluht unsrer Schuld verseiget)
> Der holden Liebe Sonnen-Strahl
> In seines Blutes Wolcken, zeiget.

This is in abominable taste. But it is from a poem, published thirteen years after Canitz's death, which was to be very

[1] *Op. cit.* p. xliv.   [2] *Ibid.* p. 21.

popular.[1] Taste, then, was faulty and sobriety was needed. No original image or striking turn of phrase breaks the smooth, polished surface of Canitz's civilised verses. There are constant echoes of the past—Horace, Boileau, Opitz—a quality which König praised. To our taste Canitz's style represents alternation between conventional images and rather dry abstraction. Aesthetically it is uninteresting; historically it is important for its very bareness. Here is another poem which at first sight seems somewhat different:

Der Hof

> Ein Schloß, da Circe schertzt mit ihren Gauckel-Possen:
> Ein Kercker, da das Glück die Sclaven hält verschlossen:
> Ein Tollhaus, da man sich durch manche Narren drängt,
> Von denen einer singt, der andre Grillen fängt.
> Ein Kloster, da man sieht die reichsten Brüder betteln:
> Ein Glückstopff, welcher meist besteht in leeren Zetteln:
> Ein Marckt, da Wind und Rauch die besten Waaren sind,
> Und wo ein Gauckel-Dieb das meiste Geld gewinnt.
> Ein angefüllt Spital, in welches einzutreten,
> Ein Krancker sich bemüht den andern todt zu beten.
> Ein stetes Fastnacht-Spiel, da Tugend wird verhönt,
> Obgleich das Laster selbst von ihr die Maske lehnt.
> Denn schmeicheln heißt man hier: sich nach der Zeit bequemen;
> Verleumden: ohnvermerckt den Gifft der Schlangen nehmen;
> Den Hochmuth: Freund und Feind frey unter Augen gehn;
> Den Geitz: mit Wolbedacht auf seine Wirthschafft sehn;
> Die Pracht: den Purpur nicht mit Niedrigkeit beflecken;
> Die Falschheit: mit Verstand des andern Sinn entdecken;
> Den Soff: ein fremdes Hertz erforschen in dem Wein;
> Die Unzucht: recht galant beym Frauenzimmer seyn.
> Eins wisse! Welcher denckt, hier tugendhafft zu handeln,
> Muß, mit Gefahr und Streit, auf dieser Strasse wandeln,
> Worauf in einem Tag mehr Ungeheuer sind,
> Als man in Africa im ödsten Reiche findt.[2]

The structure is very stylised: a series of images leading up to *Fastnacht-Spiel*, switching with the *Tugend... Laster* contrast to a succession of abstracts from *schmeicheln* to *Unzucht*, the whole

---

[1] B. H. Brockes, Passion Oratorio, 1712—his earliest published work. See below, p. 243. [2] Canitz, *ed. cit.* p. 130.

rounded off by a rather flat quatrain. The first half of the poem immediately recalls a very famous poem by Hofmannswaldau:

Die Welt

Was ist die Welt, und ihr berühmtes gläntzen?
Was ist die Welt und ihre gantze Pracht?
Ein schnöder Schein in kurzgefasten Gräntzen,
Ein schneller Blitz bey schwartzgewölckter Nacht.
Ein bundtes Feld, da Kummerdisteln grünen;
Ein schön Spital, so voller Kranckheit steckt.
Ein Sclavenhauß, da alle Menschen dienen,
Ein faules Grab, so Alabaster deckt.
Das ist der Grund, darauff wir Menschen bauen,
Und was das Fleisch für einen Abgott hält.
Komm Seele, komm, und lerne weiter schauen,
Als sich erstreckt der Zirckel dieser Welt.
Streich ab von dir derselben kurtzes Prangen,
Halt ihre Lust vor eine schwere Last.
So wirstu leicht in diesen Port gelangen,
Da Ewigkeit und Schönheit sich umbfast.[1]

Both poems have the succession of images. This was an extreme form of baroque asyndeton, much cultivated by Hofmannswaldau. One poem, entitled *Verachtung der Welt*,[2] has a list of thirty-three comparisons. The question-and-answer form is found in other poems of the same author.[3] But notice that the initial repeated question is lacking in Canitz's poem. Such rhetoric is foreign to his style. Hofmannswaldau's apostrophe to the soul has a much more modest equivalent. And the antithetical juggling with metaphor is completely lacking. At first sight some of the images seem to be common to both poems—*Sclaven, Spital*—even *Fastnacht-Spiel* seems a baroque commonplace—but they are used quite differently. Compare the antithetical *schön Spital* of the one poet with the straightforward *angefüllt Spital* of the other. Canitz's philosophy is not baroque and antithesis is not his natural

---

[1] Text from *Vermischte Gedichte* in *C.H.V.H. Deutsche Ubersetzungen und Getichte* (Breslau, 1679). British Museum copy, p. 31.

[2] Amongst the *Begräbnuß Gedichte* in the same edition, pp. 50–3.

[3] E.g. those beginning 'Was ist die Lust der Welt? nichts als ein Fastnachtsspiel etc. etc.' and 'Was ist die Welt? ein Ball voll Unbestand etc.'

mode of expression. His madhouse is full of madmen, not sages. And there is no mention of alabaster or anything so extravagant. When we reach the *Fastnacht-Spiel*, metaphor is discarded like a mask. Abstractions follow. Both poems end flatly, the one in Africa and the other in Paradise, both poetic abstractions. The similarity between the two poems is fallacious. But it would be difficult to find a better example of what the taste of the new age did with the paraphernalia it found in the property-room of poetic diction.

Benjamin Neukirch (1665–1729) began as an admirer of the Silesians but turned away from them as a result of his contact with the personality and work of Canitz. He was a Silesian by birth, published Lohenstein's *Arminius* and edited the most important of all anthologies of later seventeenth-century verse.[1] In the long preface to this anthology Neukirch attacks the fabrication of occasional verses and the German disregard of their own language and literature. He praises Opitz; but thinks that Hofmannswaldau is the model for love-poetry and Lohenstein for learned, sententious verse. He distinguishes mere versifying from galant verses and from great poetry. The first is useless; the second requires 'feurige und auffgeweckte gemüther, welche in der galanterie sehr wohl erfahren, im erfinden kurtz, in der ausarbeitung hurtig, und in allen ihren gedancken selttzam seyn' (similar, we notice, to those qualities demanded by the theorists of prose style for the middle, *sinnreich* style); but for the last, one must know many languages, be both versed in learning and experienced in the world, be full of wit and master of one's feelings —and also *vernünftig*. But this is so difficult that it is better to keep to the second, galant type of writing. This Neukirch did. The foreswearing of Silesianism comes in a poem composed in 1700:[2]

> Mein reim klingt vielen schon sehr matt und ohne krafft,
> Warum? Ich tränck' ihn nicht in muscateller-safft;

---

[1] *Herrn von Hoffmannswaldau und andrer Deutschen außerlesener und bißher ungedruckter Gedichte*, 7 parts, 1695–1727. Neukirch edited only the first two parts. I have used the British Museum copy.

[2] *Ibid*. 6. Theil, p. 95.

> Ich speis' ihn auch nicht mehr mit theuren amber-kuchen:
> Denn er ist alt genung, die nahrung selbst zu suchen.
> Zibeth und bisam hat ihm manchen dienst gethan:
> Nun will ich einmahl sehn, was er alleine kan.

The answer was: not much, except in satire. His early style had outdone Lohenstein in absurdities of metaphor and *concetti*. Here is a quite moderate example of this florid style:[1]

> Sylvia ist angenehm.
> Ihre lippen sind corallen,
> Ihre brüste zucker-ballen,
> Und ihr honigsüsses lallen
> Gleicht den jungen nachtigallen,
> Die die mutter abgericht;
> Nur ihr hertze tauget nicht.

But it would seem that this extremely precious poet, who could chide his mistress for denying him intimacies which she accorded to her fleas, was somewhat self-conscious about his artificiality even before 1700. For alongside the poem just quoted, we find the following:

> Sylvia, dein süsser mund
> Machet, wenn verdruß und plagen
> Tausend andre niederschlagen,
> Mein verwundtes hertz gesund.
> Ja, daß ich nicht gantz verbrenne,
> Daß ich mich nicht elend nenne,
> Thut, wenn ich es nur bekenne,
> Sylvia, dein süsser mund.

This is from a different poem in the same anthology.[2] It is as gauche as the other is stilted. But it shows Neukirch in his plain style. The tension must have existed before 1700. In his satire *Auf unverständige Poeten*,[3] Neukirch claimed that his abandon-

---

[1] *Hoffmannswaldau und andrer Deutschen* etc., 1. Theil, p. 329.
[2] *Op. cit.* p. 331.
[3] I quote from the text as given in *G. B. Hanckens Gedichte, Erster Theil, Nebst denen Neukirchischen Satyren*, 2nd ed. (Leipzig, 1731), pp. 450–1. British Museum copy, lines 97–105 a, 109–10.

ment of the florid style, because it represented an exchange of falsehood for truth, had lost him his popularity:

> So lang ich meinen Vers nach gleicher Art gewogen,
> Dem Bilde der Natur die Schmincke fürgezogen,
> Der Reime dürren Leib mit Purpur ausgeschmückt,
> Und abgeborgte Krafft den Wörtern angeflickt,
> So war ich auch ein Mann von hohen Dichter-Gaben;
> Allein, so bald ich nur der Spuhre nachgegraben,
> Auf der man zur Vernunfft beschämt zurücke kreucht,
> Und endlich nach und nach nur den Parnaß erreicht,
> So ist es aus mit mir....

But what should he do? Return to the fashion he had discarded?

> Was soll ich Aermster thun? Soll ich noch einmahl rasen,
> Und durch mein Haber-Rohr zum Feder-Sturme blasen?

This he cannot do. He finds consolation in study of the ancients. The language of Neukirch's satire has much more punch than that of Canitz. Even when he is not hard-hitting, the style is always lively:

> Eh nun der Tag erschien, da nach so langem Leiden
> Der treue Ritter sich in Rosen solte weiden,
> So sprach die Mutter noch vorher die Tochter an:
> Dein Glück ist nun gemacht, mein Kummer abgethan.
> Nun must du witzig seyn, und zwar von aussen prahlen,
> Doch alles also drehn, daß Muffel muß bezahlen;
> Und wenn er endlich Herr von dienen Gliedern ist,
> So mache, daß du Frau von seinem Gelde bist.[1]

It seems a pity that he did not try his hand at comedy. When his work later fell out of favour, it was asserted that he gained his fame on the rebound from Silesianism.[2] This is hardly true, for, as we have seen, the tension between plain and florid style is there

---

[1] *Wieder die Faulen* (Hancke 1, p. 446).
[2] For example in the *Hannoverisches Magazin* for 1768, pp. 87 ff.: 'Man wollte sich von dem Lohensteinischen Geschrei erholen, das so lange Deutschland betäubt hatte, und der matte Gesang eines Neukirchs schmeichelte dem verwöhnten Ohre der Deutschen zu sehr, als daß er nicht hätte Beifall finden sollen.' Quoted by Fulda in his essay in Kürschner's *Deutsche National-Litteratur*, vol. 39, p. 459.

from the beginning and he was never very comfortable in either. But his satire, as I have briefly illustrated, has definite, positive qualities. The style shows the influence of Horace, Boileau and Canitz; basically it is the same sober, sensible style as that of Canitz but it has more bite.

The attack on the Second Silesian School becomes more explicit with Christian Wernicke (1661–1725).[1] He expresses his surprise that such sensual poets should have been so interested in marble breasts and alabaster cheeks. In his preface he mocks at lines like Lohenstein's:

> Zinober krönte Milch auf ihren Zucker-Ballen.

The finest words, he says, become absurd if ill-related to the context. He refers to 'eitlen und falschen Wörtern', the pleasantness and smoothness of which tickle the ear but do not penetrate to the heart. He contrasts them with what he calls the 'nachdrückliche und Männliche Ahrt zu schreiben'.[2] The simplest words if well used can be excellent. This critical realisation that 'fine words' are not essential to poetry is a valuable contribution to the current, ill-formulated views on the nature of poetry. But this is Wernicke's only charge against the Silesians and he returns to it again and again without ever going deeper:

> (a) Ihr Tichter, wenn ein Verss aus eurer Feder quillt
> Um eure Phillis zu bedienen,
> So zeigt sich gleich ein *Marmor-Bild*,
> Ihr *Aug'* ist von *Achat*, die *Lippen* sind *Rubinen*,
> Die *Adern* aus *Saphier* gemacht,
> Und eure *Buhlschafft* wird, weil ihr sie *preisst*, *verlacht*.
>
> (b) *Artemon* hat gelernt an mehr als einem Ort
> Ein *unverständlich Nichts* durch *auffgeblasne Wort'*
> In *wollgezehlte Reim'* ohn' allen Zwang zu bringen;
> In jedem Abschnitt hört man klingen,

---

[1] The best modern edition of Wernicke's epigrams is by R. Pechel (*Palaestra*, LXXI), 1909, which reprints the third edition of 1704 and has a good introduction. I have used this edition.
[2] *Op. cit.* ed. Pechel, p. 120.

THE LANGUAGE OF POETRY

Schnee, Marmor, Alabast, Musck, Bisem und Zibeht,
Samm't, Purpur, Seid' und Gold, Stern, Sonn' und Morgenröht'.
   Die sich im Unverstand verschantzen,
   Und in geschlossner Reihe tantzen.[1]

In a note to the second of these poems Wernicke suggests that this exotic imagery of the Silesians had merely sound-value. This is certainly untrue, for their verse was more pictorial than musical. More to the point is the general charge of *Unverstand* reinforced in several other epigrams:

(a) *Der Abschnitt? gut. Der Vers? fliesst voll. Der Reim? geschickt.*
   Die Wort? in Ordnung. Nichts, als der Verstand verrückt.

(b) *Man findt, wenn man mit Fleiss die Rosen und Narzissen,*
   Die unsre deutsche Vers' anfüllen oder schliessen,
   Mit dem Verstand und Sinn des Tichters überlegt:
   Daß ein unfruchtbar Land die meiste Blumen trägt.[2]

There is the suggestion here, never very well expressed, that Wernicke appreciated that Silesian metaphor did not correspond to anything real in the poet. Wernicke's own style seems to show a constant battle with a rather intractable medium. He was always revising his verses and apparently trying to attain that compactness he so much admired in the French. But he is often wordy and flat:

   Allmosen giebt man zwar den Armen,
      Doch mehr aus Hoffarth als Erbarmen,
   Und drum erreichet hier kein Reicher Ziel und Zweck;
   Am besten geben die, die selbst im Elend wandern:
      Ein Reicher wirfft die Gabe weg,
      Ein Armer lehnet sie dem andern.

or, in the attempt to achieve compression, merely clumsy:

   Daß vor erwiesne Dienst' oft Cremon mich gepriesen,
   Ist keine Danckbarkeit, und nichts als Gauckeley;
   Er trachtet darzuthun, was er, nicht was ich sey;
   Mehr, dass er sie verdient, als dass ich sie erwiesen.

---

[1] *Ed. cit.* pp. 185–6, 215–16. My italics represent the *Sperrdruck* in Pechel's edition.
[2] *Ibid.* pp. 252, 463.

or even obscure:

> Wer der *Vernunfft Gesetz* versteht,
> Der quählt sich selber nicht durch *eigne Striem*' und *Schläge*;
> Denn beyde sind auff gleichem Wege,
> Der die *Begier beherrscht*, wie dieser der sie *tödt*.[1]

It is difficult to disagree with Herder's judgment that Wernicke was a harsh and heavy-handed writer. He has neither the verve of Neukirch nor the elegance of Canitz. But his attitude to the language of poetry was the same as theirs, and these three writers belong together as representatives of a new call for plainness and reality in the early years of the eighteenth century. Wernicke says:

> Man muss auf meinem Blatt nach keinem *Amber* suchen,
> Und meine *Mus' im Zorn* bäckt keinen *Biesem-Kuchen*;
> Ich folge *der Natur*, und schreib' auf ihre Weis':
> Vor *Kinder* ist die *Milch*, vor *Männer* starcke *Speis*'.[2]

This clumsy quatrain seems to show how difficult it was to be neat in this language; but it expresses the current attitude to baroque poetic diction.

The many lesser treatises on poetics at this time continue the attack on metaphorical diction in the name of naturalness and reason and in the same terms as the writers we have been considering. Gottsched's approach was clear from the outset. In the second volume of *Die Vernünfftigen Tadlerinnen* (1726) he quoted these lines by Pietsch:

> Der Adler zeigt sich, ihr Feinde könnt ihn schauen,
> Der Donner wältzet sich in den geschärften Klauen.
> Er trennt die finstre Lufft....

and analysed them as follows:

> Ich will hier die Redensart nicht tadeln, daß *der Donner sich wältzet*, denn vielleicht möchte noch ein Grund zu finden seyn, warum der Donnerknall mit dem Wältzen eine Aehnlichkeit hätte. Aber warum soll sich der Donner eben *in den Klauen* wältzen? Ist nicht der Donner ein Knall, der einen grossen Lufftraum erschüttert? Wie hat derselbe

---

[1] *Ed. cit.* pp. 227, 400, 140.   [2] *Ed. cit.* p. 211.

denn Raum genug, sich in den Klauen des Adlers zu wältzen? Oder, wie kan ein Thon, ein bloßer Schall mit den Klauen gehalten werden? Ferner möchte ich wissen, warum die Klauen *geschärfte* Klauen heißen? vors erste thut die Schärfe gar nichts zum Werffen des Donners; vors andre wird nichts geschärft, als was vorhin stumpf gewesen. Kan das aber von den Adler-Klauen gesagt werden? Scharf könten sie wohl heißen; aber nicht *geschärft*, wenn man nicht der Sprache Gewalt thun will.

It does not seem likely that this approach can ever result in the appreciation of poetry. Gottsched's gingerly attitude to metaphor proceeds from a pedantic mistrust of the imagination. 'Zu einem vollkommenen Poeten gehört eine gleiche Mischung von Vernunfft und Einbildungskraft.'[1] Nothing is to be left to chance. The imagination must be controlled by the reason. Consideration of some fanciful metaphors of the Silesian type leads Gottsched to draw the conclusion: 'Hieraus erhellet, wie nöthig es sey, daß ein Poete seine Einbildungs-Krafft in Ordnung halte, damit er nicht das Ansehen gewinne, als wenn es ihm an einer anderen Krafft des Verstandes fehle, so daß er zu haseliren anfange.'[2] Much the same attitude had characterised the letter sent on 18 December 1721 by the *Gesellschaft der Mahler* to the poet Besser. He is praised for the *naturalness* of his style which results from 'aufgeweckte Imagination und scharffer Verstand'.[3] These are envisaged as complementary forces, exactly in the spirit of Gottsched and of Addison. Because Besser's imagination is controlled by reason, his writing is natural and effective—in contrast to the '*falschen* Imaginations-Spiele' of Hofmannswaldau which are unnatural and ineffective. Taking up the charge of falseness, Bodmer, in the nineteenth of the first series of the *Discourse*, speaks of the frosty hearts but fervid metaphors of the Silesians. This sort of metaphor was false because it did not correspond to anything real in the mind. It was an artificial, pedantic, snobbish pose.

[1] *Op. cit.* vol. II, p. 61.
[2] *Ibid.* vol. II, p. 278. *Haseliren* = to behave foolishly. The *DWb.* connects it with a use of *Hase* to mean 'fool'.
[3] *Chronick* (see above, p. 69), ed. Vetter, p. 40.

Gottsched's *Critische Dichtkunst*, first published in 1730, has one single moment when the spirit of poetry is almost glimpsed. But the vision proves to be a mirage and never materialises into anything substantial. Poetry differs from prose, says Gottsched late on in the first half of his ponderous treatise, 'hauptsächlich in der Art zu dencken'; the distinction has nothing to do with form.[1] But Gottsched's use of the word *dencken* is already suspect, and he goes on to say that 'thinking poetically' means having plenty of *Witz* and producing constant *Einfälle*, by which he means tropes. And so we find ourselves back at the three characters of style, stated as in the *Redekunst*, with no distinction at all between prose and poetry. Elsewhere in the book this difference is given as one of degree—'noch körnigter, nachdrücklicher und kräftiger'.[2] On the really fundamental question therefore Gottsched is no better than his time. And since there is no understanding of poetry, we shall not expect, or find, any understanding of the imaginative use or creation of words. Zesen, we are told, was 'bold' and his 'absurdities' still disfigured the eighteenth century. A poet's natural gifts must be aroused and 'von ihrer anklebenden Unrichtigkeit gesaubert'[3]—apparently from a sort of aesthetic original sin! He must acquire taste and learn how to use language to best effect. He is allowed a certain freedom of words as compared with the historian, but this is not unrestricted. He may use an archaic word to good effect if the form is pleasing and the meaning clear. For the poet must avoid ordinary words (except for conscious effect) and use 'die ungemeinsten Wörter': 'Wenn z.E. gemeine Leute sagen: *Der Kopf thut mir wehe*: so spricht etwa der Poet: *Mich schmertzt das Haupt.* Jenes hört man täglich, drum klingt es nicht: Dieses hört man selten; drum ist es edler und erhabener.'[4] If we disregard the triviality of the example, this does in fact come close to the practice of elevating diction above the commonplace which Pope called 'throwing the language out of Prose'. But as theory it is no better than seven-

---

[1] I use the original edition, and quote from the copy in the Beit Library at Cambridge. This passage is on p. 283.   [2] *Ibid.* p. 238.
[3] *Ibid.* p. 87.   [4] *Ibid.* p. 190.

teenth-century advocation of metaphorical figuration. Both were means to the same end. New words Gottsched considers on the whole unnecessary: 'Man kan auch alle seine Gedancken gar leicht mit üblichen und gewöhnlichen Redensarten zu verstehen geben'[1]—which conflicts with the demand for elevated diction just noted and never for a moment considers whether poetry is anything more than conveying thought! All he concedes is that, if the poet use a neologism, then it must have 'edle Kühnheit' and be beautiful. It is clear that he still considers figuration as the essence of poetry: 'Der gröste Zierrath poetischer Ausdrückungen, besteht endlich in den tropischen, uneigentlichen und verblümten Worten und Redensarten.'[2] He notes that some, wishing to avoid Silesian bombast, had fallen into flat prose; and cites Christian Weise and Besser. As a contrast he quotes some stanzas from Flemming, 'durch ihre verblümte Redensarten weit schöner und geistreicher geworden, als wenn sie aus lauter eigentlichen [i.e. non-figurative] Ausdrückungen bestanden hätte'.[3] Good metaphors must be based on real similarity, must not involve the base or the absurd, must not be too recondite and must help to make the idea more vivid. Excessive or empty figuration must be shunned. Therefore although the poet has greater freedom of expression than the orator or the historian, he must never lose sight of 'die gesunde Vernunft'. Displacement of words from their natural prose-order should be avoided as much as possible. He cites examples from seventeenth-century authors, mentioning particularly the separation of a prefix as in Opitz's:

> Er wird mir auch verzeihen,
> Daß ich frey öffentlich als Herold *aus darf schreyen*.[4]

He instances certain 'wrong' genders. He objects to 'lengthenings' like *Genade, Gelücke, Gelauben, Grabestein, nichtes* and 'shortenings' like *'raus, 'rauf, 'rein*, to 'careless' omission of the auxiliary verb.[5] But he allows the displacement of words from prose-order for the sake of emphasis or as an expression of emotion. He

---

[1] *Ibid.* p. 199.   [2] *Ibid.* p. 212.   [3] *Ibid.* p. 216.
[4] *Ibid.* p. 243.   [5] *Ibid.* I, ch. ix.

appreciates the vigorous effect that can be obtained by such displacement. Examples are quoted from various poets, including some from Günther. There is a faint flash of insight here. But the *Critische Dichtkunst* had little influence on the development of the German language because its author had no real understanding of poetry and its language.

It is now time to turn to the poets themselves. What was their attitude to these developments in critical theory? The most explicit statement comes from the greatest of them. Günther in 1721 looks back on the style of his earlier poems:

> Da drechselt ich mit Fleiß auf einer hohen Spur
> Wort, Silben und Verstand auch wieder die Natur;
> Denn wollt ich dazumahl ein schönes Kind beschreiben,
> So lies ich ihren Mund mit Scharlachbeeren reiben.
> Erhob ich einen Kerl zuweilen um das Geld,
> So fing ich prächtig an: Orackel unsrer Welt!
> Ich flocht, wie jezt noch viel, die Nahmen vor die Lieder
> Und gieng oft um ein A. drey Stunden auf und nieder.
> Auch schift ich oftermahl auf Dielen über Meer
> Und holt ein Gleichnüßwort aus Misisippi her,
> Bestahl den Lohenstein wie andre Schulmonarchen,
> Und war kein Reim darauf, so flickt ich ihn von Parchen,
> So schlimm das Wort auch klang; Marocco, Bengala,
> Fez, Bantam, Mexico, Quinsay, Florida,
> Die alle musten mir Baum, Steine, Thiere, Linsen
> Und was nur kostbar lies in Dichterkasten zinsen.
> Da klappte mir kein Vers, der nicht auf Stelzen gieng...
> Dies thät ich, als mein Wiz noch gar zu unreif hies
> Und wie ein siedend Fett den Schaum voran verstieß.[1]

This was written in 1721, and the style Günther is here describing had prevailed in his own poetry up to about 1717. Let us now examine the language of the more interesting of the poets writing during the first half of the century.

[1] From vol. IV of the edition of his works by W. Krämer (*Bibliothek des literarischen Vereins in Stuttgart*, vol. 283), p. 238. *Parchen*=Mod.Ger. *Barchent*. The English equivalent of the meaning in this context would be 'fustian'.

VIII

THE DEVELOPMENT OF THE POETICAL MEDIUM

THE development of Günther's language is best seen in his love-poetry.[1] At first, indirect expression tends to veil delicate subject-matter:

> Gewis, die Lippe führt ein reiches Kaufmannsgut,
> Und das Gesichte zeigt ein Meer voll Milch und Blut,
> Allwo die Gratien am Ufer deiner Wangen
> So Perlen suchen gehn als Purpurschnecken fangen.[2]

This is from a poem written in 1714. It has all the exaggerated, exotic bombast of baroque figurative style. Or again:

> Verdienet denn, du Bild der keuschen Zucht,
> Ein blinder Grif den Donner deiner Strafe?
> Und zürnestu mit einem armen Schaafe,
> Das hier herum die Lilgenweide sucht....[3]

The use of *Donner* for 'anger' is a type of metaphorical decoration, common in later seventeenth-century verse. With Günther this becomes automatic and meaningless substitution: love is

---

[1] The difficulties of establishing a reliable text of Günther's poetry have been described by W. Krämer in the introduction to vol. 1 of his edition in the *Bibliothek des literarischen Vereins* (six volumes, out of the seven volumes planned, had appeared by 1937). The love-poetry is contained in the first volume of this edition, from which I quote. On Günther, see the introduction to the various volumes of Krämer's edition, the excellent essay by M. Colleville in his book, *La renaissance du lyrisme dans la poésie allemande au XVIIIe siècle* (Paris, 1936) and K. Enders, *Zeitfolge der Gedichte und Briefe J. C. Günthers* (Dortmund, 1904). The latest biography is by Krämer (Godesberg, 1950). H. Groschupp's dissertation *Die Sprache Johann Christian Günthers* (Leipzig, 1900) deals only with phonology and morphology. Krämer's own dissertation *J. C. Günther, sein Weg aus dem Barock* (Munich, 1927) and W. Dreyer, *Wandlungen im Lebensgefühl und Sprachgestaltung J. C. Günthers* (typescript diss. Frankfurt, 1951) were inaccessible to me, despite various and protracted attempts to gain sight of them.

[2] *Ed. cit.* vol. 1, p. 26.   [3] *Ibid.* p. 51.

Glut, passion is *Zunder*, bitterness is *Wermuth*, sorrow is *Aloe*, youth is *Lenz*, art is *der Kiel*, delight is *Zucker*, pain is *der Nord* and hope is *der Anker*. This results in a mannered indirectness of expression and produces absurdities like the injunction: 'Koch aus Wermuth Honigseim'[1] or this quatrain:

> Kluge Schönheit, meine Funcken
> Überreicht dir dieses Blat,
> Das mehr naßes Salz getruncken,
> Als dein Mund jezt Zucker hat.[2]

Metaphorical word-groups like *der Wollust Most, der Keuschheit Tempel, der Lippen May* lead to a characteristic type of seventeenth-century 'poetic' compound where the second element is a metaphorical image of the first. Günther expresses himself frequently by such compounds: *Angstgebürge, Kummeressig, Lästerzahn, Hoffnungsanker, Hoffnungsbaum* and *Hoffnungskleid* (both green), and the following couplet:

> Es macht mich treu und ist ein *Hofnungsschild*,
> Wenn Neid und Noth *Verfolgungssteine* schmeißen.[3]

The heart is a magnet, his lady a lodestar, his life a ship, her bosom a port, her eyes are candles or lightning shafts or mirrors, her cheeks are roses or rubies and jasmine or lilies—all the *clichés* are there and nothing is gained by this avoidance of direct expression. Metaphor is mere stucco, as we see when the homely lath-and-plaster suddenly and delightfully reveals itself:

> Der ordentliche Bau, das Uhrwerck deiner Glieder,
> Streckt wie ein Cedernbaum den wohlgesezten Leib.
> Ist nun die Majestät ein Weib,
> So giebt sie sich in dir als ihrer Tochter wieder.
> Die Ehrfurcht küst dein Bild,
> *Bey welchem die Natur geschwizet,*
> Als sie das zarte Fleisch aus Alabast geschnizet,
> Durch welchen der Saphir von Schneckenblute schwillt.[4]

---

[1] *Ed. cit.* vol. I, p. 22; cf. 'den schärfsten Wermuth mir mit Zucker überstreut', *ibid.* p. 61.
[2] *Ibid.* pp. 22–3.   [3] *Ibid.* p. 85. My italics.
[4] *Ibid.* pp. 62–3. My italics.

We find also the exotic imagery so favoured by baroque poets in their craving for sumptuousness:

> Bringt Blumen und Violen,
> Last Narden und Jasmin aus fremden Ländern holen,
> Salbt den erblasten Leib, beräuchert Gruft und Sarg
> Mit Ambra und Zibeth, ja, zieht das beste Marck
> Aus Perlen, Gold und Stein, belebt die kalten Glieder
> Mit warmen Mumien, vielleicht erwacht sie wieder.[1]

Other forms of seventeenth-century rhetoric are there too: hyperbole (his tears come in floods or cloudbursts), enumeration:

> Denn lebt ich nicht vor dich, so sucht ich meinen Tod
> Durch Feuer, Meßer, Strick, Stahl, Brunnen, Gift und Degen.[2]

antithesis:

> Uns nahm die Wärterin, wir unsre Lust in Acht.[3]

oxymoron:

> Du meines Lebens Tod und du mein todtes Leben.[4]

word-play:

> Auch unser Unverstand
> Verstand die Liebe schon.[5]

All this rhetoric and metaphor proceeds from a desire to avoid the commonplace and to be arresting. It aims consciously at effect. Between the real experience and the poem there is elaboration and gestation in terms of wit and fashion. One feels the tyranny of an established poetic style, an accepted 'poetical' way of saying things. Very occasionally there is a sign of restiveness: Günther speaks of longing, *Sehnsucht*...

> Die ohne den Kompaß und ohne Leitstern schift,
> Die ohne — doch was soll ein großes Wortgepränge?
> Dem Schmerzen ist mein Herz und mir die Welt zu enge.[6]

---

[1] *Ed. cit.* vol. I, p. 5. *Auf den Tod seiner geliebten Flavie*, 1714—the first poem in Krämer's chronological arrangement of the love-poetry.
[2] *Ibid.* p. 99.   [3] *Ibid.* p. 6.
[4] *Ibid.* p. 5.
[5] *Ibid.* p. 6.   [6] *Ibid.* p. 8.

There are moments when the poet gives this stereotyped diction his own individual twist, and we have a sudden, sharp flash of real poetry:

> (a) Die Einsamkeit sizt auf dem Steine,
> Der mir an meinem Herzen liegt.
>
> (b) Wie manche schöne Nacht sieht mich der blaße Mond
> In stiller Einsamkeit am Kummerfaden spinnen!
>
> (c) So küß ich deine Sonnenlichter
> Und mercke keinen Splitterrichter.[1]

The stone on his heart, the *Kummerfaden* and the *Sonnenlichter* step out of their usual air of polite poetic convention and become real things. The result is startling. Even a hackneyed image takes on new life in a line like:

> Auch die Rosen werden alt.

Or a commonplace of mythology in:

> Die Sonne führt die Pferde trincken.

This is metaphor ceasing to be a meaningless mode and coming back into its real expressive function. Günther's early poetry is, however, not all in this metaphorical style. Much of it has the flatness of diction which characterised the opponents of the Second Silesian School. Here are two brief examples:

> (a) Und der Hofnung, die sie liebt,
> Einfluß und Ergözung giebt.
>
> (b) Wenn die *Hauptperson* nur wüste,
> Was vor Seufzer sanfter Lüste
> Ihrer Schönheit opfern gehn.[2]

But occasionally even this abstractness produces a delightful effect:

> Ich leugne nicht die starcken Triebe
> Und seufze nach der *Gegenliebe*.[3]

The great transformation in Günther's use of language came during the years at Leipzig (1718–19) when, under the influence

---

[1] *Ed. cit.* vol. I, pp. 79, 100, 65.
[2] *Ibid.* pp. 15, 18. My italics.
[3] *Ibid.* p. 19. My italics.

THE DEVELOPMENT OF THE POETICAL MEDIUM

of Burkhard Mencke, he forswore Silesian euphuism. But the beginnings of the change are earlier. In October 1717 he writes:

> Mein Phoebus liegt noch kranck, ich hab ihn in der Cur
> Und will ihm nach und nach die schwülstige Natur,
> Die seine Jugend plagt, aus Blut und Gliedern treiben.[1]

The cure was intensive study of Latin authors, especially Horace, Ovid, Tibullus and Propertius, and certain Neo-Latin erotic poets (especially the Dutchman Johannes Secundus whom Goethe also admired) and anacreontic poetry generally. Epicurean ideas appeal to Günther's moods. He writes his famous student songs and his love-poetry takes on a new intensity in this *carpe diem* atmosphere.

> Täglich droht die Baare.[2]

His own translations of Anacreon's odes are lost but several of his poems have been shown to derive from the Greek originals. Ideas from Tibullus also occur. Thus one stanza of the famous Winter Song begins:

> Der Schönen in den Armen liegen
> Wenn draußen Nord und Regen pfeift,
> Macht so ein inniglich Vergnügen,
> Dergleichen niemand recht begreift...[3]

which derives from a passage in the first elegy of Tibullus, namely:

> Quam iuvat inmites ventos audire cubantem
> et dominam tenero continuisse sinu
> aut, gelidas hibernus aquas cum fuderit Auster,
> securum somnos imbre iuvante sequi.

Similarly the conceit:

> Ich küße den gefrornen Riegel,
> Der mir Amanden vorenthielt[4]

was doubtless suggested by

> me retinent vinctum formosae vincla puellae,
> et sedeo duras ianitor ante fores.

---

[1] *Ed. cit.* vol. III, p. 55.   [2] *Ed. cit.* vol. I, p. 293.
[3] *Ed. cit.* vol. I, p. 308.   [4] *Ibid.* p. 309.

in the same elegy. From this last example we can see that Günther has not abandoned metaphor. Reminiscences of his early figurative style occur throughout his whole work. *Kummermeer* and *Vergnügungsperlen* appear sporadically in the poems of his last years. In this middle period there is a new infectious roguishness which gives the language vitality: of his amorous conquests...

> Ich schwöre verbindlich, bis daß ich's genoßen;
> Und bin ich dann fertig, so schwenck ich den Hut
> Und gehe zur andern, die eben das thut.[1]

Things are no longer expressed through a veil of allusive, traditional metaphor. Where there is imagery, it is used to enforce, not to weaken the direct impact of the words. Artificial, 'exotic' imagery (precious stuffs and stones and perfumes) is gone. But many of the old rhetorical devices are, like metaphor, used to strengthen the direct effect. There is a certain unreality about anacreontic poetry which makes the use of euphuistic devices possible. But it is Günther's genius that gives force to an antithesis like:

> Die Angst durchwandert mir das Marck der starcken Glieder,
> Um die sie kurz vorher die falschen Armen schlang.

or a conceit like:

> Wer hat dir den Geschmack der Liebe beygebracht?[2]

This power over language increases as his genius matures. Consider the intensity of lines like the following, dated 1719:

> Der Nordwind pfeift ums Dach und heulet in den Linden,
> Ich lieg auf Eiß und Schnee, die mehr als du empfinden
>   Und selbst vor Leid zergehn.[3]

Ice and snow are familiar metaphorical substitutes in Silesian diction. But this is real ice and snow. The poet has discovered

---

[1] *Ed. cit.* vol. I, p. 132.   [2] *Ibid.* pp. 162 and 163.
[3] *Ibid.* p. 184. Enders compares Horace, *Odes* III, 10:
> 'audis quo strepitu ianua, quo nemus
> inter pulchra satum tecta remugiat
> ventis, et positas ut glaciet nives
>   puro numine Iuppiter?'

the reality of metaphorical language. Here is another example, dated 1722, of new vigour infused into conventional images—life as service, life as the progress of the seasons, life as a stream:

> Das Alter kommt mir vor den Jahren,
>   Ich habe zeitig ausgedient,
>   Mein Frühling ist in Angst vergrünt
> Und als ein Strom dahingefahren.[1]

Conventional poetic stances become bitter reality:

> (*a*) Nichts ergözt mich mehr auf Erden
>   Als das Weinen in der Nacht.
>
> (*b*) Nun Kind, ich geh. Geh auch und nimm den Kuß,
>   Wir martern nur einander durch dies Lezen.
>
> (*c*) Die Sehnsucht jaget mich
>   So wie ein schüchtern Wild;
>   Mein Schlaf ist nur ein Qualm,
>   Mein Lied ein Klagepsalm;
>   Die Angst der bangen Einsamkeit
>   Begräbt mich vor der Zeit,
>   Weil ich den Kuß
>   Entbehren muß,
>   Der so viel Lust verspricht.[2]

Poetic commonplaces all spring ultimately from something real. Somewhere in the past there was a real stirring of poetic feeling; but it had become a convention through constant repetition and imitation by craftsmen. Günther converts these conventions back into realities by the force of his own genius. This applies not only to content but also to expression. He restores to metaphor its reality as a function of language. It ceases to be a conventional mode into which poetry demands all expression to be cast. Nor is it something essentially artificial and against nature. The mature Günther avoids the excesses of both the school of Lohenstein and the German disciples of Boileau. He shows that it is possible to be metaphorical without being unnatural; and to be poetical without being metaphorical. The use of metaphor in poetic language becomes more restricted but more functional. Metaphor

[1] *Ed. cit.* vol. III, p. 165.   [2] *Ed. cit.* vol. I, pp. 203, 202, 250.

ceases to be surface figuration and enters again into its old right. It has been demonstrated that the German language could have directness and pictorialness as a poetical medium if used directly and with a true respect for images.

But Günther was an exception and the lesson of his achievement passed unheeded. Poetic diction continued in the wake either of the adherents or the detractors of the Silesian metaphorical style. The anti-metaphorical trend predominates. This, as we have seen, resulted often in verse that was little more than rhymed prose, but the movement represented a purgation necessary to the German language in this stage of its development. Consider for a moment the following two poems, both on the subject of Spring. The first (by Birken) first published in 1673, the second (by Brockes) in 1727:

(a)   Ihr Blätter-wetterspiel, ihr vortrab frischer Früchte,
Des Zephyrs Buhlgewächs, ihr leichte Lenzen-brut,
Ihr zelte, die ihr uns oft nemt in sichre hut,
Die ihr aus unsrem Geist lockt geistige Gedichte!
ihr, die ihr weidet auch das Ohr und das Gesichte,
mit lieblichem geräusch: lasst kommen mir zu gut
jetzund die freie Luft. Ach! heitert meinen muth,
und machet nun in mir die sorgen-nacht zu nichte.
Und du, Smaragden-Gras, du Sarg der blassen sorgen,
Du blumenbunter Rock der Lenzen-wöchnerin,
Der perlenträchtig sich lässt sehen alle morgen,
du Kräuterwochenbett! nim meine Glieder hin,
Und bringe sie zu ruh Laß deinen Balsam riechen:
So werden freud und lust mein krankes haupt durchkriechen.[1]

(b)   Willkommen, liebster May! Wie lieblich und wie schön
Ist alles, was wir in dir hören,
Empfinden, schmecken, riechen, sehn!
In reinen Lüften flamm't ein fast Sapphir'nes Blau,
In welchem ich mit Lust viel güld'ne Berge schau.
Der Erden runde Brust, das fette Land,

---

[1] *Der Pegnitz-Schäfere Gesellschaft-Weide und Frülings-Freude: beschrieben durch Floridan im Jahr MXCXLV* in *Pegnesis* (Nuremberg, 1673), p. 59. Text from the copy in the Nuremberg Stadtbibliothek and kindly communicated to me by the Director.

Bedeckt ein liebliches, Smaragden-gleich Gewand.
Der Bluhmen-Heer durchwirkt ein fast lebendig Grün.
Ein reines Silber blinkt in der bestral'ten Flut,
Und auch zugleich auf Bäumen, welche blühn.
Die süsse Macht der holden Liebe
Erfüll't das fast erstarrte Blut
Mit der so angenemen Gluht
Der lieblichen Vermehrungs-Triebe.
 Ach sehet, wie in den beblühmten Feldern
So manches munt're Lämmchen springt!
Ach hör't, wie in begrün'ten Wäldern
So manche Nachtigal, so manche Drossel singt!
Ach riecht die balsamir'ten Düfte!
Ach fühlt das Schmeicheln lauer Lüfte!
Ach schmeckt in Kräutern, im Spinat,
In Spargel, Hopfen und Salat
So mancherley Blut-reinigende Kraft,
So manchen angenemen Saft,
Und denkt in dieser Frühlings-Lust,
Mit Dank- und Lust-erfüll'ter Brust,
An Den, Der alle Pracht
Zu eurer Lust hervor gebracht!
Lasst euer fröhliches Gemüte
Auch Blühte tragen bey der Blühte!
Auf, lasst uns recht mit Andacht sehn
Die Dinge, die mit Emsigkeit
In dieser holden Mayen-Zeit
Zu uns'rer Lust, zu unserm Nutz geschehn!
 Man sammlet im beblühmten Mayen,
Zu mannigfalt'gen Arzeneyen,
Auf manchem Berg', in manchem Thal
Gesunde Kräuter ohne Zahl.
Es muß die beste Gersten-Sat
Im frühen May gesäet seyn,
Und um Urbani etwas spat
Buch-Weizen, Hirse, Hanf und Lein.
Die Schafe scheeret man bey holder Frühlings-Wärme,
Man rupft die Gäns', und nimmt die Schwärme
Der flücht'gen Bienen itzt absonderlich in acht.
 Ach lasst des Schöpfers Lieb' und weise Wunder-Macht,

Die wir anitzt an allen Orten spüren,
Uns doch zu Seinem Ruhm, die Seele rühren!
Bedenkt! Für so viel Gut's, für solche Wunder-Gaben
Verlangt der Schöpfer nichts, als eure Lust, zu haben.[1]

One could hardly wish for a better illustration of the difference in climate between the two centuries. The baroque poet with his *krankes haupt* greets Spring, rather feebly, as respite from the *sorgen-nacht* of Winter and of life in general. The *Aufklärung* poet jubilantly salutes the season of replenishment in an anthropocentric universe created by a wise and kindly God. Nature for Birken seems merely a background for introspective burrowings; he is more interested in his *sorgen-nacht* than its dispersion. Nature for Brockes is no poetic *coulisse*; he knows it and loves it, even down to the spinach, and relates it to his physico-teleological deism with its belief in the best of all possible worlds, eminently useful to man, which is in itself a proof of God's infinite goodness and wisdom. In Brockes we have a peculiar combination of some sense of the Sublime with a tendency to equate this with ethical and rational excellence—an Infinite which is the perfection of the Finite. There is a world of difference between these two poets as regards mood. The first has a stifled gloom and heavy gait; *nim meine Glieder hin und bringe sie zu ruh*. The other has five clear senses and a springy walk, bowels working freely (thanks to spinach, asparagus and what not) in contrast to the constipated sensuality of the first. Equally great is the difference in language. Birken's style is saturated, nay dripping with metaphor; Brockes's is direct almost to the point of baldness. Birken's poem is a taut, packed sonnet, held together by full sound and meaning, rich to the point of sickliness; Brockes's poem is a free-verse *arioso*, rhymed but otherwise loose in composition, flabby almost to the point of tastelessness. But if we look a little closer, the contrast is not quite so abrupt. If we leave aside difference of content and consider what words and stylistic devices are used, a connection becomes apparent, a linguistic connection. In the first section of

---

[1] *Irdisches Vergnügen in Gott*, vol. II, pp. 476–7, *Der May*. Text from the British Museum copy of the original edition.

the Brockes poem, the word *fast* is used three times: *ein fast Sapphir'nes Blau*; *ein fast lebendig Grün*; *das fast erstarrte Blut*. This seeming hesitancy, this desire to avoid being thought outlandish, results in a toning down of metaphor. But the basic structure of this style is the metaphorical style of seventeenth-century baroque; not the direct, unfigurative style of Canitz. It presents the paradox of a metaphorical style developed in an unmetaphorical spirit.

Many aspects of baroque rhetoric are still to be found in the language of Brockes.[1] His early works, written before 1721, consist of a translation from Marino, an oratorio on the Passion, and several occasional pieces.[2] Everywhere we find the same attempt to screw up language to a high pitch of intensity as had characterised the poetry of the Second Silesian School, and by the same familiar devices:

(a) Dem Leben sprecht ihrs Leben ab,
Des Todes Tod soll durch euch sterben.

(b) Segel, welche kaum zu zehlen,
Zu beseelen,
Fehlt es offt *dem Wind' an Wind*.[3]

When Brockes moved towards a realm of subject-matter more real to him in the *Irdisches Vergnügen in Gott* (first volume 1721;

---

[1] There is an excellent book on Brockes's language by H. W. Pfund, *Studien zu Wort und Stil bei Brockes* (New York, 1935), to which I am indebted for several ideas and examples. There are a few pages on the subject in Alois Brandl's monograph of Brockes (Innsbruck, 1878, pp. 111–25) and an article by G. Rosenhagen entitled 'Wörter und Worte beim alten Dichter Brockes' in the *Fests. Melle* (Hamburg, 1933), pp. 148–59. There is an article on Brockes and Thomson in *JEGP*, x (1911) by M. C. Stewart; and a study of Brockes and Marino by G. Zamboni in the *Atti del r. Istituto Veneto di Lettere, Scienze e Arti*, vol. 90 (1932). The best general accounts of Brockes's work are by Ludwig Fulda (in Kürschner's *Deutsche National-Litteratur*, vol. 39) and by Colleville (*op. cit.*, see above p. 233); but neither deals with his language.

[2] Weichmann's *Poesie der Niedersachsen* (1725–38) contains several poems by Brockes of various dates; more significant is the volume entitled *Verteutschter Bethlehemitischer Kindermord* (Hamburg, 1715), which contains the oratorio (published separately in 1712) and early occasional poems as well as the translation from Marino. I have used the British Museum copy of the original edition (abbreviated title *VBK*). This seems to have been a popular book; there were several reprints, the seventh and last in 1758.

[3] *VBK*, pp. 307, 324. My italics.

eight further volumes followed between 1727 and 1748), his style became less florid, but many of the old tricks remained. Here, for instance, is a rhetorical use of repetition from the last volume but one, which appeared in 1746:[1]

> Ein sanftes dunkel Gelb, ein sanftes dunkel Braun,
> Ein sanftes dunkel Roth, ein sanftes dunkel Grün,
> Sieht man licht-gelb-, licht-braun-, licht-roth-, licht-grüne Stellen,
> Wohin man sieht, erheben und erhellen;

This example shows too much striving after precision to be called baroque; but it derives from seventeenth-century rhetoric. Particularly baroque forms of this stylistic use of repetition can be found throughout the collection. Here are a few examples chosen at random:[2]

> (a) Da sich das künftge, fast mit dem vergangnen bindet,
> Und man die Gegenwart kaum kaum dazwischen findet;
>
> (b) Wie viel, wie viel, wie vielerley
> An Witterung, an Segen und an Fleiß.
>
> (c) Hier beweisen ird'sche Sterne
> Der so schön- so schönen Welt
> Einen GOtt, der sie erhält.

Particularly frequent is repetition of the word *tausend* (*tausend tausend Bluhmen*, etc.)—itself usually a hyperbole. The *des Todes Tod* type of emphasis is also frequent. It is a common trope in

---

[1] This passage is on p. 235 of the first edition of vol. VIII. Complete sets of the *Irdisches Vergnügen in Gott* are, it seems, not easy to find. The British Museum has all nine volumes, but not the first edition of all volumes. The nine volumes appeared originally in 1721, 1727, 1728, 1731, 1736, 1739, 1743, 1746 and 1748 respectively. Of vol. I I have used the first, second (1724) and seventh (1744) editions; the second edition is already revised and enlarged. Of vol. II I have used the first and fourth (1739) editions. Of vol. III I used the fourth edition of 1747, of vol. IV the third edition of 1745, of vol. V the second edition of 1740, of vol. VI the first edition, of vol. VII the edition (unnamed) of 1748, of vols. VIII and IX the first editions. All these are in the British Museum. Where more than one edition was available I have taken my examples from the earlier (except where otherwise stated). All this is very messy; but Pfund and Colleville had the same trouble and fared worse. They had apparently no access to the first edition of vol. I, the text of which varies considerably from later editions.

[2] Vol. IV, p. 440; vol. VII, p. 270; vol. I (2nd edn.), p. 12 (the poem not in 1st edn.).

THE DEVELOPMENT OF THE POETICAL MEDIUM

baroque lyrical style, and has classical and Hebrew ancestry. It is one of the rhetorical tricks which Klopstock retained in his search for the grand style. It would seem that sheer sound often led Brockes to write in this way. How else should one account for lines like:

> Des Luft-Sapphirs Sapphirnen Spiegel [1]

or:

> Durch Neuigkeit, was süß, noch süsser zu versüssen [2]

if not by that same delight in aural effects for which he was so much admired by his contemporaries? Emphatic enumeration of detached words (asyndeton) was another device of baroque rhetoric. Gryphius made striking use of it in the beginning of a poem on Hell. Brockes uses such concatenations more moderately and slips in an occasional *und*; but he likes the device and uses it to the same purpose. For example:

> Wir mögen unsern Sinn, worauf wir wollen, lencken;
> Es mögen Feld und Wald, Sand, Blumen, Holtz und Stein,
> Gebäude, Thiere, Graß, Metall, ein schnell Geflügel,
> Ein Regen-Wurm, ein Fisch, das Meer, ein Thal, ein Hügel,
> Ein Bach, das Firmament, ein Mensch, gesehen seyn;
> So stimmet alles doch hierin stets überein:
> Es ist ein Göttlich Werck, es ist von ihm entstanden. [3]

A peculiar form of asyndeton found in seventeenth-century poetry is what Strich called *Wechselsätze*.[4] This consists of a sequence of grammatical subjects followed by a sequence of verbs, each verb referring to one of the subjects and in the corresponding order. There are a few examples of this in Brockes's early work: for instance:

> Kein Strom, kein Pfeil, kein Wind, kein Dampf, kein Blitz, kein Stral,
> Verrauscht, verfleucht, verwehet,
> Verraucht, verstreicht, vergehet
> So schnell, als unsre Lebens-Zeit.[5]

---

[1] Vol. I (2nd edn.), p. 70.   [2] Vol. IV, p. 28.
[3] Vol. V, p. 196.
[4] Fritz Strich, 'Der lyrische Stil des siebzehnten Jahrhunderts' in *Abhandlungen zur deutschen Literaturgeschichte, Franz Muncker zum 60. Geburtstage dargebracht* (Munich, 1916), p. 38.   [5] *Ird. Verg.* vol. I, p. 186.

We also find emphatic use of alliteration and apostrophe. We note an instinctive tendency towards the use of emphatic modifiers like *ganz, so, recht, mehr als* with adjectives; and the superlative elements *höchst-, all-, aller-*. All these baroque devices aim at intensifying the effect of the language. Brockes feels the need of this because his subject is the infinite wonder of God and His universe.

But this theme was not a baroque preoccupation. Brockes's whole attitude to experience is quite different from that of Hofmannswaldau or Gryphius. This is clear from the impressive piece with which the vast collection opens:

Das Firmament.

Als jüngst mein Auge sich in die Saphirne Tieffe,
Die weder Grund, noch Strand, noch Ziel, noch End' umschrenckt,
Ins unerforschte Meer des holen Luft-Raums, senkt',
Und mein verschlungner Blick bald hie- bald dahin lieffe,
Doch immer tieffer sank: entsatzte sich mein Geist,
Es schwindelte mein Aug', es stockte meine Sele
Ob der unendlichen, unmässig-tieffen Höle,
Die, wol mit Recht, ein Bild der Ewigkeiten heisst,
So nur aus GOtt allein, ohn' End' und Anfang, stammen.
Es schlug des Abgrunds Raum, wie eine dicke Flut
Des Boden-losen Meers auf sinkend Eisen thut,
In einem Augenblick, auf meinen Geist zusammen.
Die ungeheure Gruft des tieffen dunkeln Lichts,
Der lichten Dunkelheit, ohn' Anfang, ohne Schranken,
Verschlang so gar die Welt, begrub selbst die Gedanken;
Mein ganzes Wesen ward ein Staub, ein Punct, ein Nichts,
Und ich verlor mich selbst. Dieß schlug mich plötzlich nieder;
Verzweiflung drohete der ganz verwirrten Brust.
Allein, o heylsams Nichts! glückseliger Verlust!
Allgegenwärt'ger GOTT, in Dir fand ich mich wieder.

This poem is a symbol of its time, beginning as it does with agonised peerings into eternity, the searchings of a mind without stable foundation—*weder Grund, noch Strand, noch Ziel, noch End*—words which seem so applicable to the spirit of the preceding age—and then, out of this experience of insecurity comes a new security, the poet loses himself to find himself again in the true knowledge of God, and life has once again a centre and a foundation. The language is full of baroque features: a jewelled image—*Saphirne Tieffe*, asyndeton in the second line, typical compounds (*Luft-Raum, unmässig-tieff*), typical word-groupings (*des Abgrunds Raum*), clashing oxymoron—*des tieffen dunkeln Lichts, / Der lichten Dunkelheit*,[1] another asyndeton—*ein Staub, ein Punct, ein Nichts*—trailing away into insignificance and building up to the dramatic terseness of the climax: *Und ich verlor mich selbst*. But the antitheses, unlike those of Hofmannswaldau, are overcome and the new certainty is expressed with majestic, triumphant strength in the straightforward simplicity of the last line. The language is inherited from baroque diction but the spirit is one that has moved beyond the baroque. This is already apparent in the handling of the language. The devices are brought to telling climaxes:

> ein Staub, ein Punct, ein Nichts,
> Und ich verlor mich selbst.

Yet there are also moments of flatness: the *wol mit Recht* in line 8, the colourless *thut* in line 11, even: *Dieß schlug mich plötzlich nieder* seems rather bald. But Brockes has a modest, unassuming mind. We can see this in the images of the poem. All forms of hyperbole are quite foreign to his nature. In personality Brockes was so very much in tune with the general climate of his age that his poetry, and his style, were bound to be influential.

His use of language was much admired by his contemporaries. In the long *Vorrede* to the first edition of the first volume, C. F. Weichmann said:

Die Schreib-Ahrt dieser Gedichte ist eben so wenig niederträchtig und leichtsinnig, so wenig man dieser Mängel überhaupt den Herrn Brockes beschuldigen kann. Vielmehr stimmet sie mit der Großmuht

---

[1] The seventh edition reads here:
> 'voll unsichtbaren Lichts,
> Voll lichter Dunckelheit'

which seems to show a reversion from the extreme repetition of the original phrase. This may well be a significant moving away from the baroque.

und Leutseligkeit ihres Verfassers völlig überein. Sie ist Majestätisch und nachdrücklich; aber doch dabey sanft und lieblich....[1]

It was the *sound* of Brockes's verse that aroused most approval. He became famous for his musical and onomatopoeic effects. Weichmann gives several examples; for instance:

> Es schien der Wald ein Meer, drin grüne *Wellen wallen*

or an 'expressive pun':

> Die, wie der Blitz, erscheinen und entstehn,
> Und *wieder, wie der* Blitz, zerplatzen und vergehn.

On the lines:

> Der Donner rollt und knallt; Blitz, Ströme, Stralen, Schlossen,
> Vermischen ihre Wut.

he comments: 'Von einem Gewitter überhaupt wird nicht leicht was stärckerers in gleicher Kürze vorkommen' and then goes on to draw attention to the combination of *l-* and *r-* sounds. Musical effects had been studied and practised by seventeenth-century poets, particularly by Harsdörffer and Zesen; but it is true to say that the poetry of the Second Silesian School was more pictorial than musical. Weichmann in this essay quotes Marino's remark about poetry and music being sisters and, applying it to Brockes, says: 'Jedwedes Seiner Gedichte ist, so zu sagen, eine Regelmässige Harmonie, und zugleich ein vollkommenes Gemählde.' The implication was that Brockes's verse was not only pictorial *but also musical*. This was the novelty which appealed to his contemporaries. And this was his most important contribution to the development of the German literary language in his period. Brockes drew attention once more to the importance of music in the language of poetry.

Sometimes music replaces metaphor as the spring of poetic effect. On the lines:

> Noch stral'te Blitz auf Blitz mit fürchterlichem Schein;
> Der Donner rollte noch mit grässlichem Gebrülle:
> Allein im Augenblick nam eine sanfte Stille
> Die fast betäubte Luft gemach von neuen ein.

[1] *Op. cit.* b. 3.

THE DEVELOPMENT OF THE POETICAL MEDIUM

Weichmann comments: 'Wie nachdrücklich die zwey ersten Zeilen: so lieblich und sanft klingen die letzten.' This example and two of the others quoted in the last paragraph are from one poem entitled *Die auf ein starkes Ungewitter erfolgte Stille*,[1] which is built entirely on the musical contrast of soft, feminine *l-* sounds and strong, masculine *r-* sounds. The last two lines are:

> Es ist die helle Sonn' ein Bild von Gottes Liebe,
> So wie des Donners Grimm die Probe Seiner Kraft.

The age was sensitive to music and admired attempts at soundpainting like Brockes's various descriptions of the song of the nightingale. Here is one:

> Jetzt quarret sie, dem Frosch im nahen Bach,
> Jetzt schnarret sie, dem Grase-König nach;
> Jetzt stimmt ihr feuriger Gesang,
> Mit dem durchdringend reinen Klang
> Metallner Glocken überein.
> Da sie bald lockt, bald schlägt, bald pfeift
> Bald stehnt, bald jauchzt, bald klagt, bald keift;[2]

Onomatopoeic verbs, we notice, are used with virtuosity. Here is the same skill applied to a different set of sounds:

> Wie schwirrt und schreit, wie knirrt und pfeifft
> Der Schnee bey iedem Tritt! Mit den ietzt trägen Naben
> Knarrt, stockt, und schleppt der Räder starres Rund....[3]

Even words which are not onomatopoeic—*träg, stockt, schleppt, starr*—take on this quality. Everything resounds. This new form of verbal virtuosity attracted an age which had sickened of metaphor. Hamburg was full of music and musicians, some of them very good; Brockes's oratorio text had been set by several of the leading musicians of the day, including Telemann and Händel.

We have seen, from our comparison between Brockes and Birken, that Brockes did not have a poetic attitude to imagery. Where he uses images, he does not do so instinctively but rather

---
[1] *Ird. Verg.* vol. I (1st edn.), pp. 109 ff. [2] Vol. VIII, p. 18.
[3] Vol. IV, p. 394.

fetches them up for the sake of exact comparison or depiction. Metaphor for Birken is a means of avoiding the obvious; Brockes uses his comparisons to get as near as possible to exact depiction. It is very characteristic that whereas Birken spoke of *Smaragden-Gras*, Brockes more cautiously refers to its *Smaragden-gleich Gewand*. Brockes has rationalised a typically baroque jewelled image. We can see here both the tradition and the manipulation of it in a spirit quite opposed to that which had produced this tradition. The tradition is still used in a traditional way in his earliest poems where he talks about *der Laster Ruß* or *der Laster Eyter-Beulen* and *Eifersuchts-Tand*, *Andachts-Oele* or *Wohlfahrts-Thau*. But this flamboyance is restrained in the *Irdisches Vergnügen in Gott* and the most that we find are rather stock formulas like *Unschulds-Seide*, *Andachts-Glut*, and *Balsam-Saft*. These diminish in frequency as the work progresses, but even in the later volumes there are occasional flash-backs.

> Will ein Verfolgungs-Nord den Baum der Ehre kürzen,
> Dich in Verachtungs-Thal, den Pful des Schimpfes stürzen,
> Und scheitert Ruhm und Glimpf, an der Verläumdung Klippen:
> So denke, daß die Ehre dieser Zeit
> Nur bloß ein leichter Hauch veränderlicher Lippen,
> Ein Dunst, ein Schatten sey, ein Bild der Eitelkeit,
> Ja nichtes gegen Gott, der allenthalben wohnt....[1]

This is from a very sober poem on the omnipresence of God. Our elderly Hamburg dignitary, prosperous senator and respected citizen, is liable to whip off a pirouette on his country walks—when he thinks no one is looking! This is not his normal behaviour. His normal use of the comparison (more often a simile than a metaphor) is represented by the following passage from a poem on the planets in volume II, which was much debated by his contemporaries:

> Es kommen, in Vergleich
> Mit dieses Lichtes weitem Reich,
> Mit diesem glänzenden unmeßlichen Revier,
> Uns die Planeten ja nicht anders für,

[1] Vol. VI, p. 533.

> Als schwümmen in dem weiten Meer,
> Damit sie wol gewaschen werden mögten,
> Nur sechszehn Erbsen hin und her...[1]

This was too homely for some tastes; and the last line but one was omitted in later editions. But it represented something real; it was not merely artifice. In these realistic comparisons of Brockes we can see the first signs of a return to a more functional use of metaphor. He draws continuously on what he sees and hears. The sea is used to express immensity or inconstancy or uncertainty; for Brockes has watched it in all its moods. A peach-tree in blossom is like a *glänzender, erhabner Pfauenschwanz*, the field and the forest drink in the sun's rays like blotting-paper. Sudden realistic flashes enliven the dullest poems:

> Das Feld war unbeschreiblich schön,
> Und fast natürlich anzusehn,
> Als ob in einem reich- und grossen Kaufmanns-Laden
> Ein bunter Schatz von güld- und silbernen Brocaden
> Zur Schau geleget war.[2]

Rich stuffs again; but how differently used from the velvet and ermine of Hofmannswaldau and Lohenstein! There is a famous example in volume IV. Speaking of Nature in autumn, Brockes says:

> Im Garten hatte sie ihr bunt gefärbt Gewand
> Schon ab-, doch auf das neu mit unsichtbarer Hand,
> Ein güldnes wieder angeleget.
> Die Bluhm' aus Africa, die güldne Blätter träget,
> Nasturtium, die gelbe Ritter-Sporen,
> Die Sonnen-Bluhm', in gleichfalls güldner Zier,
> Die kamen mir,
> Als ich sie übersah, fast gleichsam vor,
> *Als wie ein Schlaff-Rock von Drap d'or,*
> *In welchem die Natur, eh sie zur langen Ruh*
> *Die müden Glieder neigte,*
> *Annoch zu guter letzt sich halb entkleidet zeigte.*
> Damit der Schlaff-Rock auch nicht gar einfärbig schien,
> War auch demselbigen nicht nur noch etwas grün,

[1] Vol. II (1st edn.), p. 9.   [2] Vol. II (1st edn.), p. 65.

> Nein, auch von Farben Wunder-schön,
> Ein Winter-Rosen-Busch noch hier und dort zu sehn,
> An deren feurigem Rubinen-gleichen Prangen
> Das menschliche Gesicht, fast wider willen, hangen,
> Und, fast gezwungen, kleben bleibt.[1]

The lines I have italicised spring out of the flabby, conventional language of the rest with startling brilliance. The complicated syntactical *ab-...angeleget* antithesis of the first sentence, the emphatic repetition of *gülden*, and then later the complex compound *Winter-Rosen-Busch* and the epithet *Rubinen-gleich*—all these are Silesian echoes; and with them are several examples of Brockes's timidity producing flatness of expression, like *fast gleichsam, als wie, fast wider willen, fast gezwungen* and far too many colourless adverbs. Out of this cotton-wool diction there comes a flash of poetry, a sudden deeper seeing of things, the situation grasped as an image, seen not thought, seen not described. But such moments have to be sought in the poetry of Brockes. Normally his expression rarely rises above verbal felicity, and when this lets him down, we find the old Silesian devices being hauled up from the storeroom of his memory.

Brockes was much praised for his use of the characterising epithet. Epithets had degenerated into superficial additions in late seventeenth-century verse. Frequent were metaphorical epithets containing reference to precious materials and denominal past participles with prefix *be-* (*bedornt, beflammt, begrünt*, etc.). These ornamental epithets are still to be found plentifully in Brockes's verse. The poem on May, quoted above, has several examples: *Sapphir'nes Blau, güld'ne Berge, Smaragden-gleich Gewand, bestral'te Flut, beblühmte Felder, begrün'te Wälder, balsamir'te Düfte*. These epithets add nothing to the expression; they are stock accretions. But Brockes can also give an epithet real value, characterising value: *die schertzenden, geschwinden Fliegen; ein krauses Blatt; ein murmelnd Flöten; ein saftiges Gezische; ein angewürzter Duft*. Normally he is more successful with sounds than with the material of the other senses where he often seems

---

[1] Vol. IV, *ed. cit.* pp. 377–8.

at a loss for words: 'Was sind die Farben doch? Nichts, als ein blosses Nichts' he says in one poem,[1] for they vanish with the light. All he can say of the dew on a vine is *ein gefärbtes Nichts, ein gleichsam-geistig Blau*;[2] of a rosebush that it is *weisslich-roht*, and then, developing this idea, *röthlich-bleich...süß in weißer Röhte*.[3] In smells he often takes over the exotic imagery of his predecessors and talks of amber, myrrh, civet and such like—so that in one poem we are told the jonquil smells of *Mosch, Zibeth und Bisam* and in another the same terms are used of the perfume of a strawberry.[4] Breitinger was surely right in saying that Brockes defeated his object by comparing natural things with artificial rarities.[5] It was as wrong for Brockes as it would have been for Stifter to write about earthquakes. Sometimes Brockes, in the effort to be exact, proliferates the epithets to such an extent that no clear impression results:

     Mich deucht...
Es sey darin der Duft und Kraft vereint zu finden
Von Honig, Mandel-Milch, Most, Pfirsch-Kern, Zimmet-Rinden,
Und daß mit holder Süssigkeit
Ein wenig säurliches und bitt'res sich verbinden
In solchem Grad, der Herz und Hirn erfreut.[6]

It would be difficult to guess what Brockes is here depicting; in fact it is the smell of a simple viola. Or again:

Durch deren glänzend-schroffe Spitzen, durch deren glatt' und rauhe Höh'n,
Der Bau der Erden öd' und prächtig, vergnüglich-wild, entsetzlich-schön,
Gefällig-greßlich, schreckend-lieblich, zugleich auf einmahl anzusehen.[7]

which is the description of icebergs on the Elbe.

The last two examples bring us to the very root of the problem of Brockes's style in its historical perspective. The *Irdisches Vergnügen in Gott* is a large collection of poetry which is essen-

---

[1] Vol. I (1st edn.), p. 116.
[2] Vol. I (2nd edn.), p. 257; the seventh edition has *geistlich* for *geistig*.
[3] Vol. I (7th edn.), p. 82. First edition had *schön in süsser Röhte*.
[4] Vol. III, p. 579 and vol. IV, p. 181.   [5] See below, p. 291.
[6] Vol. I (2nd edn.), p. 16.   [7] Vol. VII, p. 580.

tially descriptive poetry. It is concerned with a wide variety of subjects, but all of them real things. The range is considerable—from the firmament to the flowers of the field. There is even a poem on a tooth. Everything is related by the poet to God's goodness, but this is apt to be an artificial relation as regards the form of the poem. The poems tend to fall into two distinct parts: a description and then the moral. Sometimes this is a conscious contrast, the latter section introduced by a 'nevertheless'. But more often than not the poem does not present a formal unity. There is no doubt about the sincerity of Brockes's moralising. But he was also a man of considerable ingenuity and delight in words. The description is sought after, it is not part of the original poetic experience. And here his verbal virtuosity sometimes runs away with him and words become an end in themselves—as in the two examples just quoted. In a way this is still baroque. The Silesians had striven after striking metaphors and jostled impressions in frenzied antitheses; Brockes similarly strives after more and more precise details. Form becomes an end in itself, there is no generating artistic unity in the poet's mind and, except for the finest examples, the poems remain concatenations of fragments not fused into any total impression—fragments of unreality with the Silesians, fragments of reality with Brockes. This was Lessing's objection to descriptive poetry. The mind ranges from one detail to another, but the fragments never cohere into a final whole. Brockes had greater facility in language than any of his contemporaries, he had a good eye and an even better ear, he tried to make language express what he saw and heard—but his use of language remained a conscious striving after effect, a striving to imitate reality as precisely as possible. This is not the purpose of poetry, as Breitinger was to point out. Brockes's use of language is rarely poetic. It is at most precise, rarely evocative. Precision is a prose quality. Images and rhythms do not come welling up in Brockes, conditioning the whole shape and meaning of a poem, as with Günther. But his work represents a notable attempt at bringing the German language towards a more exact denotation of sense-impressions by sound, by descriptive epithets and sometimes images. And his development away from baroque poetic style was as definite as that of Günther, although quite different. It was a development in the use of epithets and of onomatopoeia, a development towards painting and music.

The first published collection of verse by Friedrich von Hagedorn, the *Versuch einiger Gedichte* of 1729, contains experiments in all the accepted poetic styles.[1] Its very eclecticism is symptomatic of a prevailing stylistic uncertainty. The collection contains occasional pieces in the style of König or Besser, descriptive pieces showing the influence of Brockes's onomatopoeia and satires in the spirit of Canitz. In these satires we note exploitation of the symmetry offered by the two halves of the alexandrine in which a thought is presented in two parts linked by copula or variation and resulting in a balanced, rounded statement. Here are a few examples:

(*a*) Der Vorsicht Fügungs-Schluß ist stets der Klugen Wille.
(*b*) Du, Nero, quälst die Welt, und dein Gewissen dich.
(*c*) Ein unvernünft'ger Feind vernünftiger Gedancken.[2]

Metaphor, where it appears, is pallid; there are only one or two echoes of Silesianism.[3] The ode to poetry begins very bombastically, but recants:

> Doch nein. Mich treibt mein Trieb zu weit,
> Und täuschet mich mit falschen Bildern.

The ode to wine contains the words:

> Es muß, die Reben zu erhöhn,
> Nicht jedes Wort auf Steltzen gehn,
> Um Reim und Ausdruck aufzuschwellen.

This is Horatian in spirit, and Horace remained always one of

---

[1] I quote from the reprint by Sauer in the *Neudrucke* series (Heilbronn, 1883). There is a monograph by H. Badstüber, *Friedrich von Hagedorns Jugendgedichte* (Vienna, 1904). On Hagedorn's language, see K. Epting, *Der Stil in den lyrischen und didaktischen Gedichten Friedrich von Hagedorns* (Stuttgart, 1929).
[2] *Ed. cit.* pp. 52–5.
[3] E.g. 'Wer nicht vorher den Wermuht schon geschmecket,
    Weiß kaum wie süß und wol der Zucker thut.'
    (*Die Grösse eines weislich-zufriedenen Gemühtes*)

Hagedorn's favourite authors. But he was not able to achieve an elevated style which was free of bombast and yet suited to the ode. What we do find in this first collection is a tendency towards the rounded *sententia* with an elegant cultivation of symmetry. There is also delightful irony:

> Mich lehrt dein Großmuth-volles Hertz,
> Und mich vergnügt dein weiser Schertz
> Dein Umgang wird zur Kraft der Seelen...
> Du bleibst mein Engel auf der Welt,
> Und was mich dir getreu erhält
> Ist dein Verstand, wie deine Glieder.[1]

The same delight in rounding off a phrase results here in a *pointe*. This is the 'good humour' which Hagedorn (according to Gleim) introduced into German poetry. Poetry was certainly always a pleasure for him. A later poem apostrophises poetry as the playmate of his leisure hours; the ode to poetry in this first collection ends with the words:

> Sey du mein Zeit-Vertreib und Lust,
> Und heisse ferner meine Brust
> Mit dir die langen Stunden kürtzen.[2]

Hagedorn was at first not disposed to polish his verses. In 1726 we find him writing to Weichmann 'daß das viele Ausbessern demjenigen lebhaften Feuer, worauf das Salz und die Höhe der Gedanken beruht, oft mehr schadet als nutzet'.[3] But on this he changed his mind. As a result he became a writer of great smoothness and grace. Here to illustrate this progression is the opening stanza of *Der Wein* as it appears in the *Versuche* of 1729 and the *Oden und Lieder* of 1747:

> (1729) So brausender, als süsser Most!
> Du jährend Marck der schlancken Reben!
> Geschenck des Bacchus: Nectar-Kost!
> Laß Dein Verdienst den Reim erheben.
> Du feuerreicher Götter-Safft!

---

[1] *Ed. cit.* p. 92. [2] *Ibid.* p. 40.
[3] *Werke*, ed. Eschenburg (Hamburg, 1800), vol. v, p. 6.

THE DEVELOPMENT OF THE POETICAL MEDIUM

>   Auf! gib allhier den Worten Kraft:
>   Auf! laß mir Wort und Reim gelingen.
>   Und, weil dein Einfluß, Trieb und Geist
>   So oft und manche singen heist,
>   Auch hier die frohe Muse singen.
>
> (1748) Du brausender und frischer Most,
>   Du gährend Mark der milden Reben,
>   Des Herbstes Ehre, Götter-Kost!
>   Mein Lied will deinen Ruhm erheben,
>   O feuerreicher Trauben-Saft!
>   Gieb meinen Worten deine Kraft,
>   Laß sie, wie du, ans Herze dringen,
>   Und, weil dein Einfluß und dein Geist
>   Dem Witze Muth und Glück verheisst,
>   Auch mich von deinen Wundern singen.

The new version is not so restless and therefore more concentrated. The apostrophe now begins at once with the first word, the contrast between the epithets in each of the first two lines is more strongly marked, a virtual tautology is avoided in the third line, a circumlocution in the fourth, a clumsy stress (*allhier*) in the sixth with a gain in meaning by the *mein–dein* opposition and a similar strengthening of the next line, the rhythm is smoothed out in the eighth and ninth lines and there is a saving of two mythological incursions, Bacchus and the Muse. There is a general gain in tautness, smoothness and strength.

Hagedorn's next collection of verse was the *Versuch in Fabeln und Erzählungen* of 1738.[1] Interest in the fable had revived in Germany in the late seventeenth century with translations and imitations of La Fontaine. Hagedorn was steeped in French literature. In a letter to Bodmer in 1753 he said that in his youth he had read much more French literature than German and rightly so. It is perhaps because of this that we find so few traces of Silesianism in his early verse. It was Boileau and Pope, he said, who turned him against the cult of 'Italian writers'. With English

---

[1] There is a good monograph by W. Eigenbrodt, *Hagedorn und die Erzählung in Reimversen* (Berlin, 1884), and an article by Petsch 'Hagedorn und die deutsche Fabel' in the *Festschrift Melle* (Hamburg, 1933).

literature, as we shall see later, he was also acquainted. It is, however, difficult to agree with Muncker that Hagedorn modelled the *language* of his fables on La Fontaine. He has nothing of the Frenchman's colourful vocabulary, nor his vivid use of popular syntax, nor his graphic vitality. He remained a writer of grace and elegance, nothing more. He lacks the richness of characterising detail, the saucy crispness and the savage genius which we admire in La Fontaine. But his fables are smoothly told and the moral is stated neatly and well. Here again we note the delight in the pleasant rounding of an idea into a succinct and complete statement. He had learnt this from the French and the English. He admired Pope. But he had also, all his life, been reading and re-reading Horace.

He had a marked talent for the epigram. It was the natural expression for his attitude to language. Everything he wrote had something epigrammatic about it. Even when he is not being witty there is a tendency towards the balancing of words in delicate counterpoise:

> Seyd auch den Dichtern hold: Versorgt und rühmet sie;
> Nur jenes nicht zu spät, und dieses nicht zu früh![1]

His style, as Epting has noted, is naturally simple and naturally symmetrical. It demands clear structures, it avoids hypotaxis, pregnant illogicality and the more paradoxical figures of speech (oxymoron, zeugma). It is essentially paratactic, logical and uses only the simpler figures (repetition, prosopopoeia, apostrophe, rhetorical question). It is more nominal than verbal, putting the meaning into the nouns and linking them by simple copulae. The ability to write a well-turned *pointe* was something new in German verse and it is part of the grace that Hagedorn gave to the language, for it was he who perfected this device. The same grace characterises the *Oden und Lieder* of 1747 which, since they belong to the anacreontic tradition, we shall discuss in a later chapter. The same telling economy of words gives crispness to the maxims in his longer didactic poems, most of which are to be found in

[1] *Werke*, ed. Eschenburg, vol. I, p. 181.

the *Moralische Gedichte* of 1750 although many of them were published separately before that date. Here the English influence[1] is more apparent. The English didactic poem of the early eighteenth century was a verse counterpart to the moral weeklies. The ideas of Shaftesbury and other moralists were expressed by Addison in prose and by Pope in verse. The neatly turned line that stuck in the memory was an important element of Pope's style. 'Mr Pope's chief excellence', said Shenstone, 'lies in what I would term consolidating or condensing sentences, yet preserving ease and perspicuity.'[2] Albrecht von Haller, in his famous comparison of himself with Hagedorn in a letter of 1772, said of the influence of their English sojourns:

> Wir fühlten, daß man in wenigen Wörtern weit mehr sagen konnte, als man in Deutschland bis hieher gesagt hatte... und strebten beyde nach einer Stärcke, dazu wir noch keine Urbilder gehabt hatten.[3]

This is somewhat overstated; for Haller is forgetting Hagedorn's early acquaintance with Horace. There is, however, no doubt that the influence of Pope strengthened the tendency towards sententious terseness and polish which Hagedorn had already acquired from Horace;[4] for his terseness always maintains Pope's 'ease and perspicuity'. There is an Augustan ring about many of his couplets:

> (a) Der Geist, durch den ein Cato groß geworden,
> Fährt in kein Band, und ruht auf keinem Orden.
>
> (b) Was ist die Weisheit denn, die wenigen gemein?
> Sie ist die Wissenschaft, in sich beglückt zu seyn.
>
> (c) Es mag ein Sybarit auf weichen Rosen liegen,
> Die leichte Spinne kann sich zehnmal sanfter wiegen.[5]

---

[1] On this, see B. R. Coffmann's articles in *MPh.* XII and XIII (1914–16).

[2] *Works*, vol. 11 (London, 1764), p. 14.

[3] See Hirzel's edition of Haller's poems, p. 398. Germans at this time constantly praise the pregnant brevity of the English language. Thus young Sulzer to Gleim (18 November 1745): 'Ich habe angefangen, etwas aus Thomsons Englischem zu übersetzen. Es soll ein Beweis seyn, daß wir eben so kurz und nachdrücklich schreiben können, als die Engländer.' Uz (*Werke* (1768), vol. 11, pp. 313–14) refers to the English 'gedankenreiche und körnichte Art zu dichten'.

[4] The prose *Schreiben an einen Freund*, written in 1752 to justify the notes attached to the *Moralische Gedichte*, is full of quotations from Pope.

[5] *Ed. cit.* vol. 1, pp. 16, 20, 22.

Mythological allusions of a simple kind are used:

> Ein Midas trotzt auf den Besitz der Schätze,
> Um die der Geiz nach fernen Ufern reist.

This is the beginning of the poem entitled *Der Weise*, first published in 1741.[1] Characteristic is the substitution of either the mythological type (*ein Midas*) or the abstract quality (*der Geiz*) for the individual appellative. All three are represented in the couplet (with my italics):

> *Er* schläft mit Lust, wo *andrer Sorgen* wachen;
> Wann *Boreas* um Dach und Fenster heult[2]

The substitutions represent a tendency away from ordinary expression towards elevated diction. In his poem on Horace, Hagedorn said that the functions of the poet include that he should accustom the ear 'der Wörter Wahl zu lernen, / Im Ausdruck sich vom Pöbel zu entfernen'.[3] This is still the attitude of the Renaissance. It had been the attitude of Opitz. But in this cultivation of elegance Hagedorn never strayed into baroque euphuism or anything like it. His inspiration was more purely classical.

It is a commonplace to compare Hagedorn with Albrecht von Haller and to say that there is no greater contrast imaginable. Hagedorn—gay, elegant and epicurean; Haller—serious, clumsy and *kulturpessimistisch*. The relation between the two poets was considered by Haller himself in a long letter to Gemmingen, dated March 1772. By this time Hagedorn had been dead nearly twenty years and Haller had been poetically dead for some thirty-five years. Reflective assessment was therefore possible. Both of them, says Haller, were born in the same year, both educated carefully, both were left orphans, both started to write verses at an early age, both had more taste than ability. Hagedorn remodelled his early verses, Haller burned his. Both visited England and were deeply affected, both admired the terseness of English philosophical poetry and determined to imitate it. Hagedorn published his first collection in 1729, Haller in 1732. Both

---

[1] *Ed. cit.* vol. I, p. 15. [2] *Ibid.* [3] *Ed. cit.* vol. I, p. 115.

refrained from taking sides in the aesthetic debate between Leipzig and Zürich, both disliked the new rhymeless verse and the German hexameter, both had the same stylistic ideal in didactic verse: emphatic terseness. And yet they were basically different in temperament. Hagedorn was of a jovial disposition, drank his glass of wine and enjoyed company; Haller was solitary and preferred tea. A similar difference existed in the whole tone and style of their poetry. Hagedorn composed songs of love and wine which were the first German songs that could be compared with the French in quality. In *Heiterkeit* he approached Horace and surpassed Boileau; he was as correct as Boileau, as witty as Horace and as polished as Pope. Haller was a brooder and his deep feeling gave his poems a melancholy seriousness which contrasted strongly with Hagedorn's natural gaiety. Then comes an important statement on language:

> Ein anderer Vorzug des Hrn. v. Hagedorn war die Kenntnis der Sprache. Er lebte in Deutschland und war von seiner Jugend an im reinen Deutschen erzogen. Hier konnte ich ihn nicht erreichen; in meinem Vaterlande, jenseits den Gränzen des deutschen Reichs, sprechen selbst die Gelehrtesten in einer sehr unreinen Mundart; wir haben auch in unsern symbolischen Büchern und in den Staatsschriften andre Declinationen, andre Wortfügungen. Diese Unarten musste ich nach und nach ablegen, und da meine anderweitigen Arbeiten mir nicht zuließen, meine Stunden auf die Muttersprache zu wenden, so blieb mir allemahl eine gewisse Armuth im Ausdruke, die ich schon damahls am besten fühlte, wenn ich mich gegen die Leichtigkeit des Günthers verglich. Manchen Gedanken lähmte mir der Zwang der Sprache; manchen andern drükte ich mit einem unvermeidlichen Verluste an der Reinigkeit und an dem leichten Schwunge des Verses aus.

Considerable attacks were levelled at these imperfections of Haller's language. Gottsched brusquely spoke of 'Sprachschnitzer'. Haller made revisions in the text of his poems for each new edition. The first was published at Berne in 1732 and bore the title: *Versuch Schweizerischer Gedichten.*[1] Eleven editions

---

[1] The fine critical edition by Ludwig Hirzel in the *Bibliothek älterer Schriftwerke der deutschen Schweiz* (vol. III, Frauenfeld, 1882) contains in its introduction of over five hundred pages the best account of Haller's life and works. The text

were published during his lifetime, the last in the year of his death. Gottsched found the second edition of 1734 already 'weit sauberer und unanstößiger'. This had some sixty corrections.[1] The third edition of 1743 benefited from his residence in Germany. In the preface Haller said that German was to a certain extent his mother-tongue, but it was spoken less purely and less frequently in his homeland than French. He now makes over four hundred alterations. Even the last corrected edition of 1777 had a hundred and fifty changes from the preceding one. The second edition had corrected inflectional forms mainly, the third edition continued this process but also eradicated apocope and syncope, the fourth and later editions made improvements in syntax and style and replaced local expressions by words of wider currency. According to Socin, Berne was the most conservative linguistically of the towns of German-speaking Switzerland. It preferred to use its own Alemannic or French rather than the Saxon Standard German. But Haller had none of the linguistic chauvinism of Bodmer. He did not argue the point; he agreed that his language was incorrect and took pains to improve it. Following his native speech he had naturally written forms like *anderst, spat, Vatterland, Spraach, lehrnt, Forcht, förchten, dörften* and *genennt, gekennt*—although the last two already show adaptation to the *Schriftsprache* forms. Yet sometimes he used forms which were not Saxon Standard but also not Alemannic, like

follows the 1777 edition but has been somewhat regularised; readings of the earlier editions are given in the notes. I have taken my text from the original 1732 and 1777 editions (the first and the last during Haller's lifetime) using the British Museum copies. I also give parallel references to Hirzel's edition, for the convenience of my readers.

The letter to Gemmingen, quoted above, is reprinted in Hirzel, pp. 397–406. It originated as a defence of serious poetry against what Haller considered the frivolity of the Anacreontics. It remained a draft, for it was never sent.

[1] My figures and some of the other materials in this paragraph are taken from K. Zagajewski, *Albrecht von Hallers Dichtersprache* (Strassburg, 1909) (Quellen und Forschungen, vol. 105). There are two earlier treatments: W. Horák, 'Die Entwicklung der Sprache Hallers' (Programm Bielitz, Jg. xiv and xv) (Bielitz, 1890 and 1891), and H. Käslin, *Albrecht von Hallers Sprache in ihrer Entwicklung* (Diss. Freiburg i.Br. 1892). The materials of both these studies are evaluated by Zagajewski.

gläubt or *kömmt*. This shows a general uncertainty about what is correct and what is not. Hence he vacillated between three forms of one suffix: *-nuß*, *-nüß* and *-niß*. He failed to distinguish between *wenn* and *wann*, and between *denn* and *dann*. He used some quite archaic 'literary' forms like *ich sieh* and *du solt*. He had the same tendency towards a wider use of the *-en* suffix for nominative/accusative and genitive plural of nouns that we find in other Upper German prints of the first half of the eighteenth century.[1] The first edition of his poems had the title *Versuch Schweizerischer Gedichten*, the second: *Versuch Von Schweizerischen Gedichten*, and the third: *Versuch Schweizerischer Gedichte*. This speaks for itself. There was a similar uncertainty about strong or weak declension with the adjective. Flexionless attributive adjectives represented exploitation of a metrically convenient archaism. Strong preterite indicatives formed analogically from subjunctives (*fund*, *zwung*) were the sign of a speech-form which had lost the simple preterite indicative. It is clear that Haller often did not know what was correct. Even in 1772, in his letter to Gemmingen, he could write: '*Unseres* Jahrhundert ist gesellschaftlicher als alle vorhergehenden.'[2] It was this sense of insecurity which had made him beseech the help of Leipzig. In the 1748 preface there is a note of petulant desperation:

> Bey vielen Stellen habe ich auch keinen Ausweg finden können und lieber einen Sprachfehler als einen matten Gedanken stehen lassen wollen. Ich bitte diejenigen, die die Reinigkeit der Sprache zum Hauptwesen der Dichtkunst machen, nur den Opiz ohne Vorurtheil durchzusehen. Sie werden leicht gestehen, daß man mit Provinzial Wörtern, mit ungewöhnlichen Ausdrücken und mit würklichen Fehlern wider die Sprachkunst dennoch ihren eigenen Beyfall und ihre Verwunderung habe erhalten können.[3]

Nearly thirty years later, in reply to Gemmingen's statement that he preferred the first versions of Haller's poems, the old man looked back on the fruits of that poetic activity which had made

---

[1] See my article on '*The Parnassus Boicus* and the German Language' (see above, p. 142), and my article on Dornblüth (see above, p. 140).
[2] Hirzel, p. 405. My italics.   [3] *Ibid.* p. 250.

him so famous but which had stopped when he was only 28 years of age, and said:

> Meine Gedichte waren freylich a. 1732 in ihrer natürlichen Stärke, wann es eine Stärke ist, und Vieles war nicht sprachrichtig aber kernhaffter ausgedrükt. Das wollten aber die Deutschen nicht leiden, und mir fiel sowohl des Caesar's als des Boileau Ausspruch ein, wodurch die Sprachreinigkeit zum unumgänglichen Vorzuge eines guten Gedichtes gemacht wird.[1]

But even Gottsched had joined in the general acclamation of the *Stärke* of these poems. In a private letter to Haller, dated 22 October 1735, he called their language 'stark und voll Nachdruck' and added (rather unexpectedly) 'in welcher Absicht ich gern darinnen hier und da die meißnische, oft gedankenlose Zierlichkeit und leichtfließende Innigkeit vermissen will'.[2] But he was later to turn against Haller.

The other charge against Haller's language was that it was obscure. This was raised by Gottsched in the third edition of his *Critische Dichtkunst* in 1742. By this time the battle on aesthetics between Leipzig and Zürich was in full swing and Haller had become one of the contested reputations. In Gottsched's mind he became linked with Bodmer and Milton in the new-fangled cult of obscurity. The point was taken up by Cramer and Mylius in the first number of their periodical *Bemühungen zur Beförderung der Critik und des guten Geschmacks*, 1743, and the assertion made that this obscurity derived largely from Haller's use of out-of-the-way words and of participial constructions. To this Pyra replied that Haller was one of the few Germans to have a truly poetic style of writing; Breitinger defended Haller's use of participial constructions and said that he provided 'die Idee und die Probe von einer ungottschedischen Poesie'.[3] The basic objection of Cramer and Mylius was that Haller's temperament was too serious for poetry. 'In die Poesie gehören solche tiefsinnige,

---

[1] Letter of 21 September 1776. [2] Hirzel, p. cl, footnote.
[3] Pyra, *Erweis, daß die G.ttsch.dianische Secte den Geschmack verderbe*, quoted Hirzel, pp. ccxiii ff. Breitinger, *Vertheidigung der Schweitzerischen Muse Hrn. D. Albrecht Hallers* (Zürich, 1744), quoted Hirzel, pp. ccxvi ff.

philosophische Begriffe nicht.' They also chided him with having read too much English and having acquired an English manner of thinking; and as he was not concerned about beauty or correctness of style: 'so sind seine Gedichte in der That voll von einem gewissen ausländischen Erhabenen, welches die Ohren unaufhörlich verletzet und sehr oft in nichts bestehet als in der Dunkelheit englisch-barbarischer und schweizerisch-solöcismischer Ausdrückungen'.[1] Haller defended himself in his 1748 preface. Having put aside Lohenstein, he had learnt from the English poets 'die Liebe zum Denken und den Vorzug der schweren Dichtkunst'. And in order to hold the attention of the reader he had deliberately set out to pack his lines with as much meaning as possible:

Nach meinem Begriffe muß man die Aufmerksamkeit dess Lesers niemahls abnehmen lassen. Dieses geschieht ohnfehlbar auf eine mechanische Weise, sobald man ihm einige lähre Zeilen vorlegt, wobey er nichts zu denken findet. Ein Dichter muß Bilder, lebhaffte Figuren, kurze Sprüche, starke Züge und unerwartete Anmerkungen auf einander häuffen oder gewärtig sein, daß man ihn weglegt.[2]

This important passage continues:

Aber ich bin ein Schweizer, die deutsche Sprache ist mir fremd, und die Wahl der Wörter war mir fast unbekannt. Der Ueberfluß der Ausdrücke fehlte mir völlig, und die schweren Begriffe, die ich einzukleiden hatte, machten die Sprache für mich noch enger.... Bey vielen Stellen habe ich auch keinen Ausweg finden können und lieber einen Sprachfehler als einen matten Gedanken stehen lassen wollen.

This determination at all costs to avoid expression that was *matt*, is significant; it occurs already in the 1734 preface: 'Endlich habe ich mir eine Freude gemacht, alle matte Stellen auszureuten.'[3] This represents a practical realisation of the ideal Breitinger was to raise theoretically in his *Critische Dichkunst*, as we shall see. Haller risked obscurity by his cultivation of fullness instead of flatness. In 1768 he saw the situation of 1732 as follows: 'Kaniz war, bey allen seinen Naturgaben, doch etwas zu wässericht und weitläuftig. Man sagt, meine Gedichte seyen hingegen zu

---

[1] Hirzel, p. ccxxi. [2] *Ibid.* p. 249. [3] *Ibid.* p. 243.

gedrungen und die Gedanken zu kurz, die Bilder auch nicht genugsam aus einander gesetzt.'[1] Gottsched's *Sprachkunst* had had some good things to say about Haller, but opposed his participial constructions and had a general attack on *die gedrungenen Dichter*. Haller, reviewing the book for the *Göttinger Gelehrte Zeitung* defended his participles by reference to Opitz and his terseness by mentioning the pleasure it had given to most of his contemporaries. The situation is well described by the anonymous reviewer of Schönaich's *Hermann* in the same Göttingen paper in 1752. It might be Haller himself. He says:

> Deutschland ist eine Zeit daher in zwey poetische Secten vertheilt. Die eine sucht die Größe in starken Bildern, erhabenen Gedanken und gewichtigen Beiwörtern. Die andere schätzt die Gedichte nach der Reinigkeit der Sprache, nach der Deutlichkeit des Vortrages und der Flüssigkeit der Schreibart.[2]

This is the real distinction between Haller and Hagedorn.

Let us now consider in some detail this sovereign quality of Haller's language which his admirers described as terse and his detractors as obscure. 'Im Lehrgedichte', he said in the Gemmingen letter, 'haben die gleich langen Verse, *in deren jedem ein Begrif ausgeführt ist*, einen überaus deutlichen Vorzug.'[3] One idea expressed in a single line—this will naturally lead to sententiousness. Haller believed that it produced solemnity and memorability. He achieved this pregnant brevity by various means. A predicative adjective in unusual environment:

> Kein Unstern mahlt sie schwarz, kein schwülstig Glüke roht.[4]

This construction, familiar enough with *machen*, is here employed with a verb which does not need a predicate to give a complete meaning. Compare:

> Was heut noch rühmlich war, dient morgens uns zur Schmaach,
> *Ein Thor sagt lächerlich*, was ein Held weislich sprach.[5]

---

[1] Preface to 1768 edition of the poems, p. 4 (Hirzel, p. 264).
[2] *Op. cit.* (1752), pp. 123 ff. Quoted by Hirzel.
[3] Hirzel, p. 400. My italics.
[4] *Ibid.* p. 24 (text emended from the 1732 edition).
[5] *Ibid.* p. 66 (with 1732 text).

THE DEVELOPMENT OF THE POETICAL MEDIUM

The second line needs careful analysis: *lächerlich* is semi-predicate to *sagt* used in the sense of *heißt*, but *weislich* is adverbial modifier of *sprach*. What looks like a parallel construction, is therefore quite otherwise. This is confusing and obscure. Haller's gain in precision is at the expense of clarity. What is one to make of a line like:

> Die alle nennen Gott ein Wesen nur in Ohren,?

It is clearer if we consider it in its context:

> Offt dekt der Priester selbst sich mit erlernten Minen,
> Sein Herze höhnt den Gott, dem seine Lippen dienen,
> Er lachet, wann das Volk vor Gözen niederfällt,
> Die List vergöttert hat und Aberwiz erhält.
> Die alle nennen Gott ein Wesen nur in Ohren
> Dem Staat zu Nuz erdacht, und mächtig nur vor Thoren:[1]

but *in Ohren* still seems a very uncomfortable prepositional attribute. Quite often there is a real gain in intensity. Oblique cases of the noun are used instead of a prepositional phrase: 'Belohnung suchen *deiner Huld*'; '[Prometheus] findt *dem Donner* Brüder';[2] or, from the description of cheesemaking in *Die Alpen*:

> Hier kocht der zweite Raub der Milch *dem armen Volke*.[3]

All sorts of elliptical constructions are used. For instance:

> (*a*) Glückselig Volk, dem Gott zum Herrscher ihn verlieh.
> (*b*) Ein Herr der Welt zu seyn gebohren.
> (*c*) Vergangnes Leid muß wohlsein fühlen lehren.[4]

The complex effect of this style is illustrated by a passage such as:

> Dein Lieben war, mein Leid ergötzen
> Mit heimlich sorgender Geduld;
> Mein Lieben war, mich selig schätzen,
> Belohnung suchen deiner Huld.[5]

---

[1] *Ibid.* pp. 53–4 (1732 text). My italics.
[2] *Ibid.* p. 164, p. 45 (first three editions have *macht*). My italics.
[3] *Ibid.* p. 31. My italics.
[4] *Ibid.* pp. 196, 297; p. 7 (later editions).
[5] *Ibid.* p. 164 (1777 text).

Sometimes ambiguity results. A passage in the first edition of *Die Alpen*:

> Er treibt den trägen Schwarm der schwer beleibten Kühen,
> Mit freudigem Gebrüll durch den bethauten Steg,[1]

called forth the sarcastic comment: 'Wie schön der Hirt nicht brüllet!' from Schönaich, and had to be altered. A particular form of elliptical construction was the absolute use of participles, for which Haller was censured, especially by Gottsched. There is no doubt about it: the density of Haller's style was unique in German writers of the period. This was his major contribution to the development of the German language. However much he may have overdone it and however unsuccessful and unpoetical he so often was, the tautness and crowded terseness of his language was a valuable antidote against the flatness of Canitz, the verbosity of Brockes and even the extreme smoothness of Hagedorn. Many of the details of his style, such as the use of participles and of cases to replace prepositional phrases, were taken up and developed by Klopstock.

We have a few poems written by Haller before he consciously set out to develop this new style. The poem entitled *Morgen-Gedanken*, written in 1725 when Haller was sixteen, shows the influence of Brockes and Lohenstein.[2] It is constructed like a Brockes poem. The first part is descriptive; the second turns to praise of the deity for His beneficence. The first part is full of Silesian clichés—'Perlen-Thau', 'Der Lilgen Ambra-Dampff', etc.[3] The second part offers an enumeration, in Brockes's manner, of the works of God—stars, sun, moon, winds, dew, stars and eventually the elephant. A phrase like:

> Des weiten Himmel-Raums saphirene Gewölber

---

[1] Hirzel, p. 302 (1732 text).

[2] In the letter to Gemmingen of 1772, from which I have already several times quoted, Haller described his early method of composition as follows: 'Ich ahmte bald Brokes, bald Lohenstein und bald andere niedersächsische Dichter nach, indem ich eines von ihren Gedichten zum Muster vor mich nahm und ein anders ausarbeitete, das nichts von dem Muster nachschreiben und doch ihm ähnlich seyn sollte' (Hirzel, p. 398).

[3] 1732 text; cf. Hirzel, pp. 3–4.

suggests Brockes's own refashioning of the diction of Lohenstein. The *Sehnsucht nach dem Vaterlande* of 1726 shows already that use of rhetorical figures—apostrophe, repetition, antithesis and rhetorical question—which was to remain a constant feature of Haller's style. The ode *Über die Ehre*, composed in 1728 but much revised for the later editions, shows a further development of this rhetorical style with extensive use of synecdoche and mythological allusion. These two forms of indirect expression often lead to mixed images and a general effect every bit as muddled as that produced by the metaphorical substitutions of Silesian baroque. For instance:

> O Jüngling ruffte jener Weise
> Warum dringt deine Helden-Reise
>   Biß in der Sonne glühend Bett?
> Du rennst in tausend blosse Sebel
> Nur daß der Griechen müß'ger Pöbel
>   Am Tisch von deinen Thaten redt.   (1732 text)

Consider the absurd impression resulting from the following:

> Baut eitle Herrscher Sonnen-Säulen,
> Die weder Zeit noch Regen fäulen,
>   Mit des gepreßeten Volckes Blut;
> Doch wißt, daß in dem Zahn der Würmen,
> Man unter Himmel hohen Thürmen
>   Nicht besser als im Rasen ruht.[1]

This is nothing more than a sort of attenuated baroque style in which the imagery, still entirely decorative, has been spread out and weakened. All the essential elements of Haller's style are to be found in this poem, but still unfused and unmoulded. It is about this time that Haller discovered the English poets and despatched his juvenilia to the flames. The critical years are 1728 and 1729. In Basle he became friendly with the physicist Benedikt Stähelin and the botanist Karl Friedrich Drollinger. Both were intensely interested in English poetry. Stähelin corresponded in English and Drollinger had already burnt his early poems in a revulsion against the absurdities of Lohenstein. Drollinger wrote

[1] 1732 text; cf. Hirzel, p. 297.

a number of philosophical poems, modelled on the English type, which were collected and published in 1745. His translation of Pope's *Essay on Criticism* was published by Bodmer in the *Sammlung critischer Schriften* of 1741. Haller begins to learn English thoroughly. He now finds Lohenstein vapid and Brockes verbose. The subjects of poetry shall be serious, the style concise. The first effects of this are to be seen in *Die Alpen*, completed in March 1729. The prefatory note refers to the difficulties of its composition.[1] Haller chose a ten-line stanza of two quatrains with a final couplet, and endeavoured to make each stanza contain one *Gemählde* which attained its greatest vividness in the couplet. He admits that this structure gave him great difficulty, and that there were 'noch viele Spuren des Lohensteinischen Geschmacks darin'. By the latter he probably meant a passage like

> Die Lufft erfüllet sich mit lauen Ambra-Dämpffen,
>   Die Florens bunt Geschlecht gelinden Westen zollt,
> Der Blumen schekicht Heer, scheint um den Rang zu kämpffen,
>   Ein lichtes Himmel-Blau beschämt ein nahes Gold.
> Ein ganz Gebürge scheint gefirnißt von dem Regen,
>   Ein grünender Tapet, gestikt mit Regenbögen.[2]

But real meaning is restored to this conventional vocabulary when he describes the joys of country loves in the couplet:

> O dreymal Selige! Euch muß ein Fürst beneiden,
> Dann Liebe balsamt Gras, und Ekel herrscht auf Seiden.

The 'difficulty' with the couplets refers to that striving after sententiousness, often successful, which we have noted as a form of his didactic style. It is interesting to follow this through the various editions. Extra meaning is constantly being packed into the lines. Redundancies are erased and loose words strengthened.

> Dort *fliegt* ein schnelles Bley in das entfernte Weisse,
> Das blizt, und Lufft und Ziel *im gleichen nu* durchbohrt;
>
> (1732 text)

---

[1] This note is in the fourth (1748) and later editions. See Hirzel, p. 20.

[2] 1732 text; cf. Hirzel, p. 36. Comparisons with precious stones and materials are found sporadically throughout the poem.

is changed into:

> Dort *eilt* ein schnelles Bley in das entfernte Weisse,
> Das blitzt, und Luft und Ziel im gleichen *Jetzt* durchbohrt;
>
> (1777 text)

Characteristic is this preference for the general, universal expression—*ein schnelles Blei*; *das entfernte Weiße*; compare 'Dort tanzt *ein bunter Ring*...' or '*Das graue Alter* dort sitzt hin...' or 'In der verdickten Luft schwebt *ein bewegtes Grau*'—a sort of abstract metonymy sometimes approaching personification. This is characteristic, because Haller's themes are the general, typical aspects of human nature and activity. And this not only in *Die Alpen*. His subjects are the general philosophical preoccupations of the day—the corruption of society, the tyranny of superstition, reason and virtue, the origin and nature of evil, the meaning of death and eternity. Schooled by the English he has evolved a language applicable to and commensurate with his themes. *Die Alpen* is, however, not a purely philosophical poem. And in the descriptive sections we find careful attention to epithets (*futterreiche Weide*; *mauergleiche Spitzen*; *gähe Kraft*; *strudelreiche Wellen*). They are often participial (*zerstäubte Theile*; *etzend Naß*; *durchgeseufzte Nächte*; *angestorbener Grund*), sometimes representing the old baroque denominal type (*beblümt, beglänzt, bethaut, beflügelt, begrünt, beschäumt*), sometimes of a Greek-looking compound nature (*Gift-geschwollner Neid*). Perhaps it is this uneasy companionship of the reflective style stressing the general and a descriptive style stressing the particular which leads Haller to his occasional lapses into the unsuitable or even the comic. For example:

> Ihr thätig Leben stärkt der Leiber reiffe Kräfften,
> Der träge Müssiggang *schwellt niemals ihren Bauch*.
>
> (1732 text)

And the style sometimes parodies itself, as in the excessively prosopopoeic and ultra-sententious couplet:

> Begierd und Hunger würtzt, was Einfalt hat bereitet,
> Bis Schlaff und Liebe sie, umarmt zum Bett begleitet.
>
> (1732 text)

But the achievement was considerable and the style matured as Haller abandoned descriptive verse for purely didactic poems.

It was the *Gedanken über Vernunft, Aberglauben und Unglauben*, dated 1729, which finally convinced the sceptical Stähelin that philosophical poetry was possible in the German language. And not only Stähelin. For it showed the new terse, abstract style in full development. This style we have analysed above. We have seen its compression, its sententiousness and its obscurity. We have appreciated both its clumsiness and its strength. And we have acknowledged its importance as a counterweight to other influences on the German language prevalent at this time. Further analysis here would seem to be unnecessary, for no new linguistic features present themselves as the style matures in the didactic poems written between 1730 and 1736. The heroic couplet becomes Haller's natural verse-form. He had found his way towards it under the influence of his enthusiasm for the English philosophical poets, and it enables him to give his thoughts lapidary and often striking expression. But this summary terseness never rises to wit because he lacks the necessary irony and the general tone is too serious. The result is often a concatenation of maxims, with the language, as it were, constantly standing to attention. This may become wearisome; and there is little attempt by Haller to vary his style. But the mind is frequently held by striking formulations. These may be effective by their very oddness:

(*a*) Wir irren allesamt, nur jeder irret anderst.[1]

(*b*) Heut heißt ein Staat ein Zug, und morgen ein Venedig;[2]

or have a definite beauty:

(*a*)   die weiten Kreise
Der anfangslosen Dau'r...[3]

(*b*) Das Leben einer Welt, verlebt in Ungemach,
Ist nur ein schwüler Tag, wo dich die Sonne stach.[4]

---

[1] *Gedanken über Vernunft*, etc., 1777 text; cf. Hirzel, p. 56.
[2] *Die verdorbenen Sitten*, 1777 text; cf. Hirzel, p. 94.
[3] *Gedanken über Vernunft*, etc., 1777 text; cf. Hirzel, p. 57.
[4] *Antwort an Herrn Bodmer*, 1777 text; cf. Hirzel, p. 182.

THE DEVELOPMENT OF THE POETICAL MEDIUM

But original images are rare and Haller scarcely moves beyond synecdoche. The style is essentially an abstract style and remains so. It is therefore more suited to ideas than to the expression of feeling and is far too rhetorical to be suited to lyrical poetry. The famous poem on the death of his first wife Mariane, except for two moments which vaguely foreshadow the Strassburg Goethe,[1] is too much *about* feelings to be really moving. This was the substance of Schiller's criticism of Haller in *Über naive und sentimentalische Dichtung*. It is significant that Haller could go on to write a second poem, *Über eben dieselbe*, for this is a subject like any other, a subject to be *treated*. Haller is uncomfortable about expressing his feelings. 'Dieses kleine Gedicht, worinn *die Poesie schwach, und nichts als die Rührung des Herzens noch einigermassen poetisch ist*' he said of the earliest of the three Mariane poems,[2] and in a note to the *Trauerode* he says the poem has more feeling than wit and hesitantly suggests that this might be a good thing in lyrical poetry![3] The poem *Über den Ursprung des Übels* (1734) contains two unexpected but significant cast-backs. First a descriptive introduction in the manner of Brockes, containing depictive detail which is sometimes prosaic and yet sometimes quite poetical, which culminates in the usual reference to God's goodness. The form is the free but rhymed *arioso* favoured by Brockes. The poem proper then begins to unfold its argument in the usual rhetorical, abstract style and in heroic couplets. Then in the third book comes a peculiar cast-back of another kind.[4]

---

[1] (*a*) lines 25–8:
> 'Ich seh dich noch, wie du erblaßtest,
> Wie ich verzweifelnd zu dir trat,
> Wie du die letzten Kräfte faßtest,
> Um noch ein Wort, das ich erbat.'

and (*b*) lines 102–5:
> 'Ich will dich sehen, wie du giengest,
> Wie traurig, wann ich Abschied nahm;
> Wie zärtlich, wann du mich umfiengest;
> Wie freudig wann ich wieder kam.' (1777 text)

[2] Hirzel, p. 155. My italics.
[3] *Ibid.* p. 332.
[4] Lines 115 ff. and 133 ff. My italics. (1777 text.)

> Die Furcht, der Seele *Frost*, der Flammen*strom*, der Zorn,
> Die Rachsucht ohne Macht, des Kummers tiefer *Dorn*...
> Der *Brand* der Ungedult, der theure *Preis* der Freude,
> Der Liebe *Folter-Bett*...

and then a few lines later:

> Die Zeit muß seit dem Fall ihr Sandglas gäher stürzen,
> Die Mordsucht grub ein *Erzt*, die kurze Frist zu kürzen,
> Tod, Schmerz und Krankheit wird *ergraben und erschifft*,
> Und unsre Speise macht der Ueberfluß zum *Gift*,
> Der Sorgen *Wurm* verzehret den *Balsam* unsrer Säfte,
> Der Wollust *gäher Brand* verschwendet des Leibes Kräfte,
> Verwesend, abgenutzt, und nur zum Leiden stark
> Eilt er zur alten Ruh, und sinket nach dem Sark.

This attenuated Silesianism shows all too plainly the decay of a style into a meaningless mannerism. It also shows the tenacious hold of this tradition on the language. This is, by general assent, the weakest section of the poem. We note that when imagination flags, Haller—like Günther—drapes himself in the old tinsel. The highest point in the development of Haller's powerful management of the German language is represented by the unfinished ode *Über die Ewigkeit* of 1736 where he breaks through the rigidity of the heroic couplet to achieve startling effects like:

> Des Lebens lange Last erdrückt die müden Glieder;
> Die Freude flieht von mir, mit flatterndem Gefieder,
> Der Sorgen-freyen Jugend zu.[1]

or the sombre grandeur of the lines:

> Furchtbares Meer der ernsten Ewigkeit!
> Uraltes Quell von Welten und von Zeiten!
> Unendlichs Grab von Welten und von Zeit!
> Beständigs Reich der Gegenwärtigkeit!
> Die Asche der Vergangenheit
> Ist dir ein Keim von Künftigkeiten.
> Unendlichkeit! wer misset dich?[2]

Perhaps it was here that Schiller learnt the strange, evocative power of resounding abstract rhetoric.

---

[1] *Op. cit.*, 1777 text. Cf. Hirzel, p. 154.
[2] *Ibid.*, cf. Hirzel, p. 151.

THE DEVELOPMENT OF THE POETICAL MEDIUM

The four poets we have considered in this chapter all contributed in a notable way to the development of the German language as an instrument for poetry. Each of them represents a reversion from a formalistic mould of diction and the development of an individual style. In general this is a movement from a highly indirect towards a more direct mode of expression. The cult of ornamentation is abandoned, and where rhetorical figures are used they must have functional validity. The influence of Latin poetry is marked; Horace with Günther and Hagedorn, Virgil with Brockes and Haller. Brockes develops a descriptive style by skilful use of sound-values and characterising epithets. Hagedorn evolves by unceasing attention and impeccable taste an elegant, graceful style suited to light, ironical treatment. Haller perfects a lapidary, abstract medium suited to the treatment of philosophical and didactic matters. Günther finds his way eventually to a truly lyrical style, forthright and powerful in its expression of emotion. All of them start from a rejection of the manneristic use of metaphor. None of them, except Günther, found his way to a true use of metaphor. It was two critics who were to reinstate metaphor as a rightful mode of poetry.

IX

THE REVIVAL OF METAPHOR

In the critical treatises of Bodmer and Breitinger there is a strange blend of rationalism and irrationalism. This is due to their conception of the Imagination as that faculty of the mind which recognises the likeness of an imitation in art to its original in nature. Hence, although they rated the imagination higher than all else in poetry, this did not imply any rejection of reason. For the imagination was part of the reason. In their criticism of Lohenstein's imagery they applied the same principles and arrived at more or less the same conclusions as Gottsched; and yet Bodmer's great discovery and inspiration was Milton, whose imagination Gottsched considered 'disorderly'[1] by rational precepts. Bodmer could coin a phrase like *eine Imagination die sich wol cultiviert hat*[2]—which shows his quandary. With all his belief in the sovereign powers of poetic fancy he was unwilling to accept an art without laws. 'Der Enthusiasmus mag da noch so stark sein, so muß er doch allezeit von der Vernunft geleitet werden', said Breitinger.[3] Yet Bodmer found this concept of a well-cultivated imagination inadequate to embrace *Paradise Lost*. The two men worked out their problems together and their treatises are virtually of joint authorship. They tried to resolve the dissonance by reference to Leibniz's doctrine of possible worlds. The world of the poet's fancy is a possible world; poetic imagination does not therefore fly in the face of logic. History deals with the real world, poetry with a possible world. The poet brings us 'Historie aus einer andern möglichen Welt'[4] and this cannot displease the philosopher:

[1] *regellos*. Letter of 7 October 1732, quoted in Eugen Wolff (see above, p. 107, footnote). Vol. II, p. 212.
[2] *Discourse der Mahlern*, vol. I, beginning of Discours XIX.
[3] *Critische Dichtkunst*, vol. I, p. 331.
[4] *Ibid.* vol. I, p. 60.

Und Wolf, dem die Natur die Weißheit vorgezehlet,
Kan nichts darinne sehn, das selbst sich widerspricht;
Und seine Meinung gilt nicht mehr als dein Gedicht.[1]

Bodmer's idea of poetic language, as expressed in the *Discourse der Mahlern*, is that the poet 'läßt sein Herze reden' and since the poet is characterised by a particularly lively imagination (an idea taken from Addison's essay on the 'Pleasures of the Imagination'), this will give him lively, vigorous words.

In an earlier chapter we noted that Gottsched and the Swiss were at first united in their attack on poetical bombast, but that Gottsched in *Die Vernünfftigen Tadlerinnen* reproved Bodmer for himself indulging in bombast and that Bodmer had replied in the *Antipatriot*. Bodmer's reply had involved a defence of metaphorical style as providing clarification, intensification and delight. He seemed to sense that Gottsched had no feeling for metaphor, and that in attacking the exaggerations of metaphorical style (an attack in which Bodmer also joined) he had not appreciated the just value of metaphor when properly used. In the last section of the *Antipatriot* we find the statement that the writer need not limit himself to the real world but should draw on the innumerable worlds of his imagination. Of poetry it is said: 'Sie muß wahrscheinlich seyn, und sich gründen entweder auf wahrhaffte und ähnliche Begebenheiten oder wenigstens auf einen angenommenen allgemeinen Wahn.' All poetry (*Dichtung*) must have a 'mystischer Sinn', and all figures of speech must contribute to this. In this phrase *mystischer Sinn* we may assume the first obscure beginnings of the doctrine of *das Wunderbare*.

In the treatise *Von dem Einfluss und Gebrauche der Einbildungs-Krafft* (1727), we find some further consideration of diction:

Man muß die Macht und die wahre Eigenschafft der Wörter wol kennen und wissen, was für einen Unterscheid zwey obgleich ähnliche und verwandte Wörter in den Begriffen machen, und diese Wissenschafft muß sich biß auf die absonderlichsten Dinge erstrecken. Man muß alle müßige und unnöthige Wörter abschneiden, und allein die jenigen brauchen, welche der Sache gerichts zutreffen.

---

[1] Bodmer, *Character der Teutschen Gedichte* (1734), concluding lines.

Superfluous words distract and therefore weaken the force of the style: 'Ins besondere sind die Fügungs- und kleine Hilffs-Wörter auszuweichen, welche ohne Abbruch des Begrieffes wegbleiben können.'[1] The treatise ends with a striking description of poetic enthusiasm, including the statement that it is a passion which

jaget die Einbildungs-Krafft in eine ausserordentliche Hitze, und führet den Dichter gleichsam ausser sich selbst, daß er die Einbildungen von den Empfindungen nicht unterscheiden kan, die gerichts von dem Gegenstand, den wir wircklich vor dem Gesicht haben, abkommen; sondern meinet er sehe und fühle die Dinge gegenwärtig.

This is a further development of the passage on *wahrhafft* and *wahrscheinlich* in the *Antipatriot* just quoted. Both contain the germ of the central doctrine of Breitinger's lengthy but important treatise on poetry.

We are not primarily concerned here with the aesthetic theory presented in Breitinger's *Critische Dichtkunst* of 1740;[2] but if we are to appreciate what he has to say about poetic diction in the second volume of this work, some brief account of the theory of poetry presented in the first volume is an indispensable prerequisite. Breitinger still holds that the function of art is the presentation of truth in an agreeable and acceptable form. Both poetry and painting have the same purpose, 'nemlich dem Menschen abwesende Dinge als gegenwärtig vorzustellen, und ihm dieselben gleichsam zu fühlen und zu empfinden zu geben'. But the means by which this purpose is achieved, differs with each of these two arts. Painting has an immediate effect, poetry builds up its effect. Painting works on the eye, poetry on all the

---

[1] *Op. cit.* p. 24. Quoting from the copy in the Central Library at Zürich.
[2] The work is in two volumes, both published at Zürich and Leipzig simultaneously in 1740. The first volume bears the sub-title: 'worinnen die Poetische Mahlerey in Absicht auf die Erfindung Im Grunde untersuchet', the second: 'worinnen die Poetische Mahlerey in Absicht auf den Ausdruck und die Farben abgehandelt wird'. Each volume has a preface by Bodmer. This famous work never reached a second edition, and copies are not easy to come by. There is none in the British Museum. I have used the copy in the University Library at Basle. It is from this copy that I quote. There is also a copy in the Central Library at Zürich.

senses. The fundamental task of poetry is to present to the mind a picture as vivid as the visual presentation of painting. But the province of poetry is wider, for it is not restricted to the visible, existing world. All *possible* worlds, not merely the one existing *real* world, are open to poetic presentation:

> denn was ist Dichten anders, als sich in der Phantasie neue Begriffe und Vorstellungen formieren, deren Originale nicht in der gegenwärtigen Welt der würcklichen Dinge, sondern in irgend einem andern möglichen Welt-Gebäude zu suchen sind. Ein jedes wohlerfundenes Gedicht ist darum nicht anderst anzusehen, als eine Historie aus einer andern möglichen Welt...[1]

but the subjects of great poetry should be both pleasing and instructive. If a poetic presentation is to please and delight, it must have something unusual, something 'new' about it. Nothing can be more 'new' (in this sense) than the marvellous, *das Wunderbare*—for this seems to contradict our normal knowledge and experience. In this seeming contradiction lies its attraction. The contradiction is, however, only apparent, for the marvellous is nothing more than 'ein vermummetes Wahrscheinliches', that is to say it belongs to the realm of the possible (not containing within itself a logical contradiction). The following is a crucial passage:

> Die eigenthümliche Kunst des Poeten bestehet...darinnen, daß er die Sachen, die er durch seine Vorstellung angenehm machen will, von dem Ansehen der Wahrheit bis auf einen gewissen Grad künstlich entferne, jedoch allezeit in dem Maasse, daß man den Schein der Wahrheit auch in ihrer weitesten Entfernung nicht gäntzlich aus dem Gesichte verliehret. Folglich muß der Poet das Wahre als wahrscheinlich, und das Wahrscheinliche als wunderbar vorstellen, und hiemit hat das poetische Wahrscheinliche immer die Wahrheit, gleichwie das Wunderbare in der Poesie die Wahrscheinlichkeit zum Grunde.[2]

This combination of the *wunderbar* and the *wahrscheinlich* is the magic of poetry and the secret of its effect. Poetry portrays what

---

[1] *Op. cit.* vol. I, pp. 59–60. The whole work makes use of the philosophical concepts of Leibniz and Wolff.
[2] *Ibid.* vol. I, p. 139.

Nature might have been in different conditions; or if it deal with well-known, real things it must remove these somewhat from the world of reality (*Wahrheit*). The mainspring of the effect of poetry is imagery: 'Die Poesie empfängt ihre gröste Stärcke und Schönheit von der geschickten Wahl der Bilder.'[1] These give magic—'ein ungewöhnliches Licht und Leben'—to well-known phenomena of the material world. For the beauty of poetry lies between the extremes of the too ordinary and the too extraordinary—'dem Gemeinen und dem Unglaublichen' as Breitinger puts it. The whole theory is best summarised in the following passage:

> Vor einen Poeten gehöret *os magna sonaturum*; er muß mehr als gemeine, wunderbare Dinge sagen; die stärckesten, zärtlichsten und keinesweges pöbelhafte Ausdrücke brauchen; fremde Phantasie- oder Verstandes-Bildereyen erfinden; die Reden unterflechten und unterbrechen mit Ausruffen, mit Anreden, kurtzen Abweichungen, und andern affectmässigen, herrlichen und anmuthigen Figuren; mit lebhaften Metaphoren, mit unerwarteten Betrachtungen; er muß die lebhaftesten Abbildungen der Sitten, der Affecte, der Handlungen und der Urtheile der Menschen machen; jedoch daß er die Augen beständig auf das Wahre und das Anständige richte. Die Poesie muß mit einem Worte den Zuhörer aufgeweckt, erfreut und entzücket behalten.[2]

The second volume of the treatise examines poetic expression in the light of this conception of the nature and purpose of poetry. The whole success of a poet depends on his ability to arouse in the reader by words the image deduced by the subject in his, the poet's, own mind. Two things are therefore essential for good poetry: a clear image in the poet's mind, and the ability to translate this image into evocative words. Even when the first is present, the second is often lacking.

Breitinger begins his second volume with a consideration of the onomatopoeic nature of words and the possibility of exploiting this for poetic effect. He praises Brockes in this context,

---

[1] Vol. I, p. 84.
[2] Vol. I, pp. 371–2. The first word *vor* is, of course, used in the sense of modern *für*.

citing the description of the brook and of the storm from the first part of the *Irdisches Vergnügen in Gott*. The general rule is then posited that the sound of a line of verse should never conflict with the nature of its content. Yet euphony should not be overstressed; it is easy to clothe base thoughts in fine words. He then turns to the consideration of words not as mere sounds but as 'Zeichen und Dollmetscher der Gedanken'—especially to those words which express concepts with particular clarity and emphasis, the *Machtwörter*, as Breitinger calls them. These constitute the real wealth and strength of a language. They must be preserved and their number increased. It was lack of *Machtwörter* that accounted for the flabbiness (*Mattigkeit*) of German writing in his day, thinks Breitinger. As a contrast he turns to his great and constant ideal—Martin Opitz.[1] Opitz always sought pregnant expression. His poems are full of *Machtwörter*. The examples which Breitinger then gives, help to clarify his own concept. He praises the phrase *auf Pracht und Ehre gehen* as expressive of burning desire—more so than *nachjagen* which merely implies haste. He admires the expression: *den Feind bestehen*. Both, we notice, are metaphorical; both are graphic and pungent. The same applies to:

> Also ward eure That
> Beschauet bis Neptun euch *losgebürget* hat.

Here it is obviously the graphic prefix which appeals to Breitinger. His ideal is therefore condensed, vivid expression. It must be both graphic and pungent; it is always concise and often metaphorical. He approves of powerful prefixes and cites words like

---

[1] 'Opitz, den ich niemahls ohne Hochachtung nenne', *Critische Abhandlung von der Natur den Absichten und dem Gebrauche der Gleichnisse* (Zürich, 1740), p. 123. There is a great encomium on him in the IX. Stück of the *Sammlung critischer, poetischer und anderer geistvollen Schriften* (Zürich, 1743), pp. 3–41, by Bodmer. A footnote to Bodmer's translation of Mauvillon in *Sammlung critischer Schriften*, v. Stück (1742), p. 71, contains this tribute: 'Darinn besteht Opitzens Stärcke; die geschickt angebrachten Bilder, die Neuigkeit in denselben, die Zierlichkeit in den Gedanken, sein poetisches Naturell, das sich in die Ausbildung der schlechtesten Materien ergiesset, die Verbindung seiner poetischen Vorstellungen zu einem Ende, das er stets im Gesichte behält, die genaue Uebereinstimmung der Affecte, die er erwecket, mit dem Vorhaben und den Sachen; das sind die Dinge, die ihn über alle andern Poeten erheben.'

ansiegen (to win a victory over), *anfleuhen* (to take refuge with), both of which are rather extreme examples.[1] But he also singles out for approval more usual verbs like *betagen*, *anfreyen*, eines Dinges *abkommen*, das Gespräche *abreißen*, sich *ausmergeln*. Metaphorical phrases mentioned here include: *er weidet sich mit diesen Vorstellungen*; *im Antritt meiner Freuden*; *sich mit Traurigkeit schleppen*; *auf etwas fussen*; *auf etwas verpicht sein*. Some of these expressions were falling into disuse. But it was not true to say that there were equally good words to express the same thing. *Er unterhält sich mit diesen Vorstellungen* was not the same as *er weidet sich mit diesen Vorstellungen*. It was a flabby equivalent of the sense, but nothing more. It lacked the 'Nachdruck' of the *Machtwort*. The proper realm for these forceful words is poetry where more freedom in expression is permitted. Haller's poems are praised because they are 'voll Nachdruckes und voller Gedancken..., die so dicht neben einander liegen'. From *Die Alpen* he cites:

> Ein Aug das Kunst und Weißheit *schärffen*.
> Sie hat dich von der Welt mit Bergen *abgezäunet*.
> Der sorgenlose Tag wird müssig *durchgescherzt*.
> Ein sanfter Schwindel schließt die allzuschwachen Augen,
> Die den zu fernen Kreiß nicht *durchzustrahlen* taugen.

and other examples of what he considers pungent expression. We note that these always involve a metaphor or a prefix—if the latter, then usually a prefix expressing movement. In epic poetry it is particularly important that poetical expression should shun all that is ordinary and commonplace. Homer and Virgil used every means to give their language 'eine ungemeine Kraft und Schönheit', including the use of somewhat unusual *but therefore all the more expressive* words. So too Milton who in order to express the superhuman grandeur of his subject used language which had 'etwas hohes und ungewohntes' about it, and a greater freedom of syntax.

Breitinger turns next to what he calls 'gleichgültige Wörter',

[1] Adelung considers them obsolescent, although he notes their use by Opitz.

synonyms. It is wrong, he claims, to judge the wealth of a language by its richness in synonyms. In any good language there should be no synonyms: no two words should mean exactly the same thing or be used indiscriminately for each other. A rich language is one in which expressions contiguous in meaning have been semantically delimited from each other. Good progress had been made in this respect with German during the last twenty years—in the sphere of philosophy. He mentions with approval the work of Leibniz and Wolff and certain learned societies. He then proceeds to give a list of words frequently used without distinction, and tries to suggest some respective limitation of usage. For instance: 'Der *Weise* suchet den nächsten Weg, der ihn zu seinem Zwecke führen kan, und folget der Leitung seiner Vernunft: der *Kluge* wehlet den sichersten Weg, wenn es schon nicht der nächste ist, und setzet sich nicht leicht in Gefahr. Die *Weisheit* ist erleuchtet, und die *Klugheit* mißtrauisch.'[1] Or the distinction between *unnütz* ('ohne Nutzen'), *vergeblich* ('ohne Resultat') and *umsonst* ('ohne Lohn, Gewinn').

The next chapter deals with translation and includes a section on national idioms. Here Breitinger defends participial constructions (Gottsched, we remember, was to disapprove of them). Participial constructions are good, says Breitinger, because they make for concision. He notes medieval examples from an old Zürich chronicle: *des Erbs wartende sin*; *daz er den Win bas wurd gebende*.[2] He defends this verbal use with dependent object, noting useful, common phrases like *etwas betreffend, anbelangend*; *während daß er dieses zu ihr sagte*, etc. He accepts the absolute use of the past participle, saying that he definitely prefers, for instance, 'Die Diener liessen die Pferde, um den Bauch festgegürtet, an das Gestade hinunter' to 'Die Diener liessen die um die Bäuche wohlgegürteten Pferde an das Gestade hinunter'. Reason: 'es

---

[1] *Op. cit.* vol. II, p. 105.
[2] Breitinger's spelling. The examples are from the so-called *Richtebrief*, composed around 1300, which Bodmer had published in vol. II of the *Helvetische Bibliothek* (Zürich, 1736). In his comments on Mauvillon's essay on the German language, Bodmer praises participial constructions as a particular advantage of German syntax (*Sammlung critischer Schriften*, vol. V, pp. 24–5 n.).

bekömmt einen grössern und schnellern Nachdruck'.[1] He defends similar constructions with adjectives, as in:

> Was helfen dir zulezt der Weisheit hohe Lehren,
> Zu schwach sie zu verstehn, zu stoltz sie zu entbehren.

He approves constructions with postposition of adjective, citing:

> Vil werden Vursten hoh gemut
> Begunden sich da dringen [2]

and:
> Die Welt verehrte todt, wer lebend sie verheerte.

These constructions were examples of ellipsis—a phenomenon recognised in all languages and 'clear to all except the pedants'.

The next section ventures on the difficult topic of semantic change. Breitinger notes that some words lose their dignified aspect for various reasons. They descend the scale of values. They may disappear altogether. It is difficult, however, to decide finally when a word has 'disappeared'. The Saxon critic of Bodmer's translation of Milton had objected to many expressions as archaic, amongst them *Mißthöne, Ungut, Nothschickung, Heilschickung, Gespielschaft, bündig, vorbündig, vergestalten, das Mißbehagen, Unterjochen, das Mithafte, die Unbill*.[3] The following principle is then announced: 'Aus diesem allem ziehe ich nun den Schluß, daß man mit Recht kein Wort als alt und verlegen verwerffen kan, so lange man in einer Sprache nicht ein anders gleichgültiges aufweisen kan, welches dienet, den Begriff desselben in einem gleichen Lichte vollkommen auszudrücken.'[4] Breitinger is obviously anxious to preserve a rich and varied vocabulary, even if some portions of it are rarely used. He laments the pruning of the French vocabulary in the seventeenth century. For him this was not improvement but loss; and conditioned by a taste that was mollycoddled (*verzärtelt*).

---

[1] *Op. cit.* vol. II, p. 150.
[2] Breitinger's spelling! Example from Konrad von Würzburg's *Partonopier und Meliur*, a fragment of which had been discovered by Bodmer and published.
[3] My selection, representing various types, from Breitinger's examples. Some of them, we notice, have survived into the twentieth century.
[4] *Ibid.* p. 211. *gleichgültig*, used in the sense of 'synonymous', as above.

The next section of the treatise deals with epithets. Everything depends on the skilful use of epithets. They are 'die poetischen Farben, die den poetischen Schildereyen und Erzehlungen einen reitzenden Glantz mittheilen, und sie über die matte und historische Erzehlung und Beschreibung weit weit erheben'.[1] They designate either an essential quality (*wesentliche Eigenschaft*) or an occasional aspect (*zufällige Beschaffenheit*) of a person or thing. Both are important aids to the clear characterisation of the person or thing. Epithets which do not contribute to this characterisation are obscuring and distracting in their effect. The aptness and choice of epithets should be determined not so much by the nature of the subject as by the intentions of the author. In poetry the function of epithets is not so much to convey meaning as to produce a vivid, *wunderbar* impression: 'sie dienen, uns die Sachen so lebhaft vorzustellen, als ob wir sie vor Augen sähen, und uns mit unvermutheten und angenehmen Begriffen zu überraschen'.[2] Poetic epithets should assist in the production of those three qualities that are essential for poetic beauty, namely *das Wahrscheinliche, das Neue und Ungemeine*, and *das Wunderbare*. Breitinger quotes the following passage from Brockes:

> Schau, wie sich dort
> Ein *blauer* Schwarm *beschuppter* Fische
> Mit *frohem* Wimmeln reget,
> Und *wunder-schnell* sein *flüssigs* Wohnhaus trennt.[3]

and comments: 'Alle diese Beywörter sind für die Deutlichkeit des Verstandes gantz müssig' but they give the description 'eine mahlerische Kraft'. From Haller's *Die Alpen* he chooses the famous lines from the nineteenth strophe:

> Er treibt den *trägen* Schwarm der *schwer-beleibten* Kühen,
> Mit *freudigem* Gebrüll durch den *bethauten* Steg,
> Sie irren *langsam* um, wo Klee und Muttern blühen,
> Und mäh'n das *zarte* Gras mit *scharfen* Zungen weg.[4]

---

[1] *Ibid.* p. 249. *Historisch* in the sense of 'factual'.
[2] *Ibid.* p. 261.   [3] From a poem entitled *Wasser im Frühlinge*.
[4] In all these quotations I give the text as Breitinger quotes it. The word *Muttern* in this passage means the plant *ligusticum mutellina*. This is the first version of this passage, to which Schönaich objected. See above, p. 268.

and comments:

>Hier unterstützet und erkläret je ein Beywort das andere. Wenn der Poet die Kühe als *schwer-beleibt* beschreibet, so giebt er euch damit eine zulängliche Ursache, warum er sie zuvor *träg* genennet hat; und die Absicht der Natur in Formierung der Zunge der Kühe wird durch das Beywort *zart*, damit sie das *zarte* Gras abmähen konnen, vor nothwendig erkläret.

He notes with approval Brockes's use of onomatopoeic epithets to suggest sound and movement. All the passages considered so far are examples of the use of epithets to heighten *Wahrscheinlichkeit*. Breitinger then passes on, in a passage important for our considerations, to defend the use of compound epithets. He says of them: 'Diese Zusammensetzung der Wörter tauget für die Poesie auf eine besondere Weise, nicht nur weil solche die Schreibart erhöhet und verherrlichet, sondern auch, weil dadurch der Thonlaut mächtig verstärcket wird, mehr Klang und Pomp überkömmt, und die Bilder desto mehr Nachdruck erhalten, indem sie durch den Thon nachgeahmet werden.'[1] The realisation here voiced—that full-sounding words help to give emphasis—is important for the development of the grand style in German poetic diction during the eighteenth century. We find its results in poets as different as Klopstock, Schiller, Hölderlin and, at various stages in his life and in different variations, Goethe. It was realised from the outset that this was a potentiality of the German language in which it might successfully imitate Greek. Breitinger himself in this passage points to the frequent use of full-sounding, compound epithets by Homer: 'damit er seine Schreibart ungemein über die Prosa erhübe'.[2] Lastly Breitinger has something to say about those epithets which involve a contradiction. He quotes a description of skating by Brockes, in which occur the lines:

>Man sieht izt die, so Schritt-Schuh' unterziehn,
>Auf glattem Eis', auf schmalen Eisen fliehn,

---

[1] *Ibid.* p. 271–2.
[2] Cf. Pope (*Postscript to The Odyssey*, 1726): 'To throw his Language more out of Prose, Homer seems to have affected the Compound-Epithets....'

Und zwischen zackichten und starren Wasser-Hügeln,
Auf einer Bahn, in welcher sie sich spiegeln,
Mit trocknem Fuß, selbst in der Flut, mit Haufen
Auf bodenlosen Tiefen laufen.[1]

He notes that *bodenlose Tiefe* shows intensifying use of an epithet, but that *auf bodenlosen Tiefen laufen* involves a contradiction, as does also *trocknem Fuß, selbst in der Flut*. These apparent contradictions express 'das Wunderbare dieser Handlung' and do not offend against *Wahrscheinlichkeit*. Similarly when Brockes speaks of the *kühle rothe Glut* of a rose, this is 'höchst wunderbar' and therefore highly poetical. The argumentation is rather obscure; but behind it would seem to lie some understanding of poetic imagery. This is important. It is also significant to see Breitinger brought as far as a defence of the baroque oxymoron.

The next chapter deals with style in general. After a theoretical section based on the three characters of style, in which obscurity of thought, bombast, timidity of expression and wordiness are deprecated, Breitinger proceeds to a description of figurative usage. He points out that by the figurative usage of words, new powers of expression are added to a language. Words thereby increase their range of meaning and application. Ideas attain to more plastic expression. Metaphor is the crown of all figurative usage. But metaphors must not be too far-fetched (*zuweit hergeholet*) nor too mixed. The reader's attention must not be jerked too quickly from one image to another. They must not be driven too far. They must not be piled up, or else confusion may ensue. Bouhours is quoted on this matter, and other French rhetoricians who had tried to agree on a maximum sequence of metaphors. Breitinger is satisfied to leave this to the writer's taste. Metaphorical expression gives a new face to things that are well known. Hence its great value in poetic diction.

This is perhaps the climax of the treatise. The whole of Breitinger's peculiar argument about *das Wunderbare*, operating so illogically with apparently logical concepts, has culminated in an unflinching defence of metaphorical diction. This is the funda-

[1] *Schrittschuh* is the older form of *Schlittschuh*.

mental opposition to Gottsched and the central importance of this criticism.

But figurative style was not the only style recognised by Breitinger as suited to poetry. He also defended the 'pathetische, bewegliche oder hertzrührende Schreibart', the style which spoke directly to the emotions, the old 'grand' style of rhetoric. Here he would admit looser, more emotive syntax. For this language must mirror emotion. Asyndeton, aposiopesis and anacoluthia belong therefore to its very nature. Breitinger appreciates that the origin of poetic inversions is in this 'Sprache der Affecte'. (This point was later to be taken up by Herder.) He is also quite explicitly opposed to Christian Weise's demand for prose-construction in verse: 'Ich könnte hier noch des Zwanges gedenken, welcher dem deutschen Verse dadurch angethan wird, daß man ihn allzu scharf an die prosaische Construction bindet. ... Es ist ein Irrthum, wenn man gläubt, daß die deutsche Sprache von der ordentlichen und üblichen Construction in keinen Weg abweichen könne; ohne daß eine lächerliche Rede herauskomme.'[1] Breitinger suggests that poetry gets its effect either by pleasing our curiosity or by arousing our passions. Graphic concise expression and *wunderbar* content are both essential. But, given this, both *figürlich* and *pathetisch* style are possible.

Ordinary language is too weak for the poet. 'Sein gantzer Ausdruck muß darum gantz neu und wunderbar, d.i., viel sinnlicher, prächtiger, und nachdrücklicher seyn.'[2] Breitinger laments the fact that most poets of his day were unconcerned about this and 'daß ihre so genannten Gedichte überhaupt nichts anders sind, als eine gereimte Prosa'. Images are the life-blood of poetry and the faculty of lighting on them is part of one's temperament and can hardly be learnt. In the verse of his own day, Breitinger saw two extremes of absurdity: there were some so anxious not to be commonplace: 'sie können kein Ding ohne eine Metapher nennen, und zuweilen ohne eine verwegene Metapher, und eine überspannte Hyperbole', but there were others: 'welche die gekünstelte Schreibart so sorgfältig meiden, und so sehr beflissen sind,

[1] Vol. II, p. 463.   [2] *Ibid.* pp. 403–4.

THE REVIVAL OF METAPHOR

lauter natürliche und einfältige Gedancken zu sagen, daß ihre Verse zu einer gereimten Prosa werden'. We are back again at the antithesis represented by Lohenstein and Christian Weise, the antithesis which dominates the whole period like some two-headed ogre.

Both these undesirable extremes are described by Bodmer in his *Character der Teutschen Gedichte*, published in 1734.[1] He says of Hofmannswaldau:

> Er hüllet die Begriff in Gleichniß und Figur,
> Als einen Kercker ein, verbirgt uns die Natur,
> Und meidt die Deutlichkeit, die uns nichts fremdes bringet,
> Die uns mit Bantams Wahr nicht in Verwundrung singet.

Of Lohenstein:

> Er braucht ein Gleichniß nicht zu einem Leitungs-Faden,
> Nein, sondern nur den Kopf der Bürde zu entladen,
> Womit die Wissenschafft, die drinnen ungeschickt
> Auf einem Hauffen liegt, die schwache Hirnschal drückt.

Both authors, therefore, used metaphor for wrong purposes: Hofmannswaldau to confuse the reader, Lohenstein to display his learning. At the other end of the scale we find those who instinctively avoid metaphor: the timid Besser:

> Der Vers ist leicht und sanfft, die Schreib-Art so bescheiden,
> Daß sie recht furchtsam scheint, die Farben zu vermeiden...

and the prosaic König:

> Der Vers ist männlich zwar, jedoch geziert und zart,
> Ist sittsam doch behertzt, voll, doch nicht schwer und hart.
> Nur könnt' er hier und dar mehr von der Prosa weichen,
> Und öffters seine Hand der ächten Dichtung reichen.

Breitinger's ideas on metaphorical style find amplification in the *Critische Abhandlung von der Natur, den Absichten und dem Gebrauche der Gleichnisse* (Zürich, 1740),[2] which distinguishes four types of comparisons: *erleuchtende, auszierende, nachdrückliche*

---

[1] There is a modern reprint by Baechtold of this rhymed history of German poetry in *Vier kritische Gedichte von J. J. Bodmer* (Heilbronn, 1883).
[2] There is a copy in the British Museum, from which I quote.

and *lehrreiche Gleichnisse*. The first are used to make descriptions 'vernehmlich, deutlich und lebhaft'. Thus Brockes on the strawberry:

 (*a*) Der niedern Erd-Beer weisse Blüthe
   Die wie ein Schnee auf dichten Blättern lag.

 (*b*) Der reiffen Erd-Beer holdes Roth
   Vergleichet sich dem Schmuck, womit die Wangen
   Der Rosen-reichen Jugend prangen.

He refutes La Motte's objection (in the preface to his edition of the *Iliad*) that none of Homer's comparisons give a clearer, more vivid picture than his descriptions or narrations. Breitinger gives examples from the various senses and notes the phenomenon of synaesthesia.[1] Secondly: there are thoughts and concepts which are unpleasing in their naked form, having nothing unusual or *verwundersam* about them to attract and delight the mind. If these be clothed in an image they become new and unusual, the idea 'pranget in einem fremdem Schmucke' and obtains 'einen neuen Glantz'. These are *auszierende Gleichnisse*. Two excesses are to be avoided in this type of figuration: 'die Kargheit und die Verschwendung', especially the latter. The third type of comparisons—*nachdrückliche Gleichnisse*—is used to keep the attention of the reader and to intensify the general effect. *Lehrreiche Gleichnisse* involve general truths. Example: the following from Pope: 'Die thörigten Liebhaber des Thones bewundern an der liebreitzenden Muse alleine die Stimme; sie besuchen den Parnaß alleine, damit sie die Ohren kützeln, nicht damit sie den Willen verbessern; wie viele Leute in die Kirche gehen, nicht um der Predigt, sondern um des Gesanges willen.'[2] An author may combine any or all of these functions of the comparison in his writings. As regards protracted metaphors, the *comparaisons à longue queue* on which there had been much discussion in France, Breitinger refuses to discuss whether they are good or bad in

---

[1] 'Ein sanfter, klarer, grober, heller, scharffer, reiner Thon' (p. 24). This is essential, 'weil ohne ihre Hülffe die dunckeln Begriffe nicht können erkläret, noch die ungewissen angesetzet werden' (p. 38).

[2] The original is to be found in *An Essay on Criticism*, ll. 339–43.

themselves. Metaphorical expression is not suited to all subjects. It belongs to a mind in repose and is unsuited to passionate feeling or narration. This is where the Silesian poets had erred. They had used metaphor for all subjects; and the Germans, dazzled by this glut of magnificence, had forgotten what true Nature looked like. Lohenstein devalued metaphor by squandering it. Others, however, had fallen into the other extreme of flatness. How skilfully Homer had used imagery to revive the flagging attention of his readers! Some of his comparisons had been considered ignoble (souls of murdered wooers compared with bats; restless, vengeful Ulysses with a man roasting the stomach of a sacrificial animal). They were not ignoble, but expressive. Lohenstein used his images badly. They had no functional relevance. Breitinger turns aside for a moment to consider the metaphorical style of Brockes which he admires, but with reservations:

> Mich dünckot aber, daß den schönsten von seinen Beschreibungen noch öfters Fehler von dem unreinen Geschmack des Marino ankleben; daß er in der Ausbildung seiner Sachen nicht nur freygebig, sondern verschwenderisch ist; daß er seine Gemählde mehr durch die hohen und heitern Farben, als durch die künstliche Uebereinstimmung mit dem Urbild zu erheben suche, daher denn rühret, daß die überflüssige Auszierung, dadurch das wahre Maß der Natur aus der Acht gelassen wird, öfters die wesentlichen Schönheiten deren Dinge, die er beschreiben soll, nur verdunckeln.[1]

He criticises Brockes's use of exotic and unusual things as objects of comparison with ordinary and everyday things. He condemns 'das unbescheidene Prangen mit Gold, Silber, Edelgesteinen und anderen Kostbarkeiten' in poetry. Descriptions in German poetry of the period were 'überall mit Edelsteinen versezet und in Gold und Silber eingefasset'. Here speaks the plainer taste of a generation that has turned its back on the aristocratic extravagance of the world of baroque imagery! Breitinger points out quite astutely that Brockes makes a mistake in trying to demonstrate the glories of nature by comparing them with works of art:

[1] *Op. cit.* p. 430. One would expect *verdunckelt* at the end, but my text reads *verdunckeln*.

'welches gleichviel ist, als das Original eines kunstreichen Mahlers mit einer ungeschickten Copie desselben vergleichen, und dann jenem den Vorzug über diese geben'. He then returns to Lohenstein. Lohenstein's metaphors were either too learned, e.g.: 'Die Unglückseligen, da sie sich des vergangenen Uebels erinnern, sind insgemein, wie das fühlende Kraut in Egypten geartet, welches, wenn man es anrühret, seine Zweige zurücke, seine Blätter zusammen zeucht, oder gar verdorren läßt'; or too extravagant, e.g.: 'Sie ließ ihre Thränen über ihre Wangen fliessen, daß es schien, als hätten ihre Augen sich in das regnende Siebengestirne werwandelt'; or unnecessarily obstructive of the course of the action: 'Die Schönheit sey so selten keusch, als die Sonne kalt'; or offend against *bienséance*: 'Diese Gaben zohen, nicht anders als der Agtstein die Spreu, unterschiedene Helden an den Hof.' Such style is quite unsuited to the old teutonic warriors of *Arminius*. Of the women characters Breitinger says: 'Es ist euch, ihr höret jene *Pretieuses ridicules* bey Molière reden.' This remark reveals the European setting of this phenomenon.

In Bodmer's *Critische Betrachtungen über die Poetischen Gemählde der Dichter* (1741) there is a similar attack on the style of Lohenstein and his school.[1] Bodmer's criterion is quite rationalistic: their similes do not rest on any real basis of comparison. On Postel's lines:

> Doch, wenn die Lust vorbey in Jammer-Pfützen stürzt,
> Draus Thränen-Nebel steigt...

he comments: 'Alleine, was ist für Gleichheit zwischen Pfützen und dem Jammer?'[2] This sort of metamorphosis, frequent in Lohenstein and his disciples, is based on arbitrary association of dissimilar ideas and leads to obscurity. It aims at being striking, learned or sumptuous. It is self-conscious. Amongst Bodmer's examples is this purple passage from Lohenstein's *Cleopatra*:

> ...Die holden Wangen lachen,
> Auf denen Schnee und Glut zusammen Hochzeit machen,

---

[1] There is a copy in the British Museum, from which I quote.
[2] *Op. cit.* p. 111.

THE REVIVAL OF METAPHOR

Ihr himmlisch Antlitz ist ein Paradies der Lust;
Der Adern blauer Türcks durchflicht die zarte Brust;
Zinober quillt aus Milch, Blut aus den Marmel-Ballen;
Der Augen schwartze Nacht läßt tausend Blitze fallen,
Die kein behertzter Geist nicht ohne Brand empfindt.
Ihr süsser Athem ist ein eingebiesamt Wind.
Es kan der Schnecke nichts auf Zung und Muschel rinnen,
Das den Rubinen wird der Lippen abgewinnen:
Ihr wellicht Haar entfärbt der Morgen-Röthe Licht.
Es gleicht kein Helffenbein sich ihren Gliedern nicht.

He comments aptly:[1] 'Einige von diesen verblühmten Ausdrücken könnten schön heissen, wenn sie nur einzel angebracht würden, aber die hyperbolische Verschwendung derselben und die Vermischung so vieler Kostbarkeiten verwirret den Begriff.' Metaphor should aim at making a graphic impression. The imagery of Lohenstein and his disciples had no such purpose. It was far-fetched, verbose and learnedly subtle.[2] In contrast expressive imagery is quoted from Ovid, Virgil, Homer, an English poet described as 'Sasper',[3] and amongst his contemporaries, Pietsch, Brockes, König and Günther. Of earlier German poets he praises Opitz and Fischart. There is passing mention of Flemming and Gryphius; but Gryphius is censured for the artificiality of his style. Note the terms in which Bodmer praises certain passages of metaphorical writing: 'Diese Vergleichung ist nicht alleine sehr prächtig und majestätisch, sondern auch gantz ähnlich',[4] 'weit nachdrücklicher...weil sie in der Oeconomie und dem Ausdruck viel poetischer ist, massen das Wunderbare darinnen durchgehends herrschet',[5] 'sehr lebhaft beschrieben... glücklich nachgeahmet und ausgedrückt'.[6] All this receives a

---

[1] *Ibid.* p. 162.
[2] '...sie die Bilder dazu allzu weit her suchen, und mit einem weitläuftigen Gewasche und einer gelehrten Spitzfündigkeit überkleistern.' *Ibid.* p. 165.
[3] Theseus' description of his dogs. Bodmer knew it from Addison.
[4] *Ibid.* p. 182; of a description of cymbal-clashing by König. Note the last phrase.
[5] *Ibid.* p. 193. Description of an army by Pietsch. Not too much learned detail or use of technical terms.
[6] *Ibid.* p. 206. Description of workmen by König.

firmer theoretical basis when we come, in a later chapter, to his definition of figures of speech: 'Diese sind nicht anders, als verschiedene Symptomata oder Anfälle der Empfindungen, wie solche in der Rede hervorbrechen, woraus ihre Beschaffenheit, Eigenschaft, Schwung und Grade erkennet werden. Es sind gewisse Formen, in welchen die Empfindungen ihrer Art gemäß erscheinen.'[1] As an aid to effective, figurative writing Bodmer recommends the study of figures in other writers. He notes that, in the expression of passion, connecting *particulae* are a hindrance: 'Die Leidenschaft redet mit unterbrochnen Worten, und schlägt in ihren Sätzen keine Achtung auf ihre Zusammenfügung.'[2] Enumeration of the various tropes is useless to the aspiring writer. He should never attempt the *bewegliche Schreibart* unless inflamed by his subject. But then: 'Muntern Köpfen von einer feuerreichen Einbildungskraft wird es nicht schwer fallen, sich auf besagte Weise zu erhitzen, und einen gewissen Affect an sich zu nehmen; und alsdann dörfen sie sich nur der Führung desselben überlassen, und das schreiben, was derselbe ihnen in die Gedancken giebt.'[3]

Bodmer deprecates authors who choose metaphorical expression simply in order to avoid what is natural and straightforward. The aim should be not to avoid being natural, but to avoid being flat. This can be achieved either by using words which originally represented bold metaphors but are now hallowed by long usage, especially those expressions referring to everyday matters (*sich mit Unmöglichkeiten verschlagen*; *seiner ersten Liebe nachsetzen*; *die Gelegenheit aus Händen lassen* are amongst the examples he gives), or by using words not current in ordinary speech but which were used by good authors in the past. This latter class of words—words which have not become weakened by frequent use—Bodmer considers would give the language 'einen gewissen, dauerhaften Verstand' and to poetry 'ein herrliches Ansehen'.[4] This is an important idea with Bodmer and he constantly returns to it. In his preface to the second volume

[1] *Op. cit.* pp. 310–11.   [2] *Ibid.* p. 323.
[3] *Ibid.* pp. 342–3.   [4] *Ibid.* p. 94.

of Breitinger's *Critische Dichtkunst*, Bodmer claimed that there were many good old words not current in Meissen which had been preserved by other dialects:

> Wenn denn ein solches Wort oder eine Redensart in einer oder mehr Provinzen noch in seiner ersten und uralten Bedeutung üblich ist, das aber in Sachsen ins Vergessen gekommen, und mit keinem gleich so guten wieder ersetzet worden, mag man selbst urtheilen, ob jene vielmehr schuldig seyn, es wegzuwerffen, oder dieses, es verstehen zu lernen.

If such good words exist, why should they be allowed to disappear? 'Wahrhaftig die Verschiedenheit der Mundart in Sachsen gegen der Mundart in den übrigen Provinzen entsteht öfters daher, weil ienes gute alte Wörter hat untergehen lassen, die diese unverändert behalten haben.' Elsewhere he refers to the puritanical evildoers who take pains

> die Wörter, Redensarten, und Metaphern, welche die Einwohner gewisser Provintzen für ihre eigene Nothwendigkeit eingeführet, und von ihren Umständen, Sitten und Gebräuchen hergenommen haben, zu verwerffen und auszumustern; ohne Betrachtung ob sie mit der Natur der Dinge, der Sprache-Aehnlichkeit, den Stamm- und Wurzelwörtern, übereinkommen oder nicht; ob sie sich überdas mit einem ansehnlichen Alter rechtfertigen können, oder erst von gestern oder vorgestern her sind.[1]

As his medieval interests developed Bodmer became aware of the relationship between his own native dialect and the language of Middle German poetry. Hence the terms of his invitation to Klopstock:[2]

> Komm doch die Sprache zu hören, die vormals der fürstliche Hermann
> Mit dem von Veldec und Eschilbach redte.

Gottsched's mockery at the rough, untutored language of the Swiss critics led Bodmer to consider elevating his Alemannic dialect into a literary language. This plan he soon abandoned;

---

[1] In a footnote to his translation of Blackwell's *Enquiry* in the *Sammlung critischer poetischer und anderer geistvollen Schriften*, VII. Stück (Zürich, 1743), p. 15. Blackwell had referred to the *advantages* of enriching languages from provincial dialects.

[2] From the Ode *Verlangen nach Klopstocks Ankunft* (1749).

but he continued to advocate the enrichment and rejuvenation of the *Schriftsprache* by adding to it the good old words still to be found in the dialects. In 1756 we find Bodmer sponsoring the production of a Zürich idioticon. Owing to its conservatism, Alemannic was closest of all the dialects to the medieval language he had so grown to admire.

Bodmer's interest in the Middle Ages was at first more historical than aesthetic.[1] His appreciation was antiquarian and cramped by the usual prejudices of his age. It was some time before he came to realise that Middle High German literature was not merely interesting but good, and that its language was possessed not merely of period interest but of poetical strength and power against which eighteenth-century diction was colourless and effete. There are occasional medieval references in the critical treatises of 1740-1, but neither the doctrine of *das Wunderbare* nor the sharpened historical approach to literature (stimulated by Du Bos and particularly evident in the *Critische Betrachtungen über die poetischen Gemählde*) led to any immediate enthusiasm for the poetic qualities of the medieval German literary language. Breitinger's examples of *Machtwörter* are culled mainly from the seventeenth century. His quotations from older authors are mostly classical, often from Homer. It would seem that Thomas Blackwell's *Enquiry into the Life and Writings of Homer* (1735), with its characterisation of the Homeric age as transitional from barbarism to civilisation, led Bodmer to a deeper appreciation of the Hohenstauffen culture.[2] Bodmer published a translation of parts

---

[1] This subject has been admirably treated by Dorothy Knight in an M.A. thesis for the University of London: 'J. J. Bodmer's contribution to the knowledge and appreciation of Middle High German Literature', presented in 1949 and still—unfortunately—unpublished. This paragraph owes much to Miss Knight's work and advice. Burdach's excellent essay 'Die Entdeckung des Minnesangs und die deutsche Sprache' has something to say on Bodmer, but covers a wider field (written in 1918 and contained in *Vorspiel*, II, Halle, 1926). Max Wehrli, *Johann Jakob Bodmer und die Geschichte der Literatur* (Frauenfeld and Leipzig, 1937), also contains material on this topic.

[2] See Dorothy Knight, 'Thomas Blackwell and J. J. Bodmer: The Establishment of a Literary Link between Homeric Greece and Medieval Germany', *GLL*, N.S. VI (1952-3), pp. 249-58.

of Blackwell's book in the *Sammlung critischer Schriften* of 1743; and in the same year (and the same periodical) his essay 'Von den vortrefflichen Umständen für die Poesie unter den Kaisern aus dem schwäbischen Hause'.[1] In this essay he suggested that the Hohenstauffen period was an age similar to Homeric Greece as characterised by Blackwell. The Germans of that time were no longer barbaric and not yet cramped by civilisation. Such ages reveal the whole man, engage all his passions, engender 'einen freyen und hurtigen Geist', for there is much to see and much to feel. Language must keep pace with this development of human experience. It had to be 'eine reiche und nachdrükliche Sprache'. It was not yet rubbed bare by too much polish:

> Indessen war diese Sprache noch nicht so sehr auspoliert, daß sie dadurch wäre abgeschliffen und geschwächet worden. Durch die Ausputzung wird manches Wort weggeworffen, sie stekt den Menschen gleichsam in einen Sack, gestattet ihm nur eine gewisse Zahl von üblichen Redensarten, und beraubet ihn vieler nachdrucksreichen Wörter, und starker schöner Ausdrüke, welche er wagen und dabey in Gefahr stehen muß, daß sie veraltert und platt scheinen.[2]

In this description is implied a contrast with the sophisticated language of poetry in Bodmer's own day. This explains Bodmer's use of words like *natürlich*, *anmutig*, and *artig* to describe the language and literature of Middle High German times. For him this literature and this language had a naïve simplicity and a frank, sincere naturalness. They represented pristine freshness and truth: 'Es ergetzet uns dergleichen zu lesen, weil wir gerne mit Leuten umgehen, denen wir ins Hertze sehen, die nichts vor uns Verborgenes haben.' A strange judgment on a literature that included so many enigmatic writers; but comprehensible in its proper setting. Bodmer admired the strength of a language which expressed itself 'so wohl durch Metaphern von dem natürlichsten Gegenständen, als durch einen glücklichen Schatz der Sprache'.

---

[1] *Sammlung critischer Schriften*, VII. Stuck (Zürich, 1743), pp. 25–53. Reprinted in *Das geistige Zurich im 18. Jahrhundert*, ed. Max Wehrli (Zürich, 1943), pp. 67–76.

[2] *Sammlung critischer Schriften*, VII. Stück, p. 28. British Museum copy.

Strength, natural metaphors, wealth of vocabulary—these qualities recall the criteria of Breitinger's *Critische Dichtkunst*. The two critics have not changed their ground in any way. Bodmer went on to suggest that German poets might *learn* from the medieval language. The remark was introduced during his discussion of a collection of medieval fables when he recalled La Fontaine's adoption of many expressions from Clément Marot.[1] Having reached this stage in the development of his ideas, Bodmer now turned his attention towards enlisting wider interest in medieval German. Two articles appeared during 1745 in the *Freymüthige Nachrichten von neuen Büchern*, two during 1746 in the *Critische Briefe*, and several during 1749 in the *Neue Critische Briefe*.[2] Medieval literature became a recurrent theme in Bodmer's voluminous correspondence. Interest was shown by Gleim, Hagedorn, Gellert and J. E. Schlegel. In 1748 there appeared the *Proben der alten schwäbischen Poesie des dreyzehnten Jahrhunderts*, extracts from the works of eighty-two poets in the Manesse manuscript, with glossary and notes. This was the first of Bodmer's important publications of medieval works. It was followed by his own modern version in hexameters of parts of *Parzival* (*Der Parcival*, 1753), an edition of *Fabeln aus den Zeiten der Minnesinger* (1757) and of parts of the *Nibelungenlied* (as *Chriemhilden Rache und die Klage*, 1757) and the second and much larger collection of the lyrical poetry published, in collaboration with Breitinger, as *Sammlung von Minnesingern aus dem schwäbischen Zeitpuncte* in two volumes in 1758 and 1759.[3] Further essays by Bodmer on medieval literature appeared in various periodicals after 1750. His interest remained undiminished to his death in 1783.

We noted that, in the 1743 essay on the Hohenstauffen age,

[1] *Sammlung critischer Schriften*, VII. Stück (1743), pp. 52–3.

[2] These were all published at Zürich. Of them, only the *Freymüthige Nachrichten* are in the British Museum. There are copies of the other two in the Central Library at Zürich.

[3] These works, all published at Zürich, are in the British Museum; except the *Proben der alten schwäbischen Poesie* of which I have used photostats of the copy in the Central Library at Zürich. I subsequently discovered a copy in the Priebsch Collection of the Institute of Germanic Languages and Literatures of the University of London.

THE REVIVAL OF METAPHOR

Bodmer had stated that he admired the Middle High German language for its natural imagery and its rich vocabulary. These two points recur like a *leitmotif* throughout all he had to say on the medieval German language. Wolfram's *Parẓival* is told 'mit einem grossen Reichthum der Sprache und einer angenehmen Einfalt der Bilder'.[1] The latter phrase may seem to us a rather inadequate description of Wolfram's imagery, but we must remember that Bodmer came to it with a mind sickened by the luxuriant pomp of the Second Silesian School. In the preface to his own version of Wolfram's poem[2] Bodmer quoted a series of short passages to show 'daß dieser Poet gewisse gedanken und bilder gehabt hat, welche man vielleicht am wenigsten bei ihm gesucht hatte'. The text reads *hatte*, but even if this is a misprint for *hätte*, the assertion remains that the poem contained 'unexpected' images and thoughts. The passages Bodmer quotes,[3] all without comment, include:

> Da fuorten si den jungen Man
> In eine kemenaten san
> Die war also geeret
> Mit einem bet geheret
> Das mich mein armuot imer myet
> Sit die Erde all solche richheit blyet[4]

in which he found, no doubt, both the antithesis and the personification striking. Or a strong phrase like:

> Vil kerzen und die varwe sin
> Gaben ze gegenstrit schin.[5]
>
> Got noch kynste kan genuoc.[6]
>
> ..disen umbevank
> Da von min truren wirt krank.[7]

---

[1] In an essay in the appendix to *Gedichte in gereimten Versen* (1754), p. 140. British Museum copy.
[2] *Der Parcival* (1753), p. A 2. British Museum copy.
[3] I quote them in his spelling and punctuation. Bodmer used the 1477 printed version without always quoting exactly. I give references from Lachmann-Hartl for the sake of convenience.
[4] This is Lachmann-Hartl, 242, 25 ff.   [5] *Ibid.* 243, 9–10.
[6] *Ibid.* 796, 16.   [7] *Ibid.* 801, 11–12.

Or a striking simile:

> Ich lege die senewen an bogen
> Die senewe ist ein bispel
> Auch dunket mich der bogen snel
> Noch ist sneller das die senewe jaget
> Die senewe glichet meren slecht.[1]

A bold metaphor:

> Partzifal niht eine lag
> Geselliclich unz an den tag
> War bi im strenge arebeit
> Ir boten kynftige leit
> Santen im im schlafe dar.[2]

Metaphor and personification:

> Min zorn ist anders imer nywe
> Gen ir sit ich einen wank sah
> Ich bin Wolfram von Eschilbach
> Und kan ein tail mit sange
> Ich bin ein habende zange
> Mit zorne...[3]

A sprightly sentiment:

> Sy kund wol wibes try haben
> Beide syfzen und lachen
> Kund ir munt wol machen.[4]

A graphic image:

> Wan ich in dem munde trage
> Das schlos diser aventyre.[5]

A conceit:

> Do muoste kyssens vil ergan
> Dar zuo ir munt was je so rot
> Der leit von kyssen nu die not
> Das es mich myet und ist mir leit
> Das ich nicht hab solche arbeit
> Fyr si...[6]

Why were these thoughts and images 'unexpected'? Bodmer's examples speak for themselves. They have aesthetic qualities

---

[1] Lachmann-Hartl, 241, 8 ff. [2] Ibid. 245, 1 ff. [3] Ibid. 114, 10 ff.
[4] Ibid. 113, 30 ff. [5] Ibid. 734, 6–7. [6] Ibid. 807, 4 ff.

THE REVIVAL OF METAPHOR

unsuspected by an age which still considered medieval literature uncouth and barbarous.

In the curiously un-medieval invocation to the muse with which Bodmer's *Der Parcival*[1] begins, occur the following lines:

> Ob die worte von deiner sprach', ihr leben und adel,
> Unsern leuten gleich dunkel und alt und niederig scheinen,
> Seh ich die bilder darinn doch leben, und fyhl im gemythe
> Deinen ausdruk der angst und bewundre die neuen gedanken.
> Die will ich meinen zeiten entfalten....

It is the reflection of these *Bilder*, this *Ausdruck* and these *neue Gedanken* which enlivens the otherwise rather flat hexameters of this odd production. 'Hermelin war der belz; sein antlitz traurig.'[2] Or:

> Wenn sie das mæchtigste Heer bestyrmte, die leut in dem schlosse
> Gæben nicht eine nuss die gefahr von ihnen zu wenden.[3]

(the original having *niht ein brot*). A novel thought:

> ...er wæschte die hænd und das antliz,
> Jedermann dynkt', ihm glænzt' ein zweiter tag von dem antliz,
> So gar sass er untadlich in liebenswyrdiger schœnheit.[4]

But let us compare this latter example with the original:

> alte und junge wânden
> daz von in ander tac erschine.
> sus saz der minneclîche wine.
> gar vor allem tadel vrî

Bodmer's version lacks the bite of the original. Indeed, for all his admiration of the concision, pictorialness and richness of the Middle High German language, he is not very successful at rendering these qualities in modern German. Let us examine in detail a well-known passage: Parzival's first visit to Munsalvæsche. The original is constantly weakened. Thus *da man jamer vür si*

---

[1] Bodmer's version is in two cantos and only embraces a part of the whole. The first canto is based on Book v and covers the first visit to Munsalvæsche and the first part of the conversation with Sigune. The second canto consists of sections of the later adventures of Parzival from Books vi, ix, xv and xvi.
[2] *Op. cit.* p. 8. No parallel in the original.
[3] *Ibid.* p. 8; cf. Lachmann-Hartl, 226, 20 ff.
[4] *Ibid.* p. 9; cf. Lachmann-Hartl, 228, 4 ff.

truoc is rendered 'als ploetzlich ein trauriger anblik gebracht ward'; *das ich iuch bringe an die vart* by 'will ich euch melden'; *vier kint vor missewende vrî* by 'vier maedchen / Ganz untadlich'. It is perhaps significant that the *hundert bette* with the *hundert kulter* appear as 'hundert seidene Sophas'. And for the wonderful description of Amfortas:

> ez was worden wette
> zwischen im und der vröude:
> er lebte niht wan töude.

the best Bodmer can do is:

> Zwischen ihm und der freude wars quitt, er lebte nur halbig.

There are constant omissions where one suspects Bodmer has been mystified by the text. This is not to be wondered at. But he also omits things he well understood: 'röcke *grüener denne ein gras*', 'zwei mezzer *snîdende als ein grât*'. The reason would seem to be that in some passages he feels a superfluity of imagery. This is true of the second example just given: he leaves out the *grât*, but renders the line 'ez hete stahel wol versniten' which comes a little later. Similarly the beautiful lines:

> wan der grâl was der sælden vruht,
> der werlde süeze ein söhl genuht,
> er wac vil nâch gelîche
> als man saget von himelrîche.

are omitted; apparently because later we have:

> allez von des grâles craft.
> diu werde geselleschaft
> heten wirtschaft von dem grâl.

Bodmer has:
> das alles entstand von der tugend des GRALES;
> Von ihm erhielt die edle gesellschaft die theure bewirthung.

Faced with the lines:

> ich mag ez wol sprechen âne guft,
> er was noch grâwer dan der tuft.

Bodmer can do nothing with this personal intervention of the author; and the good old word *tuft* appears as 'reifen'. Some of

THE REVIVAL OF METAPHOR

the other good old words are also either not translated or incorrectly rendered. If we take as a sample the section corresponding to Lachmann-Hartl, 239,11 – 240,2, and look at the words since become obsolete, we find that *âne schranz*, *balc* and *urhap* are not translated, that *gehilze* is correctly rendered by 'heft' but *massenîe* incorrectly by 'feier'. It would seem therefore from all this evidence that Bodmer has not always been successful in rendering the particular qualities of Wolfram's style. Nevertheless the fact that he was unable to reproduce these qualities, does not mean that he was insensitive to them. His admiration for Wolfram's imagery is apparent, and he does not miss the striking moments in this part of the narrative. Repanse de Schoye:

> Trug den wunsch der erde, das reis und die wurzel des lebens.

The scornful words of the *knappe* ring out as Parzival leaves the castle precincts:

> Paket euch fort, ihr hass der sonn, ihr ganshaupt...

and this is followed by the image of the bow and the sinews which comes earlier in Wolfram:

> Ich bin der so die sehn' an den bogen leget, die sehne
> Mag wol gut seyn, wol mag der bogen geschwind seyn, noch schneller
> Ist die kraft, so die sehne vom bogen jaget; der bogen
> Ist der sehne das was der knotte der einfachen fabel.

—an unusual interpretation of a cryptic passage. Bodmer was so fascinated by the comparison of Antikonîe's waist with an ant[1] that he affixes the passage to Repanse de Schoye:

> Ich sah nicht Ameisse
> Die gelenker war, als sie da war, wo der gyrtel sie umfasst,
> Zwischen der brust und der hyfte.

This, no doubt, is an outstanding example of what Bodmer meant by *angenehme Einfalt der Bilder* or *Metaphern von den natürlichsten Gegenständen*. It was the very opposite of the jewelled imagery of the Silesians. It was homely, quaint, charming; but immensely effective, real, vivid. It gave new life to an old thought.

---

[1] Lachmann-Hartl, 410, 2 ff. (and 409, 29).

Most of the other important images of the grail episode are preserved in Bodmer's version:

(a) Mir wird mein armuth schwerer, seitdem ich weiß daß die erde
    Mit dem reichthume glænzt.

(b) Zwischen der menge der lichter und seinen leuchtenden gliedern
    Ward ein wettstreit.

(c) Aber er lag nicht allein; bei ihm im bett war die nacht durch
    Strenge arbeit.

Bodmer, we notice, does not always capture the exact meaning (as, for example, of *strengiu arbeit* in the last example), but he always appreciates the force of the image. And Sigune's reproach rings out true and clear:

Trugest du denn den giftigen zahn des wolfes im munde,
Daß du nicht mitleid hattest mit deinem großmythigen wirthe?

By this analysis of a well-known passage I have tried to show both the quality and the effect of Bodmer's appreciation of the imagery and the vocabulary of Middle High German. We have seen what he meant by the *Einfalt der Bilder*. In the language of the *Nibelungenlied* he found similar qualities: 'Schmuck, Witz, Wendungen, sind das wenigste, warum der Poet sich bekümmert hat. Man muß bey ihm nicht [sic] mehr suchen als die einfältigste Natur durch starke und bequeme Bilder ausgedrücket.'[1] Bodmer is here emphasising the contrast with the artificial writing of his own day. He returns to the point: 'Es ist etwas anziehendes in dem Gedichte, eine grosse Klarheit und Einfalt, Sachen, die bey allen Völkern und in allen Zeiten viel gegolten haben, und die sich in wenigen von unsern heutigen Stücken finden.'[2] There is no complex figuration about the style, but it has vivid pictorialness:

Es ist die eigene Sprache der Krieger, und wenn sie zierlich oder stark wird, so macht es ein Bild, eine Vorstellung, ein Umstand, welche die Sache, die Materie, sinnlich und lebhaft darstellen;...Also bekommen seine Worte ihr poetisches Ansehen nicht von ihrer figür-

---

[1] *Freymüthige Nachrichten von neuen Büchern* (Zürich, 1756), p. 93. Quoting from British Museum copy.   [2] *Ibid.* p. 94.

THE REVIVAL OF METAPHOR

lichen Gestalt, sondern daher, daß sie in dem Gemüthe, ein sinnliches Bild der Handlung, der Sache, eines kleinen Umstandes derselben entwerfen.[1]

He cites a number of examples of what he means; amongst them:[2]

> Sin vart dú wart ernúwet
> Von heizem blute naz.
>
> Mit dem scharpfen swerte
> Das im gap Rudeger
> Frumt er dú grozlichen ser
>
> Ez ist also verschranchet
> Dú Etzeln túr
> Von zweier rechen handen
> Da gent wol tusent rigel fúr

These images, he says, were probably not the invention of the poet but taken 'aus dem Umgange und dem Munde der Krieger'. The language had countless words whose figurative use became their normal use. For example: *alles trostes eine bestan*; *als im sin ellen riet*; *ʒe gelte chomen*; *den lip túren*; *sorge twang in*; *an den lip raten*. It also had 'artige Umschreibungen' like: *Man sach si hawende gan*; *Die bluot varwen degenen*; *Sigestap hiw den bluotigen bach uʒ herten ringen*; *Heú, was roter vanken ob sime helme gelac*. He finds a certain charm in groupings like *Wine der Gotelinde, Der edeln Uten Kind, Des kunen Adrianen Kind*. Similes were short. There were no *comparaisons à longue queue*. There were no *Flickwörter*. Everything was sharp and direct. For poets in those days could be direct without being considered vulgar. The same applied to their grammar: 'die Schwünge, die eigenthümlichen Wendungen, die ihre Seele waren, sind zu Sprachschnizern geworden'.[3] In the glossary to his edition of the poem,[4] Bodmer praises the concision of its language, throwing together under this heading both phonetic and stylistic qualities:

Wenn ich die Abkürzungen, die Auslassungen, Abbeissungen, Verschweigungen, Versezungen betrachte, die in dieser Sprache so

---

[1] *Ibid.* (1757), p. 106. [2] Bodmer's spelling.
[3] *Freymüthige Nachrichten* (1757), p. 159.
[4] *Chriemhilden Rache* (Zürich, 1757), Glossary, p. 63.

häufig vorkommen, so kann ich mich nicht entbrechen zu glauben, daß der Geist der Leute, welche dieselbe eingeführt und geliebt haben, ganz gelenk, fertig und feurig gewesen sey. Diese idiotischen Schwünge, diese vielfältigen Abweichungen von der pünktlichen Ordnung nicht der Wörter allein sondern der Begriffe, zeigen einen Geist, der forteilet, der den Weg sich durchhaut, der ohne Mühe ergänzet und hinzudenket, was ihm überlassen wird.

The first part of this interesting description recalls Bodmer's attack on Saxon language in *Der Mahler der Sitten*[1] which had ironically protested: 'Was nicht gelencke, tönend, kurtz ist, das ist zum Gebrauche nichts nütze.' Implied was a defence of *Abbeissung*, of apocope and syncope resulting in full-sounding monosyllables with strongly articulated consonant-clusters. Bodmer does not seem to have been at all disturbed by Mauvillon's assertion that German was a rough language. Indeed, he seems to have approved of this description; for he agreed with Mauvillon that Saxons spoke rapidly and almost with a stammer, in order to give the German language *a softness which it does not possess*.[2] The reference is to the Saxon *-e* and the preservation (as against *Abbeissung*) of secondary syllables which gave the language a more even flow and correspondingly less intensity at the stress-points. It may have been Gottsched's opposition to the harshness and monosyllabism of Upper German which engendered in Bodmer a love of linguistic roughness. Certain it is that he came to equate roughness with strength, and as his medieval studies developed he found this same quality of full-sounding compression in Middle High German. His native roughness had now acquired the patina of antiquity. It was also easy to demonstrate how much Middle High German poetry owed to this quality of its language. It was important to ward off the old charge of

---

[1] *Der Mahler der Sitten* (Zürich, 1746), vol. II, pp. 612 ff. The passage is included in Wehrli's anthology entitled *Das geistige Zürich im 18. Jahrhundert* (Zürich, 1943).

[2] 'Des Herrn von Mauvillon Brief von der Sprache der Deutschen' in *Sammlung critischer Schriften*, v. Stück (1742). It had long been agreed that the speech of Meissen was soft; testimonies are frequent in the seventeenth century, some approving of this fact, others not.

barbarism which still hung in the air. The French had used it of the Germans, the Germans of everything before Opitz. Bodmer, however, calls Middle High German 'nichts weniger als barbarisch', not at all barbaric: 'Eine Vergleichung derselben mit der gegenwärtigen Sprache wird ihr und den Dichtern...zu keinem Nachtheile gereichen. Leute von Geschmacke werden zugleich wahrnehmen, daß diese Poeten ihre so geschickte Sprache gebraucht haben, tausend artige, natürlich-einfältige, und in dem Grunde des menschlichen Herzens entsprungene Empfindungen auszubilden.'

These words are taken from his grammatical notes which form part of the preface to the *Proben der alten schwäbischen Poesie*.[1] Bodmer was anxious that this language should not be considered as imperfect and immature Modern German. It had, he said elsewhere,[2] its own *Verfassung* based on proper rules; and whether it had gained in richness, sound or other facilities from the changes undergone since the sixteenth century, was very much open to question. 'Es waren Elemente zu einer Sprache, wie diejenigen waren, die Spencer [*sic*] und *Shakespear* vor sich hatten, und die ein Kopf, wie ihrer war, mit der Geschicklichkeit, die sie in der *Faery queen* und den Tragödien angewandt haben, zu derselben Höhe hätte erheben können, in welcher die Sprache in diesen Werken gestiegen ist.'[3] But this language had declined through neglect of its literature. It had taken on a completely different *Verfassung*. It had decayed in definiteness, concision, flexibility and variety.[4] These ideas dominate Bodmer's presentation of Middle High German grammar in the preface to the *Proben der alten schwäbischen Poesie*. We are told that the genitive case was used extensively to give concision, precision and emphasis to the

---

[1] Zürich, 1748. This remark on pp. xl–xli. I quote from the copy in the Central Library at Zürich.

[2] *Sammlung von Minnesingern*, I. Theil (Zürich, 1758), p. iv.

[3] *Freymüthige Nachrichten* (1758), p. 157. Article on the *Sammlung von Minnesingern*.

[4] *Ibid.* p. 158; and *Neue Critische Briefe* (1749), p. 495. The exact words are 'an Bestimmung, an Kürze, an Geschmeidigkeit, an Mannigfaltigkeit'. I take *Bestimmung* in the sense of *Bestimmtheit*.

style. Flexibility is adduced as the reason for lack of adjectival inflection (*din gœtlich tugent*) or for the confusion between second and third plural forms in the present indicative. Richness of sound is suggested as the reason why strong verbs show fuller forms in the preterite and past participle and why the prefix *ge-* is found in all moods and tenses. Emphasis is made to account for the *s-* in *swa, swer*, and the use of *so* in *swas so mir geschach*. Much of this we should now consider unjust application of stylistic criteria to grammatical phenomena. It is, however, important for us to observe that Bodmer interpreted this grammar in the light of his aesthetic enthusiasm. To the peculiarities of Middle High German syntax he was fully alive. The pleonastic demonstrative in a construction like *si iehent der sumer der si hie* he deemed emphatic, the position of the article in *minen gedanken den vrien* was 'artig', the frequent omission of subject pronoun (even with impersonal verbs), the constant use of elliptical constructions and the looser word-order were all noted *and admired*. He observed a parallel between Middle High German: *Was ob mich ein bote versumet gar* and a similar ellipsis in English: *What tho the sun draw from the deep | More than the rivers pour?* He recognised that in prosody the contractions, elisions, expletives, enclitics and proclitics of the language resulted in rich, full-sounding verse.

Bodmer's hope was that his contemporaries would revivify their language by a return to these pristine springs of beauty and power. Many of these pregnant constructions could, he thought, be revived without doing violence to the spirit of the language. He recalled how the French had turned to Marot and Amyot, the English to Spenser and Chaucer. He advocated that linguistic societies should collect obsolete but useful words. Much could be done in this way to enrich the expressive potentialities of the language. One could collect words for which no satisfactory substitute had been found. One could observe the original meaning of a word and try to recapture some of its force. One could note good words ousted by conflict of homophones. One could observe the relationship between the figurative and the 'original' usage of words. One could compare the modern and the medieval languages in certain restricted fields of their vocabulary. This would reveal great riches which had been left unexplored.[1]

It was poetry that Bodmer had primarily in mind. At first sight it may seem strange that he should have felt an affinity between the medieval *Minnesang* and the anacreontic poetry of his own day. But there were parallels. Both dwelt with the simple joys of life and dealt with them in a pleasing, graceful manner. It is easy to understand why Bodmer so often used the word *Artigkeit* in this context if we but realise that he came to this poetry from the stuffy artificiality of the later seventeenth century. The point is made clear when the *naturalness* of medieval love-poetry is contrasted with the 'erdichtete Liebes-Briefe' of Hofmannswaldau.[2] One can see why he felt that Wolfram's comparison of a lady's waist with an ant had *naife Artigkeit*.[3] It was fresh and it was delightful; but it was also something ordinary and therefore something natural. He admired the *natyrliche Einfalt* of medieval German fables, they had 'nichts gekynsteltes, und auch nichts frostiges'.[4] In a review of Gleim's poetry, published in 1745, he said that both medieval and anacreontic poetry had *Artigkeit und Natürlichkeit*.[5] These two words recur again and again in his remarks on medieval poetry. The nearest he came to defining *Artigkeit* was in connection with the *style marotique* of La Fontaine: 'Diese Artigkeit entsteht durch die besondere Bestimmung eines Begriffes, durch das natürliche Wesen, durch die Kürtze eines Ausdruckes.'[6] Something quite similar is said of Walther von der Vogelweide: 'In seinen verliebten Liedern entsteht die Artigkeit so gerne von dem wizigen Einfalle als von der zärtlichen Empfindung.'[7] In the fanciful allegory *Das Erdmännchen*, stanzas

---

[1] The latter part of this paragraph is a summary of a remarkable passage (too long to quote) in the preface to the second volume of the *Sammlung von Minnesingern*.
[2] *Critische Briefe* (1746), p. 218.
[3] *Gedichte in Gereimten Versen*, p. 136.
[4] *Fabeln aus den Zeiten der Minnesinger* (1757), Preface.
[5] *Freymüthige Nachrichten* (1745), p. 284.
[6] *Sammlung critischer Schriften*, VII. Stück, pp. 52–3.
[7] *Proben*, p. xxxiv.

from Hagedorn are balanced antiphonally with verses from the Manesse manuscript. Both compared the joys of love with the joys of nature. Both derived their imagery from the same source. But the older poets had the advantage of their language. Words had not yet acquired the flatness imparted by centuries of common use. Words had a full, rich sound with plenty of vowels and with clipped consonants. Simple things could still be said simply and effectively.[1]

The theoretical discussion of diction in the treatises of 1740-1 had found a strange fulfilment and exemplification in these medieval studies. The connecting link had been the doctrine of the Marvellous. And Milton was the *fons et origo* of it all. In the preface to his translation of *Paradise Lost*,[2] published in 1732, Bodmer had written:

> Die besten Engelländischen Scribenten bekennen, daß ihre Sprache selbst unter Milton eingesuncken und zu schwach gewesen die erhabene Gedancken seiner Sele in ihrer vollen Kraft vorzustellen; dennoch hatte Milton den Spencer und Shakespear vor den Augen. Er hat sich unterschiedlicher Mittel bedienet, seine Rede von der Prosa zu unterscheiden, indem er Z.E. fremde Mundarten nachgeahmet, alte machtvolle Wörter an das Licht hervor gezogen, neue geprägt, die Wortfügung verändert, ungewöhnliche Metaphoren erfunden, die Absätze der Rede in einander geschlungen..., etc.

It may well be that in urging the Germans to improve their literary language by study of their own past, Bodmer had the example of Milton and the English language in mind. The passage just quoted has reference to Addison's essays on Milton in *The Spectator*, especially no. 285 dated 26 January 1712. Addison proceeded from the statement that the language of an epic poem should be 'both perspicuous and sublime'. It should deviate from the common forms and ordinary phrases of speech. All this had a strong effect on Bodmer who rejected Christian Weise's demand

---

[1] The *Erdmännchen* and these remarks are to be found in the *Neue Critische Briefe* of 1749, pp. 479–506. Copy in the Central Library at Zürich.

[2] *Johann Miltons Verlust des Paradieses, Ein Helden-Gedicht*, published anonymously, Zürich, 1732. There is a copy in the British Museum, from which I quote.

for prose-construction in verse and lamented the flat diction of verse in his own day. In his notes to the translation of Mauvillon's essay he called this lack of a sublime style 'the falling sickness'.[1] Addison had recalled those aids to the achievement of sublime style which had been enumerated by Aristotle: use of metaphor, of idioms from other tongues, of forms shorter or longer than the common forms, and of obsolescent words. Some of this, we notice, recurs in the description of Milton's diction by Bodmer in the passage just quoted. The point is developed in his essay on Milton's language in the *Sammlung critischer Schriften* ten years later.[2] He shows how Milton followed Aristotle's precepts and suggests that Germans might do the same. Foreign words can easily be adopted; archaic words might be revived to advantage. He then cites several syntactical constructions now obsolete which might well be revived; postposition of epithet, substantivation of adjective or infinitive, poetic inversion (in its widest sense: *Versezung der Wörter aus der prosaischen Fügung*[3]) and ellipsis of the auxiliary verb. This makes an interesting comparison with Addison's essay: 'Under this head may be reckoned the placing the adjective after the substantive, the transposition of words, the turning the adjective into a substantive, with several other foreign modes of speech which this poet has naturalised, to give his verse the greater sound, and throw it out of prose.' For Addison, we notice, these modes of speech were foreign; for Bodmer they were archaic. He found them in medieval German. In the preface to the second volume of the *Sammlung von Minnesingern* he enumerates four points of medieval syntax which he admires, amongst them the placing of a monosyllabic word, which completes the sense of a line, into the next line (compare 'die Absätze der Rede in einander geschlungen' from the preface to the translation of Milton), and the avoidance of normal order of words, with interpolations of considerable length.[4] This list forms an interesting

---

[1] *Sammlung critischer Schriften*, v. Stück, p. 53, footnote.
[2] *Op. cit.* III. Stück (1742), pp. 75–133.
[3] Christian Weise is expressly mentioned here, for disapproval (*op. cit.* p. 98).
[4] *Op. cit.* p. iii.

parallel with the list in the preface to the Milton translation and in the Milton essay. The dates of the three works are 1732, 1742, and 1759. Bodmer's ideas were obviously fairly constant. His enthusiasm for Middle High German is derived ultimately from Addison's essay on Milton's diction!

The doctrine of the *Machtwort* also derives from the same source. Addison quoted Aristotle's praise of metaphor as one of the means to achieve sublime style. Bodmer contrasted the strength of Milton's imagery with the absurdity of the Silesians. He accepted Addison's statement that Milton had revived metaphors from older English poets and thought the Germans might well do some salvaging from their own medieval imagery. His examples are:[1] *Seine Kunst behälligen; sich mit Reden verhauen; einen spöttisch aufziehen; ein Adler, der die Flügel leichtet; einem einen Fehltritt aufheben; einem Schrecken einspinnen; sich auf seine Macht triegen; der Reichthum ist zerronnen; in einen Anschlag gehällen; nach mißschlagender Verheissung; schwartzbraune Haare, welche sich wohl werffen; Gewand, das mit seinen Schlingungen wohl geworffen ist; das Aehrenfeld spreußt sich.* We can see, says Bodmer, how much the German language has lost in this kind of strong, vivid expression if we read sixteenth-century authors. Still more so if we go back to Hohenstauffen times. Dutch had preserved many such expressions. English had regained them through Milton. Why should not German do the same? He also advocates the invention of new words with the same sort of terse expressiveness, giving as examples: *verparadiest, Paradiesmässig, mißgeschaffen,*[2] *Mißthon, Hölleverdammt,*[2] *Verkehrtheit, Enthaltsamkeit, sonnigt, abändern, thauend, dämmernd, Unding, veredeln, überthürmen, überfliessen, schlakigt, unablänglich, Empfindniß, Nothgeschicke, abgezogen* (= 'abstract'), *bräutlich, unwillkommen, Unreife, Unform, Innigkeit, Zugethanheit, luftig* (= 'aereus'), *beschönen, unerkennbar, Begriff* (= 'grip'), *mürben* (verb), *verviel-*

---

[1] *Sammlung critischer Schriften*, vol. III, p. 114 (Milton essay). I give the examples in Bodmer's own spelling.

[2] Addison in a parallel passage has *miscreated* and *hell-doomed* amongst his examples.

fachen. Common to all these words is perspicuity and concision. Several of them show graphic prefixes. Participles are well represented. The plea for *Begriff* in this sense is a plea for a metaphor to be preserved. We shall see the effects of all this in Klopstock and the Sturm und Drang.

The conclusion of this interesting and illuminating essay, ostensibly on Milton but ranging far wider, contains an encomium on the English language. English, thought Bodmer, had preserved many features which he admired in Middle High German. He liked the monosyllabic nature of its verbs, the way it had sloughed off its inflectional endings, the freedom of its word-order. It is full of features, he says, which give light, life and strength to style. It is rich in participial constructions. It has a great facility for using intransitive verbs with transitive force[1] and transitive verbs with intransitive or passive meaning.[2] It uses the cognate accusative construction quite regularly. It has valuable gerunds and gerundial expressions whereas German now has none although it had them in the fourteenth century.

Defence of Milton had led Bodmer and Breitinger on to a consideration of poetic diction in general. It had also led Bodmer to Dante and to medieval literature in general. Here he found *das Wunderbare* and the sort of strong, poetic language he wanted. His admiration of Middle High German was coloured by his historical theories of the 'naturalness' of medieval communities and his aesthetic revulsion from seventeenth-century sophistication. It is most significant that this should have happened in Switzerland. It was natural that the Swiss should find easier access to the Middle Ages. Their history and their speech helped them. Bodmer and Breitinger made two important contributions to the development of the German language: they advocated strong, metaphorical expression and they pointed to the Middle Ages as an example.

[1] Bodmer (*op. cit.* p. 129, footnote) says that similar constructions in German would be: 'ein Pferd zu Tode *rennen*, seinen Gegner müde *schreiben*, die Zeit *wegplaudern*, einen kranck *trinken*', etc.

[2] A German parallel would be, says Bodmer: 'Er wollte nicht gern um der Religion willen *brennen*.'

X

THE GRAND MANNER

'ERSCHEINE, grosser Geist....' In the *Charakter der Teutschen Gedichte* of 1734, Bodmer had invoked the epic genius which he longed to see arise in Germany. We know that Klopstock was moved by his words, for he says so in his first letter to Bodmer dated 10 August 1748. In his excitement at the first cantos of *Der Messias* Bodmer saluted in Klopstock a spirit 'der einen gleichen Schwung mit dem Milton nehmen wird'.[1] Klopstock in his letter says that he had read his Homer and his Virgil and was inwardly displeased by the Saxon critics. Then he came upon the works of Bodmer and Breitinger and consumed them wishing that their promised treatise of the Sublime would appear. It was Bodmer's translation which had first introduced him to Milton; and it was Milton who had fanned the flame which Homer had kindled in him. At first he contemplated various secular subjects. Then he was induced by his reading of Pyra's *Tempel der wahren Dichtkunst* (first published at Halle in 1737) to treat the theme of Christ's redemption of the world. Under the spell of this influence and of his reading of Milton, Homer and Virgil, he began to think out the project while still at school. At Jena (where he matriculated in 1745) he began to write down sections of what later became the first three cantos. These were in poetical prose and have not survived. From a hint in the essay prefacing the second volume of *Der Messias*, it would appear that the style of this prose was modelled on Fénelon's *Télémaque*. In the summer of 1746 came the final decision to write the poem in hexameters and the recasting of what was already written.

---

[1] *Freymüthige Nachrichten* (1748), 25. Herbstmonath. P. Grosser, *Der junge Klopstock im Urteil seiner Zeit* (1937), is useful for the assessment of Klopstock's impact on his age. Two studies appeared while I was thinking out this chapter: M. Freivogel, *Klopstock, der heilige Dichter* (Berne, 1954) and K. A. Schleiden, *Klopstocks Dichtungstheorie* (Saarbrücken, 1954).

A happy chance brought him in touch with J. A. Cramer and the circle of the *Bremer Beyträge* who criticised and helped him to polish his poem. Doubts about publication were entertained and in 1747 the opinions were sought of Hagedorn and Bodmer. Hagedorn gave rather lukewarm approval but Bodmer reacted with immediate enthusiasm. And so the first three cantos were published in 1748. In many ways the language of the 1748 *Messias* came near to fulfilling Bodmer's ideal. It was concise, it was powerful, it avoided commonplace expression, it was even agreeably rough and shunned the smooth alternation of accented and unaccented syllables which had dominated German verse since Opitz. Bodmer liked the bumps and clashes that characterised the apparently rather gawky hexameters of these first three cantos. For him this was not clumsiness, but rhythmic power. Strength, not sweetness, was his ideal. And this he found in Klopstock.

The clumsy lines of the first three cantos can be read in two different ways according to whether the natural stress of speech or the traditional form of the hexameter is sacrificed to the other. It would seem from investigation that Klopstock consciously refashioned the hexameter, substituting trochees for spondees and making other concessions to the natural rhythms of German, but without violating normal stress and preserving the general spirit (though not the exact classical form) of the hexameter. The awkwardness of some lines in the first three cantos is due therefore not to any inability to control the form but to the fact that the work was begun in prose.[1] Klopstock decided to use hexameters sometime during the summer of 1746. By this time Ewald von Kleist's poem *Der Frühling*, which used hexameters with *Auftakt* added,[2] was well advanced in composition and we know that Klopstock was interested. He himself had enjoyed an exceptionally thorough grounding in the classics at Schulpforta and

---

[1] G. C. L. Schuchard, *Studien zur Verskunst des jungen Klopstock* (Stuttgart, 1927).

[2] This metre seems to be found first in a poem by Uz, also entitled *Der Frühling*, first published (in Schwabe's *Belustigungen des Verstandes und des Witzes*) in 1743, and written a year previously.

his library, although otherwise motley, contained full sets of all the important Greek and Latin authors. He chose the hexameter because it was more elastic than the iambic pentameter or the alexandrine. He was anxious that his verse should have maximum variety of rhythm. For similar reasons he introduced variations into the iambic pentameter in his dramas; and defended these (in the preface to *Salomo*). His free treatment of classical metres, seen also in his odes, is dictated by the desire to keep the rhythm fluid and to avoid monotony. The change to completely free rhythms in the odes (around 1754)[1] is merely a further development of an already existing situation, not a radical change. Enjambement, of stanza as well as of line, is already found in the early odes: the poem *An Fanny* of 1748 has a protasis extending over five stanzas before we reach the principal clause. He speaks in one poem of 'satzungenlose Dithyramben'. This would seem to have been his ideal. In later life he tightened up his forms, returning more and more to a rigid modern correspondence to the ancient metrical schemes and losing much of his fluidity of rhythm. The change takes place around 1760 in the odes. It is seen in the 1780 revision of *Der Messias*. It may have been a concession to hostile criticism. Schuchard thinks it was; and that it was regrettable. It may, however, have represented that revulsion against free verse which has overcome more than one poet in later life.[2]

Klopstock's metrical forms reflect and influence his whole attitude to language. This is apparent in the essay entitled *Von der Nachahmung des griechischen Sylbenmaßes im Deutschen*, prefixed to the second volume of the 1756 edition of *Der Messias*.[3] He admires the *Strom...Schwung...Feuer* of the Greek hexameter; and the alcaic strophe for *ihrem Schwunge, ihrer Fülle,*

---

[1] *Die Genesung.* The first printed poem to show this change is *Dem Allgegenwärtigen* of 1758.

[2] On the style of the Odes, see I. Böger, *Bewegung als formendes Gesetz in Klopstocks Oden* (Berlin, 1939); G. Goldbach, *Das Stilproblem der Odendichtung Klopstocks* (Diss. Munich, 1938); and E. Kaußmann, *Der Stil der Oden Klopstocks* (Diss. Leipzig, 1931).

[3] The standard edition of Klopstock's numerous essays on linguistic matters is by A. L. Back and A. R. C. Spindler in six volumes (Leipzig, 1830). These form vols. XIII–XVIII of the *Sämmtliche Werke* (Leipzig, 1823–30).

ihrem fallenden Schlage. Let us note these terms. Nowhere is there any talk of grace, clarity, *Artigkeit.* We are far from the world of Gottsched's criteria. He speaks of the wonderful *harmony* of Homer's verse: 'die itzt fließt, dann strömt, hier sanft klingt, dort majestätisch tönt'. But by 'harmony' he meant more than sweet sound; he meant 'music' in its fullest sense. Variety (*Abwechslung*) is for him an important element of *Harmonie.*[1] How far can this harmonious variety be attained in German, he wonders. 'Der wesentliche Charakter unsrer Sprache, in Absicht auf ihren Klang, scheint mir zu seyn, daß sie voll und männlich klingt, und mit einer gewissen gesetzten Stärke ausgesprochen seyn will.'[2] This description may not seem to suggest either harmony or variety. But Klopstock is determined to prove his point and proceeds to argue his way towards an assertion of the kindred nature of German and Greek. French, in comparison, has fewer full-sounding words and is too rapid in speech to be suited to periodic sentences; Italian is soft and voluptuous when compared with the full, firm accent of Latin; and English is perhaps too monosyllabic and jerky to recapture the full amplitude of Greek periods as well as German. The German hexameter loses little by its substitution of trochees for spondees. It is indeed superior to the Greek hexameter because of its greater variety of rhythm.[3] The German language is declared to be better suited to the hexameter than to Opitz's verse with its regular alternation of accented and unaccented syllables which leads to monotony and prevents the use of many poetic and even almost indispensable words. This is in an unfinished treatise on classical rhythms in

---

[1] 'Sogar *rauhe* Töne gehören, wenn sie der Inhalt erfodert, mit zum Wolklange.' *Die deutsche Gelehrtenrepublik* (original edition, Hamburg, 1774), vol. I, p. 138. There is a copy in the British Museum.

[2] Back-Spindler, III, p. 6.

[3] *Vom deutschen Hexameter*, in third volume of 1769 edition of *Der Messias.* Back-Spindler, III, pp. 68–9. In the *Gelehrtenrepublik* Klopstock has a long section on the rhythmic patterns of German. He claims that since all its stem-syllables are long, important ideas are always conveyed in long syllables (subsidiary ideas being confined to inflectional, short syllables). 'Dieses macht, daß unsre Sprache den Absichten der Verskunst angemesner ist, als es selbst die beyden alten Sprachen sind' (original edn. (Hamburg, 1774), pp. 345–6).

German included in the *Fragmente über Sprache und Dichtkunst* (Hamburg, 1779).[1] The same essay considers in some detail the relation between rhythm (*Zeitausdruck*) and sound (*Tonverhalt*):

Wenn der Dichter sagt:

> Aber da rollte der Donner von dunklen Gewölken herunter.

so wird über der Schnelligkeit des Zeitausdrucks, weil sie sich zur Sache schickt, das nicht passende Sanfte des Tonverhalts nicht bemerkt... Sagt hingegen der Dichter:

> Da die Lüfte des Lenzes mit Blüthe das Mädchen bewehten.

so hört man nur auf das Sanfte des Tonverhalts... In diesem Verse:

> Und der Donner schlug ein, und durchscholl das Geklüft.

sind Zeitausdruck und Tonverhalt vereint, und wirken daher desto stärker.[2]

In the fragmentary essay *Vom Sylbenmaße*,[3] cast in dialogue form, one of the characters mentions that German has lost many of the sounds used by the 'unpoetic Otfried' and that if he had been a poet, this harmonious language would have survived. The consonant-clusters of German make it, in most people's opinion, a less harmonious language than Greek. And yet there were unpleasant sounds in Greek which German does not possess.[4] The sound of German is strong and need not be rough. It has an advantage over Greek in that every polysyllabic word must contain at least one 'long syllable'. It naturally favours monosyllables and resents any attempt to make these disyllabic: 'Wir hören lieber *geht*, als *gehet*, und einige Ausdehnungen dulden wir gar nicht. Wir sagen niemals *läufet*, sondern allzeit *läuft*.'[5] And yet this extension does increase the number of the vowels and may therefore be permitted for particular effects. 'Das Vornehmste kommt überhaupt bey unserer Aussprache darauf an, daß wir einige Vokalen und alle Diphthongen voll; die Konsonanten zwar ganz, aber doch auch bey Häufung derselben einige etwas leise hören lassen.'[6]

---

[1] Back-Spindler, III, pp. 87 ff.   [2] *Ibid.* pp. 209–10.
[3] In the first number of the continuation of the *Briefe über Merkwürdigkeiten der Litteratur* (Hamburg and Bremen, 1770). Back-Spindler, III, pp. 227 ff.
[4] Klopstock (*ibid.* p. 231) mentions the frequent *u*- sounds, *ai* and *oi*, *phth*.
[5] *Ibid.* p. 245.   [6] *Ibid.* pp. 258–9.

But few people agreed with Klopstock that German could reproduce or even surpass the music of Greek. One of the most interesting comments comes from Haller, interesting because it draws attention to the connection between Klopstock's prosody and his vocabulary. The passage (from the preface to the 1768 edition of his poems) runs as follows:

> Da aber die Trocheen und Dactylen im Deutschen fast unmöglich den Wohlklang der Alten erlangen können, da der Spondäus im deutschen Verse fast unerträglich ist, da die vielen e, und die gehäufften Consonanten, die o, die a, die i, und u der Alten und die fliessende Abwechselung mit Selbstlautern nicht ersetzen können, so wurde der Urheber der deutschen Hexametern genöthigt, dieser alzusehr der reimlosen Rede sich nähernden Art zu dichten durch andere Mittel den über die Prose sich erhebenden Anstand der Poesie zu geben. Man führte neue, zusammengesetzte, emphatische Wörter ein: man gab selbst der Sprache eine neue Wortfügung, die mit den alten Sprachen näher übereinkömmt.[1]

Klopstock's attitude to language is best seen in the various revisions to which he subjected the text of *Der Messias*.[2] The

---

[1] Ed. Hirzel, pp. 264–5 (text corrected from original edition, copy in British Museum). Similar thoughts are expressed in the 1772 letter to Gemmingen, *ibid.* p. 400.

[2] A good deal has been written on Klopstock's language. The fundamental work was done by Friedrich Petri in his *Kritische Beiträge zur Geschichte der Dichtersprache Klopstocks* (Greifswald, 1894). Later studies include Jellinek's 'Bemerkungen über Klopstocks Dichtersprache' in the Walzel Festschrift (Wildpark-Potsdam, 1924). Walzel's article on 'Barockstil bei Klopstock' in the Jellinek Festschrift (Vienna and Leipzig, 1928), an article by Beißner, 'Klopstock als Erneuerer der deutschen Dichtersprache', in *ZfDk.* LVI (1942), and various articles by August Langen who asserts the influence of Pietism on Klopstock's vocabulary, 'Klopstocks sprachwissenschaftliche Bedeutung', *Wirkendes Wort*, VI (1952–3), the relevant section in his 'Deutsche Sprachgeschichte vom Barock bis zur Gegenwart', in *Deutsche Philologie im Aufriß* (ed. W. Stammler, vol. I, 1952), and 'Verbale Dynamik in der dichterischen Landschaftsschilderung des 18. Jhts', *ZfdPh.* LXX (1949) (which deals with Klopstock and his influence on others). Horst Engert, 'Klopstocks Dichtung und unsere Zeit', *ZfDk.* XXXV (1921), has some points on language. Max Freivogel (Berne, 1954), *Klopstock*, has a good section on poetical language. Isabella Papmehl-Rüttenauer, *Das Wort HEILIG in der deutschen Dichtersprache von Pyra bis zum jungen Herder* (Weimar, 1937), has a central chapter on Klopstock's use of the word. Two unprinted dissertations are listed by Langen, namely, W. Popp, *Wortwiederholung in*

first three cantos appeared in 1748 in the fourth volume of the
Bremer Beiträge. In 1751 the first revision appeared with cantos
four and five added. In 1755–6 the first ten cantos appeared in
a two-volume edition with prefaces to each volume. The eleventh
to fifteenth cantos were published in 1768, the remaining five in
1773. Then the whole poem was republished, with considerable
revision of the earlier sections, in 1780–1. In 1793 a second
revised edition appeared. The final text was published in 1799–
1800 in the collected works.[1] If the text of the first three cantos
in this final edition be compared with that of 1748, an interesting
picture emerges of the development of Klopstock's poetic diction.
'Veränderungen und Verbesserungen, die ein Dichter, wie Klopstock, in seinen Werken macht, verdienen nicht allein angemerkt,
sondern mit allem Fleisse studieret zu werden', said Lessing in
the nineteenth *Literaturbrief*. 'Man studieret in ihnen die feinsten
Regeln der Kunst; denn was die Meister der Kunst zu beobachten
für gut befinden, das sind Regeln.'

Let us compare two versions of a short passage from the first
canto:

(1748) Also gieng Gabriel itzt auf den mitternächtlichen Bergen,
        Und schon stand sein unsterblicher Fuß an der heiligen Pforte,
        Die sich vor ihm, wie Flügel der rauschenden Cherubim aufthat.
        Schon war sie hinter ihm wieder geschlossen. Nun gieng der
          Seraph
        In den Tiefen der Erde. Da wälzten sich Oceane
        Um ihn mit langsamer Flut zum menschenlosen Gestade.
        Alle Söhne der Oceane, gewaltige Flüsse,
        Flossen, wie Ungewitter sich aus den Wüsten heraufziehn,
        Fern und rauhtönend ihm nach.

Klopstocks Messias (Greifswald, 1923), and P. Rosenberg, *Klopstock und die deutsche Sprache* (Vienna, 1934). I. Bacon, 'Pietistische und rationalistische Elemente in Klopstocks Sprache', *JEGP*, XLIX (1950), does not seem to me to prove the case for 'rationalist' elements.

[1] The British Museum has the 1749, 1755 and 1780 editions. It also has a set of four volumes in two, of which vol. I (Cantos I–V) is 1760, vol. II (VI–X) 1756, vol. III (XI–XV) 1769 and vol. IV (XVI–XX) 1773—all published at Halle. I have used all these editions.

This becomes:

(1799) So ging Gabriel jetzt auf den mitternächtlichen Bergen,
Und schon stand des Unsterblichen Fuß an der heiligen Pforte,
Welche vor ihm, wie rauschender Cherubim Flügel, sich aufthat,
Hinter ihm wieder mit Eile sich schloß. Nun wandelt der Seraph
In der Erd' Abgründen. Da wälzten sich Oceane
Ringsum, langsamer Flut, zu menschenlosen Gestaden.
Alle Söhne der Oceane, gewaltige Ströme
Flossen, wie Ungewitter sich aus den Wüsten heraufziehn,
Tiefauftönend ihm nach.[1]

Many passages would show more elaborate refashioning. But I have purposely chosen a section where the alterations are slight, so that the general tenor and direction of this revision may emerge clearly. In several places the expression has been strengthened: *schon* becomes *mit Eile*, *gieng* becomes *wandelt*, *Tiefen* is replaced by *Abgründen*, *um* by *ringsum*. In each case a less common word replaces the everyday expression. The same can be said of the plural *Gestaden*. Similar strengthening is achieved by inversion (*rauschender Cherubim Flügel*; *In der Erd' Abgründen*), by rearrangement placing an important word in a more important rhythmical position (*Hinter ihm wieder mit Eile sich schloß*), by using a nominal case instead of a prepositional phrase (*langsamer Flut*, genitive, for *mit langsamer Flut*), by variation instead of virtual repetition (*Ströme flossen* for *Flüsse flossen*) and by the striking compound *tiefauftönend*, characteristic of Klopstock in three ways: in its being a present participle, in its combination with an adverbial modifier (*tief*) and in its use of the prefix *auf*. This is exactly the type of compound epithet which Breitinger had praised for its full-soundingness, and the same graphic use of a preposition and the same sort of participle which he had advocated as *nachdrücklich*.

---

[1] There is no critical edition of *Der Messias*. The edition by R. Hamel in Kürschner's *Deutsche National-Litteratur* is useful. It gives the 1799 text; and, in the first three cantos, faces this with the 1748 text. But there is no full variorum edition. My text is taken from Hamel, *op. cit.* pp. 48–9.

Klopstock formulated his own theory of poetic diction in the essay *Von der Sprache der Poesie*, first published in 1758 in the first volume of the periodical *Der nordische Aufseher*.[1] His basic contention is that the language of poetry must be notably different from that of prose. No nation, he asserts, has ever achieved excellence in either prose or poetry which has not observed this difference. The Greeks gave the words of prose a different sound in poetry: 'Eben das Wort, das auch in Prosa gebräuchlich war, wurde, durch eine Sylbe mehr oder weniger, durch Hinzusetzung, Wegnehmung, oder Veränderung eines Buchstabens, zum poetischen Worte gemacht.'[2] (This derives from Aristotle, possibly via Addison and Bodmer, see above, p. 311, and was in direct opposition to Gottsched's objections to 'lengthenings and shortenings'.[3]) The Italians transformed words in poetry in a similar way; and they had a whole set of words only used in poetry. Of all the great modern nations the French had made least difference between the language of poetry and prose; and many Frenchmen had regretted this. English poetic language, although markedly different from that of prose, was so full of foreign words that the associations of these in their original languages were apt to obscure the effect. In German the difference between the language of poetry and prose had been clearly demonstrated by Luther in his translation of the poetical books of the Bible; but the Germans had not followed his lead. Opitz had reminded them of this important difference, Haller did so even more strongly; but they still seemed to ignore it. Poetry has finer, nobler and broader (*vielseitigere*) thoughts to express

---

[1] Back-Spindler, IV, pp. 13 ff. *Der nordische Aufseher* was edited by J. A. Cramer and published at Copenhagen and Leipzig from 1758 to 1761. Lessing commented on this essay by Klopstock in the fifty-first of the *Literaturbriefe* (Lachmann-Muncker, VIII, p. 143). Herder praised it in the *Fragmente* (Suphan, I, p. 156) and elsewhere.

[2] *Ibid*. p. 16.

[3] In ch. IX of Part One of the *Critische Dichtkunst*. See above, p. 231. Schönaich (see below, p. 336) objects to this ironically: 'Wir haben schon oben bewundert, daß unsere heiligen Dichter berechtiget sind, den armen Wörtern bald ihren Kopf, bald ihren Schwanz zu rauben; ja das Eingeweid reissen sie ihnen aus dem Leibe' (*ed. cit.* p. 179).

than prose. It must have words to express them fully. There are some words which have lost all their force by constant usage, or never had any such force. These are useless for poetry. Others are only suitable for some types of poetry. Others are unsuitable because of sound and rhythm. The choice of words is therefore more restricted than in prose. Poetry must avoid words with base or ridiculous associations. It must use words which say something (avoiding those which merely seem to say something), words of *ausgemachter Stärke*, well-built compounds,[1] obsolescent words, even new words—so long as there are no associations with words of too ordinary or colloquial nature. Words must be placed to best effect. Poetry demands a different word-order from that conventionalised by prose. The most powerful elements in an imaginative perception (*Vorstellung*) must come first in its expression. Sound as well as meaning will play its part in this poetic arrangement of words. Klopstock is here foreshadowing Herder's justification of poetic inversion. In another essay (*Von der Darstellung*)[2] he noted: 'Unvermuthetes, scheinbare Unordnung, schnelles Abbrechen des Gedankens, erregte Erwartung, Alles dieß setzt die Seele in eine Bewegung, die sie für die Eindrücke empfänglicher macht.'[3] This recalls Breitinger's statement that the origin of poetic inversions is in the *Sprache der Affecte*.[4] The line Breitinger—Klopstock—Herder is a clear one. The essay we have been analysing continues with various details. In poetic language words should not be unnecessarily spun out into phrases. Prominent particles should be avoided. 'Ein: *dem ungeachtet*, könnte die schönste Stelle verderben.'[5] A *doch* can be omitted from the expression of a wish. But interjections are

---

[1] 'Das Zusammensetzen macht, daß man schneller denkt: und der schnellere Gedanke ist lebendiger, hat mehr Kraft', he says in the fourth of the *Grammatische Gespräche* (Back-Spindler, I, pp. 176–7).
  Since this chapter of my work was completed, a study of Klopstock's compound adjectives by Edna Purdie has appeared in *GR*, XXXI (1956), entitled, 'Some descriptive compounds in Klopstock's poetic vocabulary'. For more detailed reference to this article, see below, in the footnotes to pp. 332 ff.
[2] First published in the *Fragmente über Sprache und Dichtkunst* (Hamburg, 1779). Back-Spindler, IV, pp. 1 ff.   [3] Back-Spindler, IV, p. 6.
[4] See above, p. 288.   [5] Back-Spindler, IV, p. 25.

valuable; and participles are expressive. All this, we notice, represents a rejection of prose logic in favour of poetic expressiveness. It is *Sprache der Affecte*; and the connection with the theories of Bodmer and Breitinger is close. The German language, says Klopstock, has a certain superfluity of words. It would be good if this could be replaced by richness. This might be done in two ways: by following the direction given by Luther, Opitz and Haller and by imitation of Hebrew, Greek, Latin and some modern languages. German, he thinks, is 'männlich, gedankenvoll, oft kurz'[1] and has a certain flexibility in adopting something of the tone of other languages. In the poem *Unsre Sprache* (1767) we read:

> Den Gedanken, die Empfindung, treffend, und mit Kraft,
> Mit Wendungen der Kühnheit, zu sagen! das ist,
> Sprache des Thuiskon, Göttin, dir,
> Wie unseren Helden Eroberung, ein Spiel!

Klopstock is here asserting that his own stylistic criteria—pregnancy, forcefulness, arrestingness—are the natural qualities of the German language.

These ideas find expansion elsewhere. The arrangement of words in poetry must, he says in the essay entitled *Von der Wortfolge*,[2] be free from the conventionalised order of prose—*must*, not *may*: 'Das Abweichen ist ihm [the poet] also nicht etwa blos erlaubt, sondern es ist Pflicht.' Four principles are recognised as operative forces in poetic inversion: emotion, tension, surprise and euphony. Emotion causes first things to come first; tension and surprise lead to the delaying of some important part of the sentence which in 'cold prose' would come earlier. Poetry must 'etwas erwarten lassen'. It must stimulate expectancy and bring the unexpected. The essay *Vom edlen Ausdrucke*[3] asserts that the most difficult problem in poetic diction is to control the

---

[1] Back-Spindler, IV, p. 27. See also *Der Kranz* (1782) and *Mein Thal* (1795).
[2] Back-Spindler, II, pp. 271 ff.: This was first published in the *Fragmente über Sprache und Dichtkunst* (Hamburg, 1779).
[3] Back-Spindler, II, pp. 283 ff. Also first published in the *Fragmente*, etc. of 1779.

swarm of associations aroused by any word. This is particularly difficult with foreign words. Klopstock then amplifies his criticism of English by a ludicrous translation of the hymn to the light from *Paradise Lost* in which every non-Germanic word is rendered by a *Fremdwort*. The passage begins:[1]

> Sey gegrüßet, heiliges Licht, erstgeborner Sohn des Himmels, oder des Eternellen coeterneller Strahl! Aber darf ich dich unblamirt exprimiren? Denn Gott ist Licht, und wohnte von Eternität her nie anderswo als in unapprochirtem Lichte, wohnte in dir, helle Effluenz der hellen uncreirten Essenz. Oder hörest du lieber: Purer, ätherischer Strom, dessen Fontaine Niemand kennt? Vor der Sonne, vor den Himmeln warest du; und auf Gottes Stimme investirtest du, wie mit einem Mantel, die aus dunkeln und tiefen Wassern emporsteigende Welt, sie, die dem wüsten und formlosen Infiniten entrissen ward. Dich revisitire ich jetzo mit kühnerem Schwunge, echapirt dem stygischen Pfuhle, wie lange mich auch der obscure Sejur detinirte.

There is a footnote to the effect that the foreign words in this translation are no more clumsily used than in the English. He suggests that the English language would be made more expressive if it regained some of its old Germanic words and if it borrowed words from German and adapted them to its Anglo-Saxon forms. His attitude to language seems to have become almost racialist. He advocated enrichment of a language by the imitation of others, but he was opposed to direct borrowing. Everything was to be inbred. He makes the German Language exclaim:

> Wer mich verbrittet, ich hass' ihn! mich gallizismet, ich hass' ihn!
> Liebe dann selbst Günstlinge nicht, wenn sie mich zur Quiritinn
> Machen, und nicht, wenn sie mich verachä'n. Ein erhabnes Beispiel
> Ließ mir Hellänis: Sie bildete sich durch sich![2]

---

[1] Back-Spindler, II, p. 289; cf. *Paradise Lost*, the beginning of Book III. This essay was originally printed in Klopstock's reformed orthography, which aimed at phonetic reproduction. The first ideas for this are to be found in the *Gelehrtenrepublik* (see below, p. 326). The system is described and illustrated in the essay *Über die deutsche Rechtschreibung* (Back-Spindler, II, pp. 145–240; first published in the *Fragmente über Sprache und Dichtkunst* (Hamburg, 1779)). He ran into difficulties because there was still no agreement on correct pronunciation.

[2] *Unsere Sprache an uns* (1796). I quote Klopstock's Odes from the edition by Muncker and Pawel, 2 vols. (Stuttgart, 1889), which reprints faithfully the *final* text. This is vol. II, p. 129.

This defiant nationalism is the keynote of *Die deutsche Gelehrtenrepublik* (1774), which has much to say on language.[1] Those who despise their native language are banished from the republic. German can hold its own with all other languages. It is 'eine reichhaltige, vollblühende, fruchtschwere, tönende, gemesne, freye, bildsame, männliche, edle, und vortrefliche Sprache, der es kaum die griechische, und keine der andern Europäersprachen bieten darf'.[2] Scattered throughout the *Gelehrtenrepublik* are sections of the Grammar that Klopstock never completed. As his criterion of correctness he accepts only usage, and in doubtful cases the usage of good writers.[3] He makes certain initial proposals towards a phonetic spelling.[4] He attempts a systematic analysis of word-formation and of declensional types, using his own German names for the elements of grammar. He is bitterly opposed to *Fremdwörter*. Nowhere are they more ludicrous than in the language of poetry. In this respect he again attacks English. There is much talk of the language of poetry, of the uselessness of rules, of the sole criterion of imagination, of *Handlung* (by which he means not external action but conscious direction of will-power towards a goal) and *Leidenschaft*, of portrayal rather than description, of the dangers of polish and the value of roughness. Just the stuff for a young poet! No wonder Goethe was so enthusiastic about it.

Patriotic fervour also permeates the *Grammatische Gespräche*, written down late in Klopstock's life but planned over many years.[5] The second dialogue (*Die Aussprache*) defends 'unsere

---

[1] I quote from the original edition (Hamburg, 1774), copy in the British Museum.

[2] *Ed. cit.* p. 169.

[3] *Ibid.* p. 225. But not the *Kanzleistil*: 'Er gehört eben so wenig zur Sprache, als die Mundarten dazu gehören' (*ibid.* p. 228).

[4] *Ibid.* p. 236. Abandonment of *ph, qu, th, dt, c, y*; introduction of a sign of length; simplification of double consonants. These points were later developed into a full system, see note 1 to p. 325 above.

[5] Eleven dialogues were planned: 1. *Grammatik*; 2. *Aussprache*; 3. *Wohlklang*; 4. *Wortbildung*; 5. *Sylbenzeit*; 6. *Wortänderniß*; 7. *Kühr*; 8. *Wortänderung*; 9. *Wortfolge*; 10. *Verskunst*; 11. *Bedeutsamkeit*. Of these, nos. 1–4, no. 7 and a fragment of no. 8 were published together at Altona in 1794. These are contained in Back-Spindler, vol. I, together with a fragment of no. 10. Fragments

männliche Sprache' against French objections to its guttural sound. 'Töne, welche zu tief aus dem Halse heraufkommen, verrathen ihm [the frenchman] Barbarey; und Töne, die man mit Selbstgefallen in die Nase hinauftreibt, überfeine Kultur', Klopstock exclaims ironically.[1] The tone is petulant and almost chauvinistic. He envies the French language its universally acclaimed excellence and seeks for arguments in favour of German. It is stronger and more forthright than French, it does not 'verschleyern' and 'verschönern'. On the other hand it is timid in comparison with English and a shy cousin alongside Greek. The comparison with Greek is continued in the third dialogue (*Der Wohlklang*) where Klopstock attempts to prove that they have words in common (developing Plato's mention of the words derived by Greek from Scythian, 'dem ersten Quell des Deutschen'), shows that he knows that German originally had reduplication and dual number, and points to the ease with which both languages form compounds. Both languages can be rough-sounding on occasions, German through its consonant clusters and Greek through its diphthongs. Twofold rection of prepositions and terseness of style are claimed, in other dialogues, as properties common to both languages. The argument is insistent, monotonous and not always convincing. The third dialogue branches off rather unexpectedly into an attack on the chancery sentence, called variously *regensburger Perioden* or *Heiligerömischereichsperioden* or *Heiligerömischreichdeutschernazionsperioden*. Equally absurd, however, is what he calls the *Wasistdaswasdasistwashaftigkeit* (or *Qu'estcequec'estqueitüde*) of French. The dialogue on word-formation contains some peculiar etymologies but shows appreciation of the true nature and value of suffixes. He objects to the *-iren* suffix in verbs, and parodies the misuse of some adjectival suffixes.[2] He disapproves of *Gerngroß* and *Gernwitz* (because *seyn/haben* must be understood), of *Springins-*

---

of the others are contained in Back-Spindler, vol. II. Schleiden (*Klopstocks Dichtungstheorie*, p. 156) argues that the dialogues were written between 1780 and 1788.

[1] Back-Spindler, I, p. 20. [2] *Ibid.* pp. 163–6.

feld (because it is, he thinks, constructed on the model of *bec en l'air* and therefore unnatural to the language) and of too cumbrous compounds like *Körperundgeisterwelt* which are 'half word and half phrase or a vile cross between the two'. In the fragment of the eleventh dialogue[1] he lists a number of neologisms to which he objects, mostly with justification. But amongst them figure *Staatsbürger* and *Geschmacksurteil* which Klopstock considers tautological formations and compares jocularly with *Wasserfisch*.[2] He objects on logical grounds to *geringfügig*, which was in common usage by this time: 'Was sich fügt, das fügt sich mehr oder weniger gut: aber nichts fügt sich gering. Geringfügig kann nicht bedeuten, was es bedeuten soll.'[3] In all cases he demands respect for the natural properties of the German language.

The 1782 ode addressed to Cramer and entitled simply *Die Sprache* describes the greater expressiveness attained by poetry because of its combination of *Wohlklang* and *Verstand*. The poem begins:

> Des Gedankens Zwilling, das Wort scheint Hall nur,
> Der in die Luft hinfließt; heiliges Band
> Des Sterblichen ist es, erhebt
> Die Vernunft ihm, und das Herz ihm!

Vernunft seems to be identified for Klopstock with prose and *Herz* with poetry. The best expression of this is in the essay *Von der heiligen Poesie* to be found in the first volume of the 1760 Halle edition of *Der Messias*. The passage runs:

> Die höhere Poesie ist ein Werk des Genie; und sie soll nur selten einige Züge des Witzes, zum Ausmalen, anwenden.
> Es giebt Werke des Witzes, die Meisterstücke sind, ohne daß das Herz etwas dazu beygetragen hatte. Allein, das Genie ohne Herz, wäre nur halbes Genie. Die letzten und höchsten Wirkungen der Werke des Genie sind, daß sie die ganze Seele bewegen. Wir können hier einige Stufen der starken und der stärkern Empfindung hinaufsteigen.

---

[1] First published in the *Berlinisches Archiv der Zeit und ihres Geschmacks* for 1795. Back-Spindler, II, pp. 115 ff.
[2] The *DWb.* suggests that *Staatsbürger* is first found in Wieland (1789) and *Geschmacksurteil* in Kant (1790).
[3] Back-Spindler, II, 131.

Dieß ist der Schauplatz des Erhabenen. Wer es für einen geringen Unterschied hält, die Seele leicht rühren; oder sie ganz in allen ihren mächtigen Kräften, bewegen: der denkt nicht würdig genung von ihr.[1]

The conviction that the language of poetry is and must be quite different from that of prose is the generating force in Klopstock's use of language. Yet his avoidance of the ordinary proceeds not, as with Gottsched, from a desire to be civilised but from a determination to be powerful. In *Der Messias* he is obsessed by the problem of finding expression commensurate with his subject. Verbs like *rauben, jammern, umgeben* are not enough; they are replaced by *abzwingen, wehklagen, umfliessen* respectively. Similarly *herumtragen* becomes *umhertragen, herumsehen* becomes *ringsumhersehen*. In some places we even find *befehlen* changed to *gebieten* and *anfangen* to *beginnen*. *Den Abfall wagen* is intensified into *zur Empörung sich aufschwingen*; and *umbringen* is replaced by the absurd, though certainly expressive neologism *wegwürgen*.[2]

If we analyse long enough, we find certain recurrent types of enlivenment, some old and some new. Amongst the verbs we notice use of the simplex instead of the more usual compound. The result is sometimes a striking transitive construction, as in Christ's admonition to the daughters of Jerusalem: 'Weinet mich nicht.' Occasionally the effect is archaic and we may possibly adduce the influence of Luther whose language we know he admired.[3] This archaism is found occasionally in other poets of

---

[1] *Ibid.* IV, pp. 89–90.
[2] These examples are selected from Petri's comparison of the 1748, 1755 and 1780 versions of *Der Messias*. They are all from the second and third cantos.
[3] 'Niemand, der weiß, was eine Sprache ist,' he said in the *Gelehrtenrepublik*, 'erscheine ohne Ehrerbietung vor Luthern. Unter keinem Volke hat Ein Mann so viel an seiner Sprache gebildet' (orig. ed. (Hamburg, 1774), p. 170); and in the ode *Die deutsche Bibel*, he mocks at Luther's detractors:

> 'Weder die Sitte, noch der Sprache Weise
> Kennen sie, und es ist der reinen Keuschheit
> Ihnen Mährchen! was sich erhebt, was Kraft hat,
> Edleres, Thorheit!
>
> Dunkel auf immer ihnen jener Gipfel,
> Den du muthig erstiegst, und dort des Vater-
> Landes Sprache bildetest, zu der Engel
> Sprach', und der Menschen.' (Muncker-Pawel, II, p. 61.)

the first half of the century and is a characteristic element in Haller's terse style. Thus: 'Schmeichler *betteln* Gnaden', 'Zwar die Gelehrtheit *feilscht* hier nicht papierne Schätze', '(er) *hoffet* keinen Tod', 'Wie? sollte dich die Liebe *schrecken?* Mit Scham mag sich das Laster *decken*', 'Dort *kürzt* ein schnelles Bley den Lauf getriebner Böcken'.[1] But Klopstock makes it his own and develops it to hitherto unknown proportions, bestowing on these unexpectedly transitive verbs the most startling objects:

> Cidli, du weinest, und ich schlumre sicher,
> Wo im Sande der Weg verzogen fortschleicht;
> Auch wenn stille Nacht ihn umschattend decket,
> Schlumr' ich ihn sicher.[2]

or:
> Der Weltraum *fernt mich weit* von dir,
> So *fernt mich nicht* die Zeit.[3]

or:
> sie dachten Schönheit,[4]

or:
> der Erguß tönet Verein.[5]

As a complement to this we note the use of verbal prefixes to form new derivatives. Novelty ensures that the prefix has expressive function which it has lost in well-worn words in normal usage. Hence for Klopstock *fernen* (as we have just seen) is more expressive than *entfernen*,[6] but *entstrahlen* than *strahlen*. 'Der Abendstern *entstrahlte* dem Himmel' he writes; or, with a different type of meaning: 'Wälder *entnebeln* ihr Antlitz.'[7] This feature is also found in Haller: in casual reading I have noticed *entbauchte*

---

[1] Hirzel, pp. 78, 24, 123, 82, 302.
[2] *Furcht der Geliebten* (1753). My italics, as in all the examples which follow. Muncker-Pawel, I, p. 113.
[3] *Das Wiedersehn* (1797), *ibid.* II, p. 136.
[4] *An Giacomo Zigno* (1783), *ibid.* II, p. 53.
[5] *Die deutsche Sprache* (1783), *ibid.* II, p. 55.
[6] Also, no doubt, because the privative sense of the prefix is already implied by the meaning of the verb.
[7] In quoting from *Der Messias* I use Hamel's edition (see above, p. 321) for the 1748 text of the first three cantos and for the final, 1799, text. I have also used the copies in the British Museum of the 1755, 1769, 1773 and 1780 editions. Line-numbering is only found in Hamel and in the 1755 edition; for other editions I have therefore had to give page references. These two phrases are to be found in XV, p. 243 (1769 edn.) and I, line 606 (1748 edn., Hamel).

Hunde and *entadeln*. The prefix has powerful dynamic force. Klopstock uses other prefixes of movement in a similar way. Here are some striking examples from *Der Messias*:

(a) Schimmernd *reifte* sie *auf* im frohen Garbengefilde
(b) Seine dem Tode noch kaum *entgegenringende* Seele
(c) ...o wie reif *schimmerst* du *her*.
(d) ...den (acc.) David (subject) ....
  Gern aus den Armen des Vaters *heruntergebetet* hätte.[1]

Extensive use is also made of the prefix *er-* to form new transitives (*ergraben, erluften, erschweben*); similarly striking is a phrase like 'Friede *beascht* jetzt schlummernde Glut'.[2] Both represent the survival of a favourite linguistic feature of seventeenth-century poetic diction. Past participles in *be-*, of the old baroque type which we saw persisting in Günther and Brockes, are also found; but, according to Petri, not at all commonly in the earlier poems. This would seem to indicate conscious adoption of an archaic device in order to heighten expression.

New derivatives are not the only means employed by Klopstock towards the attainment of strong effects with verbs. He sometimes revels in unusual compounds:

Wehklagen, und bang Seufzen vom Graunthale des Abgrunds her,
Sturmheulen, und Strombrüllen, und Felskrachen, das laut niederstürzt',
Und Wuthschrein, und Rachausrufen, erscholl dumpf auf![3]

This virtuosity is not restricted to infinitives. It is also found in finite tenses: '...Gedanken *spinnwebt*', '*wehdroht* mir die Nacht'.[4] It is especially fruitful with participles. The type represented by '*ruhigschweigender* Mittler', '*geradefortlaufende* Länge', '*sanftwandelnde* Stimme'—with adverbial modifier as first element—is found already in his earliest poems.[5] Later we find bolder

[1] (a) XI, p. 27 (1769 edn.); (b) II, line 142 (1748, Hamel); (c) XX, p. 194 (1773 edn.); (d) IV, lines 400–1 (1755 edn.). My italics.
[2] *Delphi* (1782); Muncker-Pawel, II, p. 45.
[3] *Messias*, XX, p. 198 (1773 edn.). [4] Muncker-Pawel, II, 121, 55.
[5] *Messias*, II, lines 192, 270, 65 (1748, Hamel).

combinations like 'der *wankendströmende* Jordan', '*überschweng-lichtröstender* Anblick'.¹ A similar type has substantive as first element. This, according to Petri, is not frequent until the 1750's. The simpler examples are easily analysable into object + verbal governor (*abschiednehmendes* Lächeln); but later we find looser combinations where the first element is equivalent to an oblique case or prepositional phrase. Petri notes '*himmelringende* Seele', '*himmelfallende* Blitze', '*himmelfliegendes* Erstaunen', and '*himmelsteigende* Wogen' where the relationship between the two elements of the compound is different in each case.² In later cantos of *Der Messias* he notes '*grabverlangende* Blicke'; '*jammerhallende* Ufer'; and in a 1782 ode, '*kentnißdurstende* Seele'.³ In a 1796 ode, I find the phrase 'mit *schreckenrauschenden* Seilen'.⁴ Similar compounds are found with a past participle as second element. The type with adverbial modifier as first element (*hocherfreut, treugesinnt*) was nothing new; but Klopstock develops this possibility to include looser constructions like '*banggerungene* Hände', '*feuriggeflügelte* Worte' and '*schwarzbehautet*'.⁵ The pattern with substantival first element was common in the poetical language before Klopstock. We had *mit Dank- und Lust-erfüll'ter Brust* in the Brockes poem on May. Klopstock abandons hyphenation (still found in Haller who uses the type frequently)⁶ and again expands the range of the formation to embrace looser but expressive combinations: '*weisheitverlassene* Hoffnung', '*aschebedeckte* Gebeine'.⁷

We noted earlier that Hagedorn packed his meaning into the

---

¹ *Messias*, XIII, p. 122 (1769 edn.) and XIV, p. 156 (1769 edn.).

² *Ibid.* X, line 932 (1755 edn.) and XI, p. 39 (1769 edn.); Muncker-Pawel, I, p. 138 and II, p. 12. See Professor Purdie's article in *GR* (see above, p. 323, for the reference), which discusses these more fully, *ibid.* pp. 90–1.

³ *Messias*, IX, line 391 (1755 edn.); IX, line 506 (1755 edn.); Muncker-Pawel, II, p. 47.

⁴ Muncker-Pawel, II, p. 119.

⁵ *Messias*, X, line 19 (1755 edn.); XIX, p. 124 (1773 edn.); Muncker-Pawel, II, p. 99.

⁶ The type with adverbial first element also tends to show hyphenation in the early eighteenth century (*bunt-gefärbtes Licht*, etc.).

⁷ *Messias*, XI, pp. 35 and 59 (1769 edn.). On these compound past participles, see Purdie, *op. cit.* p. 91.

nouns. Klopstock, in contrast, concentrates his in verbs. Unusual formations amongst verbs include:

> Und wenn es nun gar mit ihm
> *Kleinelt* und *zwergelt*...[1]

and, representing the same depreciatory force of the suffix, *äugeln, künsteln, richteln, kunstwörtelnd*.[2] This shows development of the opportunities offered by an existing suffix. Another instance is the verb *jährigen*:

> Mit Einem Winke giebst du, und nimst du ja
> Dem Wurm, dem Stunden sind wie Jahrhunderte,
> Sein kurzes Glück; dem Wurm, der Mensch heißt,
> *Jähriget*, blühet, verblüht, und abfällt.[3]

Examples of this expansion of the productivity of a suffix could be multiplied; it is not the number of examples that matters but the principle at work. Similar exploitation of expressive potential can be seen in the sphere of syntax. Bodmer, we remember, had admired English for its ability to use intransitive verbs in certain constructions with transitive force and had suggested parallels in German. Klopstock experiments in this:

> Hör', es wiehert unten dein Roß, aus der Burg dich zu *tanzen*
> Zu der Schaar, die Schlachten uns spielt,[4]

Concentration of expression produces unusual transitive usage in a phrase like *sie lächelten Liebe*.[5] A quasi-cognate accusative, closely related in meaning to the root-meaning of the verb, may be used instead of the more normal adverb extension. There is a gain in freshness and precision. This becomes one of Klopstock's favourite constructions. Bolder examples are: *Christus blutete Gnade; sie stammeln Erwartung; schaute Verderben; die Seelen schauerten Wonne*.[6] It may be that what we have called

---

[1] Muncker-Pawel, II, p. 13.
[2] The last example is from the ode *Der Genügsame* (1796); Muncker-Pawel, II, p. 121.   [3] *An Gott* (1748); Muncker-Pawel, I, p. 74.
[4] Muncker-Pawel, II, p. 70.
[5] *Messias*, XV, p. 228 (1769 edn.); cf. XVI, p. 31 (1773 edn.).
[6] *Messias*, XVIII, p. 94 (1773 edn.); VI, lines 423 and 433 (1755 edn.) and VIII, line 480 (1755 edn.).

Haller's 'abstract metonymy' has been influential on this construction. Haller's influence may well also be detected in Klopstock's affection for participial constructions. He praises their brevity in the *Grammatische Gespräche*.[1] He also favoured their attributive use, often preferring them to normal adjectives because of their extra dimension of time. In the first canto of the 1748 *Messias* I note: 'den *grünenden* Arm', 'im *kühlenden* Erdreich', '*wandelndes* Jauchzen', 'in *donnernden* Wettern gesprochen', '*sanftthränendes* Auge', 'dein *tödtend* Gerichte'. These effects are sometimes quite extraordinary: *aus nebelndem Quell*; *die Kinder der mordenden Stadt*.[2] This last example is from the 1780 revision of *Der Messias* and replaces *die Kinder der mördrischen Stadt*. Such replacement is frequent.[3] Substantivations like *der Erlösende* for normal *der Erlöser* also form a constant element of Klopstock's later style.

Desire for saturated meaning also lies behind the contention advanced in the *Grammatische Gespräche* that 'Wehmuth, Thränen' is better than 'Wehmüthige Thränen' because it is stronger. Similarly that 'in der wüthenden Verzweiflung' is less expressive than 'in der Wuth, der Verzweiflung'. And the force should not be weakened by the insertion of an *und* after the

[1] In the seventh *Gespräch*.
[2] *Messias*, II, line 372 (1748, Hamel); III, p. 83 (1780 edn.).
[3] In the nineteenth *Literaturbrief* Lessing claims that Klopstock replaced participles which had made the verse heavy or obscure. His examples would, however, seem to be incorrectly interpreted. Thus, of Satan:

'Daß er noch durch so viele Jahrhunderte, seit der Erschaffung
In der ersten von Gott ihm gegebenen Herrlichkeit glänzte.'

becomes (second line only) in 1755:

'In der Herrlichkeit glänzte, die ihm der Donnerer anschuf.'

But surely the point of this is not to remove the participle, but to place *Herrlichkeit glänzte* in a more prominent position and to gain extra force with *Donnerer* and *anschuf*. Lessing's other example is:

'Seine von allen Göttern so lange gewünschte Zurückkunft'

becoming:

'Seine Zurückkunft, auf welche die Götter so lange schon harrten.'

I should interpret this as bringing the important word *Zurückkunft* into greater relief and replacing the pallid *wünschen* by the more active *harren*. Lachmann-Muncker, VIII, p. 50.

comma.¹ This would seem to be a peculiar lingering of the baroque love of asyndeton and pleonastic compounds; but re-interpreted in the light of a new stylistic. Striking, and again reminiscent of Haller, is the preservation of the old fuller meaning of the oblique cases. This is also a gain in concision and strength. We find the genitive in adverbial usage:

>Die er auch *frommes Herzens* begann...²

in partitive usage:
>Du sandtest
>*Deiner Krieger* hin.³

as extension of an interjection (*O der Aussicht drüben!*). The dative has also often a much fuller meaning than in normal prose usage:

>...da strahlt's von dem Frühling, der *uns* ewig
>Blüht, und duftet, und weht.⁴

or: 'nur *sich und dem Sohne* vernommen', '*dir* kaum bemerkt' and many other examples. Characteristic is the replacement of:

>...daß schon so viele Gerechte
>*Zu mir* sich sammeln, und nun bald alle Geschlechte der Menschen
>*Durch mich* geheiliget werden! (1748)

by:
>Sich *mir* sammeln, und nun bald alle Geschlechte der Menschen
>*Mir* sich heiligen werden. (1755)

which attains compression at the price of obscurity.⁵ This is what Goethe was referring to when he said, in *Dichtung und Wahrheit*, of Klopstock: 'Durch seinen Wettstreit mit den Alten, besonders dem Tacitus, sieht er sich immer mehr ins Enge genötigt, wodurch er zuletzt unverständlich und ungenießbar wird.' Very peculiar, to say the least, is the accusative in:

>Dann wird ein Tag seyn, *den* werd ich auferstehn!
>Dann wird ein Tag seyn, *den* wirst du auferstehn!⁶

---

¹ In the seventh *Gespräch*. ² *Messias*, III, p. 78 (1780 edn.).
³ Muncker-Pawel, I, p. 221. ⁴ *Ibid.* II, p. 26.
⁵ This is Canto I, lines 109 ff. of the 1748 version (Hamel).
⁶ *An Fanny* (1748), Muncker-Pawel, I, p. 64.

This would seem to be an extension of the old accusative-of-time construction (*nächsten Mittwoch*). Compare:

> Ach ist es ihnen nicht genung, auf sich selber zu donnern?
> Sich zu spießen *die Tage der Schlacht?*[1]

The originality, boldness and manneredness of this language aroused opposition in several quarters. The general criticism was that it did violence to the spirit of the German language—that it was un-German and not German. Thus Haller complains that the ode *An Gott* is 'écrit dans un allemand-latin, qui n'eut jamais son égal'.[2] Bodmer mentions that it was the 'griechische und lateinische Deutsch in der Messiade' which was the main point of attack.[3] Perhaps some such objection also lay behind Novalis's rather summary dismissal of Klopstock's work as 'größtentheils freie Übersetzungen und Bearbeitungen eines unbekannten Dichters durch einen sehr talentvollen, aber unpoetischen Philologen'.[4] Herder took a more positive view of this refashioning of German under classical influence. In the second part of *Terpsichore* (1795) he says of Klopstock's classical metres:

> Er hat uns in diesen Gedanken- und Empfindungsweisen der Alten für unsre eigensten und reinsten Empfindungen gleichsam eine neue Sprache geschaffen, und damit dem innigsten Gemüth eine Bildung, der Seele eine Selbsterkenntniß, dem Herzen einen Ausdruck, der Sprache eine Zartheit, Fülle und Wohlklang verliehen, von der man vor ihm nicht träumte.[5]

The Gottschedians objected to the strong division between prose and poetry. Schönaich, in his *Neologisches Wörterbuch* of 1754,[6] mocks at this *sehraffische Dichtkunst* whose 'divine inspiration'

---

[1] *Die Lerche, und die Nachtigall* (1796), Muncker-Pawel, II, p. 119.

[2] Letter to Tscharner of 26 January 1752. S. Levy, *Klopstock und die Antike* (Diss. Munich, 1923), considers in great detail the influence of Latin and Greek on Klopstock's word-formation and syntax. His conclusions are that Klopstock develops many of these features to an extent not found in the classical languages. Purdie (*op. cit.* p. 94) agrees and speaks of his 'imaginative daring'—which seems to me exactly the right description.

[3] *Edward Grandisons Geschichte in Görlitz*, p. 39.

[4] Works, ed. Kluckhohn and Samuel, II, p. 328.

[5] Works, ed. Suphan, XXVII, p. 172.

[6] Reprint edited by A. Köster in the *Neudrucke* series, Berlin, 1900.

rejects normal syntax and vocabulary in order to be interesting. For instance: 'So kann man nicht in der heiligen Dichtkunst sagen, *von Soldaten bewacht*. Das wäre zwar der Sprachlehre gemäß; aber es ist zu langweilig. Sprich z.E. *Nachtwächterbewacht*: das wird schön seyn.' Or again, with reference to the phrase '*dir* bäthen unsterbliche Menschen': 'Die Gebeendung ist in der heiligen Dichtkunst heilig; wie überhaupt alle mögliche Fehler wider die Sprache: ihre Regeln schaden dem Hohen: sie können sie daher nicht beobachten.'[1] Nowhere in this welter of tedious, ironic persiflage is there any appreciation of the poetic significance of Klopstock's language. Nor any desire or attempt to appreciate it. But this was hardly to be expected. Schönaich's attitude to metaphor is still that of Gottsched twenty-five years before. And his understanding of poetry is no further advanced.

Amongst the more individual elements of Klopstock's style we notice a further development of what I have called Haller's 'abstract metonymy'.[2] For example:

> ... Überall faltete noch *die tiefe Verwundrung*
> Heilige Hände vor ihm.[3]

God has just revealed the mystery of man's redemption to the worshipping angels. *Die tiefe Verwundrung* refers therefore to an assembly of persons. In this respect one recalls Schiller's criticism of Klopstock: 'Man möchte sagen, er ziehe allem, was er behandelt, den Körper aus, um es zu Geist zu machen.' The disembodied result, according to Schiller, was consciously envisaged as part of Klopstock's stylistic intentions; *um es zu Geist zu machen* is not an objective connotation of result but a subjective expression of intention. But whereas Goethe saw in this unplastic nature of Klopstock's art the absence of poetry, Schiller accepted Klopstock as a '*musikalischer* Dichter' who expresses states of mind directly without recourse to the intermediary of actions or

---

[1] *Ed. cit.* pp. 106–7 and 39. He also objects to Klopstock's forceful omission of purely grammatical elements, his great use of prefix-formations, his metaphorical language, his rhetorical use of repetition and personification.
[2] See above, p. 271; for something similar in Hagedorn, see above, p. 260.
[3] *Messias*, I, lines 467–8 (1748, Hamel; remodelled in the later versions).

things. Interesting is Erich Schmidt's suggestion[1] that this incorporeal nature of Klopstock's language represents the final extreme of reaction against the excessive imagery of the later seventeenth century. Haller's 'abstract metonymy' seemed to us to be induced by some striving after the universal. How is one to interpret this feature in Klopstock's style? Peculiar is the use of a plural in this sort of construction. For example:

> Ich muß schauen dahin, wo deine *Verwesungen* ruhen.[2]

The meaning is 'mortal remains'; and would seem to stand here for more normal 'Gebeine'. But there is a difference. Compare the following passage:

> Neben einander begrub Ein Grab vier Freunde. Dem Hügel
> War das Felsengewölbe, worunter die Leichname ruhten,
> Im Erdbeben entstürzt. Sie sahen ihre *Gebeine*
> Ueber ihrer *Verwesungen* eingesunkenen Asche
> Liegen, und segneten diese zerstreuten Trümmern des Lebens,
> Mit dem Wunsche nach Auferstehung.[3]

This meaning is vaguer and wider. It means corruption of the *whole* body. Two more examples shall serve to validate the point:

(a) Als wenn über die Schöpfung umher ein allmächtiger Tod läg,
    Und in allen Welten nur stille *Verwesungen* schliefen...

(b)   Der hangende Himmel
    Wölbt sich um Golgatha, wie um *Verwesungen* Todtengewölbe....[4]

Here is a less straightforward passage:

> Erstaunen! himmelfliegendes Erstaunen!
> Über den, der unendlich ist!
> O du *der Seligkeiten höchste*,
> Überströme du meine ganze Seele
>
> Mit deinem heiligen Feuer!
> Und laß sie, du Seligkeit,
> So oft, und so hoch die Endliche kann,
> Aufflammen in *Entzückungen*![5]

---

[1] *Lessing*, 4th edn. (Berlin, 1923), vol. II, p. 531.
[2] *Messias*, V, line 552 (1755 edn.).   [3] *Messias*, XI, p. 51 (1769 edn.).
[4] (a) *Messias*, VIII, lines 254–5 (1755 edn.); (b) *Messias*, VIII, lines 486–7 (1755 edn.).   [5] *Der Erbarmer* (1759); Muncker-Pawel, I, p. 138.

The figure here occurs twice: the first time as normal baroque emphasis, the second time, however, with much more individual colouring and equivalent to 'states of ecstasy'. This use recalls Middle High German 'daz wære ein unmanheit' etc., with similar individualised sense. Klopstock even addressed his abstract as an individual, *du Seligkeit*; and the plural *Entzückungen* is a logical outcome of this individualisation. Use of a plural abstract to denote individual occurrences of a state or quality is found regularly in Klopstock. For instance:

> (*a*)   Wie hat uns der Mittler
> Mit *Barmherzigkeiten*, mit Huld, mit Gnade beseligt!
>
> (*b*)   Ich maß mein daurendes Leben
> Nach der Ewigkeit ab, und zählte die seligen Tage
> Nach der Zahl der *Erbarmungen* Gottes.[1]

Or again, this time from one of the most celebrated of his shorter poems:

> Wenn der Schimmer von dem Monde nun herab
> In die Wälder sich ergießt, und Gerüche
> Mit den Düften von der Linde
> In den *Kühlungen* wehn:[2]

The sense would seem, at first sight, to be 'cool places'; and as a formation one might compare English 'clearings'. The effect is quite charming. And the abstractness seems to enhance the effect. There is a coolness everywhere which is, in fact, various sorts of coolness, produced by different contributory factors in different sets of circumstances. Coolnesses. The word has an embracing power. It is something more than 'cool *places*'; coolnesses. There are coolnesses everywhere, all pervaded by scents and perfumes. Each different in itself, but each cool. And all of them transfigured by the calm light of the summer moon and brought to coolness by it; so that the forest is an amalgam of coolnesses. The plural and the abstractness are essential to the peculiar nature of the poetic idea. It would seem therefore that although this

---

[1] (*a*) *Messias*, XI, p. 13 (1769 edn.); (*b*) *Messias*, XIX, p. 123 (1773 edn.).
[2] *Die Sommernacht* (1766); Muncker-Pawel, I, p. 179.

element of abstractness in Klopstock's poetic vocabulary may seem at first acquaintance to conflict with his general striving after pungent, vivid expression, it is part of his conscious avoidance of prose. Like many other features of Klopstock's language it tends to become a mannerism. But it can—as we have just seen—be the expression of a poetic sensibility of great charm and distinction.

This cultivation of abstractness distinguishes Klopstock sharply from Milton. Temperamentally and stylistically the two writers have very little in common, and it is important that we should realise this. Both certainly strove after elevated expression such as is demanded by the epic. But we must not let talk of 'Miltonic diction' and 'the Miltonic vague' suggest that there is any deep stylistic affinity between Milton and Klopstock. In both, the search for noble expression was largely guided by intense affection for the classics. Thus we shall find in Milton a love of participles— particularly of compound participles—such as we have already noted in Klopstock (*sceptred* angels, *grazed* ox, *straw-built* citadel, *all-ruling* sire, *heaven-warring* champions, *night-warbling* bird, *love-laboured* song, *star-paved* heaven, *night-foundered* skiff).[1] We shall also find hosts of unusual (often, one suspects, invented) words. Many of them are of highly Latinate appearance (*concoctive, intelligential, eternise, umbrageous, hyacinthine, irriguous, opacous, orbicular, horrent*), others show development of native material along native lines (*unbottomed, imbosomed, inwove, imbrowned, slumberous, unsmooth, disrelished, unwiser*).[2] There is often a Latinate quality about the syntax of both writers. In interpreting difficult passages in Klopstock, Lessing admitted: 'ich mußte hier und da die lateinische Sprache mit zu Hülfe nehmen.'[3] Similar comments were, and still are, made concerning the language of Milton. Both were classically nourished. Both

---

[1] My examples in this section are taken entirely from *Paradise Lost*.

[2] It is interesting to note that an early draft for the poem bore the title: 'Adam Unparadized.'

[3] Review of *Der Messias* in second part of *Schrifften*, Berlin, 1753. Lachmann-Muncker, v, p. 90.

delighted in grand, full-sounding words. Both abhorred and instinctively avoided the commonplace. But here the resemblance stops. For Milton is an immensely graphic, concrete writer. Where in Klopstock does one find epithets like: 'the sleepy drench / Of that forgetful lake', 'the sport and prey / Of racking whirlwinds', 'the amorous descant of the nightingale', 'the spicy forest', 'the shrub unfumed' or 'the madding wheels of brazen chariots'? There is nothing akin to those dazzling comparisons with the leaves of Vallombrosa, the locusts of Egypt, the pines of Norway, bees in springtime, summer's noontide air, the cany waggons of the Chineses, or those 'who sail / Beyond the Cape of Hope, and now are past / Mozambic'. Nothing to approach the way in which words are made graphic by unusual contexts:

> A thousand demi-gods on golden seats
> *Frequent* and full...

or the tree of life

> High eminent, blooming ambrosial fruit
> Of *vegetable* gold.

or the other trees in the garden

> ...whose fruit, burnished with golden rind
> Hung *amiable*.

No matter how immense the scene or the character, everything seems to be envisaged with knife-edge clarity in Milton's imagination. His hosts of Hell move 'in perfect phalanx to the Dorian mood / Of flutes and soft recorders'. The battle of the angels, the creation of the world and the Garden of Eden are all presented with a wealth of colourful and precise detail. By this means his supernatural beings are brought quite close to ordinary men and women. His angels eat and sleep, sing and dance—'like the Greek gods' says a German critic at the end of the eighteenth century. The implication is that such conduct was unworthy of Christian angels. This critic, one C. F. Benkowitz in a prize essay entitled *Der Messias von Klopstok* [sic], *aesthetisch beurtheilt und verglichen mit der Iliade, der Aeneide und dem verlohrnen Paradiese*

(Breslau, 1797),[1] compares Abbadona's description of his former bliss in Canto XIX of Klopstock's poem:

> Mit schattendem Flügel
> Deckte mich ewiges Heil! In jeder Aussicht sah ich
> Seligkeiten um mich! Mir jauchzt' ich in meiner Entzückung,
> Daß ich geschaffen war, zu. Ich war, geliebet zu werden
> Von dem Besten der Wesen! Ich maß mein dauerndes Leben
> Nach der Ewigkeit ab, und zählte die seligen Tage
> Nach der Zahl der Erbarmungen Gottes!² [2]

and comments: 'Der Dichter lässt sich nicht auf das Specielle der Seligkeit ein, aber er vermeidet auch, unwahrscheinlich zu werden, und unter der Würde seines Gegenstandes zu schreiben.'[3] He therefore prefers Klopstock for the reason that we prefer Milton. This may well be an interesting clue to the reason for Klopstock's abstractness. It may well have been induced by the desire to be reverent. Earthly comparisons would be blasphemous, concreteness incompatible with the sublime. Benkowitz's essay is a defence of the *style noble*. Comparing Homer and Klopstock describing the washing of hands, he finds that the German has 'geschmücktere Ausdrücke'. He attains greater sublimity by avoiding the ordinary terms of human experience. Homer has 'nichts als unverschönerte Natur'. He describes the blinding of Polyphemus with revolting detail. But Klopstock is reticent in scenes of physical violence like the flagellation:

> Doch mir sinket die Hand die Harf herab, ich vermag nicht,
> Alle Leiden des ewigen Sohns, sie alle zu singen![4]

Whereas Homer describes Hera boxing the ears of Artemis, Klopstock avoids direct expression of Christ being struck by the officer of the High Priest. All he says is:

> da that ein Knecht, mit knechtischer Seele,
> Eine That, die niedrig genung war, Unmenschlichkeiten
> Zu verkündigen.[5]

---

[1] Copy in the British Museum. Benkowitz lived from 1764 to 1807 and was a minor novelist of the period.
[2] 1799 text; Hamel, lines 164 ff.   [3] *Op. cit.* p. 58.
[4] *Messias*, VII, lines 816–17 (1755 edn.).
[5] *Messias*, VI, lines 180–2 (1755 edn.).

Milton is too precise. He expresses himself too much in the language of *human* experience. Like Homer and Virgil describing Olympus, Milton creates his Heaven out of his imagination and in terms of earthly palaces. It even has a staircase. Whereas Klopstock 'lässt die Einbildungskraft aus dem Spiel, und stellt ihn so dar, wie er wirklich seyn kann, *wie die Verstand ihn haben will*'. That is to say: Heaven is described according to what it represents in Christian doctrine. 'Klopstok schildert alles, wie es der Grösse Gottes gemäss ist.' It may well be that Benkowitz has correctly appreciated the motive force behind Klopstock's disembodiedness. His treatise represents the obverse of Goethe's comments to Eckermann. Both arrive by the same arguments at opposite conclusions. Both establish that Klopstock is lacking in concreteness and plasticity. For Goethe this is unpoetic, for Benkowitz it is the sublime.

We have now seen Klopstock's conception of poetic language and analysed it into its constituent elements. It has been suggested by quite recent research that some of these elements might have come from pietism.[1] One can, however, show that of all his predecessors it was Haller who had most in common stylistically with Klopstock. Neither Haller nor Klopstock were pietists; and a recent biographer has demonstrated that there is nothing specifically pietist about the theology of *Der Messias*.[2] But it is possible to be influenced by the vocabulary of ideologies one does not subscribe to—as we of the twentieth century know to our embarrassment. It has been suggested that the dynamic, verbal nature of Klopstock's language derives from pietism. It has been shown that the basic situation of pietism is one where two extremes are striving towards fusion, 'das Gegenüber und Entgegen von Gott und Seele',[3] and that this finds expression in language where verbs

---

[1] See especially August Langen, *Der Wortschatz des deutschen Pietismus* (Tübingen, 1954). An earlier article by Sperber, 'Der Einfluß des Pietismus auf die deutsche Sprache', *Dt.Vjs.* VIII (1930) is full of valuable observations.

[2] Karl Kindt, *Klopstock* (Berlin, 1941).

[3] Langen, *op. cit.* p. 376. On *entgegen-* in verbal compounds see Sperber's article 'Beiträge zur Geschichte der deutschen Sprache im achtzehnten Jahrhundert', *ZfdPh.* LII (1927), pp. 331–45.

and prefixes of movement abound, especially movement towards, into and through. The fulcrum of this style is the verb; and this affects other parts of speech. Hence the frequency of verbal epithets and verbal nouns—of participles, substantivised infinitives and deverbative abstracts. The most striking aspect of all this is an extension of the prefix-formations of baroque mysticism; especially verbs with *durch-*, *ein-* and *hinein-*. Metaphor is often embodied in these formations, particularly when the basic verb is not a verb of movement but becomes one by the addition of the prefix (*sich einglauben, durchbekehren, nacharten, zusterben*). There is no doubt that this latter feature is common to both pietism and Klopstock. Indeed, he seems to have developed it to the point of almost unbearable virtuosity. Especially is this so with descriptive verbs which he activises by dynamic prefixes: *empordenken, dahinzittern, herunterschimmern, aufweinen, zusegnen, heruntertrauern, herschäumen, hineinlügen, hinseufzen*.[1] But this is the only salient feature of Klopstock's style which can be related at all certainly to pietism. Even the predilection for participles, common to both, does not present a real parallel; for it is the constant use of the *present* participle which is so striking in Klopstock and yet this is admittedly fairly uncommon amongst the pietists—nothing like so common, we are told, as with the medieval mystics.[2] Transitive use of normally intransitive verbs is also rare in pietist writing.[3] On the other side of the scale one must realise that several of the most colourful peculiarities of pietist style are not found frequently, if at all, in Klopstock's style. He does not use those characteristic 'negative abstracts' which pietism had inherited from medieval mysticism (*Unlauterkeit*,

---

[1] Schönaich ridicules this: 'Wir lernen alle Tage je mehr und mehr, daß auch eine einzige Sylbe einen Vers verengeln kann' (*ed. cit.* p. 36). There is an interesting remark in a letter of Rabener to Cramer, dated 7 May 1752, in which he blames the use of 'gewisser Redensarten Klopstocks' and continues: 'Das *schläft sie zu Gott hin* ist ein Ausdruck, der mich ehedem betäubt hat, und nun glaube ich kaum, daß er richtig gedacht sey. Kann ich *dahin schlafen*, so kann ich auch *einher wachen*' (quoted Langen, *op. cit.* pp. 446–7).

[2] Langen, p. 384.

[3] *Ibid.* p. 389: 'Dieses Stilmittel scheint Klopstocks Eigenleistung zu sein.'

Ungestorbenheit, Ungrund, Lieblosheit). And although abstracts are frequent, one is not conscious of eccentric neologisms like *Totenhaftigkeit, Todigkeit, Schwerigkeit, Gemütszartigkeit, Nahbeiheit, Vielheit, Selbstheit, Meinheit, Deinheit, Lieblosheit, Hingesunkenheit* or, perhaps even more startling, the deverbatives *Einwohnung, Verlassung, Absterbung, Vergessung, Ersinkung, Anklebung, Verlierung* or *Schmeckung*.[1] This sort of outlandishness is not part of Klopstock's style. Nor, in fact, is the predilection for the substantivised infinitive which Klopstock in his mature style used only for special effect (as in the passage from the last canto of *Der Messias*, quoted above on p. 331). Such infinitives are commoner in his earlier poems, but he often excised them in revising *Der Messias* and later called the construction 'cold'.[2] There seems to be no parallel in pietism to Klopstock's metonymous use of plural abstracts. This struck his admirer and biographer Cramer as unusual;[3] but plural abstracts had been common enough in baroque verse (although not with the particular effect achieved by Klopstock). It would seem therefore that some of the most salient features of the style of Klopstock are not found in pietist writings, and that there are certain stylistic predilections of pietism which he does not share. What the two have in common is a dynamic, verbal style with great use of prefix-formations. But this is not specifically pietist; it is found fully developed in baroque mysticism and has its roots in the medieval German mystics. We can see it gone to seed already in the *Kühlpsalter* of Quirinus Kuhlmann, published in 1684. The most one can say is that these linguistic features were in the air at the time. No one would wish to deny Klopstock's linguistic genius. He took what he found and used it with telling effect.

---

[1] Examples selected from the much longer lists of Langen.

[2] In the seventh of the *Grammatische Gespräche* (Back-Spindler, 1, p. 252): 'Das Trösten ist kälter, als Der Trost.'

[3] 'Klopstock ist sehr kühn in der Bildung manches neuen Plurals bei Wörtern, die, ich weiß nicht aus welchem närrischen Eigensinn der Sprache, vorher keinen unter uns hatten, wenn gleich ihr Begriff die Mehrzahl gern zuließ. Die Ehren, die Frühen, die Tode, und nicht selten bei solchen, wo nur der Dichter sich ihn erlauben darf: Ewigkeiten, Verwesungen, Einsamkeiten u.a.' Quoted by Langen.

And wherever the individual elements may ultimately have come from (if indeed that be ascertainable with any degree of conviction) it was their combination and the *bravura* with which they were employed that constitute Klopstock's linguistic originality. The purpose, result and effect were far more important than the origins and antecedents.

The purpose, as we have seen, was the revivification of German verse by demonstrating the essential difference between the language of poetry and that of what he called 'cold prose'. The result was sometimes an astonishing obscurity. One poem begins:

> Ferner Gestade, die Woge schnell,
> Dem Blicke gehellt bis zum Kiesel ist,
> Das Gebüsch blinket er durch, oder wallt
> In die Luft, hohes Gewölk duftend, der Strom;[1]

The obscurity is hardly lightened by the knowledge that the poem is entitled *Die deutsche Sprache*. It was written in 1783 when Klopstock's style had reached its full maturity. If we analyse this stanza, we find that tautness is achieved by means of several of the devices we have noted. Thus an adverbial genitive of place *ferner Gestade* (cf. *aller Orten*) is used instead of a prepositional phrase,[2] this is followed by an absolute phrase *die Woge schnell* (cf. '*Voll die Brust* von süßen Liedern / Naht er schon dem frohen Ziele'), a striking participle *gehellt* (in meaning equivalent to an intensified *hell*) is preceded by a terse dative extension without preposition to explain the relationship (the verb *hellen* is itself an unusual simplex variant for the more usual *aufhellen, aushellen* or *erhellen* as Adelung tells us), 'blinket er *durch*' and 'wallt in *die* Luft' show expressive use of prepositions of motion, *Gebüsch* and *Gewölk* show movement away from reality towards the abstract, *duftend* is used transitively with object *Gewölk* (in the sense of

---

[1] Muncker-Pawel, II, p. 54.

[2] But in what meaning? One sense would seem to be 'from distant shores'; but this use of the genitive would be quite exceptional. Düntzer suggests that *Gestade* refers to the banks of the river and gives the meaning as 'im breiten Flußbett'. That it could have such a meaning is clear from Adelung's definition: 'das Ufer des Meeres *oder eines Flusses*'.

düften, ausdüften) and then, delayed to the very end, a good example of 'etwas erwarten lassen', the subject, *der Strom*.

Attention is projected most strangely on to the word *der Strom* by this extraordinary build-up. In an admirable study of the rhythmic patterns of Klopstock's Odes, Irmgard Böger suggests that in this style the separate existence of certain individual words is emphasised rather than the connections between words. She says, very truly: 'Stellen wir dem fließenden Rhythmus eines Eichendorffschen Liedes die harte Fügung einer Klopstockschen Hymne gegenüber, so kennzeichnet sich der Rhythmus hier darin, daß er die Wörter nicht ineinander übergleiten läßt zu einer Melodie, sondern sie gliedernd gegeneinander abhebt... Er reißt die Wortmassen durch deutlich geprägte Stillstandsmomente auseinander.'[1] The term *harte Fügung* was, I think, first used by Norbert von Hellingrath and with reference to Hölderlin. It has since been applied to other German poets, especially to George and the later Rilke. It designates a quality which recurs in German verse, a mode naturally engendered by the German language in hieratic state, and here with Klopstock we have perhaps its first great flowering. This style is full of pent-up energy. It stammers in repetition, interrupts itself with interjections, intensifies itself by variations—all in order to hold back the rhythm, to prevent it from becoming fluid and to throw some element still to come into startling relief:

> Der Liebe Schmerzen, nicht der erwartenden
> Noch ungeliebten, die Schmerzen nicht,
> Denn ich liebe, so liebte
> Keiner! so werd' ich geliebt!
>
> Die sanftern Schmerzen, welche zum Wiedersehn
> Hinblicken, welche zum Wiedersehn
> Tief aufathmen, doch lispelt
> Stammelnde Freude mit auf!
> Die Schmerzen wollt ich singen.[2]

[1] Irmgard Böger (see above, footnote to p. 316), p. 20.
[2] *Gegenwart der Abwesenden* (1753), Muncker-Pawel, I, p. 119. There is an interesting analysis of this passage in Kaußmann's dissertation (see above, p. 316, n.) on pp. 115–16.

Consider the extraordinary halting effect of the word *oder* in:

> Von des schimmernden Sees Traubengestaden her,
> *Oder*, flohest du schon wieder zum Himmel auf,
> Kom in röthendem Strale
> Auf dem Flügel der Abendluft,
> Kom, und lehre mein Lied jugendlich heiter seyn,
> Süße Freude....[1]

The result is to throw emphasis on to the delayed subject. But other parts of the sentence can be thrown into relief by this means. For instance:

> (a) Auch hier stand die Natur, da sie aus reicher Hand
> Über Hügel und Thal lebende Schönheit goß,
> Mit verweilendem Tritte,
> Diese Thäler zu schmücken, *still*.[2]
>
> (b) Nicht in den Ozean der Welten alle
> Will ich mich stürzen! schweben *nicht*,...[3]
>
> (c) So wend' ich mich seitwärts, und nehme des Barden Telyn,
> Und sing, o Vaterland, *dich dir*![4]
>
> (d) Will mit Gespielen euch, mit Thränenweiden,
> Rings umpflanzen, daß einst, wenn nun die Sonne
> Sinkt, in eurer Kühle, durchhaucht von Abend-
> Lüften, ihr Laub *sich*
>   Leise bewege....[5]
>
> (e) Es schleichet der Tod nun hier, nun dort *hin*.[6]
>
> (f)   ...Sturmwinde
> Rauschen, und Meere dann *her*![7]

The result of all this is an effect of breaking away entirely from the rhythms of prose. Sometimes one feels that the whole natural stress-system of German is being violated. Contemporary critics were right in asserting that this language was un-German. But

---

[1] *Der Zürchersee* (1750), Muncker-Pawel, I, p. 83. There is a detailed analysis of this ode by Beissner (Münster-Cologne, 1952), and by Emil Staiger in *M. Heideggers Einfluß auf die Wissenschaften* (1950).

[2] Muncker-Pawel, I, p. 91.   [3] *Ibid*. I, p. 133.
[4] *Ibid*. I, p. 220.   [5] *Ibid*. II, p. 14.
[6] *Ibid*. II, p. 59.   [7] *Ibid*. I, p. 164.

the question is, was this gain or loss? The elements of the sentence seem to be all over the place:

> Denn im Haine brauset' es her gehobnes
> Halses, und sprang, Flug die Mähne, dahin
> Das heilige Roß, und ein Spott
> War der Sturm ihm, und der Strom ihm![1]

Everything seems to be disjointed, like the constituent parts in a Picasso portrait of the 1940's. Our attention is pulled hither and thither to the very confines of the canvas, teeth and eyes pop up in the most unexpected places. The very shape of the parts may be unusually distorted, giving either the concentrated essence or an eccentric variation of a form. But the result, with Klopstock as with Picasso, is an extra intensity of illumination on these apparently scattered parts. And we are forced by the power of the experience to fit the parts together, to realise their inner connection which external dislocation cannot destroy but rather heightens. And the resultant whole is something clearer and stronger than life; or, with Klopstock, than prose.

In the detailed analysis of poetic fragments there is some danger of losing sight of poems as individual wholes. Let us therefore in conclusion see how Klopstock's expression can sustain an idea throughout a whole poem. Here is an ode written in 1784:

Der Frohsinn

> Voller Gefühl des Jünglings, weil' ich Tage
> Auf dem Roß', und dem Stahl',[2] ich seh des Lenzes
> Grüne Bäume froh dann, und froh des Winters
> Dürre beblütet.
>
> Und der geflohnen Sonnen, die ich sahe,
> Sind so wenig doch nicht, und auf dem Scheitel
> Blühet mir es winterlich schon, auch ist es
> Hier und da öde.
>
> Wenn ich dieß frische Leben regsam athme;
> Hör' ich dich denn auch wohl, mit Geistes Ohre,
> Dich dein Tröpfchen leises Geräusches träufeln,
> Weinende Weide.

---

[1] *Weissagung* (1773), Muncker-Pawel, II, p. 4.   [2] I.e. 'skates'.

> Nicht die Zipresse, denn nur traurig ist sie;
> Du bist traurig und schön, du ihre Schwester,
> O es pflanze dich an das Grab der Freund mir,
> Weide der Thränen!
>
> Jünglinge schlummern hin, und Greise bleiben
> Wach. Es schleichet der Tod nun hier, nun dort hin,
> Hebt die Sichel, eilt, daß er schneide, wartet
> Oft nicht der Ähre.
>
> Weiß auch der Mensch, wenn ihm des Todes Ruf schallt?
> Seine Antwort darauf? Wer dann mich klagen
> Hört, verzeih' dem Thoren sein Ach: denn glücklich
> War ich durch Frohsinn.[1]

After quoting such a poem, it would seem hardly necessary to underline the debt of Hölderlin to Klopstock. The extraordinary emphasis which fixes itself so unexpectedly on to the words like *dann* (in the third line) or *schon* (in the third line of the second stanza) or *mir* (at the end of the third line of the fourth stanza), the whole formation of the phrases, the sad lingering grandeur of the sound—all remind one of Hölderlin. So do other features I have mentioned earlier—such as *tiefauftönend*. But sometimes Klopstock's dislocation of language suggests rather the frenzied intensity of the Expressionists, as does also his concentration of meaning and his *harte Fügung*. The strange evocative way in which he uses abstract words and his use of unexpected objects to intransitive verbs often suggest the Rilke of the Duino Elegies. The fact is that the influence of Klopstock on German elevated poetic diction has been lasting. It was he who laid the foundations of a new grand style, giving to the German language a whole new register of voice. It was he who by his dislocation of language freed it from the accretion of conventionalised contexts.

[1] Muncker-Pawel, II, p. 59.

XI

THE PROSE OF MATURITY

It is generally recognised that German prose reached its maturity in the second half of the 1750's; and this recognition is usually coupled with the name of Lessing. Histories of literature are full of vague statements such as that German prose begins with Lessing or (more precise but no more accurate) that his is the first German prose that shows individual character or that his is the first *good* German prose. Lessing certainly did write magnificent prose, of a definite type. But he did not create modern German prose, individually, out of nothing, by the sheer, inventive power of his supreme, solitary genius. His prose grows out of the traditions of good prose-writing which we have seen establishing themselves in the first half of the century. And he was not the only writer of good German prose at this period. In the late fifties something very definite is achieved in the development of German as a prose medium. And this achievement is the crown of a development stretching back over several decades.

Lessing was intensely interested in language.[1] He followed

---

[1] There is no really satisfactory account of Lessing's views on language and no full analysis of his own use of language. Erich Schmidt, in his biography, has a chapter packed with examples, but arranged rather unsystematically and entirely without references. This remains the fullest account to date; but the lack of references to such a voluminous writer makes it difficult to use. Earlier work includes: A. Lehmann, *Forschungen über Lessings Sprache* (Brunswick, 1875) and C. Behschnitt, *Lessings Ansichten von der deutschen Sprache* (Diss. Breslau, 1915). More restricted studies include M. von Waldberg, *Studien zu Lessings Stil in der Hamburgischen Dramaturgie* (Berlin, 1882); O. Immisch, 'Beiträge zur Beurteilung der stilistischen Kunst in Lessings Prosa, insonderheit der Streitschriften' (said to be good but unavailable to me), Jahn's *Jahrbücher für Philologie* (Leipzig, 1887); F. Tyrol, *Lessings sprachliche Revision seiner Jugenddramen* (Berlin, 1893); W. Metzger, *Die Entwicklung von Lessings Briefstil* (Giessen, 1927); and F. J. Stopp's typescript dissertation *The art of exposition in Lessing's prose-works* (dealing specifically with the polemical writings) presented at the University of London in 1948. The account of Lessing in Langen's *Deutsche Sprachgeschichte*, etc. in Stammler's *Deutsche Philologie im Aufriß* (Berlin Biele-

with critical attention the linguistic activities of his contemporaries. He was deeply concerned about the establishment of an accepted norm of the German language with the production of an adequate grammar and dictionary. He knew the work of foreign grammarians and constantly quoted from the dictionaries of Ménage and Dr Johnson. He greeted the first appearance of Gottsched's grammar with a sympathetic though not uncritical review.[1] He made notes in an interleaved copy of Steinbach's dictionary (Latin-German, Breslau, 1725), collected material between 1759 and 1774 towards the production of a dictionary of his own; but abandoned this on the appearance of Adelung's first volume (although he was not entirely satisfied with this). In temperament he had much of the antiquarian about him. This included a passion for etymologising. There is an amusing reference to this in the *Briefe antiquarischen Inhalts*:

Ich bekenne Ihnen meine Schwäche: mir ist es selten genug, daß ich ein Ding kenne, und weis, wie dieses Ding heißt; ich möchte sehr oft auch gern wissen, warum dieses Ding so und nicht anders heißt. Kurz, ich bin einer von den entschlossensten Wortgrüblern; und so lächerlich als vielen das etymologische Studium vorkömmt, so geringfügig mir es selbst, mit dem Studio der Dinge verglichen, erscheinet, so erpicht bin ich gleichwohl darauf. Der Geist ist dabey in einer so faulen Thätigkeit; er ist so geschäftig und zugleich so ruhig, daß ich mir für eine gemächliche Neugierde keine wollüstigere Arbeit denken kann. Man schmeichelt sich mit dem Suchen, ohne an den Werth des Dinges zu denken, das man sucht: man freuet sich über das Finden,

---

feld, 1952) is necessarily brief but has some good points and there is an excellent stylistic analysis of the second *Anti-Goeze* in Hans Hafen, *Studien zur Geschichte der deutschen Prosa im 18. Jahrhundert* (St Gall, 1952). I have not been able to see Markwardt's articles on Lessing's prose style in the *Wiss. Zs. d. Univ. Greifswald* (1953-4 and subsequently).

[1] In the *Berlinische privilegierte Zeitung* for 1748, doubting the validity as linguistic models of some of Gottsched's *gute Scribenten*, criticising his use of the word *Sprachkunst* instead of *Sprachlehre*, and pointing to the lack of logical basis, e.g.: 'Woher will man aber beweisen, daß diese Provinz [where the best German is spoken] allemal gerade in die Mitte müsse zu liegen kommen?' (Lachmann-Muncker, IV, p. 7). Except where otherwise stated, I quote Lessing's works from the Lachmann-Muncker ed. (Stuttgart and Leipzig, 1886-1924, 23 vols.—abbreviated L-M).

ohne sich darüber zu ärgern, daß es ein Nichts ist, was man nun endlich nach vieler Mühe gefunden hat.¹

His procedure had all the enthusiasm of the amateur. He notes the connection between *sitzen* and *setzen*, and that 'die bloße Veränderung des Vocalis *i* in *e*' gives the differentiation. Then moving on to a consideration of *sinken-senken, blicken-blecken*, and *trinken-tränken*, he arrives at an appreciation of the factitive meaning without calling it such.² Elsewhere he broods on the pairs *der Gruß—grüssen, der Kuß—küssen* but *der Fluß—fliessen* and *der Guß—giessen* 'Woher dieser Unterschied?' He decides that those verbs with *-o-* in the 'imperfect' have *-ie-* in the infinitive, whereas those with *-ü-* or *-u-* in the imperfect have *-ü-* in the infinitive.³ One feels the lack of proper analysis and terminology. One feels it even more in the following:

Die ganze Verderbung der alten Sprachen rühret von vier Hauptquellen her, welche von Zeit zu Zeit neue Sprachen hervorbringen; und diese vier Quellen betreffen alle die Veränderung der Buchstaben; denn nach dem dieselben verwechselt, zugesetzt, weggenommen und versetzt werden, nach dem entstehen neue Wörter, welche wie verkleidet sind, und welche man Mühe hat, zu kennen.⁴

This is not cold science. There are overtones of emotion in the vocabulary. The *Wortgrübeln* is that of an artist. Etymology had for him a practical end: 'die Wissenschaft der Etymologie, dieses heißt, die Sprache bereichern.'⁵ In his extensive reading he was constantly noting old words that appealed to him—words which were good words, words that should not have been allowed to fall into misuse. His interest is never purely antiquarian; aesthetic considerations always contribute something.

We see this clearly in the edition of Logau's poems which Lessing published with Ramler in 1759. Lessing admires the

---

¹ *Briefe antiquarischen Inhalts*, no. 47. L–M, x, p. 391–2.
² This is amongst the *Collectanea* (L–M, xv, p. 377).
³ L–M, xv, pp. 335–6. Amongst his examples is *mußte*; but he does not appreciate that this is of a different type from the others.
⁴ In his review of Ménage's dictionary for the *Critische Nachrichten aus dem Reiche der Gelehrsamkeit* in 1751. (L–M, iv, p. 215.)
⁵ L–M, iv, p. 212.

language of Logau. His style was always suited to his subject-matter and varied accordingly. He did not use foreign words when he could use a German word; but he was not exaggerated in his purism and he mocked at the absurdities of Zesen. Recent authors, anxious to enrich the language, had imitated French and English, rather than revive many a good old German word. Logau's poems were full of such words, and it was in the hope of persuading authors of repute to reintroduce these words into the language that he, Lessing, had appended a glossary to the text. He recognised that there were provincial features in Logau's vocabulary.[1] He had noted them in other Silesian authors. He would like to see a deeper study of Silesian language. But let us note why: 'Die Schlesische Mundart ist deswegen einer kritischen Aufmerksamkeit, vor allen anderen Mundarten, würdig, weil wir in ihr die ersten guten Dichter bekommen haben.'[2] Lessing is only interested in those words which have proved their worth by being effectively used in writing. He enumerates some general Silesian peculiarities: not an exhaustive list but merely those from which Logau had drawn use and modern writers might perhaps draw some advantage. These are mostly aids to conciseness, both syntactical (omission of article; omission of subject pronoun; flexionless attributive adjective; use of flexionless adjective as substantive) and lexical (more adjectives in -*ley*; omission of *ge-* in *Würze, Schmach, Ruch, nießen, linde, bracht*; omission of *be-* in *sonders, müht* and *hausen*). Separation of prefix from verb (*ich wills ihm ein noch treiben*) and partitive genitive after cardinal numbers help the rhythm of verse.[3] Detailed examination of Lessing's glossary reveals a variety of factors attracting him to words. Only very rarely does he note with disapproval: '*tummelhaftig*...wovon man die Endsylbe *ig* besser wegläßt.'[4] Many of the words commended are shorter than their normal counterparts. *Drang* (Drangsal), *Gedieg* (Gediegenheit), *Belieb* (Belieben), *plotz*

---

[1] Review of this edition in the *Literaturbriefe*; see L–M, VIII, p. 119.

[2] L–M, VII, p. 354. This was an added reason for his detailed study of Steinbach's dictionary.

[3] L–M, VII, pp. 355–7.   [4] *Ibid.* p. 403.

(plötzlich), *verkünden* (verkündigen) and *dannen* (von dannen) show sloughing of valueless grammatical suffixes. *Halt* (Hinterhalt), *Kerb* (Kerbholz) and *Blick* (Augenblick) avoid the tautology of their modern equivalents.[1] *Allengefallenheit*, meaning 'the endeavour to please everybody' might well be adopted by theologians as a rendering of St Paul's ἀρεσκεια: it obviously appealed to Lessing because of its compactness. The word *vervielen* is useful and should not be allowed to become obsolete: '*Vermehren, vervielen, vervielfältigen*, sind drey Wörter, welche dienen, das verschiedene Zunehmen der Dinge an Größe, Anzahl und Eigenschaften genauer zu bestimmen. Z.E. Das Wasser vermehrt sich; alle Blumen vervielen sich; einige Blumen verfielfältigen sich.' A similar acute distinction is made to justify the retention of *wirthlich* alongside *wirthschaftlich*.[2] Etymological speculation causes him to note *Deube* (Diebstahl), *güteln, erlusten, frevelich* (rather than 'freventlich'), *Schwesterschaft* (on the model of 'Brüderschaft'), *hahnen* (zu Hahnrei machen), *prachten, Ihrzen* and *duzen, von etwas feyern* (in the sense of 'aufhören damit'), *wächsig* and *Gebruch* (from *gebrechen*). The *selbander, selbdritt* type of pronoun appealed to him for both etymological and aesthetic reasons: still current only in certain provinces and not used by the best authors it would save 'more than one useless word'. Expressive formations like *Gedenkkunst, Gerneklug* (he compares *Gernegroß* and the English use of *would-be* in phrases of similar type of meaning), *Ortgedächtnis* and *blitzlich* attract him. *Arzung* is archaic but has found no adequate equivalent: 'Heilung kann nur von äußerlichen Schaden gesagt werden; und die *Curirung*, die *Gesundmachung* — welche Wörter!' He notes some useful terms used by Logau instead of foreign words current in the German of his day: *Durchschnitt* (Profil), *Fußgicht* (Podagra), *Hauptgut* (Capital), *Beylaut* (Accentus), *Fundregister* (Inventarium), *Wiederzins* (Anatocismus). Lessing commends

[1] In each case I cite Logau's form first and then (in brackets) the normal form as given by Lessing.
[2] '*Wirthlich* geht die Person, den Wirth an; *wirthschaftlich* geht die Sache, die Wirthschaft an. Also sagt man: wirthschaftliche Gebäude, und wirthliche Leute' (L–M, VII, p. 409).

moderation in this as in other linguistic matters. He notes the activating prefix in: 'Wenn ein redlich frommer Christ *hin* sich sichert in das Grab' and comments: 'Einige Neuere haben dergleichen Wörter ohne Unterschied getadelt, andere haben dergleichen bis zum Ekel gemacht. Dichter von gutem Geschmacke halten das Mittel.' He no doubt appreciated the graphic value of such formations for he recommends *hergesippt* and *zugesippt* as worthy of adoption. Graphic uses of familiar words, such as *grün* in the sense of 'fresh, healthy' or *greis* to mean 'grey' (or 'gray'), *Knechterey* in the sense of 'enslavement' are commended. Metaphor plays some part here, as it does in *schlägefaul, verschildwacht* (applied to the conscience), *verbürgen* and *jemandem die Husche geben*. But apart from these few examples and a few nonce-words (*Flammenschütze* for 'love', *Ausgleicher* for 'death' and *Bilderbogen* for 'zodiac') we do not observe that Lessing was attracted to old metaphorical words to the same extent as Bodmer and Breitinger. Far too often we find him recommending a word simply because it is old. Hence *befahren* is a 'good, old word'. So are *Degen* (in the sense of 'hero'), *frommen, gach, Gaden, Geding, gumpen, kiefeln, kosen* and *Thurst*. It is difficult to see why *Geding* should be preferable to *Hoffnung*, *kosen* to *reden* or *Thurst* to *Mut*. This is Lessing's antiquarianism coming out. At one point, when he praises *bieder* as 'dieses alte, der deutschen Redlichkeit so angemessene Wort' one seems to sense that same somewhat 'bardic' enthusiasm which pervaded his praise of Gleim's grenadier songs and his more sweeping rejections of French taste. This is in conflict with his normal aesthetic attitude towards vocabulary, and might perhaps explain why he himself used so few of these old words in his own writings.

The beginnings of Lessing's interest in provincial and archaic vocabulary seem to go back to his review of Richey's famous *Idioticon Hamburgense* in the *Berlinische Privilegierte Zeitung* during 1754. Here occur the words:

Es ist eher an kein etymologisches Lexicon... zu denken, bevor wir nicht die eignen Wörter aller Provinzen gesammelt, und sie unter einander verglichen haben. Dieses aber würde vielleicht noch zu erhalten seyn, wenn sich nur mehrere Gelehrte bemühen wollten, dem Exempel des Herrn Prof. Richeys zu folgen.[1]

In the Logau edition occur the words:

Aehnliche Wörterbücher über alle unsere guten Schriftsteller, würden, ohne Zweifel, der erste nähere Schritt zu einem allgemeinen Wörterbuche unsrer Sprache seyn.[2]

Two quite different intentions are combined here. The Logau glossary had, as we have seen, the practical purpose of enriching the literary language; the wider plan of an etymological dictionary represented the more scholarly undertaking of cataloguing the lexical riches of the language. The former proceeds from Lessing the artist, the latter from Lessing the antiquarian. His wish for more dialect dictionaries was fulfilled during the second half of the century;[3] and he himself turned his attention to the vocabulary of other individual authors, especially Silesians. He prepared an edition of Andreas Scultetus, the disciple of Opitz, which was published in 1771. He finds his language 'so reich, so stark, so mahlerisch... daß sie nur mit der Opitzischen verglichen zu werden verdienet'.[4] Amongst the notes to the poems we find commendation of the phrase *kein Muttermensch* (which he thinks is specifically Silesian, like *mutterseelenallein*), of the 'good, old word' *bekleiben*, of the adverbial genitive *jener Zeit* ('bey den Schlesischen Dichtern sehr gebräuchlich'), the emphatic word *selbselbst* (a Silesianism, he thinks) and the metaphorical use of *kochen* to express anxiety, the metaphorical phrase *Unterschleif des Krämervolkes* to describe the money-changers in the temple ('dieses Wort hier sehr gut gebraucht') and the metaphor in:

> Der Lazar wird erweckt
> Und dankt den Würmen ab.

('sehr nachdrücklich').[5] Such comments may seem to us to show doubtful judgment, but they are only properly appreciable within

---

[1] L–M, v, p. 447.   [2] L–M, vii, p. 131.
[3] 1765, Osnabrückisch; 1766–71, Bremisch-Niedersächsisch; 1781, Plattdeutsch-Pommersch; 1781, Schlesisch; 1785, Preussisch; 1802 ff., Holsteinisch.
[4] L–M, xi, p. 173.   [5] *Ibid.* pp. 174, 176, 178, 183, 182.

the wider context of his general stylistic ideals. Jottings from his reading of other Silesian authors (Opitz, Fleming, Tscherning, Zincgref) and of Steinbach's dictionary (which had a marked Silesian flavour), together with words noted during his reading of Luther for his theological controversies and from medieval and early modern fable-writers perused for his treatise on the Fable, even some notes on words in Bodmer's editions of medieval texts, are to be found amongst his posthumous papers. A large amount of this material has been lost;[1] but what remains is still quite bulky. He seems to have started collecting material in 1759 or soon after. The jottings in the interleaved copy of Steinbach's dictionary belong to this period[2] and show the same combination of antiquarian and aesthetic values as the Logau glossary of the same year. Thus the use of *eilend* in *eilende Fälle*, and the words *Ehrensache* and *Ehrenhandel* are praised as 'alt und schön'. But the French-sounding use of *erst* in 'Ich habe die erste gesündiget' (Geßner) is simply described as 'nicht neu, sondern alt, und wäre daher wohl nachzubrauchen'. Why *daher*, one may ask? Similarly, in his notes on medieval fables, he comments on the Middle High German genitive extension with verbs: 'Und dieser *Genit.* bey besinnen, bedenken ist ohne Zweifel beßer als die Construction mit *auf*.'[3] Why *beßer*? Is this *ohne Zweifel*? It is slightly terser; but the real reason would seem to be that it was older. This is made quite clear in the jottings on Luther when, noting Adelung's objection to the construction *einem* (instead of *von einem*) *abfällig werden*, Lessing remarks: 'Warum sollen nicht Zeitwörter und davon gemachte Participia und Adjectiva auch ohne Präposition einen Casum eben so gut regieren als im Lateinischen und Griechischen.'[4] Age gives respectability! The comparison with Latin and Greek is significant. When, in the Steinbach notes, he commends *verreitzen* (to entice) as 'ein altes *aber* schönes Wort' (my italics) Lessing seems to be half-aware

---

[1] See Lachmann-Muncker, vol. XVI, notes by Muncker on pp. 3–4, 42–4; and Arthur Hübner, 'Lessings Plan eines Deutschen Wörterbuches' in *Kleine Schriften* (Berlin, 1940) (originally a lecture delivered in 1936).

[2] Some additional notes are later, for they refer to Adelung's first volume.

[3] L–M, XVI, p. 170.   [4] *Ibid.* p. 92.

of his inconsistency.¹ Amongst the motley jottings gathered together as *Beyträge zu einem Deutschen Glossarium* by Fülleborn² we find the entry: '*Aehren, Nachähren, Nachährer*, alte gute Wörter für Nachlese.'³ The obvious connection with *Ähre* appeals to the etymologist in him. Simple and clear relationship to a native root-word is one of the features that attracts him to words. Hence he praises *ernsten* (to be earnest) and suggests that *schlinden* (from *Schlund*) is more correct than *schlingen*.⁴ *Drehseln*, he says, is 'wohlklingender *und der Ableitung gemäßer* [my italics] als *drechseln*'. For similar reasons the older form *widerspännig* is preferable to *widerspänstig*.⁵ One jotting gives an explicit statement on root-relationship: 'Die Provinzialismen, welche der Schriftsteller brauchen kann, müssen nächst ihren andern zu bestimmenden Eigenschaften auch diese haben: daß man ihren Stamm in einer von den Quellen der Sprache zeigen, und sonach gewiß seyn kann, daß sie keine Aftergeburten des Dialects in neuern Zeiten sind.'⁶ It was generally known that Lessing was working on a dictionary. Ebert referred to the plan in 1768 and Nicolai tried to buy Lessing's collection of words in 1769. In November 1773 Karl Lessing reported having heard in Berlin that his brother was 'sweating night and day over the completion of a German dictionary'. But Lessing in his reply, dated 2 February 1774, said that he had abandoned the idea. Adelung's first volume had just appeared. Lessing was not entirely satisfied and spoke of giving 'eine kleine Probe' of what his own dictionary would have been like. But this has not survived, although we have some pages of comment on the entries under letter A in Adelung. Lessing criticises some of Adelung's statements and rejects some of his definitions. Adelung had stated that *aber* as a temporal adverb (meaning 'again') was obsolete except in certain compound words and in Upper Swabian speech, and that its current use was only colloquial; Lessing points out that it was also used

---

¹ L–M, xvi, p. 29.
² In the third volume of Karl Lessing's edition of the life and posthumous papers, published in 1795.
³ L–M, xvi, p. 44. ⁴ *Ibid.* pp. 48, 58.
⁵ *Ibid.* pp. 47, 63. ⁶ *Ibid.* p. 84.

in Upper Saxon speech and that its literary use could be 'feyerlich' as in *Und aber erklang die Trommete* or *Und aber schoß ein Strahl herab*, where the more usual *abermahl* would be 'höchst schleppend' and the equivalent *wiederum* would be 'sehr kahl'.[1] The word appeals to him because it is more concise and less hackneyed. Among these various jottings there are several proposals for clearly-built, graphic words to replace some of the more commonly used foreign words. There is an interesting example amongst these notes on Adelung. He rejects Adelung's definition of *Abbild* as 'Abriß, Bild' and suggests instead 'Bild von einem Bilde', contrasting it with *Urbild*. *Abbild*, he thinks, would be a good replacement for *Kopie*; and he might have used the contrast *Bild—Abbild* in *Emilia Galotti* instead of 'die *Schilderey* selbst, wovor sie gesessen, hat ihr abwesender Vater bekommen. Aber diese *Kopie*...' (Act I, Scene iv). Might have...'wenn es im Dramatischen nicht mehr darauf ankäme, der Person *ihr angemessene*, als *gute* Worte in den Mund zu legen'.[2] It would seem that we owe the word *empfindsam* to Lessing, for he recommends it as an equivalent for English 'sentimental' in a letter during the summer of 1768 to Bode who was translating Sterne's *Sentimental Journey*: 'War es Sternen erlaubt, sich ein neues Wort zu bilden: so muß es eben darum auch seinem Uebersetzer erlaubt seyn.... Wenn eine *mühsame* Reise eine Reise heißt, bey der viel Mühe ist; so kann ja auch eine *empfindsame* Reise eine Reise heissen, bey der viel Empfindung war.'[3] In his translations from Frederick the Great and from Voltaire, made in the early and mid 1750's, he often uses a new-sounding German word where the French word was current in Germany: *Schenktisch* (buffet), *Gewissenszweifel* (scrupule), *Gnadengeld* (pension), *Denkwürdigkeit* (mémoire).[4] On the matter of foreign words Lessing, like his admired Logau, was no extreme purist. But if a good German word could be found, he would prefer to use it. This is why he chided Wieland, in the fourteenth *Literaturbrief*, for using so many *unnecessary* French words—'*Linge*, sagt Herr Wieland so

[1] L–M, xvi, p. 84. [2] *Ibid.* p. 85.
[3] L–M, xvii, p. 256. [4] Quoted in Behschnitt, *op. cit.*

gar'—whereas there were so many 'good words' current in Swiss usage and waiting to be brought into Germany.[1] Swiss translations, though clumsy in sentence-structure, were 'ungemein reich an guten nachdrücklichen Wörtern, an körnichten Redensarten'.[2] Later he came to admire Wieland's bold use of words and we are told that he often spoke of Wieland's 'glückliche Wörterfabrik'.[3]

In his preface to a French translation of the *Laokoon* (date uncertain; Erich Schmidt thinks 1770) Lessing wrote: 'La langue allemande...est...encore à former, à creer meme, pour plusieurs genres de composition, dont celui-ci n'est pas le moindre.'[4] He believed that a writer of real genius could form his native language, whichever it may be: 'Für ein Genie sind die Sprachen alle von einer Natur.'[5] But in the *Laokoon* he argued that German was, in one respect at least, inferior to Greek. For Greek permitted a closer combination of epithets:

Wir sagen zwar 'die runden, ehernen, achtspeichigten' — aber 'Räder' schleppt hinten nach.... Der Grieche verbindet das Subject gleich mit dem ersten Prädicate, und läßt die andern nachfolgen; er sagt: 'runde Räder, eherne, achtspeichigte'. So wissen wir mit eins wovon er redet, und werden, der natürlichen Ordnung des Denkens gemäß, erst mit dem Dinge, und dann mit seinen Zufälligkeiten bekannt. Diesen Vortheil hat unsere Sprache nicht. Oder soll ich sagen, sie hat ihn, und kann ihn nur selten ohne Zweydeutigkeit nutzen? Beydes ist eins. Denn wenn wir Beywörter hintennach setzen wollen, so müssen sie im *statu absoluto* stehen; wir müssen sagen: runde Räder, ehern und achtspeichigt. Allein in diesem *statu* kommen unsere Adjectiva völlig mit den Adverbiis überein, und müssen, wenn man sie als solche zu dem nächsten Zeitworte, das von dem Dinge prädiciret wird, ziehet, nicht selten einen ganz falschen, allezeit aber einen sehr schielenden Sinn verursachen.[6]

This is an important passage because it contains the essence of Lessing's whole attitude to language. The feature he is praising is both clear and concise; one might say that it is clear because

---

[1] L–M, VIII, p. 31. [2] *Ibid.* p. 81.
[3] Fülleborn; quoted L–M, XVI, p. 81. [4] L–M, XIV, p. 440.
[5] L–M, VII, p. 472. A similar idea is expressed in Diderot's *Lettre sur les Sourds et Muets* (1751), reviewed by Lessing in *Das Neueste aus dem Reiche des Witzes* (L–M, IV, p. 422). [6] L–M, IX, pp. 110–11.

it is concise. German, in trying to reproduce it, is either concise but not clear, or clear but not concise. Clear conciseness is Lessing's sovereign stylistic ideal. It is also his sole stylistic ideal. We see it in his objection to the 'platte Schwatzhaftigkeit' of his brother's plays.[1] We see it in his judgments on his contemporaries: Pope's genius defined as 'den reichsten, triftigsten Sinn in die wenigsten, wohlklingendsten Worte zu legen',[2] Gleim praised for his 'glückliche Kürze',[3] Cronegk for his 'nachdrückliche Kürze',[4] Klopstock blamed that his lines are sometimes not 'dunkel' enough.[5] We can see it in his lasting affection for Horace. We can see it in his predilection for the fable and the epigram. We can see it in all that word-grubbing which we have already discussed. We can see it in his rejection of the 'labyrinthische Perioden' of chancery style—the very opposite of all he stood for. We can see it in his objection to that 'kalte Vollständigkeit' and 'langweilige Deutlichkeit' which made Frau Gottsched turn 'J'en jouirai, je vous rendrai tous heureux' into 'Alsdenn werde ich meiner Güter erst recht genießen, wenn ich euch beide dadurch werde glücklich gemacht haben'. Note his comment: 'Dieses Alsdenn, mit seinem Schwanze von Wenn; dieses Erst; dieses Recht; dieses Dadurch: lauter Bestimmungen, die dem Ausbruche des Herzens alle Bedenklichkeiten der Ueberlegung geben, und *eine warme Empfindung in eine frostige Schlußrede verwandeln.*'[6] We can see it in his defence of pithy colloquialisms against the *style noble.* We can, I think, even see it in his approach to poetry.

There is, in the fifty-second *Literaturbrief*, high praise for Klopstock's essay on the difference between the language of poetry and that of prose. And there is, in the *Laokoon*, the statement: 'Der Poet will nicht bloß verständlich werden, seine

---

[1] L–M, XVII, p. 293.   [2] L–M, VIII, p. 5.
[3] L–M, VII, p. 106.   [4] L–M, IX, p. 191.
[5] 'Wir mußten es oft genug hören, der Messias sey nicht zu verstehen, und ich mußte mich oft genug auslachen lassen, wenn ich sagte, ich wollte, daß er noch ein wenig dunkler wäre.' He points out that the line: 'Die der Messias auf Erden in seiner Menschheit vollendet' says one thing thrice. This is in the review of the poem in the *Schrifften*, Second Part, 1753. L–M, v, p. 90.
[6] L–M, IX, p. 266. My italics.

Vorstellungen sollen nicht bloß klar und deutlich seyn; hiermit begnügt sich der Prosaist.'[1] But we are not told what extra qualities poetry demands, except for a statement (in the paralipomena to the same work) that 'natural' speech-signs give music to poetry and 'arbitrary' speech-signs must be elevated in poetry to the value of natural signs *by metaphor*.[2] Lessing seems hardly to have progressed beyond Breitinger's conception of the *Machtwort*. Poetry is for him a particularly pregnant form of expression; but nothing more. He never shows any appreciation of those other, less tangible qualities which make up the communication of poetry. One wonders what he would have made of Eichendorff. As for sound: 'Für mich ist schon die möglichste Kürze Wohlklang.'[3] And then there is that statement in one of the *Literaturbriefe*: 'Die Sprache kann alles ausdrücken, was wir deutlich denken; daß sie aber alle Nüancen der Empfindung sollte ausdrücken können, das ist eben so unmöglich, als es unnöthig seyn würde.'[4] One does not know exactly what he means by *ausdrücken* or how much stress is meant to fall on *alles* and *alle*. But the statement does not seem to indicate great feeling for poetry. And this might go some distance towards explaining why he liked Scultetus's: *Der Lazar wird erweckt / Und dankt den Würmen ab* and why he thought that Gottsched might have become a poet if his opinions and taste had broadened and clarified themselves with the opinions and taste of his age.[5] One cannot but conclude that Lessing was essentially a prose-writer with a prose-writer's demands on language.

His own prose was at first fairly conventional and rather cumbrous, but he soon began to develop more point and power as a result, no doubt, of his reading and translating from the French. His earliest works show a considerable number of provincial words current in his home district. These decrease with time but words like *abluxen* (to deprive by guile), *ausgattern* (to espy),

---

[1] L–M, IX, p. 101.
[2] L–M, XIV, pp. 428–9. Using 'natural' and 'arbitrary' in Plato's sense, see below, p. 462.
[3] L–M, XVI, p. 92.
[4] L–M, VIII, pp. 132–3.
[5] L–M, X, p. 128.

ruscheln (to scamp), *stankern* (to rummage about) and *begeizen* (to begrudge) are still to be found in his mature works, especially in the polemical writings where he is out after a direct, hard-hitting effect. We also find homely words, not provincialisms, but not accepted as 'literary' at the time: such as *aufmutzen* (to point out), *aushunzen* (to rebuke), *verhunzen* (to bungle) or *ausfenstern, ausfilzen* (to scold). Adelung objected both to these provincial and to these colloquial elements in Lessing's vocabulary as 'unedel'. Lessing never shied at a good, strong word so long as it were appropriate to its context. He defended his use of the word *Hure* in *Minna von Barnhelm*.[1] He was opposed to all artificial diction. Hence his attacks on *Schwulst* and the *style noble*. 'Bey einer gesuchten, kostbaren, schwülstigen Sprache kann niemals Empfindung seyn'; 'Die edelsten Worte sind eben deswegen, weil sie die edelsten sind, fast niemals zugleich diejenigen, die uns in der Geschwindigkeit, und besonders im Affecte, zu erst beyfallen.'[2] The ideal should be 'nicht das edelste, sondern das nachdrücklichste Wort'. In sentence-construction Lessing shows many of the anti-Ciceronian features evolved by Gottsched and advanced by Gellert. In his attack on chancery style in the *Literaturbriefe*, he pointed out that when Cicero used elaborate periods there was always symmetry of words and symmetry of ideas; but now the form had lost all real functional shape and had degenerated into labyrinthine confusion. He admired the naturalness of Gellert. But his great ideal was the style of Voltaire. Voltaire in his *Conseils à un journaliste* had attacked the padding of Ciceronian style. Lessing reacted so strongly in the other direction that his dialogue in *Emilia Galotti* was elliptic and laconic, a fact noted by Goethe. He always retained the ability to unfold a complex period when it was needed. But he does not use superfluous particles to give his period conventionalised shape. ('Für mich ist die möglichste Kürze Wohlklang. Wenigstens ist dem Wohlklange leicht nichts hinderlicher, als überflüßige Partikeln.' 'Das *fast* ist ein recht nützliches Wörtchen, wenn man etwas ungereimtes sagen, und zugleich auch nicht

[1] L-M, xv, pp. 61–2.   [2] L-M, x, p. 31 and viii, p. 145.

sagen will'¹ etc.) With masterly control of every conceivable rhetorical and rhythmic device Lessing projects a sentence firmly towards its climax. The result is that his prose is less verbose than Gottsched's and less insipid than Gellert's. It has more concentration and more bite. Heine spoke of its 'höchste Solidität bei der höchsten Einfachheit; gleich Quadersteinen, ruhen die Sätze aufeinander',² and says that logical progression binds them together. Herder (in his obituary notice for *Der Teutsche Merkur*, October 1781) spoke of Lessing's 'Geschlankigkeit des Ausdruks', and paid tribute to his dialogue style 'in dem er die durchdachtesten Sachen mit Neckerey und Leichtigkeit gleichsam nur hinzuwerfen wußte'. His writing had nothing 'von der plumpen Art, von dem steifen Gange, den man ihr [the German language] zum Nationaleigenthum machen will'.³

It is interesting to face these statements with what Lessing himself said in the thirteenth *Literaturbrief* about the French language: 'Die Franzosen, ohne Zweifel, haben eine blühendere Sprache; sie zeigen mehr Witz, mehr Einbildungskraft; der *Virtuose* spricht mehr aus ihnen.'⁴ More than the Germans, is the implication. Lessing was always on his guard against surface brilliance. There is a most important reference to this in the second *Anti-Goeze*, where he says:

> Was kann ich dafür, daß ich nun einmal keinen andern Stil habe? Daß ich ihn nicht erkünstle, bin ich mir bewußt. Auch bin ich mir bewußt, daß er gerade dann die ungewöhnlichsten Cascaden zu machen geneigt ist, wenn ich der Sache am reifsten nachgedacht habe. Er spielt mit der Materie oft um so muthwilliger, je mehr ich erst durch kaltes Nachdenken derselben mächtig zu werden gesucht habe.
>
> Es kömmt wenig darauf an, wie wir schreiben: aber viel, wie wir denken.... Ich kenne keinen blendenden Stil, der seinen Glanz nicht von der Wahrheit mehr oder weniger entlehnet. Wahrheit allein gibt echten Glanz; und muß auch bey Spötterey und Posse, wenigstens als Folie, unterliegen.⁵

---

¹ L–M, XVI, p. 92; V, p. 298.
² In *Zur Geschichte der Religion und Philosophie in Deutschland*, Zweites Buch.
³ Original edition, p. 4.   ⁴ L–M, VIII, p. 28.
⁵ L–M, XIII, pp. 149–50.

The realisation of the temptation towards virtuosity was accompanied by the strength to resist it, a strength based on his ideal of truth. This stylistic criterion of truth is not very different from Gellert's cultured naturalness. Talking of letter-writing Lessing said elsewhere that the best manual of that art should prove that no manual was necessary and that the whole art of letter-writing was to write without art: 'Allein wie viel seltne Eigenschaften setzt diese Vermeidung der Kunst voraus? Gesunde Ordnung im Denken, lebhafter Wiz, Kenntniß der Welt, ein empfindliches Herze, Leichtigkeit des Ausdrucks.'[1] He shared the current conception that a letter should be a natural dialogue with an absent person. Dialogue (with or without the other person's reply) is Lessing's fundamental form of expression. Not only in the drama but in the critical writings. Someone is being addressed nearly all the time.[2] It is a vivid style punctuated by accents of arraignment or appeal. An orator pleading a case, ridiculing an enemy, tickling the responses of the public. It is a persuasive style and therefore rhetorical devices are in place in it. We note the use of interjections, rhetorical questions, sudden apostrophes (sometimes to the reader), intensification by repetition or variation or enumeration, the anaphoric taking-up of an idea and spinning it further, the casting of a word into unusual relief by unusual word-order and the brilliant use of punctuation in which the very dots and dashes speak. We encounter all sorts of old friends from the chancery style: omission of auxiliary verb, use of a pair of synonyms instead of one word, constant play with antitheses and even the protasis if-clause. There is altogether a tendency to stress the main clause by leading up to it: 'Daß ich ihn nicht erkünstle, bin ich mir bewußt.' These devices and many others give shape to the thoughts, tension to the arrangement and persuasiveness to the argument. Dr Stopp has shown how Lessing's obsession with *clarity* leads him into an analytic attention to words, to constant definitions and distinctions; and how his addiction to

---

[1] Review of Gellert's work, 1751. L–M, IV, p. 315.
[2] The eleventh *Literaturbrief* contains an encomium of the Socratic method and a recommendation for its use in the establishment of definitions.

emphasis leads him into various forms of amplification, either cumulative (giving gradation) or accumulative (giving breadth). He has revealed that there is a strong tendency in Lessing for doublets 'to multiply weed-like throughout a passage', doublets which, if undifferentiated, give breadth but if differentiated, give elegance; and that, to some degree, this elegant variation unites within itself the opposite values of clarity and emphasis. Dr Stopp is only speaking of the polemical writings; but because of this restriction of the field and the functional type of analysis employed, his study goes far deeper than anything else written on Lessing's language and its conclusions would seem to be relatable to the observations we ourselves have already made in this study. This rhetorical expansiveness is not confined to the polemical writings; it is found in other works of Lessing but together with the opposite tendency, that tendency towards laconic, elliptic writing noted by Goethe. Both forms of expression—terse as well as broad—are natural to Lessing. How is this to be accounted for? I think by the fact that the ideal of graphic conciseness contains two disparate elements which are sometimes in harmony but also sometimes in conflict. Concision is one form of emphasis; but expansiveness is another. One can get a point home by saying it sharply or by saying it repeatedly. It would seem that for Lessing the sharp type of emphasis, the saying much in few words, was the highest ideal. But he recognised that this was not always attainable, and that breadth was sometimes necessary. His comparison of Greek and German in the *Laokoon* suggested, as we saw, that sharp emphasis was less easily attainable in German; and it was this that he was searching for in his word-grubbings. But normally, for emphatic and persuasive writing, he needed breadth and all the figures of *anaphora* and *amplificatio*. His rhetoric is highly artistic, but it never degenerates into mere virtuosity. The end is clarity and emphasis. The style never becomes an end in itself. In that sense it is not *erkünstelt*.

With these observations in mind, let us conclude our consideration of Lessing by examining some samples of his prose. First of all a very familiar passage:

'Niemand, sagen die Verfasser der Bibliothek, wird leugnen, daß die deutsche Schaubühne einen grossen Theil ihrer ersten Verbesserung dem Herrn Professor *Gottsched* zu danken habe.'

Ich bin dieser Niemand; ich leugne es gerade zu. Es wäre zu wünschen, daß sich Herr *Gottsched* niemals mit dem Theater vermengt hätte. Seine vermeinten Verbesserungen betreffen entweder entbehrliche Kleinigkeiten, oder sind wahre Verschlimmerungen.

Als die *Neuberin* blühte, und so mancher den Beruf fühlte, sich um sie und die Bühne verdient zu machen, sahe es freylich mit unserer dramatischen Poesie sehr elend aus. Man kannte keine Regeln; man bekümmerte sich um keine Muster. Unsre *Staats- und Helden-Actionen* waren voller Unsinn, Bombast, Schmutz und Pöbelwitz. Unsre *Lustpiele* bestanden in Verkleidungen und Zaubereyen; und Prügel waren die witzigsten Einfälle derselben. Dieses Verderbniß einzusehen, brauchte man eben nicht der feinste und gröste Geist zu seyn. Auch war Herr *Gottsched* nicht der erste, der es einsahe; er war nur der erste, der sich Kräfte genug zutraute, ihm abzuhelfen. Und wie ging er damit zu Werke? Er verstand ein wenig Französisch und fing an zu übersetzen; er ermunterte alles, was reimen und *Oui Monsieur* verstehen konnte, gleichfalls zu übersetzen; er verfertigte, wie ein Schweitzerischer Kunstrichter sagt, mit *Kleister und Scheere* seinen *Cato*; er ließ den *Darius* und die *Austern*, die *Elise* und den *Bock im Processe*, den *Aurelius* und den *Wizling*, die *Banise* und den *Hypocondristen*, ohne Kleister und Scheere machen; er legte seinen Fluch auf das extemporiren; er ließ den Harlequin feyerlich vom Theater vertreiben, welches selbst die größte Harlequinade war, die jemals gespielt worden; kurz, er wollte nicht sowohl unser altes Theater verbessern, als der Schöpfer eines ganz neuen seyn. Und was für eines neuen? Eines Französirenden; ohne zu untersuchen, ob dieses französirende Theater der deutschen Denkungsart angemessen sey, oder nicht.[1]

We note the effect of the punctuation ('Ich bin dieser Niemand; ich leugne es gerade zu'; 'Man kannte keine Regeln; man bekümmerte sich um keine Muster.') and the skilful paragraphisation. We note the use of rhetorical balance ('entbehrliche Kleinigkeiten...wahre Verschlimmerungen') of enumeration ('Unsinn, Bombast, Schmutz und Pöbelwitz'), of inversion of clauses for emphasis ('Dieses Verderbnis einzusehen, brauchte

[1] L–M, VIII, pp. 41–2.

man eben nicht der feinste und gröste Geist zu sein'), anaphora and repetition ('der erste, der es einsahe...der erste, der...') and of rhetorical question ('Und wie ging er damit zu Werke?') There follows a succession of parallel clauses ('Er verstand... er ermunterte... er verfertigte... er ließ... er legte seinen Fluch... er ließ...') and the enumeration of play-titles, working up to the sudden discharge of tension with *kurz*—comma—and then a perfectly balanced two-part sentence with a *nicht sowohl— als* linkage. Then comes another anaphora expressed in a rhetorical question, a crisp sharp ellipsis *ohne zu untersuchen*, and then a most effective comma pushing the stress on to the final *nicht*. Analysed in this way the style seems very conscious. It certainly was always well-considered. 'Man muß nie schreiben, was einem zuerst in den Kopf kommt', Lessing wrote to his brother;[1] and he warned the critic about language: 'Er muß wissen, welche Wirkung er damit hervor bringen will, und es ist nothwendig, daß er seine Worte nach dieser Wirkung abwäget.'[2] But Lessing's point in saying that his style was not *erkünstelt*, was that he was not aiming to dazzle but to convince, not aiming at style but at truth. Here, in contrast, is a passage with more complex sentence-structures:

Ohne hier zu untersuchen, wie weit es dem Dichter gelingen kann, körperliche Schönheit zu schildern: so ist so viel unstreitig, daß, da das ganze unermeßliche Reich der Vollkommenheit seiner Nachahmung offen stehet, diese sichtbare Hülle, unter welcher Vollkommenheit zu Schönheit wird, nur eines von den geringsten Mitteln seyn kann, durch die er uns für Personen zu intereßiren weis. Oft vernachläßiget er dieses Mittel gänzlich; versichert, daß wenn sein Held einmal unsere Gewogenheit gewonnen, uns dessen edlere Eigenschaften entweder so beschäftigen, daß wir an die körperliche Gestalt gar nicht denken, oder, wenn wir daran denken, uns so bestechen, daß wir ihm von selbst wo nicht eine schöne, doch eine gleichgültige ertheilen. Am wenigsten wird er bey jedem einzeln Zuge, der nicht ausdrücklich für das Gesicht bestimmet ist, seine Rücksicht dennoch auf diesen Sinn nehmen dürffen.[3]

Despite its complexity this prose is neither obscure nor heavy. The vivid, ejaculatory style of the attack on Gottsched would

---

[1] L–M, XVII, p. 294. [2] L–M, X, p. 436.
[3] From chapter IV of the *Laokoon*, L–M, IX, p. 22.

obviously have been unsuited to this reflective, considered content, which finds suitably measured expression. It is not wordy. The links are functional. The participle *versichert* is elliptic. A few lines later, when occasion demands, he returns to a more graphic style:

> Wer tadelt ihn [the poet] also noch? Wer muß nicht vielmehr bekennen: wenn der Künstler wohl that, daß er den Laokoon nicht schreyen ließ, so that der Dichter eben so wohl, daß er ihn schreyen ließ?
>
> Aber Virgil ist hier bloß ein erzehlender Dichter. Wird in seiner Rechtfertigung auch der dramatische Dichter mit begriffen seyn? Einen andern Eindruck macht die Erzehlung von jemands Geschrey; einen andern dieses Geschrey selbst. Das Drama, welches für die lebendige Mahlerey des Schauspielers bestimmt ist, dürfte vielleicht eben deswegen sich an die Gesetze der materiellen Mahlerey strenger halten müssen. In ihm glauben wir nicht bloß einen schreyenden Philoktet zu sehen und zu hören; wir hören und sehen wirklich schreyen.[1]

Note how in the following passage measured reflection is succeeded by graphic description with a return to reflection in the last sentence:

> Wenn in einer heftigen Situation die Seele sich auf einmal zu sammeln scheinet, um einen überlegenden Blick auf sich, oder auf das, was sie umgiebt, zu werfen; so ist es natürlich, daß sie allen Bewegungen des Körpers, die von ihrem bloßen Willen abhangen, gebieten wird. Nicht die Stimme allein wird gelassener; die Glieder alle gerathen in einen Stand der Ruhe, um die innere Ruhe auszudrücken, ohne die das Auge der Vernunft nicht wohl um sich schauen kann. Mit eins tritt der fortschreitende Fuß fest auf, die Arme sinken, der ganze Körper zieht sich in den wagrechten Stand; eine Pause — und dann die Reflexion. Der Mann steht da, in einer feyerlichen Stille, als ob er sich nicht stöhren wollte, sich selbst zu hören. Die Reflexion ist aus, — wieder eine Pause — und so wie die Reflexion abgezielet, seine Leidenschaft entweder zu mäßigen, oder zu befeuern, bricht er entweder auf einmal wieder los, oder setzet allmälig das Spiel seiner Glieder wieder in Gang. Nur auf dem Gesichte bleiben, während der Reflexion, die Spuren des Affekts; Mine und Auge sind noch in Bewegung und Feuer; denn wir haben Mine und Auge nicht so urplötzlich in unserer

[1] L–M, IX, p. 23.

Gewalt, als Fuß und Hand. Und hierinn dann, in diesen ausdrückenden Minen, in diesem entbrannten Auge, und in dem Ruhestande des ganzen übrigen Körpers, bestehet die Mischung von Feuer und Kälte, mit welcher ich glaube, daß die Moral in heftigen Situationen gesprochen seyn will.[1]

It is this combination of the reflective and the vivid, the indirect and the direct, the abstract and the concrete—and the ability to pass from one to the other with equal verbal mastery that constitutes the individuality of Lessing's style. It represents the consummation of an attitude to and use of language which we have observed maturing in German prose since the time of Leibniz: the overthrow of a rigid Ciceronian sentence-mould in favour of greater variety in structure and rhythm but still representing a predominantly rationalistic view of language as the logical and ordered conveyance of thought. Lessing brings to this the persuasiveness of the orator and the directness of the dramatist. His language is therefore both rhetorical and vivid.

Herder, in a famous passage, says that Lessing's style is like his view of poetry—thought and image evolve as we read.[2] He contrasts this with the style of Winckelmann. If Lessing's style is progressive, Winckelmann's is static. A static style, a style that deals with objects rather than with processes, would seem to be well suited to a historian of the plastic arts. Recently Hans Hafen, in a penetrating analysis of the first section of Winckelmann's *Beschreibung des Torso im Belvedere zu Rom* (1759), has drawn attention to the 'plastic' nature of this style, the greater importance given to nouns than to verbs, the calmness of the rhythmic flow. Implied is a contrast between this plastic, nominal, static style of Winckelmann and the dramatic, verbal, dynamic style of Lessing.[3] Hafen shows how Winckelmann's language

---

[1] From the third number of the *Hamburgische Dramaturgie*, L–M, IX, pp. 196–7.   [2] First *Kritisches Wäldchen*; Suphan, III, p. 12.

[3] Hans Hafen, *op. cit.* (see above, p. 352), pp. 51–7. The third opposition of *Ruhe*—*Bewegung* is difficult to render adjectivally in English. There are two typescript dissertations on Winckelmann's language: Hans G. Evers, *Studien zu Winckelmanns Stil* (Göttingen, 1924), and Maria Müller, *Untersuchungen zur Sprache Winckelmanns* (Leipzig, 1926) which considers only accidence.

throws all the emphasis on to things rather than actions. An appositional phrase following a noun throws it into sharper relief, illustrative comparisons clarify the mental picture, pairs of synonyms achieve emphasis by variative repetition, verbs resolve themselves into periphrases with nominal elements (participles or infinitives) which can then be stressed. It is the style of a man concerned about solid things. In this it differs from the equally nominal style of Hagedorn. But two features, both noted by Hafen, seem not to conform with this characterisation: the many abstract words and the heavy particles. Hafen submits that the former failing is counteracted by concreteness of subject, the latter by general clarity of style. But this is not good enough. These features are not occasional blemishes, they are constant elements of the style. They must be taken into full account in any adequate description of Winckelmann's language. Let us now examine a few samples of his prose.

First, an example of the melodiousness and measuredness of his prose, achieved by the felicitous placing of well-sounding words:

Je ruhiger der Stand des Cörpers ist, desto geschickter ist er, den wahren Character der Seele zu schildern: in allen Stellungen, die von dem Stand der Ruhe zu sehr abweichen, befindet sich die Seele nicht in dem Zustand, der ihr der eigentlichste ist, sondern in einem gewaltsamen und erzwungenen Zustand. Kentlicher und bezeichnender wird die Seele in heftigen Leidenschaften; groß aber und edel ist sie in dem Stand der Einheit, in dem Stand der Ruhe. Im Laocoon würde der Schmertz, allein gebildet, Parenthyrsus gewesen seyn; der Künstler gab ihm daher, um das Bezeichnende und das Edle der Seele in eins zu vereinigen, eine Action, die dem Stand der Ruhe in solchem Schmertz der nächste war. Aber in dieser Ruhe muß die Seele durch Züge, die ihr und keiner andern Seele eigen sind, bezeichnet werden, um sie ruhig, aber zugleich wircksam, stille, aber nicht gleichgültig oder schläfrig zu bilden.[1]

[1] From the *Gedanken über die Nachahmung der griechischen Kunstwerke* (1755), ed. Urlichs, Stuttgart, 1885 (*Neudrucke*, no. 20), p. 25. The word *Parenthyrsus* is glossed in Fernow's edition of Winckelmann's works (Dresden, 1808) as 'das höchste Pathos an der unrechten Stelle'.

Note that the passage is entirely abstract. The rhythm corresponds to the *Ruhe* it is describing. Historically this prose represents the type of language established by Gellert, now raised to extreme refinement. It shows the same cultivation of balanced clauses with the same types of linkage (*Je...desto*; *nicht in dem Zustand... sondern*). The same 'Ruhe in der Bewegung' produces synonymic doublets (*gewaltsam und erzwungen*; *kentlicher und bezeichnender*), repetition (*in dem Stand...in dem Stand*), and even one tautology (*in eins zu vereinigen*). The verbs are colourless, almost inadequate: *schildern* in the first sentence seems inexact, *sich befinden* equally so and the rest are mostly periphrases with *werden* or *sein*, casting emphasis on to the nominal elements. The one exception is the peculiar but characteristic use of *bilden* at the very end, a verb which is always on the dividing line between abstract and concrete, and partakes of both. Let us now recall the most famous passage Winckelmann ever wrote:

> Das allgemeine vorzügliche Kennzeichen der Griechischen Meisterstücke ist endlich eine edle Einfalt, und eine stille Grösse, so wohl in der Stellung als im Ausdruck. So wie die Tiefe des Meers allezeit ruhig bleibt, die Oberfläche mag noch so wüten, eben so zeiget der Ausdruck in den Figuren der Griechen bey allen Leidenschaften eine grosse und gesetzte Seele.
>
> Diese Seele schildert sich in dem Gesicht des Laocoons, und nicht in dem Gesicht allein, bey dem heftigsten Leiden. Der Schmertz, welcher sich in allen Muskeln und Sehnen des Cörpers entdecket, und den man gantz allein, ohne das Gesicht und andere Theile zu betrachten, an den schmertzlich eingezogenen Unter-Leib beynahe selbst zu empfinden glaubet; dieser Schmertz, sage ich, äussert sich dennoch mit keiner Wuth in dem Gesichte und in der gantzen Stellung. Er erhebet kein schreckliches Geschrey, wie Virgil von seinem Laocoon singet: Die Oeffnung des Mundes gestattet es nicht; es ist vielmehr ein ängstliches und beklemmtes Seufzen, wie es Sadolet beschreibet. Der Schmertz des Cörpers und die Grösse der Seele sind durch den gantzen Bau der Figur mit gleicher Stärcke ausgetheilet, und gleichsam abgewogen.[1]

Abgewogen would seem to be the very word to describe Winckelmann's language. This passage shows the same cultivation of

---

[1] *Ed. cit.* p. 24.

balance as the one we have just analysed (note the steadying comma after *Einfalt*!). But whereas the first passage was entirely abstract, this one proceeds from abstract to concrete by way of an illustrative comparison. The terms of the comparison *die Tiefe des Meers*,...*die Oberfläche* are, in form, abstract; but in meaning, concrete. *Die Tiefe des Meers* is equivalent to *das tiefe Meer*; but an abstract form of statement is used, because quality is being compared with quality. *Oberfläche* is half-abstract, half-concrete. *Oeffnung* later in the passage looks abstract but is obviously concrete, because it refers to the shape of the mouth, not the action of opening it. This use of abstract words with almost, sometimes completely, concrete force seems to me fundamental in Winckelmann's language. In this early work he had not solved the relationship between abstract and concrete. He was always at a loss for a verb to express the relationship between the general and the particular. We noted in the last passage how imprecise seemed the verb *schildern* to express the relationship between soul and body: here we have 'der Ausdruck *zeiget*...eine Seele; die Seele *schildert* sich in dem Gesicht...; der Schmertz *entdecket* sich in allen Muskeln...*äussert* sich in dem Gesichte'. Indeed, an investigation of Winckelmann's verbs led me to the conclusion that, apart from virtual synonyms of *sein*, they are largely attempts to express this relationship.[1] The connection between abstract quality and concrete work of art remains ill-defined. The result is that abstract qualities often acquire plasticity by directed illumination. Hence '*eine* edle Einfalt...*eine* stille Grösse'. The distinction between the quality and its manifestation is slight. This is why abstract words occur so frequently in such a plastic style without appearing incongruous.

The heaviness in Winckelmann's prose is illustrated by the following passage, in which I italicise certain words:

Diese beyden Mumien sind über die gewöhnlichen leinenen Binden, womit *dergleichen* Körper unzählige mahl *pflegen bewunden zu seyn*, und

[1] For instance: *malen, zeigen, ausdrücken, andeuten, vorstellen, bilden, anwenden, bezeichnen, deuten*. By 'virtual synonyms of *sein*', I mean words like *scheinen, erscheinen, bedeuten, sich (be)finden, däfür gehalten werden, beruhen auf, als etwas angesehen werden, für etwas genommen werden, gehören zu*.

welche nach Art eines Barrecan gewebet worden, in verschiedene (und wie jemand an einer Mumie in England *bemerken wollen*, in drey) Arten von gröberer Leinwand eingewickelt. Diese Leinwand ist durch besondere Bänder, fast wie Gurte, jedoch schmäler, gearbeitet, befestiget, *dergestalt, daß* nicht die geringste Erhobenheit eines Theils des Gesichts zu sehen. Die oberste Decke ist eine feine Leinwand, *welche* mit einem gewissen dünnen Grund übertragen, häufig vergoldet, und mit allerhand Figuren gezieret ist: auf *derselben* ist die Figur des Verstorbenen gemalet.[1]

No comment is necessary. One recognises these elements for what they are and one knows their provenance. The heaviness seems to increase when Winckelmann is trying to be polite (as in prefaces and dedications) or trying to be pedantic (as in reporting his opponents' views).[2] The most common elements are the recurrent use of *welcher* as his relative and *derselbe* as his demonstrative pronoun, the use of certain 'long forms' of pronouns already rather archaic in those days (*denenjenigen*) and some rather archaic adverbial forms (*nunmehro, itzo, sonderlich, daselbst*, etc.) and heavier-sounding unsyncopated forms of verbs (*saget, dienet, spielet, erreichet, erleget*). These features are clearly to be interpreted as part of his extremely refined and elevated diction.[3]

When Winckelmann's first work appeared (*Gedanken über die Nachahmung der griechischen Kunstwerke*, 1755) Nicolai praised the exceptional concentration of its style: 'Der Ausdruck ist nachdrucksvoll und körnig, man wird niemals ein Wort finden, welches unnötig wäre.'[4] Evers describes this style as 'schroff...

[1] *Werke*, ed. Fernow, I, p. 119. Slightly modernised text.

[2] For instance, in the preface to the *Anmerkungen über die Baukunst der Alten* (1760) and the imagined rejoinder to his *Gedanken über die Nachahmung* which he published together with it, and with a reply, in 1766.

[3] Hafen recognises Winckelmann's 'Weglassung alles Banalen, Gewöhnlichen', but fails to relate this stiffness to that general observation. The fuller forms *saget, dienet*, etc. were allowed by Gottsched. Maria Müller (*op. cit.* p. 9) notes that these forms give Winckelmann's language 'einen edlen und feierlich gemessenen Klang', and that they contrast with the syncopated forms to be found in his letters. Their use in his works would therefore seem to be consciously stylistic.

[4] Review in the *Bibliothek der schönen Wissenschaften und der freyen Künste*, quoted on p. 214 of vol. I of Fernow's edition of Winckelmann's works (Dresden, 1808).

markante Prägung... energisches Auftreten... preussisch, streng, unpersönlich... gehackt... körnig'.[1] This is only partly true, for there is also careful cultivation of balance and symmetry, as we have seen. But Evers notes in it also the beginning of that copulative alignment of phrases which (as with Hagedorn, we may add) becomes a recurrent feature of this essentially nominal style. In drafts of his later work, especially for the *Geschichte der Kunst des Alterthums*, we observe hypotaxis being replaced by parataxis. His favourite type of sentence becomes a two-part parataxis connected by *und*. Sometimes an idea is divided into two such parts to attain clarification. Sometimes we find a relative clause succeeding a main clause, not with real subordination, but as extension of the idea in the main clause. Considerations of elegance and symmetry also play their part. This matured style appears at its best in the description of the Apollo Belvedere in the *Geschichte der Kunst des Alterthums*, Part Two (Dresden, 1764). Here is part of it:

> Ueber die Menschheit erhaben ist sein Gewächs, und sein Stand zeuget von der ihn erfüllenden Größe. Ein ewiger Frühling, wie in dem glücklichen Elysien, bekleidet die reizende Männlichkeit vollkommener Jahre mit gefälliger Jugend, und spielet mit sanften Zärtlichkeiten auf dem stolzen Gebäude seiner Glieder. Gehe mit deinem Geiste in das Reich unkörperlicher Schönheiten, und versuche ein Schöpfer einer Himmlischen Natur zu werden, um den Geist mit Schönheiten, die sich über die Natur erheben, zu erfüllen: denn hier ist nichts Sterbliches, noch was die Menschliche Dürftigkeit erfordert. Keine Adern noch Sehnen erhitzen und regen diesen Körper, sondern ein Himmlischer Geist, der sich wie ein sanfter Strohm ergossen, hat gleichsam die ganze Umschreibung dieser Figur erfüllet. Er hat den Python, wider welchen er zuerst seinen Bogen gebraucht, verfolget, und sein mächtiger Schritt hat ihn erreichet und erleget. Von der Höhe seiner Genugsamkeit geht sein erhabener Blick, wie ins Unendliche, weit über seinen Sieg hinaus: Verachtung sitzt auf seinen Lippen, und der Unmuth, welcher er in sich zieht, blähet sich in den Nüssen seiner Nase, und tritt bis in die stolze Stirn hinauf. Aber der Friede, welcher

---

[1] *Op. cit.* pp. 47–9.

in einer seligen Stille auf derselben schwebet, bleibt ungestört, und sein Auge ist voll Süßigkeit, wie unter den Musen, die ihn zu umarmen suchen.[1]

We notice that the verbs are no longer ciphers and that repetition and variation are no longer found. Everything is much tauter. The hovering between abstract and concrete has now developed into a fascinating interplay between the two: there are 'Zärtlichkeit*en*' and 'Schönheit*en*', there is '*ein* Frühling' and '*eine* Natur', a heavenly spirit fills an 'Umschreibung' and his 'Genugsamkeit' is a hill. And that certain ponderousness (which I prefer to call *weightiness*, for it is a positive quality in his style), appears in the relatives and demonstratives of the second half of the piece, but seems to be there in order to remind us that we are in the presence of no ordinary mortal but of the very god himself.

The vocabulary and rhythms of both Lessing's and Winckelmann's writing are essentially those of prose, and magnificently so. Never is there any suggestion of the half-lights or music of poetry. Never is there anything approaching *Sprache des Affekts* in Breitinger's sense—for Lessing's most impassioned utterances never abandon the logic of prose for more than a momentary ejaculation and Winckelmann never allows his enthusiasm to disrupt his reverence for shape and order. Meanwhile, however, something different was stirring in German prose, something that was to prove quite infectious:

O du! die du lieblicher bist, als der thauende Morgen, du mit den grossen schwarzen Augen; schön wallet dein dunkles Haar unter dem Blumenkranz weg, und spielt mit den Winden. Lieblich ists, wenn deine rothen Lippen zum Lachen sich öfnen, lieblicher noch, wenn sie zum Singen sich öfnen. Ich habe dich behorcht, Chloe! o ich habe dich behorcht! da du an jenem Morgen beym Brunnen sangest, den die zwo Eichen beschatten; böse daß die Vögel nicht schwiegen, böse daß die Quelle rauschte hab ich dich behorcht.

In this language there is no logical principle of sentence-construction. Sound and rhythm are its governing factors. Linkage

---

[1] *Op. cit.* quoting from the original edition (pp. 392–3). There is a copy in the British Museum.

is provided by sound, shape is conditioned by rhythm. Repetition is used to a degree that would seem poverty-stricken in the prose of normal argument, narrative or description. Here it is used with suggestive, not informative value. One clause is so strongly rhythmical that it falls into a regular metrical pattern ('die du lieblicher bist, als der thauende Morgen'). The section after the last semi-colon, almost devoid of grammatical assemblage, is given meaning by the echoing return of a former phrase. This is musical prose with a musical structure.

It is taken from one of Salomon Geßner's idylls published in 1756.[1] The influence of Klopstock is visible in 'der *thauende Morgen*', in 'wallet dein Haar *weg*' and perhaps in the meaning given to *beschatten*. But otherwise it is difficult to relate this language to anything we have encountered so far. Let us consider another sample:

> O wenn die frohen Lieder dir gefielen! die meine Muse oft dem Hirten abhorcht; auch oft belauschet sie in dichten Hainen der Bäume Nymphen und den Ziegenfüß'gen Wald-Gott, und Schilfbekränzte Nymphen in den Grotten; und oft besuchet sie bemooste Hütten, um die der Landmann stille Schatten pflanzet, und bringt Geschichten her, von Großmuth und von Tugend, und von der immer frohen Unschuld. Auch oft beschleichet sie der Gott der Liebe, in grünen Grotten dichtverwebner Sträuche, und oft im Weidenbusch an kleinen Bächen. Er horchet dann ihr Lied, und kränzt ihr fliegend Haar, wenn sie von Liebe singt und frohem Scherz.[2]

Ziegenfüßig, schilfbekränzt and *dichtverweben* suggest Greek *via* Klopstock; and *bemoost* and the transitive use of *kränzen* also point to Klopstock (or Haller). Nowhere else, however, would one find such a characteristic breaking of normal word-order for the sake of sound as 'bringt Geschichten her, *von Großmuth und von Tugend, und von der immer frohen Unschuld*' (some editions omit the commas; note the propelling force of the repeated *und*),

---

[1] *Idyllen von dem Verfasser des Daphnis* (Leipzig, 1760), quoting from the British Museum copy. This passage is on p. 16 and is the beginning of *Milon*. This German edition was a pirated reprint of the Zürich 1759 edition.

[2] *Ed. cit.* pp. 14–15.

or: 'wenn sie von Liebe singt *und frohem Scherz*'. Except perhaps in Winckelmann; but there for plastic, not musical effect. Note also the use of full, unsyncopated forms like *belauschet, besuchet, pflanzet*. We saw how Winckelmann achieved weightiness by this means; Geßner is merely concerned with melody, and hence he will also use uninflected (*fliegend Haar*) or clipped forms (*ziegenfüß'gen*) when they suit him. He avoids hiatus by elision or by use of a final *-e* where occasion demands; but he will retain or even enforce it where he wishes to break the regularity of the rhythm for some purpose. All this shows a highly sensitive ear. Sometimes the effect is quite magical, as in the beautiful opening of *Mirtil*:

Bey stillem Abend hatte Mirtil noch den Mondbeglänzten Sumpf besucht, die stille Gegend im Mondschein und das Lied der Nachtigall hatten ihn in stillem Entzüken aufgehalten. Aber izt kam er zurük, in die grüne Laube von Reben vor seiner einsamen Hütte, und fand seinen alten Vater sanftschlummernd am Mondschein, hingesunken, sein graues Haupt auf den einen Arm hingelehnt.[1]

The patterning is most subtle: the insistent *still* in the first sentence prepares the mood, *die grüne Laube von Reben* gives weight by its wordiness. Repetition and circumlocution, indefensible in a logical stylistic, are shown to have musical value. The rest is a languorous rhythmical sequence of careful composition. With Geßner's idylls sound and rhythm have become meaningful elements in German prose.[2] This is achieved by a very delicate extra accentuation of normal rhythms, sustained and controlled by a refined sensitivity and impeccable taste. It represents a gentle approximation of prose towards verse, involving perhaps a disrespect for the medium of prose, which may be considered theoretically unjustified. But historically it was of immense importance; for here in this highly rhythmical prose is the foundation

---

[1] *Ed. cit.* p. 28.
[2] Zimmermann wrote to Geßner on 4 August 1769: 'Sie haben zuerst der Welt gezeiget, daß die deutsche Sprache der feinsten Harmonie und des Ausdruckes der zärtlichsten Empfindungen fähig ist.'

of the prose of *Werther* and *Hyperion*. The vocabulary, apart from Klopstockian epithets, remains the vocabulary of prose; and the rhythms always avoid sustained regularity. The language never becomes verse, not even free verse. It is essentially prose, but a prose which is more highly charged emotionally. *Sprache des Affekts* achieved not by *Machtwörter* but by sound and rhythm. The historical accident is that another stream of highly rhythmical and highly emotional prose came into German literature at just this time—the prose of Ossian. Reinforced by the example of Ossian this type of prose appealed to the new generation as something in which the rhythm of their heart-beats could find direct expression without being transmuted into the logic of prose-statement.

The similarity between the prose of Geßner and that of Ossian was noted already by Coleridge in 1802: 'I have discovered that the poetical parts of the Bible and the best parts of Ossian are little more than slovenly hexameters, and the rhythmical prose of Gessner is still more so.'[1] The *Quarterly Review* for 1814 even suggested a real connection between the two.[2] This is hardly possible; for the first translation of Geßner into English was *The Death of Abel* in 1761 and Macpherson had published his *Fragments of ancient Poetry* in 1760. It seems unlikely that the German Geßner would have influenced his English rhythms, even supposing that Macpherson knew German. It seems more likely that the two had some inspiration in common. Macpherson's language would seem to have some direct connection with the English Bible. Much of it suggests the parallelism of Hebrew poetry. Coleridge, in the remark quoted above, suggests this connection; indeed it was almost acknowledged by Macpherson himself in the passages he quotes in his notes. But it is difficult to connect this,

---

[1] Letter to William Sotheby, dated 26 August 1802.

[2] 'The Death of Abel was probably one of the models upon which Macpherson formed his Ossianic style', *op. cit.* vol. XI, p. 78. The article states that the book's popularity in England was due in large measure to its style. The first translation was by Mrs Collyer. Geßner was well known to Scott, Byron and Wordsworth. See Bertha Reed, *The Influence of Solomon* [sic] *Gessner upon English Literature* (Philadelphia, 1905). The idylls were first translated in 1762.

or correspondingly Luther's Bible, with Geßner. The rhythms of Luther's translation are quite different from those of the Authorised Version, and in reading Geßner—or the idylls at least —one is not aware of anything resembling Luther's language. One might suspect classical influence. But Geßner, it would appear, relied on translations for his knowledge of Greek authors, although he did know Latin.[1] Of the modern languages he knew French, but not English.[2] The origins of Geßner's style are therefore somewhat obscure. Wölfflin suggests that he may have got it from a translation of Shaftesbury's hymn to Nature (in 'number'd prose') in *The Moralists*. It seems to me fairly clear, however, that it developed out of Geßner's own rather poor verses.

The information we have about Geßner's early literary affections is piecemeal and not very revealing; it is no surprise to learn that he devoured *Robinson Crusoe*, read Brockes 'with pleasure and profit' and confessed to a liking for the verses of Gleim and Hagedorn.[3] His earliest writings were described by his first biographer as 'Gedichte mit und ohne Reimen, Prose mit Versen untermischt, Fabeln, Erzählungen, Satyren und Anakreontische Lieder'—in fact all the genres cultivated by Gleim and his friends. One poem preserved from this period, the *Lied eines Schweizers an sein bewaffnetes Mädchen* published in 1750, is

---

[1] In the obituary notice of Geßner in the *Schweitzer Museum* for 1788 we read: 'Umsonst bemühte sich sein Lehrer ihm Latein und Griechisch beyzubringen, obgleich er in spätern Jahren jenes verstand und beydes hochschätzte.'

[2] Geßner to Tscharner, 8 January 1763: 'Ich verstehe kein Englisch, und kenne die Engländer nur aus Übersetzungen.'

[3] The first biography of Geßner was by J. H. Hottinger and published in 1796. There is an essay by A. Frey in the volume devoted to Geßner of Kürschner's *Deutsche National-Litteratur*. Other works include monographs by H. Wölfflin (1889) and F. Bergemann (1913). The fullest and most recent study is by P. Leemann-van Elck (Zürich and Leipzig, 1930). In 1930, the two-hundredth anniversary of Geßner's birth, a *Gedenkbuch* was published at Zürich which contains articles by Ermatinger and by Baldensperger (the latter entitled: 'L'épisode de Gessner dans la littérature européenne'). A Heidelberg diss. by Rudolf Strasser, *Stilprobleme in Geßners Kunst und Dichtung* (1936), makes interesting comparisons between Geßner's writing and painting. See also Erich Schmidt, 'Salomon Geßners rhythmische Prosa', *ZfdA*, XXI (1877), pp. 303 ff.

in unrhymed quatrains in ballad-metre, and culminates in a typical anacreontic *pointe*:

> Des frechen Feindes scharfer Pfeil
> Zisch' yber dir vorbey;
> Dich treffe nur der sanfte Pfeil
> Vom kleinen Liebes-Gott.[1]

It seems that some time in 1749, when Geßner was in Berlin, Ramler advised him to abandon writing in strict forms. He seems to have had no facility in versifying. In a letter to a friend of 19 May 1752, he said of his prose-poem *Der Frühling*: 'Ich soll ihn versifizieren, das ist mir ohnmöglich, ich habs versuchen wollen, aber ich brachte nicht drei Linien zusammen.' Wölfflin thinks it strange that Ramler should have advised him against verse, seeing that Ramler himself was such a formalist and later translated some of the idylls and *Der erste Schiffer* into hexameters. But this is not the point: Ramler was not disapproving of verse, he merely saw that Geßner would express himself better in a less regular medium which made full use of rhythmical variety. Wölfflin tells us (without examples) that translations published at Zürich at this time were often in rhythmical prose and it was this sort of prose that set Geßner off. But surely we have only to transpose Geßner's very loose-limbed, unrhymed verse into prose to get the basis of his style; and surely Ramler is indicating this when, in the dedication to his hexametric translation of Geßner's idylls, he recalls the early Berlin days in words which Wölfflin quotes without grasping their full significance:

> Damals wußtest du selten dein Lied in Bande zu zwingen:
> Immer floß es frei durch mannigfaltige Strophen
> Jede melodisch und jede von selbst erfundenem Versmaß...

From these lines we get a fairly clear idea of what these lost verses were like. Melodious, but irregular. It is from these verses that his prose developed.

---

[1] Text, with Bodmerian orthography, from the 1762 Zürich edition of the *Schriften*, British Museum copy, Part III, p. 141.

THE PROSE OF MATURITY

It is fascinating to watch it grow. The prose-poem *Die Nacht*, published anonymously in 1753, already has some features of his mature style: rhythmical use of repetition:

(*a*) Stille Nacht! Wie lieblich überfällst du mich hier! hier am bemoosten Stein.

(*b*) Flammen hüpfen daher, mit hüpfenden Flammen, sie wollen sich haschen...[1]

breaking of normal word-order ('Ich will hingehn aus dem Hain') and Klopstockian participles (*dichtbelaubt, sternebesäet, hochgewölbt*). One passage in the work, later remodelled, parodied a passage in Bodmer's *Syndflut*. Bodmer recognised this and the Klopstockian influence.[2] Geßner later called the work 'une carricature composée dans une heure de folie ou d'ivresse'. It is difficult to know what to make of it, especially as the original edition is so hard to come by and later editions have a revised text. The pastoral *Daphnis* (1754) shows the influence of Klopstock even more markedly. Thus in the first few paragraphs we have *dahinreißen, daherschwimmen, umherlächeln, aufwachsen, umherschwärmen, hingegossen,* and *einhergehen* as well as the usual participles. Later on we find *freundlichlächelnd* and *schmachtendlächelnd* (printed with divisions in some editions); *aufbeben; Wem rauschen die Quellen Vergnügen; er athmet Entzücken; befalten* (in the sense of 'to cover with folds') and, several times, the word *thränend*. The prose shows complete absence of incapsulation:

Der trat er hinein zu seinem alten Vater, der freudig seinem Sohn entgegen lachte und von dem Fest ihn fragte, und dann erzehlte, wie oft er gesehen, daß der wilde Fluß das Ufer weggerissen, Bäume voll reiffer Früchte auf wütenden Wellen weggetragen, wie er schon Nachen umgerissen und Hirten enträkt hat. Daphnis höret ihm stillschweigend zu, und geht dann aus der Hütte, und bleibt unter den

---

[1] Quoting from Frey's text in Kürschner's *Deutsche National-Litteratur*.

[2] Bodmer to Sulzer, 23 April 1753: 'Der junge Geßner hat in seiner Nacht, einem Gedicht in Prosa, das er auf Weihnacht publiziert hat, die geweihtesten Ausdrücke der Messiade auf die profansten Sujets applicirt.' Bergemann, however, does not think Geßner was being malicious, but rather attempting to conciliate Bodmer. I am not convinced.

Bäumen die vor seiner Hütte stehen, und sieht die ganze Gegend im düstern Mondlicht, da steht er traurig und seufzt.[1]

Copulative conjunctions are frequent and subordination is of the simplest. Inside the sentence the elements follow each other in simple, uninterrupted succession:

aber itzt sang er nicht, | er gieng still aus der Hütte, | und trieb seine kleine Herde | staunend | vor sich her | auf die Flur.[2]

Whole sequences are paratactic:

  Oft saß Daphnis traurig am Bach oder im Hain, dann sank er wachend in Träume hin, er sah sein Mädchen, er erzehlt ihr seine Liebe, sie wird schamroth, er drückt ihr die Hand, und küßt sie, will fliehn, er umfaßt ihre Knie und weint, sie seufzt und lächelt, sie setzt sich neben ihn, er küßt sie unersättlich, sie küßt ihn wieder, er drückt sie an seine Brust, dann drängt sich der traurige Gedanke hervor, daß...[3]

It may well be that, as Bergemann suggests, Amyot's translation of Longus induced this paratactic structure; I should prefer 'helped to induce', for the form seems so natural to Geßner's style. We have now reached the extreme opposite of the *Kanzleistil*. The attendant danger is monotony. But there are already the beginnings of simple rhythmic patternings: 'Dann sucht' er einen Nachen, und fuhr aus andre Ufer und suchte sein Mädchen, lief dem Ufer nach, und stieg auf die Hügel und suchte sein Mädchen...'[4] or: 'Ach! dann, dann pochet mein Herz, dann seh ich nicht Frühling, dann riech ich nicht Blumen, ach! dann fühl ich nur, dann fühl ich nur deinen Kuß.'[5] or: 'Ich will hinfliehn, hinfliehn will ich'; 'Alles freute sich itzt, nur Daphnis konnte sich nicht freuen'. The last example has just that touch of clumsiness which would not pass muster in the Idylls. The rhythm

---

[1] I have been unable to see the original edition, but quote from the German 1756 reprint of it (British Museum copy). This is on p. 14. The word *die* in line 10 of my quotation is absent from some later editions of the text.

[2] *Ibid.* p. 16. My division.

[3] *Ibid.* p. 18. Strasser, *op. cit.* pp. 35 ff. points out that Geßner's *dass-*, *wenn-* and *wie-*clauses often do not represent real subordination. He also notes that parallelism is persistent and characteristic.

[4] *Op. cit.* p. 18.   [5] *Ibid.* p. 53.

THE PROSE OF MATURITY

collapses in a sentence like: 'Dann stör ich die Ruhe des grauen Alters durch Unmuth und Verdruß', or: 'Ach! dich nicht mehr sehn und unglücklich seyn, unglücklich seyn mein Leben durch!' On the other hand there is a conscious, though not consistent, attempt to avoid hiatus; for example: 'Ich könnt ihm nicht danken, ich konnte nur weinen.' This might account for the use of the forms *grösseste* and *höheste*. One can feel the maturing of a style in *Daphnis* and one can see quite clearly the direction in which it is developing. The influence of Klopstock is indisputable; the presence of phrases like *Wem rauschen die Quellen Vergnügen* or *Er athmet Entzücken* and the repeated use of two of Klopstock's favourite words *thränend* and *dahinfließen* point to this. There is even more evidence in the *Idyllen*, where we find the compound participles, the prefix-compounds and occasionally the transitive use of normally intransitive verbs. When a phrase falls into regular metrical form, this can usually be construed as hexametric.[1] He must have known something of *Der Messias*. This is the only outside influence to be perceived in Geßner's language, and even this must not be overstated. His vocabulary has nothing of Klopstock's adventurousness and he never comes anywhere near being obscure.[2] The sound-pattern is totally different from that of Klopstock. It remains a highly individual style; and if we take it right back to include *Die Nacht* it would seem to have developed steadily in the search for melodic perfection and consistently out of his own abandonment of verse-forms. There is not much development beyond the first collection of *Idyllen*. *Der Tod Abels* (1758) has, in the outbursts of Cain, some forebodings of the ejaculatory style of *Sturm und Drang* drama; for instance:

Kain stund in betäubendem Schrecken todblaß, kalter Schweiß umfloß die bebenden Glieder; er sah des Erschlagenen letzte krampfichte Bewegung und das rinnende, zu ihm aufrauchende Blut. 'Verfluchter

---

[1] For example: 'Ach dann schwellt mir die Brust und häufige Thränen...'; or: 'Dann soll es seyn wie ein Hain voll süsser Gerüche.'

[2] In a letter to Ramler dated 12 February 1775, Geßner repudiates the 'abentheuerliche hieroglyphische Heldensprache' of Klopstock. Klopstock, in a letter to Azerbi of November 1800, called Geßner 'trivial' (*Deutsche Rundschau*, April, 1894).

Schlag! rief er, Bruder! — erwache — erwache Bruder! Wie blaß ist sein Gesicht! wie starr sein Auge! wie das Blut um sein Haupt hinfließt! — Ich Elender! — o was ahnt mir! — Höllische Schrecken! so brüllt er und warf wütend die blutbespritzte Keule weit weg, und schlug die starke Faust wider seine Stirne. Itzt wankt' er zum Erschlagnen hin und wollt' ihn von der Erd' aufheben; Abel! — Bruder! — erwache! Ha! — Höllenangst faßt mich! wie sein blutträufelndes Haupt hängt! wie ohnmächtig! — Tot — o Höllenangst, er ist tot! Ich will fliehen! Eilet, wankende Knie!' So brüllt er, und floh ins nahe Gebüsche.[1]

But it lives mainly on its idyllic and its lyrical passages, and there is an uncomfortable contrast between the pointed rhythmical expression of the various apostrophes and the prosaic narration where rhythm is not used consciously. The later works, especially *Der erste Schiffer* (1762) and the second collection of idylls (1772), show a falling-away in style with an abandonment of his earlier, highly individual manipulation of rhythms, although the language always retains a certain melodiousness. There is a quaint but correct statement on Geßner's significance for his time in the *Critical Review* for 1769:

Upon the whole there is something so original, new and pleasing in these elegant poems, as sufficiently to evince that genius is confined to no country, and that Germany can produce poets as well as Great Britain, France or Italy. If we may judge from some later influences in the fine arts, particularly music and poetry, taste is daily gaining ground in Germany on that heavy literature which used to distinguish the subjects of the empire. Gessner and the melodious Abel are alone sufficient to rescue that nation from the injudicious censure of dullness and insensibility.

Certainly as far as prose was concerned, Germany had now shown that she had a language that would compare with the other literary languages of Europe, a language that had outgrown a conventionalised prose-style and shown itself capable of individual handling to great effect by three such different personalities as those we have considered in this chapter.

[1] Works, ed. Frey, p. 154.

XII

THE CULTURE OF WIT AND FEELING

In his praise of the poems of Theocritus, Geßner had contrasted their sincerity and simplicity with the 'epigrammatic pointed wit' fashionable in his own day.[1] This was an important component of the eighteenth-century atmosphere. Indeed, Professor Böckmann claims that it was the predominant element in the culture of *Aufklärung* Germany.[2] Baroque literature had cultivated *Zierlichkeit*; the succeeding age rejected this as external bombast and advocated more attention to content. Wernicke praised 'sinnreiche Gedanken und Einfälle' rather than 'balsamierte und vergüldte Redensarten'. Christian Weise said much the same. Wernicke and Thomasius had advocated the French ideal of the *bel esprit*; and Wernicke, in referring to Bouhours's allegations about the Germans, had used the word *Witz* to designate that *esprit* they were supposed to lack. Bouhours had said that in the *bel esprit* there was a combination of intelligence and imagination; Christian Wolff described *Witz* as a mixture of *Einbildungskraft* and *Scharfsinnigkeit*. Basing himself on Locke's distinction between wit as the observation of likenesses and judgment as the observation of differences, Wolff defined *Witz* as 'die Leichtigkeit, die Ähnlichkeiten wahrzunehmen' but he considered judgment (*Scharfsinnigkeit*) as part of this. Wit was really the discovery of *hidden* likenesses, and for this judgment was needed. Wolff said in his Metaphysics:

Wer scharfsinnig ist, der kann sich deutlich vorstellen, auch was in den Dingen verborgen ist und von andern übersehen wird. Wenn nun

---

[1] Preface to the 1756 collection of *Idyllen*.
[2] P. Böckmann, 'Das Formprinzip des Witzes in der Frühzeit der deutschen Aufklärung', *Jahrbuch des Freien Deutschen Hochstifts* (Frankfurt am Main, 1932–3), pp. 52–130; and the same author's *Formgeschichte der deutschen Dichtung*, vol. I (Hamburg, 1949), pp. 471–546. For an objection that this formulation is too narrow, see Bruno Markwardt, *Geschichte der deutschen Poetik*, vol. II (Berlin, 1956), pp. 27–9.

die Einbildungskraft andere Dinge hervorbringet..., welche mit den gegenwärtigen etwas gemein haben, so erkennet er... ihre Ähnlichkeit. Derowegen da die Leichtigkeit die Ähnlichkeit wahrzunehmen der Witz ist, so ist klar, daß *Witz* aus einer *Scharfsinnigkeit* und guten *Einbildungskraft* und Gedächtnis entstehet.[1]

Into this English analysis of 'wit' has gone much of the French ideal of *esprit*. For Wolff it was *scharfsinnige Einbildungskraft* and from it sprang all literary creation. It could be found, he thought, in language as well as in content. Böckmann suggests that this ideal really lies behind Gottsched's *Critische Dichtkunst*. He notes that according to Gottsched the poet must possess 'starke Einbildungskraft, viel Scharfsinnigkeit und einen großen Witz'.[2] *Witz* was also Gottsched's specification of the essence of the *poetische Schreibart*. Gottsched's followers called their organ *Belustigungen des Verstandes und des Witzes*. It was a conscious attempt to refute Bouhours's allegation, more recently restated by Mauvillon in his *Lettres françaises et germaniques* of 1740. The *Belustigungen* brought instructive material in amusing and ironical form. Anacreontic poetry stemmed from the same ideal of *Witz*. In G. F. Meier's *Gedanken von Scherzen* (Halle, 1744), a work which we know to have been influential on Gleim and his friends, there is constant reference to 'Aufheiterung des Gemüts' as the purpose of art and of 'scharfsinniger Witz' as the means to achieve this end. The artistic form is *Scherz*, a highly conscious, intellectual medium: 'Ich rate daher einem jedweden witzigen Kopfe, nicht gleich einen jeden sinnreichen Einfall für einen Scherz zu halten und auszugeben, sondern jederzeit zu bedenken, ob der Witz durch die nötige Scharfsinnigkeit unterstützt worden.'[3] Markwardt sees in this concept of *Scherz* 'ein Versuch, das Frostige des Witzig-Geistreichen erwärmend und belebend

---

[1] *Op. cit.* sect. 858. See above (p. 100) for Bodmer's discussion of this point.

[2] *Op. cit.* ch. 11. See above, p. 230: *Witz* and *Einfälle*.

[3] *Op. cit.* p. 64. See Böckmann, 'Das Formprinzip des Witzes', p. 129, and *Formgeschichte*, pp. 526 ff. Meier relates *Scherz* to the concepts of *iocus* and *facetia* found in Cicero and Quintilian, and is careful to distinguish it from mere *Narrenspossen*.

zu zerschmelzen'.[1] It connotes the essence of rococo as against *Aufklärung*. Related to it are the concepts of *das Gefällige, das Graciöse* and *das Niedliche*. The whole atmosphere is warmer, more humane, less intellectual. *Gefällig* stands to *artig* as *Scherz* to *Witz*. One of its meanings is 'flexible, pliable'. Society is there in the background influencing this concept. Art becomes more concerned with *delectare* than *prodesse*.

Essential to the workings of *Witz* is the ability of the author to detach himself from his subject, to stand back and observe it with a quizzing-glass. If his passions become involved, the form is shattered. A certain playfulness is essential to this style. It must never demand to be taken seriously. If it does, it becomes absurd or repulsive. This is what happened when serious moralising invaded the sophisticated playfulness of English Restoration drama. Böckmann shows how the form is beginning to break down in Lessing's comedies, especially in *Minna von Barnhelm*. The effect is a rather uncomfortable seriousness. The heart begins to make its demands, although playfulness and true *Witz* remain in the language most of the time. In a letter Lessing had noted the 'dangers' of displaying too much wit: 'Ein Dichter, der Witz und Lebhaftigkeit besitzet, kann sehr leicht in diesen Fehler fallen, der aber dem wahren Ausdruck der Leidenschaften ungemein zuwider ist.'[2] It depends, of course, on whether one wishes to attain 'den wahren Ausdruck der Leidenschaften'. *Minna* does. The pure culture of wit did not. Nothing was further from its purpose, as we shall see in discussing the anacreontics. But Lessing felt too deeply about certain subjects for him to remain comfortably within the culture of wit. This explains his uneasiness about the 'cascades' he was prone to. Klopstock, in a passage we have already quoted, realised to the full this

---

[1] *Geschichte der deutsche Poetik*, vol. II, pp. 243 ff. This whole section, 'Das Kunstwollen des Rokoko', forms an interesting extension to Böckmann. It is by far the best treatment of the aesthetics of German anacreonticism and has some interesting things to say on Wieland (although I do not entirely agree with his presentation of Wieland, as I indicate below).

[2] *Briefwechsel mit Mendelssohn und Nicolai über das Trauerspiel*, ed. Petsch (Leipzig, 1910), p. 41.

contrast between *Witz* and *Herz*: 'Die höhere Poesie ist ein Werk des Genie; und sie soll nur selten einige Züge des Witzes, zum Ausmalen, anwenden. Es giebt Werke des Witzes, die Meisterstücke sind, ohne daß das Herz etwas dazu beygetragen hatte.'[1] Spener had made a moral contrast between the *einfältige Herz* and the *lüsternden Ingeniorum fürwitz*. Breitinger had contrasted subjects able 'unsern Vorwitz zu stillen' with those able 'das Herz zu rühren'.[2] Klopstock is saying that *Witz* and *Herz* are incompatible. They are each destructive of the other.

Anacreontic poetry is the poetry of wit. It cultivated ingenious conceits and pleasing comparisons. But it was not purely cerebral. It appealed also to the feelings. 'Was für süße Empfindungen habe ich Ihnen zu danken' wrote Geßner to Gleim about his poetry; it contained 'die feinsten Empfindungen', he was 'der feinste Dichter der Freude'.[3] Note the epithets. Feeling appears in this poetry not as passion but as sentiment. It is refined; and the characteristic adjectives applied to it are *süß, fein* and *angenehm*. 'Witz und Empfindung, zwey so ungleichartige und doch so nahe verwandte Dinge', exclaimed Wieland.[4] This is the real answer to Klopstock's assertion of the incompatibility of *Witz* and *Herz*. *Witz* embodies refinement, a refinement of the reason; *Herz* is naked and direct expression of the emotions. Only when it has undergone similar refinement, can it coexist with *Witz*. The word used to denote this refinement of feeling is *Empfindung*. This stands in the same relation to *Herz* as *Witz* to *Vernunft*. The refinement is to a certain extent socially conditioned: *Witz* and *Empfindung* are therefore hallmarks of civilisation. The connection between these two cultures has not been sufficiently recognised by historians of eighteenth-century German literature. It is this omission of the culture of feeling which makes Böckmann's analysis, for all its clarity, incomplete. Similarly, writers on *Empfindsamkeit*, tend to present the culture of feeling as a later reaction

[1] See above, p. 328.
[2] Spener, *Pia desideria* (quoted Böckmann, *Formgeschichte*, p. 563); Breitinger, *Critische Dichtkunst*, I, p. 85 (quoted Böckmann, *op. cit.* p. 571).
[3] Letters to Gleim dated 16 June 1767 and 18 April 1772.
[4] In the second of the *Briefe an einen jungen Dichter*, 1782.

against or simultaneous countercurrent to the culture of reason. Both are inherently connected as different aspects of the movement towards sophistication in a country which needed it. The connection becomes apparent when we view the situation linguistically.

A taste for anacreontic verse had established itself in Germany during the seventeenth century. Its civilised indirectness had appealed to the courtly artificiality of that day, and its description of simple pleasures was not irreconcilable with *carpe diem* or *vanitas vanitatum*, given the right emphasis and integration. Opitz, Weckherlin and Moscherosch had been attracted to these poems, and the first full translation into German of the Greek anacreontica (having little or nothing to do with Anacreon of Teos, and published at Paris in 1554) appeared in 1698. Günther's translation is lost, but we know that the anacreontica helped him to achieve simplicity. This was a quality much praised in anacreontic poetry by the eighteenth century. It seemed engagingly simple after the age of *Schwulst*; yet to that age it had also appealed, both by its artificiality and by its innocence.[1] The enthusiasm of Mencke and his friends did not result in any immediate outburst of anacreontic poetry. The decisive impulse came from a group of enthusiasts in Halle during the winter of 1739–40 who were stimulated by Gottsched's *Versuch einer Übersetzung Anacreons in reimlose Verse* (in the *Gedichte* of 1736). Amongst them were Gleim, Uz and Götz. A translation of the 'Odes of Anacreon' by Uz and Götz was published in 1746. Meanwhile verses in the spirit of Anacreon had appeared in Hagedorn's *Oden und Lieder* (the first part of which was published at Hamburg in 1742, the second part in 1744; the third part was added for the edition of 1752), in Gleim's *Versuch in scherzhaften Liedern* (two

[1] There is no study of the language of German anacreontic verse. Langen treats it very briefly in his article in Stammler's *Aufriß*. Most critics (including recently Böckmann and Markwardt) have stressed the importance of anacreontic poetry in the development of German as a literary medium but this importance has never been analysed. The best general account of this poetry still seems to me that by J. Lees, *The Anacreontic poetry of Germany in the eighteenth century* (Aberdeen, 1911).

parts, published anonymously at Berlin in 1744 and 1745), and in Götz's *Versuch eines Wormsers in Gedichten* (1745). Later collections of anacreontic verse included Uz's *Lyrische Gedichte* of 1749 and Lessing's *Kleinigkeiten* of 1751. Almost every German author of the fifties and sixties tried his hand at verse of this kind. Most of them outgrew it. But the fascination of the mode was irresistible while it lasted.

In his preface to the 1744 *Oden und Lieder* Hagedorn stressed the social aspect of anacreontic poetry.[1] His odes were to be of the pleasing rather than the lofty kind; he accepted as his ideal the *iuvenum curas et libera vina* of his master Horace. He paid tribute here to 'die Lebhaftigkeit und der zärtliche Geschmack' of the French, but deprecated 'die allzu epigrammatischen und zu sinnreichen Einfälle des spielenden Witzes' in some French songs. This is interesting. Wit shall not be an end in itself. Hagedorn means that it should be allied with *Empfindung*. He wishes to delight and engage our fancy, not merely to dazzle our brains. His subjects are therefore never lofty or profound. His muse is not stirring, but soothing:

> O Dichtkunst, die das Leben lindert!
> Wie manchen Gram hast du vermindert,
> Wie manche Fröhlichkeit vermehrt![2]

This recalls Meier's description of *Scherz* which 'kann unser Gemüt dergestalt aufheitern, daß dadurch alle bange Ernsthaftigkeit aus der Seele vertrieben wird'.[3] Hagedorn's poems are 'Kleinigkeiten'. There is talk of 'halbentblößten Busen' and 'Was Hannens Mieder deckt', but the sensuality never luxuriates into licentious detail and the indulgence never degenerates into excess. Love is not a consuming passion but a pleasant sensation. The disappointed lover does not commit suicide; he creeps back

---

[1] I have used the British Museum copy of the 1747 Hamburg edition. On Hagedorn's connection with the anacreontics, see G. Witkowski, *Vorläufer der anakreontischen Dichtung und Friedrich von Hagedorn* (Leipzig, 1889).

[2] *Ed. cit.* p. 2.

[3] *Gedanken von Scherzen* (Halle, 1744), p. 105; quoted Böckmann, *Formgeschichte*, p. 527.

to his bed. Hagedorn's goddess of Joy does not make men *feuertrunken*; she 'erheitert die Vernunft'.

All this is mirrored in the language of these poems. There is no striving after intense expression, because intensity would be out of place. There are no *Machtwörter*, for they would disturb the graceful composure of the form. The range of images is generally restricted to the conventionalised environment. The vocabulary is polite. We find a reticent use of abstracts like: 'der Helden Trefflichkeiten', 'seine Zärtlichkeiten andeuten', 'Beförd'rer vieler Lustbarkeiten'. Or the ironical use of *précieux* synonyms: 'Für dich muß ich noch heut' *erblassen*', 'will nunmehr durch Gift *erbleichen*'. Along with this we have a bucolic strain which brings a fresh realism of language into Hagedorn's verses. In the poem *Der verliebte Bauer* we have 'reifer Schlee', 'die Tenne knarrte recht', 'schäkern', a 'Schallmey', a 'Kehraus', 'verplempert' and a girl who calls her lover 'Büfchen' (Bübchen). This realism is not anacreontic; it is Hagedorn's own individual variation of the mode. In *Der May* we have an almost Brockeslike precision:

>Nun singet die steigende Lerche,
>Nun klappern die reisenden Störche,
>Nun schwatzet der gauklende Staar.

This poem shows a combination of realism with stylisation. It begins with the nightingale, but proceeds to the lark, the storks and the starling. The second stanza begins with conventional shepherds, but continues with ducks and drakes and even sparrows. We then have Zephyr and Flora, with 'Sprossen und Garben', but we rush on to bullrushes, rustling springs and the peasants dancing. The final stanza with its reference to the Sabines and its *beatus ille* attempts to bring the poem back into the conventional mould. For this realism and colour is quite opposed to anacreonticism which flourishes on artificiality. Truly anacreontic, however, is the infectious gaiety of the rhythm, the concentration on the two themes of love and wine, the cultivation of wit and, above all, the lightness of touch. We have seen this in other spheres of Hagedorn's poetry and we have recognised it for what it was—

a fundamentally French ideal coming to him either direct from French or by way of English. Linguistically it acted as a counterweight to other tendencies towards obscurity (Haller) and towards the disruption of forms (Klopstock). It was valuable to show in these times that the German language could be a vehicle for gaiety, wit and good manners.

All the poets proudly protested that the subjects of their verse bore no resemblance to the contents of their lives. 'Was auch die Philosophen dawider sagen mögen', writes Gleim to Jacobi, 'die wahren Empfindungen nicht, sondern die angenommenen machen den Dichter.'[1] There is no question of *Erlebnislyrik*. Gleim, in a letter to Bodmer, complained of those stupid people who cannot separate the man from the poet; he and his brother poets 'characterisiren sich nicht, wie sie sind, sondern wie es die Art der Gedichte erfodert, und sie nehmen das Systema am liebsten an, welches am meisten Gelegenheit giebt, witzig zu seyn'.[2] There was no question of *Notdrang des Inhalts*; poetry for these poets was a pastime and never intended to be anything else. Outbursts of moral indignation like Hettner's 'Erlogene anakreontische Heiterkeit wurde schöngeistige Mode' are completely beside the point. This poetry makes no claim to veracity or to spontaneity. It is consciously artificial poetry which delights in its own artificiality.

Consider the first poem of Gleim's *Versuch in scherzhaften Liedern*:

> Anakreon, mein Lehrer,
> Singt nur von Wein und Liebe;
> Er salbt den Bart mit Salben,
> Und singt von Wein und Liebe;
> Er krönt sein Haupt mit Rosen,
> Und singt von Wein und Liebe;
> Er paaret sich im Garten,
> Und singt von Wein und Liebe;
> Er wird beim Trunk ein König,

---

[1] Letter dated 28 January 1768.
[2] *Versuch in scherzhaften Liedern*, Zweiter Theil (Berlin, 1745), pp. xx–xxi. British Museum copy of original edition. It is possible that this preface may be by Naumann, not by Gleim.

> Und singt von Wein und Liebe;
> Er spielt mit seinen Göttern,
> Er lacht mit seinen Freunden,
> Vertreibt sich Gram und Sorgen,
> Verschmäht den reichen Pöbel,
> Verwirft das Lob der Helden,
> Und singt von Wein und Liebe;
> Soll denn sein treuer Schüler
> Von Haß und Wasser singen?[1]

There is, we notice, a sort of *pointe* at the end, to which the poem builds up rhythmically with the punctuating refrain emphasising the succession of parallel clauses, until we double the tempo with 'Vertreibt... Verschmäht... Verwirft' to increase the tension before the last recurrence of the refrain leads into the final couplet. The verse is rhymeless and heptasyllabic.[2] Each line tends to be complete in itself. Enjambement is found in this poetry but never the sustaining of an idea for any length of time. Anything expansive is automatically excluded as too heavy for the form. We are usually presented with the other extreme, a series of fragments, sometimes (as in this poem) arranged towards some sort of climax, but more often as a mere catalogue of parallel ideas. For instance:

> Für mich bestrahlt die Sonne
> Die Wälder und die Auen!
> Für mich sind diese Schatten
> So kühl, und diese Rasen
> So sanft, und diese Quellen
> So rein, und jene Thäler
> So lieblich anzusehen!
> Für mich bist du, o Rose!
> Die Königin der Blumen;
> Für mich bist du, Gewölbe!

---

[1] Quoting from the British Museum copy of the original edition (Berlin, n.d. (1744)).

[2] In England John Phillips (1631–1706) had laid down the rule that an 'anacreontic' line should consist of seven syllables, without being tied to any law of quantity. Bodmer's defence of unrhymed verse had been taken up by Pyra. He transmitted the idea to Gleim and his friends (see W. Körte, *Gleims Leben* (Halberstadt, 1811), p. 20), who favoured lighter verse to illustrate the potentialities of the unrhymed form.

> Des Himmels aufgerichtet;
> Für mich glänzt in dem Wasser
> Der Mond, wie helles Silber;
> Für mich singt die Sirene
> Des Waldes, ihre Lieder;
> Nicht für den reichen Milon...[1]

And so on, and so on. The determination to avoid heaviness and longwindedness has resulted in emptiness and extreme shortwindedness, which is equally verbose and *schwatzhaft*. The jaunty jingle becomes a set mould:

> Ich bin noch nicht gestorben,
> Und wenn ich einmal sterbe,
> Dann will man mich begraben...

The rhythm seems highly unsuitable to this subject. But even this gross disagreement of form and content is made into a point and allowed to beget its own display of badinage. The poem continues:

> Und dann soll ich vermodern,
> Und nicht noch einmal tanzen.
> Jetzt, da ich noch nicht modre,
> Muß ich noch Rosen pflükken,
> Weil ich den Duft noch rieche;
> Jetzt, da ich noch nicht modre,
> Muß ich noch Mädchen küssen,
> Weil ich den Kuß noch fühle;
> Jetzt, da ich noch nicht modre,
> Muß ich den Wein verbrauchen.
> Werd ich im Grab auch dursten?[2]

Death has no fears for this poet; he is merely concerned with making capital out of it:

> *An den Tod*
>
> Tod, kannst du dich auch verlieben?
> Warum holst du denn mein Mädchen?
> Kannst du nicht die Mutter holen?

---

[1] *Sieben Gedichte nach dem Anakreon* (Amsterdam, 1767).
[2] *Versuch in scherzhaften Liedern*, First Part, p. 5. Poem entitled *Todesgedanken*.

> Denn die sieht dir doch noch ähnlich.
> Frische rosenrote Wangen,
> Die mein Wunsch so schön gefärbet,
> Blühen nicht vor blasse Knochen,
> Blühen nicht vor deine Lippen.
> Tod, was willst du mit dem Mädchen?
> Mit den Zähnen ohne Lippen
> Kannst du es ja doch nicht küssen.[1]

What a strange metamorphosis of baroque *guignol*! The dogged determination to be jolly even extends to bombs:

> Ach Prag, ich will dir rathen,
> Verspare deine Thaten.
> Ergib dich an uns Preussen,
> Eh wir die Bomben schmeissen,
> Sonst fallen deine Mauren,
> Und deine Kinder trauren,
> Wenn wir, auf deinen Gassen,
> Die Bomben toben lassen, etc., etc.[2]

The tone and the rhythms soon provoked parody. Here is the satirist A. G. Kästner summing up the situation:

> Was Henker soll ich machen
> Daß ich ein Dichter werde?
> Gedankenleere Prose
> In ungereimten Zeilen
> In Dreiquerfingerzeilen,
> Von Mägdchen und von Weine,
> Von Weine und von Mägdchen,
> Von Trinken und von Küssen,
> Von Küssen und von Trinken,
> Und wieder Wein und Mägdchen,
> Und wieder Kuß und Trinken,
> Und lauter Wein und Mägdchen,
> Und lauter Kuß und Trinken,
> Und nichts als Wein und Mägdchen,
> Und nichts als Kuß und Trinken,

---

[1] *Versuch in scherzhaften Liedern*, First Part, p. 40.
[2] *Ibid.* Second Part, p. 73. Quoting from British Museum copy of the original edition of 1745.

Und immer so gekindert,
Will ich halbschlafend schreiben.
Das heißen unsre Zeiten
Anakreontisch dichten.[1]

The parody points brutally to the monotony and flatness of the language of this poetry. Its appeal lay entirely in its facile and infectious gaiety. It was their lack of seriousness that made these poems popular. We find the young J. G. Jacobi defending his 'playful poems' against the contemporary taste for seriousness.[2] Uz makes the point indirectly when referring ironically to 'Magister Duns, das grosse Licht,/Der deutschen Dichtkunst Ehre' who mixes metaphysics with courting and addresses his Chloris in terms of monads, sufficient reason and the best of all possible worlds; but Chloris prefers the cheerful (*heiter*) songs of the shepherd-boy.[3] It was *Heiterkeit* which Haller admired in Hagedorn. Himself a serious and philosophical poet and lacking in *Heiterkeit*, he admitted in late life that he was not without feeling for 'die leichten Schwünge des lächelnden Anacreons', although he questioned the moral effect of the banishment of serious poetry by 'diese fröliche Secte'.[4] Haller did not appreciate that it was the amorality, not the immorality of this anacreontic poetry which constituted its appeal for an age too much fed on serious moralising. It was this lack of philosophical brooding and the straightforward acceptance of earthly joys that struck the age as 'simple' and 'naïve'. Lessing spoke of the 'besondere Naivite' of Gleim's *Lieder*; and elsewhere of the 'naive Zärtlichkeit' of Matthew Prior.[5] Geßner, writing to Gleim, even speaks of the latter's 'innocence'. The passage is revealing: 'Wie liebenswürdig ist ein Dichter, der die leichten

---

[1] Quoted by Muncker in the introduction to his volume *Anakreontiker und preußisch-patriotische Lyriker* in Kürschner's *Deutsche National-Litteratur*.

[2] J. G. Jacobi, *Sämmtliche Werke* (Zürich, 1819), I, p. 29; cf. *ibid.* p. 112, where he expresses disinclination for the melancholy verses of the imitators of Young's *Night Thoughts*.

[3] Uz, *Sämmtliche Poetische Werke* (Neudrucke no. 33, Stuttgart, 1890), ed. Sauer, p. 34.

[4] Poems, ed. Hirzel, pp. 405–6. Letter to Gemmingen, 1772.

[5] L–M, VII, 106; VIII, 80.

Freuden so fein und so unschuldig malt. Solche Empfindungen machen doch einen grossen Theil unserer Glückseligkeit aus, aber nur dann, wenn sie so unschuldvoll sind, wie Sie dieselben schildern.'[1] This was the appeal of anacreontic poetry: it was *liebenswürdig*, it painted the *leichten Freuden* and in a manner that was *fein* and *unschuldig*. It made people feel happy.

Psychologically this is poetry expressing refinement and modification. Linguistically its characteristic essence is to be found not in the nouns and verbs but in the modifying parts of speech, in the adjectives and adverbs. Consider for a moment the passage by Gleim quoted above on p. 395; note the emphasised succession 'so kühl...so sanft...so rein...so lieblich'. These are the epithets of refinement, agreeable epithets. They recur constantly, along with others of similar hue: *artig, froh, fröhlich, vergnügt, verliebt, anmuthsvoll, zart, schamhaft, zärtlich, mild, leise, hold, heiter, still, heimlich, gelinde* and the ubiquitous *süß*. The range is not wide and in some poems even the slight emotional colouring of these epithets is lacking. Everything about this poetry is pleasant. It appeals to the intellect through its pleasant felicities of phrase, it appeals to the heart by the pleasant feelings it describes and arouses. Geßner writes to Gleim of a translation from Anacreon: 'Wie viel *angenehme* Bilderchen haben Sie nachgebracht, wie vielen die *angenehmste* Wendung und lachende Mienen gegeben...Sie haben mit ungemeiner *Annehmlichkeit* die Sätze oft durch einander fließen lassen.'[2] Gleim himself protested: 'mir geschähe das größte Unrecht, wenn man mich unter diejenigen zählte, die den Endzweck aller Poesie im *Angenehmen* suchen; ich würde lieber Shakespeare seyn, als Anakreon'[3]—but this was tantamount to an admission that the keyword to describe anacreontic poetry was *angenehm*. There is no trace of the occasional earthiness of Hagedorn or the paroxysmic splendour of Klopstock. The one would be too real, the other too unreal; and both too serious. The whole is an elaborate game, never allowed to absorb the deeper feelings but always engaging the intelligence

---

[1] Letter to Gleim of 2 October 1755. [2] 2 October 1755 (my italics).
[3] In a letter written in February 1755.

and the desire for entertainment. One recalls Goethe's exclamation at such a poem: 'Ich dächte aber, es wäre gut! Es drückt den Zustand artig aus und bleibt hübsch im Gleichnis.'[1] He never lost his delight in anacreontic poetry.

Uz was much too interested in philosophical questions to cultivate carefreeness and too much concerned with moral values to maintain that amoral innocence essential to the mode. But he was steeped in the Greek originals and in his early anacreontic verse he spoke the same language as Gleim.[2] He objected to the emptiness and gossipiness of much anacreontic verse:

> Ihr träger Witz gebiert nur wörterreiche Sätze.
> Nie war dein Freund Anacreon
> So schwatzhaft, ob gleich alt; und Amor haßt Geschwätze.[3]

but he defended the mode against its detractors:

> Welch schwacher Geist, hört ich die Muse sagen,
> Will von Parnaß die Grazien verjagen?
> Ist niemand weis, als wer nur immer weint,
> Ein finstrer Kopf, dem Schwermuth Tugend scheint?[4]

and gave a pronouncement on poetic language:

> Schleift alles Rauhe weg! wählt; aber künstelt nicht!
> Auch der wird lächerlich, der nie, wie andre, spricht:
> Der bald ein schimmelnd Wort bejahrter Nacht entreisset,
> Das niemand itzt mehr kennt, bald neue werden heisset;
> Die kühnsten Tropen häuft, versetzt, verstümmelt, wagt,
> Und doch nicht schöner sagt, was andre längst gesagt.[5]

---

[1] Conversations with Eckermann, 5 April 1829.

[2] There are, however, occasional relicts of baroque diction, especially participles with *be-* (*beperlt, beblümt, bedornt, bepurpert*) and exotic imagery (*ambrareiche* Lüfte; *smaragdene* Flur) which, by the form in which they appear, suggest the influence of Brockes. In his first published poem, *Der Frühling*, published in 1743 but written in 1741, we find these features together with *siegbegierig, siegprangend* and two examples of activated prefixes, namely: 'Vor dir scherzt Hebe *dahin*' and 'Es lachen lauere Lüfte/Dich, Kind der Sonne, gefälliger *an*'. This is too early for any influence of Klopstock to have made itself felt. One must therefore assume influence of Greek (in the compound participles) and of pietism possibly (in the prefix compounds). There may be influence of the diction of Pyra and Lange. The poem is not anacreontic.

[3] *An Venus*, p. 70 in Sauer's edition.

[4] *Brief an Herrn Kanonikus Gleim* (1757), Sauer, p. 379.

[5] *Brief an Herrn Hofrat Christ* (1754), Sauer, p. 372.

which is not a plea for plainness but for polished ('Schleift alles *Rauhe* weg!') simplicity. But even during his period of most complete addiction to this world of artificial expression—for such it is—we find with Uz that his seriousness leads him out of the mode, as if he were unwilling to play and wishes to speak his heart for a moment:

> Die Erde drückt ein tiefer Schnee:
> Es glänzt ein blendend Weiß um ihre nackten Glieder:
> Es glänzen Wald, Gefild und See.
> Kein muntrer Vogel singt:
> Die trübe Schwermuth schwingt
> Ihr trauriges Gefieder.[1]

This is an anacreonticism which has outgrown itself. It has abandoned that essentially unreal and lighthearted attitude and replaced wit by passion, so that the language rises to an unheard-of pitch of intensity and a reality which is quite improper to, and indeed destructive of, the mode. The idea of the first two lines is a characteristic example of anacreontic wit, but in reverse. Here it is in normal position:

> Phyllis, dein entblößter Busen
> Gleicht — wem soll ich ihn vergleichen? —
> Gleicht mit Schnee bedeckten Hügeln.
> Doch ich irre: es ist weißer.
> Ist er auch für mich noch kälter?[2]

With Uz the earth is his subject and the lady is only the term of comparison. Hence the conceit about 'hills' becomes a description of a real landscape. He has left the world of artificial diction in a momentary vision which demanded much more compelling language to rivet in on to the paper. By this contrast the true nature of the anacreontic style is revealed.

On the sixth of July 1737 Frederick of Prussia had written to Voltaire about the Germans as follows: 'Si on pouvait les corriger

---

[1] Sauer, pp. 105-6.
[2] By Ewald von Kleist, one of his earliest poems and contained in a letter from him to Gleim dated 4 December 1743.

de leur pesanteur et les familiariser un peu plus avec les Grâces, je ne désespérais pas que ma nation ne produisît de grands hommes.' This was achieved in anacreontic poetry; and this is its great importance in the history of the language. 'Wie leicht und gelenk wird unter Ihren Händen unsere Sprache' wrote Geßner to Gleim; and to Kleist: 'Wie wird die Sprache unter Ihren Händen so sanft.'[1] It was a continuation of the achievement of Hagedorn, a reaction against the *Geist der Schwere* which was already besetting the Germans. One can, I think, easily understand the appeal to a public fed on didactic poetry of the breezy, cheerful language of the following:

Abschied von Chloris

Ihr Schönen zittert gar zu leicht,
Wenn Amor euch bekriegt;
Denn, eh euch noch sein Pfeil erreicht,
Hat er euch schon besiegt.

Die mich nicht haßt, eh sie mich liebt,
Die mir nicht wiedersteht,
Die sich, wie Leipzig, leicht ergiebt,
Die wird von mir verschmäht.

Ich fragte Chloris: Willst du mich?
Da sprach sie gleich: Ich will!
Schnell regten meine Lippen sich,
Und ihre hielten still.

Ich küßte sie ein hundert mahl,
Da sagte sie: Halt ein!
Dir muß noch eine größre Zahl
Von mir gegeben seyn.

Sie fing mit hundert Küssen an,
Und hundert folgten drauf.
Sie sprach: Mein liebster künftger Mann!
Ich aber sprach: Hör auf![2]

In such a poem the attentive reader will catch accents anticipating Heine. And it also does not need much historical imagination to

---

[1] Letters dated 2 October 1755 and 28 March 1758.
[2] Gleim, *Lieder* (1758), pp. 8–9.

appreciate the appeal of the following to a public fed on the disembodiedness of Klopstock:

> *Belinde*
>
> Das leztere leichtflatternde Gewand
> Sank; welch ein Blick! die artige Belinde
> Ward um und um ein Spiel der sanften Winde,
> Wo sie, wie Venus einst auf Ida, stand.
>
> Durch ihren Reitz, durch ihre zarte Hand,
> Von der ich noch den sanften Scherz empfinde,
> Durch alles, was an ihr mein Auge fand,
> Floß in mein Herz das süsse Gift der Sünde.
>
> Erstaunt, entzückt, mir selber unbewust,
> Bemächtigte sich die Gewalt der Sinnen
> Ach, alzubald der Tugend meiner Brust.
>
> Du, der du sagst: Ich will den Sieg gewinnen;
> Ach laß doch nie das süsse Gift der Lust,
> Laß es doch nie nach deinem Herzen rinnen.[1]

This poem reveals quite clearly the connection between anacreonticism and sentimentalism. Nothing could be further removed in content from the middle-class moralising of a Richardson or a Gellert. This is *Spiel* and *Scherz*. Both words occur at crucial points in the poem. But the pivotal oxymoron *das süsse Gift*, on which the whole poem is built, represents a type which belongs just as much to sentimentalism as to anacreonticism. Epithets like *artig, sanft, zart, süß* (all of which occur in the poem) represent that culture of feeling which is common to both. The water-images (*floß, rinnen*) and the ecstatic participles (*erstaunt, entzückt, unbewust*) are characteristic of sentimentalism rather than anacreonticism. And *das süße Gift* is not really a witty conceit; it is a typical 'mixed feeling' of sentimentalism.

Sentimentalism has developed contemporaneously and similarly in England and Germany. It seems at first sight to run counter to the spirit of the age of rationalism, yet has to be accepted as

---

[1] Quoted from the 1749 Zürich edition of the *Lieder* of Gleim (British Museum copy; there was a Halberstadt edition of 1745), but I have changed the punctuation of the third and fourth lines which is nonsensical in the original.

one of its salient features. The bridge between feeling and reason is Shaftesbury's concept of 'moral sense' as the ethical force within man, based on inner feeling but appealing to the mind. Feelings which do not pass through the mind are rejected as 'enthusiasm'. One should therefore cultivate one's feelings as well as one's reason. What we have in this ethical system is an ultimate criterion in which head and heart are in partnership. A German critic has suggested the term *Fühldenken* to describe it.[1] In the initial stage (represented by Shaftesbury) the mind predominated in this complex and the word 'sentimental' meant (for instance in Richardson) 'engaged in moral sentiments'. But, according to Professor Willey, feeling became the predominant partner in the 1750's and for this Hume was largely responsible.[2] Hume's ethics are also based on the notion of 'sentiment', which is one of the key-words of the period. It connotes not feeling, but (according to the *N.E.D.*) 'a thought or reflection coloured by or proceeding from emotion'. In 1762 we find Lord Kames stating: 'Every thought prompted by passion [i.e. feeling] is termed sentiment.' Mind and heart are still wedded in the concept; but the stress seems now to be more on the origin than the nature of 'sentiments'. Hence feeling comes to dominate the partnership and the word 'sentimental' shifts to a meaning approaching to 'capable of refined feeling'.[3] Behind the ethics of Shaftesbury or Hume is the assumption that man's natural feelings are good. Sympathy is said to correspond to gravitation in the physical world. Virtuous conduct becomes dependent on cultivation of feeling; therefore refinement of feeling becomes a touchstone of moral worth. This quality appears in the heroines of Richardson's novels. Their steadfastness in temptation and suffering has been related to the tradition of English puritanism; but the general spirit of sentimentalism had little in common with puritanism except a strong moral sense. For puritanism did not

---

[1] R. Haferkorn, 'Zum Begriff des Sentimentalen', *Fests. Deutschbein* (Leipzig, 1936).

[2] Basil Willey, *The Eighteenth Century Background* (London, 1940).

[3] For the semantic history of 'sentimental' see Erik Erämetsä's works (titles below on p. 406).

believe in the essential goodness of human nature. The connections of German *Empfindsamkeit* with pietism are much more obvious. But the religious element in both should not be lost sight of, for this has affected the language. *Empfindsamkeit* has been presented by some critics as a secularisation of pietism. But the influence of English sentimentalism cannot be ignored; nor perhaps that of French *sensibilité* (especially through the *comédie larmoyante*), although the linguistic aspect of this has not been investigated.

It is essential that one should distinguish between the culture and the cultivation of feeling, between refinement and indulgence. Refinement of feeling is sentimentalism; indulgence of feeling is sentimentality. The former degenerated into the latter and is often confused with it. But in its original form sentimentalism represented refinement and was a positive value. At first it had ethical and religious connections; refinement of feeling was a sign of virtue and led to ultimate reward by God. Later, when the moral connections weakened, the ability to feel more acutely or more deeply remained a positive quality. Even in Sterne, who more than anyone else made sensibility into a fashionable affectation and thus precipitated the trend from sentimentalism into sentimentality, we can see this positive value. Note the following passage from the *Journal to Eliza*, written in 1767: 'What a Stupid, selfish, unsentimental set of Beings are the Bulk of our Sex! by Heaven! no one man out of 50, informd with feelings or endow'd either with heads or hearts able to possess and fill the mind of such a Being as thee, with one Vibration like its own.'[1] The vibrations can proceed from and to heads or hearts. The connection between wit and sentimentalism in Sterne is obvious. Indeed, it would seem that the word 'sentimental' as used in his *Sentimental Journey* can mean 'witty' as well as 'delicate'. For it connotes the arousing of 'vibrations', an appeal causing some pleasurable stimulus of either head or heart.

The vocabulary of sentimentalism and *Empfindsamkeit* has

---

[1] *Op. cit.* Everyman's Library edition (London, 1927), p. 177.

been examined by the Finnish scholar Erik Erämetsä.[1] He finds that the English word 'sentimental', with some derivatives, are new words but that otherwise English sentimentalism is characterised more by semantic reorientation of existing terms than by the invention of new words. Nouns and adjectives constitute the significant elements of the sentence and there is considerable use of adverbial constructions. There would seem to be a predilection for compounds with *half-*, *over-*, *self-* and *un-*. Hyperbole, intensification (including use of synonymous doublets or triads), enumeration and typographical emphasis are the most noticeable stylistic features, apart from plural abstracts. Of these features, the compounds with *self-* had been frequent in Puritan literature,[2] the use of synonymous doublets was a tradition of English prose since the Renaissance,[3] and hyperbole, emphasis and enumeration are figures used by all men in all ages. Really characteristic of this language would seem to be a preference for hyperbolic compound adjectives with *all-* and *ever-* (*all-attracting*; *all-cheering*; *ever-adorable*; *ever-charming*—all from Richardson) and for the use of *a hundred* or *a thousand* with similar function; also the use of compounds with *half-* and *over-* (yielding some unusual and significant examples like 'his more than *half-menage*'; 'my *half-severe* friend'; '*over-lively*'; '*over-persuasions*'; 'some *half-ungenerous* advantage'—all from Richardson); the use of *un-* compounds to denote not the presence of evil but the absence of a pleasing, 'sentimental' quality (*ungenerous*, *uncheerful*, *undaughterly*); and, possibly, the plural abstracts ('*Indifferences*, if not *disgusts*, will arise in every wedded life'; 'these fruitless *gloominesses*'; 'a few *livelinesses* on her side at dinner-time'—all from Richardson). In addition to these propensities we note a

[1] E. Erämetsä, *A study of the word 'sentimental' and of other linguistic characteristics of eighteenth century sentimentalism in England* (1951); 'Sentimental — sentimentalisch — empfindsam' in *Festschrift Emil Öhmann* (1954); *Englische Lehnprägungen in der deutschen Empfindsamkeit des achtzehnten Jahrhunderts* (1955)—all in the *Annales Academiae Scientiarum Fennicae* (Series B, vols. 74, 84, 98). The same author has an article on 'Der sprachliche Einfluß Richardsons auf Goethes *Werther*' in *NM*, LVII (1956), pp. 118–25.

[2] Erämetsä refers us to K. Waentig, *Die self-Komposita der Puritanersprache* (Diss. Leipzig, 1932).   [3] See above, p. 83.

new feeling-tone attaching itself to words; thus *weakness* has a positive sense when it arises from sensibility, *pity* (in the words of *The Spectator*) is 'a kind of pleasing anguish, as well as a generous sympathy, that knits mankind together';[1] *delicacy* is given by Dr Johnson as a synonym of 'sensibility', *generosity* as not only 'noble of mind' but also 'open of heart'. Certain words occur with increased frequency, begetting sentimental clichés like the 'feeling', 'melting', 'tender' or 'swelling' heart, 'sympathetic tears' or the 'luxury of grief'.

In German we note similar semantic colouring with similar effects. Langen draws attention to the use of *edel-* as a modifier (*edeldenkend, Edelmut* and *edelmütig*—all expressing 'Fühldenken') and parallel use of *fein* (with both *feiner Geist* and *Feinheit der Empfindung*).[2] Many of the terms seem to be supplied by pietism: thus *Munterkeit* and *Heiterkeit* (for Addison's 'chearfulness', classed with 'good-nature' as 'the two great Ornaments of Virtue'),[3] *Empfindlichkeit, Entzücken,* water-metaphors like *Überfluß, Ergießung, strömen, schwellen* (also *schmelzend*) and the development of both derivatives and compounds from *Herz*. Many more had been part of the religious vocabulary for centuries and many of these stem ultimately from the Bible. This is one of the major difficulties in dealing with the vocabulary of pietism and one which Langen has not satisfactorily overcome: much of this vocabulary (and particularly its images) is 'new' only in the sense that it embodies a new and deeper acquaintance with the Bible. Erämetsä asserts that in much of the vocabulary of German *Empfindsamkeit* we have words of pietistic origin or with pietistic feeling-tone, strengthened by the influence of English sentimentalism. Thus *Schwachheit* takes on the sentimental associations of *weakness* noted above, and *Mitleid* becomes a 'pleasing anguish' and tends to go with *Zärtlichkeit* (=*tenderness*, also a positive quality). We also find a similar sentimental use of *un-*

[1] *Op. cit.* no. 397.
[2] *Deutsche Sprachgeschichte*, etc. in Stammler's *Aufriß*, 1222–3, examples from Sophie von Laroche, *Das Fräulein von Sternheim.*
[3] *Spectator*, no. 243, Everyman edn., ed. Gregory Smith (London, 1906), II, p. 278.

adjectives: *ungroßmüthig, ungütig, unedelmüthig*—note 'ein *nicht unedelmüthiges* Herz' for 'a mind not ungenerous' in *Grandison*. (Pietism knew *ungelassen* and *unempfindlich*.) English influence might be made accountable for emphatic use of *tausend, ausnehmend* and compounds with *ewig-*; on the other hand composition with *selbst-* is found in pietism, with *halb-, ganz-* and *über-* much earlier. The situation is obviously complex.[1]

But the argument for English influence is often very hard-pressed. Many of the 'loan-formations' listed by Erämetsä are very literal, possibly even bad translations. These words have not become part of the German language, they did not even have temporary currency. Neither did the literal renderings of obvious nonce-words like 'precept-giver', 'benefit-conferrer', 'rememberer'. The fact that similar formations are found in Klopstock proves merely that he realised the potentialities of this type of formation. It is part of his activism and proceeds from quite different impulses than these fundamentally ironical appellations of sentimentalism. His whole attitude to language was quite different. But his influence on the language of *Empfindsamkeit* should not be (but has been) underestimated. My impression is that more came from him than from sentimentalism or pietism.

There remains the vexed question of the plural abstracts. Deutschbein noted their use in Old English *either* to denote the recurrence of an action or state *or* for intensification. The former use represents concretisation; the latter, which has no real plural sense, he termed *Gefühlsplural*, instancing Modern English uses like 'such dreads and terrors' and noting the frequency of this feature in Shakespeare.[2] Havers gives various examples of this emotional plural (which he calls *Intensitätsplural*), noting the Latin 'poetic plural' (*irae, laetitiae, fortitudines*) and the presence of emotional plurals in all the early Germanic dialects (such as the plural of a word for 'death' to signify 'violent death').[3]

[1] See above, p. 244, for similar use of *tausend* in Brockes, and p. 246 for his use of other intensifiers.
[2] M. Deutschbein, *System der neuenglischen Syntax* (Cöthen, 1917).
[3] W. Havers, 'Zur Bedeutung des Plurals' in *Festschrift Kretschmer* (Vienna, 1926).

Öhmann shows that, although incidence of this feature in medieval German may often be stimulated by the Latin use, it often occurs without Latin parallel, suggesting that it was native to German.[1] A similar phenomenon occurs in French, becoming a stylistic feature in the sixteenth and seventeenth centuries.[2] Ménage was of the opinion that this use of the plural 'ne contribue pas peu à la sublimité de l'oraison'. Brunot quotes from Mlle de Gournay and Guez de Balzac to suggest that this degenerated into a fashion. We find grammarians around 1650 castigating it, yet it seems to have persisted into the eighteenth century. Öhmann notes that emotional plurals of abstracts are common in eighteenth-century German and adduces French influence; Erämetsä adduces English influence. Since this feature seems to be widespread at various periods in (at least) English, French and German, and since it has parallels in Latin and Greek, it would seem more likely that it represents a basic stylistic use of the plural. Havers agrees with Wundt that plural number originally denoted whole or mass and therefore embraced not only the meaning of number but also that of intensity. He notes that the plural can be used for definiteness ('the clergy took their seats') as well as indefiniteness (Latin *numina*).[3] Each may be a required form of intensity. Luise Thon (for Impressionism) and Petri (for Klopstock) have instanced usage of the emotional plural to express finer gradations.[4] But finer gradations are also a form of intensification, just as individual manifestations of an abstract quality tend to be. The two uses distinguished by Deutschbein for Old English can therefore be subsumed under a prime purpose of intensification. Luise Thon mentions *enttypisieren*; we have seen something similar in Klopstock. Another way of looking at it would be to say that this

---

[1] E. Öhmann, 'Über die Pluralbildung von abstrakten Substantiven im Deutschen', *PBB*, LXV (1941), pp. 134–52. In the course of this article he criticises Sister A. R. Lingl's diss. *Über den Gebrauch der Abstrakta im Plural im Althochdeutschen und im Mittelhochdeutschen* (Munich, 1934).
[2] Th. Haas, *Die Plural der Abstrakta im Französischen* (Erlangen, 1884); F. Brunot, *Histoire de la langue française*, vol. III, pp. 461–3.
[3] Havers, *Handbuch der erklärenden Syntax* (Heidelberg, 1931), pp. 106 and 150.
[4] Luise Thon, *Die Sprache des Impressionismus* (Munich, 1928); Petri, *op. cit.* (see above, p. 319).

represents intensification of the abstract idea by personifying it in individual manifestations. Klopstock's *Kühlungen* (which contains both definiteness and indefiniteness) would fit in here; so would the examples we noted in Winckelmann. In general it would seem that this was a stylistic potentiality which has been used by authors of all times and countries. Its prevalence in eighteenth-century Germany cannot be ascribed to any one influence. In part it was a straight heritage from the baroque.[1] Klopstock's use may well have affected others. But each author made something individual out of it and the 'emotional plural' of abstracts never became a meaningless *cliché*.

The whole vocabulary of sentimentalism appears in Wieland's first *Agathon* (1766–7).[2] 'Can you read Homer?' Hippias asks Agathon. 'Ich kann lesen', he replies, 'und ich meyne, daß ich den Homer *empfinden* könne.'[3] *Empfindliche Seelen* are those which feel more acutely than others, they are *gefühlvoll*. Feeling is their test of truth, it is akin to seeing: 'Ich sehe die Sonne, sie ist also; ich empfinde mich selbst, ich bin also; ich empfinde, ich sehe diesen obersten Geist, er ist also.'[4] Those who have not this quality are *unempfindlich*, like the Cilician pirates at the beginning of the book who have a *mehr als stoische Unempfindlichkeit* towards the tears, supplications and *Reizungen* of their beautiful captives. Those with *Empfindlichkeit* have *innere Sinne*, they experience *angenehmes Staunen* at the beauty of Nature, their *gepreßtes Herz* is relieved by a *Strom* of tears, experiencing *Wollust* at this liberation, and their ecstasy is a prolonged moment, the *fortdaurender Augenblick der Entzükung*, of *sprachlose Stille*:

> Der Gebrauch der Sprache hört auf, wenn sich die Seelen einander unmittelbar mittheilen, sich unmittelbar anschauen und berühren, und in einem Augenblick mehr empfinden, als die Zunge der Musen selbst in ganzen Jahren auszusprechen vermöchte.[5]

---

[1] See above, p. 246, for an example of *Ewigkeiten* in Brockes.
[2] I use the British Museum copy of the original edition, concentrating on the first of its two volumes. Where the comparison is significant for our considerations, I have also referred to the considerably revised second edition of 1773 (also using the British Museum copy).
[3] *Ed. cit.* I, p. 37.   [4] *Ibid.* I, p. 63.   [5] *Ibid.* I, p. 15.

THE CULTURE OF WIT AND FEELING

Such a moment is described by Agathon in these words:

> Die allgemeine Stille, der Mondschein, die rührende Schönheit der schlummernden Natur, die mit den Ausdünstungen der Blumen durchwürzte Nachtluft, tausend angenehme Empfindungen, deren liebliche Verwirrung meine Seele trunken machte, sezte sie in eine Art von Entzükung, worinnen ein andrer Schauplaz von unbekannten Schönheiten sich vor mir aufthat; es war nur ein Augenblik, aber ein Augenblik, den ich um eines von den Jahren des Königs von Persien nicht vertauschen wollte.[1]

Note the *angenehme Empfindungen*. Music can induce such a state:

> Er liebte eine Music, welche die Leidenschaften besänftigte, und die Seele in ein angenehmes Staunen wiegte, oder das Lob der Unsterblichen mit einen feurigen Schwung von Begeistrung sang, wodurch das Herz in heiliges Entzüken und in ein schauervolles Gefühl der gegenwärtigen Gottheit gesezt wurde; und wenn sie Zärtlichkeit und Freude ausdrükte, so sollte es die Zärtlichkeit der Unschuld und die rührende Freude der einfältigen Natur seyn.[2]

Certain seraphic elements (*Schwung von Begeistrung*, *heiliges Entzüken*; *schauervolles Gefühl*) show how Klopstock's language naturally affects descriptions of rapture; but the fundamental tone is *empfindsam*. *Angenehm* once again is a key-word. *Angenehme Empfindungen* also bulk largely in the philosophy of the sophist Hippias and *Empfindlichkeit* is necessary for their enjoyment. *Zärtlichkeit der Empfindung* and *Stärke der Seele* which enables man to control his passions lead to that state of pleasurable content which is *Glükseligkeit*, says Hippias.[3] For him, the eudaimonistic sensualist, this *Empfindlichkeit* consists in response to provocative *Reizungen*; Agathon's problem is to find a spiritually satisfying approach to love without returning to his priggish platonism which is presented ironically. The love he had felt at seventeen for the priestess at Delphi was like that aroused by good roast beef in a hungry man; but this 'animalische Liebe', as the 1773 edition calls it, gave way to the *Zärtlichkeit* inspired by Psyche, 'eine Liebe der *Sympathie*, eine *Harmonie* der Herzen, eine

---

[1] *Ed. cit.* I, pp. 57–8.   [2] *Ibid.* I, p. 52.
[3] *Ibid.* I, p. 80.

geheime *Verwandschaft* der Seelen'.[1] In such a state the soul *zerfließt*, loses its apartness, sheds *sympathetische Thränen* and *zärtliche Ergiessungen*. In Danae's great seduction-scene, the cantata sings of the precedence of love based on *Empfindung* over that based on mere desire, it expresses *die rührenden Schmerzen* of true love which find in this pain *ein melancholisches Vergnügen* (oxymoron!). Her voice makes *alle Sayten* of his heart *widerhallen* (compare Sterne's 'vibrations'). Agathon *zerfließt* in the *Empfindungen* expressed by the music and rushes to *aushauchen* his *in Enzükung und Liebe zerschmolzene Seele* at her feet.

When the hero of *Don Sylvio von Rosalva* (Wieland's other novel of the 1760's) experiences real, as against imagined love, this is described in terms similar to those already noted:

> Ihr erster Blick, der dem seinigen begegnete, schien ihre Seelen auszutauschen. Die ganze Gewalt dieser unbeschreiblichen Entzückung, womit eine sympathetische Liebe, zumahl wenn es die erste ist, bey Erblickung ihres Gegenstandes, eine empfindliche und zu dieser glücklichen Art von Schwärmerey aufgelegte Seele berauschen kann, durchdrang, erfüllte, überwältigte sein ganzes Wesen. Alle seine vorigen Ideen schienen ausgelöscht; neue Sinnen schienen plötzlich in seinem Innersten sich zu entwickeln, um alle diese unzählige Reizungen aufzufassen, die ihm entgegen stralten.[2]

And in *Aspasia* the Platonist overcome by *Empfindsamkeit* describes his feelings in similar language:

> Wenn dort ein Geist den andern ganz durchstrahlet,
> Ihn ganz durchdringt, erfüllt, mit ihm in Eins zerfließt,
> Und ewig unerschöpft, sich mittheilt und genießt.[3]

This is ironical; but the terms are the same. Note the verbs; and compare Agathon's description of Nature:

> welche ich mir als einen Spiegel vorstellte, aus welchem das Wesentliche, Unvergängliche und Göttliche in unsern Geist *zurükstrale*, und ihn nach und nach eben so *durchdringe* und *erfülle* wie die Sonne einen angestralten Wasser-Tropfen.[4]

---

[1] 1st edn. I, p. 170. The comparison with roast beef is from Fielding, as Wieland himself tells us.   [2] Second edition (see below, p. 419), II, pp. 53–4.
[3] *Sämmtliche Werke*, ed. Gruber (Leipzig, 1819), VII, p. 155.
[4] *Ed. cit.* I, pp. 275–6. My italics.

The image knits together these terms which are all frequently used in pietistic literature to describe states of mystical communication or rapture.[1] This is a clear case of secularisation of religious vocabulary. None of these words is claimed by Erämetsä as characteristic of sentimentalism. Indeed, they would seem to denote a much intenser and deeper attitude to feeling. First impressions would suggest that there is more emphasis on states of rapture in German *Empfindsamkeit* than in English sentimentalism. This, I would suggest, is due to its deeper religious affinities and above all to the influence of Klopstock, for the seraphic strain in the vocabulary of *Empfindsamkeit* is never absent for long. Thus, when Danae begins to be affected by Agathon's *Empfindsamkeit*, not only is she *zu Thränen gerührt* by the *zärtliche Klagen der Nachtigal in stillheitern Nächten* but dreams *süße Träume von bessern Welten*, experiences in the midst of love's joys certain *Gedanken von Gräbern und Urnen*, gazes at the starry heavens and rhapsodises on the *Wonne der Unsterblichen*, on *unvergängliche Schönheiten* and *himmlische Welten*.[2]

The *Agathon* is permeated by that mingling of mind and heart which is the essence of sentimentalism. 'Jeder neue Gedanke, der sich in mir entwikelte, wurde zu einer Empfindung meines Herzens; und so lebte ich in einem stillen und lichtvollen Zustand des Gemüths' says Agathon.[3] *Zärtlichkeit des Herzens*, says, Wieland in one of his direct talks to the reader, is the 'Anlage zu jeder Tugend', it goes with the 'Sinn für das sittliche Schöne'.[4] This is an important statement. It attests the positive value of sensibility in the opinion of its age. Sensibility was the opposite of brutish insensitivity, of roast-beef love and the Cilician pirates. It was a state of mind, of the *Gemüth*, induced by culture of feeling.

[1] See Langen, *Wortschatz des deutschen Pietismus*, 99 (*durchdringen*), 24 (*erfüllen*, also biblical), 392 (*überwältigen*, literal in Luther), 85 (*entgegenstrahlen*), 101 (*durchstrahlen*, influence of Klopstock?), 291 (*zerfließen*, also medieval mystics); *sich mitteilen* is not noted by Langen.
[2] *Ed. cit.* I, p. 219.   [3] *Ibid.* I, p. 276.
[4] *Ibid.* I, pp. 210, 214.

In Wieland's tale *Combabus* (1770) there occurs this description of the hero:

> Und dann sein Geist, wie groß! Sein Herz
> Wie schön, wie sanft, wie edelmüthig!
> Wie fein sein Witz, wie gefallend sein Scherz![1]

This man combines *Herz* with *Witz*, and harmoniously. Note the epithets applied to the heart; this is a civilised heart, beautiful and delicate and *edelmüthig*. The heart, so Wieland would say, can exist alongside wit if it is refined. Then we have an interplay such as is described in 'Wie fein sein Witz, wie gefallend sein Scherz'. Later in the same poem we find wit aligned with beauty, and wit opposed to *Verstand*:

> Und Dummkopf lobet Gott aus voller Brust,
> Der was an *Witz* ihm fehlt, ihm an *Verstand* gegeben.[2]

This opposition between *Witz* and *Verstand* is between what Tristram Shandy called 'refined parts' and 'good plain household understanding'. Rationalism had been made civilised and socially acceptable in the culture of wit. Now here, with Wieland, we have a socially acceptable culture of feeling. Tendencies towards excessive use of the reason or excessive indulgence in the feelings are curbed by combining the culture of wit with the culture of feeling in an overall ideal of grace, *Grazie*. This is most clearly expounded in the work entitled *Die Grazien* (1770). In the introduction Wieland associates himself with the anacreontic poets as having embraced the Graces and taken as mistress of their minds 'die freundliche Weisheit' which combines *Witz* with *Empfindung*.[3] Apollo, disguised as Seladon amongst the shepherds, refined their rude pleasures by his *Witz*.[4] The Graces come to men in order 'ihren Witz zugleich mit ihrem Gefühl zu verfeinern';[5] when Amor comes amongst the Graces: 'seine Empfindungen verfeinerten sich'.[6] The Arcadian shepherds are good fellows but do not know the charms of refined society, 'den

---

[1] Quoting from the British Museum copy of the original edition, p. 31.
[2] *Ibid.* p. 55, italics represent heavy type in original.
[3] I quote from the British Museum copy of the original edition (Leipzig, 1770). This is pp. 8–9. [4] *Ibid.* p. 21.
[5] *Ibid.* p. 23. [6] *Ibid.* p. 74.

züchtigen Scherz und das witzige Lachen' (note the combination of mind and feeling) until the Graces come.¹ Phyllis is 'eine junge Unempfindliche'.² The connection with *Empfindsamkeit* is clear, for only an *empfindsam* basis can be refined. *Grazie* is the magic 'wozu die empfindsamen Seelen einen eigenen Sinn haben'.³ But when the Graces come to Arcady, Daphnis loves as never before—'die feurigste Liebe, von der zärtlichsten Ehrerbietung gefesselt'. This, says the author, is how one loves 'wenn die Grazien mit Amorn die Herrschaft über unsre Herzen theilen'.⁴ They refine the heart by controlling it; they also refine the mind by controlling the mind: 'Allein unter den Händen der Grazien verliert die Weisheit und die Tugend der Sterblichen das Uebertriebene und Aufgedunsene, das Herbe, Steife und Eckichte.'⁵ This is what Musarion taught. How could one fail to understand her? The upshot of Wieland's philosophy was civilisation, and it was civilisation that he brought to the German language. There is no strong linguistic tendency in any direction, nothing highly individual and, of course, nothing intense. But a beautiful balance between wit and feeling. Nothing could be further from the truth than Markwardt's statement that there is *tension* between wit and feeling in Wieland and that he hovered 'uncertainly' between the 'Kaltsinnigkeit der Aufklärung' and the 'Enthusiasmus der Geniezeit'.⁶ This is a harmonious, not a tense style; and it is not at all uncertain. Sengle says of some of the verse-tales: 'Hier platzten naturalistische Kraßheit und feinste Formkunst, plumpste Sinnlichkeit und elegantester Schliff am schärfsten aufeinander.'⁷

¹ *Ibid.* p. 92.   ² *Ibid.* p. 98.   ³ *Ibid.* p. 64.
⁴ *Ibid.* p. 106.   ⁵ *Ibid.* p. 163.
⁶ *Op. cit.* II, p. 279: 'Die starke Spannung von Witz und Empfindung, die nach entspannendem Ausgleich in Wielands eigenem Wesen und Werk — letztlich vergeblich — rang.... Wieland durchlebt jenen Zwiespalt von "Witz" und "Empfindung" gleichsam als Erbe der Geschmacksepoche, in der er zuletzt doch befangen blieb.... Er geriet zwischen Kaltsinnigkeit der Aufklärung und Enthusiasmus der Geniezeit...ohne sich klar entscheiden zu können.'
⁷ Friedrich Sengle, *Wieland* (Stuttgart, 1949), pp. 178 ff. This excellent book is the first really thorough study of Wieland and is likely to be the standard biography for some time to come. The criticism I offer concerns merely an infelicity of phrase and should not be taken to imply any disapproval of this most scholarly and valuable book.

One can hardly think of a more unsuitable word to apply to Wieland than *platzen*. It is not the language of a genius; but it is the language of a very cultured man in which nothing *platzt*. Wieland arrived at this style after much vacillation between the seraphic and the anacreontic. Technical facility and a fascination with difficult forms came to him early. It was, however, some time before he found his way to those forms which suited him best. During this formative period we observe a deep knowledge of classical literature trying to fuse with strong pietistic origins. He begins by serious didactic poems in heavy forms; then he turns to lighter forms under the spell of his first infection with anacreonticism but is unable to rid himself entirely of Klopstockian transcendentalism. Sengle quotes this example of seraphic combining with anacreontic on an *empfindsam* background:

> Komm Doris! laß uns küssen,
> Da alles scherzt und küsset
> Und die Natur empfindet.
> . . . . . .
> Wie süß sind diese Küsse?
> Wie fühlt die ganze Seele?
> Wie taumelt sie in Freuden?
> . . . . . .
> So trunken von Entzückung
> Wallt nicht mein fühlend Herz auf,
> Wenn Milton Even singet,
> Als wenn mich Doris küsset;
> Ja, seine Paradiese
> Die wären vor mich wüste
> Wenn ich in ihren Lauben
> Nicht Doris küssen könnte.

This was written sometime in 1750 or 1751. In 1752 we find him speaking of 'diese naive Annehmlichkeiten, dieser natürliche Witz, die anmutige, einfältige Sprache' of the verse of Hagedorn and Gellert; but Klopstock soon reclaims his affections and we find almost every feature of Klopstock's style permeating the

THE CULTURE OF WIT AND FEELING

works he wrote between 1752 and 1756. Beck[1] lists plural abstracts (including *Reizungen, Ewigkeiten, Geistigkeiten, Seligkeiten*), *nomina agentis* in *-er*, participial *nomina agentis*, compound epithets (some embodying oxymoron), prefix-formations in verbs and use of the comparative adjective with intensifying function. Amongst syntactical features he notes use of simplex for prefix-verb, use of descriptive verbs as verbs of motion (*zittern, tönen, glänzen*, etc. with prepositional extension), 'full' use of oblique cases of the noun and a predilection for present participles. Between 1756 and 1758 Wieland's mental attitude crystallized into irony. In November 1758 we find him turning against Klopstock: 'Sein Ausdruck ist ungleich, zuweilen schwülstig, zuweilen matt. Er affektierte gewisse Bilder, die er unaufhörlich wiederholt. Alles lächelt und weint und staunt und umarmt sich und wallet und zerfliesset in seinen Gedichten. Er raffiniert zu viel in Sentiment.'[2] An interesting statement. Nevertheless, as we have seen, Wieland continued to use the language of sentiment—although always combining it with irony.

It is as irony that the culture of wit appears in Wieland. This irony maintains a counterpoise to his culture of feeling which we have already examined. The first *Agathon* is full of irony. We see it in the Fielding-like addresses to the reader, discussing the morality of the hero's actions; we see it in Agathon's narration to Danae of Pythia's unsuccessful attempts to seduce him; we see it in Agathon's exposition of platonic love to Pythia during her attempts at seduction: 'In der That konnte im Prospect eines so schönen Busens als ich vor mir sahe, nichts seltsamers seyn, als eine Lobrede auf die intellectualische Liebe.' No doubt Danae was meant to smile at this. The constant envisagement of an audience is essential to irony. For the author, irony is a guard against self-importance and also self-immolation. Nothing could be further from Wieland's art than the passionate outpourings of

---

[1] G. Beck, *Die Sprache des jungen Wieland* (Diss. Heidelberg, 1913). The first part of this (dealing with the influence of Klopstock) was published at Bucharest in 1913.
[2] *Ausgewählte Briefe*, ed. Gessner (Zürich, 1815), vol. I, pp. 306 ff.

Erlebnislyrik. It would have embarrassed him. There is always someone looking, someone to nudge, to wink at, to appeal to for opinion or support. This is apparent in the *Comische Erzählungen* (1765) which may well have had a definite audience in mind, the entourage of Count Stadion at Warthausen.[1] Nerves are kept in suspended titillation by the constant delaying-tactics: inner monologues (Diana on the possible consequences of kissing Endymion), interruptions from imaginary listeners and replies from the author, arguments with the characters, ironical references to authority (such as to Helvétius, Buffon and Albertus Magnus to corroborate that young girls like young boys), ironical *variatio* of an obvious point ('Daß ihn die Mädchen gerne sahen; / Zum mindsten lieffen sie nie wenn er kam davon'),[2] sham coyness before a juicier episode ('The Muses hold back...'; 'Look it up in Plato...'; 'The Greek word is better', etc.)—all this serves the same purpose of awaking the appetite and results in the same tendency to long-windedness. Even the old cumbersome chancery-sentence is used with stylistic effect. *Endymion* begins with a sentence extending over twenty-one lines of verse: the main clause is delayed, the pattern of the structure being 'In jener Zeit...; als...und...; eh' noch...; und kurz, in jener Zeit, da...: in dieser Zeit lebt' ...ein junger Hirt...'. The delay gives impetus, the repetition gives lucidity and *kurz* is effectively ironical. An interesting study could be made of Wieland's use of *kurz* in such sentences; it is a constantly recurring feature in both his prose and his verse. The language of the *Comische Erzählungen* hardly ventures outside the range of conventional anacreontic vocabulary. For Wieland's Paris the three goddesses are merely 'schön und schlank und glatt'.[3] Most other things are *süß, froh, hold, artig, reitzend, gelind, zärtlich, schalkhaft* or *lieblich. Zärtlich*, a key-word, occurs in sentimentalist environments like *zärtliche Gedanken, zärtliches*

---

[1] I quote from the earliest edition to which I had access, the second revised impression of 1768 (no place on title-page; Goedeke gives Zürich), using the copy in the Bavarian State Library at Munich.

[2] *Ed. cit.* p. 48.

[3] Variant of later revision. See *Sämmtliche Werke*, ed. Gruber (Leipzig, 1819), VII, p. 53.

Ungestüm or *zärtliche Entzückung*. The anacreontic *angenehm* occurs in a wide range of contexts, including *angenehmes Erstaunen* and *angenehmes Erschrecken*. The oxymoron becomes meaningful with Wieland, designating either a mixed feeling ('Wie angenehm sie erschrack, als sie unter den Blumen den kleinen Gott erblickte') or a divided impression ('Wie angenehm erblaßt... / Ihr Rosenmund' with the adverb referring to the observer not the sufferer). The more normal type (*süßer Schmerz*; *süßes Schrecken*; *geliebte Feindinn*; *reitzende Grimassen*) occurs frequently. The imagery is conventional. Occasionally there is a witty *pointe*. But the fun depends mainly on the ironical spirit of the whole conception.

A characteristic form of this is represented by the following passage, from *Aspasia* (1773):

> Und, wenn sie sich zur Ruh begab, versank
> Die schöne Last der wohl gepflegten Lenden
> In Schwanenpflaum: und doch, bey frischem Blut
> Und blühendem Gesicht, schlief sie — nur selten gut.[1]

The author has caught us out. Following after a voluptuous flight of the imagination we are brought back to earth by a prick of the bubble, a check to our fanciful meanderings, a halt to our *Schwärmerey*.

This recalls the famous opening to *Don Sylvio von Rosalva* (1764):[2]

> In einem alten baufälligen Schlosse der Spanischen Provinz Valencia lebte vor einigen Jahren ein Frauenzimmer von Stande, die zu der-

[1] *Sämmtliche Werke*, ed. Gruber, VII, pp. 143–4.
[2] The first edition was published at Ulm in 1764. This is full of crass misprints (*Pyrenäe* for *Pyrenäen*, *Sapphes* for *Sappho's*, *Postel* for *Pastell*) and Southern forms and spellings (*Kien* for *Kinn*, *Dienste* for *Dünste*, *ungeräumt* for *ungereimt*, *stoßte*, *tretten*, *kan*, *trift*, *Landgutsche*). A statement after the corrigenda says that the editor (i.e. author, for the work is published anonymously ås though it were a true story) was not able to do the corrections. The second edition (Leipzig, 1772), in two parts with separate pagination, has a preface referring to the 'imperfect' state of the first edition. I have therefore followed the second edition as better representing Wieland's intentions, comparing it with the first edition. I have used the British Museum copies of both editions.

jenigen Zeit, da sie in der folgenden Geschichte ihre Rolle spielte, bereits über ein halbes Jahrhundert unter dem Namen Donna Mencia von Rosalva sehr wenig Aufsehens in der Welt gemacht hatte.

The conclusion is unexpected, a sort of *pointe*. Something sounding grand turns out to be something quite ordinary. Things are not what they seem. Note the way the sentence pulls up before plunging into the final disillusionment. A dash is inserted at this point in the finally revised text, making the pull-up even stronger. We continue:

Die Dame hatte die Hoffnung, sich durch ihre persönliche Annehmlichkeiten zu unterscheiden, schon seit dem Succeßions-Kriege aufgegeben, in dessen Zeiten sie zwar jung und nicht ungeneigt gewesen war, einen würdigen Liebhaber glücklich zu machen, aber immer so empfindliche Kränkungen von der Kaltsinnigkeit der Mannspersonen erfahren hatte, daß sie mehr als einmal in Versuchung gerathen war, in der Abgeschiedenheit einer Kloster-Celle ein Herz, dessen die Welt sich so unwürdig bezeugte, dem Himmel aufzuopfern.

The old heavy type of sentence has become a thing of sophistication at the hands of an artist. The effect is irony. It is interesting to reflect that another great ironist, Thomas Mann, uses similar sentences to similar effect. What is there in the form to promote this? Let us examine Wieland's sentence more closely. Note how abstract periphrasis ('persönliche Annehmlichkeiten', 'empfindliche Kränkungen von der Kaltsinnigkeit der Mannspersonen'), polite understatement ('nicht ungeneigt') and impersonalisation ('*ein* Herz') are turned from conventional trappings into characterising features. This indirectness and also the constantly interrupted flow which we noted above as characteristic of chancery style here become expressive values—the indirectness giving politeness and poise, the interruptions permitting reflection and modification by the author.[1] This style of reticent assertion demands the utmost tact and elegance and the most delicate and sure control of associations. Wieland has all this; it is the very essence of his urbanity. It avoids crass outspokenness. It hints. And it

---

[1] Note also that the abstract periphrasis of chancery style appears here with eighteenth-century plural abstracts.

demands sympathetic and alert readers to take the hint. It presupposes an audience. This is the essential situation in Wieland's art and it is a characteristic he shares with the anacreontics. There is an agreed *rapport* between author and reader. The author talks to us as we read. He does not hurry or stumble or get heated. He takes his time. Wieland knew he was denied 'das Talent des Laconisme und die Kunst, mit wenigem viel zu sagen'.[1] His contemporaries attested to his longwindedness in conversation, his addiction to the gradual unfolding of ideas in elaborate sentences. During his Erfurt lectures the audience sometimes had to help him out when he lost the thread of his sentence. He justified this prolixity as a desire for maximum clarity: 'Ich weiß es, daß sie [his sentences] oft zu sehr mit eingeschobenen Sätzen angefüllt sind. Allein mein Bestreben nach Deutlichkeit und Bestimmtheit gestattet mirs nicht anders.'[2] But there were other reasons. He realised the satisfying completeness of a well-rounded periodic sentence. Its weightiness could give mock solemnity, expressive of pretence and humbug. The casting of personal everydayness in the depersonalised ceremoniousness of this form suggests simulation and hypocrisy. He also appreciated that surprise which is attained by delaying some important element until the end when it can appear as a sort of *pointe*. And the subordinate clauses gave endless opportunities for those asides, winks and nudges to his invited audience which he loved so much.

Here again is Donna Mencia:

> Sie wurde eine Spröde, und nahm sich vor, ihre beleidigten Reizungen an allen den Unglückseligen zu rächen, welche sie als Wolken ansah, die den Glanz derselben aufgefangen und unkräftig gemacht hatten, sie erklärte sich öffentlich für eine abgesagte Feindin der Schönheit und Liebe, und warf sich hingegen zur Beschützerin aller dieser ehrwürdigen Vestalen auf, denen die Natur die Gabe der transitiven Keuschheit mitgetheilt hat, von Geschöpfen, deren bloßer Anblick hinlänglich wäre, den muthwilligsten Faun — weise zu machen.

[1] *Auswahl denkwürdiger Briefe*, ed. Ludwig Wieland, vol. II (Vienna, 1815), p. 149.
[2] Böttiger, *Literarische Zustände und Zeitgenossen*, vol. I (Leipzig, 1838), p. 259.

We have the same stylistic features: circumlocutions, pull-up, *pointe*. Even *derselben* is used to effect. An aside to the listener appears in the shape of a learned footnote on the interesting property of transitive virginity.[1] A few pages later on we come across this nice sentence:

> Denn ihre erstaunliche Belesenheit in Chroniken und Ritterbüchern, und die Beredsamkeit, womit sie ihre tiefen Einsichten in die Staatswissenschaft und Sittenlehre bey der Mahlzeit und bey andern Gelegenheiten auszulegen pflegte, hatten ihm eine desto größere Meynung von ihrem Verstande beygebracht, je weniger seine eigene martialische Lebensart ihm Zeit gelassen hatte, eine mehrere Kenntniß von dem, was man die polite Gelehrtheit heißt, zu erwerben, als etwan das wenige seyn mochte, was ihm aus seinen Schuljahren in einem nicht allzugetreuen Gedächtniß übrig geblieben war.

Thus ends the first chapter. It is a testimony to the solidity of such sentences that Wieland should so often end a chapter in this way, usually with a verbal complex at the very end. Indeed, he has a tendency to end most sentences (except in spoken dialogue) with a compound verb or verbal complex.[2] He signs off with a flourish.

The old heavy sentence is used, then, by Wieland to achieve mock solemnity and mock finality; and to preserve *rapport* between author and audience by permitting constant interruption. In chapter ten of the first book Don Sylvio upbraids Pedrillo for constantly interrupting him—which is casting irony on an ironical device. Later Don Sylvio charges Pedrillo with being longwinded; things take time to tell, says Pedrillo; 'aber mußt du', says Don Sylvio, 'alle diese nichts bedeutenden Umstände mit dazu nehmen, wodurch deine Erzählung so schleppend und einschläfernd wird als wie ein altes Kunkelstuben-Mährchen?'[3] Double irony again. Periphrases smelling of the chancery give Don Sylvio's speech

---

[1] Characteristic of the imperfections of the first edition is that this appears there as *transcendental* virginity!

[2] In the first four pages of Chapter Nine of Book Three (a random sample) we have sentences ending in 'zu betrachten schienen', 'zu erscheinen pflegten', 'sehen kann', 'gesehen habe', 'übertroffen wurde', 'halten konnte', 'aufgestiegen waren', 'werden würde' and 'sich baden wollen'.

[3] Second edition, I, pp. 331–3.

a priggish and pedantic unreality (which contrasts admirably with the malapropisms, oaths and conversational turns of Pedrillo). Here he is reflecting on the fact that he has no sword:

> Ohne Degen auf Abentheuer auszugehen, däuchte ihm eine Unanständigkeit, die nicht zu entschuldigen wäre. Ob ich gleich hoffen darf, dachte er, daß mir die Fee Radiante im Fall der Noth einen diamantnen geben würde, so würde es doch das Ansehen einer Zagheit haben, wenn ich kein andres Gewehr führen wollte als ein bezaubertes.[1]

Note the impersonalisation (*auszugehen...däuchte ihm...zu entschuldigen wäre*), then a brief personal interruption, then (with *so würde es*) return to the impersonal, then the distancing of the personal statement by a *wollte*. The *würde—würde—wollte* pattern is striking. The clumsiness is characterising. But this is not always the simple fact. Take the following example:

> Der kleine Schrecken, den diese Stimme unsern Schönen machte, weil sie nicht gleich sahen, woher sie kam, verschwand augenblicklich, wie sie nun den Pedrillo ansichtig wurden, der, ungeachtet seines nicht sehr schimmernden Aufzugs, ein junger Pursche von einer glücklichen Physionomie und von einer Figur war, die einem sprödern Mädchen als die schöne Laura zu seyn schien, hätte Anfechtungen machen können.[2]

This is not expressive of character. Yet the heavy sentence has a different stylistic value. It describes a situation with a touch of pretence about it. This is only a '*kleine* Schrecken', and for all the polite wrappings of *ansichtig wurden, ungeachtet* and *zu seyn schien* they are pleased to see him. The stately progress of the sentence makes possible the monumental indirectness of *hätte Anfechtungen machen können* at which it finally arrives, and towards which it has been projected from the start. Involved and indirect sentences are therefore used by Wieland both to characterise persons of a pedantic, hypocritical or affected nature (in speech and reflection), and also (in narrative or author's comments) with wider stylistic functions to contribute to the ironical atmosphere of the whole. The full flower of this irony is to be seen in *Die Abderiten*.

But I have concentrated on works written during the 1760's because it was in this decade that Wieland demonstrated his

[1] *Ibid.* I, pp. 171–2.   [2] *Ibid.* p. 284.

civilisation of the German language. In his first attempt at *ottava rima*, *Idris und Zenide* (1767), we find an interesting revival of baroque linguistic features. In the first canto we have limbs described as 'unbefleckter Schnee, getuscht mit Rosenblut', a bosom 'so kalt wie Alpenschnee...und härter als der Diamant', 'Klauen von Smaragd' and 'Augen von Achat'.[1] We even find our old friend 'die braune Nacht', but ironically caparisoned with homely prosaicness:

> Sie kämpfen noch, da schon die braune Nacht
> Die halbe Welt von Mohnsaft trunken macht,
> Und Titans Zug, in Amphitritens Grotten,
> Von seinem Tagewerk, den Himmel durchzu*trotten*,
> Auf einer Liljenstreu *verschnaubt*,
> Und aus der Nymphen Hand ambrosisch *Futter* raubt.[2]

Along with all this we find sententious couplets reminiscent of English Augustanism and Hagedorn:

> Wo Tugend und Natur sich bis aufs Leben gehn,
> Verzehrt der Widerstand die Kraft zum Widerstehn.

or again:

> Man muß im Sieg nur nachzugeben wissen,
> Ihr Zorn verzehrt sich selbst, und stirbt zuletzt in Küssen.[3]

Intensified expressions ('ganze Thränenregen'; 'flammenschwangre Drachen') always have a touch of irony about them in this poem. The general atmosphere is mock-heroic. Sentimental oxymoron also occurs:

> Der Liebe süßes Gift und schmerzendes Entzücken.

Yet there is no tension, no *platzen* in this combination of baroque, Augustan and sentimental features. All seem to fit naturally into the ironical world of the poem, the many sub-narratives of which

---

[1] I quote from the Berne reprint of 1775, British Museum copy, pp. 12, 15, 41, 68. Compare: 'Marmorwangen' (98), 'Lüfte, die von Zimmt- und Amberdüften wallten' (143), 'Balsamschlaf' (169—Beck notes several compounds with *Balsam*- in the early works showing Klopstock's influence), 'Mund von lebenden Corallen' (173), etc., etc.

[2] *Ed. cit.* p. 49, my italics. 'Die braune Nacht' appears again in *Die erste Liebe* (1774): 'Vergebens hofften wir den Flug der braunen Nacht...festzuhalten.' [3] *Ibid.* pp. 38 and 67.

are like so many vast incapsulated clauses. Everything is controlled with surety and grace. Even an occasional odd word ('ihr *electrisch* Blut'; 'Herzen von *Asbest*') becomes a delight. It was a stunning effect to use the old jewelled imagery to describe the actual jewelled palaces of fairyland, just as it had been to use the anacreontic paraphernalia to describe an actual anacreontic tableau in *Agathon*.[1] Ironically the metaphor suddenly ceases to be one. We are actually in a land where 'die Edelsteine keimen', where 'eßbares Gold reift auf smaragdnen Bäumen'.[2]

In the course of various articles in the *Teutsche Merkur*, mostly written after the period we are studying but significant as representing his general views on language, Wieland compared German with other literary languages.[3] It was inferior to most in euphony; but it could express strong emotion and was rich in onomatopoeic words. Compared with Greek it lacked the flexibility given by a rich verb-system. Compared with Latin it had difficulty in approaching the urbanity of Catullus, the terseness of Horace or the 'Frischheit, Wärme, Glanz und Grazie' of Virgil. English had a rich vocabulary and the strength that comes from concentration. Italian had more 'Geschmeidigkeit', more subtly-coloured words to give grace and variety to its verse. But French had a wealth of 'versüßenden und einwickelnden Redensarten, die der leidenden Eitelkeit zu Hülfe kommen und einen sanft bedeckenden Schatten auf Theile legen, denen ein volles Licht nicht günstig wäre';[4] and also the supreme ability 'Witz und Empfindung (zwey so ungleichartige und doch so nahe verwandte Dinge) bis auf den äußersten Grad der Feinheit auszuspinnen und zu verweben'.[5] In thus admiring French for its civilised indirectness and its refinement of wit and feeling Wieland was voicing his own stylistic principles.

---

[1] I mean the passage on pp. 229–30 of vol. I of the first edition.
[2] *Ed. cit.* p. 257; cf. the description in Canto IX of *Der neue Amadis* (1771), original edition, vol. I, pp. 241–2. Copy in the British Museum.
[3] See Ernst Richter, 'Wielands sprachliche Ansichten im Teutschen Merkur', *ZfdPh*. 58 (1933), pp. 266–96.
[4] 1784, I, p. 162. Contrast Klopstock (see above, p. 327) who considered this a disadvantage of French!   [5] 1782, IV, p. 64.

XIII

THE MYSTICAL APPROACH

WIELAND's irony had accepted the dichotomy of head and heart; and his ethic amounted to a civilised fusing of the two in a culture of wit and feeling. We must now turn to one who would not accept the dichotomy, nor the influence of wit on feeling. 'Ich verstehe von allem, das zur artigen Welt und schönen Natur gehört, nicht ein lebendiges Wort', wrote Johann Georg Hamann in 1786, towards the end of his life;[1] thereby reiterating that opposition to all rationalistic criteria which he had expressed some twenty years before, in 1763, when he had spoken of 'die Chimäre der schönen Natur, des guten Geschmacks und der gesunden Vernunft'.[2] It was Hamann who categorically rejected the culture of wit. 'Lügen ist die Muttersprache unserer Vernunft und Witzes', he wrote to Kant on 27 July 1759. In this moral, impassioned atmosphere the culture of wit cannot survive.

Hamann wrote a considerable amount about language and even when he was not specifically dealing with language, reference to it or analogy with it was always making itself felt.[3] His own use

---

[1] Letter to Jacobi, 8 June 1786.
[2] In the second of the *Fünf Hirtenbriefe das Schuldrama betreffend*, Works, ed. Nadler, vol. II, p. 356. Nadler's edition (six vols., Vienna, 1949–57) is much fuller than the earlier editions of F. Roth (eight vols., Berlin, 1821–43) and C. H. Gildemeister (six vols., Gotha, 1857–73); but it has been severely criticised for misprints and other errors of detail by W. Boehlich in *Euph.* L (1956), pp. 341–56. Unless otherwise stated, my references to Hamann's *works* are to Nadler's edition. His *letters* I quote, wherever possible, from the definitive edition of W. Ziesemer and A. Henkel (Wiesbaden, 1955–), but as this is still in progress I have had to use Roth or Gildemeister for the later letters. An annotated edition of Hamann's *Hauptschriften* with elaborate commentaries has begun to appear (Gütersloh, 1956– , seven vols. planned) but none of the works on language had appeared in this edition by the time I was composing this chapter. The first volume of this edition contains a very full bibliography of works on Hamann and a historical survey of Hamann criticism.
[3] On Hamann's views on language, see R. Unger, *Hamanns Sprachtheorie im*

of language developed into a highly individual, bizarre style which infected a few (Hippel, Jean Paul) and fascinated many (Herder, Goethe, Hegel, Grillparzer, Hebbel and Kierkegaard amongst them). But it was primarily his strange approach to language which was so influential on the development of German as a literary language.

At the age of twenty-eight Hamann found himself destitute and dejected in London. He was in a state of spiritual anguish which no activity of his well-cultivated reason could dispel. He was full of a sense of failure and of mystery at the whole purpose and meaning of life. In this mood he stumbled on the Bible. Finding his own problems clarified in the history of the Jewish people he wrote down his *Biblische Betrachtungen eines Christen* as a sort of spiritual diary.[1] The year is 1758. He feels God speaking to him through the incidents and persons of the Bible, through Cain, through the Tower of Babel, through Jeremiah. In his reflections he returns constantly to St Paul's statement that the 'foolishness of God is wiser than men' and its corollary: 'God hath chosen the foolish things of the world, to confound the wise.'[2] Jeremiah was rescued from prison by old cast clouts and

---

Zusammenhänge seines Denkens (Munich, 1905). This is expanded into a long chapter on language and style in Unger's later work *Hamann und die Aufklärung* (Halle, 1925). The treatment, though full of information, is unsatisfactory because in a welter of detail it does not distinguish sufficiently between important statements and momentary opinions, and the overriding pattern of Hamann's attitude to language does not emerge. Indeed, Unger denies that he had any consistent philosophy of language. Nadler, in his biography of Hamann (Salzburg, 1949, referred to in this chapter as Nadler, *Hamann*), is more successful in relating Hamann's conception of language to his general thought and has four splendid pages on Hamann's style (462–5). More detail on Hamann's style is to be found in Nadler's earlier work *Die Hamannausgabe*, 1930 (*Schriften der Königsberger Gelehrten Gesellschaft*, 7. Jahr, Heft 6). Recently J. C. O'Flaherty, *Unity and Language: A Study in the Philosophy of Johann Georg Hamann* (Chapel Hill, 1952) (=Univ. of North Carolina Studies in the Germanic Languages and Literatures, no. 6), has argued that Hamann had a consistent and original philosophy of language which is of historical importance. No one, so far as I can see, has considered Hamann's own use of language against the background of then prevailing styles and stylistics.

[1] As the original title, *Tagebuch eines Christen*, indicates. The full text is published for the first time by Nadler in vol. 1 of his edition of Hamann's works.
[2] I Corinthians i. 25 and 27.

old rotten rags; the blind man was cured by dust and spittle. Philosophers might expect God to speak in more intellectual terms; but the fact is that the Bible speaks in simple, everyday images and examples. When we read of the aged Asa that 'he was diseased in his feet' we should not, says Hamann, be put off: this remark confirms 'wie Gott durch keine andere Zeichen mit uns reden kann, als durch körperliche oder sinnliche, so hat er durch die Natur des Leibes das Verderben unsern [*sic*] Seelen ausgedrückt'.¹ It is through such pregnant images that God speaks to man; the 'foolishness' of God, to use St Paul's phrase, is revealed in this unintellectual but graphic language and those unsophisticated and simple people which He chose for His revelation. 'Wie ist in den geringsten Bildern ein Sinn, ein Verstand, der sich aufschließt, wenn wir mit Einfalt und Demuth Gottes Wort lesen', exclaims Hamann, 'mit eben der Einfalt und Demuth, die Gottes Geist angenommen, da er sich den Menschen durch dasselbe entdeckt hat.'² The cardinal demonstration of God's humility was His incarnation as Christ. God's humility in the language of the scriptures is therefore parallel and akin to His incarnation. Hamann states the incarnation in the well-known terms of the logos: God 'ist, wo sein Wort ist, er ist, wo sein Sohn ist. Ist sein Wort in uns, so ist sein Sohn in uns, ist sein Wort in uns, so ist der Geist dieses Worts in uns'.³ But he concentrates more on the linguistic than on the theological implications. There was nothing new in interpreting the logos as a statement about the incarnation; what was new was to interpret the logos as a statement about language in terms of the incarnation. This Hamann seized on with the cry: 'Gott — ein Schriftsteller!'

'Gott offenbart sich — der Schöpfer der Welt ein Schriftsteller!' Hamann, like Francis Bacon whose works he came to know well, believed in a twofold revelation: 'Gott hat sich geoffenbart den Menschen in der Natur und seinem Wort.'⁴ These two revelations must be consonant with each other. Nature

---

¹ Nadler, Works, vol. I, p. 121. The reference is to I Kings xv. 23.
² *Ed. cit.* I, p. 102.   ³ *Ibid.* p. 64.   ⁴ *Ibid.* p. 8.

is organised in a similar way to the Word. 'Die ganze Natur ist voller Zeichen, und siehe, so wie die Schrift ist';[1] 'Alle Werke Gottes sind Zeichen und Ausdrücke seiner Eigenschaften; und so, scheint es, ist die ganze körperliche Natur ein Ausdruck, ein Gleichnis, der Geisterwelt.'[2] We finite men can only comprehend truth and reality through the medium of images, *Gleichnisse*: 'Die Schrift kann mit uns Menschen nicht anders reden, als in Gleichnissen, weil alle unsere Erkenntnis sinnlich, figürlich und der Verstand und die Vernunft die Bilder der äußerlichen Dinge allenthalben zu Allegorien und Zeichen abstracter, geistiger und höherer Begriffe macht.'[3]

Hamann constantly marvels at the power of this imagery. God's comparison of Himself with a wilderness (Jeremiah ii. 31) calls forth the comment: 'Was kann die Sprache kühner ausdrücken'; His use of the phrase 'cleanness of teeth...and want of bread' to denote hunger (Amos iv. 6) is beautiful in its 'natural likeness and figurative sense'.[4] Hamann explains the full force of the images in 'the new wine is ashamed, the oil languisheth' (Joel i. 10): 'Der neue Wein ist beschämt —— ein Schamhafter zeigt sich nicht; er verbirgt sich, so viel er kann; er darf weder reden noch sich rühren. Stumm und ungeschickt, ohne Lippen, ohne Geist und Leben. Das Öl ist matt als ein siecher, hat keine Kraft, keine Farbe',[5] and the extreme relevance of the word 'spin' in 'Consider the lilies of the field...': 'Die Sorge der Kleidung ist dem weiblichen Geschlecht besonders eigen. Daher scheint unser Heyland den Lilien eine weibliche Beschäftigung, das Spinnen, zuzuschreiben.'[6] It may be that some of this came to him from the English theological works (by James Hervey and others) which he acquired in London. It is important that we should remember the English background; for Hamann was reading the Bible not in German but in our own

---

[1] *Ibid.* p. 68.   [2] *Ibid.* p. 112.
[3] *Ibid.* pp. 157–8. Unger suggests that this passage shows how Hamann's appreciation of imagery had grown out of the allegorical-mystical Biblical exegesis favoured by pietists (with which he was familiar).
[4] *Ed. cit.* I, pp. 175 and 185.   [5] *Ibid.* p. 183.
[6] *Ibid.* p. 198.

Authorised Version.[1] Often we find him adopting marginal readings, as when he notes the images in Zephaniah iii. 9: 'For then I will turn to the people a pure *lip*, that they may all call upon the name of the Lord, to serve him with one *shoulder*.' Hamann is particularly fascinated by images connected with speech—the still, small voice 'die wir mit Zittern in Gottes Wort und in unserm Herzen hören' and the phrase in St Mark's gospel: 'Unto you that *hear* shall more be given' (iv. 24) on which he has an entry headed 'Hören und haben'.[2] Hamann interprets incidents as images of higher truths: the burning bush is Israel, the 'first rain and latter rain' of Deuteronomy xi. 14 refers perhaps to the advent of the Messiah and the outpouring of the Holy Spirit, the fleshhook of three teeth in the story of Eli's sons is the threepronged fork of Satan (so too are the fowls, the stony places and the thorns in the parable of the sower), the twelve pieces into which the Levite of Mount Ephraim divided his concubine are the twelve apostles (so too are the twelve baskets of bread left after the feeding of the five thousand). The tradition of medieval tropology has contributed much here; so has the interpretation of the Bible as prophesying future events.[3] The basic attitude is constant: language works through imagery which gives words deeper and richer meanings than their surface significance.

At one point Hamann notes the use of repetition to attain emphasis and ventures the following opinion: 'Die Wiederholung eben desselben Worts in der hebräischen Sprache ist sehr vielbedeutend. Sie trieb die Gewißheit, die Größe, die Güte einer Sache an.'[4] We should retain such tropes in translation '...und

---

[1] Probably in the 1755 Oxford edition, of which a copy was amongst his books when he drew up the catalogue for auction in 1776.   [2] *Ibid.* pp. 121, 208.

[3] Sometimes Hamann drives this rather far, as when St Paul's shipwreck on the unknown island is interpreted as a prophecy of the advent of Christianity to America, on the grounds that the soldiers' counsel to kill the prisoners foreshadows the violence shown towards the natives of the New World and that the 'fourteenth night' corresponds to a similar moment in the voyage of the discoverers.

[4] *Ed. cit.* I, p. 124. The passage in question is II Kings xxv. 15: 'such things as [were] of gold, [in] gold, and of silver, [in] silver'. Words in square brackets are italicised in the A.V.

lieber stark als rein...übersetzen'. He praises the 'Stärke' of expression in the book of Proverbs, strength attained by few and simple words.[1] The gospel is 'die stärkste, sinnlichste und überschwenglichste Offenbarung der Natur des göttlichen Willens'.[2] In a letter written soon after his return from London he wrote: 'Stark und schön ist alles, was ich bey einem Gedichte fordere.'[3] He realised that the language of the Bible defies and transcends all the criteria of rationalistic prose:

> In der Bibel finden wir eben die *regelmäßige Unordnung*, die wir in der Natur entdecken. Alle Methoden sind als Gängelwagen der Vernunft anzusehen und als Krücken derselben. Die Einbildungskraft der Dichter hat einen Faden, der dem gemeinen Auge unsichtbar ist und den Kennern ein Meisterstück zu seyn scheint. Alle verborgene Kunst ist bey ihm Natur. Die heilige Schrift ist in diesem Stück das gröste Muster und der feinste Probierstein aller menschlichen Kritik.[4]

Here in this most important passage we have the core of Hamann's irrationalism. Let us note the parallel between language and Nature, and the striking phrase which I have italicised. Let us note the scorn of method and the homage to imagination. And let us note the acknowledgement of the Bible as the highest authority in poetry.

The *Biblische Betrachtungen* are full of scornful references to *Vernunft* and *Witz*. The book of Ecclesiastes demonstrates the limitations and abuses of Reason, says Hamann, which works painfully, losing itself in labyrinths and finding defects everywhere because it examines too closely to permit a sense of the whole. 'Der Unterricht Gottes im Schlaf und im Traume macht uns weiser und glücklicher als das Wachen der Vernunft', he says with reference to Joseph's dream in Matthew i. 20–1.[5] The voice of Heaven proclaiming the glorification of the Son of Man (John xii. 29) was interpreted by men as a natural phenomenon (thunder) or a lesser miracle (angel)—two characteristic and lasting errors of the Reason.[6] Reason is foolish and unable to put right the evil

---
[1] *Ibid.* p. 165. [2] *Ibid.* p. 226.
[3] To J. G. Lindner, dated 8 August 1759. Ziesemer and Henkel, I, p. 390.
[4] Works, I, pp. 229–30. [5] *Ibid.* p. 194.
[6] *Ibid.* p. 217.

of our hearts.¹ The Tower of Babel is a 'Thurm der Vernunft', thrusting *upward* as a symbol of man's pride and contrasting bitterly with God's humility in coming *down* to earth for our salvation.² *Witz* is put to shame by a teaching like St Paul's 'to preach the gospel not with wisdom of words lest the cross of Christ should be made of none effect' which Hamann calls 'profound' and 'more powerful than all miracles'.³ Wit can even be a bad quality. The devil has 'überlegener Witz'.⁴

In all this we see the most immediate effect of Hamann's religious experience—the reaction against the culture of wit. We see this in his letters to his former pupil Baron von Witten written during October 1758 immediately after his return from London. Thus: 'Deutlichkeit, Einfalt des Ausdrucks, Zusammenhang sind mehr werth *als drey seltene Worte und noch einmal so viel sinnreiche Einfälle*', 'Es würde mir niemals gelingen den mürrischen Ernst meiner Vernunfft in den *gaukelnden Witz* eines Stutzers umzugießen' and 'Ich will mir also die lächerliche und schädliche Eitelkeit nicht in den Sinn kommen laßen gelehrte, *witzige und schöne* Briefe zu schmieden'.⁵ 'Schwung, Witz und alle das Zeug sind entzückende Dinge, und sehr willkommene Vorzüge, wenn wir die erste, die beste Leiche oder Schönheit zu besingen haben [i.e. for occasional pieces]', he writes to J. G. Lindner in July 1759, 'wenn Witz, Schwung und alle das Zeug aber zu höheren Gegenständen gebraucht wird...so ist es eine vernünftige Raserey und eine extatische Selbstliebe — ein eccentrischer Stoltz'.⁶ This colours his attitude to *Aufklärung* literature. Lessing, for instance, was too 'philosophisch und witzig'; 'der Scharfsinn' was 'sein böser Dämon'.⁷

A glance at Hamann's earliest writings shows that he had begun in the school of wit, but his native seriousness was a disturbing factor.⁸ His contributions to the journal *Daphne* accept the

---

[1] Works, I, p. 18.   [2] Ibid. p. 30.
[3] Ibid. pp. 234–5. The reference is to I Corinthians i. 17.   [4] Ibid. p. 54.
[5] Ziesemer and Henkel, I, pp. 256, 267, 268. My italics.
[6] Ziesemer and Henkel, I, p. 354.
[7] Ziesemer and Henkel, II, p. 17; Roth, VII, p. 243.
[8] See my article, 'The Young Hamann' in *GLL*, N.S. IX, pp. 277–80 (July 1956).

THE MYSTICAL APPROACH

validity of wit but only when it is conjoined with good feelings, not when it becomes an end in itself.[1] He chides the author of the *Lettre à Uranie* for using wit against religion, but approves of the combination of wit and 'das beste Herz von der Welt' in Gellert, of wit and 'Empfindung' in Hagedorn. 'Wer überhaupt die Schönheiten witziger Schriften nicht empfindet, der straft sich selbst'; but an evil fate awaits those 'die aus dem Witz ein Handwerk zu treiben suchen'.[2] The implication is that wit should not be used for serious matters—the same attitude as is revealed in the letter to Lindner quoted in the last paragraph. In his earliest letters we find two styles kept quite separate: wit for the gayer moments, *gravitas* for more serious stuff. His solemn style is cumbrous and stilted: thus writing to his father in 1752:

> Sie kennen die Neigung, die ich Ihnen mehr als einmal entdeckt habe; und ich versichere Sie, daß ich niemals mit mir zufrieden seyn könnte, in welchen Stand ich auch gesetzt würde, wenn ich auf der Welt seyn müste ohne von derselben mehr als mein Vaterland zu kennen. Ich habe diesem Triebe zu reisen gemäs mein Studieren eingerichtet, v mich daher nicht so wohl auf eine besondere Wißenschaft, die mir zum Handwerk dienen könnte, sondern vielmehr auf einen guten Geschmack in der Gelehrsamkeit überhaupt gelegt. So sehr wir Ursache haben Gott für das Gute zu danken, das er uns durch Sie hat zuflüßen laßen, so reicht doch weder ihr Vermögen zu, daß ich meinen Vorsatz auf Ihre Unkosten ausführen könnte, v ich

---

[1] *Daphne* appeared from March 1749 to June 1750. For the circumstances of its composition, see Nadler, *Hamann*, pp. 39 ff. Berens, one of its founders, claimed that people said he had 'einen feinen Witz...der schöne Einfälle leicht und unvermuthet hervorbrächte'. This pleased him: 'Das wäre doch ein vieles.' In the fifty-seventh number it was claimed of Hamann: 'seine Schreibart geräth ihm wo nicht witzig, so doch ausgesucht'. The periodical accepted the ideal of wit and this was appreciated. A friend in Berlin wrote to Hamann on 20 August 1751: 'Die Daphne gefällt mir ungemein, und Königsberg kann es den witzigen Verfaßern dieser Sittenschrift nicht genug verdanken, daß Sie die Quellen eines gereinigten Witzes zuerst nach Preußen geleitet haben. Nach gerade wäre es Zeit, daß man den gothischen Geschmack, der so lange in Preußen geherrscht hat, verbannete, und die leichte und blühende Schreibart der Frantzosen mehr nach ahmete' (Ziesemer and Henkel, 1, p. 1).

[2] Nadler claims to have identified the sections written by Hamann (reasoning, see *Die Hamannausgabe*, pp. 34–5 and *Hamann*, p. 42) and has published these in vol. 4 of his edition. See there pp. 19, 27, 29 for my quotations.

halte mein Alter selbst noch nicht reif genung dazu.... Sie werden...
von selbst einsehen, daß mir eine kleine Ausflucht am besten dienen
würde, mich selbst führen zu lernen, indem ich mich andere zu führen
brauchen laße.[1]

On the other hand we find him writing to a 'Galanter Freund'
a spirited defence of *Artigkeit* and appending a poem by Gresset.
These early letters are spiced with consciously witty remarks.
But Hamann has as yet no style. The formal and the frivolous
modes do not blend; and, as with wine, the presence of two tastes
is a sign of immaturity. Add to this a constant uncertainty about
whether to use Dative or Accusative, or auxiliary *sein* or *haben*,
and regarding the correct form of a preterite indicative or a past
participle, and one can appreciate his regret that no one had ever
instructed him in the art of writing.[2]

Much of this is still true of the prose of the *Biblische Betrachtungen*. The grammatical uncertainty remains.[3] The wit has
gone; but we now get a violent awareness of imagery conflicting
with a basic cumbrousness. The result is often a strange mixture
of colourless solemnity and striking vigour. We encounter occasionally a hideous word like *Unhinlänglichkeit* or *Geschöpfaus-*

---

[1] Ziesemer and Henkel, I, pp. 9–10.

[2] For the defence of *Artigkeit*, see Ziesemer and Henkel, I, p. 5; for examples of the witty remarks see my article 'The Young Hamann'; for regrets at having never been taught how to write, see Gildemeister, V, p. 445 (letter to Jacobi, 7. xii. 1786). His letters are full of grammatical corrections. Even so he could leave a sentence like: 'Er hat mich gedroht mich bey Sie zu verklagen' (Ziesemer and Henkel, I, p. 5) and use *eingeladet* as past participle (*ibid.* p. 33). He wrote to his brother *à propos* of the Dangeuil translation: 'Sey ein scharfer Corrector, v sieh auf Sprachfehler; ich bin nicht sicher darüber, Du hast noch wohl Gottscheds Grammatic, die preuß. Constructiones Dat. für den Accus. hängen mir an' (Ziesemer and Henkel, I, p. 155).

[3] We find the preterites *bedung* (189), *ausbedung* (245) and *verbund* (211). In the *Gedanken über meinen Lebenslauf* (also 1758) he uses *drung* (*ed. cit.* II, p. 47); in the *Wolken* (1761) we find *gelung* (*ed. cit.* II, p. 107). Even in the late work *Golgotha und Scheblimini* (1784) there occurs the form *hung*! (*ed. cit.* III, p. 314). Complete confusion reigns on whether the attributive adjective is to be declined weak or strong—an uncertainty which goes beyond what we find in other writers of the period. Hamann's handwriting may have misled editors. Nadler admits that it is difficult to distinguish always between *dem* and *den* (*ed. cit.* I, p. 325). It seems hardly possible that Hamann could have written 'das heiligen Abendmahl' (*ed. cit.* I, p. 216) or 'zur Nachtheil' (*ibid.* p. 131).

THE MYSTICAL APPROACH

drücke, or almost incomprehensible gibberish like: 'und dieser Alte gab gleichfalls eine Lügen für eine Erscheinung und sprach hierauf, was Gott thun wollte wie Herodes that, was Gott durch seine Propheten versprochen hatte'. The form *Lügen* (accusative singular) is but one example of a frequent use of archaisms (*in der Wüsten*; genitive plural *der Monden*; genitive singular *der Kirchen*; preterite singulars *sahe*, *litte* and many others with paragogic *-e*; the use of a double pronoun *sich einander*; and the forms *empfahen*, *ohnstreitig* and *genung*).[1] All this makes for a certain mustiness. Along with this we have frequent use of Biblical imagery. We must not forget that this is a private document, not intended for publication. It is therefore less consciously written than his other works. But in its stylistic tension between conventional ciceronianism and a highly irrational use of Biblical imagery we have the roots of Hamann's style.

Sometimes we encounter already his characteristic use of a concatenation of clashing images used as intensifiers but not adding up to any composite picture: 'Eine Scherbe von Thon — Lazarus hatte Hunde, die seine Füße leckten; der arme Hiob hatte nichts als eine Scherbe von Thon, ein zweifelhaftes, unvollkommenes, trübes Tocht der Vernunft, ein zerbrochenes Rohr zu seiner Stütze; einen Schein der Natur, der ungewiß, todt und kalt war wie die wandelbare Bleiche des Mondes.'[2] It was this technique of emphatic variation by equivalent images which Hamann admired in the poetic books of the Old Testament, especially Proverbs. It is a form of indirect expression, involving

---

[1] For any reader interested in following up these details, the references are: (*ed. cit.* I), p. 147, line 5; p. 173, line 12; p. 195; p. 199, line 34; p. 209, line 23; p. 225, line 14: preterites with *-e passim*; *sich einander*, p. 185, line 31 and p. 182, line 38 and p. 229, line 24 (and continuing right into his last works. I have noted several examples in *Golgotha und Schleblimini*). The other forms: p. 169, line 20 (*et passim*); p. 172, line 23; p. 199, line 24.

[2] *Ed. cit.* I, pp. 144–5; on Job ii. 8—Job smitten with boils—'And he took him a potsherd to scrape himself withal; and he sat down among the ashes.' The reference to Lazarus is Luke xvi. 21. The *Tocht* and the *Rohr* come probably from Isaiah xlii. 3; 'bruised reed...smoking [marginal variant: dimly burning] flax' (Luther uses *Tocht* here). The application of flax to *Vernunft* would seem to be Hamann's own. The pale, fickle moon is almost a *cliché* in English.

substitution; but the substitution is emphatic, not decorative, in function. In this it differs from baroque image-series such as we considered above. With Hamann the images are connected by a common allegorical reference—thus Job's potsherd and Lazarus's dogs both symbolise the desolation of suffering. But the connection has to be realised.

Sometimes the reference is very oblique and the full meaning yields itself with difficulty. Consider the following:

Die Aussicht einer dürren Wüste, worinn ich mich von Wasser und Ähren verlassen sehe, ist mir jetzt näher als jemals. Die Wissenschaften und jene Freunde meiner Vernunft scheinen gleich Hiobs mehr meine Geduld auf die Probe zu stellen, anstatt mich zu trösten, und mehr die Wunden meiner Erfahrung blutend zu machen, als ihren Schmerz zu lindern. Die Natur hat in alle Körper ein Saltz gelegt, das die Scheidekünstler auszuziehen wissen, und die Vorsehung, es scheint, in allen Wiederwärtigkeiten einen moralischen Urstoff, den wir aufzulösen und abzusondern haben und den wir mit Nutzen als ein Hülfsmittel gegen die Krankheiten unserer Natur und gegen unsere Gemüthsübel verwenden können. Wenn wir Gott bey Sonnenschein in der Wolkensäule übersehen, so erscheint uns seine Gegenwart des Nachts in der Feuersäule sichtbarer und nachdrücklicher.[1]

The wilderness of Christ's temptation, the false friends of Job, the wounds of him who fell among thieves—all these align themselves easily in Hamann's imagination as symbols of suffering. Salt which may lose its savour, the salt of the earth—this is the positive force against despair. Salt and fire are contrasted in St Mark's gospel.[2] There are pillars of salt and pillars of fire. There are pillars of fire by night and pillars of cloud by day.[3]

---

[1] *Ed. cit.* I, p. 7.
[2] Mark ix. 49, 50: 'For every one shall be salted with fire, and every sacrifice shall be salted with salt. Salt is good: but if the salt have lost his saltness, wherewith will ye season it? Have salt in yourselves, and have peace one with another.' Hamann comments on this passage (*ibid.* p. 210): 'Kein Opfer ist also angenehm, zu dem das rechte Saltz desselben fehlt, die Empfindung unserer Sünde und der Glaube an den, der das Feuer der Sünde ausgelöscht.' The identification of salt with a sense of sin and belief in redemption adds further significance to the passage we are analysing.
[3] Exodus xiii. 21.

THE MYSTICAL APPROACH

This is how Hamann's image-series evolve. When all the terms are Biblical, elucidation is relatively easy. But his mature style draws on a much wider field and is more elliptic. The common term has to be sought in an elusive cross-reference. Reading him becomes like solving a crossword puzzle. His style would seem to be a learned game, were it not intensely serious and backed by a mystical attitude to language which sees in the Incarnation the supreme act of that basic irony of God which is also revealed in the everydayness of the language of his Word.

Irony for Hamann is a divine attribute, a mystical quality and therefore opposed to all rationalism. He was familiar with Shaftesbury's defence of the 'free play of the mind' and Hume's advocation of the 'careless disposition'. Socrates became for him the symbol of this attitude. He was 'full of Hume' when he wrote the *Sokratische Denkwürdigkeiten* (1759). Socrates was the philosopher who took pride in not knowing and trusted his daimon rather than his reason. 'Die Analogie war die Seele seiner Schlüsse, und er gab ihnen die Ironie zu ihrem Leibe.'[1] Socrates never became a writer; but if he had, his style would have been like mine, implies Hamann, for the critics did not like his references nor his comparisons. Nor did they like Hamann's. This first entry of his into the field of letters was greeted with mystification and ridicule. One notice described him as 'überwitzig und unphilosophisch' because he tried to be witty and philosophical at the same time. His style was 'unverständlich, dunkel und ausschweifend'.[2] Hamann replied with sublime disdain in *Wolken* (1761) in which most features of his ironical-imagist style are present.

Mottos (with *sous-entendus*) in Latin, Greek, Hebrew and English; constant cross-references to the Bible and classical authors in which the common term is either an image or a pun; explanatory footnotes which explain nothing and seem to laugh

---

[1] *Ed. cit.* II, p. 61.
[2] In no. 57 of the *Hamburgische Nachrichten aus dem Reiche der Gelehrsamkeit*, reprinted as the 'Erster Aufzug' of *Wolken* (*ed. cit.* II, pp. 86–9). Hamann thought this notice was inspired by Berens (who wanted him to remain a publicist) and Kant (who wanted him to translate from the *Encyclopédie*).

in one's face; those parallels of which Goethe said: 'Schlägt man sie auf, so gibt es abermals ein zweideutiges Doppellicht, das uns höchst angenehm erscheint, nur muß man durchaus auf das Verzicht thun, was man gewöhnlich Verstehen nennt';[1] sibylline utterances with the operative words in *Sperrdruck*; cultivation of what is known as *cento* (a patchwork of quotations from other works, often in various languages) and the *reductio ad absurdum* of other people's arguments by presenting them himself in exaggerated form or providing them with ridiculous footnotes. Analogy and irony, those twin pillars of the Socratic style, seem to have run riot here:

> Alle lang- und kurz-weilige Schriftsteller, sie mögen seyn, wes Standes, Alters und Statur sie wollen; — Schöpfer oder Schöpse, Dichter oder hinkende Boten, Weltweise oder Bettelmönche, Kunstrichter oder Zahnbrecher; — — die sich durch ihren *Bart* oder durch ihr *Milchkinn* der Welt bestens empfehlen; — — die, gleich den *Schriftgelehrten*, in Mänteln und weissen Denksäumen, oder wie *Scarron* in seinem am Ellbogen zurißnen Brustwamms, sich selbst gefallen; — — die aus dem Faß des Cynikers oder auf dem Lehnstuhl gesetzlicher Vernunft *lästern, da sie nichts von wissen*; — — die ihren *Stab*, wie der Gesetzgeber von schwerer Sprache und schwerer Zunge, oder wie *Bileam*, der Sohn *Beor* von *Pethor*, zu führen wissen; — sämtlich und sonders! — alle Thiere auf dem Felde, denen ein Gerücht von der Sprachkunde, den Ränken, der Verschwiegenheit, den Reisen, dem heiligen Magen, der güldenen Hüfte des *krotonischen* Sittenlehrers Pythagoras, durch ihre Vorfahren zu Ohren gekommen; alle Vögel unter dem Himmel vom *königlichen Geschmack* des *Adlers*, werden zur offenen Tafel des Hamburgischen Nachrichters eingeladen, der seine Gäste im Feyerkleide eines *griechischen Herolden* zu bewirthen, selbst erscheinen soll.[2]

The pun *Schöpfer—Schöpse* is 'explained' by a quotation from Horace, the references for the armchair, the staff and the Greek herald are given. But the rest we have to work out for ourselves, including the comparison of Moses and Hamann in the phrase

---

[1] *Dichtung und Wahrheit*, Part Three, Book Twelve. Weimar edn. XXVIII, p. 110.

[2] *Ed. cit.* II, p. 85. Words given here in italics are in *Sperrdruck* in the original.

'Gesetzgeber von schwerer Sprache und schwerer Zunge' (Hamann stuttered). This style cannot be said to have any aesthetic effect other than the certain delight at its ingenuity when one has 'got it all out'. But one cannot help being arrested by the absurd power of some of its more lapidary phrases: 'Schöpfer und Schöpse', 'Gesetzgeber von schwerer Sprache und schwerer Zunge'. Or consider the astonishing exhortation: 'Sucht keine Blonde unter den Gespielinnen des Apolls'—his attendants will be dark-skinned because the sun of genius has burned them (cf. Song of Solomon i. 6: 'I am black because the sun hath looked upon me'). At the end he implores his 'wunderliche Muse' to send a youth to confound the scribes (rationalistic philosophers) like the infant Christ, to confound them with genius, with arguments more like *Heuschrecken* than *Blindschleichen*.[1]

The *Kreuzzüge des Philologen* (1762) show Hamann's style in full flower, and contains in the section entitled *Aesthetica in nuce* a further development of his views on language. Not a reasoned statement, for Hamann himself reasoned like a grasshopper; but, as he calls it, a 'rhapsody in cabbalistic prose'. The mood is set by three mottos. First a phrase from the Song of Deborah: 'a spoil of divers colours of embroidery'. Then the words of Elihu to Job and his three friends: 'Behold, my belly is as wine which hath no vent; it is ready to burst like new bottles. I will speak that I may be refreshed: I will open my lips, and answer. Let me not, I pray you, accept or respect any man's person; neither let me give flattering titles... in so doing my maker would soon take me away.' Finally Horace's 'odi...' with its 'carmina non prius audita'. The author, then, is inflamed, defiant and no respecter of persons; his song is new and iconoclastic, its form an embroidery 'meet for the neck of the spoiler' as Deborah continues—but her image is ironical for the spoiler is Sisera and Sisera is slain, nailed to the ground. Hers is a song of triumph.

[1] The image recurs in a letter to Kant of July 1769: 'Jedes Thier hat im denken und schreiben seinen Gang. Der eine geht in Sätzen und Bogen wie eine Heuschrecke; der andere in einer zusammenhängenden Verbindung wie eine Blindschleiche im Fahrgleise, der Sicherheit wegen, die sein Bau nöthig haben soll. Der eine gerade, der andere krumm' (Ziesemer and Henkel, I, p. 379).

A note of destruction and triumph is therefore struck from the outset. We begin:

> Nicht Leyer! — noch Pinsel! — eine Wurfschaufel für meine Muse, die Tenne heiliger Litteratur zu fegen! — — Heil dem Erzengel über die Reliquien der Sprache Kanaans! — auf schönen Eselinnen siegt er im Wettlauf; — aber der weise Idiot Griechenlands borgt Euthyphrons stolze Hengste zum philologischen Wortwechsel.[1]

Two footnotes refer us to Judges for the she-asses and to Plato's *Cratylus* for the stallions. We need also to realise that the 'archangel' is J. D. Michaelis (pun!), the distinguished orientalist whose rationalistic disapproval of the language of the Old Testament had aroused Hamann's wrath, and that the 'relics of the language of Canaan' reflect the title of one of his works.[2] The 'beautiful asses' are the seat of those 'that sit in judgment'. The 'wise idiot of Greece' is Socrates who, in Plato's dialogue, ironically refers to a certain Euthyphro as his authority. After etymologising the names of the Gods Socrates says: 'Ask about anything but them, and thou shalt see how the steeds of Euthyphro shall prance.' Euthyphro was subject to possession (ἐνθουσιασμός) and Socrates claimed to be inspired by him. It would seem that for Hamann this imaged the philosopher inspired by the poetic afflatus and borrowing the horses of Apollo. The contrast is between the docile white asses of scholarship and the fiery stallions of visionary enthusiasm.

This is a good example of elliptic cross-reference in Hamann's style. Hamann's muse shall have a winnowing-fan (image from Jeremiah li. 2) to sweep clean the threshing-floor, to 'purge the floor' (Matthew iii. 12) of sacred literature from rationalistic interpretation which does not appreciate the divine function of imagery.

[1] I quote the *Aesthetica* from the text in the second volume of Nadler's edition where it is to be found on pp. 195–217. I shall not give more detailed references.

[2] *Beurtheilung der Mittel, die ausgestorbene hebräische Sprache zu verstehen* (1757). It was Michaelis pre-eminently who introduced deistic exegesis into Germany. He added notes to the German edition of Robert Lowth's treatise on Hebrew poetry. He rejected symbolical exegesis such as Hamann favoured. Hamann called on the authority of Bacon's defence of 'parabolical poetry' in the thirteenth chapter of the second book of *De dignitate et augmentis scientiarum*: 'there was an infused mystery in many of the ancient Fables of the Poets' (Gilbert Wats's translation (Oxford, 1640), p. 108).

Poesie ist die Muttersprache des menschlichen Geschlechts; wie der Gartenbau, älter als der Acker: Malerey, — als Schrift: Gesang, — als Deklamation: Gleichnisse, — als Schlüsse: Tausch, — als Handel. Ein tieferer Schlaf war die Ruhe unsrer Urahnen; und ihre Bewegung, ein taumelnder Tanz. Sieben Tage im Stillschweigen des Nachsinns oder Erstaunens saßen sie; —— und thaten ihren Mund auf — zu geflügelten Sprüchen.

Sinne und Leidenschaften reden und verstehen nichts als Bilder. In Bildern besteht der ganze Schatz menschlicher Erkenntniß und Glückseligkeit. Der erste Ausbruch der Schöpfung, und der erste Eindruck ihres Geschichtschreibers; —— die erste Erscheinung und der erste Genuß der Natur vereinigen sich in dem Worte: Es werde Licht! hiemit fängt sich die Empfindung von der Gegenwart der Dinge an.

This passage is an extension of ideas expressed in the *Biblische Betrachtungen*. A footnote refers us to 'Bacon, mein Euthyphron'. This is Hamann's great asseveration of the primacy of poetry over prose, and of pictorial language as the medium of all knowledge and revelation. The creation of the world began with a command in figurative language. For Hamann the 'Light' of the first chapter of Genesis was linked with the 'Light' of the first chapter of St John. The Word = God produces Light = Creation (and, in the second revelation, Redemption) by speaking. An act of language is therefore the primal act of the Deity. And this act is pictorial, involves an image, is poetry.

Hence the next thread in Hamann's 'needlework': 'Rede, daß ich Dich sehe! —— Dieser Wunsch wurde durch die Schöpfung erfüllt, die eine Rede an die Kreatur durch die Kreatur ist; denn ein Tag sagts dem andern, und eine Nacht thuts kund der andern.' Nature is the stuff of poetry presenting itself to man: 'Wir haben an der Natur nichts als Turbatverse und *disiecti membra poetae* zu unserm Gebrauch übrig. Diese zu sammeln ist des Gelehrten; sie auszulegen, des Philosophen; sie nachzuahmen — oder noch kühner! —— sie in Geschick zu bringen des Poeten bescheiden Theil.' 'Sie in Geschick zu bringen'—a strange phrase; the meaning is presumably 'to bring them alive' and give them 'destiny' by assembling them into a meaningful whole: 'Reden ist übersetzen — aus einer Engelsprache in eine Menschensprache, das heist, Gedanken in Worte, — Sachen in Namen, — Bilder in Zeichen; die poetisch oder kyriologisch, historisch, oder symbolisch oder hieroglyphisch — — und philosophisch oder charakteristisch seyn können.' By *reden* Hamann here obviously means not the creative act of God (as in: 'Rede, daß ich Dich sehe!') but the language of human beings. Such ambiguity is an ironical ambiguity essential to his mystical conception of language. Just as God is man in Christ, so God is language in the Word—and this Word is both the Bible and God himself. Creation is both an activity and its result, and this activity is linguistic both in God's spoken command which created the world and in the poet's creation from the *disiecti membra poetae* of that world.

The terminology *kyriologisch* (using pictures)—*hieroglyphisch* (using symbolic signs)—*charakteristisch* (using arbitrary signs) is from J. G. Wachter, as Hamann tells us.[1] The alternative trichotomy (poetical—historical—philosophical) would seem to be his own. Note that it is poetry which preserves the pictorial nature of language, whereas philosophy has moved farthest away from it. But if poetry is imitation of Nature, this Nature must not be destroyed by philosophers, for they, according to Bacon, had destroyed Nature by their abstractions. 'Die Natur würkt durch Sinne und Leidenschaften. Wer ihre Werkzeuge verstümmelt, wie mag der empfinden?' Nature without God is colourless and meaningless. We must always remain aware of the 'analogy' of God with His creation. This, and only this, gives the world meaning.

O eine Muse wie das Feuer des Goldschmieds, und wie die Seife der Wäscher! — — Sie wird es wagen, den natürlichen Gebrauch der Sinne von dem unnatürlichen Gebrauch der Abstractionen zu läutern, wodurch unsere Begriffe von den Dingen eben so sehr verstümmelt werden, als der Name des Schöpfers unterdrückt und gelästert wird.[2]

---

[1] J. G. Wachter, *Naturae et scripturae concordia* (Leipzig, 1752).
[2] The images in the first sentence are from Malachi iii. 2: 'He is like a refiner's fire, and like fullers' sope.' The passage continues: 'And he shall sit as a refiner and purifier of silver; and he shall purify the sons of Levi, and purge them as gold and silver.'

This is the climax of the *Aesthetica*. In our context we can see that it links on to much that had been said by Bodmer and Breitinger; but here it is flung out as a challenge to philosophy and a testimony to religious faith. Language cannot exist for Hamann without philosophical and religious reference.

Why this mistrust of emotion in our rationalistic age, he asks: 'Wenn die Leidenschaften Glieder der Unehre sind, hören sie deswegen auf, Waffen der Mannheit zu seyn?...Leidenschaft allein giebt Abstractionen sowohl als Hypothesen Hände, Füße, Flügel; — Bildern und Zeichen Geist, Leben und Zunge.' Why are we always referred to the Greeks and not farther back to the living springs of real antiquity? 'Das Heil kommt von den Juden.' We shall only revive language from its moribund state by pilgrimages to Arabia, crusades to the East and by regaining that magic which Bacon said consisted in noting the secret relations of things.[1]

The contrast between all this and the generally respected ideal of language at the time is illustrated by Moses Mendelssohn's assertion that the author of the *Kreuzzüge des Philologen* was so determined to be original that his writing lacked good taste, 'Leichtigkeit' and 'nachdrückliche Kürze'; he had cultivated whimsicality to the point of obscurity. Hamann replied by asserting that 'Leichtigkeit' and 'Kürze' were mutually exclusive qualities, and that 'Geschmack' was but a 'mathematical teacher of the aesthetic average' for whom style consisted in the amusing idea and the witty reference.[2] The mathematical spirit makes for rigidity in language, he asserted elsewhere in the *Kreuzzüge*.[3] But

[1] In the first chapter of the third book of *De Dignitate et Augmentis Scientiarum*: 'And indeed the Persian Magique...consists chiefly in this; to observe the respondency in the Architectures, and Fabriques of things Natural; & of things Civile.' Such resemblances are not 'meere Similitudes only...but one and the very same footsteps, and seales of Nature, printed upon severall subjects or matters' (translated Gilbert Wats (Oxford, 1640), p. 135).
[2] Mendelssohn's review was in no. 254 of the *Litteraturbriefe*. It was republished by Hamann with an ironic commentary (see Nadler's edition of the works, vol. II, pp. 257–74).
[3] *Ed. cit.* II, p. 124; in the *Versuch über eine akademische Frage*, stimulated by Michaelis's prize essay for the Berlin academy on the influence of language on opinions and *vice versa*.

the mathematical spirit, as we have seen from our consideration of Christian Wolff, is the essence of rationalism. It embodies the spirit of observation and Hamann contrasts it with poetry which embodies the spirit of prophecy. 'Die wahre Poesie ist eine natürliche Art der Prophezeyung' he had written in the *Biblische Betrachtungen*; later, in a letter, he pointed the contrast with the spirit of observation.[1] Then, right at the end of his life, he related this opposition to the opposition of philosophy and poetry:

Geist der Beobachtung und Geist der Weissagung sind die Fittige des menschlichen Geistes. Zum Gebiete der ersteren gehört alles Gegenwärtige; zum Gebiete des [sic] letzteren alles Abwesende, der Vergangenheit und Zukunft. Das *philosophische* Genie äussert seine Macht dadurch, daß es, vermittelst der Abstraction, das Gegenwärtige abwesend zu machen sich bemüht; wirkliche Gegenstände zu nackten Begriffen und bloß denkbaren Merkmalen, zu reinen Erscheinungen und Phänomenen entkleidet. Das *poetische* Genie äussert seine Macht dadurch, daß es, vermittelst der Fiction, die Visionen abwesender Vergangenheit und Zukunft zu gegenwärtigen Darstellungen verklärt.[2]

Hamann deplored the way in which the mathematical spirit had impoverished and fettered the French language: 'Die Reinigkeit einer Sprache entzieht ihrem Reichthum; eine gar zu gefesselte Richtigkeit, ihrer Stärke und Mannheit.'[3] Against the regulated word-order of French he placed the free word-order of Latin. The possibility of inversion as a stylistic value should not be abandoned for considerations of regularity. 'Die deutsche Sprache ist ihrer Natur nach vor andern dieser Inversionen fähig; und ihre Kühnheit trägt mit zum Ansehn unserer poetischen Schreibart bey.'[4] An Academy may adjudicate on what is 'lauter und artig',

---

[1] 'Was wäre alle Erkenntniß des Gegenwärtigen ohne eine Göttliche Erinnerung des Vergangenen und ohne eine noch glücklichere Ahndung des Künftigen, wie Socrates seinem Dämon verdankte? Was wäre der Geist der Beobachtung ohne den Geist der Weissagung und seine Leitfäden der Vergangenheit und Zukunft?' (to Jacobi, 8 June 1786, Gildemeister, v, pp. 351–2).

[2] *Ed. cit.* III, pp. 382 and 384. From the first version of the *Fliegender Brief an Niemand, den Kundbaren* (1786), my italics.

[3] *Ed. cit.* II, p. 136.

[4] *Ibid.* pp. 130–1. In this essay Hamann draws on the comparison between French and Latin word-order in Pluche, *La méchanique des Langues* (Paris, 1751), which had mentioned the almost total lack of inversion in French. Diderot

but only genius can use the treasury of a language with wisdom or increase it with skill. In France genius 'grovelled before the tinsel of fashion', the supreme authority of genius had been replaced by the pale substitute of 'gesunde Vernunft' which inhibits feeling and spontaneity:

> Wenn unsere Vernunft Fleisch und Blut hat, haben muß, und eine Wäscherin oder Sirene wird; wie wollen sie es den Leidenschaften verbieten? Wie wollen Sie den erstgebornen Affect der menschlichen Seele dem Joch der Beschneidung unterwerfen? Kannst du mit ihm spielen wie mit einem Vogel? oder ihn deinen Regeln binden? Sehen Sie nicht, daß Sie hiedurch alle Leuchtthürme niederreissen, die Ihnen selbst und andern zur Richtschnur dienen müssen.[1]

The language of the Bible seems foolish, shallow and ignoble to these rationalists; this proves their criteria to be inadequate. Clarity?—'Die Deutlichkeit gewisser Bücher ist oft Betrug und Mangel, auch vielem Misbrauch ausgesetzt'; and he agreed that 'Gedanken durch die Deutlichkeit einen großen Theil ihrer Neuheit, Kühnheit und Wahrheit verlieren können'.[2] *Bon Sens?*—did this produce the great legislators of humanity? 'Les dix commandemens, les douze tables & les Codes ne furent pas compilés pour les gens du bon sens; mais pour inspirer au vulgaire la belle passion d'horreur pour les gens d'esprit sans pieté & sans religion.'[3] Taste?—the rationalist philosophers, the *philosophes*

---

in the introduction to his *Lettre sur les sourds et muets*, also 1751, had drawn a distinction between natural and artificial order. Other points in this essay are taken from Restaut, *Principes généraux et raisonnés de la Grammaire françoise* (Paris, 1730) and the *Grammaire de Port Royal*. See Unger, *Sprachtheorie*, pp. 190 ff.

[1] *Ed. cit.* II, p. 164. The bird is a reference to Job xl. 24 in Luther's numbering, which reads: 'Kanstu mit ihm [the Leviathan] spielen / wie mit einen Vogel / oder ihn deinen Dirnen binden.' Note the equation of feeling with Leviathan and rules with handmaidens.

[2] *Ibid.* p. 183. In his ironical footnotes to a review of the *Kreuzzüge* in the *Hamburgische Nachricht*, Hamann speaks of the 'deutliche Waschhaftigkeit eines Kräuterweibes' (*ed. cit.* II, p. 248). In a letter to Herder dated 3 August 1786 there is the striking statement: 'Ich traue eben so wenig den deutlichen als den dunkeln Begriffen; man kann sich durch beide hinters Licht führen lassen' (Roth, VII, p. 333).

[3] *Ed. cit.* II, p. 293. In the *Glose Philippique* (1762) aimed at the Berlin academy and its rationalistic spirit.

serpens 'marchent au rocher du Génie sur leur ventre & mangent la poussiere par Gout'.[1] And concerning Rules in general there is a terrific utterance in the fourth of the *Hirtenbriefe*, couched in the usual biblical imagery:

Ein Engel fuhr herab zu seiner Zeit und bewegte den Teich Bethesda, in dessen fünf Hallen viel Kranke, Blinde, Lahme, Dürre lagen und warteten, wenn sich das Wasser bewegte — Eben so muß ein Genie sich herablaßen Regeln zu erschüttern; sonst bleiben sie Wasser: — und man muß der erste seyn hereinzusteigen, nachdem das Wasser bewegt wird, wenn man die Wirkung und Kraft der Regeln, selbst erleben will.[2]

In rejecting clarity as an absolute criterion of style Hamann found support in St Augustine and proudly noted the fact in a letter of June 1759.[3] He quotes two passages which I give here abbreviated and in Pusey's translation. Speaking of Moses, St Augustine says:

I would then, had I been what he was, and been enjoined by Thee to write the book of Genesis, have desired such a power of expression and such a style to be given me, that neither they who cannot yet understand how God created, might reject the sayings, as beyond their capacity; and they who had attained thereto, might find what true opinion soever they had by thought arrived at, not passed over in those few words of that Thy servant: and should another man by the light of truth have discovered another, neither should that fail of being discoverable in those same words.

There follows a metaphor. Then again:

For I certainly, were I to indite any thing to have supreme authority, I should prefer so to write, that whatever truth any could apprehend on those matters, might be conveyed in my words, rather than set down my own meaning so clearly as to exclude the rest, which not being false, could not offend me. I will not therefore, O my God, be so rash, as not to believe, that Thou vouchsafedst as much to that great man. He without doubt, when he wrote those words, perceived and thought on what truth soever we have been able to find, yea and whatsoever we have not been able, nor yet are, but which may be found in them.[4]

---

[1] *Ed. cit.* II, p. 289.   [2] *Ibid.* p. 362.
[3] Ziesemer and Henkel, I, pp. 334–6.
[4] *Confessions*, Book XII, §§ xxvi and xxxi.

THE MYSTICAL APPROACH

Hamann notes that these ideas run counter to normally accepted ideas of good style because they admit that truth can subsist in manifold interpretations of a single thing; and 'nach den Gedanken des Augustinus von der Schreibart, sollte man den grösten Fehler in eine Schönheit verwandelt sehen; die Klarheit in einen unbestimmten vieldeutigen Sinn'. Fullness of meaning, manifold application and interpretation—not singleness of reference—is the stylistic principle advocated. This is a tremendously important statement, a stylistic with irony as its cardinal virtue, ambivalence as its content and ambiguity as its basic form.

The obscurity of Hamann's style derives therefore from a conscious stylistic and not merely from inarticulateness. Disorderliness was, he admitted, the prime failing of his nature. He could not sustain an argument. He tended towards the aphorism as his natural means of expression.[1] This was transmuted into a conscious stylistic when he realised that concentration was a positive contrast to rationalist verbosity and concreteness to rationalist abstractness. Concentration gave multiple reference such as was admired by St Augustine; concreteness gave force and irony such as he admired in the Bible. In a letter written in October 1783 to his son he mentioned the 'threefold repetition of a term by Demosthenes'. This was ὑπόκρισις, action. In the preface to the *Kreuzzüge* he had mentioned this and contrasted the author 'der Handlung liebt' with one 'der ins Gras beissen muß'. A few months earlier he had written to Lindner: 'Handlung soll meinem Styl in nichts nachgeben, wenn es so weit kommen wird.'[2] He adapted Demosthenes to his own purpose: 'Leidenschaft — Leidenschaft — Leidenschaft wie des Demosthenes *actio*.'[3] Passion and vigour would therefore seem to be what he understood by *Handlung*. Hence his opposition to abstract lan-

---

[1] *Ed. cit.* II, p. 21: 'Unordnung, der allgemeine Grundfehler meiner Gemüthsart.' *Ibid.* p. 14: 'Ich finde mich in vieler Mühe meine Gedanken mündlich und schriftlich in Ordnung zu sammeln und mit Leichtigkeit auszudrücken.' Roth, VII, p. 309: 'Zum *formale* habe ich mein ganzes Leben nicht getaugt in keinem einzigen Stück.' Ziesemer and Henkel, I, p. 431: 'Wahrheiten, Grundsätze, Systems bin ich nicht gewachsen. Brocken, Fragmente, Grillen, Einfälle. Ein jeder nach seinem Grund und Boden.'

[2] Ziesemer and Henkel, II, p. 67.   [3] Gildemeister, V, p. 501.

guage which he never tired of maintaining. 'Nur keine geläuterte, und abgezogene und leere Wörter—die scheu ich, wie tiefe stille Wasser und glattes Eis.'[1] His opposition to verbosity led to ellipsis, his hatred of abstraction to figurative allegory—a combination sustained by his love of irony. It was as early as August 1759 that he made his famous statement: 'Meine Briefe sind vielleicht schwer, weil ich elliptisch wie ein Griech, und allegorisch wie ein Morgenländer schreibe.'[2] Less often quoted is the statement slightly later in the same letter that he argued 'bald κατ' ἀνθρωπον bald κατ' ἐξοχην'—now like a man, now like a God. This surely is the recognition that irony was the guiding spirit; but an irony very different from the extremely human irony of Wieland.

Ellipsis led to his 'verfluchter Wurststyl',[3] allegory to the riot of images. In the famous first letter to Kant he referred ironically to the 'spectacles of his imagination with which he had to fortify the feeble eyes of his reason'. Sometimes we find disparate ideas expressed by connected images; sometimes disparate images connected by related ideas. Sometimes the idea embodied in the image is stated: 'Genie ist eine Dornenkrone und der Geschmack ein Purpurmantel, der einen zerfleischten Rücken deckt';[4] sometimes indicated: 'Der Geburtstag eines Genies wird, wie gewöhnlich, von einem Märtyrerfest unschuldiger Kinder begleitet';[5] sometimes left for us to work out: 'Warum flechten wir nun Schürze von Feigenblättern, wenn Röcke von Fellen fertig auf uns warten?'[6] These are three progressive stages of compression. It is the last that gives Hamann's style its individuality. It produces memorable amalgams like 'Ballet hinkender Hypothesen', 'Caviar des Leviathans' or the description of *der, die, das* as 'etymologische Pudenda'.[7] Eccentric statements like: 'Optimus Maximus verlangt keine Kopfschmerzen sondern Pulsschläge' or

---

[1] Gildemeister, v, p. 16. [2] Ziesemer and Henkel, I, p. 396.
[3] 'der von Verstopfung herkömmt' (Gildemeister, v, p. 186, drawing a contrast with 'Lavaters Durchfall'). Hamann suffered from constipation.
[4] Ziesemer and Henkel, II, p. 168.
[5] Works, *ed. cit.* II, p. 214. [6] Works, *ed. cit.* II, p. 362.
[7] Works, *ed. cit.* II, p. 189; *ibid.* III, p. 202; *ibid.* III, p. 209.

THE MYSTICAL APPROACH

'Der Beweiß ist der Despotismus des Apolls; die Parabel schmeckt nach der Aristokratie der Musen' or the description of Voltaire as 'Arouet Falstaff, der unverschämteste Spermolog und Virtuose, Hiero- und Sykophant seines Jahrhunderts' show a brilliant control of language.[1] His style is pungent, momentary, switching. It is the very opposite of systematic. But must we all be systematic? Is there not room for silkworms as well as spiders?: 'Spinnen und ihrem Bewunderer Spinoza [pun!] ist die geometrische Bauart natürlich? Können wir alle Systematicker seyn? Und wo bleiben die Seiden Würmer, diese Lieblinge unseres Salomo [Frederick the Great]?'[2]

In his later works Hamann sometimes showed himself capable of more systematic expression. His exposition was still apt to jump like a grasshopper, but there are short passages of connected argument (like the passage quoted above on p. 444). His imagery became more predominantly sexual as he came to think of everything in terms of life and its creation. Biblical influence on this 'spermologischer Styl', as he called it, is apparent. The Song of Solomon was for him the 'navel' of the Bible.[3] But there were other influences as well: Hellenistic authors, mystical writers, Rabelais and Sterne. The idea of the *logos spermatikos* came from the Stoics and combined with Paracelsian alchemy to serve Hamann with a whole set of images to explain the transition from God to man. But this lies outside our sphere of enquiry in this book. We are not concerned with Hamann's theology nor his late works. It was the earlier works which really influenced his generation, and it was his earlier style which made history.

Amongst these later works there is a vigorous dismissal of the rationalistic approach to language in the *Neue Apologie des Buchstabens h* (1773). Unger treats this as a tract on spelling reform; but it is far more than that and deserves brief mention here.

---

[1] Gildemeister, v, p. 197; Ziesemer and Henkel, II, p. 128; Works, *ed. cit.* III, p. 144.
[2] Ziesemer and Henkel, II, p. 197. For a fuller study of Hamann's use of imagery, see my paper to the English Goethe Society, 'Irony and Imagery in Hamann', *Publications*, XXVI (1957).
[3] Roth, VI, p. 60. For the phrase 'spermologischer Styl', see Roth, VI, p. 122.

Hamann uses someone's passing objection to the silent *h* in German to launch an attack on rationalistic deism which derives God only from what is seen and heard.[1] The letter *h*—'Hauch, spiritum'—is a symbol of the true, invisible God who is not of this world and whose 'language' cannot be understood by those who only observe His 'external' works. 'Der Geist ist es, der lebendig macht; der Buchstabe ist Fleisch, und eure Wörterbücher sind Heu!'[2] He rejects the phonetic criterion for spelling, on the grounds that this would produce regional orthographies; the silent *h* was merely a convenient sign for indicating a long vowel or differentiating homophones. In the *Zweifel und Einfälle über eine vermischte Nachricht* (1776) he ridicules the 'infallible rule of three' of rationalist grammar—best pronunciation, best provinces, best authors—which 'ein dreyfaches Beste als bereits gefunden voraus setzt, davon das gesuchte Gute eine sehr unbeträchtliche Kleinigkeit'.[3] Attacking Klopstock's reformed orthography in *Zwey Scherflein zur neuesten Deutschen Litteratur* (1780) he pointed out the vicious circle in the phonetic argument. The whole 'platonic' ideal of an ideal and abstract orthography disregards the fact that language is a living thing which cannot be schematically petrified. Desire to stabilise fluctuations and to prune superfluities produces sterility in language. Speech is something more than the articulation of blind sounds, and writing than the alignment of 'their dumb stadtholders'; the visual and the aural are inextricably interrelated in language, both acting as levers to our thoughts. The orthography of a language expresses its individuality, the 'Begriffe, Meinungen, Vorurtheile eines Volks'. It was not enough to go back to pre-*Kanzleisprache*. 'Wer nicht in die Gebärmutter der Sprache...eingeht, ist nicht geschickt zur Geistestaufe einer Kirchen- und Staatsreformation.' It was time to return to origins.

[1] The work in question was C. F. Damm, *Betrachtungen über die Religion* (1773). Hamann's little treatise is to be found in volume III of Nadler's edition of the works, pp. 89–107.

[2] *Ed. cit.* III, p. 107; cf., in *Konxompax* (1779): 'Der Geist aber rechtfertigt und macht lebendig. Fleisch und Buch ohne Geist ist kein Nütze' (*ed. cit.* III, p. 227).   [3] *Ed. cit.* III, p. 184.

XIV

THE RETURN TO ORIGINS

HAMANN'S attitude to language represents a counterblast to rationalistic mistrust which, in its extreme form, had declared that language impeded reason and that philosophy should try to do without language altogether. Hamann objected that without language we should have no reason; that language represents the pattern of experience; that language is essential for cognition; and that although language is not the only means for the objectivation of thought it is the most effective because God is a speaking God and man was created in His image. Herder's early works are dominated by this question of the relation between language and thought; and in them we find embedded many of Hamann's ideas. The two men were well acquainted and there was a fruitful exchange of ideas during the gestative period of Herder's first important work, the *Fragmente über die neuere deutsche Litteratur* (1766–7).[1]

Herder approaches language not from theology but from literature. 'Wer über die Litteratur eines Landes schreibt, muß ihre Sprache auch nicht aus der Acht lassen.... Der Genius der Sprache ist also auch der Genius von der Litteratur einer Nation.... Ihr könnt also die Litteratur eines Volks ohne ihre Sprache nicht übersehen': for both progressed simultaneously.[2] Hamann's trifold division of language reappears as 'poetische Sprache...biegsame Sprache...genaue Sprache': but Herder presents poetry, prose and philosophy as three successive stages in

---

[1] For more detail on Hamann's correspondence with Herder in these years, see my article 'Hamann in the Doldrums' in *GLL*, N.S. x (July 1957). On their community of ideas in these years, see J. Haussmann, 'Der junge Herder und Hamann', *JEGP*, VI (1906–7), pp. 606–48.

[2] I shall quote Herder's works from the edition of B. Suphan (and others), 33 vols. (Berlin, 1877–1913). These sentences are taken from the opening of the first *Fragment*, ed. cit. I, pp. 147–8.

language which develops like an organism: 'keimt, trägt Knospen, blüht und verblüht'. In the first, natural stage of language (which precedes poetry) man utters sharp sounds, mostly monosyllabic and strongly accented and high-pitched, as the expression of his immediate reactions to sense-stimuli. These sounds are mere emotional reflexes. As he grows out of this first childhood, man's fear and terror at his surroundings gradually subside and he begins to give things names. These are at first onomatopoeic; but visual impressions have also to be named (a knotty point, which Herder skates over for the moment). Man's whole vocabulary was, in this early stage, *sinnlich* (by which Herder means that it represented direct sound-reactions to sense-impressions).[1] Language was accompanied by mime and gesture. It was rhapsodic. Primitive man sang. Then, as 'die Wildheit senkte sich zur Politischen Ruhe', speech became smoother, less ejaculatory. Non-sensual concepts, abstract ideas, begin to enter the language; but these were expressed by means of sense-imagery. And mythology arose to explain the wonder of the universe. What was this mythology but metaphor? With its imagery and metaphor, this second stage of language was full of poetry and mythology. 'Die stärksten Machtwörter, die reichste Fruchtbarkeit, kühne Inversionen, einfache Partikeln, der klingendste Rhythmus, die stärkste Declamation — alles belebte sie, um ihr einen sinnlichen Nachdruck zu geben, um sie zur Poetischen zu erheben.' As language grew older it became reasoned and logical, inversions dropped into misuse, idioms were weakened, *Machtwörter* paraphrased. Language became more perfect but less poetic. This is the age of prose. 'Statt der Sprache der Leidenschaft ward sie eine Sprache des mitlern Wizzes: und endlich des Verstandes.' In the old-age of language beauty is replaced as a criterion by correctness and exactness. This is the language of philosophy, rejecting synonymic variation for the sake of clarity and regulating syntax to avoid ambiguity, perfect for the philosopher but bad for the poet.

[1] R. T. Clark, *Herder* (Berkeley and Los Angeles, 1955), p. 17, claims that this was G. F. Meier's rendering of Baumgarten's term *sensitivus*, meaning 'pertaining to the faculties of sensation'. Poetry, according to Baumgarten, was *oratio perfecta sensitiva*.

THE RETURN TO ORIGINS

It has been remarked that this represents a fusion of heterogeneous contemporary ideas into a shape derived from Rousseau.[1] Herder's envisagement of the earliest stage of language came from Condillac (via Rousseau)[2] and Diderot, his enthusiasm for the 'poetic' age of language from Hamann and Lowth, and the conception of progressive stages of language from Blackwell. But Blackwell's progression was towards perfection, Herder's towards decay and therefore similar to Winckelmann's view of the development of Greek art. Rousseau showed the political relevance of such a view of history; Herder translates this into terms of literature: 'Lernet also, ihr Kunstrichter! eure Sprache kennen: und sucht sie zur Poesie, zur Weltweisheit und zur Prose zu bereiten.'

The question one naturally asks is: in which of these stages did Herder consider the German language to be? Answer: the age of prose. It therefore looked towards poetry with one face and towards philosophy with the other. He believed that the language could be improved in either direction: the poetic aspect by translation from more *sinnlich* languages, the philosophical aspect by reflection on how best to use such material to enrich, not overload, the existing lexicon of the language. He praised the Swiss for salvaging so much valuable obsolescent vocabulary. This is part of the idiom of a language. *Idiotismen* are 'patronymic beauties', embodying the essence of a language. For every language embodies a national character, a national way of thinking; and this is what makes translation so difficult. Every language has its own genius (*Genie*). Much violence had been done to the *Genie* of the German language by Gottsched and his followers. They had emasculated it, robbed it of its personal idioms. By acting against this the Swiss, for all their faults, had enriched the

[1] Hans M. Wolff, 'Der junge Herder und die Entwicklungsidee Rousseaus', *PMLA*, LVII (1942), pp. 753–819.
[2] A note in the *Nachschrift* to the third collection of *Fragmente* suggests that Herder's direct acquaintance with Condillac's work began *after* he had composed the first series. But he knew Rousseau's description in the second *Discours*, which owes much to Condillac. On Herder's debt to Diderot, see K.-G. Gerold, *Herder und Diderot* (Frankfurt am Main, 1941); and R. Mortier, *Diderot en Allemagne* (Brussels, 1954).

language. More should be done in this way. For obsolescent idioms lead one into hidden veins of riches in the language. Like Hamann, Herder calls for cleansing (*läutern*) and rejuvenating (*verjüngen*).[1] An individual genius will show his worth by the boldness of his idiom, breaking his way through heavy ceremoniousness down into the bowels of the language, down through rocky clefts to find gold. Even if what he finds is but a shapeless lump, there may be opportunity for chemistry. Would there were many such miners and smelters in Germany! Did not the great Leibniz tell us that German was the language of miners and hunters?

It is difficult to render in one's own language the individuality of another. How impossible for Modern German to reproduce the *Machtwörter* and the inversions of Ancient Greek! Inversions —i.e. free word-order—are an important aspect of primitive language for Herder. He discusses this topic in sections twelve and thirteen of the first series of the *Fragmente*. The rational ideal of prose results in a stereotyped word-order aiming at clear exposition of ideas. But this is inadequate to express strong emotion:

> Nun stellet euch zwei sinnliche Geschöpfe vor, davon der eine spricht, der andre höret: Dem ersten ist das Auge die Quelle seiner Begriffe; und jeden Gegenstand kann er in verschiedenen Gesichtspunkten sehen; dem andern zeiget er diesen Gegenstand, und es kann auf eben so verschiedenen Seiten geschehen. Nun betrachtet die Rede, als ein Zeichen dieser Gegenstände: so habt ihr den Ursprung der Inversionen. Je mehr sich also die Aufmerksamkeit, die Empfindung, der Affekt auf einen Augenpunkt heftet: je mehr will er dem andern auch eben diese Seite zeigen, am ersten zeigen, im hellesten Lichte zeigen — und dies ist der Ursprung der Inversionen. Ein Beispiel: *Fleuch* die Schlange! ruft mir jemand zu, der mein fliehen zu seinem Hauptaugenmerk hat, wenn ich nicht fliehen wollte. — *Die Schlange* fleuch! ruft ein anderer, der nichts geschwinder will, als mir die Schlange zeigen; fliehen werd ich von selbst, so bald ich von ihr höre.[2]

---

[1] *Ed. cit.* II, pp. 57, 160, 283.
[2] *Ed. cit.* I, pp. 191–2. The example is taken from Diderot's *Lettres sur les sourds et muets* (1751).

THE RETURN TO ORIGINS

Inversions, therefore, translate emotional emphasis into linguistic emphasis. They depend on accent and possibly gesture (Condillac!). They are therefore frequent in the early stages of language. They preceded grammar; but recede when written language evolves a fixed word-order. 'Aber für das Poetische Genie ist diese Sprache der Vernunft ein Fluch.' French shows this; and some Frenchmen realised how enslaved their language was by its logical word-order.

Herder refers us to Diderot. But the point had already been made by Hamann, who had drawn on other French opinions.[1] Seventeenth-century French grammarians had claimed that the *ordre direct* was the 'natural order'; but some authors felt a certain sense of restriction. 'On est esclave de la construction', said La Bruyère; and Fénelon, in his *Lettre à l'Académie* of 1714, dared to suggest that the *ordre direct* had 'appauvri, desséché, et gêné notre langue'. As the eighteenth century unfolds we find Batteux and others recognising emotional as well as logical order. It was pointed out that Latin order was different from that of French. Which then was 'natural'? Neither, said Diderot; both, said Condillac.—'Il y a des esprits qui ne recherchent que l'ordre et la plus grande clarté; il y en a d'autres qui préfèrent la variété et la vivacité.'[2] Interest became centred on the point whether inversion could usefully be permitted in modern prose style. Some thought it helped in the attainment of *clarté*. Many agreed that the insistence on *ordre direct* made French prose monotonous.[3] Condillac's criterion of *la liaison des idées* and his insistence on *rapidité* as part of this, helped to boost emotional order. His assertion that there are 'tours propres au sentiment' was developed by Rapin and Batteux. 'Je dirais que nous avons gagné, à n'avoir point d'inversions, de la netteté, de la clarté, de la précision, qualités essentielles au discours', said Diderot, 'et que nous y avons

---

[1] See above, p. 444. Nevertheless the parallel with Diderot is closest.
[2] Condillac, *Oeuvres* (Paris, 1798), vol. I, p. 415. The conclusion of his discussion on inversions in the *Essai sur l'origine des connoissances humaines*.
[3] For examples, see vol. VI of Brunot's *Histoire de la langue française*, by Alexis François, pp. 1937 ff.

perdu de la chaleur, de l'éloquence et de l'énergie.'[1] Elsewhere Diderot recognised the existence of a language of the heart 'mille fois plus variée que celle de l'esprit'.[2] Against the strict classical conception of harmony, a wider *harmonie expressive* begins to assert itself in French prose; and this concept allowed more varied sentence-rhythms. For the time being, inversions were still considered as deviations from an established norm. Herder's praise of inversions would therefore seem to be more positive than anything advocated in France; for although Condillac justified head-position of the object in ancient languages as representing gesture towards the object affected, he did not advocate its revival. But Herder's attitude merely represented a development of Breitinger's which, as we have seen, stemmed ultimately from Addison. Important, however, is the developing emphasis: from being something permitted, inversions become useful and then vital. For Herder they are the soul of poetry.

In other respects Herder differed sharply from Breitinger. Thus on the matter of synonyms, Breitinger (see above, p. 283) had considered synonymic wealth a failing and praised rationalistic delimitation. Herder considers the wide range of synonyms in primitive languages as part of their poetic quality and deplores rationalistic delimitation: 'Noch blieben aber Synonymen! Aber der Philosoph suchte feine Unterschiede in sie zu legen, und sie also als neue, gültige Wörter zu gebrauchen.' But the poet: 'Der Dichter muß rasend werden, wenn du ihm die Synonyme raubst; er lebt vom Ueberfluß.'[3] This is a striking example of the conflict between poetical and philosophical perfection in language. It was this above all which rationalism had failed to realise. Nicolai had expressly stated that definiteness and exactness were the most beautiful properties of a language; Sulzer had demanded that German poetry should develop logical clarity. To this end Sulzer had proposed removal of synonyms, idioms and inversions

---

[1] Diderot, *Oeuvres*, ed. Assézat and Tourneux (Paris, 1875–9), vol. I, p. 371.
[2] Quoted by Charles Bruneau in his *Petite histoire de la langue française*, vol. I (Paris, 1955), p. 260.
[3] *Ed. cit.* I, p. 170 and II, p. 103.

and the regulation of language by philosophical principles.[1] Herder maintains that poetry makes different demands on language from philosophy. Following Klopstock he asserts that these are conflicting criteria. He does not accept Hamann's complete rejection of rationalist criteria of language; but he asserts that they apply only to philosophy.

Herder was justified in echoing Hamann's view that German was more capable of inversions than French. In other respects, however, he still thought French superior. It was supreme as a language for prose, for it had that lightness and brilliance which escaped the Germans in their excessive striving for clarity. (Again an idea from Hamann.) There was still much to be learnt from the 'strength' of English. But we must remember that each language embodies *Nationalgeist* and *Nationalvorurteile*. Surface imitation without imitation of the spirit is therefore valueless. The 'short, parabolic tone' of Hebrew tends to be falsely transposed into German periodic structure, with relation rather than parallelism of images.[2] This is more Greek than Hebrew. But German had suffered also from false imitation of Greek. Useless to imitate Homer's imagery without having his way of looking at things; useless to imitate the bold compounds and illogical constructions of Pindar without the true dithyrambic spirit; useless to imitate Anacreon's conceits without his *naïveté*. The worst harm, however, had been done by enslavement to Latin.

The German language, says Herder, had declined since the sixteenth century; it had lost bite. Gottsched's reform was far too Latin in spirit. 'Man verachtete die alte Deutsche Kernsprache.' The much-vaunted 'Ciceronian' style was a wrongheaded attempt to impose periodicity (which Latin needed because of the shortness of its words) on German (where it resulted in a dragging heaviness). German was full of strongly accented syllables, heavy conjunctions and relatives, and auxiliary verbs—all

[1] See R. T. Clark, *op. cit.* pp. 22, 64, 66.
[2] 'Wir müssen...jene zerstückte Bilder, die sich wiederholen, zu einem Ganzen ordnen, und sie in einem gebildeten Poetischen Perioden mehr in der Perspektiv eines Gleichnisses zeichnen', i.e. convert image-series into progressive metaphor. *Ed. cit.* I, p. 271.

of which helped to slow down style. Amplitude was therefore not a perfection it should strive after. In the second part of his unfinished memorial to Thomas Abbt, Herder makes a distinction between periodic sentence and periodic style: the former belongs to Latin but not to German, for German depends on the latter. The distinction is not made very clear but it would seem to be that between *connexio verbalis* and *connexio realis* with which we are already familiar—except that Herder would undoubtedly lay more importance on rhythmical and emphatic devices in establishing connection. The Latin period was 'ein fortschreitendes Ganze', whereas the German periodic sentence was 'ein verkettetes Ding' and nothing more.[1] It trailed away into a *hätte werden können* or some such verbal concatenation. It had to, because of the fixed word-order of German. But German had its own way of assembling members. It had its own type of *circumductio*; but the ideal of amplitude, *ambitus*, was foreign to its spirit. On the whole, he thinks Tacitus a more useful model for his countrymen than Cicero or Livy. For Germans tend naturally towards diffuseness. He admires the style of Thomas Abbt for combining Tacitean precision with French lightness and English colourfulness. English colourfulness is for Herder the extreme opposite of Greek simplicity. He thinks that German style was either excessively infected by French elegance or by English richness. 'Das Mittel zwischen einem Engländer und Franzosen ist ohngefähr—ein Deutscher.'[2] This is an interesting remark when considered against the background of the conflicting linguistic ideals which had inspired Germans since the beginning of the century.

It is not my intention here to examine Herder's own style in any detail. It was his ideas on language rather than his own use of language which were influential. His style displeased some who were in general sympathy with his ideas; notably Hamann who found the language of the first *Fragmente* 'an einigen Stellen zu *petillant*, und die periodische Form durch Fragen, Ausruffungen, *Interjectio*nen gar zu zerrißen'. Herder defended himself by reference to his immaturity and to the fact 'daß ich das Phlegma

[1] *Ed. cit.* II, p. 339.   [2] *Ibid.* p. 360.

eines *homme d'esprit*, noch gar nicht mit dem Enthusiasmus des Genies zu verbinden weiß' (which sounds self-satisfied but is probably ironical or even sarcastic). 'Meine Studien sind wie Zweige, die durch ein Ungewitter mit einemal ausgetrieben worden.... Stellen Sie sich meine Pein vor, die ich haben muß, um einen Gedanken auszubilden, zehn jüngere zu verlieren.'[1] It was the misfortune of having too much to say and too strong an impulse to say it. Coupled with this sense of compelling urgency there was in Herder an instinctive dislike of cold, reasoned exposition. For both these reasons he found language inadequate and transformed it into a highly emotional, graphic, unsystematic style. He shared Hamann's hatred of systems. 'Vor nichts graut mir mehr als vor dem Erbfehler der Deutschen, Systeme zu zimmern.'[2] And he admitted that he sometimes wrote hastily, impelled by the heat of the moment.[3] He was unwilling to consider this a fault; for spontaneity was one of his main demands on authors. But Hamann was unconvinced, and in a letter of December 1774 we find him writing: 'Die Gräuel der Verwüstung in Ansehung der deutschen Sprache, die alcibiadischen Verhunzungen des Artikels, die monstrosen Wort-Kuppeleyen, der dithyrambische Syntax und alle übrige *licentiae poeticae* verdienen eine öffentliche Ahndung, und verrathen eine so spasmodische Denkungsart, daß dem Unfuge auf eine oder andere Art gesteuert werden muß.'[4] Herder's style was not careless; it embodied, as Hamann here suggests and Herder himself had admitted in the passage quoted above, his own manner of thought. It also embodied his own views on language—a fascinating topic which I have developed elsewhere.[5] We must content ourselves here with some rather general remarks.

Noticeable is a steady progress away from the periodic sentence.

---

[1] Ziesemer and Henkel, II, p. 377 (Hamann to Herder, 12 August 1766) and pp. 381–2 (Herder to Hamann, undated).
[2] Letter to Scheffner, 31 October 1767.
[3] 'Hitze des Schreibens', referring to the essay on the origin of language, letter to Formey, 28 August 1771.   [4] Roth, v, pp. 120–1.
[5] See my paper to members of the Germanic Institute of the University of London on 'The imprint of Herder's linguistic theory upon his early prose style', to be published shortly.

Parataxis rather than hypotaxis renders thoughts which often come in successive gusts, each amplifying and perhaps clarifying the last. It is interesting to relate this to Herder's praise of parallelism in Hebrew poetry, and to his later appreciation of symmetry as a constructive principle in the Ossian essay. Clauses tend to be short and heavily punctuated, especially with colons, semi-colons and dashes. The dash is often used emotionally as a dramatic pause, sometimes to break off a statement or rhetorical question. Graphic use is also made of marks of interrogation and exclamation, dots, *Sperrdruck* and interjections. Frequent are the apparent addresses or appeals to the reader; apparent, because Herder is really talking to himself, thinking aloud, advancing and retracting, working his way towards a satisfactory statement. Ejaculatory as this style becomes at its most ebullient (as in the essay on the Origin of Language and the contributions to *Von deutscher Art und Kunst*) it is never incoherent. The clauses sometimes proliferate in apparent circumambiency, but there is always a general surge forwards. Connections are provided by emphasis rather than by particles: inversion, elision, repetition, variation, enumeration, punctuation and even shouts are used to throw connecting ideas into relief and project the reader on to the next stage. It is an excited style, difficult to sustain and exhausting to read. One can appreciate Hamann's dig about 'dithyrambic syntax'; but one can also understand Herder's desire to get away from the flatness of rationalistic, excessively connected prose. This results in a conscious suppression of merely grammatical elements which add nothing to the meaning or vigour of the expression. He will omit an auxiliary verb, a subject pronoun, an article as occasion suggests; he will break stereotyped word-order to gain emphasis; he favours the flexionless form of adjectives. He uses many of the highly concentrated forms shown by Klopstock (simplex for compound, prefix-formations, compound adjectives, transitive use of normally intransitive verbs, oblique case for prepositional phrase, participial constructions).[1] Sometimes the

---

[1] This fact is not recognised by J. Haußmann, *Untersuchungen über Sprache und Stil des jungen Herder* (Leipzig, 1907), who has good material but does not

THE RETURN TO ORIGINS

result is compression to the point of grittiness. Sometimes the use of emphatic connection results in almost impromptu looseness of structure. But always one is conscious of a highly individual mind using language with the greatest freedom, vivacity and punch. In the second version of the first collection of *Fragmente* (1768) Herder attempts to describe the national individuality of the German language. It is sonorous and stately. Consonant clusters prevent elision and give measured gait; wealth of vowels gives sonority. German is full of 'Klangworte', many of which are *Machtwörter*. And the older language had still more, as Bodmer had shown. Herder sums up as follows: 'Männlich und stark ist also unsere Sprache in ihren Elementen — rauh und vest in ihren Sylbenmaaßen — gesetzt und langsam in ihren Wortverkehrungen — nachdrücklich und ernsthaft in ihren Idiotismen: soll ich also unserer ganzen Schreibart Charakter geben: so nehme ich diese Stücke zusammen, und sage: ernsthafte Prose, tiefsinnige Poesie.'[1] His stylistic ideal is expressed as follows: 'Aber Deutsche Schriftsteller, die vielleicht bei tausend Fehlern ihrer Sprache mächtig, auf eine gewisse eigene Art dieselbe behandeln — die sind mir theuer.'[2] The important word is *eigen*. Style is the individual handling of the national character of a language. This was achieved by Thomas Abbt: 'Er kennet das Schroot und Korn der unsrigen [Sprache], und sucht starke Worte zu prägen, alte Machtworte hervorzusuchen, die Wortfügung nach seinem Zweck und der Eigenheit unsrer Sprache zu lenken.'[3] Contrast Bodmer: 'Bei Bodmern gattet sich der Orientalische Parenthyrsus mit Griechischer Einfalt und Nordischer Trockenheit: eine Zaubergegend des Uebertriebnen, neben dem blühenden Garten

---

interpret it adequately with regard to Herder's linguistic theory nor to the state of language and linguistic theory at the time. Burdach deals with several points in his article 'Die grammatische Verjüngung der Sprache', in *Die Wissenschaft von deutscher Sprache* (Berlin and Leipzig, 1934). There is a Cologne typescript diss. by E. Saffenreuther, *Der Prosastil Johann Gottfried Herders in seinen Wandlungen bis zur Weimar Zeit* (1941)—full of interesting material presented in a rather bitty way. [1] *Ed. cit.* II, p. 50; cf. Klopstock, see above, p. 317.
[2] *Ibid.* II, p. 54. [3] *Ibid.* II, p. 281.

der Natur, und einer durch Frost beblühmten Fensterscheibe....'¹
If it be true that the German language has lost in 'inner strength' since the sixteenth century and that it should be refreshed by study of old authors, no better place to start than Luther's Bible. Herder looks forward to the time when the German language will return 'zur alten Deutschen Einfalt und rauhen Stärke', reject unnecessary borrowed 'gems', 'und daß ich mich zum Voraus auf eine Ernte Prosaischer Originalschriftsteller freue, von denen jeder *seinen* Stil haben kann'.²

Herder developed his conception of primitive language in his prize-essay *Über den Ursprung der Sprache*. The question of the origin of language was a speculative problem which greatly occupied the eighteenth century.³ There was obviously some relationship between language and thought, and the philosophers set themselves to define it. The basic problem had already been debated by Plato in the *Cratylus*: did words represent names arbitrarily imposed to ensure delineation of concepts or were they given in accordance with some quality or aspect of the object signified? In short, are words 'conventional' or 'natural' names? The Middle Ages had accepted the account given in Genesis: that God named things in the act of creating them. Alongside this there is in Genesis the statement that God brought to Adam the beasts of the field and the fowls of the air 'to see what he [i.e. Adam] would call them: and whatsoever Adam called every living creature, that was the name thereof'. A new problem there-

---

¹ *Ed. cit.* II, p. 169.
² *Ibid.* II, p. 288. For information on Herder's attitude to German authors of the past, see Hildegard Brüggemann's typescript diss., *Die Anschauungen Herders über das Verhältnis älterer deutscher Dichter zur Sprache* (Munich, 1920).
³ For my description in this paragraph of the background to Herder's essay I have drawn on J. H. W. Rosteutscher, *The History of the German Controversy on the Origin of Language*, typescript diss. (Cambridge, 1937). A shorter but good statement is more easily accessible in H. A. Salmony, *Die Philosophie des jungen Herder* (Zürich, 1949) (written obviously in ignorance of Rosteutscher's thesis). See also W. Sturm, *Herders Sprachphilosophie in ihrem Entwicklungsgang und ihrer historischen Stellung* (Breslau, 1927); G. Konrad, *Herders Sprachproblem im Zusammenhang der Geistesgeschichte* (Berlin, 1937) and Hanna Weber, *Herders Sprachphilosophie, eine Interpretation in Hinblick auf die moderne Sprachphilosophie* (Berlin, 1939).

fore arises: was language of divine or of human origin? When Hobbes restates the biblical account (in chapter 4 of the *Leviathan*) he bridges the gulf between these two statements in Genesis:

> The first author of Speech was God himself, that instructed Adam how to name such creatures as he presented to his sight.... This was sufficient to direct him to adde more names, as the experience and use of the creatures should give him occasion... and so by succession of time, so much language might be gotten, as he had found use for.

But all this was lost after the Tower of Babel. Hence names must be conventional. Locke's view was that God 'having designed man for a social creature... furnished him also with language.... Man, therefore, had by nature his organs so fashioned as to be fit to frame articulate sounds, which we call words.'[1] The sounds articulated by man are 'signs of internal conceptions', 'marks for the ideas within his own mind, whereby they might be made known to others'. Leibniz quarrelled with Locke's statement that God furnished man with *language*; in his view, man was provided only with the faculty of producing language. Both, however, represented the 'conventional' theory. The theory of divine origin survived into the eighteenth century. It is restated in England by Warburton and Leland, in Germany (amongst others) by J. P. Süssmilch who argued teleologically from the completeness and orderliness of language to its origination in a first cause possessed of perfect reason. Words were conventional names: 'Werk des Verstandes und freien Wahl, dabei nichts von einer natürlichen und notwendigen Bestimmung wahrzunehmen ist.' This was in his *Versuch eines Beweises, daß die erste Sprache ihren Ursprung nicht vom Menschen, sondern allein vom Schöpfer erhalten habe*, presented to the Berlin academy in 1756. It was intended as a refutation of the *Dissertation sur les différents moyens dont les hommes se sont servis pour exprimer leurs idées* presented by Maupertuis to the same body two years earlier. Maupertuis rejected divine origin in favour of the view that language was invented by man as a social necessity. Meanwhile Lessing,

[1] See the beginning of the third book of the *Essay concerning Human Understanding* (1690).

Wieland and Thomas Abbt had rejected Süssmilch's version of the 'higher hypothesis'. The Academy seems still to have been divided. So in 1759 a prize is offered for an essay on the influence of language on opinions, which was won by Michaelis with an essay which, as we have seen, aroused Hamann's disapproval. In 1767 a refutation of Süssmilch was published by J. G. Sulzer entitled *L'influence de la raison sur le langage et du langage sur la raison*, arguing that, since only clear concepts can be named, man must bring some order into the chaos of impressions invading him before language is formed. To give a name, man must detach one impression from the mass and distinguish it from the others. The first names, Sulzer thought, were probably onomatopoeic; then came the names for non-sounding things which were formed by association or metaphor. The intellect therefore marks out concepts by giving them sounding names. This represented in part a revival of the 'natural' theory. In 1769 the academy set the following question: 'En supposant les hommes abandonnés à leurs facultés naturelles, sont-ils en état d'inventer le langage? et par quels moyens parviendront-ils d'eux-mêmes à cette invention?' Herder composed his essay at Strassburg in the last days of 1770, and won the prize.

In his essay Herder refers not only to the views of those we have already mentioned, but also to the important contributions made to the discussion by Condillac, Rousseau and Moses Mendelssohn. Condillac, in the second part of his *Essai sur l'origine des connoissances humaines* (Amsterdam, 1746–55), propounded what is usually known as the 'sensualist' theory: language originated in symbolic movement of the body, in expressive gesture and mime accompanying passional cries similar to the cries of animals. This *langage d'action* was then replaced by differences of intonation and accent. Two valuable contributions to the discussion were made by this sensualist theory: the appreciation of the emotional origins of language and the envisagement of language as a developing phenomenon. The first was a counterweight to the rationalist theory, the second to the static mechanism of Locke. Spoken language for Condillac is obviously dependent on the existence of society. Rousseau disagreed on this point, asserting (in the *Discours sur l'inégalité*, published 1755) that since the earliest language hardly differed from animal cries, the origins of language were prompted not by social needs but by passional outbursts, and were therefore anterior to the establishment of society. Language, he argued, was a faculty possessed by man 'en puissance' (i.e. as a potentiality) which became a reality in social converse.[1] Mendelssohn translated Rousseau's essay and sent it to Lessing with a criticism in 1756 (*Sendschreiben an den Herrn Magister Lessing in Leipzig*). In this he stressed the importance of 'association' (a concept developed by English empiricism) in the emergence of language, a fairly elementary faculty of the mind which, in forming words, associates certain imitative sounds with certain impressions. No highly developed stage of the reason, therefore, is necessary for the birth of language. This was aimed at breaking the vicious circle which haunted Rousseau ('Si les hommes ont eu besoin de la parole pour apprendre à penser, ils ont eu bien plus besoin encore de savoir penser pour trouver l'art de la parole') and had led him to postulate *réflexion en puissance*; it deals also with the objection that Condillac's theory presupposed highly developed emotions. Herder's statement on language in the *Fragmente* obviously owed more to Condillac and Rousseau than to anyone else. His characterisation of the poetical stage of language can be closely paralleled from Condillac. And his statement of the basic problem: 'Wie weit hat die Kunst zu denken, die Kunst zu sprechen, und diese jene gebildet und ausgebildet?'[2] is a restatement of Rousseau's vicious circle.

So was the theme proposed by the Academy. Herder claims that the higher hypothesis does not explain the origin of language but merely restates the vicious circle. If man was taught language by God, then he must already have possessed reason. Herder is concerned to show the simultaneous emergence of language and

[1] Rousseau developed and to some extent modified his attitude in the posthumously published *Essai sur l'origine des langues* (1782).
[2] *Ed. cit.* II, p. 63.

reason. Divine transmission, passional cries, social needs, *refléxion en puissance*, association—none of these in Herder's opinion show *how* language emerged. Language cannot have arisen by agreement amongst members of a society because one can only agree on something which is already there. The sensualist theory he rejects by the assertion that language is something different *in kind*, not in degree, from animal noises; it could therefore not evolve from passional cries, for no animals show anything like language. Language is the essentially human attribute, a natural attribute and therefore not produced by something artificial like society. He therefore counters Condillac's statement that two children put into a desert before they learnt to speak would needs evolve language, by the assertion that the beginnings of language are already found in the new-born babe. It is by language that man is distinguished from the animals.

Herder leads up to this by a consideration of the differences between animals and man. Animals have stronger instincts than men; and some animals have stronger instincts than others.[1] The stronger the instincts, the more restricted is the field of activity and the greater the achievement therein. He instances bees, spiders and other insects. Correspondingly the wider this field of activity, the weaker the instincts and the skill. The instincts, skill and works of animals would therefore seem to be in inverse ratio to the size and manifoldness of their spheres of activity. But man has a much wider sphere of activity than any animal. Therefore his sense-reactions to any individual stimulus are weaker than those of any animal, for his senses are not so sharp. All this is a distinction of degree. But man also has the power of freeing himself from his sensations. This is a distinction of kind and has no correspondence in the animal world. The noises emitted by animals are instinctive reactions to sense-stimuli. The broader their spheres of activity, the more they 'need' these noises. Hence man, with the broadest sphere, needs something more than grunts and whines. He needs language. This is produced by man's power of disposing over his perceptions, by a co-ordinating

[1] This was an idea already advanced by Shaftesbury and by Buffon.

THE RETURN TO ORIGINS

power which some call 'reason' and others 'consciousness'. Leibniz had called it 'apperception'. Herder uses the term *Besonnenheit*, the power of reflection. It is not really a faculty. It is the marshalling and control of all man's faculties 'die seiner Gattung eigene Richtung aller Kräfte'.[1] It directs his powers as instinct does those of animals. Hence, as instinct is the essential power in animals, *Besonnenheit* is that in man. But *Besonnenheit* is not an extension of animal instinct. Nor is it *réflexion en puissance* but a positive, active force.

How does it work and how does it produce language? Here is Herder's own description: 'Der Mensch beweiset Reflexion, wenn die Kraft seiner Seele so frei würket, daß sie in dem ganzen Ocean von Empfindungen, der sie durch alle Sinnen durchrauschet, Eine Welle, wenn ich so sagen darf, absondern, sie anhalten, die Aufmerksamkeit auf sie richten, und sich bewußt seyn kann, daß sie aufmerke.'[2] This concentration on one impression out of the flood of impressions constantly impinging on man's senses, leads to the observation of a certain characteristic (*Merkmal*) which distinguishes it from other impressions. The detachment of such a *Merkmal* is the beginning of language. It is a 'Wort der Seele'. Suppose a lamb comes into sight. Man will not be affected by instinct, as would a wolf, a lion, a ram:

> So bald er in die Bedürfniß kommt, das Schaaf kennen zu lernen: so störet ihn kein Instinkt: so reißt ihn kein Sinn auf dasselbe zu nahe hin, oder davon ab: es steht da, ganz wie es sich seinen Sinnen äußert. Weiß, sanft, wollicht — seine besonnen sich übende Seele sucht ein Merkmal, — das Schaaf *blöcket*! sie hat Merkmal gefunden. Der innere Sinn würket. Dies Blöken, das ihr am stärksten Eindruck macht, das sich von allen andern Eigenschaften des Beschauens und Betastens losriß, hervorsprang, am tiefsten eindrang, bleibt ihr. Das Schaaf kommt wieder. Weiß, sanft, wollicht — sie steht, tastet, besinnet sich, sucht Merkmal — es blöckt, und nun erkennet sies wieder! 'Ha! du bist das Blöckende!' fühlt sie innerlich, sie hat es *Menschlich* erkannt, da sies deutlich, das ist, mit einem Merkmal erkennet und nennet....[3]

---
[1] *Ed. cit.* v, p. 31. Herder also uses the word *Reflexion* as a synonym of *Besonnenheit*.   [2] *Ed. cit.* v, pp. 34–5.
[3] *Ed. cit.* v, p. 36. Italics correspond to *Sperrdruck* of the original.

Such a *Merkmal* is 'ein innerliches Merkwort'. The earliest language is an assemblage of such words, it is *innere Sprache*. Thus does language come into being: 'eben so natürlich und dem Menschen nothwendig erfunden, als der Mensch ein Mensch war'. Language is therefore man's reaction to his environment. The birth of a word is simultaneous with the birth of a concept. Rousseau's vicious circle has been broken by Herder's individual manipulation of ideas from Condillac, Mendelssohn and Sulzer.[1] The first of these 'words of the soul' to become articulated were sound-words. Bleating gave the *Merkmal* for the sheep, barking for the dog, cooing for the dove. In all languages we distinguish most carefully between the noises emitted by various animals. The first words would have been verbs denoting sound, *tönende Verba*. (This was a new idea, for the mental picture of God teaching Adam the names of things had suggested that the first words were nouns.) The further development of language mirrors the development of man's mind, 'die Geschichte seiner Entdeckungen'. From the verb *blöken*, a noun is formed: *der Blökende*. This is the first stage in abstraction, an important stage in the development of thought. Mythology is born of such abstraction. And with it poetry: 'Was war diese erste Sprache als eine Sammlung von Elementen der Poesie? Nachahmung der tönenden, handelnden, sich regenden Natur!'[2]

So far, so good. But now comes the tricky point in the argument, the knotty point which he had sheered away from in the *Fragmente*. How does man form words for non-sounding things? Are these natural or conventional names? Mendelssohn had dealt with this through his example of the bleating sheep:

Das wirkliche oder nachgeahmte Blöken der Schafe rief nicht allein das Bild dieser Thiere in unser Gedächtniß zurück; sondern man

---

[1] Hanna Weber (*op. cit.* p. 17) points out that by calling language both the 'organ' and the 'product' of *Besonnenheit*, Herder lands himself in a contradiction by which language is the product of *Besonnenheit* which only comes into existence with language! This leads him later (in the *Metakritik*) to assert the *identity* of language and reason.

The example of the bleating sheep comes from Mendelssohn, but is used differently. [2] *Ed. cit.* v, p. 56.

THE RETURN TO ORIGINS

dachte zugleich an die Wiese, darauf diese Schafe geweidet hatten, und an die Blumen, mit welchen diese Wiese häufig geschmückt war.... Man brauchte alsdann nur die mittleren Glieder, die Schafe und die Wiese, wegzulassen, um bei Anhörung eines ursprünglich nachahmenden Tones an die Blumen zu gedenken, in Ansehung deren dieser Laut ein bloß willkürliches Zeichen genannt werden kann.[1]

A valiant attempt to reconcile the 'natural' with the 'conventional' theory! But horribly imprecise. What is meant by *weglassen*? How is this achieved? By what psychological process does it take place? Herder attacks the problem quite differently. He turns to a consideration of our sense-apparatus. Man is a 'thinking *sensorium commune*' assailed from all sides by stimuli. He receives a wave of impressions which attack various senses simultaneously. Touch is man's strongest sense, embracing everything and correspondingly vague; sight gives too many *Merkmale*. Hearing is the middle sense between sight and touch, 'die eigentliche Thür zur Seele, und das Verbindungsband der übrigen Sinne'.[2] By means of hearing, all our senses become *sprachfähig*. 'Wir sehen, wir fühlen; aber die gesehene, gefühlte Natur tönet.' When a sensation is predominantly non-sounding, a sound is produced to correspond to the effect on the other senses. Thus tactile impressions are rendered by words which sound like the object felt (*hart, rauh, weich, wolligt, starr*). So also with visual impressions: 'Der Blitz schallet nicht: wenn er nun aber ausgedrückt werden soll,...natürlich wirds ein Wort machen, das durch Hülfe eines Mittelgefühls dem Ohr die Empfindung des Urplötzlichschnellen gibt, die das Auge hatte — Blitz!'[3]

This may not seem a very satisfactory explanation of why a tree is called a tree and a stone a stone. But we are not concerned here with the merits of this work as a contribution to linguistics, but solely with its place in the development of the German language. Herder's appreciation of synaesthesia in language was an important strengthening of his assertion that imagery and metaphor were primal qualities in language. He goes on, in the

---

[1] Moses Mendelssohn, *Gesammelte Schriften* (Leipzig, 1843), vol. I, pp. 396–7.
[2] *Ed. cit.* v, p. 64.   [3] *Ibid.* v, p. 63.

prize-essay, to state that the older the language, the greater is the incidence of this *Analogie der Sinne* and the more the senses *sich durchkreuzen*:

> Man schlage das Erste, beste Morgenländische Wörterbuch auf, und man wird den Drang sehen, sich ausdrücken zu wollen! Wie der Erfinder Ideen aus Einem Gefühl hinausriß und für ein anderes borgte! wie er bei den schwersten, kältesten, deutlichsten Sinnen am meisten borgte! wie Alles Gefühl und Laut werden muste, um Ausdruck zu werden! Daher die starken kühnen Metaphern in den Wurzeln der Worte! daher die Übertragungen aus Gefühl in Gefühl, so daß die Bedeutungen eines Stammworts, und noch mehr seiner Abstammungen gegen Einander gesetzt, das buntschäckichste Gemälde werden.[1]

Consequently we find that in primitive languages feelings are not clearly distinguished and concepts not delineated. There is a wealth of overlapping synonyms. Abstracts are few and tend to have a sensual quality. For Eastern people, spirit was a wind, a breath, a storm. Missionaries report the lack of abstract words amongst savage tribes. The more primitive the language, the less grammar. But it will make up for lack of inflections by gesture and synonyms. It will be full of *tönende Verba*. As Herder proceeds with his description, it becomes once again clear that this is the language he prefers to all other.

Primitive language had been described by Herder in the *Fragmente* as developing from strong passional cries accompanied by expressive gesture into articulate speech retaining rhythm and pitch as expressive values (inversions; proximity to song). It is full of *lebender Ausdruck* (verbs; idioms) and *sinnliche Gestaltung* (images).[2] Now, in the prize-essay, its salient features are described as *tönende Verba*, synonyms and *Analogie der Sinne*, immediacy and strength its nature. The description of it as *lebender Ausdruck* and *sinnliche Gestaltung* can therefore still stand. New

---

[1] *Ed. cit.* v, p. 71.
[2] The fullest description is to be found in the revised edition of the first collection, see *ed. cit.* II, pp. 70 ff. Note also this statement on verbs: 'Ein Nomen stellt immer nur die Sache todt dar: das Verbum setzt sie in Handlung, diese erregt Empfindung, denn sie ist selbst gleichsam mit Geist beseelet' (*ed. cit.* XI, p. 227).

THE RETURN TO ORIGINS

is the statement that language does not develop from animal cries but from human *Besonnenheit*. It is therefore not instinctive reaction but creative action. Language, by isolating *Merkmale*, gives shape and meaning to experience. In this sense it is poetry. It was this conception of the poet as *Sprachschöpfer* which fired Herder's younger contemporaries, the writers of the Storm and Stress. Correlative was the second idea that in language man fulfilled his essential destiny and expressed his whole being, not merely one faculty. Language was 'die seiner Gattung eigene Richtung aller Kräfte'. Here the idea of the 'Genius einer Sprache' crystallising the spirit of a nation, has widened into a more general and at the same time more individual statement. Behind both stands the concept of language as something elemental, springing from origins: *Ursprünglichkeit*. Primitive language shows this: but every language at every period, Herder would assert, should be conscious of its origins and essence. The poets have always shown this awareness. They have always used language with immediacy and strength. They have known the value of rhythm and pitch, of images and synonyms, of senseanalogy and *Sinnlichkeit*.

In the first *Kritisches Wäldchen* (1769) Herder arrives at the statement: 'Kraft ist das Wesen der Poesie.'[1] He makes a distinction between *Energie* and *Kraft*, but does not explain it. The concept of *Kraft* plays a large part in Herder's thought, and he himself admitted that it was difficult to define.[2] Professor R. T. Clark points out that Aristotle in his *Metaphysics* had distinguished between ἐντελέχεια (completed actualisation), ἐνέργεια (process of actualisation) and δύναμις (force producing the process of actualisation). This survived into the Middle Ages with δύναμις rendered by Latin *vis* and Middle High German *kraft*. Superior and inferior faculties or *vires* were recognised by scholastic psychology. Herder's distinction between *Energie* and *Kraft* derives primarily from James Harris (*Three Treatises*, London,

---
[1] *Ed. cit.* III, p. 137.
[2] *Ibid.* VIII, p. 177. See R. T. Clark, 'Herder's conception of *Kraft*', *PMLA*, LVII (1942), pp. 737–52.

1744) whose opposition energy–power corresponds roughly to Aristotle's ἐνέργεια–δύναμις distinction. Herder uses *Kraft* for Harris's *power*; but he also quite frequently uses *Kräfte* for the scholastic *vires* (or faculties) which survived in eighteenth-century rationalism and protestant theology. Hence a statement like: 'Alle Kräfte unsrer Seele sind nur *Eine* Kraft, wie unsere Seele nur *Eine* Seele ist';[1] or the description of God as 'die Urkraft aller Kräfte' in *Gott, Einige Gespräche* (1787).[2] The first *Kritisches Wäldchen* posits a classification of the arts corresponding to the *Raum-Zeit-Kraft* scheme of metaphysics. Herder combines Lessing's place-time contrast with Harris's distinction between arts 'die ein *Werk* liefern' (plastic arts; gardening) and those 'die durch *Energie* wirken' (music; dance). But he adds *Kraft* (poetry). We thus end up with a trichotomy which looks like Aristotle's applied to aesthetics. *Kraft* is far more elemental than *Energie* or *Werk*, it is presumably the power which produces *Energie* which in turn produces *Werk*. It would seem that the concept of *Kraft* is similar to (and perhaps identical with) that of *Besonnenheit* 'die seiner Gattung eigene Richtung aller *Kräfte*', for *Richtung* in this definition is a verbal noun. It represents the essential power in man which energises one or more of his faculties (*Kräfte*) into action. Poetry as the art of *Kraft* proceeds from and acts upon the very essence of the soul. Hence Herder's characterisation of it as 'die einzige schöne Kunst unmittelbar für die Seele'.[3] The others work through one of the senses, but poetry is bound to none. It appeals directly to the whole man, embodying the vital force of personality which experiences and creates as an integrated whole through *Kraft*.

The concepts of *Kraft* and *Ursprünglichkeit* are closely connected with that of *Genie*.[4] There is the genius of the language—that we have already considered. But there is also individual genius producing a style which is *eigen* and yet born of the

[1] *Ed. cit.* IX, p. 295.   [2] *Ibid.* XVI, p. 453.
[3] *Ibid.* IV, p. 163.
[4] Herman Wolf, 'Die Genielehre des jungen Herder', *Dt.Vjs.* III (1925), pp. 401–30; P. Grappin, *La théorie du génie dans le préclassicisme allemand* (Paris, 1952), especially pp. 221–50.

THE RETURN TO ORIGINS

national genius of the language. Geniuses 'entstehen'; they are thrown up by the nation, in them speaks and is concentrated the *Volk*. So it is with the anonymous folksong. Folksong and individual geniuses embody the national spirit. Both are *ursprünglich*. Hence their connection in Herder's mind and their juxtaposition in his contributions to *Von deutscher Art und Kunst*, begun soon after the treatise on the origin of language.[1] Language embodying man's inmost being and creating through *Besonnenheit*, poetry creating from the basic force of *Kraft*, primitive language embodying *lebender Ausdruck* and *sinnliche Gestaltung*, national language embodying national character—all these ideas are related in Herder's mind. *Besonnenheit*, *Kraft*, poetry and national character all embody *Ursprünglichkeit*; this is the quality both of primitive language and poetic language. Creating from origins is *Genie*. There is *Genie eines Volkes* and *Originalgenie*. No wonder Herder could pass so easily from Ossian to folksong to Shakespeare.

The Shakespeare essay is a hymn to genius, to *Originalgenie*, pictured at the beginning as a sublimely indifferent Promethean figure, enveloped by storm and sea, but haloed by heavenly brightness. In the course of the essay *Genie* is opposed to *Philosophie*, and *Schöpfer* to *Zergliederer*. Originality is contrasted with *Regelnvorrath*, spontaneity ('die unmittelbaren, ersten, ungeschminkten Regungen, wie sie Worte suchen und endlich finden') to indirectness ('Gemälde der Empfindung von dritter, fremder Hand') and to 'Zuschnitt, Inhalt, Bilderwirthschaft, Glanz, Witz, Philosophie'. Shakespeare is presented as moulding the material of experience as he found it in his own time and place, moulding it from *Urkraft*, moulding 'das Verschiedenartigste Zeug zu einem Wunderganzen', to 'Begebenheit...Eräugniß'. Herder distinguishes between the individual 'Handlung' of a Greek drama and the manifold 'Begebenheit' ('Eräugniß') of a play by

[1] In what follows I take my text from Suphan, vol. v; but I have also used with profit the excellent critical edition by Edna Purdie (Oxford, 1924). On Herder's use of the word *ursprünglich*, see Professor Purdie's article 'Some Word-Associations in the Writings of Hamann and Herder' in *German Studies presented to Leonard Ashley Willoughby* (Oxford, 1952), especially p. 150.

Shakespeare, between the style of the former and the styles of the latter. But he does not discuss Shakespeare's language. It is in the other essay, *Ossian und die Lieder alter Völker*, that he gives his most detailed analysis of primitive, poetical language. This represents the culmination of all he had written so far. It was also of the greatest importance for the future of the German language. We must therefore observe in detail the terms of this description.

Denis's translation of Ossian into hexameters lacked the 'Ton, Farbe, die schnelleste Empfindung von Eigenheit des Orts, des Zwecks' of the original which was 'kurz, stark, männlich, abgebrochen in Bildern und Empfindungen'.[1] To render these 'Lieder, Lieder des Volks, Lieder eines ungebildeten sinnlichen Volks' into an expansive manner and metre was disregarding their lyrical style. For lyrical style depends not only on sense but on sound, rhyme, word-position and the 'dunkler Gang der Melodie'. This Herder illustrates by quoting *Come away, come away, Death!* and speaks of the 'Abdruck des Äussern, des Sinnlichen, in Form, Klang, Ton, Melodie, alles des Dunklen, Unnennbaren, was uns mit dem Gesange Stromweise in die Seele fliesset', pointing to the close connection between poetry and song. This relationship is essential and elemental; it is therefore closest in the oldest poetry. The more primitive a people, the 'lebendiger, freier, sinnlicher, lyrisch handelnder' are its songs. This lyrical quality embraces strong rhythms ('Tanzmäßige des Gesanges'), living (i.e. not conventional) images, 'Nothdrang des Inhalts, der Empfindungen', symmetry of words and syllables and letters (i.e. refrain, assonance, alliteration) and 'Gang der Melodie'. By 'Nothdrang des Inhalts' Herder means that inner unity imposed by what, in the Shakespeare essay, he had called the *Begebenheit*. The whole phrase reads: 'Zusammenhang und gleichsam Nothdrang des Inhalts, der Empfindungen.' *Nothdrang* is therefore an intenser form of *Zusammenhang*: emotional unity rather than logical connectedness. Melody is also something more basic than

---

[1] As my commentary follows the course of the essay, I have not thought it necessary to give specific references. The text is from Suphan, vol. v.

THE RETURN TO ORIGINS

metrical form: it is 'sinnlicher Rhythmus', 'wilder Gang'. Rhythms in these old songs are varied and manifold, governed by the 'fühlbaren Takt des Ohrs', pointed by alliterative 'Losungen zum Schlag des Takts'. Everything is 'Schälle, Laute eines lebenden Gesanges, Wecker des Takts und der Erinnerung'. Everything 'klopfte, und stieß und schallte zusammen!'

A first point has been established: the importance of sound in general and of rhythm in particular in primitive poetry. Herder recognises the irrational nature of this quality and implicitly contrasts it with rationalistic criteria of language. Important is the observation that in such poetry language is jagged, jerky and organised not logically but rhythmically.

He then proceeds to examples. First a Peruvian serenade showing alliteration, repetition and elision as constructive elements:

> Schlummre, schlummr', o Mädchen,
> Sanft in meine Lieder,
> Mitternachts, o Mädchen,
> Weck' ich dich schon wieder!

Note the emotionally defensible but illogical construction of the second line. Then a longer song in Spanish trochaic rhythm, using refrain and repetition and containing two striking examples of 'strong' style. First a cognate accusative:

> Daß es wettert
> Ungewitter,
> Blitz und Donner!

So strong was the linguistic influence of Klopstock that he appears in this primitive environment! The second example contains an inversion and in its ecstatic stammering again recalls Klopstock:

> Denn so hat dir
> Er der Weltgeist!
> Er der Weltgott!
> Virakocha!
> Macht gegeben
> Amt gegeben!

This is *Nothdrang des Inhalts* resulting in a rhythmical tension which is structure, although without *connexio*. Herder praises its

'Symmetrie des Rhythmus, des Sangbaren'. Symmetry of sound instead of order according to sense—this is a whole new attitude to language and was to transform German style.

Herder continues his demonstration of rhythmic tension as a structural force by two rather more extreme examples. First a Lapp song containing elaborate use of repetition and elision to give rhythmic pressure, with meaning pent up by omission of links:

> Was ist stärker, *als Flechte Sehnen?* als eisene, mächtige Ketten? So feßelt uns die Liebe, *die Umschafferinn Sinns und Willens*:

(my italics), or drawn out by inversions:

> Ich würde den Fichtengipfel ersteigen, könnt'ich schauen den Orra-See! Ich würd' ihn ersteigen, den Gipfel...

or concentrated by a *Machtwort* as in 'Zweige *stümmeln*' (for *verstümmeln*). Herder comments on the way all the elements of imagery in this poem are drawn together by reference to the Lapplander's girl. (This is *Begebenheit*, in the sense of the Shakespeare essay.) Then comes the *Edward* ballad. Here rhythmic elements abound. The refrain, the repeated ejaculatory *O!*, elision, omission of subject pronoun:

> Dein Schwert, wie ists von Blut so roth
> Und gehst so traurig da! — O!

or again:

> Dein Roß war alt und hasts nicht noth!

Illogical but meaningful sequences. The rhythm demands a meaningful monosyllable at the end of the line: it must be meaningful because it rhymes and is strongly accented, it must contain a dark vowel because of the general mood, although there is a switch to *-i-* in the rhymes of the penultimate stanza, which enhances the return to the prevailing mood in the last verse. Inversion of the type 'Ich hab geschlagen meinen Geyer todt' is therefore recurrent and powerfully effective.

At this point Herder breaks off to pay homage to the hard, bardic language of Klopstock in his later works. 'Kurz...stark und abgebrochen' he calls it, using exactly the same terms as he had earlier applied to Ossian. His word-formation is 'so Dramatisch, so Deutsch!', his style full of 'kurzer, Dramatischer Dialog und Wurf der Gedanken'. Herder now illustrates the *dramatic* quality of early poetry from two Old Norse lays. Each of these is 'eine fortgehende, handelnde, lebendige Scene'. There is no rhyme, the lines are short, the first syllable is unaccented *Auftakt*. Hence the important word is thrown into second position to catch the stress, which means that we find inversion working in the opposite way from that in the Edward ballad, and we find either elision or some rather unimportant word at the beginning of the line. This may be an anticipatory impersonal pronoun ('Es erhub sich Odin') or an emotionally valueless grammatical element like an article or a subject pronoun or even a connecting particle. Interesting is the use of a repeated *Und* to increase pace. Here is the first section of *Odins Höllenfahrt*:

> Es erhub sich Odin
> Der Menschen höchster!
> Und nahm sein Roß
> Und schwang sich aufs Roß
> Und ritt hinunter
> Zu der Höllen Thor.
> Da kam ihm entgegen
> Der Höllenhund!

Note the Klopstockian delaying of *Höllenhund*. The rhythmical pattern is broken occasionally by a stressed first syllable:

> Blutbespritzt
> War seine Brust!

The result is often a compound *Machtwort* (*Höllenschloß*; *Todtenerweckenden*; *Gräbergesang*; *Todtenstimme*; *Drei-Riesen-Mutter*). Characteristic is suppression of article in

> Ein Wandrer bin ich,
> Kriegerssohn.

Sometimes there is a highly elliptic construction:

> O du kein Wandrer,
> Wie ich erst gewähnt!

Unusual accentuation of prepositions and adverbs of motion impels the flight of the verse. The second lay begins:

> Umher wirds dunkel
> Von Pfeilgewölken!
> Sie breiten umher sich
> Wetterverkündend!
> Es regnet Blut!
> Auf!...

Later we have:

> Hinaus, hinaus
> An die Schaaren hinan,
> Wo...

with more *Machtwörter* ('Schlachtgewebe', 'Sieggarn', 'Blutwolken'), assonance and alliteration ('Und Irrland wird / Trauer treffen') and even melodic use of proper names:

> Sie kommen zu weben
> Mit nackten Schwerdtern,
> Hild', Hiorthrimul,
> Sangrida, Svipul...

Herder praises the rough simplicity, the festive magic-like grandeur and the deep impression made by every 'starkgesagte Wort' and the 'freie Wurf' of it all.

Having provided us with splendid examples Herder now draws some theoretical conclusions. In this poetry there is nothing abstract, contrived, slow or premeditated. A whole thought is expressed by a whole word. Everything is plastic, alive, spontaneous, immediate; full of 'Thätigkeit', 'Sicherheit', 'Vestigkeit'. In the course of his remarks he uses a number of words to express the opposite of what he is praising (and, ultimately, advocating). These are 'Pedanten...methodisch...Apotheker ...Spekulation...Quantitäten von Sylben kennen zu lernen... nach Regeln zu arbeiten...über Gegenstände zu dichten... Falschheit, Schwäche und Künstelei'. The section culminates in this lament: 'Wir sehen und fühlen kaum mehr, sondern denken und grübeln nur; wir dichten nicht über und in lebendiger Welt, im Sturm und im Zusammenstrom solcher Gegenstände, solcher

THE RETURN TO ORIGINS

Empfindungen; sondern erkünsteln uns entweder Thema, oder Art, das Thema zu behandeln, oder gar beides....' So much for *cultiver sa raison*, and for the culture of wit and feeling! It is in the true sense of the word an epoch-making statement; for it marks the watershed between two epochs of literary and linguistic endeavour.

Herder is fond of the word *impromptus*. He uses it to apply to Greek dithyrambs, Homer's 'rhapsodies' and Ossian's lays. It connotes that immediacy which he demands from poetry, the opposite of ratiocination. He does not condone slapdash writing; but he observes that no amount of polishing will 'improve' a poem which has not emerged as a whole. This may be from thought or feeling; but 'lange und stark und lebendig gedacht, oder schnell und würksam empfunden — im Punkt der Thätigkeit wird beides *impromptu*, oder bekömmt die Vestigkeit, Wahrheit, Lebhaftigkeit und Sicherheit desselben'. This leads him on to folksong.

Folksongs are full of 'Sprünge und Würfe'. They do not expound logically and connectedly. But this is not to be sneered at as 'unverständlich, kühn, Dithyrambisch'! It is part of the reality, the immediacy of folksong. It is its very nature. He quotes *Sweet William's Ghost* in a translation full of the features he had praised in primitive lays. It is emphasis which provides connection:

> Zu Hannchens Thür, da kam ein Geist...

or again:

> Und drückt' am Schloß und kehrt' am Schloß
> Und ächzte traurig nach.

Inversion goes even farther than anything he has quoted before. For instance:

> (*a*) Oder ists Wilhelm, mein Bräutigam!
> Aus Schottland kommen an?
>
> (*b*) Ausstreckt sie ihre Liljenhand...

Once the construction is completely broken:

> 'Ach, Hannchen, nun, nun kommt die Zeit,
> Zu scheiden weg von dir!'
> Der Geist — und mehr, mehr sprach er nicht...

Double negative occurs at one point and so does elision in *Auftakt*:

'S ist, süsses Hannchen, nur mein Geist...

To this point Herder returns later.[1] For the moment he proceeds to several German songs, showing that they have all these features. First a love-song with extreme display of inversion, very loose clause-connection, numerous elisions, double negative and archaic *geit, leit* for 'gibt, liegt'. Comment: 'Ist das Sylbenmaaß nicht schön, die Sprache nicht stark, der Ausdruck empfunden?' Then a fable with much looser rhythm than anything quoted before, stanzaic but with most of the lines in *Knüttelvers* irregular metre. It is full of archaisms of vocabulary and syntax. Amongst the latter are apocopated forms (*hab*; *thät*; *Sach*; *Wett*), the word *baß*, syncopated *in Kopf* (for *inn Kopf* from *in den Kopf*), flexionless adjective (*gut Choral*), postposition (*im Sinne sein*) and the periphrastic past *thäten anschlagen*; *thät nennen*. The colloquial nature of this last feature, together with an obvious colloquial phrase like 'Du machst mirs kraus' suggest an extension of Herder's concept of immediacy to include dialect and speech material. He finds the fable 'fest und tief erzählt', 'lustig und stark und treffend in jedem Wort, in jeder Wendung'. And defends its 'gedrängten oder lebhaften Styl' against 'Griechische Lauterkeit! Ciceronische Wohlberedtheit'.

Then comes *Haidenröslein*, full of elisions and with 'das kindische Ritornell' as a refrain. But Herder is uncertain of himself here. He may be quoting from memory. In fact his version collapses in the second part with a *jedoch* and an *aber* connecting the clauses in an oddly logical and entirely *stilfremd* way. 'Ist das nicht Kinderton?' Herder asks; 'No!' one must answer. But he goes on to praise elision in *Auftakt* (''s Rösslein') as giving the noun more 'Poetische Substantialität und Persönlichkeit'; and to contrast elision in general with 'schleppende Artikel, Partikeln u.s.w.' which slow down the progress of sense or feeling. Despite

---

[1] He had defended this against Bodmer's charge of vulgarity by the assertion that it was convenient and gave strength (in his review of Bodmer's grammar, see *ed. cit.* IV, pp. 301–2).

THE RETURN TO ORIGINS

the *jedoch* and *aber* above, this is a valuable point and leads on to the statement that the *Sprünge und Würfe* of folksong correspond to similar leaps and jerks in the imagination. They are not part of an assumed style. The only structure in song is that of the *Begebenheit* itself. Even moral lessons are transposed into *sinnlich* expression in folksong. We are given only 'Blumen der Moral', not coherent exposition. The moral is pointed by symmetry and refrain, not analytically and dogmatically.

To illustrate this he turns to one of Luther's hymns, pointing out that they contain things bolder than any 'Klopstocksche Wendung'. How powerful are his transitions and inversions! 'Ursprünglich, unentnervt, frei und männlich' (contrast 'die schläfrigsten Zeilen, die erkünsteltsten Partikeln, die mattesten Reime'). The example he gives embodies all the features he has discussed and illustrated from primitive and folk poetry in this essay. Sixteenth-century German still had all these features. The essay therefore ends with a plea for their revival, for a return to 'volle, gesunde, blühende Weltjugend', to 'Herz' instead of 'Regelncodex', to harmony which means not 'aufgezähltes Harmonienkunststück' but 'Bewegung! Melodie des Herzens! Tanz!'

XV

THE GOLDEN TOUCH

IN the Frankfurt of his childhood Goethe was surrounded by buildings and customs which had survived almost unchanged from the sixteenth century. The house on the Hirschgraben was old, dark and full of corners; his grandfather's house had been a castle and still looked like one; the rows of benches in the town-hall symbolised the ancient constitution and the portraits of emperors the historical importance of the Free City; its festivals preserved in their forms and patterns a living link with the past; the skull of a traitor executed in 1616 still adorned the bridge-tower; and the boy was even present at the burning of a book. A taste for the past was encouraged by the woodcuts and engravings in his father's house and by the reading of old chronicles. He also devoured the chapbooks—Eulenspiegel, Melusine, Octavianus, Magelone, Fortunatus and the rest, including the Wandering Jew. Of his grandfather's house and library Goethe said:

> Alles was ihn umgab war alterthümlich. In seiner getäfelten Stube habe ich niemals irgend eine Neuerung wahrgenommen. Seine Bibliothek enthielt außer juristischen Werken nur die ersten Reisebeschreibungen, Seefahrten und Länder-Entdeckungen. Überhaupt erinnere ich mich keines Zustandes, der so wie dieser das Gefühl eines unverbrüchlichen Friedens und einer ewigen Dauer gegeben hätte.[1]

Both by what he saw around him and by what he read Goethe was made aware of a living continuance of the past. The culmination was the coronation of Joseph the Second as *römischer König* in 1764, in which the world of the old chronicles came alive before his eyes. No wonder Goethe was an *Augenmensch*. No wonder he thought naturally in images. No wonder he found it easier than anyone else to return to the sixteenth century.

The linguistic environment of his youth was equally archaic.

---

[1] Weimar ed. XXVI, p. 57.

Frankfurt had preserved a certain detachment from the linguistic endeavours of the first half of the century. As the Free City in which emperors were crowned it naturally had strong links with the Imperial Chancery and had preserved old scribal traditions. Works published or written at Frankfurt in the eighteenth century show the influence of this. Thus a German grammar published there by one Weber in 1759, when Goethe was ten years old, although it is based on Gottsched, maintains a certain independence and shows a somewhat more archaic standpoint. The influence of Luther's Bible, the catechism and the hymns was strong in this city governed by Protestant burghers. It was in this cosily old-fashioned atmosphere that Goethe learnt to speak and write.[1]

His early exercises in copper-plate were from dictated biblical texts. In this wise archaic forms were early impressed upon his mind. In these texts we find the old participles *kommen* and *funden*, syncopated *ichs*, verbal forms with a medial weak *-e-* (*erwürgete, gehet, fehlete*), adverb *feste* and predicative adjective *enge*. Spellings like *Vatter, vergiese, Hofnung, tödten, Gedancken, Hertz, gros, begienge, ungedultig* and *bekomt* may account for the fact that he did not always get the first prize; but even when he did, the sample contains the form *wenns* and the spellings *geniesen, komts* and *Blutvergiesen*. Having made allowances for the fact that this is the work of a child who is only eight years old, one can nevertheless feel the presence of a strong local tradition. The same forms recur in the exercises given him for translation into foreign languages by various Frankfurt schoolmasters. We only have these in Goethe's transcription, but leaving apart obvious errors, we note a complete uncertainty about double consonants alongside some odd notations of length (*gefrohrnen, gelerhrt*), doubts about *Umlaut* (*unbestendig, Kreuter, gezelet*), complete lack of distinction between *vor* and *für*, hyphenation in compound

---

[1] Throughout this chapter I shall quote from *Der junge Goethe*, ed. Max Morris, 6 vols. (Leipzig, 1909–12), which contains everything Goethe wrote up to his departure for Weimar in 1775. For works and letters after that date I quote from the Weimar edition. On the language of the young Goethe, see S. Waetzoldt, *Die Jugendsprache Goethes* (Berlin, 1888); Burdach's article in *Vorspiel*, II; and H. G. Heun, *Der Satzbau in der Prosa des jungen Goethe* (Berlin, 1930).

nouns (*Glatt-Eiß*; even *Sieben-Uhr*), apocopated and, less frequently, syncopated forms (*Ursach, Knab, Gemüß*; *aufgericht* for 'aufgerichtet'), uncertainty about declension of the attributive adjective (*die hohe Berge*; but *die lieben Kinder*), a tendency to spell the adjectival suffix as *-ig* (*höflig, glücklig*) and occasional archaisms of syntax like *nachdem ich bin arm worden*.[1] The little dialogues, doubtless of his own composition, are conversational but the words given to his father show stiff forms like *dermalen, jezuweilen* and *dermaleinst* which occasionally flow over into the words of the *filius*. The tenacity of the old curial style is clearly seen in the astonishingly musty language of the texts given him by Conrector Reinhard for translation into Latin in imitation of Justin. These contain almost medieval spellings like *Babst, Ungelück* and *zehenden*, paragogic preterite *-e* (*thate, sahe, galte*), characteristic chancery forms like *vorhero, dahero, bishero*, heavy links like *derohalben, sintemahlen* and *derowegen*, the spellings *Gleichnüß, Erkändnüß* and various archaisms of morphology like *worden, es seye, viele Jahrhundert*, relative *so, genennet* and *niemahlen*. The style often sounds more like the sixteenth century than the eighteenth: 'Ob nun dieses falsch war, so wurde es doch von vielen Leicht-Glaubigen vor wahr angenommen. Allein die besser unterrichtet waren haben ihn billig als ein Göttliches Geschenck ausgenommen und ist bey seiner Ankunft eine grose Begierde bei iederman entstanden.'[2] A similar dusty pedantry pervades the texts given him by Johann Jakob Gottlieb Scherbius for translation into Greek, together with arrant archaisms like *viel Volcks* and *auf daß* for 'damit'. His first letters, as a boy of fifteen, show the influence of all this: *Betrübtnuß, Gleichnüß, Geheimnüß, ohngefähr, Briefgen, nemlich, Merckmahle, gantz, Graß, Persohn* and *Weeg*. The replies of Buri, who lived near Offenbach am Main, show similar archaic features—plenty of consonant-heaping and the form *törigt* amongst them. Linguistically this was a good old conservative corner of Germany.

---

[1] My examples are taken from the first few pages of the text (Morris, I, pp. 7–12), but the same features recur throughout the rest of the exercises.
[2] Morris, I, p. 43.

THE GOLDEN TOUCH

Grammar, Goethe tells us in *Dichtung und Wahrheit*, displeased him because it seemed arbitrary, rules because they were denied by so many exceptions. But rhetoric he took to, although linguistic mistakes often occurred in his exercises. From earliest years he had a passion for versifying. Canitz, Hagedorn, Drollinger, Gellert and Haller were in his father's library; but his father would have no truck with the rhymeless verse of Klopstock, so *Der Messias* had to be read on the sly and learnt by heart, both the tender and the violent passages. French occupation during 1759 and the succeeding two years introduced him to the grace of the French language and the sophistication of French manners. He learnt French, English, Italian, Latin, Greek and Hebrew as a child and was soon trying his hand at a polyglot novel. His imagination was strongly captivated by the Old Testament. His literary taste extends now to religious odes and anacreontic verse, and he experiments in both. 'Give him a theme and he will make you a poem on the spot', said one of his friends. Even an *artig* love-letter, half *Knüttelvers* and half madrigal. The mixture of galant and *altdeutsch* is significant. On the whole he avoids the galant world. But he has a hankering after it. He is growing up; and growing away from the old-world atmosphere of Frankfurt. After the Gretchen episode, everything turns to gall: 'Wie mir meine alten Mauern und Thürme nach und nach verleideten, so mißfiel mir auch die Verfassung der Stadt.'[1]

When he arrived in Leipzig in 1765 he found a new world. The *Messe* was on and this provided an apparent link with Frankfurt; but immediately he felt the contrast: 'Leipzig ruft dem Beschauer keine alterthümliche Zeit zurück; es ist eine neue, kurz vergangene, von Handelsthätigkeit, Wohlhabenheit, Reichthum zeugende Epoche, die sich uns in diesen Denkmalen ankündet.'[2] His lady-friends told him he looked 'wie aus einer fremden Welt hereingeschneit'. And his speech! Despite his father's attempts to make him speak 'purely' Goethe had consciously preserved some local features 'weil sie mir ihrer Naivetät wegen gefielen', especially a tendency to use figurative expressions

[1] Weimar ed. XXVII, p. 41.   [2] *Ibid.* p. 49.

and proverbial phrases, some of which were rather forthright. But now:

> Mir sollten die Anspielungen auf biblische Kernstellen untersagt sein, sowie die Benutzung treuherziger Chroniken-Ausdrücke. Ich sollte vergessen, daß ich den Geiler von Kaisersberg gelesen hatte und des Gebrauchs der Sprüchwörter entbehren, die doch, statt vieles Hin- und Herfackelns, den Nagel gleich auf den Kopf treffen; alles dieß, das ich mir mit jugendlicher Heftigkeit angeeignet, sollte ich missen, ich fühlte mich in meinem Innersten paralysirt und wußte kaum mehr, wie ich mich über die gemeinsten Dinge zu äußern hatte.[1]

Gottsched—old, fat and remarried—had become a laughing-stock. But Gellert was still a respected authority and to him Goethe turned for help. He attended his course on style and was told to write as he spoke. His friends told him to speak as he wrote. Here then was a bewildering situation for one who, as he himself confesses, had always carefully differentiated between speaking and writing. Verse was banned in Gellert's classes, but even his prose displeased the master. His subjects were too passionate, 'der Stil ging über die gewöhnliche Prose hinaus'. Gellert splashed the red ink about; but no one gave him any standard of judgment. 'Ich befand mich in dem schlimmen Falle, in den man gesetzt ist, wenn eine vollkommene Sinnesänderung verlangt wird, eine Entsagung alles dessen, was man bisher geliebt und für gut befunden hat.'[2] He burns all his literary productions to date.

His first letters from Leipzig still contain forms like *seye*, *ohngefähr*, *würklich* and *heut*. The uncertainty about spelling persists (*hingesezt*, *Blate*, *Commöedie* and two lines later *Commödie*, *binn*, *mann*, *Tißh*, *Küchenzettul*, *Hüner*, *Endten*, *tuht*). One might have expected a student to do better than *Catehder*, *retohrisch* and *Teolog*! Some progress is, however, noticeable. He addresses his sister first as 'Liebes Schwestergen' or 'Mädgen' but this soon gives way to 'Liebe Schwester' or 'Chere Soeur'. He works off on her the strictures of Gellert. 'Mercke diß; schreibe nur wie du reden würdest.' He puts her through a course on style,

[1] Weimar ed. XXVII, p. 59.   [2] Ibid. p. 68.

objecting to participial phrases, 'curial' words and expressions, omissions of auxiliary verb, French words, *davor* for *dafür*, and so on. Soon he has got her to the stage where her letter is 'si joliment, si poliment ecrite'; but 'j'aurois attendu une lettre plus naife, plus vive...tout sent le premedite'.[1] This is Gellert's criterion of cultured naturalness. It shows the envisagement of an audience. We feel this in Goethe's own letters when he breaks into verse or a flight of rhetoric like:

> Tantot me promenant, dans des vastes et sombres allees, encore impenetrable au soleil quoique depouillees par l'hiver, tantot assis au pieds d'une statue qui ornoit un berceau, d'une verdure qui ne meurt jamais, tantot debout, regardant d'un seul coup d'oil l'entree de six diverses allees sans pouvoir atteindre des yieux la sortie d'aucune; Ce sont les situations aux quelle je passai mon apres midi.[2]

Ungrammatical as this is, it shows a delight in words. It is probably pieced together from phrases which had stuck in his mind from his reading. Dodd's *Beauties of Shakespear* acts on him in the same way. Linguistically he is in a highly impressionable state. Once we seem to catch a heartbeat:

> Einsam, einsam, ganz einsam...diese Einsamkeit hat, so eine gewisse Traurigkeit, in meine Seele geprägt.
>
> > Es ist mein einziges Vergnügen,
> > Wenn ich entfernt von jedermann,
> > Am Bache, bey den Büschen liegen,
> > An meine Lieben dencken kann.[3]

But this is also affectation. It is English spleen. 'Many time I become a melancholical one. I know not whence it comes. Then I look on every man with a starring owl like countenance. Then I go in woods, to streams, I look on the pyed daisies...etc., etc.' At times he feels 'bien revenu de la folie de me croire poete'. At others he feels that he has qualities necessary to a poet and that he could become one by application, *Fleiß*.[4] He is drawn towards anacreonticism. He cannot therefore show his poems to the moralist Gellert. He would rather be judged by a girl than

---
[1] Morris, I, p. 133. Goethe's French scorns accents!
[2] Morris, I, p. 128.   [3] *Ibid.* p. 125.   [4] *Ibid.* I, pp. 130, 143, 159.

a critic. But even here there is affectation. There is constant talk of *sujets*. 'De l'amour seulement nous sommes amoureux.' He restates completely the anacreontic ideal: 'Pour l'amour veritable, il ne faut pas, qu'un Poete en sente, il doit peindre en ses poesies, ou des filles ideales, parfaites, ou mauvaises, comme elles sont, au lieu desquelles il peindra s'il est amoureux, sa maitresse, comme Seekatz sa femme, quand il falut des princesses.'[1] There is a tension here. For Goethe was really in love, passionately in love with Käthchen Schönkopf, as we can see from his letters to Behrisch.

The tension pervades his Leipzig poems. For all his admonitions to Cornelie to write naturally, he himself was caught in an artificial mode. 'Manchmal mach' ich Madrigals, und das sind meistenteils Naivetäten von meinem Mädgen und Freunden.' But there was nothing naive about these poems. In true anacreontic style, the audience is constantly envisaged:

> Mädgen sezzt euch zu mir nieder
> Niemand stöhrt hier unsre Ruh,
> Seht es kommt der Frühling wieder
> Wekkt die Blumen und die Lieder,
> Ihn zu ehren hört mir zu.

Or again:

> Euer Beyfall macht mich freyer,
> Mädgen, hört ein neues Lied...

The culture of wit appears in the final *pointe*:

> Jüngst schlich ich meinem Mädgen nach,
> Und ohne Hindernüß
> Umfasst' ich sie im Hayn; sie sprach:
> Laß mich, ich schrey gewiß.
> Da droht' ich trozzig: Ha, ich will
> Den tödten, der uns stöhrt.
> Still, winkt sie lispelnd, Liebster, still,
> Damit dich niemand hört.

The culture of feeling appears in 'Ziblis jung und schön, zur Liebe, / Zu der Zärtlichkeit gemacht' and her would-be ravisher: 'Zärtlich lacht das Ungeheuer.' It is Wieland's influence that is

[1] Morris, I, p. 161.

THE GOLDEN TOUCH

strongest in these verse-tales and their language contains much of his vocabulary with its characteristic mixture of seraphic and sentimental: *taumelndes* (or *feuriges*) *Entzükken, heisse Glut, Fühlbarkeit, Wonnestrahl, durchgeküßt, Freudbethränt* and *thränend*. The language of these poems is derived, their gestures charmingly artificial. But the tension between feeling and the convention is always breaking through:

> Mädgen, fürchtet rauher Leute
> Buhlerische Wollust nie.
> Die im ehrfurchtsvollen Kleide
> Viel von unschuldsvoller Freude
> Reden, Mädgen, fürchtet die.[1]

Here speaks the hobbledehoy, ill at ease in the world of *Artigkeit*. It is the mood that made him translate the first scene of *Le Menteur*. Flashes of reality appear disruptingly and portentously in these poems:

> Rings um sie her lag feyerliches Schweigen,
> Als wären sie auf dieser Welt allein.[2]

This is not the language of anacreonticism. Nor is the second line of

> Des Busens volle Blüten wies
> Sie dem verschwiegnen kalten Spiegel...[3]

It is in such moments that Goethe's genius as a word-artist begins to announce itself. But he only comes to such moments from the language of anacreonticism.

The poem entitled *Die Nacht* must have been very dear to Goethe, for there are three Leipzig versions preserved of which this is probably the earliest:

> Gern verlass' ich diese Hütte,
> Meiner Liebsten Aufenthalt,
> Wandle mit verhülltem Tritte
> Durch den ausgestorbnen Wald.
> Luna bricht die Nacht der Eichen,
> Zephirs melden ihren Lauf,
> Und die Bircken streun mit Neigen
> Ihr den süssten Weihrauch auf.

[1] Morris, I, p. 215.   [2] *Ibid.* p. 222.   [3] *Ibid.* p. 223.

> Schauer, der das Herze fühlen,
> Der die Seele schmelzen macht,
> Flüstert durch's Gebüsch im Kühlen.
> Welche süße, schöne Nacht!
> Freude, Wollust kaum zu fassen!
> Und doch wollt ich Himmel Dir
> Tausend solcher Nächte lassen,
> Ließ mein Mädgen eine mir.[1]

Ostensibly this is the language of wit, building up to a joke at the end; a pseudo-apostrophe to Heaven which is really directed to the audience. But there is a disturbing reality about this 'ausgestorbnen Wald', a life amidst its death, something forcing its way to expression in the last two lines of the first stanza. The world of Luna and Zephirs, normally so petrified and static, has burst into life. The result is rather frightening. We are not far away from the forest of *Willkommen und Abschied*, especially in the feverish intensity of the second stanza. There are no *Machtwörter*, the over-all form is still artificial and bitty; but there is an uncomfortable contrast between Luna, the property-moon, and the 'Nacht der Eichen' it is supposed to, but cannot possibly, break.

Another anacreontic poem sent to Behrisch begins as follows:

> Im Schlafgemach, fern von dem Feste,
> Sitzt Amor Dir getreu, und wacht,
> Daß nicht die List muhtwill'ger Gäste,
> Das Brautbett dir unsicher macht.
> Er harrt auf dich. Der Fackel Schimmer
> Umglänzt ihn, und ihr flammend Gold
> Treibt Weihrauchdamf der durch das Zimmer
> In wollustvollen Wirbeln rollt.[2]

The last four lines show Klopstock's diction breaking the spell that this delicate art demands. When the poem is published in the *Neue Lieder* of 1769, the lines appear recast as follows:

---

[1] Morris, VI, p. 41—sent in a letter of May 1768 to Behrisch. The other versions are in the *Lieder* for Friederike Oeser (Morris, I, p. 244) and in the *Neue Lieder* of 1769 (*ibid*. pp. 351–2). Goethe remodelled it extensively for the 1789 edition of his poems.

[2] Morris, I, pp. 169–70.

> Es blinkt mit mystisch heil'gem Schimmer
> Vor ihm der Flammen blaßes Gold,
> Ein Weihrauchwirbel füllt das Zimmer,
> Damit ihr recht genießen sollt.

Morris observes that the room is now 'von Menschenhand parfümiert und obendrein der Zweck unnütz deutlich ausgesprochen'.[1] The last line is certainly weak. Significant is, however, the way in which Goethe has made something of his own out of this borrowed language. The same can be observed in the 1767 Odes to Behrisch. The *Höllenfahrt* poem of his boyhood shows superficial influence of Klopstock's language;[2] in the Odes to Behrisch we see the full extent of the infection. Participles abound:

> Der Erde aussaugendem Geitze,
> Der Luft verderbender Fäulniß...

> Sieht triumphirend,
> Wie das Mädgen schaurend,
> Der Jüngling iammernd,
> Vorübergeht.

These are sometimes compound in form (*leichtbewegt, sorgenverwiegend, elendtragend, flammengezüngt*). We also encounter compound adjectives (*lichtgrün, vielkünstlich*). *Machtwörter* are frequent: *Prachtfeindinn, Ocktobernebel, Gebärort, Blumenfesseln, Flügelspeichen, Mörderhülle* and characteristic compounds with 'silver' (*Silberglanz, Silberblätter*). But here again we can see how Goethe's touch has turned what he found to advantage:

> Da geht der Raupe,
> Klagt der listigen Spinne
> Des Baums Unverwelcklichkeit.

The abstract word, as object to an intransitive verb—since Klopstock almost a *cliché*; but here given power and reality by

---

[1] Morris, VI, p. 70.
[2] There is an emphasis on *Jauchzen*, a *Tausend Millionen*, a few conventional abstract plurals (*Himmel, Trohnen, Gewitter, Donner, Fernen, Welten, Lüffte*), a certain activism ('Sterne *zittern*', 'Sonne *bebt*') and intensification ('*tausendfache* Qual', '*ewig* finstre Nacht') and some infinitives used substantivally ('Dein Siegen', 'ihrem Wüthen', 'Sein Sprechen').

transmutation into imagery. And look what has become of Klopstock's so-conscious use of participles in

> Auf Kieseln im Bache, da lieg ich, wie helle,
> Verbreite die Arme der kommenden Welle,
> Und buhlerisch drückt sie die sehnende Brust.

The second version goes even further:

> Im spielenden Bache da lieg ich wie helle!
> Verbreite die Arme der kommenden Welle,
> Und buhlerisch drückt sie die sehnende Brust.[1]

Both anacreontic and seraphic language respond to Goethe's golden touch. We can also feel the proximity of Hagedorn's waggishness as well as his sententiousness. Goethe is allowing himself to be influenced by every style and form. Even French alexandrines contribute their measure. In the final version of *Die Mitschuldigen* an incongruous mixture of *style noble* and homely colloquialism is brilliantly used for comic effect.[2] Even Wieland makes a modest contribution: 'Sympatie, dies schwimmende Gefühl', also modulated into:

> *Sophie.* Ein sympathetisch Herz wie deines fand ich nie.
> *Söller.* Wenn ihr zusammen gähnt das nennt ihr Sympathie.[3]

This is written at a time of great admiration for Wieland, when Wieland's worldliness and grace crystallised all Goethe's dislike of abstract philosophy, dead languages and formalistic law. He was back at Frankfurt, recovering from Leipzig. It was a period of taking stock. Restrained by illness he did little more than touch up some poems and *Die Mitschuldigen*. But he had plenty of time to reflect on what Leipzig had given him. The academic side had got him nowhere. In literature he had learnt to value 'das Bedeutende des Stoffs und das Konzise der Behandlung'. In his behaviour, and to a certain extent in his writing, he had achieved some degree of 'Gewandtheit'. This is how he saw things later from the vantage-point of *Dichtung und Wahrheit*.

---

[1] Morris, I, pp. 243 and 358.
[2] For more detail, see my forthcoming article on 'The language of Goethe's *Die Mitschuldigen*'.   [3] Morris, I, pp. 397, 392.

It is true that the revision of his poems shows a maturing sense of language. But it would be a mistake to think that Leipzig had killed the old Frankfurt self. Even the Annette poems are studded with Frankfurt forms and spellings. It was as if he could toe the line when speaking or writing to others but relapsed into his linguistic self when writing for his own delight. Not, of course, into the old lusty 'Kernstellen'; Leipzig taste prevented that. But the essential linguistic substratum was still intact and was always forcing its way to the surface. Indeed, to read his letters from Frankfurt to his Leipzig friends, one would think he had hardly changed at all linguistically. We still find *tuhn, Schue, Empfelungen, bißgen, Käthgen, dencken, würcklich, Lebhafftigkeit, Schicksaal, binn* and the rest. He is quite unable (or unwilling) to distinguish between *malen* and *mahlen*. Alongside this we find him telling Käthchen Schönkopf to write *gespielt* and not *gespiehlt, geschickt* and not *geschückt*—and *freilig* but not *freilich*! He objects to her *Profezeihung* and *Comoetigen Zettel*; but himself writes *Famielie, Bibliotheck* and *Reflecktiohnen*. Is this an unwillingness to write foreign spellings? Or is it simply a general uncertainty about language? He constantly protests that he is starved of culture in 'Franckfurt', that he is out of 'Connexion mit allen schönen Geistern', that he would go to Paris to learn French and become *artig*, that what Leipzig thinks today Frankfurt thinks three months later, that he lives in a famine of good taste; but he had outgrown Leipzig and found his way back to where he belonged.

Basically he was still his old, passionate self: 'das habe ich mit allen tragischen Helden gemein, dass meine Leidenschafft sich sehr gerne in Tiraden ergiesst, und wehe dem der meiner Lava in den Weeg kömmt'.[1] It was this lava which had disturbed Gellert. It was not the stuff for Leipzig:

> Allein es sitzt zu tief im Herzen,
> Und Spott vertreibt die Liebe nicht.[2]

His friend Horn put it like this: 'Goethe...ist sehr stipide geworden, die Reichslufft hat ihn schon recht angesteckt.' Goethe

[1] Morris, I, p. 310.   [2] Ibid. p. 360.

himself wrote to Käthchen Schönkopf: 'Es war eine Zeit da ich nicht fertig werden konnte mit Ihnen zu reden, und ietzt will all mein Witz nicht hinreichen, eine Seite an Sie zu schreiben. Denn ich kann mir nichts dencken was Ihnen angenehm seyn könnte.'[1] The truth was that he was no longer interested in being *angenehm*. He had outgrown the culture of wit.

Goethe's Strassburg period is sometimes presented as a discovery of content; in fact, it was a discovery of form. It was not a shift from feigned to real feeling, but from borrowed to real form. Nothing could illustrate this better than *Mit einem gemalten Bande*:

> Kleine Blumen, kleine Blätter
> Streuen mir mit leichter Hand
> Gute iunge Frühlings Götter
> Tändlend auf ein luftig Band.
>
> Zephir nimms auf deine Flügel,
> Schlings um meiner Liebsten Kleid!
> Und dann tritt sie für den Spiegel
> Mit zufriedener Munterkeit.
>
> Sieht mit Rosen sich umgeben,
> Sie, wie eine Rose iung
> — Einen Kuß! geliebtes Leben,
> Und ich bin belohnt genung.
>
> Schicksaal seegne diese Triebe,
> Lass mich ihr und lass sie mein,
> Lass das Leben unsrer Liebe
> Doch kein Rosen Leben seyn.
>
> Mädgen das wie ich empfindet,
> Reich mir deine liebe Hand,
> Und das Band das uns verbindet
> Sey kein schwaches Rosen Band.

A strange kind of *pointe*! The poem ends by denying its own subject. In these last two lines we have the perfect image of Goethe's break with anacreonticism. No more *schwaches Rosen Band*; things will have a stronger coherence and more lasting

[1] Morris, I, pp. 440, 334.

form in future. But note how the poem divides in the middle. After a perfect rococo beginning—'*kleine* Blumen...*leichter* Hand...iunge Frühlings Götter...tändelnd...luftig Band'— Zephir delivers the usual garland and the girl decks herself. Then suddenly an idea:

> Sieht mit Rosen sich umgeben

echoes into

> Sie wie eine Rose iung...

Illogical, magical, musical—and from then on, a leap, a *Sprung und Wurf*:

> Einen Kuß! geliebtes Leben,
> Und ich bin belohnt genung.

The echoing image providing an emotional and musical link, this is *Sprache des Affekts*. Music, rhythm and intensity have come into their own. Note the Klopstockian substantivised infinitive *Leben*; and the Herderian use of *Und*. But the golden touch is at work. The poem is unmistakably and completely Goethe.

Looking back on his meeting with Herder, Goethe recognised in it the turning-point of his poetic life. The first effect was destructive. Herder was 'always scolding and blaming', rejecting much of what Goethe thought should be admired. The fact that his attack was so effective and disarming, shows that Goethe had little defence to offer. It was a liberating experience after the restricting effect of Leipzig, a liberation which he was ready to receive. Whole new realms of poetry swept into his impressionable mind—Hebrew poetry, primitive poetry, folk-poetry. Herder talked to him about the origins of language, about the beginnings of poetry, about genius, about Shakespeare; he persuaded him to read Hamann; he encouraged him to collect folksongs. He freed him from obsession with content, with *sujets*. He showed him, by means of *The Vicar of Wakefield*, that some measure of detachment was essential to art—not rococo glancing at the audience, but the detachment which was form. Form was a world of variety. Form did not mean regularity. French form was not German form. Goethe's eyes were opened. The seeming 'monster' of the Strassburg minster had its own form which gave unity to its variety. Goethe did not attain to any real understanding of Gothic form, for he applied to it the neo-classical principles he had imbibed from Oeser.[1] He preferred to call the minster 'German' rather than Gothic. The proposal to replace the twisting German streets of Strassburg by French straight lines he considered preposterous. There was something fundamentally German about the parsonage at Sesenheim. The Brion sisters when they came to town were 'die einzigen in der Gesellschaft, welche sich deutsch trugen'. His interest in German antiquities revived. He profited from conversations with Schöpflin and his friends, visited museums, went on antiquarian expeditions, studied medieval remains and documents, became interested in medieval German poetry. But the Middle Ages were too remote.[2] It was the sixteenth century, the period of the birth of German form and style, which drew him. Like Herder he realised that there was more to be gleaned here than from the more distant past, more of immediate value to him and his age. But for Goethe it was not a voyage of discovery. It was a return to the world of his childhood. He studied Luther's Bible and Schade's glossary. He collected *Machtwörter*: '*Spännungen* Irrungen...*Stumpfreden* Schimpfreden...*Das Geraib* alles Eingeweide der abgeschlachten Tiere oder vielmehr alles was nicht als Fleischstück verkauft wird ...*Ringerung*...*Gaffeln* Zünften.'[3] He was full of 'die Deutschheit des sechzehnten Jahrhunderts'.

This was accompanied by a rejection of the sophisticated taste of eighteenth-century France. 'Schon früher und wiederholt auf die Natur gewiesen, wollten wir daher nichts gelten lassen als Wahrheit und Aufrichtigkeit des Gefuhls, *und der rasche derbe Ausdruck desselben*.'[4] Once again it was the reaction against French assertions that Germans were barbarous: but this time

---

[1] See W. D. Robson-Scott's paper on 'Goethe and the Gothic revival', *Publications of the English Goethe Society*, N.S. vol. xxv (1956).

[2] 'Die Minnesänger lagen zu weit von uns ab; die Sprache hätte man erst studiren müssen und das war nicht unsre Sache: wir wollten leben und nicht lernen.' Weimar ed., xxix, p. 83.

[3] Morris, II, pp. 49–50.

[4] Weimar ed., xxviii, p. 57. My italics.

THE GOLDEN TOUCH

strengthened by Herder's praise of primitive poetry. The linguistic features admired by Herder abound in the folksongs which Goethe collected. They are all ballads, and unprepared switches into direct speech, *Sprünge und Würfe*, are frequent:

> Sie ging den Thurm wohl um und wieder um,
> Feinslieb bist du darinnen?

Note the repetition in the first line; and compare:

> Seyd still seyd still liebe Mutter mein
> Der Reden seyd ihr stille.

The lack of punctuation is doubtless intended to suggest spontaneity. Rhythmical emphasis casting words into relief produces postposition of adjective ('liebe Mutter mein', 'Pfalzgraf hübsch und fein'), colloquial periphrases ('thu mich selber nennen', 'thät mich verdriessen') and inversion:

> Hast du gelitten den bittern Todt
> So will ich leiden Schmerzen.

Alliterative formulae ('über Stock und Stiel'), shouts and use of refrain occur. Sometimes the structure is quite loose, with no attempt at linkage:

> Wohl aus dem Land da zieh ich nicht,
> Hab niemand was gestohlen...

or:

> Es stund nicht länger als drey Tag an,
> Die iunge Gräfinn gefahren kam.

Purely grammatical elements are often lacking: subject pronoun, inflection of adjectives, even inflections of the noun:

> Es schlafen alle Leute,
> Es schlafen alle Leut.

Apocope (*Stund, Leich, nein* for 'hinein', *Umständ*), syncope (*es reit, mi'm*) and even an occasional *Machtwort* (*reitenswehrt, wunderselten*) give punch. There is a good deal of archaic vocabulary (*Turn, Maidel, Bule, lohn* for 'lassen', *han* for 'haben', *herauser, ummer, drunnen, Schwörin* for 'mother-in-law') and many colourful colloquial words and expressions ('Du lose Plapperzung', 'ein iunges Blut', 'Das Kalb muss leiden mit der Kuh'). Occasionally the expression rises to unusual poetic intensity as in the phrase: 'Es taget nach unserem Wille' in the dawn-song, or in the strange power of *inniglich* in the following:

> Wie ist deine liebe Braut so bleich
> Als ob sie ein Kindlein hat gesäugt.
> Wie ist sie also inniglich,
> Ob sie mit einem Kindlein schwanger ist.

All the same qualities are to be found in Goethe's Sesenheim poems. Perhaps the most celebrated of all *Sprünge und Würfe* is:

> Es schlug mein Herz, geschwind zu Pferde,
> Und fort! wild wie ein Held zur Schlacht.

Mayfest leaps from one poetic idea to the next with the utmost exuberance. Rhythmic intensity produces concentrated *Machtwörter* (*ängsten*, *Wolkenhügel*, *Blütendampfe*, *Morgenblumen*, *morgenschön*), elision (*hats*; *nimms*; *'s Röslein*), apocope ('seh ich', 'umarm ich'), postposition ('Röslein roth', 'Volle Freude süss und rein'), refrain ('Röslein auf der Heiden'), repetition ('Lange hab ich nicht gesungen / Lange liebe Liebe lang'), ejaculations ('Doch ach! schon mit der Morgensonne'; 'O Erd O Sonne', with 'spontaneous' commalessness) and inversions ('Sah ein Knab...', 'Daß du ewig denkst an mich'). Purely grammatical elements are often lacking: subject pronoun ('War so jung und morgenschön'), auxiliary verb ('was ich gereimt'), repetition of main verb:

> So liebt die Lerche
> Gesang und Luft,
> Und Morgenblumen
> Den Himmels Duft,

and adjectival inflection ('luftig Band', 'sanft Geflüster', 'mein geliebt Geschwister'). The definite article departs, leaving one with a world peopled with persons:

> Wo Finsterniss aus dem Gesträuche
> Mit hundert schwarzen Augen sah.

THE GOLDEN TOUCH

Hundert embodies a Klopstockian (or sentimental) intensifier; so does 'tausend Stimmen'. But the convention seems to have taken on a new reality. It is capable of startling extension:

> Die Nacht schuf tausend Ungeheuer —
> Doch tausendfacher war mein Muth.

Also redolent of Klopstock is: 'es zittert Morgenschimmer' and the 'gethürmter Riese' who later becomes 'aufgethürmt'. It is language full of movement:

> Der Abend wiegte schon die Erde...

the full realisation of Herder's demand for 'Bewegung! Melodie des Herzens! Tanz!'

In *Wanderers Sturmlied*, composed sometime in 1772, we find this language developed almost to breaking-point. Cultivation of the *Machtwort* is intensified by Goethe's new-found enthusiasm for Pindar.[1] 'Ich wohne ietzt in Pindar', he wrote to Herder in July 1772. 'Wenn er die Pfeile ein übern andern nach dem Wolkenziel schiest steh ich freylich noch da und gaffe.' Pindar's image of 'taming emotions' is recast by Goethe into the poet's struggle with language:

> Wenn du kühn im Wagen stehst, und vier neue Pferde wild unordentlich sich an deinen Zügeln bäumen, du ihre Krafft lenckst, den austretenden herbey, den aufbäumenden hinabpeitschest, und iagst und lenckst und wendest, peitschest, hältst, und wieder ausjagst biss alle sechzehn Füsse in einem Tackt ans ziel tragen. Das ist Meisterschafft, επικρατειν, Virtuosität. Wenn ich nun aber überall herumspaziert binn, überall nur drein geguckt habe. Nirgends zugegriffen. Dreingreiffen, packen ist das Wesen ieder meisterschafft.[2]

But the effect of Pindar was merely to intensify the new-found language of Strassburg. Goethe's translation of the fifth Olympian Ode contains the nouns *Zwillingsaltäre, Springrosse, Völkerschützerinn* and *Ruhmnahme,* compound adjectives: *freudewarm,*

---

[1] Nouns: *Schlossensturm, Schlammpfad, Feuerflügel, Blumenfüsse, fluthschlamm,* etc.; participles include *neidgetroffen, siegdurchglüht, sturmathmend, bienensingend;* there is a compound adjective *blumenglücklich.*

[2] Morris, II, p. 294.

mannswert, freudmutig, compound participles: *preiserwerbend, neubewohnt, herwandelnd, gefahrumhüllt, wolckentrohnend,* a tendency towards monosyllabic contractions (*rauf, Müh, tret*), a participial construction: ('dir aber siegend / lieblichen Ruhm bereitete') and an anacoluthon at the close:

> Wem gesunder Reichtuhm zufloss
> und Besitztums Fülle häuffte,
> und Ruhmnahmen drein erwarb
> wünsche nicht ein Gott zu seyn.[1]

But all these features were, as we have seen, in Klopstock's language and many of them formed part of Herder's envisagement of primitive language. Pindar merely reinforced the development of Goethe's language in the direction it had already taken. The free strophic form of *Wanderers Sturmlied* certainly derives from Pindar; but otherwise its language is Goethe's Strassburg language applied to a grander theme. It contains refrain ('Wen du nicht verlässest Genius'), repetition ('Nach der Wärme ziehn sich Musen / Nach der Wärme Charitinnen'), emphatic delayal ('Göttergleich'; 'Jupiter Pluvius'; 'sturmathmende Gottheit'; 'Theokrit'), powerful inversions ('Mit den Feuerflügeln / Wandeln wird er'; 'Soll der zurückkehren mutig'), propelling prefixes ('entgegensingen', 'glüh ihm entgegen'), apostrophes and ejaculations—all producing a tremendous rhythmical surge and intensity, tearing itself from one highly-charged syllable to the next, clipping words into punching monosyllables ('Ros'; 'Stirn'; 'Phöb'), sweeping over commas, ignoring subject-pronouns ('Wirst die wollnen Flügel unterspreiten'; 'Wird der Regen Wolcke...entgegensingen') adjectival inflections ('hell-leuchtend unwärmend Feuer') and auxiliary verbs ('ich den ihr begleitet'), and breaking at the climaxes into stammering breathlessness: 'Python tödtend leicht gros'...'Weh weh innre Wärme / Seelen Wärme / Mittelpunckt'. Mr Trevelyan, in his authoritative study of *Goethe and the Greeks*, maintains that constructions like: 'Dich dich strömt mein Lied' or 'Glühte deine

[1] Morris, III, p. 84.

Seel Gefahren' are not only 'grammatically impossible' but not Pindaric.[1] Considering them in the setting of the German eighteenth century, we can more easily appreciate their provenance. They represent Klopstock's transitive use of normally intransitive verbs. In this, as in so much else, Goethe's poem represents the full fruit of Klopstock's endeavours to make the German language more expressive. Herder's investigations into early poetry had caused him to find and praise in it many linguistic features which Klopstock had arrived at from different premises. Here the full possibilities are exploited by a poet.

The exploitation is continued gloriously in the poems which Goethe wrote between 1773 and 1775. It would be too tedious to analyse this fully: but some of the great passages appear in an interesting new light when viewed in this context. The splendour of Goethe's imaginative power over language is not thereby diminished; it seems all the greater when one sees what he made out of what came at him from all sides. One pauses with new admiration and perhaps heightened understanding at pungent apocopes like: 'Ich kenn nichts ärmers / Unter der Sonn...', at words like *Götterselbstgefühl*, *Muttergegenwart*, *schlangewandelnd* or *jünglingfrisch*, at forceful verbs:

>Ein Zauber bleyt mich nieder,
>Ein Zauber häckelt mich wieder...

and infinitives:
>Da gehts an ein Picken
>An ein Schlürfen, ein Hacken.

One marvels at the expressive use of participles:

>Auf der Welle blincken
>Tausend schwebende Sterne
>Liebe Nebel trincken
>Rings die türmende Ferne
>Morgenwind umflügelt
>Die beschattete Bucht
>Und im See bespiegelt
>Sich die reifende Frucht.

[1] Humphry Trevelyan, *Goethe and the Greeks* (Cambridge, 1941), p. 55.

and their personification:

> Hast du die Schmerzen gelindert
> Je des Beladenen
> Hast du die Tränen gestillt
> Je des Geängsteten.

The inversion in this last example is very typical of the graphic way in which elements are thrust into relief. What more powerful delaying effect could there be than the end of *Ganymed* with its tremendous surge through ellipses, repetitions and ejaculations?:

> Hinauf, hinauf strebts
> Es schweben die Wolcken!
> Abwärts die Wolcken!
> Neigen sich der sehnenden Liebe
> Mir! Mir! —
> In deinem Schoose
> Aufwärts!
> Umfangend umfangen,
> Aufwärts
> An deinem Busen
> Allfreundlicher Vater!

What more gripping 'Melodie des Herzens' than the opening anacolutha of *An Schwager Kronos*?:

> Spude dich Kronos
> Fort den rasselnden Trott!
> Berg ab gleitet der Weeg
> Ekles Schwindeln zögert
> Mir vor die Stirne dein Haudern.

What more 'sinnlich' imagery than

> Ich saug an meiner Nabelschnur
> Nun Nahrung aus der Welt.
> Und herrlich rings ist die Natur
> Die mich am Busen hält.

What more amazing paucity of punctuation than

> Hier sitz ich forme Menschen
> Nach meinem Bilde
> Ein Geschlecht das mir gleich sey

> Zu leiden weinen
> Geniessen und zu freuen sich,
> Und dein nicht zu achten
> Wie ich.

What more heart-rending exclamation than

> Warum ziehst du mich unwiederstehlich,
> Ach! in iene Pracht?

What more concentrated ellipsis than: 'Ich dich ehren? Wofür?'? What more emphatic omission of subject pronoun than: 'Musst mir eine Erde / Doch lassen stehen'? What more striking use of flexionless adjective than 'heilig glühend Herz'? All these linguistic features seem to be concentrated, symbolically as it were, in what was perhaps the last poem he completed before his departure for Weimar, *Im Herbst 1775*:

> Fetter grüne du Laub
> Das Rebengeländer
> Hier mein Fenster herauf.
> Gedrängter quillet
> Zwillingsbeeren, und reifet
> Schneller und glänzend voller.
> Euch brütet der Mutter Sonne
> Scheideblick, euch umsäuselt
> Des holden Himmels
> Fruchtende Fülle.
> Euch kühlet des Monds
> Freundlicher Zauberhauch
> Und euch bethauen, Ach!
> Aus diesen Augen
> Der ewig belebenden Liebe
> Vollschwellende Trähnen.

No one reading this could say that the German language was any longer barbaric or inexpressive. It has attained its full maturity as a poetic medium.

We find also in some of these poems a conscious striving for folk-simplicity. This is the natural succession to the Strassburg folksongs and also partly the result of his interest in sixteenth-century, 'German' style. He realises, quite rightly, that *Knüttelvers* is an essentially German style; and he appreciates its possibilities as an expressive medium. He has learnt from Hans Sachs that its elastic rhythms can be used to good comic effect. And so when he is out for a lark, he tends to write in *Knüttelvers*. For example:

> Da hatt ich einen Kerl zu Gast,
> Er war mir eben nicht zur Last,
> Ich hatt so mein gewöhnlich Essen.
> Hat sich der Mensch pump satt gefressen
> Zum Nachtisch was ich gespeichert hatt!

The mode tends naturally to loose and archaic syntax, to apocope, flexionless and expressive inversions (as in the fourth line, with its characteristic head-position of the verb). The poem continues:

> Und kaum ist mir der Kerl so satt,
> Thut ihn der Teufel zum Nachbar führen,
> Über mein Essen zu raisonniren.
> Die Supp hätt können gewürzter seyn,
> Der Braten brauner, firner der Wein.
> Der tausend Sackerment!
> Schlagt ihn todt den Hund! Es ist ein Recensent.[1]

This shows a combination of colloquial and archaic features. They blend quite naturally because Goethe's own speech contained many elements which, by Saxon standards, were archaic. But there is also conscious imitation of the bald expression of sixteenth-century *Knüttelvers*. In it he found that stark alignment of statements and absence of purely grammatical connections which, under Herder's influence, he had admired in folksong. Its elastic rhythms permitted constant variety of movement and frequent inversions. It was the very opposite of that regularity he had come to scorn as artificial. It was German. Full realisation of the potentialities of the form, realisation that it was a form and not merely uncouthness, came to him only with his discovery of Hans Sachs. But he had been feeling his way towards such a form for some time. The regular tetrameters (inspired probably by Hagedorn) of his anacreontic verse are interspersed with trimeters and pentameters in the verse-letter to Friederike Oeser of

[1] Morris, III, p. 88; cf. IV, pp. 31–2.

THE GOLDEN TOUCH

November 1768.¹ The *Neue Lieder* of 1769 contain some verses in *Bänkelgesang* rhythm. The first essay at *Knüttelvers* which I have noted occurs in a letter to Kestner of January 1773.² From then on we find him using it regularly for occasional verses. Then the series of *Schwänke* sets in with the *Jahrmarktsfest zu Plundersweilen* and *Pater Brey*. The language is full of ellipses, inversions and contractions. The archaic features of the form are developed to embrace modern colloquialisms. The tone is predominantly waggish. Satire looms large and in *Satyros* we find mockery of sentimentalism (in the language of Psyche) and of Herderism (in the language of Satyros himself).³ Implied is the contrast with simplicity and reality. Goethe's golden touch is at work, extending the expressiveness of the form in accordance with its essential spirit. Here are two short examples:

(a) In Judäa dem heiligen Land
War einst ein Schuster wohl bekanndt
Wegen seiner Herz Frömmigkeit
Zur gar verdorbnen Kirchenzeit.

War halb Essener halb Methodist,
Herrnhuter mehr Separatist,
Denn er hielt viel auf Kreuz und Quaal
Genug er war Original
Und aus Originalität
Er andern Narren gleichen thät.   (*Der ewige Jude*)

(b) Hab aber auch die Kunst verstanden
Auszuposaunen in allen Landen
Ohne just die Backen aufzupausen
Wie ich thät meinen Telemach lausen
Dass in ihm werde dargestellt

---

¹ Morris, I, pp. 303–9.   ² *Ibid.* III, p. 23.
³ Psyche (Caroline Flachsland?) 'stirbt für Entzücken', her heart 'stirbt in Seligkeit', she experiences the mixed feeling of 'Wonn und Weh'...'Und aller Seligkeit Wahntraumbild / Fühl ich erbebend voll erfüllt'. Satyros (Herder?) produces *Machtwörter* (*HundeLagerstätt, schattenkühl, liebebang, TugendWahrheitsLicht, LiebeHimmelsWonnewarm*), discourses on *Krafft* and 'Wie im Unding das Urding erquoll.... All durchdringend, all durchdrungen', and indulges ecstatically in ellipsis: 'Dein Leben Herz für wen erglüht? / Dein Adler Auge was ersieht?'

505

>   Das Muster aller künftgen Welt.
>   Hab dazu Weiber wohlgebraucht
>   Die's Alter hett wie Schinken geraucht
>   Denen aber von speckigen Jugendtrieben
>   Nur zähes Leder überblieben. (*Hanswursts Hochzeit*)

This is the spirit of sixteenth-century *Knüttelvers* speaking in eighteenth-century terms through Goethe's imagination. *Der ewige Jude*, in the fragments we have of it, is a strange mixture of comic and serious; but here and there are moments of moving, simple expression which foreshadow the astonishing range of expression which Goethe was to draw from this old form in *Faust*.

Conscious striving for heightened expressiveness is to be found in the first version of *Götz von Berlichingen*.[1] Right at the beginning we have the following exchange:

> *2. Reuter.* Ich kann nicht begreiffen wo der von Weisling hingekommen ist. Es ist als wenn er in die Erd geschlupft wäre. Zu Nershem hat er gestern übernachtet, da sollt er heute auf Crailsheim gangen seyn, das ist seine Stras, und da wär er morgen früh durch den Winsdorfer Wald gekommen, wo wir ihm wollten aufgepasst und für's weitere Nacht Quartier gesorgt haben; unser Herr wird wild seyn, und ich binn's selbst dass er uns entgangen ist, iust da wir glaubten wir hätten ihn schon.
>
> *1. Reuter.* Vielleicht hat er den Braten gerochen, denn selten dass er mit Schnuppen behafft ist. Und ist einen andern Weeg gezogen.

We note apocope (*Erd, sollt, Stras*), contraction (*für's, binn's, behafft*), archaic form *gangen*, archaic order: 'wo wir ihm wollten aufgepasst...haben', and colloquial images (*Braten...Schnuppen*). The intention is to achieve sixteenth-century patina and also 'raschen, derben Ausdruck' (see above, p. 496). I say 'intention', for the effect remains highly intentional. Normal prose is spiked with archaisms and colloquialisms. There are inconsistencies like *gangen* alongside *gekommen* and *gezogen*, and un-sixteenth-century '*seine* Stras'. The 'speech' has a 'literary' flavour: the image of the *Braten* is taken from Götz's autobiography and the order of

---

[1] For more detailed consideration of this topic, see my paper 'The language of Goethe's *Götz von Berlichingen*', to be published shortly.

'Und ist einen anderen Weeg gezogen' is chap-book style. But the purpose is clear. Aristocrats, we are told a little later, are 'iust die artigsten' when they want something; this is intended to portray the opposite of *artig*—good, plain bluntness of speech. As the scene proceeds we encounter *ihr fahrt, liebe Freund* (plural), *'s Trinckgeld, gearbeit, die Meng und die Füll, der nächst und best Weeg, an der Nasen, nich* and *nit*. Also lusty phrases: 'Dancks ihm ein spitz Holz', colloquial words (*scheren* in the sense of 'to rob', *schnorren, pfiffig*) and ellipses: 'Das wär!'; 'denn im dunckeln über die Furt ist gefährlich'; 'wenn nicht Wein und Bier gäb sich manchmal die Grillen wegzuschwemmen'. But one is pulled up by a bookish sentence like: 'und wenn wir nicht gewollt hätten, würd er uns haben wollen machen'. Similar structures in the mouth of Olearius have some characterising force; but this is spoken by a carter! Götz speaking to Weislingen uses *Nächt, Männlin, Trepp, eisern Gelenderlin, stund*, past participle *geben, ich wett*, preterite *hört* and ellipsis 'Und wärs!'. Typical of his speech are such linkless alignments as: 'Wäre euer Gelübde nicht so heilig ich wollt euch bereden...' or 'Ich hab iust noch ein hübsches Kleid ist nicht kostbaar nur von leinen aber sauber'. The Abbot of Fulda splutters out 'Ey!' or 'Potz!', 'ein schön Buch', 'so stecken einen die Kerl am End in Sack'. And in Act Three we have a good old blunt Emperor who scorns any idea of sentence-construction:

> Ich will euch die Köpfe zurecht setzen! Wofür binn ich Kayser. Soll ich nur Strohmann seyn, und die Vögel von euern Gärten scheuchen, keinen eignen Willen haben, bildets euch nicht ein. Ich will eine Contribution von Geld und Mannschafft wider den Türcken, das will ich sag ich euch und keiner unterstehe sich darwider zu reden.

The aim is language belonging to good, plain men of action. Not gasbags, hair-splitters, intellectuals or fops—but men who get things done, men who act and speak from the heart to the heart. But unfortunately Goethe is sometimes stifled by his own reading. How can one believe that Götz's wife was 'mit Cartoffeln und Rüben erzogen' when she has just used an image from Shakespeare?[1] Even Götz himself lets slip one *demohngeachtet*. Marie sometimes talks as though she were reading out of a chapbook.[2] Other features, such as the Shakespearean word-play of Liebetraut or the rhetoric of Weislingen and Adelheid or the Ossianic landscaping of the gipsy boy, seem out of place in the sixteenth-century German atmosphere. But it cannot be said that Goethe was aiming at absolute realism of language. All he wanted was something with punch.

The work is full of dramatic strength, imaginative power and Shakespearean breadth. Herder's remark that Shakespeare had 'quite spoilt' Goethe must be understood in connection with his other stricture: 'Es ist alles nur gedacht.' In reporting these criticisms Goethe may have been overstating; for Herder was not blind to the power of the work, and to Caroline Flachsland he said: 'Es ist ungemein viel Deutsche Stärke, Tiefe und Wahrheit drin, obgleich hin und wieder es auch nur gedacht ist.'[3] Shakespeareanism was merely part of the consciousness of its language. It was hard criticism to accept; but Goethe accepted it. And although the second *Götz* is in some ways imaginatively inferior to the first, it does show a great advance towards individuality and reality of language. Goethe's sureness of touch seems to have become infallible. He has seen the point, and acted. In 1773 he protests: 'Ich hasse alle Spezialkritik von Stellen und Worten.... Ich kann leiden, wenn meine Freunde eine Arbeit von mir zu Feuer verdammen, umgegossen oder verbrannt zu werden; aber sie sollen mir keine Worte rücken, keine Buchstaben versetzen.' But in the same letter he has been talking about curses and oaths in drama:

Wenn gemeine Leute streiten, ist die Exposition der Gerechtsame sehr kurz, es geht in's Fluchen, Schimpfen und Schlagen über, und

[1] 'Leute die ihren Urin nicht halten können', Morris, II, p. 152 (cf. *The Merchant of Venice*).
[2] For example: 'Ich läugne nicht dass er denen die von ungerechten Fürsten bedrängt werden, mehr als Heiliger ist, denn seine Hülfe ist sichtbaarer, wurf er aber nicht dem Schneider zu helfen drey Cölnische Kaufleute nieder, und waren dann nicht auch die Bedrängte, waren die nicht auch unschuldig', Morris, II, p. 153. [3] *Ibid*. p. 319; cf. Goethe to Herder, *ibid*. p. 295.

der Vorhang fällt zu. Leute von Sitten werden höchstens in einen Anfall von Leidenschaft in einen Fluch ausbrechen, und das sind die beiden Arten die ich dem Drama vergönnen mögte, doch nur als Gewürz, und dass sie nothwendig stehen müssen und sie niemand herausnehmen könnte ohne dem Ausdruck zu schaden.[1]

There was a good deal in *Götz* which was not *nothwendig*, and which could be taken out 'ohne dem Ausdruck zu schaden'. He proceeded to take it out. He discards most of what was 'literary' or bookish about the language. There is a general progress towards directness and spontaneity.

For instance, Weislingen left alone after talking with Götz:

> Abzuhängen! Ein verdammtes Wort, und doch scheint es als wenn ich dazu bestimmt wäre. Ich enntfernte mich von Gottfrieden um frey zu seyn; und ietzt fühl ich erst wie sehr ich von denen kleinen Menschen abhange die ich zu regieren schien.

This is now too rhetorical for Goethe: he replaces it by the more spontaneous outcry:

> Wie ich von den elenden Menschen abhieng die ich zu beherrschen glaubte....[2]

Or take Franz's description of Adelheid:

> Inzwischen dass Adel und Freundlichkeit gleich einem Majestätischen Ehpaar über den schwarzen Augenbrauen herrschten, und die duncklen haare gleich einem Prachtvorhang um die königliche Herrlichkeit herum wallten.

Far too *gedacht* for the expression of enthusiasm; and not likely to whet Weislingen's appetite! Goethe transforms it into this:

> Adel und Freundlichkeit herrschten auf ihrer Stirne. Und das blendende Licht des Angesichts und des Busens wie es von den finstern Haaren erhoben ward![3]

This, like the former example, shows the flight away from contrived metaphor and contrived structure. Goethe also became

---

[1] Morris, III, pp. 29–32, letter to Salzmann.
[2] *Ibid.* II, p. 171 and III, p. 201.
[3] *Ibid.* II, p. 173 and III, p. 203.

GERMAN AS A LITERARY LANGUAGE

aware of a tendency towards artificial sententiousness: thus when the *Knecht* falls into the marsh, his companion exclaims:

> Michel! O weh er ist versuncken. Michel! er hört mich nicht er ist erstickt. So lauert der Todt auf den Feigen, und reisst ihn in ein unrühmlich Grab.

In the revision, the last sentence is excised.[1] It is interesting to note how in passage after passage Goethe seizes on the point where reality moves over into artificiality; and he cuts it short. Sometimes there are too many images, sometimes too much straining after emphasis, sometimes too elaborate a sentence, or too forthright a *Machtwort* (for he realises that compression or lustiness can also be artificial). Metzler's language in Act Five is much more convincing than the rant of the first version. Ossianic moods and Herderesque balladry are seen to be unnatural in the mouths of illiterate sixteenth-century gipsies. Even in Götz's dying words there is a sensitive strengthening. 'Lass meine Seele nun' becomes 'Löse meine Seele nun', and 'Die Schwachen werden regieren, mit List' becomes 'Die Nichtswürdigen werden regiern mit List'. An abstract comment like 'Sein Todt war Belohnung' (of Georg) or the nets of the weak 'womit die Feigheit die Pfade verwebt' is banished as rhetorical and *gedacht*. The result of all this is that Goethe's consciously rough language now gains in expressiveness by not being surrounded with rhetoric and bookishness.

Part of the bookishness, as we have seen, was Ossianic. A translation from Ossian has survived from Goethe's Strassburg days.[2] Here is the beginning:

> Stern der niedersinckenden Nacht! Schön ist dein Licht im Westen! Du hebest dein lockiges Haupt aus deiner Wolke: ruhig wandelst du über deinen Hügel. Was siehst du nach der Ebne? Es ruhen die

---

[1] Morris, II, p. 204; cf. III, p. 232.
[2] *Ibid.* II, pp. 84–91. For the background of this translation, see A. Gillies, *Herder und Ossian* (Berlin, 1933). The analysis of the style of this translation (and Goethe's later revision of it) by E. Büscher in her *Ossian in der Sprache des achtzehnten Jahrhunderts* (Köslin, 1937) is inadequate because it is not related to the linguistic background.

stürmischen Winde. Das Murmeln der Ströme kommt aus der Ferne. Brüllende Wellen klettern den entlegenen Felsen hinan. Die Fligen des Abends schweben auf ihren zarten Schwingen, das Summen ihres Zug's ist über dem Feld. Wo nach blickst du, schönes Licht? Aber du lächlest und gehst. Fahrewohl du schweigender Stral. Dass das Licht in Ossians Seele heraufsteige.

The striking fact about this language is the presence of features we have associated with Klopstock. The use of present participles as epithets ('nidersinckenden Nacht', 'brüllende Wellen', 'schweigender Stral'), of substantivised infinitives ('das Murmeln', 'das Summen') and of dynamic prefixes ('klettern... hinan', 'heraufsteige'). This is set in a rhythmic patterning reminiscent of Geßner (without ever becoming completely hexametric) with apostrophes and emphases such as were advocated by Herder. We noted above the strange way in which Klopstockian features occur in Herder's description of primitive language. Here is the reason. For 'Ossian', though deemed to be primitive, was not; and it was nourished from Homeric epithets and Biblical parallelism, both of which had strongly affected Klopstock. In the original, the passage runs as follows:

Star of the descending night! fair is thy light in the west! thou liftest thy unshorn head from thy cloud: thy steps are stately on thy hill. What dost thou behold in the plain? The stormy winds are laid. The murmur of the torrent comes from afar. Roaring waves climb the distant rock. The flies of evening are on their feeble wings, and the hum of their course is on the field. What dost thou behold, fair light? But thou dost smile and depart. [The waves come with joy around thee, and they bathe thy lovely hair.] Farewel, thou silent beam! — — — Let the light of Ossian's soul arise.[1]

Goethe's translation, although close, moves away significantly in several places, and always in the spirit of Klopstock or Herder. *Das Murmeln...hinan...das Summen...schweigend* show that Klopstock had taught him how to render forcefully in German something said rather differently in English. The effect seems

---

[1] I do not know why Goethe omitted the sentence which I place in square brackets. My text is from the London 1765 edition of *The Works of Ossian*, where this is vol. I, pp. 291–2.

absolutely natural to the language. So does the powerful stress on '*ruhig* wandelst du...' or the striking relief of 'es ruhen *die stürmischen Winde*'. The golden touch is seen in the rendering of 'The flies of evening are on their feeble wings' by the much more powerful 'Die Fligen des Abends *schweben* auf ihren *zarten* Schwingen'. The same affinities with Klopstock and Herder recur in the rest of the translation. We have epithets like *sanftlispelnd, weisbusig, halbverweht, seeumgeben, graubefiedert, seeumstürmt*: they correspond exactly to phrases in the original but they are also exactly of the types advocated by Klopstock. We note inversions like 'da sie allein sas am Hügel' or 'verloren auf dem stürmischen Hügel' or 'Ist denn kein Licht das mich führe zum Platz wo mein Liebster ausruht von der Mühe der Jagd!'. These correspond only roughly to the original;[1] but exactly to the type practised by Geßner or praised by Herder. We find emotional repetitions, ejaculations and elisions. And everywhere the attempt, not always successful, to reproduce the mournful rhythms of the original.

Goethe was aware of the connection between Klopstock and Ossian. In a description of skating in *Dichtung und Wahrheit* he mentions how the 'Ossianische Szenen' prompted him and his friends to declaim Klopstock's odes.[2] The period is immediately after his return from Strassburg. The connection is also present in the underlying pattern of *Die Leiden des jungen Werthers*. Klopstockian tones are struck in the very first pages: 'Die Einsamkeit ist meinem Herzen köstlicher Balsam in dieser paradisischen Gegend, und diese Jahrszeit der Jugend wärmt mit aller Fülle mein oft schauderndes Herz.' 'In dem Meer von Wohlgerüchen...ein fühlendes Herz...Gegenwart des Allmächtigen ...Wehen des Allliebenden...in ewiger Wonne schwebend... ich erliege unter der Gewalt der Herrlichkeit dieser Erscheinungen'—it is ecstatic sentimentalism with strong seraphic overtones.[3] Characteristic words recur: 'paradisisch', emphatic

---

[1] 'When she sat alone on the hill'; 'forlorn on the hill of winds'; 'Lead me, some light, to the place where my love rests from the toil of the chace'.
[2] Weimar ed., XXVIII, p. 122. [3] Morris, IV, pp. 221–2.

'tausend', 'Wonne', 'Seele'. Conflicting with this ecstasy is an earthiness, the love of simple country things, patriarchalism, linear reality, symbolised in Werther's drawing and in Homer. Homer, Goethe tells us in *Dichtung und Wahrheit*, stood in his mind at this time for 'die abgespiegelte Wahrheit einer uralten Gegenwart'.¹ Werther reads Homer as he recovers from a love-affair full of 'feinster Empfindung, schärfstem Witze'. Homer, therefore, is the antidote to the culture of wit and feeling. But even this latter had shown 'Modifikationen bis zur Unart alle mit dem Stempel des Genies bezeichnet'. He now sways between ecstasy and 'Natur', between Klopstock and Homer. Each in its way represents the reaction against civilisation, convention, 'Regeln', 'Ordnung', 'garstiges Gewäsche', 'leidige Abstraktionen'. The terror and refreshment of the storm culminates in Lotte's outcry: 'Klopstock!'; and in this mystic word their relationship achieves foundation with an immediate 'Strom von Empfindungen' and 'wonnevolleste Thränen'. But the tension is still there. Landscape is 'ein grosses dämmerndes Ganze' into which feeling 'verschwimmt sich' and we long 'uns mit all der Wonne eines einzigen grossen herrlichen Gefühls ausfüllen zu lassen'; but as we rush into it its grandeur fades, we long for something more stable and certain and we shell peas and read Homer. This patriarchal feeling, this 'simple harmlose Wonne' is without affectation, says Werther. But he deludes himself; it is as much an affectation as the culture of wit and feeling. There then comes the first mention of Ossian: 'Gefällt! das Wort haß ich in Tod. Was muß das für ein Kerl seyn, dem Lotte gefällt, dem sie nicht alle Sinnen, alle Empfindungen ausfüllt. Gefällt! Neulich fragte mich einer, wie mir Ossian gefiele.'² The connection between Klopstock ('alle Sinnen, alle Empfindungen ausfüllt') and Ossian is here established; it is later to become significant.

    Meanwhile the novel and Werther are moving towards greater individuality. There are references to tales from Goethe's childhood, there are images that grip the mind (like that of kneading language like potter's clay), there is a defence of boldness against

---

¹ Weimar ed., XXVIII, p. 145.   ² Morris, IV, p. 250.

those who always add a 'zwar...', a defence of 'Leidenschaft! Trunkenheit! Wahnsinn!' against 'ihr vernünftigen Leute...ihr sittlichen Menschen', *gelassen* is used as a term of disapproval, Albert's praise of *Verstand* leaves Werther confirmed in his *Leidenschaft*. He has found his real self. The first climax is reached. The language is still ecstatic, but the mood is changing: 'Das volle warme Gefühl meines Herzens an der lebendigen Natur, das mich mit so viel Wonne überströmte, das rings umher die Welt mir zu einem Paradiese schuf, wird mir jezt zu einem unerträglichen Peiniger, zu einem quälenden Geiste, der mich auf allen Wegen verfolgt.'[1] The Klopstockian rapture of the past ('das innere glühende heilige Leben der Natur...unendliche Fülle...alllebend...Geist des Ewigschaffenden...Ufer des ungemessenen Meeres...schäumender Becher des Unendlichen... schwellende Lebenswonne') is supplanted by the 'Abgrund des ewig offenen Grabes'. He reels 'beängstet', weeps 'trostlos einer finstern Zukunft entgegen'. 'Schauer der Einsamkeit' in the 'düstern Cabinette' in Lotte's garden darken the mood: 'Niemals geh ich im Mondenlichte spazieren, niemals daß mir nicht der Gedanke an meine Verstorbenen begegnete, daß nicht das Gefühl von Tod, von Zukunft über mich käme.' It is Lotte speaking, but it is Werther reporting. It is the graveyard mood of sentimentalism and grows quite naturally out of the ecstatic rapture of before. But all Werther's attempts to escape are fruitless. He cannot forswear his self, once he has found it. Life with the Ambassador merely accentuates his individuality. 'Ich arbeite gern leicht weg, und wie's steht so steht's', but the Ambassador wants better particles, better punctuation and no inversions. Werther tries to be 'artig', to have 'viel Witz', 'fein zu loben'— but it does not work. He writes to Lotte from a 'Hütte', in 'Einsamkeit' with snow and hail beating against the window. He still tries to escape to Homer, but now this will not work. Turbulence invades his mind and language. His sentences become disjointed. He becomes addicted to dashes. 'Ossian hat in meinem Herzen den Homer verdrängt.'

[1] Morris, IV, p. 264.

THE GOLDEN TOUCH

The magnificent passage that follows is full of illogical sentence-structures, of graphic prefixes, participles and infinitives, of inversions, repetitions and ejaculations. Characteristic is the protasis which seems to lead to no apodosis; but this comes many lines later as a delayed main clause of marvellous and overwhelming finality. As the novel proceeds, the language becomes increasingly passionate: constant exclamations and apostrophes, constant use of Herderian *und*, constant protases with delayed apodosis. It is as if the *wenn* represented his uncertainty and the *und* his inability to arrange things. 'Keine Entzückungen mehr', his heart is dead, his eyes dry, his senses anxiously furrowing his brow. Firm hard imagery replaces earlier transcendentalism: 'ein lackirt Bildgen...ein versiegter Brunn...ein verlechter Eymer'. The mad boy, poised between Ophelia and Hölderlin ('Ich suche Blumen — und finde keine') is the most powerful symbol of all. Ossianic moods recur. Ossian is the accompaniment to the last meeting of Werther and Lotte. The Strassburg translation reappears, marvellously transfigured. Here is the beginning:

> Stern der dämmernden Nacht, schön funkelst du im Westen. Hebst dein strahlend Haupt aus deiner Wolke. Wandelst stattlich deinen Hügel hin. Wornach blickst du auf die Haide? Die stürmende Winde haben sich gelegt. Von ferne kommt des Giesbachs Murmeln. Rauschende Wellen spielen am Felsen ferne. Das Gesumme der Abendfliegen schwärmet über's Feld. Wornach siehst du, schönes Licht? Aber du lächelst und gehst, freudig umgeben dich die Wellen und baden dein liebliches Haar. Lebe wohl ruhiger Strahl. Erscheine du herrliches Licht von Ossians Seele.[1]

The expression has been strengthened but in different directions. There is greater use of verbs in *funkelst* for 'ist dein Licht' and *strahlend* for 'lockig', *stürmend* for 'stürmisch'; on the other hand *ruhig* replaces 'schweigender [Strahl]' and *erscheine* the more dynamic verb 'heraufsteige'. How is one to interpret this? It would seem that, instead of following slavishly, Goethe has now penetrated to the real meaning and value of the extended expressiveness Klopstock had given to the language. Verbs and

[1] Morris, IV, p. 313; cf. above, pp. 510–11.

deverbatives are used where action and motion are required, but not where the stress is on state or appearance. '*Ruhiger* Strahl' is more effective because the emphasis is on the thing, not the action; so too in the next sentence, as Goethe indicates by strengthening the nominal (i.e. non-verbal) content with *herrlich*. The linguistic stress is now not on *schweigend* and *heraufsteige* but on *Strahl* and *herrliches Licht*—and this renders more potently the emphasis of the thought. *Dämmernd* is more emotionally charged than 'niedersinckend', omission of subject-pronoun in *Hebst...Wandelst* more impelling, *stattlich* more meaningful in the context than 'ruhig' (as well as closer to the English). The non-delayal of *stürmende Winde* and the delayal of *des Giesbachs Murmeln* show individual and creative reaction to another possibility exploited by Klopstock. Everywhere one is conscious of possibilities used with value and individuality. Nothing is allowed to become a manner. Thus the Herderian omission of subject-pronoun in 'Wandelst stattlich deinen Hügel hin', so effective in its way, is followed by 'Wornach *blickst du* auf die Haide?'. *Brüllend* is a rare epithet but '*rauschende* Wellen' is more evocative even though less original. 'Klettern hinan' is dynamic and literal, but *spielen* creates a more real impression, both aurally and visually. In later parts of the translation we note that Goethe retains some of his Klopstockian epithets, but rejects others (*grau* replacing *grauharig*, *weiss* replacing *weisbusig*), sometimes breaking them up into two words (*sanftlispelnd* becomes *schwach lispelnd*, *graubefiedert* becomes *grau befiedert*). Similarly he retains some inversions but not others, for what had been almost a mannerism becomes something real. Thus: 'As she sat alone on the hill', in the first version 'da sie allein sas am Hügel', now becomes 'da sie auf dem Hügel allein saß' (because the stress is on 'alone', not the hill). But 'Es ist Nacht; — Ich binn allein verlohren auf dem stürmischen Hügel' is retained (with the addition of an effective comma after *allein*) because here the stress is on 'hill'.

As the novel moves swiftly to its close this individual mastery of language becomes increasingly apparent. The golden touch turns a passage from Ossian into this marvellous prelude to death:

'Aber die Zeit meines Welkens ist nah, nah der Sturm, der meine Blätter herabstört! Morgen wird der Wanderer kommen, kommen der mich sah in meiner Schönheit, rings wird sein Aug im Felde mich suchen, und wird mich nicht finden.'[1] There is a moment of feverish disjointedness, punctuated by those dashes once again. Then a moment of recollective sentimentalism: 'Ich habe sie in ihrer ganzen Himmelswonne geschmeckt diese Sünde, habe Lebensbalsam und Kraft in mein Herz gesaugt' and an echo of Klopstock's Ode to Fanny. Ossianic storm-clouds race across the sky, the image of the chariot alarmingly appears, the culture of feeling wells up for one last time in 'Trunkenheit...Seligkeit ...Tausend, tausend Küsse...All! All! so sind all die Wünsche und Hoffnungen meines Lebens erfüllt', a 'blaßrothe Schleife' goes with him to the grave, and the work ends in stark, sharp prose such as has never appeared before in the whole history of the German language.

If *Werther* represents Goethe working his way from Klopstock through Ossian to a language of tremendous individual intensity, then the *Urfaust* represents this language in its first full flowering. It may seem conventional for a book on German studies to end with *Faust*, but this is the natural culmination of our subject. This is the next and last stage of our considerations, and I therefore leave aside the other works of Goethe's youth in order to pass clearly and firmly towards it.

We are plunged into sixteenth-century Germany by *Knüttelvers*. The language is crisp and firm, full of concentrating elisions and with an occasional inversion ('studirt mit heisser Müh') and passionate exclamation. Archaic forms seem to sit naturally in the rhythm and style. So, however, also do the characteristic elements of sentimentalist vocabulary which appear in the apostrophe to the moon ('trübseelger Freund...lieben Lichte... mit Geistern schweben...in deinem Dämmer weben'). They

---

[1] Morris, IV, pp. 319-20. Macpherson's text reads: 'The time of my fading is near, and the blast that shall scatter my leaves. To-morrow shall the traveller come, he that saw me in my beauty shall come; his eyes will search the field, but they will not find me' (*ed. cit.* I, p. 357).

recur in the excitement inspired by the sign of the macrocosm ('Wonne...Glut...webt') with definite recollections of Klopstock in 'Eimer', 'Seegenduftend' and 'Harmonisch all das All durchklingen'. Meanwhile the verse has broadened out into pentameters at the first moment of excitement, becoming freer as it grows and finally in the invocation and dialogue with the Earth Spirit it becomes quite free. But there is no stylistic break; the old *Knüttelvers* has been bent to the imagination of the poet, expanding and contracting as the mood demands. When Wagner arrives on the scene the same metre is used to satirise the pedant, combining naïve expression with fine foreign words ('deklamiren ...profitiren'). In the student scene its rhythms take on a jauntiness, with a good deal of rough, popular expression ('Feines Mägdlein drinn aufwarten thut') and homely images ('Als säs Heishunger in iedem Haus', 'Als ging mir ein Mühlrad im Kopf herum'). Mephistopheles is both mock-galant ('logiren', 'dressirt') and mock-learned ('Studiosi', 'reduziren', 'klassifiziren', 'preparirt', 'Paragraphos einstudirt', 'dicktirt'); and these fancy words combine waggishly with coarseness, nonce-words ('vertripplistreichelt', 'Gänsestuhlgang', 'Schwärmerian', 'irrlichtelire'), and expressive imagery ('Will einer an unserm Speichel sich lezzen, / Den thun wir zu unsrer Rechten sezzen', 'Bohrt sich selbst eine Esel und weis nicht wie'). Goethe's habit of expressing himself in a combination of images (commented on by so many of his friends) gives the scene its telling climax in

> Grau, theurer Freund, ist alle Theorie
> Und grün des Lebens goldner Baum.

When Mephistopheles reaches his own moment of excitement (the excitement of being his own, devilish self) the verse, as in Faust's moments of exaltation, expands and retracts, yet never losing its basic relation to *Knüttelvers*, for this is maintained by rhyme. In Auerbachs Keller the popular aspect of the form is accentuated to characterise laughable simplicity, extending into broken drastic prose for the dialogue and contracting into trimeters for the Song of the Flea. In Gretchen's language the same form is used to express lovable simplicity, with no ironical undertones. One has only to compare

with
>Es war einmal ein König,
>Der hett einen grossen Floh
>
>Es war ein König in Tule,
>Einen goldnen Becher er hett

to see what a wide range of expression Goethe has extracted from this bumpy old metre. Her ballad too represents retraction into trimeters, but its relation to the loose tetrameters of *Knüttelvers* is clear and effective. She speaks mostly in *Knüttelvers*; but, like the other characters, extends and retracts it under the effect of deep emotion. True folk-language, such as Goethe had never achieved before, is here to be found—not naturalistically reproduced but with its real essence transmuted into poetry. A telling simplicity of vocabulary (Faust is 'wacker' and 'keck') and syntax ('Bin doch ein törig furchtsam Weib') which flows quite naturally into the sententiousness of 'Nach Golde drängt / Am Golde hängt / Doch alles!' or the assumed refinement of 'Inkommodirt euch nicht' or 'in allen Stücken / So accurat' when she is talking to a gentleman, being afraid that her 'arm Gespräch' cannot possibly entertain him, it being as rough as her hands. In her language we find most of the features which Herder and Goethe had admired in folk-language. Her great moment of ecstasy is full of 'Sinnlichkeit':

>Mein Schoos! Gott! drängt
>Sich nach ihm hin.
>Ach dürft ich fassen
>Und halten ihn
>Und küssen ihn
>So wie ich wollt,
>An seinen Küssen
>Vergehen sollt!

How different from Faust's

>Sich hinzugeben ganz und eine Wonne
>Zu fühlen die ewig seyn muss!

He is indeed, as Mephistopheles says, an 'übersinnlicher, sinnlicher Freyer'.

The basic form of the language of the *Urfaust* is therefore the old *Knüttelvers*. But it has been transformed into a medium of rich, varied expression.[1] The old jauntiness is used to effect with the student, the satirical possibilities (already developed in Goethe's *Schwänke*) are exploited in Wagner (and Frau Marthe) and intensified into savage irony with Mephistopheles, the simple tellingness of its un-Latinate syntax in Faust's opening monologue and in Gretchen, and the freedom of its rhythms is allowed to contract into song or expand into excitement everywhere. Herder's interpretation of folk-language and his praise of its stylistic means have become so much a part of Goethe's consciousness that they are everywhere apparent—even in Faust's advice to Wagner: 'Mein Herr Magister, hab er Krafft!' This is just what the language of the *Urfaust* has. The artificiality of the first *Götz* is gone. This language seems entirely German, spontaneous and poetic.

In the great ecstatic moments we feel also the effect of Klopstock and the culture of feeling. It is present in the *wallen* and *weben* and the 'ewges Meer' of the song of the Earth Spirit. We sense the 'mixed feelings' of sentimentalism behind the 'süsse Liebespein', the 'In dieser Armuth welche Fülle!', the 'Wonnegraus' which Faust experiences on entering Gretchen's room, in the 'Glut von der ich brenne / Unendlich, ewig, ewig nenne' of Faust's confession to Mephistopheles. Most of all, however, in the passage on religion, the great seraphic moment of the play: 'Der Allumfasser...Der Allerhalter...Und drängt nicht alles...und webt...Unsichtbaar sichtbaar...in dem Gefühle seelig....'. But here as everywhere Goethe has transformed what he has absorbed into something essentially his own, something far greater than ever before. Who else could have written a line like: 'Umnebelnd Himmels Glut'?

In the last three scenes of the fragment we seem to encounter

---

[1] O. Flohr, *Geschichte des Knittelverses vom 17. Jahrhundert bis zur Jugend Goethes* (Berlin, 1893), shows how between Opitz and Goethe the form is only used for humorous and grotesque expression.

something new. Here is prose of a passionate intensity which would seem to represent an entirely new dimension of the German language. This is true; but only because the hand is Goethe's. For there are antecedents. And this prose represents the climax of all the movement away from rationalistic expression which we have been following. The scene between Faust and Mephistopheles, later headed *Trüber Tag*, is in prose alternating between eruptive directness (exclamations, imperatives, apostrophes) and more expansive lamentations. In the eruptive passages almost every sentence ends with an exclamation-mark. It is the expression of turbulent anguish. It is highly accentual, with ringing cries, graphic inversions and prepositions and participles, elliptical constructions representing successive gusts of anger and despair; and its concentrated power is intensified by the contrast with the more rhetorical general laments and cursings which often have a roll about them that suggests Geßner or Ossian ('Im unwiederbringlichen Elend bösen Geistern übergeben, und der richtenden gefühllosen Menschheit!'). But there is a subtle difference between the language of Faust and that of Mephistopheles in this scene. Whereas Faust is grandiloquent even in his despair, Mephistopheles is completely without rhetoric: 'Willst fliegen und der Kopf wird dir schwindlich. Eh! Drangen wir uns dir auf oder du dich uns?' The cold starkness of the ellipsis sends shivers down the spine. To Faust's gesturing curse: 'Den entsezlichsten Fluch über dich auf Jahrtausende', he replies with the shattering taunt: 'Greiffst du nach dem Donner? Wohl, dass er euch elenden Sterblichen nicht gegeben ward.' It is essentially dramatic language in its give-and-take, its contrasting dialogue, adding and taking away, referring back and passing on.

As an expression of deep emotion the scene is very powerful. The exclamatory aspect of this prose is something which was to be developed to the point of inarticulateness by the lesser Sturm und Drang writers, particularly by Klinger.[1] And it is often, as

---

[1] See F. Beissner's article 'Studien zur Sprache des Sturms und Drangs', *GRM*, XXII (1934), pp. 417–29; and my paper to the 1957 congress of the Fédération des Langues et Littératures Modernes, 'The Language of Sturm und Drang'.

here, combined with rhetorical apostrophes, curses and reflections. The ejaculatory element would seem to be a prose-correspondence to Klopstock's ecstatic stammerings, his progressive groping towards expression, encouraged by Herder's affection for all direct expression of emotion, and with the same disjointedness and dashes which we noted in the latter part of *Werther*. In its use of asyndeton and paratactic sequences it goes back ultimately to the curt and loose forms of Senecan style, transferred here, as Breitinger realised they could be, to the direct expression of *Affekt*. The nearest approach we have seen to this is in Geßner's *Der Tod Abels* and in Herder's evocative style. The rhetorical strain has a longer history and represents the last remnants of the classical 'grand' style as well as the sententiousness of the earlier eighteenth century. The two strains were combined in the prose of Gerstenberg's *Ugolino* (for instance, in the final speech), a play much admired by Goethe.[1] The rhetoric appears in *Götz*, more strongly in the ranting passages of the first version, but not the ejaculatory style. The two are found in juxtaposition in the impassioned moments of *Clavigo*, for example:

> Luft! Luft! — Das hat dich überrascht, angepackt wie einen Knaben. — Wo bist du, Clavigo? Wie willst du das enden? — Ein schröcklicher Zustand, in den dich deine Thorheit, deine Verrätherey gestürzt hat! (*Er greift nach dem Degen auf dem Tisch*) Ha! Kurz und gut! — (*Er läßt ihn liegen*)

or:

> Er verräth uns! (*an die Stirn schlagend und auf die Brust*) Hier! hier! es ist alles so dumpf so todt vor meiner Seele, als hätt ein Donnerschlag meine Sinnen gelähmt. Marie! Marie! du bist verrathen! — Und ich stehe hier! — Wohin — was — Ich sehe nichts, nichts! Keinen Weg! Keine Rettung (*er wirft sich in Sessel*).[2]

In Clavigo's monologue in Act Five we have the two strains combined, with broken cries interspersed with longer meditations in which there are echoes of transcendental sentimentalism:

> Todt! Marie todt! Die Fackeln dort! ihre traurigen Begleiter! — Es ist ein Zauberspiel, ein Nachtgesicht, das mich erschröckt, das mir

---

[1] See Morris, I, 323 and III, 388.   [2] *Ibid.* IV, pp. 184 and 211.

einen Spiegel vorhält, darinn ich das Ende meiner Verräthereyen ahndungsweise erkennen soll. — Noch ist es Zeit! Noch! — Ich bebe, mein Herz zerfließt in Schauer! Nein! Nein! du sollst nicht sterben. Ich komme! Ich komme! — Verschwindet, Geister der Nacht, die ihr euch mit ängstlichen Schrecknissen mir in Weg stellt — (*er geht auf sie los*) Verschwindet! — Sie stehen! Ha! sie sehen sich nach mir um! Weh! Weh mir! es sind Menschen wie ich. — Es ist wahr — Wahr — Kannst du's fassen! — Sie ist todt — Es ergreift mich mit allem Schauer der Nacht das Gefühl, sie ist todt.[1]

The same juxtaposition is found in *Stella*, a play much admired by Klinger.[2] The ecstasy of love is here expressed continually in the language of the culture of feeling. For instance:

> Sie machen uns glücklich und elend! Mit welchen Ahndungen von Seeligkeit erfüllen sie unser Herz, welche neue und unbekandte Gefühle und Hoffnungen schwellen unsere Seele, wenn ihre stürmende Leidenschafft sich ieder unserer Nerven mittheilt.

but this alternates with excited stammering:

> Sag ihm, er soll kommen, kommen! geschwind! geschwind! — Wär das überstanden! — Hätt ich ihn in diesen, in — Du betrügst dich, es ist unmöglich — Lasst mich, ihr Lieben! Lasst mich allein! —[3]

and with rhetorical apostrophes, to Venus, to nightingales, even to *Verwesung*.[4] Two monologues in the last act show the combination of these two strains most clearly. Stella begins with an apostrophe to the fullness of night, breaking immediately into 'umgieb mich! fasse mich! leite mich! ich weis nicht wohin ich trete! — — Ich muss, ich will hinaus in die weite Welt! Wohin? Ach wohin? —', then turns her address to 'Stätte meines Grabs', passing into 'Wehmuth...Wonne...dämmert...schweben... schmachtend', then outcries and dashes and a third apostrophe, this time to Fernando, with a 'Ha!', some dynamic prefixes ('entgegen sprang...aufschloss...bebtest zurück'), a second

---

[1] *Ibid.* IV, p. 215. The 'Menschen' referred to are the corpse-bearers. A comparison of this monologue with the grave-yard scene in *Hamlet* (with which it has obvious affinities of content) shows how totally different this Sturm und Drang language is from that of Shakespeare.
[2] See for instance Morris, v, p. 471.
[3] *Ibid.* v, pp. 88 and 92.   [4] *Ibid.* pp. 94, 98, 109–10.

'Ha!' and then complete dissolution into stammering inarticulateness. Fernando begins equally pointedly: 'Lass mich! Lass mich! Sieh...', soon reaches a 'Ha!', two phrases begin with the characteristic *Und*,[1] but then comes the rhetorical combination of 'Diese drei beste weibliche Geschöpfe der Erde — elend durch mich! — elend ohne mich! — Ach noch elender mit mir —' until he too breaks into stumbling disjointedness with:

> Cezilie! Mein Weib! o mein Weib! —— Elend! Elend! tiefes Elend! — Welche Seeligkeiten vereinigen sich um mich elend zu machen! — Gatte! Vater! Geliebter! — Die besten edelsten weiblichen Geschöpfe! — dein! — Dein! — kannst du das fassen, die dreifache, unsägliche Wonne? — und nur die ist's, die dich so ergreifft, die dich zerreisst! — Jede fordert mich ganz — Und ich? — Hier ist's zu! — tief! unergründlich.[2]

The two strains are there. But nowhere are they used to set off each other, nowhere with the same shattering contrast as in these final scenes of the *Urfaust*. And nothing so far has come anywhere near the fearful intensity of the final scene in Gretchen's prison. The contrast is made immediately when Faust's 'Schauer', his 'inneres Grauen der Menschheit', his Klopstockian 'zögert den Todt heran' and Gretchen's complete lack of any ecstatic generalities, her absorption in her individual fate, her simple broken sentences and cries, and the absence of all rhetoric except for Biblical echoes ('Heulen und Zähnklappen', 'Erbarme dich mein', 'Ihr heilige Engel, bewahret meine Seele!') and one recollection of past bliss: 'Wie sonst ein ganzer Himmel mit deiner Umarmung gewaltig über mich eindrang!' What a contrast between Faust's generality: 'wir entgehen dem schröcklichen Schicksaal' and her reply: 'Küsse mich! Küsse mich!', between his 'inneres Grauen der Menschheit' and her terrible cry: 'Mir graut's vor dir, Heinrich!'

---

[1] We have noted this use of *und* in Herder's analysis of folk-language and we have encountered it in *Werther*. Goethe often uses it to snap out of an ejaculatory sequence. For instance: 'Hölle! Tod! und Teufel, und du willst sie heurathen?' (Morris, IV, p. 202). This recurs in the scene later called *Trüber Tag*.

[2] Morris, V, p. 122.

THE GOLDEN TOUCH

A tragic note on which to end our considerations. But this in itself is significant. The German language has here achieved a tragic dimension which not even Lessing had attained. In this last chapter I have purposely said nothing about other writers (such as Hölty, Bürger, Gerstenberg, Lenz and Klinger) who were in part moving in the same direction, in order not to dissipate our concentration on Goethe. For Goethe represents more fully and more magnificently than they the climax of our study. German developed more rapidly and (with the exception of Russian) later than the other great literary languages of Europe. We have seen the language vindicated and then stabilised. We have watched it shaking off the shackles of Latin and the periodic sentence. We have noted the beneficial influence of French and English in the evolution of a clear and lively prose style culminating in rationalistic prose of a high order. We have traced the revolt against the absolutism of rationalist criteria and the emergence of a deeper understanding of the poetic potentialities of language. We have seen refinement balanced by a return to origins. And, in our last chapter, we have witnessed German taking its place amongst the great literary languages of the world.

GENERAL INDEX

Abbt, Thomas, 458, 461, 464
Abstract metonymy, 271, 334, 337 ff.
Abstractness, 171, 203, 221, 223, 236, 273, 338 ff., 372 ff., 442, 448
Abstracts, plural, *see* Plural abstracts
Academy planned by Leibniz (*see also* Prussian Academy), 7
Accusative and dative confused, 55, 130, 133, 138, 433
Accusative, cognate, *see* Cognate accusative
Acta Eruditorum, 51 ff.
Addison, 66–7, 70–1, 80, 259, 277, 310 ff., 322, 456
Addison and Steele, influence of their journals, 50, 60 ff., 65, 67 ff., 196
Adjective, attributive, *see* Attributive adjective
Adjectives, compound, *see* Compound adjectives
Adjectives, substantivation of, *see* Substantivation
Adverbial -*en* suffix, 143, 148
Affekts, Sprache des, 288, 323–4, 377, 380, 495, 522
Alemannic, 114, 295–6
Alliteration, 246, 475, 478, 497
Ambiguity, 157, 268, 442, 446 ff., 452
Amplificatio, 164, 367
Anacoluthia, 168, 288, 500, 502
Anacreon, 237, 391, 457
Anacreontic poetry, 309, 388, 390 ff., 402, 414
Anacreonticism, 393, 401, 403, 416, 487 ff., 494
Analogie der Sinne, 470
Analogy, 124, 126–7, 133–5, 141, 437–8
Anaphora, 366, 367, 369
Angenehm, 157, 390, 399, 411, 419, 494
Anglicisms, 119
Anmuth, 204, 208, 297
Antithesis, 222, 235, 247, 252, 254, 269, 299, 366
Apocope, 128, 135, 144, 306, 480, 484, 497–8, 501, 504, 506
Aposiopesis, 288
Apostrophe, 246, 257–8, 269, 366, 460, 500, 511, 515, 521 ff.

Archaisms, 157, 165, 181 ff., 214, 263, 284, 311, 323, 329, 331, 480, 483 ff., 497, 504, 506, 517
Aristotle, 311, 322, 471–2
Article, omission of, 354, 460, 477, 498
Artig, Artigkeit, 18, 121, 297, 305, 309 ff., 317, 399, 403, 433, 489, 507, 514
Association, 465 ff.
Asyndeton, 191, 222, 245, 247, 288, 335, 522
Attributive adjective, declension of, 133, 263, 484
Augustine, St, 152, 446
Auxiliary verbs, omission of, 138, 231, 278, 311, 366, 460, 487, 498, 500

Bacon, Francis, 428, 440 n., 443
Balance, 66, 83, 91–2, 208, 258, 368, 373–4
Balzac, Guez de, 53, 167, 200, 204, 409
Batteux, 455
Baumgarten, 452 n.
Bayle, 57
Begriff, 29–30, 36
Bel esprit, 14, 166, 387
Benkowitz, C. F., 341 ff.
Besonnenheit, 467 ff., 471 ff.
Besser, J. von, 85, 155, 216, 219, 229, 231, 255, 289
Birken, S. von, 218, 240 ff.
Blackwell, Thomas, 296, 453
Bluntness, 507
Bödiker, J., 132
Bodmer, 70, 74, 96–7, 112 ff., 257, 264, Chapter IX *passim*, 314–15, 322, 324, 333, 336, 356, 358, 383, 443, 461
Antipatriot, 97 ff., 113, 277
Character der Teutschen Gedichte, 289, 314
Discourse der Mahlern, 71 ff.
Poetische Gemählde, 292 ff.
Works on M.H.G. literature, 298 ff.
on Milton, 310 ff.
Böhme, Jakob, 34–5
Boileau, 161, 163, 218–19, 221, 226, 239, 257

GENERAL INDEX

Bombast, 94, 157–8, 172, 202, 219, 231, 233, 287, 364, 387
Bon sens, 445
Bouhours, 161, 168, 171, 174, 287, 387–8
Bourdaloue, 75 n.
Braun, H. B., 145
Breitinger, 68, 70, 163, 172–3, 253, 265, Chapter IX *passim*, 321, 323–4, 356, 363, 443, 456, 522
   Critische Dichtkunst, 278 ff.
   Diogenes, 68
   Discourse der Mahlern, 73 ff.
   Einbildungskrafft, 97 ff., 277 ff.
   Gleichnisse, 289 ff.
Brockes, B. H., 82, 172, 240 ff., 255, 268, 270, 273, 280–1, 287, 290–1, 293, 381
Burlesque, 70–1

Canitz, 155, 216, 219 ff., 223, 225–6, 255, 268, 485
Cento, 438
Chancery language as ideal, 140, 148, 203
Chancery sentence used with stylistic effect, 418, 420 ff.
Chancery style, 63, 121, 162 ff., 166, 175 ff., Chapter VI *passim*, 327, 362, 366, 384, 484
Chapbooks, 482
Chapbook style, 46, 192, 507
Characters of style, *see* Three styles
Cicero, 24
Ciceronian style, Ciceronianism, 150 ff., 164, 166, 168, 176, 184, 187, 198, 199, 203, 364, 371, 457
Circumlocution, 162, 165, 188, 191, 257, 305, 379, 422
Clarity (*Deutlichkeit*), 8, 16 ff., 46, 64, 74, 86, 90, 113, 120, 145, 157, 167–8, 172, 180, 204, 281, 317, 361 ff., 366 ff., 445, 452
Clauder, J. C., 112–13
Cognate accusative, 313, 333, 475
Coleridge, 380
Colloquialism, 23, 44, 53 ff., 90–1, 189, 192, 194, 202, 305, 362, 480, 492, 498, 504–6
Colons, 460
Complimentation, 64, 93–4, 199
Composition, 165, 323, 327, 331
Compound adjectives, 136, 158, 271, 286, 321, 378, 417, 460, 491, 500

Compounds embodying metaphor, 234, 247, 250, 356
Compound participles, 331 ff., 383, 385, 491, 500
Concetti, 224, 237, 300
Conciseness, 163, 165, 167–9, 204, 281, 283, 301, 305, 307, 313, 315, 335, 354 ff., 360 ff., 367, 443, 474
Condillac, 453, 455, 456, 464 ff.
Conjunctions, 68, 72, 163, 175, 178, 184, 202, 207, 484
Connexio, 164, 169, 175, 178, 184–5, 188, 208, 458, 475
Contraction, 480, 484, 497, 506
Contrast, 72, 74
Conventional names, 462 ff., 468 ff.
Correctness, 102 ff., 326
Cöthener Logik, 25, 33
Coupé, style, 167, 169
Crusca, Accademia della, 6
Cultured naturalness, *see* Naturalness, cultured

Dashes, 460, 514, 517, 522, 523
Dative and Accusative confused, 55, 130
Decentia, 16
Decorum, 162, 165
Delayal, 324, 347, 348, 418, 477, 500, 502, 515
Demosthenes, 447
Descartes, 26
Deutlichkeit, *see* Clarity
Deutsche Gesellschaft, of Leipzig, 107
Dialects and dialectal features, 7, 82, 112, 122–3, 144, 295, 357
Dialect dictionaries, 357 (and footnote)
Dialogue, 81, 366
Dictionary, German, 7, 110, 352, 358 ff.
Diderot, 453, 455–6
Dignitas, 165
Diminutive endings, 130
Discourse der Mahlern, 69 ff.
Dodd's *Beauties of Shakespeare*, 487
Dornblüth, 139 ff., 145 ff., 173 ff., 177, 183 ff.
Doublets, 23, 83, 189, 191–2, 208, 366, 373, 406
Drollinger, K. F., 129, 269, 485
Dürer, Albrecht, 27, 29

Ease (*ungezwungen*), 17, 163
East Middle German *Gemeinsprache*, 104, 123 ff., 143

528

GENERAL INDEX

Edelmann, J. C., 47
Ejaculations, *see* Interjections
Elegance (*elegantia*), 157, 162, 166, 208, 258, 260, 367, 420
Elevated diction, 230, 260, 340, 375
Elision, 475 ff., 498, 512, 517
Elision in *Auftakt*, 480, 498
Ellipsis, 114 n., 169, 267, 284, 308, 369, 448, 477, 502, 503, 505, 507, 521
Empfindsam, 360
Empfindsamkeit (*see also* Sentimentalism), 390, 413, 415
Empfindung, 390, 392, 412, 414, 513
Emphasis, 68, 72, 120, 192, 215, 231, 281, 308, 348, 367 ff., 479, 510, 511
Emphatic connections, 460
Emphatic enumeration, 84, 245, 366
Emphatic modifiers, 246
Emphatic repetition, 72, 252, 366, 430
Emphatic terseness, 261
Emphatic variation, 72, 83, 366
English influence, 259, 408
English language, 313, 317, 322, 327, 425, 457, 458
English prose and German, 62 ff., 193 ff.
Enjambement, 316, 395
Enumeration, 84, 164, 168, 235, 368, 406, 460
Epigram, 258, 362
Epistolary style, 197 ff.
Epithets, 165, 167, 252 ff., 271, 285 ff., 361, 399, 403, 512, 516
Epithet, postposition of, *see* Postposition
Euclid, 27, 28
Euphony, 119, 165, 215, 281, 324, 425
Exotic (jewelled) imagery, 235, 238, 247, 250, 252, 291, 303, 424–5
Expressionism, 350
Expressiveness, 113, 212, 312, 324, 328, 506

fast, 243, 252, 364
Feeling, culture of, 414 ff., 488 ff., 517, 520, 523
Fénelon, 314, 455
Figuration, figures of speech, 158, 214, 231, 287, 294
Fischart, 8, 10, 293
Flatness, 216, 220, 227, 231, 236, 247, 252, 268, 294, 310–11, 398, 460
Flexionless adjective, 263, 308, 354, 379, 460, 480, 497, 498, 500, 503, 504
Folksong, 473 ff., 495 ff.
Foreign adulteration of English vocabulary, 65, 326
Foreign words in German, 4 ff., 22 ff., 25 ff., 28, 37 ff., 84 ff., 94, 117–19, 157, 178, 311, 325–6, 354, 360, 518
Frederick I of Prussia, 109 ff.
Frederick II (the Great) of Prussia, 47, 111, 401
Free rhythms, 316
French adulteration of German syntax, 118, 136, 141, 176, 184, 186
French adulteration of German vocabulary, 6, 64, 72, 76–7, 85, 117, 141, 487
French as stylistic model, 160 ff., 227, 392, 457
French ideals, 13, 394
French language, 317, 322, 327, 425
French prose and Addison, 61
French prose and German, 61, 365
French vocabulary impoverished, 284, 444
Frisch, J. L., 132
Fruchtbringende Gesellschaft, 14, 29 n., 111 n., 157, 182
Furetière's dictionary, 8 n.

Gaiety, 57, 64, 90, 189, 261, 394
Galant, 45, 52, 95–6, 161, 199, 223, 485, 518
Gefällige, das, 389
Gegenstand (*see also* Object), 25, 35 ff., 147
Gellert, 200 ff., 298, 373, 403, 416, 433, 485 ff.
Gemeinsprache, 103–4
Gender, 130, 135, 231
Genie, concept of, 472 ff., 495
Genius (of a language), 75, 453, 471
George, Stefan, 347
Gerunds and gerundial expressions, 186, 313
Geßner, Salomon, 378 ff., 390, 399, 402, 511, 521–2
Girard, 146
Gleim, 298, 309, 362, 381, 391, 394 ff.
Goethe, 273, 286, 326, 337, 343, 367, 400, 438, and Chapter XV
Clavigo, 522–3
Frankfurt poems, 501 ff.

GENERAL INDEX

Goethe (cont.)
   Götz, 506 ff.
   Leipzig poems, 488 ff.
   Mitschuldigen, Die, 492
   Odes to Behrisch, 491 ff.
   Schwänke, 505 ff.
   Stella, 523–4
   Strassburg poems, 494 ff.
   Urfaust, 517 ff.
   Werther, 512 ff.
Good taste, 219, 220, 445
Gottsched, 47–8, 50–1, 77, 79, 82, 88 ff., Chapter IV *passim*, 153 ff., 171 ff., 180 ff., 202, 228 ff., 261 ff., 276–7, 295, 317, 352, 388, 391, 453, 457, 483, 486
   Beobachtungen, 145 ff., 182–3
   Beyträge, 68 n., 111 ff., 132
   Biedermann, 98 ff., 180
   Critische Dichtkunst, 230 ff.
   Erste Gründe der gesammten Weltweisheit, 48
   Redekunst, 153 ff.
   Sprachkunst, 114 ff.
   Vernünfftigen Tadlerinnen, Die, 88 ff., 117, 228
Götz, J. N., 391–2
Grace (see also Anmuth and *Grazie*), 90, 256, 258, 317
Gracian, Balthasar, 12
Grand style, see High style
Gravitas, 16, 433
Grazie, 414 ff.
Greek and German, 11, 144, 165, 286, 317, 327, 361, 425, 457
Grimarest, 200, 203
Gryphius, 293
Günther, 233 ff., 293, 391

Hagedorn, 255 ff., 268, 298, 310, 315, 332, 372, 381, 391 ff., 398–9, 402, 416, 424, 433, 485, 492
Haller, Albrecht von, 113, 176–7, 259 ff., 282, 319, 322, 324, 330, 332, 334, 336, 343, 398, 485
Hamann, 426 ff., 451, 453, 458, 495
   Biblische Betrachtungen, 427 ff.
   Kreuzzüge, 439 ff.
   Sokratische Denkwürdigkeiten, 437
   Wolken, 437–9
Handlung, 326, 447
Harmony, 317
Harris, James, 471 ff.
Harsdörffer, 28, 199, 218, 248

Harte Fügung, 347
Hebrew, 324, 380, 430–1, 457, 460, 495
Hegel, 46 ff.
Heldensprache motif, 120–1, 144, 145
Helveticisms, 113, 262 ff.
Hemmer, J. J., 144 ff.
Herder, 228, 323, 336, 365, 371, 451 ff., 495 ff., 508, 511, 522
   Fragmente, 451 ff.
   Gott, 472
   First *Kritisches Wäldchen*, 471–2
   Ossian essay, 474 ff.
   Shakespeare essay, 473
   Ursprung der Sprache, 462 ff.
Heroic couplet, 272
Hexameter, 315 ff.
High (grand) style, 16, 151, 158, 176, 288, 522
Hobbes, Thomas, 463
Hofmannswaldau, 96, 105, 159, 160, 216, 222–3, 229, 247, 251, 289, 309
Hölderlin, 286, 347, 350
Homer, 282, 286, 290, 291, 293, 296, 314, 317, 342–3, 457, 479, 511, 513 ff.
Horace, 219, 221, 226, 237, 238, 255 ff., 362, 392, 425, 439
Hume, 404, 437
Hunold, C. F., 106, 159, 161, 200
Hunting expressions in German, 5, 11 n., 119
Hyperbole, 174, 235, 244, 247, 406
Hyphenation in compounds, 131, 332, 483–4

Idioms, 452 ff.
Imagery essential to poetry, 280, 288
Imagery, exotic, jewelled, see Exotic imagery
Imagination, 27, 70, 229, 276–7, 326, 431
Imperatives, 521
Impromptus, 479
Incapsulation, 43, 54, 63, 76, 78, 169, 184, 185 ff., 383
Ingenieuse Inventionen, 214
Insel Felsenburg, 189 ff.
Intensification, 406, 408–9, 499
Interjections, 323, 347, 366, 460, 476, 498, 500, 502, 503, 512, 515, 517, 521 ff.
Intransitive verb with object, 313, 330, 333, 344, 350, 383, 385, 460, 491, 501

GENERAL INDEX

Inversion, 169, 311, 321, 323, 444, 452, 454 ff., 475 ff., 497, 498, 500, 504, 505, 512, 514–17, 521
Irony, 91, 256, 408, 412, 417 ff., 437 ff., 447–8
Irrationalism, 276, 431, 475
Italian language, 317, 322, 425

Jablonski, 110
Jacobi, J. G., 398
Jesuit schools, 112
Jewelled imagery, *see* Exotic imagery
Johnson, Dr, 352, 407
Journal des Sçavans, 50
Juvenal, 219

Kant, 26, 426, 439 n.
Kepler, 27, 28
Klopstock, 268, 286, 295, 313, Chapter X *passim*, 362, 378, 380, 385, 399, 402, 408, 410, 411, 413, 416 ff., 450, 460, 475 ff., 481, 485, 490 ff., 499 ff., 510 ff., 518, 520, 522
Gelehrtenrepublik, 326
Grammatische Gespräche, 326 ff.
Der Messias, 319 ff.
Odes, 347 ff.
Knüttelvers, 480, 485, 503 ff., 517 ff.
König, J. U., 216, 218, 220, 255, 289, 293
Kraft, kräftig (*see also* Strength), 121, 142, 230, 315, 417 ff., 473, 505 n.

La Bruyère, 455
La Fontaine, 257–8, 298, 309
Language above the dialects, 103, 108, 125
La Serre, 200
Latin language, 317, 425
Latin, tyranny of, 15, 457 ff.
Lectures in German, 12
Leibniz, 2 ff., 19, 34 ff., 51, 109 ff., 116, 120, 276, 283, 454, 463
De optima philosophi dictione, 8 ff.
Ermahnung, 2 ff.
Unvorgreiffliche Gedanken, 5 ff., 132
Von dem höchsten Gute, 34 ff.
Leidenschaft, 326, 447, 514
Leipziger Spectateur, Der, 67 ff.
Lengthenings and shortenings, 231, 310, 322
Letter-writing, 160–1, 180, 197 ff., 366
Lessing, 320, 351 ff., 463, 465, 472
Liaison des idées, 169, 455

Lightness, 63
Light style, development of, 54, 60, 74, 81, 90
Linkage, *see* Connexio
Locke, 387, 463
Logau, 105, 354 ff.
Lohenstein, 96, 154 ff., 158 ff., 196, 202, 204–5, 216, 219, 223, 224, 226, 239, 251, 265, 268, 269, 270, 273, 289, 291–3
Low (plain) style, 16, 151, 176, 202
Low German features, 123, 146
Low Saxon, 112, 136, 138, 139
Lowth, 440 n., 453
Luther, 8, 104, 131 ff., 146, 159, 185, 322, 324, 329, 358, 381, 462, 481, 483, 496

Machtwörter, 281, 296, 312 ff., 363, 380, 393, 452, 454 ff., 461, 476 ff., 491, 497, 498, 501, 510
Mahler der Sitten, Der, 114
Mahlern, Discourse der, 69 ff.
Manliness
  of Upper German, 142
  of German, generally, 317, 324, 327, 461
  of Ossian, 474
Mann, Thomas, 420
Marino and *marinismo*, 218, 219, 243, 248
Marot, 298, 308
Mathematical method and mathematics, 27 ff.
Mattheson, J., 60
Maupertuis, 110, 463
Mauvillon, 306, 311, 388
Meissen usage, 102 ff., 112, 123–4, 141
Ménage, 8 n., 352, 409
Mencke, Burkhard, 107, 110, 215, 237
Mencke, Otto, 51
Mendelssohn, Moses, 443, 464, 468
Metaphor
  abuse of, 158, 227, 254, 287, 288
  defence of, 277, 281–2, 287 ff.
  rejection of, 96, 171 ff., 216 ff., 228 ff.
Metaphor as clarification, 100, 231, 277, 290
Metaphor as emphasis, 100, 277, 281
Michaelis, J. D., 440, 464
Middle-class public, 49, 59 ff., 85
Middle High German, 295 ff., 358
Middle style, 16, 151, 158, 176, 202
Milton, 264, 276, 282, 284, 310 ff., 314, 325, 340 ff.

GENERAL INDEX

Mining expressions in German, 5, 11 n., 119
Minnesang, 309
'Mixed feelings', 403, 419, 520
Monosyllabism, 144, 306, 313, 318, 500
Morhof, 159, 166, 215, 218
Moscherosch, 218, 391
Musical prose-structure, 378
Mystical attitude to language, 437
Mystical vocabulary, 34 ff.
Mysticism, baroque, 344, 345
Mystics, medieval, 33, 344

Nachdruck, nachdrücklich, 16, 88, 120, 121, 145, 157, 163, 230, 264, 282, 284, 293, 297, 321, 357, 361, 364
Nasal, weakening of final, 128 ff.
Nationalism, 326 ff.
'Natural' imagery, 297 ff., 303
Natural names, 462 ff., 468 ff.
'Natural' order of words, 119, 169, 444 n.
Naturalisation of foreign words, 22, 27, 118
Naturalness, 96, 99, 149, 162, 165, 166, 201, 228, 294, 297, 309
Naturalness, cultured, 176, 199 ff., 209, 364, 366, 487
Neologisms, 157, 164, 181 ff., 231, 323, 328, 345
Neukirch, B., 159, 200, 202, 223 ff.
-niß/ -nuß/ -nüß, 135, 263, 484
Nizolius, 8
Nominal style, 258, 371 ff.
Nothdrang des Inhalts, 474
Novalis, 336

Object (*see also Gegenstand*), 26, 33
Oblique cases, 'full' use of, 321, 335, 346, 417, 460
Obscurity, 16, 163, 180, 228, 264 ff., 287, 292, 335, 346, 362, 394, 443, 447
Onomatopoeia, 248 ff., 280–1, 425, 452, 464
Opitz, 7 n., 8, 80, 105, 116, 121, 132, 137, 153, 159, 165, 177, 217, 219, 221, 223, 231, 260, 266, 281, 293, 317, 322, 324, 358, 391
Oratorical style, 72, 366 ff.
Order of words, 75, 112, 119, 121, 133, 214–15, 231, 308, 313, 323, 366, 444 n., 506 ff.

Orderliness, 157, 167, 180–1, 185–6
Ordre direct, 169, 455 ff.
Origin of language, 462 ff., 495
Orthography, 110, 125 ff., 128, 144, 325 n., 326, 449 ff.
Ossian, 380, 473 ff., 508, 510 ff., 515 ff., 521
Overcompensation, 129
Oxymoron, 172, 235, 247, 258, 287, 403, 419, 425

Pairs of words as stylistic device, 63, 66
Paracelsus, 8, 12
Parallelism, 189, 380, 460, 511
Parataxis, 191, 258, 376, 384, 460, 522
Parenthesis, 204, 207
Participial constructions, 56, 114 n., 131, 176 ff., 179, 188, 192, 194, 264, 266, 283 ff., 313, 334, 460, 487, 500
Participles, 313, 321, 323, 331, 340, 344, 346, 383, 403, 417, 490, 491, 501, 511, 515, 521
Particles (*particulae*), 74 ff., 78, 81, 168, 184, 186, 294, 323, 364, 372, 480, 514
Particles, omission of, 278
Patriot, Der, 82 ff., 88
Paul, St, 152, 428, 432
Periodic sentence, 180 ff., 184 ff., 188, 203–4, 207, 317, 421, 457
Periodic sentence and periodic style, 458
Periphrasis, 162, 165, 167, 178, 202, 207, 372, 373
Periphrasis, poetic, 217
Personification, 258, 271, 299, 300, 502
Perspicuity, 310, 313, 359
Philosophical terminology, 24 ff.
Philosophical transactions of the Royal Society, 51
Pietism, 190, 343 ff., 405, 407–8, 413
Pindar, 457, 499 ff.
Pirckenstein's Euclid, 28
Plainness, 218 ff., 224, 228
Plain style, *see* Low style
Plasticity, *see* Vividness
Plato, 440, 462
Pleonastic compounds, 335
Plural abstracts, 339, 345, 406, 408 ff., 417
Plural *-n* in nouns, 113, 131, 263
Poetry and prose, 212 ff., 230 ff., 322 ff. 362 ff.

GENERAL INDEX

Pointe, 163, 256, 258, 382, 395, 419 ff., 488 ff., 494
Polished simplicity, 401
Polishing, 256, 297, 326
Politeness, 162, 178, 198, 203, 393, 420
Pope, Alexander, 217, 257, 259, 270, 362
Postposition of epithet, 215, 284, 311, 480, 497, 498
Preciosity, 58, 165, 166, 198, 199, 393
Precision, 64, 119, 254, 333
Prefixes, 281, 313, 321, 330, 344, 346
Prefix-formations, 344, 356, 383, 385, 417, 460, 500, 511, 515, 523
Preterite -*e* in strong verbs, 132, 435, 484
Primitive language, 470, 500, 511
Prosopopoeia, *see* Personification
Provincialisms, 157, 363–4
Prussian Academy, 109 ff., 445 n., 463 ff.
Punctuation, 366, 368, 460, 514
Punctuation, lack of, 497, 500, 502
Purification of French vocabulary, 5
Purism, 14, 117, 354
Purity, 84 ff., 88, 90, 94
Pyra, 314

Querelle des Anciens et des Modernes, 161
Question, rhetorical, 258, 269, 366, 369, 460
Quintilian, 151, 152

Rabelais, 8, 449
Rabener, 201
Ramler, 382
Ratichius, W., 12 n.
Rationalism and rationalistic criteria, 135, 166, 216, 218, 250, 276, 292, 371, 437 ff., 457, 475
Reason scorned, 431 ff.
Reasonableness, 96, 99, 158
Refinement of vocabulary, 90
Réflexion en puissance, 465
Reflexive pronoun, 133, 137
Refrain, 475 ff., 498, 500
Reichstag documents, 8
Reineke Fuchs, 8
Relief, 347, 348, 366, 372, 460, 502, 512
Repetition, 42, 72, 164, 167, 168, 215, 244, 258, 269, 347, 369, 373, 377 ff., 383, 460, 475, 476, 497, 498, 500, 502, 512, 515

Reyher, Samuel, 28, 30 n.
Rhetoric, 66, 72, 74, 78, 154, 222, 235, 244, 274, 366, 371, 485, 521 ff.
Rhythmical emphasis, 497
Rhythmical tension, 475 ff.
Richardson, Samuel, 197, 403, 404, 406
Richelet, 200
Richey, M., 61 n., 82, 356
Richness, 301, 307, 308, 310, 357
Richness of vocabulary, 164, 281, 284, 297 ff., 324
Rilke, 347, 350
Robinson Crusoe, 191 ff., 196, 381
Rollenhagen, 8
Rondeur, 167
Roughness, 144, 306, 315, 318, 326, 327, 478, 510
Rousseau, 453, 464 ff.

Sachs, Hans, 8, 159, 504 ff.
Santa Clara, Abraham a, 55, 57, 99
Scaliger, 153
Scherz, 57 ff., 142, 388, 392
Schiller, 273, 274, 286, 337
Schlegel, J. E., 298
Scholastic philosophy, language of, 8, 9
Schönaich, 266, 268, 336
Schottelius, 10 ff., 25 n., 128, 143
Schupp, J. B., 12
Scriptures in German, 4
Scultetus, A. 357, 363
Seafaring words in German, 5, 120
Senecan style, 150 ff., 164, 167, 169, 176, 187, 203, 522
Sententiousness, 259, 266, 270, 510, 519, 522
Sentimentalism, 403 ff., 489, 505, 512, 517, 522
'Seraphic' vocabulary, 411, 413, 416, 489, 512, 520
Shaftesbury, 259, 381, 404, 437, 466
Shakespeare, 293, 307, 399, 473 ff., 495, 508
Silesian, 104 ff., 112, 114, 126, 130, 354, 357
Simplex for compound verb, 329, 346, 417, 460
Simplicity, 297, 387, 391, 478, 505
sinnlich, 452, 453, 470, 474 ff., 481, 502, 519
sinnreich, 99–100, 154, 202, 204, 223, 392
Sixteenth-century German, 312, 457, 462, 481, 496 ff., 503 ff.
Smoothness, 256, 268, 315

533

GENERAL INDEX

so as relative, 133, 137, 484
Sobriety, 221
Societät der Wissenschaften, see Prussian Academy
Socrates, 437, 440
sollt, du, 132, 263,
Spectator, The, 60 ff., 79, 196, 310 ff., 407
Spener, 390
Spenser, 307, 308
s-plurals, 130
Sprünge und Würfe, 479, 481, 495, 497, 498
Stammering style, 347, 475, 500, 522 ff.
Steinbach dictionary, 112, 352, 358
Sterne, 405, 414, 449
Stoff, 25, 35
Strength, strengthening (*see also Kraft*), 306, 317, 318, 321, 323, 334, 335, 357, 457, 474
Strong verbs, 112
Sturm, J. C., 28, 29 n., 30 n.
Sturm, L. C., 28
Sturm und Drang, 313, 385, 471, 521
Subject pronoun, omission of, 138, 162, 308, 354, 460, 476, 497, 498, 500, 503, 516
Substantivation of adjectives, 136, 171, 311, 334, 354
Substantivation of infinitive, 344, 345, 495, 511, 515
Sulzer, J. G., 456, 464
Süssmilch, J. P., 463–4
Syllogism, 21, 26, 42
Symmetry, 256, 258, 364, 376, 460, 476, 481
Synaesthesia, 290, 469
Synonyms, 36, 163, 165, 167, 168, 283, 456, 470
Synonymous doublets, *see* Doublets

Taste, good, *see* Good taste
Tatler, The, 60, 61 n.
tausend, 244, 408, 499, 513
Technical words, 11, 23, 27, 118, 157
Tension, 324, 369
Terseness, 259, 266 ff., 312, 327, 358
Thirty Years War, Effects of, 4, 6, 11, 49
Thomasius, 12 ff., 19 ff., 50 ff., 95–6, 116, 121, 155, 159, 177, 189, 387
Ethics, 17, 44 ff.
Introductio ad Philosophiam Aulicam, 21 ff., 32

Logic, 15, 19 ff., 43 ff.
Monatsgespräche, 50 ff., 177
Programm of 1687, 13 ff.
Three styles of antique rhetoric, 16, 151, 162, 176, 202, 287
Tibullus, 237
Tieck, 189
Timidity of expression, 287, 327
tönende Verba, 468, 470
Tschirnhausen, 19, 26, 51, 57
tun in periphrastic tenses, 133, 480, 497
Typographical emphasis, 406

Umlaut, lack of, 128, 141, 483
und, 477, 495, 515, 524
Unsyncopated verbal forms, 375, 379, 483
Urbanity, 21, 58–9, 60, 64, 90, 420
Upper German as norm, 114, 141 ff.
Upper German features, 128–9, 146 ff., 263
Upper German *Gemeinsprache*, 104, 143
Ursprünglichkeit, 471, 473
Uz, 391–2, 398, 400 ff.

Variation (*variatio*), 72, 164, 167, 168, 178, 321, 347, 367, 372, 377, 418, 435, 452, 460
Variety, 316, 317, 371
Verbal style, 258, 333, 344–5, 371, 470 n.
Verbosity, 268, 287, 293, 365, 396, 448
Verbs as the first words, 468
Vernünftler, Der, 60 ff.
Virgil, 275, 282, 293, 314, 343, 425
Virtuosity, 254, 331, 344, 365 ff.
Vividness, 87, 90, 169, 204, 279, 281, 285, 304, 366
Voiture, 200, 204

Wahrscheinliche, das, 278 ff., 286–7
Walter von der Vogelweide, 309
ward–wurde, 134
Wechselsätze, 245
Weckherlin, 391
Weise, Christian, 25, 46, 99, 103, 153, 155 ff., 164, 166, 180, 192, 194, 197, 200, 202, 204, 214 ff., 231, 288, 289, 310, 387
Weitenauer, I., 143 ff.
Wernicke, 219, 226 ff., 387
Wieland, 360–1, 410 ff., 464, 488, 492
Agathon, 410 ff.
Aspasia, 412, 419

GENERAL INDEX

Wieland (*cont.*)
  Combabus, 414
  Comische Erzählungen, 418 ff.
  Don Sylvio, 412, 419 ff.
  Idris, 424 ff.
  willt, du, 132
Winckelmann, 371 ff., 379, 410, 453
Winkler, J. H., 112, 113, 172
Wit (*Witz*), 100, 198, 214, 223, 230, 235, 387 ff., 426, 431 ff., 488 ff., 513
Wolff, Christian, 26 ff., 116, 283, 387
  Ausführliche Nachricht, 37, 47
  Autobiographical sketch, 40 ff.
  Ethics, 45, 50
  Logic, 30 ff., 39 ff.
  Mathematics, 26 ff.
  Politics, 43
Wolfram von Eschenbach, 299 ff., 309
Women, 79, 88, 90, 201
Word-order, *see* Order of words
Word-play, 163, 235
Words, 'good, old', 296, 303, 353 ff., 357
Wunderbare, das, 277, 279 ff., 285, 287, 310

Zesen, 8, 25 n., 104, 127, 164, 230, 248, 354
Ziegler, 154, 158, 196, 218
Zierlichkeit, 16, 88, 163, 264, 387

INDEX TO SECONDARY LITERATURE

Details of works by these authors are given in footnotes on the quoted pages.

Auerbach, E.
  Mimesis, 152
  'Sermo humilis', 152

Back, A. L. and Spindler, A. R. C., 316
Bacon, I., 320
Badstüber, H., 255
Baldensperger, F., 381
Bateson, F. W., 217
Beck, G., 417
Behschnitt, C., 351
Beißner, F.
  Klopstock, 319
  Sturm und Drang, 521
  Zürchersee, 348
Belaval, Y., 3
Bergemann, F., 381
Blackall, E. A.
  Dornblüth, 140
  Götz, 506
  Hamann, 432, 449, 451
  Herder, 459
  Die Mitschuldigen, 492
  Parnassus Boicus, 143
  Sturm und Drang, 521
Böckmann, P.
  Formgeschichte, 5
  Witz, 161
Bodmer-Denkschrift, 70
Boehlich, W., 426
Böger, I., 316
Boucke, E., 143
Brandl, A., 243
Bray, R., 166
Brüggemann, H., 462
Bruneau, C., 456
Brunot, F., 409
Burdach, K.
  Goethe, 483
  Gottsched, 104
  Minnesang, 296
  Verjüngung, 461
Büscher, E., 510

Clark, R. T.
  Herder, 452
  Kraft, 471
Coffmann, B. R., 259
Colleville, M., 233
Croll, M. W.
  Attic, 151
  Baroque, 151
Curtius, E. R., 152

Danzel, T. W., 107
Deutschbein, M., 408
Dreyer, W., 233

Eigenbrodt, W., 257
Enders, K., 233
Engert, H., 319
Epting, K., 255
Erämetsä, E.
  Empfindsamkeit, 406
  'sentimental', 406
  sentimentalism, 406
  Werther, 406
Ermatinger, E., 381
Eucken, R., 24
Evers, H. G., 371

Flohr, O., 520
François, A., 216
Freivogel, M., 314
Frey, A., 381
Fulda, L., 225, 243

Gerold, K.-G., 453
Geßner Gedenkbuch, 381
Gillies, A., 510
Goldbach, G., 316
Götze, A., 27
Grappin, P., 472
Groschupp, H., 233
Grosser, P., 314

Haas, T., 409

INDEX TO SECONDARY LITERATURE

Hafen, H., 352
Haferkorn, R., 404
Harnack, A., 109
Haussmann, J., 451, 460
Havers, W.
  plural, 408
  syntax, 409
Hegel, G. W. F.
  Wolff, 46
Hendrickson, G. L.
  characters of style, 151
  peripatetic mean, 151
Heun, H. G., 483
Highet, G., 151
Hirzel, L., 261
Hodermann, R.
  Thomasius, 12
  Universitätsvorlesungen in deutscher Sprache, 12
Horák, W., 262
Hottinger, J. H., 381
Hübner, A., 358
Hummerich, H., 125

Immisch, O., 351

Jellinek, M. H.
  grammar, 124
  Klopstock, 319

Kaiser, K., 103, 128
Käslin, H., 262
Kaußmann, E., 316
Kawczyński, M., 67
Kettler, H. K., 159
Kindt, K., 343
Knight, D.
  Blackwell and Bodmer, 296
  Bodmer and MHG, 296
Körte, W., 395
Konrad, G., 462
Krämer, W., 233

Lange, A., 117
Langen, A.
  Klopstock, 319
  pietism, 343
  Sprachgeschichte, 319
  Verbale Dynamik, 319
Lanson, G., 166
Leemann-van Elck, P., 381
Lees, J., 391
Lehmann, A., 351
Lévy, P., 161

Levy, S., 336
Lingl, A. R., 409
Lüdtke and Götze
  Altfränkisch, 165

Markwardt, B.
  Lessing, 352
  poetics, 159
May, K., 156
Mensing, O., 61
Metzger, W., 351
Mornet, D., 166
Mortier, R., 453
Moser, V., 129
Mourgues, O. de, 166
Müller, F., 27
Müller, Maria, 371
Muncker, F.
  anacreontics, 398
  Lessing, 358

Nadler, J.
  Die Hamannausgabe, 427
  Hamann edition, 426
  Hamann biography, 427
Neumann, F., 107
Noack, L., 47

O'Flaherty, J. C., 427
Öhmann, E., 409

Papmehl-Rüttenauer, I., 319
Paul, H., 129
Petri, F., 319
Petsch, R., 257
Pfund, H. W., 243
Pietsch, P., 3, 5
Piur, P., 33
Popp, W., 319
Prutz, R., 51
Purdie, E.
  Hamann and Herder, 473
  Klopstock, 323
  Von deutscher Art und Kunst, 473

Reed, B., 380
Reichel, E., 107
Reis, H., 129
Richey, M., 61
Richter, E., 425
Robson-Scott, W. D., 496
Rosenberg, P., 320
Rosenhagen, G., 243
Rosteutscher, J. H. W., 462

INDEX TO SECONDARY LITERATURE

Saffenreuther, E., 461
Saintsbury, G., 83
Salmony, H. A., 462
Salomon, L., 51
Schimansky, G., 107
Schirmer, A., 27
Schleiden, K. A., 314
Schmarsow, A., 3
Schmidt, E.
  Geßner, 381
  Lessing, 351
Schuchard, G. C. L., 315
Schulenburg, S. von der, 7
Sengle, F., 415
Slangen, J. H., 146
Sokol, A. E., 3
Sperber, H.
  Entgegen-, 343
  pietism, 343
Spindler, A. R. C. (and Back, A. L.), 316
Staiger, E., 348
Steinhausen, G., 178, 197
Stewart, M. C., 243
Stopp, F. J., 351
Strasser, R., 381
Strich, F., 245
Sturm, W., 462

Thon, L., 409
Trevelyan, H., 501
Tyrol, F., 351

Unger, R.
  Aufklärung, 427
  Sprachtheorie, 426

Urbach, A., 129

Vetter, T.
  Bodmer, 70
  Chronick, 69
  Spectator, 70

Waentig, K., 406
Waetzoldt, S., 483
Waldberg, M. von
  Bouhours, 161
  Lessing, 351
Walzel, O., 319
Waniek, G., 107
Weber, H., 462
Wechsler, G., 154
Wehrli, M.
  Bodmer, 296
  Zürich, 114
Weinhold, K., 104
Wendland, U., 154, 159
Werner, K., 190
Willey, B., 404
Williamson, G.
  Senecan style, 151
  'The Senecan Amble', 151
Wilson, F. P., 151
Witkowski, G., 392
Wolf, H., 472
Wolff, E., 107
Wolff, H. M., 453
Wölfflin, H., 381
Wuttke, H., 40

Zagajewski, K., 262
Zamboni, G., 243